CONTEMPORARY
Black
Biography

ISSN-1058-1316

CONTEMPORARY

Black

Biography

Profiles from the International Black Community

Volume 73

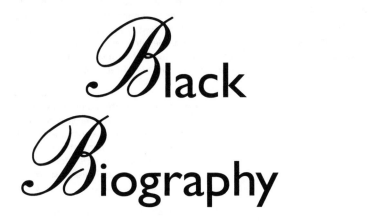

 GALE
CENGAGE Learning™

Detroit • New York • San Francisco • New Haven, Conn • Waterville, Maine • London

Contemporary Black Biography, Volume 73

Kepos Media, Inc.: Derek Jacques, Janice Jorgensen, and Paula Kepos, editors

Project Editor: Margaret Mazurkiewicz

Image Research and Acquisitions: Leitha Etheridge-Sims

Editorial Support Services: Nataliya Mikheyeva

Rights and Permissions: Margaret Abendroth, Jackie Jones

Manufacturing: Rita Wimberley

Composition and Prepress: Mary Beth Trimper, Gary Leach

Imaging: John Watkins

For product information and technology assistance, contact us at
Gale Customer Support, 1-800-877-4253.
For permission to use material from this text or product,
submit all requests online at **www.cengage.com/permissions.**
Further permissions questions can be emailed to
permissionrequest@cengage.com

While every effort has been made to ensure the reliability of the information presented in this publication, Gale, a part of Cengage Learning, does not guarantee the accuracy of the data contained herein. Gale accepts no payment for listing; and inclusion in the publication of any organization, agency, institution, publication, service, or individual does not imply endorsement of the editors or publisher. Errors brought to the attention of the publisher and verified to the satisfaction of the publisher will be corrected in future editions.

EDITORIAL DATA PRIVACY POLICY. Does this publication contain information about you as an individual? If so, for more information about our editorial data privacy policies, please see our Privacy Statement at www.gale.cengage.com.

Gale
27500 Drake Rd.
Farmington Hills, MI, 48331-3535

ISBN-13: 978-1-4144-3441-4
ISBN-10: 1-4144-3441-3

ISSN 1058-1316

This title is also available as an e-book.
ISBN 13: 978-1-4144-5690-4
ISBN-10: 1-4144-5690-5
Contact your Gale sales representative for ordering information.

Printed in the United States of America
1 2 3 4 5 6 7 13 12 11 10 09

Advisory Board

Contents

Introduction ix

Cumulative Nationality Index 165

Cumulative Occupation Index 181

Cumulative Subject Index 205

Cumulative Name Index 257

Tatyana Ali 1
  Noted television and film actress
Halima Bashir 4
  Darfur rape survivor and human rights activist
Charles M. Blow 6
  Visual journalist and op-ed writer
Usain Bolt 8
  Gold medal–winning Olympian sprinter
Melanie Brown 11
  "Scary" Spice Girl
Nappy Brown 14
  R&B pioneer
Nick Cannon 17
  Talented actor, comedian, and musician
J. L. Chestnut Jr. 20
  Dedicated civil rights lawyer and activist
Zoanne Clack 22
  ER physician and television producer
Lisa Cooper 25
  MacArthur-winning doctor and researcher
Ulysses Currie 28
  Popular Maryland state legislator
Tirunesh Dibaba 31
  Record-setting long-distance runner
Bobby Durham 34
  Legendary jazz drummer
Samuel Eto'o 36
  Top-scoring Cameroonian soccer star

Patrick Ewing 39
  Hall of Fame NBA center
Capers C. Funnye Jr. 43
  Popular Chicago rabbi related to Michelle Obama
Ken Griffey Jr. 46
  Second-generation baseball great
Danai Gurira 50
  Multitalented playwright and actress
Corey Harris 53
  Trailblazing blues musician
Isaac Hayes 56
  Iconic soul composer and performer
Arlene Holt Baker 60
  American labor executive
Mary Jackson 62
  Highly regarded basket maker
Valerie Jarrett 64
  White House senior adviser
Cullen Jones 67
  Olympic athlete and swimming activist
Seu Jorge 69
  Acclaimed Brazilian musician and actor
John Keene 72
  Innovative poet and fiction writer
Jakaya Mrisho Kikwete 75
  Dedicated president of Tanzania
Wendo Kolosoy 78
  Influential Congolese musician
K-Swift 80
  Beloved Baltimore radio host and club DJ
Ledisi 82
  Versatile R&B and jazz singer
Lisa Leslie 85
  Olympic gold medalist and professional basketball player
Nancy Hicks Maynard 89
  Prominent journalist and publisher

Thabo Mbeki 92

    Former South African president

Chi McBride 98

    Engaging film and television actor

Jaunel McKenzie 101

    Jamaican supermodel

Breno Mello 103

    Brazilian actor in Black Orpheus

Russ Mitchell 105

    Hard-working CBS broadcaster

Art Monk 108

    Record-breaking NFL wide receiver

Otto Neals 111

    New York–based sculptor and painter

Lorraine O'Grady 113

    Admired performance artist

Jackie Ormes 116

    Pioneering cartoonist

Joseph C. Phillips 118

    Actor and conservative social commentator

Run 121

    Legendary hip-hop artist

Nikkole Salter...124

    Gifted playwright and actress

Kimbo Slice...127

    Mixed martial arts sensation

Tasha Smith 129

    Former drug abuser turned successful actress and role model

Michael Steele 132

    High-ranking Republican official

Charles R. Stith 136

    Industrious minister and ambassador

Carl Stokes 139

    First black mayor of a major U.S. city

T-Pain..144

    Rising rap artist

Richard Wesley..147

    Distinguished playwright and screenwriter

Norman Whitfield 150

    Motown producer of "psychedelic soul"

Michelle Williams 153

    Chart-topping R&B and gospel singer

Serena Williams...156

    Tennis champion and top-earning female athlete

Maury Wills 162

    Record-setting shortstop

Introduction

Contemporary Black Biography provides informative biographical profiles of the important and influential persons of African heritage who form the international black community: men and women who have changed today's world and are shaping tomorrow's. *Contemporary Black Biography* covers persons of various nationalities in a wide variety of fields, including architecture, art, business, dance, education, fashion, film, industry, journalism, law, literature, medicine, music, politics and government, publishing, religion, science and technology, social issues, sports, television, theater, and others. In addition to in-depth coverage of names found in today's headlines, *Contemporary Black Biography* provides coverage of selected individuals from earlier in this century whose influence continues to impact on contemporary life. *Contemporary Black Biography* also provides coverage of important and influential persons who are not yet household names and are therefore likely to be ignored by other biographical reference series. Each volume also includes listee updates on names previously appearing in *CBB*.

Designed for Quick Research and Interesting Reading

- **Attractive page design** incorporates textual subheads, making it easy to find the information you're looking for.

- **Easy-to-locate data sections** provide quick access to vital personal statistics, career information, major awards, and mailing addresses, when available.

- **Informative biographical essays** trace the subject's personal and professional life with the kind of in-depth analysis you need.

- **To further enhance your appreciation** of the subject, most entries include photographic portraits.

- **Sources for additional information** direct the user to selected books, magazines, and newspapers where more information on the individuals can be obtained.

Helpful Indexes Make It Easy to Find the Information You Need

Contemporary Black Biography includes cumulative Nationality, Occupation, Subject, and Name indexes that make it easy to locate entries in a variety of useful ways.

Available in Electronic Formats

Diskette/Magnetic Tape. Contemporary Black Biography is available for licensing on magnetic tape or diskette in a fielded format. Either the complete database or a custom selection of entries may be ordered. The database is available for internal data processing and nonpublishing purposes only. For more information, call (800) 877-GALE.

On-line. Contemporary Black Biography is available on-line through Mead Data Central's NEXIS Service in the NEXIS, PEOPLE and SPORTS Libraries in the GALBIO file and Gale's Biography Resource Center.

Disclaimer

Contemporary Black Biography uses and lists websites as sources and these websites may become obsolete.

We Welcome Your Suggestions

The editors welcome your comments and suggestions for enhancing and improving *Contemporary Black Biography*. If you would like to suggest persons for inclusion in the series, please submit these names to the editors. Mail comments or suggestions to:

The Editor

Contemporary Black Biography

Gale, Cengage Learning

27500 Drake Rd.

Farmington Hills, MI 48331-3535

Phone: (800) 347-4253

Tatyana Ali

1979—

Actor, singer

Tatyana Ali first gained fame as one of the family members in the hit NBC sitcom *The Fresh Prince of Bel-Air* in the 1990s. After six seasons on the series that launched her costar Will Smith's acting career, Ali took a break from show business to enter Harvard University and earned her degree in 2002. More than a decade after the top-rated *Fresh Prince* ended its run, it was still seen daily in syndicated television reruns, and Ali was still recognized for her role as little Ashley Banks. "People grab me and hug me," she told *People* in 2006"When you're in people's living rooms every day, they feel like you're family."

Ali was born on January 24, 1979, in Brooklyn, New York, to Sonia Ali, a nurse of Panamanian heritage, and Sheriff Ali, a New York City police detective of Indian and Trinidadian ethnicity. The first of three daughters, Ali had an innate performing ability that brought her to the attention of producers of the popular preschoolers' television staple *Sesame Street*. Between 1985 and 1990 she appeared several times on the show under her own name. At the age of seven she won two rounds of the popular television talent contest *Star Search,* and went on to serve the role of understudy for Karima Miller, when the latter played the part of Raynell in the original 1987 Broadway production of August Wilson's *Fences*. That same year, Ali also won a part in a sketch scene in comedian Eddie Murphy's *Raw,* then a bit part in *"Crocodile" Dundee II.* In 1989 she was cast in a short-lived television series called *Wally and the Valentines.*

Ali's career proved so promising that her parents decided to move to Los Angeles to be nearer to the film

and television industry. In 1990 she beat out several other youngsters for the role of the youngest daughter of the Banks family on a new NBC sitcom called *The Fresh Prince of Bel-Air.* The series featured a young rapper-turned-actor Will Smith, who leaves behind his gritty Philadelphia neighborhood to come and live with his rich uncle in a wealthy enclave of Los Angeles. The top-rated *Fresh Prince* also starred James Avery as Philip Banks, the attorney-father, and Janet Hubert-Whitten as Aunt Vivian. Their on-screen children were the teenagers Hilary (Karyn Parsons) and Carlton (Alfonso Ribeiro), with Ali's Ashley as the youngest—and equally spoiled—offspring.

The new sitcom benefited from Smith's already established fame as one-half of the rap duo DJ Jazzy Jeff and the Fresh Prince, but its fortunes were further boosted by a strong marketing push from NBC in anticipation of its fall of 1990 debut. Larry Rohter in the *New York Times* hailed *Fresh Prince* as the first to introduce rap and hip-hop culture to a mainstream American audience. "The primary focus of the series is not tension between blacks and whites, but the cultural differences and misunderstandings that separate Fresh Prince and the black bourgeoisie, represented by his relatives," Rohter noted. "Imagine the domestic bliss of the Huxtable family on 'The Cosby Show' interrupted by a good-natured but coarse and noisy intruder from the streets, and you have 'Fresh Prince' in a nutshell." Two seasons in, *Fresh Prince* continued to be a hit with audiences and critics alike. "I'm convinced that one reason Fresh Prince's ratings have improved since its debut two years ago," wrote Ken Tucker in *Entertain-*

At a Glance . . .

Born Tatyana Marisol Ali on January 24, 1979, in Brooklyn, NY; daughter of Sheriff (a police detective) and Sonia (a nurse) Ali. *Education:* Harvard University, BA, government and African-American studies, 2002.

Career: Made television debut on *Sesame Street,* 1985; cast as an understudy in the original Broadway production of *Fences,* 1987; made film debut in *Eddie Murphy: Raw,* 1987; signed to Will Smith's production company; released first album, *Kiss the Sky,* 1998.

Addresses: *Agent*—Innovative Artists Talent and Literary Agency Inc., 1505 10th St., Santa Monica, CA 90401-2805.

ment Weekly in 1992, "is that the series is one of the few on TV that consistently acknowledges a full range of African-American lives—all social and economic classes are represented, and they eye each other with both suspicion and sympathy."

Though Ali had been cast for her acting abilities, she once sang at a cast party, and producers were so impressed that they wrote a performance part for her into one of the scripts. The song was the Aretha Franklin classic "Respect," and Ali later told writer Chuck Taylor in *Billboard,* "I'm glad I did it now, because Will was one of the people that came up to me after that show and said, 'Oh my God, you want to do this, don't you?' I'd never shared that with anybody but my mother." Smith signed her to his production company, which negotiated a recording deal for her with MJJ, the Michael Jackson–owned label that was part of the Sony media empire. Her debut album, *Kiss the Sky,* was released in 1998 and yielded two hit singles, "Daydreamin'" and "Boy You Knock Me Out," the latter a duet with Smith.

Ali put her show-business career on hold for a time after graduating from a private high school in Los Angeles and winning a spot in the Harvard University class of 2002. She moved to Cambridge, Massachusetts, in the fall of 1998, and into a Harvard dormitory building, where many of her new classmates had watched her grow up on *Fresh Prince* over its six-season run. The transition from Hollywood player to Ivy League freshman was a little difficult, she told Fred Shuster in the *Los Angeles Daily News* in 1999, explaining that during the first few weeks some of her new classmates asked to have their pictures taken with her. "I remember I told this one girl, 'I'm going to graduate with you. We're going to take classes together

and be in study groups together and party together. It's really not that much of a big deal,'" she said. "They got over it, especially the people I live with who see me in my robe walking down the hall with my toothbrush."

After graduating from Harvard with a degree in government and African-American studies in 2002, Ali returned to California to resume her acting career. Her most prominent part came in the 2006 basketball drama *Glory Road* in which she played the girlfriend of Derek Luke. She also landed a recurring role as Roxanne on the CBS daytime drama *The Young and the Restless,* which gave her ample time to work on a new collection of songs for a second album, tentatively titled *The Light.*

In 2008 Ali joined several other performers for "Yes We Can," a will.i.am single released to support the Democratic presidential campaign of then Illinois senator Barack Obama. Ali also appeared at voter-registration drives on the campuses of historically black colleges and universities to urge students to become involved in the campaign's efforts. At one stop at North Carolina Central University, she was interviewed by a local reporter for the *Durham Herald-Sun* and explained that her college major, which focused on the civil rights era in U.S. history, had been a profound influence on her. "That was a time when we had leaders, and people who weren't afraid to tackle very difficult issues," she told Dan E. Way. "Like Obama, they were more concerned about the impact of their actions on their constituents, not on their personal political careers."

Selected works

Albums

Kiss the Sky, MJJ, 1998.

Films

Eddie Murphy Raw, 1987.
"Crocodile" Dundee II, 1988.
Fakin' da Funk, 1997.
Kiss the Girls, 1997.
Jawbreaker, 1999.
The Brothers, 2001.
Nora's Hair Salon, 2004.
Back in the Day, 2005.
Glory Road, 2006.
The List, 2007.
Nora's Hair Salon II, 2008.
Hotel California, 2008.
Locker 13, 2009.
Privileged, 2009.

Television

Sesame Street, PBS, 1985–90.
Wally and the Valentines, NBC, 1989.

The Fresh Prince of Bel-Air, NBC, 1990–96.
Fall into Darkness (movie), NBC, 1996.
The Young and the Restless, CBS, 2007—.

Sources

Periodicals

Billboard, September 12, 1998, p. 118.
Durham Herald-Sun, April 11, 2008.

Ebony, February 1995, p. 128.
Entertainment Weekly, April 17, 1992, p. 44; November 22, 1996, p. 115.
Los Angeles Daily News, January 12, 1999, p. L3.
New York Times, September 17, 1990.
People, July 8, 1996, p. 61; January 23, 2006, p. 92.
St. Louis Post-Dispatch, April 2, 1999, p. E1.

—Carol Brennan

Halima Bashir

1979—

Physician, memoirist, activist

Halima Bashir is a memoirist and physician whose painful account of her own wartime experiences has done much to focus attention on a brutal conflict in one of the most remote regions of the world. Bashir is a native of Darfur, a vast and arid region in the North African nation of Sudan. The civil war that broke out there in 2003, just as she was beginning her medical career, has claimed hundreds of thousands of lives. Bashir's account, *Tears of the Desert: A Memoir of Survival in Darfur,* focuses not on the death toll, horrific as that is, but on the systematic rape of women and children by militias allied with the Sudanese government. As a victim of that crime herself, and as a physician, she understands the physical and emotional trauma it causes. Moreover, as a native of the region, she is also acutely familiar with the cultural factors there that stigmatize rape victims and discourage them from speaking out. Bashir, however, has bravely done precisely that. As she told Arlene Getz in *Newsweek,* "I'm writing my story for the people who can't write it for themselves."

Few concrete details are available concerning Bashir's early life. Though she has written evocatively of this period, she has changed many identifying details out of necessity, for the Sudanese government has frequently punished the friends and family of its critics. The name Halima Bashir is itself a pseudonym. The outline of her life is nevertheless clear. She was born in 1979 in a small Darfuri village where her father, a livestock trader, was one of the most prominent and prosperous inhabitants. Her family belonged to the Zaghawa tribe, a seminomadic Moslem people. Though issues of racial

and ethnic identity in Darfur are complicated, most inhabitants of the region consider the Zaghawa to be "African," in contrast to the "Arab" peoples who have long dominated the government and military. This distinction was to have devastating consequences with the outbreak of civil war.

As early as primary school, Bashir had distinguished herself as a student. Her success prompted her father to send her to a distant city for further study. It was a rare opportunity for a girl in rural Darfur, and Bashir took full advantage. Despite frequent racial taunts from classmates with lighter complexions, Bashir continued to excel, eventually winning entrance to medical school. After completing her studies there in 2003, she returned to her native village and began practicing. At the age of twenty-four, she was the area's first and only formally trained physician.

Bashir began her medical career just as Darfur was exploding into armed conflict. In 2003 rebel forces consisting predominately of "African" Darfuris took up arms against the government and its local "Arab" allies. These allies quickly mobilized their informal militias, known as the *janjaweed.* Heavily armed and mobile, the *janjaweed* soon gained a reputation for brutality, particularly against civilians. Bashir, alone in her clinic, treated dozens of victims, including many children. It was in this period that a visiting journalist quoted her remarks on the complexities and frustrations of the situation. Angered by what it took to be criticism of its Darfur policies, the Sudanese government banished her to a village even more remote. And it was there, in

At a Glance . . .

Born in 1979 in the Darfur region of Sudan; daughter of a livestock dealer; adopted the pseudonym Halima Bashir; married; children: two. *Religion:* Muslim. *Education:* Completed medical school in Sudan, 2003.

Career: Worked as a physician in rural Sudan, 2003–06; memoirist and activist, 2006—.

Addresses: *Office*—c/o Publicity Department, Random House Publishing Group, 1745 Broadway, Eighteenth Fl., New York, NY 10019.

the settlement known as Mazkhabad, that Bashir's sufferings really began.

In her memoir Bashir describes what happened when the *janjaweed* descended on Mazkhabad. Her account, which has been corroborated by physical evidence and other eyewitnesses, focuses on an incident at a girls' primary school in the village. There, militiamen repeatedly raped more than forty girls, some as young as eight years old, and their teachers. As the only doctor in the area, Bashir faced the enormous task of treating their wounds and trauma by herself. As word spread of the attack, two United Nations officials arrived to collect evidence. Though she had been warned not to give any more interviews, she told the investigators what had happened. A few days later she was kidnapped by government agents and repeatedly raped herself. Confident that they had broken her spirit, they let her go, and she made her way back to her own village. Her sufferings continued, however, as the *janjaweed* soon burned her village to the ground. Her father, to whom she was particularly close, died in the attack, and the rest of her family disappeared. It was only in 2008, several years later, that she learned her mother and sister had survived and were living a precarious existence in a refugee camp across the border in Chad. Her brothers remained missing.

Bashir herself was luckier. In the chaos that followed the attack, she managed to find some gold her family had hidden for emergencies. She used it to immigrate to the United Kingdom, where she was given perma-

nent asylum as a victim of torture. It was then, in a small apartment in London, that her career as a memoirist began with a simple record of her experiences. The act of remembering was a painful one, but she felt a compelling need to alert the world to the systematic abuse of civilians in Darfur. As she told Nicholas D. Kristof in the *New York Times,* "I am a well-educated woman, so I can speak up and send a message to the world." With the help of British journalist Damien Lewis, Bashir organized her memories into a narrative that quickly drew the attention of publishers. *Tears of the Desert* was published in 2008 by Hodder & Stoughton in the United Kingdom and by Ballantine Books, a division of Random House, in the United States. Kristof called the book "extraordinary," while Getz noted its value in helping readers comprehend the reality of the war in Darfur. "It's still hard for us to get a real sense of the hideousness that has taken place there," Getz wrote. "Halima Bashir might be the person who finally pulls us through that barrier."

As of early 2009 Bashir was playing an increasingly prominent role in the global, grassroots effort to end the conflict in her native land. Though she had addressed groups in New York and other cities around the world, her base remained London, where she lived with her husband, also from Darfur, and two children. Her husband's application for permanent asylum was pending.

Selected writings

(With Damien Lewis) *Tears of the Desert: A Memoir of Survival in Darfur,* One World Ballantine Books, 2008.

Sources

Periodicals

Independent (London), December 10, 2006.
New York Times, August 31, 2008.
Newsweek, October 29, 2008.

Online

"Darfur Women Scarred by Fighting," National Public Radio, October 23, 2008, http://www.npr.org/templates/story/story.php?storyId=96023425 (accessed November 28, 2008).

—R. Anthony Kugler

Charles M. Blow

1968(?)—

Journalist

In 2008 Charles M. Blow became the first visual op-ed columnist in the history of the *New York Times.* His columns were published every other Saturday and examined current-event topics from a unique perspective, that of a visual journalist. Customarily, visual journalists create graphs and other items to accompany news stories. Using those features as the starting point for an opinion piece was something new, for both Blow and the *Times.* "We call it a visual columnist," Blow explained in an interview with George Rorick on the journalism Web site Poynter.org. "What I'm doing is using visual evidence to support arguments in persuasive essay. I use charts and maps and diagrams to support my positions." "I love it," he told Rorick. "I think it's the best job I've ever had in my life."

Blow was born in northern Louisiana, where he grew up in a family of five boys. He studied mass communications at Grambling State University, earning an honors degree and completing internships at the Wilmington (Delaware) *News Journal,* the Shreveport (Louisiana) *Times,* and the *New York Times.* His first job was as a graphic artist with the *Detroit News,* where he spent nearly two years before being offered the position of graphics editor at the *New York Times* in 1994. Over the next nine years, he rose to become director of graphics and design director for news. In the latter role Blow helped the paper to win a Best of Show award from the Society of News Design for information graphics coverage related to the September 11, 2001, terror attacks on the United States.

Blow was elevated to deputy design director at the *New York Times* but left that job in 2006 for the position of art director at *National Geographic* magazine. He returned to the *New York Times* in 2008, this time as the visual op-ed columnist, a newly created position. There were a number of op-ed writers at the paper, but Blow's column was unique in its focus on charts, graphs, and other visual means of data analysis. Blow's essays explained the information conveyed by the graphics and how they sometimes required repeated levels of examination. For example, in his column "Skirting Appalachia" in May of 2008, Blow used maps of the Appalachian states outlining their counties to discuss Democratic primary returns there. Depicting election results by color-coding the counties, he observed that Democratic Party hopeful U.S. Senator Barack Obama lost overwhelmingly to U.S. Senator Hillary Clinton in that region. Although Clinton was then predicting that she could win half the Appalachian states in the general election, Blow pointed out that Obama could carry the election without the bulk of Appalachia if he offset his losses there with wins in Virginia and Florida. "Clinton said in her [West Virginia] victory speech on Tuesday night that no Democrat has won the White House since 1916 without taking West Virginia," wrote Blow. "True. But they all could have won without it. The margins of victory in those races ranged from 23 to 515 electoral votes. West Virginia has five."

For much of 2008, Blow's twice-monthly columns centered on the presidential race and the related opinion-poll results and demographic data that come along with a major national election. In August of 2008 his column "Racism and the Race" described the results

At a Glance . . .

Born in 1968(?) in Louisiana; divorced; children: three. *Education:* Grambling State University, BA (magna cum laude).

Career: *Detroit News,* graphic artist, 1992(?)–94; *New York Times,* began as graphics editor, 1994, became director of graphics and design director for news; *National Geographic* magazine, art director, 2006–08; *New York Times,* visual op-ed columnist, 2008—.

Addresses: *Home*—Brooklyn, NY. *Office*—New York Times, 620 Eighth Ave., New York, NY 10018.

of a poll conducted at that time by the *New York Times* and CBS News. The poll asked white respondents if they would vote for an African-American candidate. Five percent said they would not; but to a second question—Would most of the people they know vote for a black candidate?—nineteen percent said that those they knew would not vote for a black candidate. "Depending on how many people they know and how well they know them, this universe of voters could be substantial," Blow wrote. The poll also asked white participants such questions as whether "in recent years, too much has been made of the problems facing blacks" (27% agreed), and whether "an Obama administration would favor blacks over whites" (16% agreed). Using a simple and elegant model of proportionately sized boxes, Blow was able to depict the variation in racial attitudes depending on the presentation of the questions. "Welcome to the murky world of modern racism," wrote Blow, "where most of the open animus has been replaced by a shadowy bias that is difficult to measure."

Blow received hundreds of e-mails in response to the essay. As he explained to Rorick, "I was bracing for some kind of a backlash on that piece. But, most of the people who responded were readers who identified themselves as white and who were basically confessing that they also knew people who refused to vote for Obama simply because he is black—and those people would not say it in public." A month later, Blow's column "Lipstick Bungle,"about Republican vice presidential candidate Sarah Palin, offered bar charts depicting the features that Republican voters most liked and disliked about the Alaskan governor. Another *New York Times*/CBS News poll, had found that most Republican voters rated Palin satisfactory. "But when asked what specifically they liked about her," Blow reported, their top five reasons were that she was honest, tough, caring, outspoken and fresh-faced. "Sounds like a talk-show host, not a vice president. (By the way, her intelligence was in a three-way tie for eighth place, right behind 'I just like her.')"

Writing three days before the election, Blow correctly predicted that Obama would win the contest on November 4. He cited as reasons the major tactical errors made by the McCain/Palin campaign in the final weeks and also former U.S. Secretary of State Colin Powell's endorsement of Obama, which crossed party lines. Blow summed up the GOP strategy as "a calamity of missteps and misfortunes. Of course, anything could happen. There are three days left. McCain could still win. And, a drunk man wearing a blindfold could get a puck past [the National Hockey League goalie] Marc-André Fleury. Yeah, unlikely. It's a wrap. Fade to black." Three days later, the NYTimes.com Web site posted a blog comment from Blow just after it was apparent Obama had won the election. He wrote, "History will record this as the night the souls of black folk, living and dead, wept—and laughed, screamed and danced—releasing 400 years of pent up emotion."

Sources

Periodicals

Essence, June 2006, p. 182.
New York Times, August 9, 2008, p. A19; September 19, 2008, p. A19; November 1, 2008, p. A23.

Online

Blow, Charles M., "And Then They Wept," NYTimes. com, November 4, 2008, http://blow.blogs. nytimes.com/2008/11/04/people-wept/ (accessed December 10, 2008).
"Columnist Biography: Charles M. Blow," NYTimes. com, 2008, http://www.nytimes.com/ref/opinion/ CHBLOW-BIO.html (accessed December 10, 2008).
Quinn, Sara Dickenson, "NYT Columnist Uses Visual Evidence to Support Persuasive Arguments" [interview by George Rorick], Poynter.org, August 28, 2008, http://www.poynter.org/column.asp?id=47 &aid=149462 (accessed December 10, 2008).

—Carol Brennan

Usain Bolt

1986—

Sprinter

Bolt, Usain, photograph. Michael Buholzer/Reuters/Landov.

Jamaican sprinter Usain Bolt electrified the world with three record-breaking performances in the 2008 Summer Olympics in Beijing, China. While Bolt also anchored the Jamaican squad that shattered the world record in the four-hundred-meter relay, it was his performance in the one-hundred- and two-hundred-meter sprints that proved most memorable. Michael Johnson, the previous record holder for the two-hundred-meter distance, said in a BBC editorial that Bolt's time of 19.30 seconds in that event "was simply incredible. This guy is Superman II."

Bolt was born in August of 1986 in Trelawny, a rural area on Jamaica's northern coast, near the tourist resorts of Montego Bay. His parents ran a small grocery store that attracted a steady stream of local children. These visitors, together with his own sister and brother, would be Bolt's companions in the impromptu games and athletic contests that dominated his childhood. "When I was young I didn't really think about anything other than sports," he told Andrew Longmore in the London *Times.* "I played cricket and football [soccer] before I turned to track and field." He made that switch shortly after entering William Knibb

Memorial High School, an institution with a distinguished track-and-field tradition.

Bolt's enormous talent, even at this early stage, was obvious. His first coach, Pablo McNeil, himself a former Olympic sprinter, had only to teach a few points of strategy and technique before the young sprinter was distinguishing himself in high school competitions across the Caribbean. For example, in 2001 he won silver medals in both the two-hundred- and four-hundred-meter sprints at the Caribbean Free Trade Association (CARIFTA) Games, an annual competition for junior athletes from Caribbean nations. That year also saw his first appearance at a competition outside the Caribbean, the 2001 World Youth Championships in Debrecen, Hungary. While he failed to qualify for the finals there, his time in the two-hundred-meter sprint was the fastest he'd ever achieved. He continued to improve steadily, and when he returned to the CARIFTA Games in 2002, he won gold medals in both the two-hundred- and four-hundred-meter events. Then, at the Central American and Caribbean Junior Championships in Bridgetown, Barbados, he set a world junior record of 20.61 seconds in the two-hundred-meter sprint. He would match that time in the 2002 World Junior

Championships (WJC), which were held in his homeland. He was still only fifteen years old.

The Jamaican media's heavy coverage of Bolt's WJC triumph drew the attention of P. J. Patterson, then the nation's prime minister. Patterson arranged for the young sprinter to move from Trelawny to Kingston, the capital, so that he could use the training facilities of the Jamaica Amateur Athletic Association. The move coincided with a coaching change, as Glen Mills, a legendary coach who had worked with Jamaica's finest runners for more than three decades, took over from McNeil.

Bolt's training throughout this period was not without its challenges. As perhaps was to be expected with someone so young, Bolt sometimes balked at the strict training regimen imposed by his coaches. Injuries, too, were also a problem. For example, even though he qualified for the two-hundred-meter sprint at the Athens Olympics in 2004, the lingering effects of a hamstring injury contributed to a disappointing performance there. However, over the next four years he steadily improved his technique, a change that both improved his performances and lessened his risk of injury. Among his most notable races during this period was the two-hundred-meter sprint at the 2007 World Championships in Osaka, Japan. While he finished second behind American Tyson Gay, his time of 19.91 seconds offered clear indication of his continued improvement. His first world record came only months later. On May 31, 2008, at the Reebok Grand Prix in New York City, Bolt ran the one-hundred-meter sprint in 9.72 seconds, breaking the mark set by his friend and compatriot Asafa Powell. While Bolt's performance in New York gave him considerable momentum as he finalized his preparations for the Olympics, it also added considerable pressure. No longer just an up-and-coming youngster, Bolt was now the man to beat.

He entered three events in Beijing: the one-hundred- and two-hundred-meter sprints and, with three team-

mates, the four-hundred-meter relay. Not only would Bolt win gold medals in all three events but also he would set—or, in the case of the relay, help to set—new world records in all three. The first event was the one-hundred-meter sprint, which Bolt won easily in 9.69 seconds. In fact, toward the end of the race, Bolt was so far ahead of his opponents that he began celebrating before reaching the finish line. This unorthodox behavior, which included looking toward the crowd and thumping his chest, caused considerable controversy. Jacques Rogge, president of the International Olympic Committee, said publicly that Bolt showed a lack of sportsmanship and a disregard for the feelings of his opponents. Bolt's supporters, however, saw his actions as an expression of joy and youthful exuberance, not an insult. Edmund Bartlett, a member of the Jamaican Parliament, expressed this view succinctly, telling Raf Casert of the Associated Press, "We have to allow the personality of youth to express itself." The controversy quickly dissipated when Bolt's opponents failed to echo Rogge's criticism.

Of Bolt's three records in Beijing, his time of 19.30 seconds in the two-hundred-meter sprint was particularly impressive. The previous mark of 19.32 seconds, set by Johnson at the 1996 Summer Olympics in Atlanta, Georgia, had been deemed one of the most difficult to break in all of track and field. "When I saw his start, and then three or four strides out," Johnson told Tim Layden in *Sports Illustrated,* "I knew with the way he was running the record was gone." This time, Bolt waited until the race was over before exulting.

As of early 2009 the future of the man called "the Lightning Bolt" was bright. At only twenty-two years old, he had many years of racing ahead of him. In the meantime, his Olympic success had brought him a number of lucrative endorsement deals, including a large bonus from Puma, a sneaker manufacturer. Whatever the course of his future career, his place in the history of track and field was assured. Stephen Francis, Powell's coach, expressed the feelings of all who watched Bolt's Beijing performances. "You have people who are exceptions," he told Lynn Zinser in the *New York Times.* "You have Einstein. You have Isaac Newton. You have Beethoven. You have Usain Bolt. It's not explainable how and what they do."

Sources

Periodicals

Associated Press, August 23, 2008.
New York Times, August 20, 2008.
Sports Illustrated, September 1, 2008.
Times (London), August 24, 2008.

Online

"Athletes: Usain Bolt—Bio," NBC Universal, http://www.nbcolympics.com/athletes/athlete=271/bio/ (accessed November 28, 2008).

Johnson, Michael, "Michael Johnson on Usain Bolt," *BBC News,* August 20, 2008, http://news.bbc.co.uk/sport2/hi/olympics/athletics/7572854.stm (accessed November 28, 2008).

"Usain Bolt," ESPN, http://sports.espn.go.com/oly/summer08/fanguide/athlete?athlete=52386 (accessed November 30, 2008).

—R. Anthony Kugler

Melanie Brown

1975—

Singer, actor

Brown, Melanie, photograph. AP Images.

As part of the British pop act the Spice Girls, Melanie Brown was known as Scary Spice during her run at the top of the music charts in the mid-1990s. At the time, the Spice Girls were the most successful all-female pop act in recording history, and all five members of the group became immensely wealthy from their record sales, movies, concert tours, and merchandising tie-ins. "People always used to say that we were manufactured, but in actual fact we were the ones that did all the shouting and made all our own rules," Brown told Libby Brooks in the (London) *Guardian.*

Brown was born in 1975 in Leeds, one of the larger cities in the north of England. Her father was of African Caribbean heritage and her mother was white. Brown grew up on a council estate, as public housing is known in Britain, and recalled that as a child she was troubled by her biracial heritage. "You can't pick up a book of mixed-race culture and identify with it because there isn't one," she said in the *Guardian* interview. "I was searching to feel that identity connection with a colour, a race, a culture, anything."

Found Success with the Spice Girls

Brown became friends with Geri Halliwell and Victoria Adams when the trio were picked for a planned all-female pop act after each answered a newspaper ad for singers and dancers in early 1994. They were soon joined by another Melanie—Melanie Chisholm, also known as "Mel C."—and then recruited a fifth member, Emma Bunton. After a falling-out with the management team that had originally auditioned them, the quintet took some demo songs they had already recorded and began searching for new promoters. They secured the services of music impresario Simon Fuller, who negotiated an advantageous deal with Virgin Records in September of 1995. The singer's stage names—Scary Spice (Brown), Baby Spice (Bunton), Posh Spice (Adams), Ginger Spice (Halliwell), and Sporty Spice (Chisholm)—were bestowed by a music magazine. "I've got a loud laugh and I'm lively, so they called me Scary," Brown explained in an interview with Lester Middlehurst in the (London) *Daily Mail.* "I never quite understood why, but it worked because people were

At a Glance . . .

Born Melanie Janine Brown on May 29, 1975, in Leeds, West Yorkshire, England; married Jimmy Gulzar (a dancer), September 13, 1998 (divorced, 2001); married Stephen Belafonte (a film and television producer), June 6, 2007; children: (first marriage) Phoenix Chi; (with Eddie Murphy) Angel Iris Murphy.

Career: Founding member of the Spice Girls, 1994; signed to Virgin Records, 1995; with group, released debut LP, *Spice,* 1996, and made feature film debut in *Spice World,* 1997; released first solo record, *Hot,* in 2000; co-hosted the TLC television program *The Singing Office* with Joey Fatone, for which she was executive producer with Stephen Belafonte, 2008—.

Addresses: *Home*—Los Angeles, CA. *Agent*—Creative Artists Agency, 2000 Avenue of the Stars, Los Angeles, CA 90067. *Publicist*—The Outside Organization, Butler House, 177–178 Tottenham Court Rd., London W1T 7BY, England.

scared of me before I even spoke to them. It acted as a good deterrent so people didn't try to mess with me."

The Spice Girls' debut single and video, "Wannabe," was released in July of 1996 and made them England's biggest pop stars virtually overnight. Its catchy, infectious lyrics conveyed a message of quasi-feminist unity and verve which they called "Girl Power": " If you wanna be my lover, you gotta get with my friends / Make it last forever, friendship never ends / If you wanna be my lover, you have got to give / Taking is too easy, but that's the way it is." The song spent seven weeks in the No. 1 spot on the British singles chart, and helped propel their debut album, *Spice,* to worldwide sales of twenty-three million units, the highest ever achieved by an all-female group.

In early 1997 Brown and her bandmates set out to conquer America, where *Spice* also peaked at No. 1 and sold seven million copies. Part of the group's appeal, theorized Christopher John Farley in *Time* magazine, was the fact that they seemed accessible. "Perhaps it's because they are just shy of gorgeous that they are so popular," Farley wrote. "They are earthly beings, approachable, and could almost exist in real life." Musically, they were not breaking any new ground, Farley asserted. "On record, as vocalists, the girls are harder to tell apart. Only Mel B., whose voice has a bit of grit, stands out; the rest have bright, slight voices, more light than heat, more Wilson Phillips than

En Vogue. It's also disconcerting that the Girls' accents disappear when they sing, only to reappear during spoken-word segments."

Embarked on a Solo Career

Spice produced a few other hit singles, including "Say You'll Be There," and remained in the top ten of the U.K. album charts for more than a year. Brown and her bandmates earned millions from record sales, merchandising tie-ins, and video sales. Their follow-up album, *Spice World,* was released in the fall of 1997 and was accompanied by a lighthearted feature film of the same name. The second LP spent three weeks at the No. 1 spot on the British album charts, and the film earned more than $10 million in its opening weekend in the United States. Yet despite these successes, the group decided to fire their manager, Simon Fuller, and take over his duties themselves. Brown and Halliwell were reportedly unhappy with Fuller and convinced the other three to side with them in ousting him. Then in May of 1998, Halliwell quit the band. The remaining four kept their final tour dates, but did not film further videos because of Halliwell's absence. The group did not maintain the momentum of its early chart success, and in 2001 the Spice Girls issued a statement explaining that they would be taking a break to concentrate on solo projects.

Brown had already released her solo debut album, *Hot,* on Virgin Records in the fall of 2000, but critics drubbed it, and it peaked at No. 28 in Britain. A music video for its third single featuring her infant daughter, Phoenix, was roundly criticized in the British press. Virgin dropped her, and little more was heard from Brown until the spring of 2004, when she was cast as Mimi in the hit Broadway musical *Rent.* A year later, her second solo record, *L.A. State of Mind,* released on Amber Café Records, fared even worse on the charts than its predecessor.

Brown's private life was also marked by personal difficulties during this time. In September of 1998 she wed dancer Jimmy Gulzar. Their daughter Phoenix was born in February of 1999, but the union with Gulzar ended in 2000, and Brown reportedly paid him a large settlement to secure permanent custody of their daughter.

Performed in Reality Television Projects

By 2003 Brown was living in Los Angeles, where she was able to lead a more anonymous life than she would have in Britain. The singer reappeared in the gossip columns in 2007 when she gave birth to a second daughter, named Angel Iris, whose father, Brown divulged, was comedian Eddie Murphy. The pair had dated during the summer of 2006. Murphy denied that he was the father, but genetic testing proved that he was. Brown filed suit in California for child support, telling Marti Parham in *Jet,* "I have nothing bad to say about him—for the guy that he was when I was with him. He was nice. Really nice."

In June of 2007 Brown wed film producer Stephen Belafonte, whom she had known for several years. A year later, their jointly produced reality-television series, *The Singing Office,* premiered on the basic cable channel TLC. Brown also appeared on the hit ABC series *Dancing with the Stars,* where she and partner Maksim Chmerkovskiy reached the finals before losing to Hélio Castroneves and Julianne Hough.

In December of 2007 the Spice Girls reunited for an eleven-concert tour that countered persistent rumors of alienation among the group members. "The fact is that we are all still good friends," Brown told Middlehurst in the *Daily Mail,* "and we do speak to each other, although, perhaps, not as much as we should."

Selected works

Albums, with Spice Girls

Spice, Virgin Records, 1996.
Spice World, Virgin Records, 1997.
Forever, Virgin Records, 2000.

Albums, solo

Hot, Virgin Records, 2000.
L.A. State of Mind, Amber Café Records, 2005.

Films

Spice World, 1997.
Spice Power, 1997.
The Spice Girls in America: A Tour Story, 1999.
LD 50 Lethal Dose, 2003.
The Seat Filler, 2004.
Telling Lies, 2006.
Love Thy Neighbor, 2006.

Theater

The Vagina Monologues, Ambassador Theater, London, 2002.
Rent, Nederlander Theatre, New York City, 2004.

Books

Catch a Fire: The Autobiography, Headline Books, 2002.

Sources

Periodicals

Daily Mail (London), June 4, 2005, p. 6.
Forbes, September 22, 1997, p. 186.
Guardian (London), March 19, 2002, p. 8.
Jet, October 1, 2007, p. 62.
Newsweek, November 12, 2007, p. 89.
People, August 20, 2007, p. 70.
Time, February 3, 1997, p. 68.

—Carol Brennan

Nappy Brown

1929–2008

Vocalist

Brown, Nappy, photograph. Michael Ochs Archives/Getty Images.

Though Nappy Brown grew up singing gospel hymns, it was as a singer of the blues that he first rose to national prominence in the 1950s. His lush arrangements and innovative vocal style were major influences in the development of rhythm and blues (R&B), a genre then in its infancy. After dropping out of the music business in 1962, he lived a private life for two decades, emerging again only at the behest of fans in the early 1980s. While the strength of that comeback eventually waned, the release of the critically acclaimed album *Long Time Coming* in 2007 revived his fortunes again, and at the time of his death the following year he was enjoying some of the greatest success of his career.

Born Napoleon Brown Goodson Culp in October of 1929 in Charlotte, North Carolina, he would live in that city for most of his life. His exposure to music began with church services in early childhood. His father sang in the choir of Charlotte's First Mount Zion Baptist Church, and the rhythms and cadences of the gospel music he heard there as a boy would have a lifelong influence. His own vocal abilities were quickly recognized, and by the age of nine he had taken his place in the choir alongside his father. As a teenager, he formed a gospel group, the Golden Crowns, with some cousins. "That was the first group I had," Brown would later tell music critic Bill Dahl in a profile posted on the Blind Pig Records Web site. "I was real young then. I was about 16 years old." After moving on to another gospel group, the Golden Bell Quintet, Brown joined one of the genre's best-known groups, the Selah Jubilee Singers, then based in Raleigh, North Carolina. Though the group made a number of recordings and was often heard on radio broadcasts, Brown and the other members often had to take odd jobs to make ends meet.

In 1954 Brown's fortunes improved dramatically when he was invited to Newark, New Jersey, to join the Heavenly Light Gospel Singers. Shortly after his arrival, the group had an audition with Herman Lubinsky, owner of the Savoy record label. After listening to Brown's powerful and resonant voice, Lubinsky asked him if he would consider switching from gospel to the blues. "I was just a poor boy from the South and wanted to make some money," Brown would later recall in remarks quoted by Tony Russell in the London *Guardian*. "So I said yes." Brown was a gospel singer

At a Glance . . .

Born Napoleon Brown Goodson Culp on October 12, 1929, in Charlotte, NC; died on September 20, 2008, in Charlotte; children: four.

Career: Vocalist with various gospel groups, 1940s–54; solo recording artist for Savoy Records, 1954–62; solo performer, 1980s–2008.

Awards: Nominated for Blues Music Award for traditional blues album of the year and traditional blues male artist of the year, Blues Foundation, 2008, for *Long Time Coming.*

by training, but he had long enjoyed listening to the blues, which lacked gospel's religious overtones but shared its emphasis on vocal strength and its ability to evoke raw emotion. Among the blues performers Brown would later cite as a major influence was Charles Brown, a California singer who preferred lush, jazzlike orchestral arrangements to the spare, guitar-driven style that was typical at the time. Nappy Brown also preferred a fuller sound. Therefore, like his slightly older namesake, he is often considered a pioneer of R&B.

With the backing of several highly regarded session musicians, notably saxophonist Sam Taylor, Brown quickly made a number of recordings for Savoy, including his first major hit, 1954's *Don't Be Angry,* which rose to number twenty-five on *Billboard*'s pop chart and to number two on its R&B chart. The album featured the wordplay and idiosyncratic pronunciations that would become Brown's trademark, including his habit of adding "-li" or "-la" to the ends of words. While these extra syllables undoubtedly helped him synchronize the lyrics with the rhythm of the music, they also served to set his records apart in an increasingly crowded and competitive market. According to Ben Sisario in the *New York Times,* Brown conceived the idea while listening to foreign-language radio broadcasts.

Brown would remain with Savoy until the end of 1962. While a number of the songs he arranged and recorded for the company became hits, he never achieved the celebrity status of other performers in the blues tradition, notably pianist and vocalist Ray Charles. Perhaps the most striking example of this dichotomy came in 1959, when Charles had a major hit with the song "(Night Time Is) The Right Time," which Brown had written and recorded earlier with only modest success. Brown would later attribute Charles's achievement to the pianist's use of female backup singers instead of the

male gospel chorus he himself had used. In his recollection of the incident to Gene Tomko in *Charlotte Magazine,* Brown said, "It felt good [Charles] had covered it. That still was good for me." Tomko added that Brown made these comments "with a sly wink and a jingle of his pocket, signifying the royalties he's received."

In 1962 Brown left Savoy and returned to private life in North Carolina. The reasons for his abrupt departure have never been entirely clear, but Brown would later say that he had simply tired of the music business. After returning to his hometown, he held a variety of jobs, including circus elephant handler. His musical activities, meanwhile, were limited to occasional, noncommercial gospel performances. After roughly two decades of relative obscurity, however, he enjoyed a remarkable comeback in the early 1980s, when European fans of his Savoy recordings convinced him to go on a number of overseas tours. A series of U.S. concerts followed, as did the release of several new albums, including 1987's highly regarded *Something Gonna Jump out the Bushes.* He continued to release albums throughout the 1990s, but they were less successful, both critically and commercially.

In 2007 he staged a second comeback with the release of *Long Time Coming,* which Scott Yanow on the allmusic Web site called a "spirited set" that showed the singer "at the top of his game." At the age of seventy-eight Brown found himself in the spotlight once more, with a prominent appearance on the popular National Public Radio program *Prairie Home Companion* and two Blues Music Award nominations from the Blues Foundation. His performance at the foundation's award ceremony in May of 2008 proved to be one of his last. After several months of hospitalization, he died of respiratory failure on September 20, 2008. Surviving him were two sons, two daughters, and several grandchildren. Toward the end of his life he often expressed his gratitude to critics and fans for their renewed interest in his work. As his producer, Scott Cable, told Russell, Brown "always felt very lucky to have a second chance."

Selected discography

Don't Be Angry, Savoy Jazz, 1954.
Nappy Brown Sings, Savoy, 1955.
The Right Time, Savoy, 1958.
I Done Got Over, Stockholm, 1983.
Tore Up, Alligator, 1984.
Something Gonna Jump out the Bushes, Black Top, 1987.
Apples & Lemons, Ichiban, 1990.
I'm a Wild Man, New Moon, 1995.
Who's Been Foolin' You, New Moon, 1997.
Long Time Coming, Blind Pig, 2007.

Sources

Periodicals

Charlotte Magazine, March 1, 2008.
Guardian (London), September 26, 2008.
New York Times, September 25, 2008.

Online

Dahl, Bill, "Nappy Brown," Blind Pig Records, http://www.blindpigrecords.com/index.cfm?section=art ists&artistid=82 (accessed December 1, 2008).
Dahl, Bill, "Nappy Brown: Biography," allmusic, http://allmusic.com/cg/amg.dll?p=amg&sql=11:gifoxq 95ldje~T1 (accessed December 1, 2008).
Yanow, Scott, "*Long Time Coming*: Review," allmusic, http://allmusic.com/cg/amg.dll?p=amg&sql=10:gifrxzrhldte (accessed December 1, 2008).

—R. Anthony Kugler

Nick Cannon

1980—

Actor, comedian, musician

Nick Cannon is a multitalented entertainer whose broad appeal has led to his success in films and television and music. In addition to performing, he has also written and produced material for television and film and has written and recorded an album. Attractive, charming, and a self-described workaholic, Cannon "has the looks, talent and intelligence to be a star for as long as he wants," according to *Jet*.

Started as a Stand-up Comic

Cannon, Nick, photograph. AP Images.

Born on October 17, 1980, in San Diego, California, Cannon was raised there by his mother, Beth Hackett, and his paternal grandmother. He also spent time with his father, James Cannon, in North Carolina. A natural performer, he auditioned for the television program *It's Showtime at the Apollo* when he was eleven years old. Soon afterward he made his first appearance as a stand-up comic on his father's religion program on public access television. "People probably thought I was cute more than they thought my jokes were funny," he recalled to Soren Baker in the *Los Angeles Times*.

During his teens Cannon lived in California with his mother. Though he was attracted to show business, his mother insisted that he finish high school before trying to launch his entertainment career. He graduated from Monte Vista High School in 1998, and began to appear in comedy clubs in Los Angeles. An agent discovered him there and got him a job with the Nickelodeon television network, where he appeared as a warm-up act performing for studio audiences at tapings of the hit series *All That*. Cannon was such a success that Nickelodeon gave him his own comedy show in 2002. He served as a writer and executive producer for the *Nick Cannon Show,* and also wrote for such programs as *Keenan & Kel* and *Cousin Skeeter.*

Cannon's stand-up appearances also caught the eye of actor and producer Will Smith, who got the young performer a small role in the hit movie *Men in Black II.* Smith also produced a TV pilot starring Cannon for the WB network.

Won Acclaim in Drumline Role

Cannon landed his first starring role in the film *Drumline* (2002). Cannon played Devon Miles, a drummer

At a Glance . . .

Born Nicholas Scott Cannon on October 17, 1980, in San Diego, CA; son of James Cannon (a minister) and Beth Hackett (an accountant); married Mariah Carey (a singer), April 30, 2008.

Career: Actor, comedian, and musician, 1998—; Nick Cannon Youth Foundation, founder and director.

Addresses: *Agent*—c/o Miramax, 375 Greenwich St., New York, NY 10013.

from Harlem who receives a scholarship to the fictitious Atlanta A&T University, a historically black university with a marching band that needs some new energy. Devon is a bright talent, but resists the authority of the band director and provokes a fierce competition with the team's lead drummer. He also develops a romantic interest in the head cheerleader. "Obviously, he's kicked off the team," wrote Wesley Morris in the *Boston Globe,* "and obviously, he'll be redeemed in time for the Classic."

Despite *Drumline*'s predictable plot, critics found much to praise in the film, particularly its focus on African-American college life—a subject rarely seen in contemporary cinema. In the *New York Times,* reviewer A. O. Scott judged Cannon an "engaging lead actor," and in the *Los Angeles Times* Kenneth Turan noted that the filmmakers were "smart in picking its lively, likable cast, starting with Nick Cannon."

Drumline proved Cannon's potential as an actor, but also established his crossover appeal. The film, which grossed $13 million in its opening weekend and totaled more than $55 million domestically, drew an audience that was about 60 percent black and 40 percent non-black. According to Baker in the *Los Angeles Times,* the film was part of a "seismic shift in the way young black men are portrayed in cinema" and "helped show that young black men could carry a drama that focused on driven college kids rather than gangs and guns."

Found Further Success in Film

Cannon again played a wholesome character in his next film, *Love Don't Cost a Thing.* He portrayed Alvin Johnson, a gifted student from a supportive family, who pays a popular girl to let him date her so that he can gain friends and status at his high school. Reviewers admired Cannon's ability to show how Alvin changes from an awkward and earnest young man to an obnoxious showoff once he becomes popular. Baker wrote that Cannon brought "a good deal of

charm to both Johnson incarnations, making it hard to dislike the guy who abandons his lifelong friends, disobeys his supportive mother and even turns on [the girl] once his popularity swells." Cannon explained to Baker that he enjoyed finding depth in this character: "I always try to figure out, even if he's a bad character or a jerk: What can you love about this character? If you can find that good, innocent side within that character, then that's where the money is."

In 2007 Cannon played a supporting role in *Even Money,* a grim film chronicling gambling addition. Cannon portrayed Godfrey, a college basketball star who is pressured by his brother Clyde (Forrest Whitaker) to shave points in order to clear a debt to a bookie. Stephen Holden in the *New York Times* praised Cannon's performance in what he otherwise considered a mediocre film: "The volatile mix of devotion and desperation in Clyde and Godfrey's fraternal bond has a raw poignancy that is missing from the rest of the movie."

Cannon continued to act in film projects in 2008 and 2009, including performances in *Day of the Dead, Ball Don't Lie,* and the dramatic thriller*The Killing Room. American Son,* in which Cannon played a Marine on a four-day Thanksgiving leave, premiered at the Sundance Film Festival in 2008.

Pursued Music, Writing, Film Production

Cannon, who plays drums, synthesizer, and harmonica, has also incorporated his music into his many of his creative ventures. He composed the theme song to his self-titled TV series, and also wrote "Shorty Put It to the Floor" for *Love Don't Cost a Thing.* His cover of "Parents Just Don't Understand" was included on the soundtrack to Nickelodeon's feature film *Jimmy Neutron: Boy Genius* (2001). His song "I'm Scared of You" was included on the *Drumline* soundtrack.

In 2003 Cannon released his first compact disc, *Nick Cannon.* Singles from the album, including "Your Pops Don't Like Me" and "Feelin' Freaky," received considerable airplay on music cable channels, as did the hit song and video "Gigolo."

In addition to his music and acting, Cannon worked as a film producer and screenwriter. He executive-produced and wrote the treatment for *The Underclassman,* an action-comedy in which he also starred. He also served as executive producer for *The Beltway,* a political thriller that provided him a change of pace from his usual comedic roles.

Shared His Success with Others

Cannon told Linda Lee in the *New York Times* that "If I stay in one place too long or do one thing too long, my bones ache." Though he enjoyed partying in his teens, he now prefers sharper focus on his work. "I can't go out anymore," he explained. "Now I'm a workaholic." In fact, Cannon shows no signs of slowing his performing pace.

With the help of his father, a minister and motivational speaker, Cannon established the Nick Cannon Youth Foundation, which hosts inspirational conventions for young men. The actor hopes to inspire young people to aim for creative success while maintaining a positive life. "I'm taking my career into my own hands," he told *Ebony.* "I have a focus and a vision [now] that nobody can bring to pass but me."

In 2008 Cannon married singer Mariah Carey in a private ceremony at her estate on Windermere Island in the Bahamas. Though some cynics predicted a short union, the couple spoke glowingly of each other in January of 2009 as each debuted movies at the Sundance Film Festival. Carey told Jerry Penacoli on ExtraTV, "The secret to me is realizing when you meet the right person and being brave enough to dive in and say this is the right person for me. We have fun like nobody's business." Cannon praised his wife, saying, "I'm blessed to have a partner that's truly one of those people that affect the world."

Selected works

Films

Whatever It Takes, 2000.
Men in Black II, 2002.
Drumline, 2002.
Love Don't Cost a Thing, 2003.
Shall We Dance?, 2004.
Garfield, 2004.
The Beltway, 2005.
Roll Bounce, 2005.
The Underclassman, 2005.
Bobby, 2006.

Monster House, 2006.
Even Money, 2007.
American Son, 2008.

Television

All That, 1998–2000.
The Nick Cannon Show, 2002.
Nick Cannon Presents Wild 'n' Out, 2005–07.
Nick Cannon Presents: Short Circuitz, 2007.

Recordings

Nick Cannon, Jive Records, 2003.

Sources

Periodicals

Boston Globe, December 13, 2002, p. E7; December 12, 2003, p. E5.
Ebony, February 2004, p. 22.
Jet, January 12, 2004, p. 65.
Los Angeles Times, January 19, 2002, p. F30; December 13, 2002, p. E12; December 16, 2002, p. E1; December 11, 2003, p. E20.
New York Times, December 13, 2002; December 22, 2002; December 12, 2003; July 21, 2006; May 18, 2007.
People, May 2, 2008; May 8, 2008.

Online

"Mariah: Is She or Isn't She," ExtraTV, January 19, 2009, http://extratv.warnerbros.com/2009/01/mariah_is_she_or_isnt_she.php (accessed January 25, 2009).
Murray, Rebecca, "Hard-Working Nick Cannon on Life, Work, and Staying Grounded," About.com, 2004, http://movies.about.com/od/irobot/a/robotnc070704.htm (accessed January 26, 2009).

—E. Shostak and Melissa Doak

J. L. Chestnut Jr.

1930–2008

Lawyer, civil rights activist

An unsung hero of the civil rights movement, J. L. Chestnut Jr. provided crucial legal services to hundreds of peaceful protestors arrested in and around his birthplace of Selma, Alabama. As their courtroom representative, Chestnut was frequently called on to articulate their grievances before antagonistic, even hostile, judges. While best known for his courageous behavior during the dramatic and often violent confrontations that erupted in Selma in 1965, Chestnut exhibited a commitment to equality for all citizens that would continue for another four decades.

J. L. Chestnut Jr.—the initials were not abbreviations—was born in December of 1930. His parents, a grocery store owner and a schoolteacher, were respected leaders of Selma's close-knit African-American community. Known around town as a mischievous child and talented saxophone player, Chestnut attended schools in a segregated education system he quickly grew to detest for its fundamental unfairness. In high school he encountered teacher John F. Shields, who, after hearing Chestnut's frustrations with the outdated textbooks and inferior facilities that were characteristic of segregation, advised him to become an attorney and fight for equality through the courts. Chestnut never forgot the advice, which would shape the course of his life.

After high school he entered Dillard University, a predominately African-American institution in New Orleans, Louisiana, and graduated with a bachelor's degree in 1953. He then traveled north to Washington, DC, where he entered law school at Howard University, another African-American institution. He did so just as Thurgood Marshall and other African-American lawyers were preparing to present their case, *Brown v. Board of Education,* before the U.S. Supreme Court. The Court's 1954 decision in that case would declare racial segregation in education unconstitutional. While he was inspired by this victory, Chestnut knew that it was only a beginning and that much of the work to achieve racial equality would have to be done not in Washington but deep in the rural South. Therefore, after receiving his law degree in 1958, he decided to forego a lucrative career in the North and return to Selma.

Chestnut would be the first African-American attorney in the town's history, and one of only five in the state of Alabama at the time. His arrival "in eerily placid Selma," wrote Diane McWhorter in the *New York Times,* was like that of "a rogue elephant." White opposition to his presence was formidable. Chestnut would later recall, for example, that the local bar association conspired with the town's banks to deny him a loan he needed to establish his practice. He persisted, however, and quickly became known for his legal acumen, personal charisma, and effective courtroom technique. While white judges often tried to humiliate him by, for example, forcing him to sit in the rear of the courtroom, he took care to maintain his composure.

The most difficult test of Chestnut's skills and fortitude would come in the mid-1960s, when Selma became the epicenter of the civil rights struggle. The reasons for the town's prominence in this regard were complex, but a major factor was the presence of a particularly brutal sheriff, Jim Clark, who was systematically repressing the voting rights of African Americans. Therefore, as the struggle began to shift from segregation to voting rights, Selma seemed a logical place to start. Activists from Martin Luther King Jr.'s Southern Christian Leadership Conference and other organizations descended on the town to register voters and draw attention to Clark's abuses. Hundreds were thrown into jail, and it was Chestnut, by and large, who got them released and represented them in county courts. The turning point in the campaign came on March 7, 1965, when Clark's forces used violence to stop a peaceful march across Selma's Edmund Pettus Bridge. Known as Bloody Sunday, the event outraged the nation and galvanized support in Congress for what became the Voting Rights Act of 1965.

As crucial as Chestnut's efforts were to the success of the Selma campaign, his career was not without difficulties during this period. Most notable was a serious drinking problem, which he discussed forthrightly in a 1990 autobiography he wrote with the assistance of Julia Cass. By 1972 he had overcome his addiction and was able to begin the next phase of his career with the founding of Chestnut, Sanders, and Sanders (later Chestnut, Sanders, Sanders, and Pettway), which would be the largest African-American law firm in the state for many years. Civil rights issues continued to be a focus of his practice, and he filed a number of lawsuits to force the implementation of the gains won in principle during the active phase of the struggle. Among these were suits to desegregate the public schools in and around Selma and to increase the presence of African Americans on local juries. In the 1990s he was the lead attorney in a major antidiscrimi-

nation lawsuit against the U.S. Department of Agriculture (USDA). Known as *Pigford v. Glickman,* the suit charged that the USDA had denied agricultural subsidies to more than sixty thousand African-American farmers solely on the basis of race. Chestnut obtained a settlement, approved by a federal judge in 2000, that resulted in almost $1 billion in compensation for the plaintiffs.

As he grew older, Chestnut became increasingly involved in politics and public affairs. For example, in 1985 he joined with one of his law partners, Hank Sanders, to build the first radio station in Selma aimed at African-American audiences. He hosted a call-in talk show about politics that quickly became one of the station's most popular programs. Three years later he was a founding chair of the Alabama New South Coalition, an organization aimed at increasing the involvement of African Americans at all levels of state government.

Chestnut died of kidney failure on September 30, 2008, in Birmingham, Alabama, at the age of seventy-seven. Surviving him were his wife, Vivian, six children, and a number of grandchildren and great-grandchildren. News of his death prompted tributes from across the nation. U.S. representative John Lewis, himself a veteran of the civil rights movement, told Bruce Weber in the *New York Times,* "I don't know what would have happened to us in Selma if it wasn't for Chestnut," adding that Chestnut "was a brave and courageous man" who "used the law to help liberate the black folk of Alabama."

Selected works

(With Julia Cass) *Black in Selma: The Uncommon Life of J. L. Chestnut Jr.,* Farrar, Straus, and Giroux, 1990.

Sources

Periodicals

Montgomery Advertiser (Montgomery, AL), October 21, 2008.
New York Times, August 26, 1990; October 1, 2008.
Washington Post, October 2, 2008, p. B7.

Online

"J. L. Chestnut," *George Wallace: Settin' the Woods on Fire,* 2000, http://www.pbs.org/wgbh/amex/wallace/filmmore/reference/interview/chestnut01.html (accessed December 1, 2008).

—R. Anthony Kugler

Zoanne Clack

1968(?)—

Physician, television screenplay writer, editor, producer

Zoanne Clack has managed to combine two very different professions, medicine and entertainment, to a degree few can rival. After medical school Clack used her training in a variety of settings, from the emergency rooms of local hospitals to remote Pacific islands where few such facilities existed. She nevertheless felt unfulfilled, so in 2000 she moved to Hollywood, California, to start a new career as a television executive. There, she quickly found that her medical expertise was in high demand among the producers of medical dramas, one of television's most successful genres. As of early 2009 the program to which she had the closest ties remained *Grey's Anatomy,* a popular and long-running series on ABC.

Clack was born in about 1968 in Missouri City, Texas, a suburb of Houston. The only child of a single mother who often had to work two jobs, Clack spent a good deal of time alone as a child. She quickly grew fond of reading and television. "I was raised by television," Clack told Manuel Mendoza in the *Dallas Morning News.* "TV was my friend. It was nurturing." After high school she entered Northwestern University, where her interest in television led her to declare a major in radio, television, and film soon after her arrival. After consulting with her mother, however, Clack came to the conclusion that television was an uncertain industry and that her education should therefore be directed toward the relative stability of a career in medicine. She changed her major accordingly, and the degree she received upon graduation in 1990 was a bachelor's in communication studies, with a concentration in neurobiology.

Following graduation, Clack immediately entered medical school at the University of Texas, Southwestern, as that university system's medical campus in Dallas is known. While there, she developed an interest in emergency medicine, and it was in that field that she did her residency, after receiving her medical degree in 1994. The site of that training, Emory University in Atlanta, would remain her home for several years, for after completing her residency she won an Emory fellowship to study injury prevention. That study, in turn, led to a master's of public health in behavioral sciences from Emory's Rollins School of Public Health. Clack then spent roughly a year working for the federal government's Centers for Disease Control and Prevention (CDC). Her work for the CDC involved improving emergency medicine programs in two international locations. One was Palau, an isolated island nation in the Pacific; the other was the East African nation of Tanzania. The need for improvement in the latter was particularly clear after terrorists bombed the U.S. embassy there in August of 1998. Nearly a dozen people died, several of whom might have survived if emergency procedures in the Tanzanian capital of Dar es Salaam had been up to international standards. In this challenging environment Clack helped local administrators improve their response to natural and manmade disasters.

Despite an awareness of the importance of her medical work, Clack felt unfulfilled professionally, particularly after she left the CDC and began taking shifts in the emergency rooms of local hospitals. "I wasn't finding my niche in medicine. It wasn't where I thought I

At a Glance . . .

Born in Missouri City, TX, in 1968(?). *Education:* Northwestern University, BA, communication studies (concentration in neurobiology), 1990; University of Texas, Southwestern, MD, 1994; Emory University, MPH, behavioral sciences, 1996; University of California, Los Angeles, several courses in acting, screenwriting, and television producing, 2000–02.

Career: Emory University, residency in emergency medicine, 1994–95, medical fellowship (injury prevention), 1995–96; Centers for Disease Control and Prevention, Program in International Emergency Medicine, 1998; Beverly Hospital, Montebello, CA, emergency room physician, early 2000s—; *Presidio Med* (television series), writer, 2002; *ER* (television series), medical supervisor, 2003–04; *Grey's Anatomy* (television series), writer, 2004—, story editor, 2005, executive story editor, 2005–06, coproducer, 2006–07, producer, 2007—.

Memberships: American College of Emergency Physicians, Student National Medical Association (board member).

Awards: Scroll of Merit Award, National Medical Association, 2006; Writers Guild Award for best new television series (cowinner), Writers Guild of America, 2006, for *Grey's Anatomy;* Alpha Kappa Alpha Sorority, honorary membership, 2008.

Addresses: *Office*—c/o Emergency Department, Beverly Hospital, 309 W. Beverly Blvd., Montebello, CA 90640.

written on speculation. The series proved short lived, but it brought her to the attention of the producers of *ER,* another medical drama that was then one of the longest-running shows on television. Clack would serve for several seasons as *ER*'s medical supervisor, working to ensure that the medical procedures depicted on screen were accurate and the outcomes plausible. That position led to Clack's involvement in the program for which she later become best known: *Grey's Anatomy.*

In 2004 programming executives at ABC decided to capitalize on the public's continued interest in programs such as *ER* with a hospital show of their own. Called *Grey's Anatomy* after a famous medical school textbook, it would focus on the personal and professional lives of surgeons in a large Seattle hospital. Clack was hired as a writer while the show was still in the planning stages. She quickly received a series of promotions, though she would continue to write scripts occasionally. By 2007 she had served as a story editor, executive story editor, coproducer, and producer. The show, meanwhile, proved a critical and commercial success, winning a number of Emmy awards and other honors. One of these, the 2006 Writers Guild Award for best new television series, specifically honored Clack and her fellow scriptwriters. Two years later Clack won honorary membership into the Alpha Kappa Alpha Sorority (AKA), one of the nation's oldest and best-known organizations of African-American women. According to the AKA, Clack was recognized for her "commitment to service," particularly her willingness to incorporate important public health messages into *Grey's Anatomy* storylines. The AKA also applauded her leadership as a board member of the Student National Medical Association, an organization devoted to improving diversity and cultural sensitivity in medicine and medical education.

As it began its fifth season in the fall of 2008, *Grey's Anatomy* remained one of the most prominent dramas on network television, and Clack's position in the entertainment industry seemed assured. She also continued to work regularly at Beverly Hospital. Though these shifts have placed heavy demands on her schedule, they have also enabled her to portray the world of medicine on television with a vivid, sometimes gritty, realism that has captivated viewers across the nation.

Sources

Periodicals

Dallas Morning News, August 8, 2006.

Online

"Centennial Honorary Members," Alpha Kappa Alpha Sorority, 2008, http://www.aka1908.com/news/2008honorary/ (accessed December 1, 2008).
"Dr. Zoanne Clack," Northwestern University, http://www.northwestern.edu/aasa/clack_bio.doc (accessed December 1, 2008).

wanted to be," she told Mendoza. Realizing that her interest in entertainment, particularly in television, was still strong, she moved to Hollywood in 2000 and began taking classes in acting, scriptwriting, and television production at the University of California, Los Angeles. To support herself and to maintain her medical training, she took a job as an emergency room physician at Beverly Hospital, a small community facility in Montebello, east of Hollywood.

Her first major success in her new career came in 2002, when the producers of *Presidio Med,* a new television series set in a San Francisco hospital, hired her as a staff writer on the basis of two scripts she had

"Zoanne Clack," Black Voices, December 12, 2005, http://www.blackvoices.com/black_entertainment/ television_features_reviews_clips/featurecanvas/_a/ zoanne-clack/20051212153309990001 (accessed December 1, 2008).

"Zoanne Clack," Northwestern Luminaries, February 15, 2008, http://nuluminaries.blogspot.com/2008 /02/zoanne-clack.html (accessed December 1, 2008).

—R. Anthony Kugler

Lisa Cooper

1963—

Physician, educator

Lisa Cooper is an internationally recognized physician who has conducted groundbreaking studies of the crucial role that race and ethnicity play in doctor–patient relationships and the way clinical communication influences medical treatment. Even in the twenty-first century, African Americans continue to experience very different health outcomes from white Americans: They experience shorter life expectancies, die of cancer and heart disease at higher rates, and are less likely to seek needed medical care. These health disparities are the focus of Cooper's medical research. For her pioneering work, she received a coveted "genius grant" from the MacArthur Foundation in 2007, placing her among the nation's top creative minds.

Lisa Angeline Cooper was born on April 12, 1963, in Monrovia, the capital city of Liberia, located on the coast of West Africa. She grew up in a wealthy household in Liberia, where her mother worked as a research librarian and her father was a prominent surgeon. During her childhood Cooper watched her father care for patients at his clinic, many of them young and poor, and that experience sparked an early interest in medicine. "I'd see children come in who didn't feel well and I thought, 'I'm going to be a doctor and take care of children.'" Cooper attended an international high school in Switzerland, dreaming of one day studying medicine and becoming a pediatrician.

Political unrest forced Cooper to flee Liberia in 1980. On April 12 of that year—Cooper's seventeenth birthday—Liberian president William R. Tolbert Jr. was assassinated and his government overthrown in a violent military takeover. In the succeeding days, members of Tolbert's cabinet, many of whom were friends of the Cooper family, were executed. Cooper's father, who had been the president's personal physician, sensed the danger to his family and sent his daughter to the United States, where her older brother was then living. Cooper's parents later made it out of the country safely.

In the United States, Cooper studied chemistry at Emory University in Atlanta, receiving a bachelor's degree in 1984. She earned a medical degree at the University of North Carolina at Chapel Hill in 1988 and trained as a resident in internal medicine at the University of Maryland Hospital in Baltimore. She went on to complete a research fellowship in general internal medicine and, in 1993, a master's degree in public health at Johns Hopkins University. Though Cooper had intended to return to Liberia to practice medicine, the country remained in the grips of a bloody civil war, making it unsafe to go home. Instead she stayed on at Johns Hopkins as an instructor in the School of Medicine.

Cooper had entered medical school with an eye toward becoming a pediatrician, but she found it difficult to watch children suffer. Drawn to internal medicine, she was especially interested in the ways in which doctors and patients interact and how their communication affects patients' health. During her residency training, she had noticed important differences in the attitudes of white patients and minority patients toward health care. "I felt minority patients were often misunderstood," she said in an interview with the Robert Wood

Johnson Foundation. "There's a lot of blaming patients for their problems by health professionals. As a result, patients don't really feel trusting of the system." Cooper began to research these attitudes, wondering how factors such as race and ethnicity might affect the doctor–patient relationship and, in turn, patients' health outcomes.

In her research on the treatment of depression, Cooper found that, compared to white patients, African-American patients were more reluctant to seek treatment from a mental health provider, preferring a more intimate relationship with their primary care physician. In addition, African Americans tended to view depres-

sion as a spiritual illness rather than a medical one, and often rejected antidepressant medications because they feared addiction. Based on these findings, Cooper concluded that social and cultural factors play a key role in whether and where patients seek treatment for mental illness.

Following this line of inquiry, Cooper broadened her focus to consider the barriers that contribute to health disparities between white and minority patients. In a landmark study published in 1999 in the *Journal of the American Medical Association,* Cooper found that African-American patients viewed their doctor's decision-making style as less cooperative than white patients. Not only that, when African-American patients were treated by doctors of the same race, they talked more, asked more questions, and felt more involved in their care than those treated by white doctors, resulting in more effective treatment. For Cooper, patient-centered communication is the key to improving care and reducing health disparities. For example, in subsequent research, she found that when doctors employed communication skills such as listening, involving patients in treatment, providing language assistance services, and addressing health literacy, patients were more likely to keep follow-up appointments, take medications as prescribed, and follow diet and exercise regimes.

It is this kind of innovative work that led the John D. and Catherine T. MacArthur Foundation to name Cooper as one of its twenty-four fellows in 2007. The prestigious "genius grant," as it is known, recognizes individuals who demonstrate exceptional creativity, insight, and potential for future advances. The fellowship comes with a $500,000 award that may be used in any way the recipient chooses. Cooper hoped to use the award to extend her research beyond the United States to consider doctor–patient communication in economically and socially disadvantaged regions of the world. "I hope that I can expand my work in some new directions and that I can learn more about the reasons for the different types of communication problems that exist," she said in an interview in *Diverse Issues in Higher Education.* "Maybe then I can look to solutions that would apply not only in the U.S. but in the developing world in a place like Africa, where I grew up."

In addition to the MacArthur grant, Cooper has been recognized with many awards and fellowships. She received support from the Commonwealth Fund as a Picker/Commonwealth Scholar in Patient-Centered Care from 1995 to 1997 and from the Robert Wood Johnson Foundation as a Harold Amos Scholar from 1996 to 2000. For her commitment to cultural diversity in medicine and her efforts to improve communication in health care she also received the Herbert W. Nickens Award from the Society of General and Internal Medicine in 2006 and the George L. Engel Award from the American Academy on Communication in Healthcare in 2008.

In 2007 Cooper was promoted to professor of medicine in the Division of Internal Medicine at the Johns Hopkins University School of Medicine, becoming the first African-American woman in the university's history to achieve the rank of full professor. She held a joint appointment in the Departments of Epidemiology and Health Policy and Management in the university's Bloomberg School of Public Health.

Sources

Books

Diverse Issues in Higher Education, November 1, 2007.
Dome (Johns Hopkins Medicine), November 2007.
EmoryWire (Emory University), October 2007.
New York Times, September 25, 2007.

Online

"Developing Insights into Disparities," Robert Wood Johnson Foundation, November 1, 2007, http://www.rwjf.org/about/product.jsp?id=23292 (accessed January 15, 2009).
Ireland, Corydon, "Cooper: Doctor-Patient Relations Cause Health Disparities," *Harvard University Gazette Online,* October 23, 2008, http://www.news.harvard.edu/gazette/2008/10.23/11-disparities.html (accessed January 15, 2009).
"MacArthur Fellows 2007: Lisa Cooper," John D. and Catherine T. MacArthur Foundation, September 2007, http://www.macfound.org/site/c.lkLXJ8MQKrH/b.2913825/apps/nl/content2.asp?content_id=&notoc=1 (accessed January 15, 2009).

Other

Johns Hopkins University, "MacArthur 'Genius' Award Honors Expert on Minority Health at Johns Hopkins," news release, September 25, 2007. http://www.hopkinsmedicine.org/Press_releases/2007/09_25_07.html (accessed January 15, 2009).

—Deborah A. Ring

Ulysses Currie

1937—

Politician

Currie, Ulysses, photograph. AP Images.

Ulysses Currie had a long and distinguished career in education before winning election to Maryland's House of Delegates in 1986. The popular Democrat went on to serve several more years in the state senate, where he represented the largely African-American middle-class enclave of Prince George's County. The son of sharecroppers, Currie was ever mindful of the immense changes that he had witnessed in his lifetime. When he was in college, African Americans in the South still faced difficulty even in registering to vote. "My whole life growing up was a totally segregated world," he told Jennifer Skalka in the *Baltimore Sun*. "It was white-only. It was back of the bus. It was you couldn't go to the bathroom. You couldn't eat in a restaurant."

Currie was born on July 10, 1937, in Whiteville, North Carolina, in the eastern part of the state. His parents worked in the tobacco fields as sharecroppers, and both he and his sister picked blooms as children to contribute to the meager household earnings. Their home did not have electricity or running water until the early 1950s, around the time Currie entered high school. Despite these circumstances, the future teacher

and politician did not view his family's plight as a particularly difficult one. "We were all farmers, blacks and whites alike," he told Skalka in the *Baltimore Sun* interview. "So there was not the divide. We were all very poor. We called ourselves dirt poor."

By the time Currie finished high school, he had saved $120 from various part-time jobs in order to pay his first semester's expenses at North Carolina Agricultural & Technical State College, a historically black college in Greensboro. He became the first person in his family to go to college and supported himself by working at the Woman's College of the University of North Carolina, an all-white school that was also located in Greensboro, but on the other side of town. He worked in the cafeteria seven days a week and mopped dormitory floors on weekends. In 1958 he attended an event at Bennett College—another school in Greensboro—where the Reverend Martin Luther King Jr. was the featured speaker, which Currie later said awakened his interest in the civil rights movement.

After earning his degree in social studies and history in 1959, Currie enlisted in the U.S. Army and was stationed at Fort Dix, New Jersey, and at an American military base in what was then West Germany. Back in civilian life, he became a teacher with the public school system of Prince George's County, Maryland, which is home to several suburban communities of Washington, DC. He eventually earned a master's degree in education from American University in Washington, DC. For a time, he directed the federally funded preschool program, Head Start, in the district and also served as a school principal.

Currie began his career in politics when he was elected to the Maryland House of Delegates from Prince George's County in 1986 on the Democratic Party ticket. He was reelected to the lower house of the state legislature several more times, and in 1994 he made a successful bid for the Maryland State Senate from Prince George's County. Voters regularly returned him to his seat in Annapolis, the state capital, every four years, and in 1999 he became deputy majority whip for the Democrats in the chamber. In 2002 Maryland State Senate President Thomas V. Mike Miller Jr. named

Currie to serve as chair of the Budget and Taxation Committee, a powerful post in the legislature with oversight of the state's $31 billion budget.

During his twenty-plus years in public service, Currie was known as a respected, diligent lawmaker who rarely courted the press, did most of his campaigning by going door-to-door, and gave few interviews. Even in the Senate he took the floor only infrequently to make a speech. There were a few exceptions to this, however, as Lisa Rein wrote in the *Washington Post* in June of 2008, including an incident in which Currie "rose to express his outrage over an exploding population of troubled teenagers that the state was sending to largely unregulated group homes. He has spoken out against payday loans, which he argued hurt the poor. And as the national move to abolish welfare took hold in Maryland in the late 1990s, he pushed for an innovative tax-credit program to encourage businesses to hire welfare recipients."

Because of this unblemished record, Currie's constituents and colleagues were stunned when the public corruption investigation unit of the Federal Bureau of Investigation (FBI) announced in the spring of 2008 that Currie was a target of a special probe. In May of that year, both his family home in Forestville in Prince George's County and his Annapolis office were raided and documents carted off. Federal agents were scrutinizing Currie's work as a paid consultant to Shoppers Food & Pharmacy, a supermarket chain based in Lanham, Maryland, whose parent company, Super-Valu Inc. of Minnesota, owned other national grocery-store chains such as Jewel/Osco and Albertson's. The charges against him involved financial compensation that Currie had accepted totaling about $200,000 over a four-year period in the 1990s, which he had reported as income on his tax returns.

At issue was that Currie failed to disclose the consultancy work on forms he was required to file with the ethics office of the Maryland General Assembly. This was viewed as a potential conflict of interest, for the veteran lawmaker "arranged meetings and contacted city and state officials at critical junctures when Shoppers was seeking public financing and other concessions as part of the multimillion-dollar redevelopment of Mondawmin Mall in West Baltimore," explained investigative reporters Gadi Dechter and Laura Smitherman in the *Baltimore Sun* in July of 2008. "He also interceded on the company's behalf on routine transportation projects such as traffic signals and road improvements near Shoppers stores." Furthermore, Currie had voted on some pieces of legislation involving the company, including the transfer of one unit's liquor license to another store. According to Dechter and Smitherman's *Baltimore Sun* article, FBI sources claimed that Currie "was in frequent contact with Shoppers representatives and the county's chief liquor inspector at a time when local approval of the transfer had drawn fierce opposition."

There were some calls for Currie to resign from his chairmanship of the Budget and Taxation Committee in advance of the 2009 session, but Miller, who was still president of the Maryland State Senate, remarked in August of 2008 that the investigation was still underway and Currie had not been found guilty. "Senator Currie, in my opinion, is guilty of making a terrible mistake," Miller told Dechter and journalist, David Nitkin in the *Baltimore Sun.* "Knowing him, I believe it was absent-mindedness."

Sources

Periodicals

Baltimore Sun, March 3, 2007; July 25, 2008; August 5, 2008; August 27, 2008.
Supermarket News, June 9, 2008.
Washington Post, June 1, 2008, p. C1.

Online

"Ulysses Currie," Maryland Senate, http://www.msa.md.gov/msa/mdmanual/05sen/html/msa12163.html (accessed November 15, 2008).

—Carol Brennan

Tirunesh Dibaba

1985—

Athlete

Dibaba, Tirunesh, photograph. Terry Schmitt/UPI/Landov.

At the 2008 Summer Olympics in Beijing, China, Tirunesh Dibaba made Olympic history as the first woman to win gold medals in both the 5,000- and 10,000-meter track events at the same Olympics. The diminutive runner from Ethiopia was one of a talented new generation of long-distance runners of African birth who took first place in marathons and other long-distance events, and two of her sisters and a brother were also top competitors on the international circuit. In fact, in 1992 Dibaba's cousin Derartu Tulu was the first black African woman ever to win a gold medal in an Olympic sport. "I wanted to become someone too," Dibaba told Simon Turnbull in the (London) *Independent on Sunday,* "but I never thought I would be strong enough to be like Derartu."

Of Oromo ethnicity, Dibaba was born in 1985 in Bekoji, a village in Ethiopia's Arsi State in what is known as the Arsi Zone. This is a high-altitude region, with elevations of 10,000 feet above sea level in some parts, and has produced a number of outstanding runners. Because there is less oxygen at such high altitudes, athletes who train there develop extremely efficient cardiovascular systems. The Arsi Zone is also a fertile area whose soil produces wheat and teff, a type of millet, and Dibaba grew up in a farming family as the fourth of six children, all of whom helped out in the fields from an early age. "When we finished school, I would do a few chores, fetch water, make coffee," Dibaba recalled in an interview with Doug Gillon in the Glasgow *Herald.* "It was not far to get water—only a kilometre. That's not a long distance in our culture. Sometimes I'd look after the animals."

Home for Dibaba was a traditional cone-shaped mud hut that had no electricity. When her cousin Tulu went to Barcelona for the 1992 Summer Olympic Games, making history when she won gold in the 10,000-meter event, Dibaba's family went to a nearby hotel in order to see Tulu's race on television. Dibaba did not begin training seriously until she turned fourteen. A year later, she moved to Addis Ababa, Ethiopia's capital, in order to live with her older sister Ejegayehu, known as "Gigi" and enroll in high school. "I missed the school registration deadline, and if I had gone back home my parents would have given me away in marriage," she explained to Turnbull.

At a Glance . . .

Born on June 1, 1985, in Bekoji, Arsi, Ethiopia; daughter of farmers; married to Sileshi Sihine (an athlete), 2008.

Career: Won her first international track event, World Championship in Athletics, Paris, 2003; member, Ethiopian Olympic track and field teams, 2004 and 2008.

Addresses: *Manager*—Mark Wetmore, Global Athletics & Marketing, Inc., 80 Dartmouth St., Boston, MA 02116.

Dibaba signed on with a local running club and competed in her first international event at Ostend, Belgium, the host city for the 2001 World Cross Country Championships. She came in fifth place in the junior race; in 2002 she won second place at the same event in Dublin, Ireland. Still competing as a junior in March of 2003, she won her first gold medal at the World Cross Country Championships in Lausanne, Switzerland. Five months later, at the 2003 World Championship in Athletics in Paris, Dibaba became the youngest winner in the 5,000-meter race in the history of the event with a time of 14:51.72. She was just eighteen years and three months old, and began to train in earnest for the 2004 Summer Olympics in Athens, Greece. There she won the bronze medal in the women's 5,000-meter event, bested by two other top African runners—fellow Ethiopian Meseret Defar, who won the gold, and Isabella Ochichi of Kenya, the second-place finisher.

Dibaba's breakout year came in 2005, when she set several world records. The first came in January at the VisitScotland Great Edinburgh International Cross-country Meet; later that year she won two gold medals in the 5,000-meter and 10,000-meter races at the World Outdoor Track & Field championships in Helsinki, Finland. Returning to Edinburgh for the annual Cross-country Meet in January of 2006, however, Dibaba and her sister Gigi were delayed when their flight into London's Heathrow Airport arrived several hours behind schedule, causing them to miss their connecting flight to Edinburgh. Despite the fact that they both had valid visas for the United Kingdom, they were not allowed to leave Terminal 3, where all food concessions had shut down for the night. "We slept on the floor," Dibaba told Gillon, in the Glasgow *Herald.* "We were freezing. We had to use our T-shirts as blankets." Dibaba and her sister arrived in Edinburgh a half-hour before the start of the race, not having eaten in twenty-six hours. Nevertheless, Dibaba came in third in her event. Race organizers lodged a formal com-

plaint with Britain's Home Secretary about the treatment of the sisters by immigration and airport officials.

In 2007 Dibaba broke her own world indoor record at the Reebok Boston Indoor Games in the 5,000-meter event. In August she triumphed in the 10,000-meter event in Osaka, Japan, at the World Championship in Athletics despite a stomach ailment and a minor collision with teammate Mestawat Tufa, winning with a time of 31:55.41. "I have never been challenged as much as this," the *Weekend Argus,* a South African newspaper, quoted her as saying. "If it had not been a matter for representing my country, I would have dropped out." Her health problems did force her to cancel several other events that season, but in June of 2008 she set a new world record in the 5,000-meter race with a finish of 14:11.15 at a Golden League meet organized by the International Association of Athletics Federations (IAAF).

A little more than two months later, at the Beijing Olympics, Dibaba won a gold medal in the 10,000-meter event, setting a new Olympic record time of 29:54.66 and breaking the one set by Tulu, her cousin, in 2000. Seven days later, Dibaba took another gold medal for her first-place win in the 5,000-meter race, making her the first woman to win gold in the 5,000- and 10,000-meter events in the same Olympics.

In 2008 Dibaba married another Ethiopian runner, Sileshi Sihine, who won the silver medal in the men's 10,000-meter race in Beijing. He was also the silver medalist in the 2004 Athens Olympics, while Dibaba's sister Gigi took silver in the same women's event that year. Their younger sister, Genzebe, was also a promising track athlete, and all three sisters trained together in Addis Ababa. "Genzebe is so young and talented," Dibaba told Matthew Brown in an article that appeared on the IAAF Athletics Web site in 2008. "In time I expect she'll become even stronger and quicker than me."

Sources

Periodicals

Boston Herald, January 27, 2006, p. 92.
Herald (Glasgow, Scotland), January 14, 2006, p. 10; January 16, 2006, p. 3.
Independent on Sunday (London), March 13, 2005, p. 17.
New York Times, February 3, 2007, p. D4; August 16, 2008, p. D2; August 23, 2008, p. D4.
Weekend Argus (South Africa), August 26, 2007, p. 38.

Online

Brown, Matthew, "Dibaba Sisters Make It a Family Affair—Edinburgh 2008," IAAF.org, March 30, 2008, http://www.iaaf.org/WXC08/news/kind=100/newsid=s44263.html (accessed December 10, 2008).

Tanser, Toby, "Spend a Day with Tirunesh Dibaba," RunnersWorld.com, February 7, 2007, http://www. runnersworld.com/article/0,7120,s6-243-297–11496-0,00.html (accessed December 10, 2008).

—Carol Brennan

Bobby Durham

1937–2008

Musician

Legendary jazz drummer Bobby Durham passed away in the summer of 2008 in Genoa, Italy, where he had lived for the previous several years. The Philadelphia native also had a home in Basel, Switzerland, which is a hub for many American expatriate jazz musicians, along with other European cities where the music form still thrives in live-performance settings. The writer of a tribute that appeared in the *New York Sun,* Will Friedwald, described Durham as a "drummer known for his energetic, propulsive style, as well as for the high-flying musical company that he kept." Durham's career included stints with the Count Basie and Duke Ellington orchestras, and he also kept time for Ella Fitzgerald, Oscar Peterson, Lionel Hampton, Sonny Rollins, and many other jazz greats.

Born in Philadelphia in 1937, Durham grew up in a musical family: Both of his parents were tap dancers, and his father also played the jazz trumpet. Durham picked up tap at an early age, then took up the drums for a time before experimenting with the trombone, vibraphone, and double bass. He joined his first band at the age of sixteen—a pioneering Philly doo-wop act called the Orioles—but eventually left when drafted into the U.S. Marines. During his stint in uniform he played with a military band that provided him with further musical training. After his discharge he moved to New York City in 1960 and joined the city's swinging jazz and cabaret scene. He found steady work in the clubs and cut his first record in 1963 with tenor saxophonist Red Holloway under the title *The Burner.*

In March of 1967 Durham was invited to join the Duke Ellington Orchestra, led by one of the pioneers in American jazz. It was actually Ellington's son Mercer who recruited Durham, and the famous bandleader and upstart drummer—both strong personalities—had some notable skirmishes. "Maybe Bobby was arrogant, but he knew his work," Mercer Ellington said, according to London's *Independent* newspaper. "There was nothing about him that was not great and really right for the band." Eventually, Durham was fired from Ellington's group but stayed to fill out the remaining two weeks. After that, the younger Ellington recalled, Durham "stopped trying to impress Duke and relaxed and played what he played and that was it. And Duke said 'How come he never played like that before?' And then he told me to get him back. He hadn't been out of that band for 10 minutes before he was hired by Oscar Peterson," the jazz pianist. Durham joined a short list of names to have been fired by Ellington, for only he and jazz great Charlie Mingus shared that honor.

Durham spent three years with Peterson's outfit and returned to it on other occasions over the course of his long career. He served as drummer for Peterson's exciting live shows and appeared on several recordings, including *Exclusively for My Friends* and *Saturday Night at the Blue Note.* A writer for another London newspaper, the *Guardian,* reported that in his autobiography Peterson referred to Durham as "'Thug,' because he was 'a tough cookie.'" Yet Peterson also commended Durham's "'tremendous drive and equal dexterity across his drums.' He was also clear about Durham's sometimes combative nature. This culminated in a hilarious episode when the 5[-foot] 6[-inch] drummer squared up to Peterson's 6[-foot] bassist Sam

Jones, a far gentler individual, until the massive pianist intervened and threatened to swamp them both." Of that time with Peterson, the *Times* of London asserted that Jones's "accuracy and swing was an ideal complement to Durham's prodding urgency and Peterson's devastating technique."

In the early 1970s Durham signed on with the Jamaican pianist Monty Alexander for a few years, and then joined the legendary jazz singer Ella Fitzgerald when she embarked on a lengthy world tour with the Count Basie Orchestra. The latter assignment also put Durham in close contact with jazz pianist Tommy Flanagan, with whom he also had a long professional association. "When Fitzgerald sang with Basie's band, the Flanagan trio usually became the rhythm section, and some of Durham's best-known recordings were made from Basie's drum chair, backing Fitzgerald's scat-singing vocals, and driving along the big band in full cry," noted Durham's *Times* of London obituary.

Durham was also recruited by stellar names outside the jazz pantheon to play onstage and was one of the few jazz percussionists whose credits included backing a range of vocalists from Frank Sinatra and Ray Charles to Marvin Gaye and James Brown. He also played regularly with the "Jazz at the Philharmonic" series in New York City, which was run by Norman Granz, and Granz also recruited Durham for recordings on his label, Pablo Records. During his time with the Basie Orchestra, Durham met trombonist Al Grey, and joined his New Al Grey Quintet, which issued a self-titled 1988 release on which Durham appears.

In the early 1990s Durham served as the house drummer at the Birdland Club in New York City, and the new acid-jazz movement that erupted that decade rekindled interest in his work among a younger generation of musicians. In his later years he settled in Basel, home to a number of outstanding musical talents whose services were in demand throughout Europe. "During his later career Durham pursued the freelance life, playing with figures such as the vibraphone player Lionel Hampton, and sometimes leading his own small band," noted his *Daily Telegraph* obituary. "He developed the ability to sing while drumming and even wrote his own humorous, semi-scat songs. The most celebrated of these was The Airplane Song, with lyrics based on the safety instruction sheet provided to passengers."

Durham also had a home near Genoa, Italy, where he established an annual jazz festival in the town, called Isola del Cantone, in 2004. He died in a Genoa hospital from lung cancer and emphysema on July 6, 2008, at the age of seventy-one. He was predeceased by his wife, Betsy Perkins Durham, who died in 1996, and two of his four children; his surviving offspring were Valarie and Robbin. He was also the grandfather of four.

Selected discography

(With Red Holloway) *The Burner,* Prestige, 1963.
The New Al Grey Quintet, Chiaroscuro, 1988.
(With Oscar Peterson) *Saturday Night at the Blue Note,* Telarc, 1990.
(With Oscar Peterson) *Exclusively for My Friends,* Island, 1992.
Domani's Blues, Azzura, 2005.
For Lovers Only, Azzura, 2005.
We Three Plus Friends, Azzura, 2005.
(With Massimo Farao and Lorenzo Conte) *An Enchanted Evening Piano,* Direct Source, 2006.

Sources

Periodicals

Daily Telegraph (London), July 15, 2008.
Guardian (London), August 9, 2008, p. 37.
Independent (London), July 12, 2008.
New York Sun, July 10, 2008, p. 8.
Times (London), July 17, 2008, p. 62.

Online

Chadbourne, Eugene, "Bob Durham," Verve Records, http://www.vervemusicgroup.com/artist/default.aspx?aid=6199 (accessed November 15, 2008).

—Carol Brennan

Samuel Eto'o

1981—

Professional soccer player

Eto'o, Samuel, photograph. AP Images.

Samuel Eto'o is a Cameroonian-born Spanish soccer player who is known for his exceptional goal-scoring skills. In his first four seasons with FC Barcelona, one of the premier clubs in Spanish soccer, he ranked among the top scorers in the league, developing a reputation as a fearsome striker—the forward whose main job is putting in goals. In addition to his impressive record in Europe, Eto'o also became a legend in his home country, leading the Cameroonian national team to victory in Olympic competition and in the Africa Cup of Nations and earning the title African Footballer of the Year three years in a row.

Samuel Eto'o (pronounced eh-TOH) was born on March 10, 1981, in Nkon, Cameroon. Growing up in a country that is mad for soccer (called football outside the United States), he could not help but develop a love for the game. The year after Eto'o was born, Cameroon, long distinguished among African nations for its prowess on the pitch, became the first country in sub-Saharan Africa to have an undefeated run in World Cup competition. As a boy, Eto'o looked up to fellow Cameroonian Roger Milla, one of the first African soccer players to become widely known in international play. "He was my idol, and I feel lucky to have him as that," Eto'o recalled in the London *Times*. "He was a leader, not just for Cameroon but for Africa."

Eto'o attended the Kadji Sports Academy, an elite training facility in Cameroon. At age fifteen, he garnered national attention while playing for the second-division club UCB Douala in the 1996 Cup of Cameroon, displaying his trademark speed and accurate shooting technique. Already considered a prodigy at home, Eto'o was invited by Real Madrid, one of the top clubs in Europe, to travel to Spain for a trial. However, when the young Eto'o arrived at Madrid's Barajas Airport alone, no one from the club was there to meet him. Not speaking a word of Spanish, Eto'o approached the first African he saw, and with the good samaritan's help, he was on his way to Santiago Bernabéu Stadium. Eto'o joined Real Madrid the following year.

Eto'o's first impression of Madrid would prove to be a harbinger of his rocky relationship with the club. Though he was touted as a top prospect, upon arriving at Madrid, Eto'o was promptly loaned out to the second-division club Léganes during the 1997–98 season, and then to the first-division Espanyol de Barcelona in 1998–99. (In association soccer, teams loan players to one another for periods lasting from a few weeks to an entire season. Unlike the trades that are common in American sports such as baseball, the loaning team retains "ownership" of the player.) Seeing little play with Espanyol, Eto'o returned to Madrid, only to be loaned out once again, this time to Real Mallorca, during the 1999–2000 season.

Frustrated and disappointed, the talented Eto'o languished in reserves until the 2000–01 season, when he played twenty-eight games at Mallorca, becoming the club's top scorer with eleven goals. In June of 2001 Real Mallorca struck a deal to acquire Eto'o permanently, paying a club record $6.4 million but allowing Real Madrid to retain 50 percent ownership. In his five seasons with Real Mallorca, Eto'o made a name for himself as one of the most accurate strikers in the game. He racked up an impressive fifty-four goals, making him the highest league scorer in the club's history. In 2003 Eto'o led Mallorca to a 3–0 victory at the Spanish Cup (Copa del Rey).

After lengthy negotiations with Madrid and Mallorca, Eto'o signed with FC Barcelona, a powerhouse in the Spanish League, for a transfer fee of $38 million. He made his debut with the Barcelona club, popularly known as "Bar̗a," in the 2004–05 season opener at Ràcing Santander. In his first season with the club, Eto'o scored twenty-five goals. In championship play, he made a key goal against Levante that clinched the Spanish League title for Barcelona for the first time in

six years. Taking the opportunity to get revenge on his former team, Eto'o turned to the fans and television cameras and chanted, "Madrid, cabrón, saluda al campeon," loosely translated as, "Madrid, you bastards, hail the champion!" Eto'o was fined by the Spanish Football Federation for his comments and later apologized, saying, "If it hadn't been for Real Madrid I would never have got this far, so I beg forgiveness and hope that people will understand me," according to BBC Sport.

The following season, 2005–06, Eto'o tallied twenty-six goals, capturing the league's Pichichi Trophy, the award for top goal scorer of the season, and becoming the first player since the 1990s to score fifty goals in two seasons in the Spanish League. That year, Barcelona again took the Spanish League title, as well as the Spanish Supercup and the European Champions League prize.

In addition to his impressive record in the Spanish League, Eto'o has distinguished himself as a top international player for Cameroon's national team, nicknamed the Indomitable Lions. In 1998, at age seventeen, Eto'o was the youngest player ever to appear in FIFA World Cup competition. He played again in the 2002 World Cup, but missed in 2006 when Cameroon failed to make the tournament for the first time in twenty years. Eto'o was thrice named African Footballer of the Year by the Confederation of African Football, in 2003, 2004, and 2005, the only player ever to earn the title three years running, and in 2008 he tied the record for all-time goals scored at the Africa Cup of Nations.

Despite Eto'o's goal-scoring prowess, his career has been marred by repeated incidents of racist abuse. During a notorious match at Real Zaragoza in 2006, home-team fans taunted Eto'o by chanting monkey sounds. Too much for Eto'o to take, he told the referee, "No more. No more. No more!" and began to walk off the pitch. Barcelona coach Frank Rijkaard turned Eto'o back toward the field, while players from both teams rushed to him, urging him not to give in to the bigots. He returned to play, and Barcelona scored two goals—one put in by Eto'o—to win the match. Reflecting on the incident, Eto'o told CNN, "In that moment you start thinking whether there is something wrong with being black.... But I think we are all humans, everyone's blood is the same color, and we all have the same heart. I don't see any differences in color." Though Real Zaragoza was fined nearly $14,000 for the abuse, the Spanish league did not implement any further measures to combat racism. Eto'o reported to CNN that the taunts had become so widespread that he no longer felt safe taking his family to matches.

In 2008 Barcelona's new coach, Josep Guardiola, told Eto'o he was free to leave the club, though his contract extended through 2010. Eto'o was courted by many other leading clubs, including Chelsea and Tottenham Hotspur in the United Kingdom and AC Milan in Italy, but as of 2009 was still playing for Barcelona.

Sources

Periodicals

The Independent, February 20, 2005.
International Herald Tribune, March 1, 2006.
The Times (London), February 19, 2006; June 17, 2008.

Online

"Eto'o Apologises for Outburst," BBC Sport, May 16, 2005, http://news.bbc.co.uk/sport2/hi/football/africa/4553179.stm (accessed January 19, 2009).
FC Barcelona, "Samuel Eto'o Fils," http://www.fcbarcelona.cat/web/english/futbol/temporada_07-08/plantilla/jugadors/etoo.html (accessed January 19, 2009).

Hooper, Simon, "Eto'o: We Can't Wait until a Black Player Gets Killed," CNN, June 13, 2008, http://edition.cnn.com/2008/SPORT/football/06/13/etoo.interview/index.html (accessed January 19, 2009).
Mira, Luis, "Report: Tottenham Wants Barcelona's Eto'o," Sports Illustrated, April 22, 2008, http://sportsillustrated.cnn.com/2008/soccer/04/22/eto/ (accessed January 19, 2009).
Samuel Eto'o (official Web site), http://www.samueletoo.name/ (accessed January 19, 2009).
"Samuel Eto'o: The Best Is Yet to Come," FIFA.com, November 30, 2005, http://www.fifa.com/classic football/awards/gala/news/newsid=101618.html (accessed January 19, 2009).

—Deborah A. Ring

Patrick Ewing

1962—

Basketball player, artist, coach

Ewing, Patrick, photograph. AP Images.

Center Patrick Ewing is one of the greatest basketball players of all time. His career was record-breaking at every juncture: While at Georgetown University, he led the Hoyas to the National Collegiate Athletic Association (NCAA) Finals three times and won the NCAA Championship in his junior year. He was named the most outstanding player in the NCAA Finals and was awarded the Naismith Award as the nation's top college player in 1985. After moving to the National Basketball Association (NBA), Ewing was named Rookie of the Year in 1986 and was an NBA All-Star for most of his professional career. In 1997 he was named among the top fifty NBA players of all time and the top twenty leading scorers. A two-time Olympic gold medal winner, after retiring from the league Ewing used his considerable basketball skills as a coach for such teams as the Houston Rockets and the Orlando Magic.

Became Famous as High School Athlete

Patrick Ewing was born on August 5, 1962, in Kingston, Jamaica. When his parents emigrated from Ja-

maica, money was so scarce that Ewing remained on the island for four years, arriving in the United States, as did each of his six siblings, only when family funds permitted. Ewing shared a five-room Cambridge, Massachusetts, house with his mother, father, brother, and five sisters.

Education was the primary focus for Carl and Dorothy Ewing's seven children. Ewing entered elementary school with such a marked Jamaican accent that some peers and teachers could not easily understand him. He was determined to succeed, however, and sought extra instruction in summer school and from tutors. His parents left no doubt that Ewing's education would not stop with high school. By the time he was a senior in high school, two of his siblings had already graduated from college.

Ewing did not start playing basketball until he was twelve years old, when he joined in a pick-up game in his neighborhood. A veteran player of soccer and cricket, he quickly learned the game. In fact, a friend once commented that Ewing seemed to have been born for the basketball court. By eighth grade he had already grown to six feet six inches in height and drawn the eye of prep coaches. As a high school student at

At a Glance . . .

Born Patrick Aloysius Ewing on August 5, 1962, in Kingston, Jamaica; son of Carl Ewing (a mechanic) and Dorothy Ewing; married Rita Williams, 1990 (divorced, 1998); children: (with Sharon Stanford) Patrick Jr.; (with Williams) Randi, Corey. *Education:* Georgetown University, BA, fine arts, 1985.

Career: Center, New York Knicks, 1985–2000, Seattle Supersonics, 2000–01, Orlando Magic, 2001–02; assistant coach, Washington Wizards, 2002–03, Houston Rockets, 2003–06, Orlando Magic, 2007–09.

Memberships: NBA Players Association, president, 1997–2001.

Awards: Most Outstanding Player, NCAA Final Four, 1984; College Player of the Year, *Sporting News,* 1985; Gold Medal, Olympic games, 1984, 1992; Naismith Award, NCAA, 1985; Rookie of the Year, NBA, 1986; named among 50 Greatest NBA Players in history, eleven-time NBA All-Star, seven-time Knick of the Year, 1987–92; honor, National Committee for Prevention of Child Abuse, 1992–93.

Addresses: *Office*—Orlando Magic, 8701 Maitland Summit Blvd., Orlando, FL 32810.

Cambridge's Rindge and Latin School, Ewing not only led his team to three state championships, he also tried out for the 1980 Olympic team. Although Ewing would have to wait until the 1984 Olympics to represent the United States, no other high school athlete had ever been invited to Olympic basketball tryouts.

Recruited by Top College Teams

Every college coach in the United States had his eye on Ewing. After all, how many high school athletes were featured in *Sports Illustrated* and the *New York Times*? During Ewing'senior year, his high school coach, Mike Jarvis, sent 150 Division I schools a letter, now called the "Ewing Letter." In it Jarvis explained that Ewing had only lived in the United States for six years. He said Ewing was a hard worker, but he struggled academically and would need special tutoring and academic support. Jarvis, as a mentor and friend as well as coach, tried to ensure that Ewing would succeed both on the basketball court and in the classroom.

Jarvis meant well, but his letter had unanticipated negative results for Ewing. High school players taunted Ewing, saying he was illiterate. Once, during a high-scoring game in which Ewing led a victorious team he saw someone holding up a sign that said "Ewing can't read." According to *Sports Illustrated*, Ewing quietly commented, "I sure can count. And someday I'm going to be in the pros and counting my money all the way to the bank!"

Eighty schools responded to Jarvis' letter, often offering the special academic help Jarvis had mentioned. However, Ewing chose Georgetown University in Washington, DC. Georgetown coach John Thompson offered Ewing no academic assistance. He said his players must meet academic standards on their own—no special help other than the support of faculty advisers would be given. Still, Ewing and his parents were impressed by Thompson's no-nonsense coaching and pleased to find a team coached by an African American. Thompson said Ewing's best bet was a college education; few college athletes make careers of professional sports. Carl and Dorothy Ewing agreed.

Led Georgetown to National Championship

At Georgetown Ewing was a team leader as he had been in high school. His aggressive play and quiet confidence spurred fellow players to be more determined. In 1984 the Georgetown Hoyas, led by Ewing, became the NCAA champions. Ewing was chosen Outstanding Player of the tournament over the great center Hakeem Olajuwon. During that same year Ewing tried out for and made the U.S. Olympic basketball team and won a gold medal at the summer games in Los Angeles.

On the court Ewing was an intimidating giant. His scowl and aggressive play earned him a reputation as personally and athletically tough. Coach Thompson and his fellow Hoyas called Ewing "The Warrior," but fans from opposing teams made fun of Ewing's serious, no-holds-barred playing style, dubbing him the "Darth Vader of Basketball."

Ewing avoided the press and was criticized for being aloof. He protected himself and his family from media attention. He felt uncomfortable that other Hoya players were not asked for autographs and refused to sign himself unless his teammates were also asked. Some people thought he was shy, but Thompson said in *Sports Illustrated*, "This boy is not shy. He's private. There's a difference."

Off the court Ewing's personal life was a struggle. In 1983 his mother, a woman who had worked long hours at physically demanding, low-paying jobs to build a better life for her children, died at age fifty-five from a massive heart attack. Not long afterward, his high school sweetheart, Sharon Stanford, became pregnant. When their son, Patrick Aloysius Ewing Jr., was born on May 21, 1984, Ewing was not ready for fatherhood or marriage, but he persevered, turning down endorsements and millions of dollars to keep the promise he made to his mother that he would graduate from college. He met Rita Williams, a Howard University student and summer intern for U.S. Senator Bill Bradley, when he worked as a summer congressional intern for U.S. Senator Bob Dole. Ewing and Williams were married in 1990 and had two daughters, Randi and Corey. They divorced in 1998.

Drafted by NBA New York Knicks

Ewing graduated from college in 1985. Because he would be the first pick in the draft that year, the NBA held a lottery in which the seven worst teams would each have an equal chance to get first pick. The New York Knicks won the lottery and as expected picked Ewing on June 18. He signed a ten-year, $30-million contract, the most ever given to a rookie in the NBA.

During his first year with the Knicks, Ewing was named the Rookie of the Year and was an All-Star. The Knicks did not reach the playoffs until the 1987–88 season, when the team lost in the first round to the Boston Celtics. The team achieved more success once Pat Riley took over as head coach in 1991. Both Ewing's morale and his career began an upswing. Riley came from the Los Angeles Lakers armed with four NBA championships in nine years. When reporters panned Riley for holding "grueling" practice sessions and for open, often public criticism of his players, Ewing instead saw in Riley a man who wanted to win as much as he did.

However, despite trips to the playoffs several times over the next few years, the Knicks never succeeded in winning an NBA championship during the time Ewing played for the team. In 1993 the Knicks lost to Chicago in the conference finals; in 1994 the team reached the championship game but came up short against the Houston Rockets; in 1996 the Knicks fell to the Indiana Pacers in the conference semifinals; and in 1997 the Knicks lost the conference semifinals against the Miami Heat when several veteran players, including Ewing, were suspended for two games for leaving the bench during a fight.

In 1995 *Sport Magazine* asked if Ewing, at age thirty-two, should retire. The following year he scored his 20,000th point. In March of 1997 he surpassed 21,000 points. He then signed a lucrative contract for four additional years, making Ewing a New York Knick until past his fortieth birthday. However, in 2000 the Knicks refused to give Ewing a two-year contract extension and traded him to the Seattle Supersonics. NBA.com stated, "Knicks fans had mixed emotions about Ewing's departure. Some could never forgive him for not bringing the title back to New York, or his sense of privacy that limited a personal connection with the fans. Others appreciated his productive work ethic, the excitement he brought to the Garden and his commitment to the franchise." After one year in Seattle, Ewing signed a free agent contract with the Orlando Magic in 2001 for one more year of play before announcing his retirement.

Headed NBA Players Association

Although Ewing never signed autographs—he preferred to shake hands—or gave many interviews, he was recognized by peers, NBA team owners, and coaches alike as a leader in his profession. His fellow NBA players elected him president of the National Basketball Association Players Association in 1997. He was named one of the fifty greatest players in NBA history during the league's fiftieth anniversary season in 1996–97. He played on another Olympic gold medal basketball team in 1992. Ewing served as an assistant coach on several NBA teams after his retirement, including the Washington Wizards, the Houston Rockets, and the Orlando Magic. In 2008 he was elected to the Naismith Memorial Basketball Hall of Fame along with his beloved coach, Pat Riley.

In addition to professional basketball, Ewing pursued a rare dual career as an artist in print and poster design. A fine arts major at Georgetown, he created art for Discover's Private Issue credit card and exhibited some of his work. Together with Columbia University instructor Linda L. Louis, Ewing coauthored *In the Paint* (1999), an Abbeville Press book on children's art offering practical instruction to students and advice to parents and teachers.

Ewing also devoted his time to charitable works benefiting children. As chair of the Knicks' Stay in School program, host of Children's Aid Society fundraisers, and leader of the Knicks' Frontline against Crime gun exchange and awareness program, Ewing lived out his commitment to inner-city youth. He also conducted youth basketball clinics in South Africa along with Dikembe Mutombo and Alonzo Mourning in the summer of 1994. He single-handedly raised nearly $50,000 for the community outreach programs at Hale House in Harlem and participated in exhibition performances with other NBA stars to raise money for the American Cancer Society, Boys' and Girls' Clubs, and the Children's Health Fund.

Selected works

Books

(With Linda L. Louis) *In the Paint*, 1999.

Sources

Books

Kavanagh, Jack, *Sports Great: Patrick Ewing* (Sports Great Books), Enslow Publishers, 1992.

Wiener, Paul, *Patrick Ewing* (Basketball Legends), Chelsea House Publishers, 1996.

Periodicals

Jet, April 16, 1990; June 24, 1991.

Newsweek, March 27, 1985, p. 63.

New York Times, July 3, 1997; April 8, 2008.

Orlando Sentinel, November 17, 2008.

Sport, February, 1995.

Sporting News, May 13, 1996; May 16, 1994.

Sports Illustrated, January 22, 1990; January 17, 1994.

Time, August 6, 1990.

Online

"Magic Name Assistant Coaches," OrlandoMagic.com, July 3, 2007, http://www.nba.com/magic/news/Magic_Name_Assistant_Coaches-230608-800.html (accessed January 26, 2009).

"Patrick Ewing," NBA Encyclopedia, http://www.nba.com/history/players/ewing_bio.html (accessed January 26, 2009).

"Report: Ewing Resigns as Rockets' Assistant Coach," ESPN.com, August 30, 2006, http://sports.espn.go.com/nba/news/story?id=2565770 (accessed January 26, 2009).

Other

Additional information for this profile was provided by the New York Knicks.

—Julia Pferderhirt and Melissa Doak

Capers C. Funnye Jr.

1952(?)—

Rabbi

Funnye, Capers C., Jr., photograph. AP Images.

Ordained as a rabbi in 1985, Capers C. Funnye Jr. became the leader of a predominantly black religious community at Beth Shalom B'nai Zaken Ethiopian Hebrew Congregation on Chicago's South Side. His name began appearing in newspaper reports during the 2008 presidential campaign of the Illinois senator Barack Obama, whose wife, Michelle Obama, is Funnye's cousin. Stories about the family connection pointed out the relatively small number of African-American Jews, who are sometimes known as either black Hebrews or Israelites, but Funnye explained that he was drawn to the faith because of its universal aspects. "I am a Jew," he told Niko Koppel in the *New York Times,* "and that breaks through all color and ethnic barriers."

Funnye was born in the early 1950s, the son of Verdelle Robinson Funnye, whose brother was the grandfather of First Lady Michelle Robinson Obama. Like many other African Americans, Funnye was raised in the African Methodist Episcopal (AME) faith, and as a youngster even his pastor believed he was destined for the ministry. Yet as Funnye grew into a young adult, he began to have questions about Christianity and sought out other religions for answers to uncertainties about his own faith. His investigations included Islam, but he settled on Judaism because of its intellectual component, in which adherents are encouraged to both question and debate spiritual tenets. He was profoundly influenced by the teachings of Wentworth Arthur Matthew, a Nigerian who founded what is believed to be the first congregation of black Jews in America in Harlem in 1919. This group is sometimes referred to as the Cushites, a term used for ancient peoples of Sudan and Ethiopia who were supposedly descended from Ham, the son of Noah of biblical-flood fame. In the Old Testament's book of Numbers, a reference is made to a Cushite woman, Tharbis, who was the first wife of the prophet Moses, but it is unclear what became of her. In the Kebra Nagast, a religious text dating from the medieval period, Ethiopian Jews are described as the descendants of one of the tribes of Israel that fled across the Arabian Peninsula to Africa around 800 or 900 BCE.

Funnye earned his undergraduate degree in Jewish studies from the Spertus Institute of Jewish Studies in Chicago, and went on to fulfill requirements for a master's of science degree in human service adminis-

At a Glance . . .

Born Capers Charles Funnye Jr. in 1952(?); surname pronounced "fun-AY"; son of Verdelle Robinson Funnye and Capers Charles Funnye; married; wife's name, Mary; children: four. *Religion:* Jewish. *Education:* Spertus Institute of Jewish Studies, BA, Jewish studies, and MS, human service administration.

Career: Ordained rabbi, 1985; Beth Shalom B'nai Zaken Ethiopian Hebrew Congregation, head rabbi. Institute for Jewish and Community Research, founder, 1985; Alliance of Black Jews, cofounder, 1995; Chicago Board of Rabbis, member.

Memberships: Jewish Council on Urban Affairs, board of directors; American Jewish Congress of the Midwest, board of directors.

Addresses: *Office*—Beth Shalom B'nai Zaken Ethiopian Hebrew Congregation, 6601 S. Kedzie Ave., Chicago, IL 60629-3432.

tration from the same school. He was ordained a rabbi in 1985 by the Israelite Rabbinical Academy of Queens, New York, a school for black Hebrews, and later underwent a second ordination supervised by members of a rabbinical council made up of Orthodox and Conservative rabbis. In Chicago he became head of the Beth Shalom B'nai Zaken Ethiopian Hebrew Congregation, which was originally known as the Ethiopian Hebrew Settlement Workers Association when it was founded in 1918 by Rabbi Horace Hasan, a native of Bombay (now Mumbai), India. In later years the Beth Shalom congregation moved to a former Ashkenazi synagogue on South Kedzie Avenue in the far southwest corner of the city. Funnye presides as head rabbi of a racially integrated religious community, though the majority of its members are African American. Many are converts to Judaism, but both Rabbi Matthew and Funnye have referred to this as "reversion" instead of conversion, because they are instead returning to their ancestral faith.

There are no concrete statistics detailing the numbers of black Jews in America, only an estimate that they make up a little less than 1 percent of the 5.3 million Americans who identify themselves as Jewish. The two hundred members of Funnye's congregation are among these fifty thousand or so black Jews. He has admitted that he has periodically encountered astonishment when his religious affiliation becomes known, such as the times that he and his wife notified school officials that their daughters would be missing class because of the Jewish religious holidays. Being African American, he has said, is secondary to being Jewish. "My main concern for my kids," he told Donna Halper in an article that appeared on the Web site of the United Jewish Communities, "is that they carry on the Jewish tradition, and that they marry Jews. I don't care what color the Jews are—just so long as the Jewish tradition is kept alive." In that same article he made reference to a belief once voiced by Rabbi Matthew generations before, that the white Jewish community might find it difficult to accept black Jews. For this reason, many black Jews worship in their own organizations. "I can understand why some black Jews almost prefer to find an all-black congregation—it's not a desire for segregation, but a desire to pray without people staring at you because you look different from everyone else," Funnye told Halper.

Funnye was the first African American to sit on the Chicago Board of Rabbis, and he also joined the boards of the Jewish Council on Urban Affairs and the American Jewish Congress of the Midwest. In Chicago he and his community have made an effort to reach out to their neighbors. "We're not going anywhere," he told Koppel in the *New York Times.* "I'm going to reach out until you reach back." He also cofounded the Alliance of Black Jews, an organization that forged connections between African-American Jews and communities of black Hebrews in Ethiopia and Nigeria.

Funnye's connection to Democratic presidential candidate Barack Obama was first reported by the *Chicago Jewish News* in August of 2008, and the story was then picked up by the *Wall Street Journal*; even Koppel's article, which ran in the *New York Times* in March of 2008, had failed to mention the connection. Both Funnye and Michelle Obama grew up in the same South Side area, though he was twelve years older. They saw one another regularly at family gatherings, and Funnye said that his mother and Michelle Obama's grandfather were part of a close-knit group of siblings. "I know that her grandfather and her father and my mom and all of our relatives that are now deceased would be so very, very proud of both of them," he told Anthony Weiss in the Jewish newspaper the *Forward,* not long after Barack Obama officially became the Democratic Party nominee for president. Funnye attended the 1992 wedding of his first cousin once removed to the future U.S. president, but he told Weiss that Obama "really jumped on everyone's radar after the 2004 convention. That's when some people said, 'Isn't he related to you or something?' I said, 'Yeah, he's married to my cousin, and she's making him everything that he is.'"

Sources

Periodicals

New York Times, March 16, 2008, p. A29.

Online

"Biography of Rabbi Caper C. Funnye Jr.," Beth Shalom Temple, http://www.bethshalombz.org/files/Biography_of_Rav_Funnye.pdf (accessed November 15, 2008).

Halper, Donna, "Black Jews: A Minority within a Minority," United Jewish Communities, http://www.ujc.org/page.aspx?id=26506 (accessed November 15, 2008).

Weiss, Anthony, "Michelle Obama Has a Rabbi in Her Family," *Forward,* September 2, 2008, http://www.forward.com/articles/14121/ (accessed November 15, 2008).

—Carol Brennan

Ken Griffey Jr.

1969—

Baseball player

Griffey, Ken, Jr., photograph. G. Fiume/Getty Images.

Tagged as a top-level prospect when he was only seventeen years old, Ken Griffey Jr. joined Major League Baseball in 1989 at age nineteen. His father, Ken Griffey Sr., was a baseball superstar in his own right and was still an active player when his son joined the American League. The Griffeys made history as the first father and son to play major league baseball simultaneously. Their fame in this regard reached a peak in the 1990 season, when they both worked for the Mariners. A hard-hitting center fielder for the Seattle Mariners until 2000, Griffey was a significant force behind that team's emergence as an American League division champion. He could dominate on offense or defense, and his engaging personality brought him widespread fan approval in a time when most major league baseball players were perceived as spoiled and arrogant. *Atlanta Journal-Constitution* reporter Terence Moore called Griffey "the Hank Aaron, Willie Mays and Roberto Clemente of our time." In 2000 Griffey dismissed his potential to negotiate an extravagant contract as a free agent and returned instead to Cincinnati to play for his hometown team, the Reds, for a comparatively modest sum of $116.5 million over nine years. On July 31, 2008, the trade deadline in that year, the Reds traded Griffey to the Chicago White Sox. After a loss to Tampa in the postseason, the White Sox declined to take Griffey's $16.5 million contract option for 2009, making Griffey a free agent.

Learned Game from Baseball-Player Father

The same year George Kenneth Griffey Jr. was born, his father signed to play baseball with the Cincinnati Reds organization. In fact, Ken Jr. was born during the autumn after his father's first season of play in the Reds' minor league system. The family then lived in the Griffey hometown of Donora, Pennsylvania, but as Ken Sr.'s career took off, "Junior" and his brother moved with their parents through a series of minor league towns. Their travels came to an end in 1973 when Griffey Sr. made the parent club, which happened to be one of the best major league baseball has ever seen—the famed Cincinnati "Big Red Machine."

The demands of major league baseball are not necessarily compatible with fatherhood. Baseball players travel frequently and pursue their trade at odd hours.

At a Glance . . .

Born George Kenneth Griffey Jr. on November 21, 1969, in Donora, PA; son of George Kenneth (a baseball player) and Alberta Griffey; married Melissa; children: Trey Kenneth, Taryn Kennedy, Tevin.

Career: Professional baseball player, 1987—. Signed with Seattle Mariners as first choice in first round of 1987 amateur draft; minor leaguer in Mariners' system, 1987–89; outfielder, Seattle Mariners, 1989–2000, Cincinnati Reds, 2000–08, Chicago White Sox, 2008.

Awards: All-Star, American League, 1990–99, named All-Star Game Most Valuable Player, 1992; Gold Glove awards, 1990–99; Player of the Year and American League MVP, 1997; All-Star, National League, 2000, 2004, 2007; Comeback Player of the Year, National League, 2005.

Addresses: *Home*—Orlando, FL.

They work weekends and evenings. Nevertheless, Griffey recalled in the *Chicago Tribune*: "My dad was a dad first and a baseball player second." The elder Griffey taught his sons to hit a baseball as soon as they could hold a bat. He took them to Reds batting practice, where they hobnobbed with the likes of Pete Rose, Johnny Bench, and Tony Perez. When the Reds played in the World Series in 1975 and 1976, young Griffey looked on from the best seats in the stadium. "I watched my dad play for years," he told *People*. "I talked to him every day about the game. There isn't one thing I've seen so far that he hasn't told me about beforehand."

When Ken Griffey Sr. was traded to the New York Yankees in 1981, his wife and sons stayed behind in Cincinnati. The separations were even more prolonged and difficult than they had been before, and in the odd moments when Griffey Sr. could catch one of his son's Little League or school games, he was mobbed for autographs and pictures. Father and son never let the circumstances alter their relationship, however. Griffey Jr. told *Ebony*: "If I needed to talk to [my father], I would call him after the game, and we'd talk. If I did something wrong [on the field], he'd fly me to New York and say, 'You can't do that!' Then he would send me home the next day, and I'd play baseball." Interestingly enough, the younger Griffey recalled in the *Chicago Tribune* that he often played at his worst when his father was in the stands. "I was always trying to impress him by hitting the ball 600 feet," he said.

It was talent, not family connections, that enabled Griffey to join Cincinnati's competitive Connie Mack League, a summer amateur program composed mostly of high school graduates. Even though at sixteen years old he was among the very youngest of the players, Griffey was such a success in the league that his team advanced to the Connie Mack World Series—and he hit three home runs in the championship match. He also played high school baseball and was such a good running back with the Moeller High School football team that he was offered a football scholarship to the University of Oklahoma. He turned the scholarship down and made himself available for the 1987 baseball draft. Defending his decision, he told the *Chicago Tribune* that baseball "is a lot safer and you last longer."

Signed to Seattle Mariners Organization

Griffey was the number-one pick in major league baseball's 1987 amateur draft. He was chosen by the Seattle Mariners and signed with a $160,000 bonus. In a show of youthful bravado, the seventeen-year-old player announced that he would make the major leagues within two or three years. No one expected him to live up to that boast—even his father had spent four-and-a-half years on farm teams. Nevertheless, the exuberant Griffey Jr. began his professional career in Bellingham, Washington, batting .320, hitting 14 home runs, and completing 13 steals.

The transition to major league play was not completely smooth, however. Griffey experienced adjustment problems when faced with the pressures of professional baseball. He was far from home, and his father was busy with his own career. Years later Griffey revealed that he attempted suicide by swallowing more than 270 aspirin tablets one night during that rookie season. "I got depressed, I got angry. I didn't want to live," he explained in *Jet* magazine. "The aspirin thing was the only time I acted. It was such a dumb thing."

Griffey found his stride during his second minor league season when, despite injuries, he was voted the top major-league prospect in the California League. As the 1989 spring training season began, Griffey was determined to find a spot on the Seattle Mariners' roster. He studied the opposing pitchers, practiced his fielding diligently, and wound up batting .359 with two home runs and 21 runs batted in during spring training games. He earned a place on the team, and when he took the field for his first major league game, he was nineteen years old—one of the youngest men ever to make the majors.

Newspapers and magazines seized upon the Griffey family story. While Ken Jr. was making his debut with the Mariners in Seattle, his father was returning to the Reds and marking his twentieth anniversary in professional sports. It was a historic moment for baseball, surpassed only in 1990 when the two men both played for the Mariners simultaneously. The extra attention might have proven difficult for some rookie players, but Griffey Jr. took it all in stride. "Once he stepped onto the field," wrote E. M. Swift in *Sports Illustrated,* "the kid seemed to relate best to destiny. From the start he showed an almost preposterous flair for the dramatic. He doubled in his first official big-league at-bat. He hit an opposite-field homer on his first swing before the hometown fans in the Kingdome. He hit a game-winning two-run homer in his first pinch-hitting appearance in May 1989." Only a late-season injury robbed Griffey of the statistics necessary to earn Rookie of the Year honors. He finished third in the balloting.

Griffey put the Mariners on the baseball map in 1990, batting .300 and earning his first of ten consecutive Gold Glove awards. He also became the second youngest player ever to start an All-Star Game. That same season saw both Griffeys playing for the Mariners—an historic first for baseball that may never be repeated. Griffey Sr. joined the Mariners late in the season after being released by the Reds. Jim Lefebvre, the Mariners' manager at the time, told the *Los Angeles Times* that the teaming-up of the two Griffey stars was "a great day for baseball." Lefebvre commented: "Here he is a father, a veteran player ending his career, and the son is a brilliant young talent, just like his father was when he was first starting his career, and they're both going to be out there together."

By 1992 the days of father and son playing for the same team were over, and the era of Ken Griffey Jr. had begun. In 1992 Griffey batted .308, hit 27 home runs, and was named Most Valuable Player at the All-Star Game after turning in a three-for-four evening with a home run. He also charmed fans and the media alike with his willingness to grant interviews and his obvious love of baseball. Not surprisingly, observers began to predict a Hall of Fame career for the young star. Griffey made light of these predictions, telling *Sport* magazine: "I just want to go out there and contribute. No matter what happens, you got to be lucky to get in the Hall of Fame. You got to have a long, healthy career."

Helped Mariners Win Divisional Title

Hall of Fame prospects are also boosted by postseason play. During the early years of Griffey's major league career, his talents seemed wasted on a struggling team like the Seattle Mariners, but the circumstances changed. The Mariners moved into contender position, with the perennially strong Griffey leading the way. The team took off in the spring of 1995, showing playoff possibilities under the new divisional rankings. Ironically, Griffey almost missed the postseason show. On May 26, 1995, he broke both bones in his wrist when he crashed into the Kingdome wall while chasing down a fly ball. The injury required the installation of seven screws and a four-inch metal plate in his left wrist, and he was expected to miss at least three months of play. Nevertheless, he returned to the lineup August 15 and, after struggling through the season's later weeks, found his stride again in time for the divisional and league playoffs.

The 1995 American League divisional playoffs pitted the Mariners against the Yankees in a best-of-five series. It was during the fifth and deciding game that Griffey had his defining moment as a potential baseball immortal. The game went into extra innings, and the Yankees took a 5–4 lead in the top of the eleventh inning. When the Mariners came to bat, Griffey hit a single with a man on base to place runners at first and third. Then Edgar Martinez hit a hard shot into the left field corner. The man on third scored easily to tie the game, but Griffey was not to be denied. Turning on the base-running speed for which he is known, he streaked around the diamond and slid across home plate just in front of the outfielder's throw. Griffey's feat brought the Mariners their first divisional title and the right to meet the Cleveland Indians in the 1995 American League Playoffs.

Griffey signed to play for the Mariners through the 1996 season and extended through 2000. He expressed little interest in leaving Seattle until he was offered a contract with the Cincinnati Reds in 2000.

Plagued by Injuries in Late Career

However, once Griffey began playing with the Reds, he was plagued with a series of injuries; although his statistics were still good, they were below the level he was truly capable of. Injuries ended his seasons prematurely in 2002, 2003, and 2004. In addition, he lost strength because of the effect of all the injuries, lowering his bat speed and leading to an average of .264 in 2002. From 2002 to 2004, he missed 250 of 486 games.

In 2004 he avoided being injured long enough to become the twentieth player to hit 500 career home runs. The 500th homer occurred on June 20 during a Father's Day game with the St. Louis Cardinals, and his own father was in the stands watching him when he hit it. The home run also tied him with his father for career hits, with 2,143. Unfortunately, he suffered a torn hamstring later in the summer, and the injury kept him out of the All-Star game. After a complicated surgery and a lengthy recovery, Griffey returned to the field in 2005, and his play was much improved, with thirty-five home runs, the highest number since he had joined the Reds. In September of 2005 he was benched again with another injury to his left knee. He also had surgery to repair scars left from his earlier hamstring operation. Nevertheless, in 2005 he was named the National League Comeback Player of the Year.

In 2006 Griffey was again fighting injuries, but he had some memorable moments. Among these were hitting his 537th home run, which topped Mickey Mantle's position as number twelve on the all-time home run list. On June 27, he hit his 550th career home run, surpassing Mike Schmidt on the all-time list. He tied Reggie Jackson for the tenth spot on the list on September 25, 2006, with his 563rd hit.

Surpassed the 600 Home-Run Mark

In 2007 Griffey made the All-Star team for the thirteenth time in his career. In 2008 he hit a combined .249 and 71 RBIs in 143 games with the Cincinnati Reds and the White Sox. He became the sixth player to hit 600 home runs on June 9, 2008. Unlike other homerun hitters, Griffey was never tainted with suspicions of using performance-enhancing drugs.

He was traded to the White Sox on July 31 of that year for the opportunity to play in the postseason; the White Sox lost in the first round of the American League playoffs to Tampa Bay. During that season he passed Sammy Sosa for fifth on the all-time home-run list, with 611 at the end of the season. In October of 2008 Griffey had surgery on his left knee to repair a torn meniscus and cartilage. In the same month, the Chicago White Sox declined to take Griffey's $16.5 million contract option for 2009, making Griffey a free agent. At that time, the White Sox general manager said, "He will undoubtedly help some club, both on the field and in the clubhouse. Pure class."

Baseball, Griffey told the *Chicago Tribune,* "is never work. Work is something you have to go do and you don't want to. If you do something that's fun, you can't call it work." Griffey stated in 2007 that he would like to retire with the Seattle Mariners. At that time Mariners President Chuck Armstrong said, "I think everybody in Seattle would like to see him retire in a Mariners uniform. He was born a Mariner. And I'd like to see him finish up as a Mariner." However, as of early 2009 the Mariners had not signed Griffey.

Sources

Periodicals

Atlanta Journal-Constitution, July 13, 1994, p. E2.
Boston Globe, October 13, 1995, p. 93.
Chicago Tribune, April 17, 1992, p. C1.
Ebony, September 1989, pp. 78–82; July 2000, p. 46.
Jet, April 6, 1992.
Los Angeles Times, September 1, 1990, p. C1.
People, July 17, 1989, pp. 77–78.
Sport, March 1991, pp. 38–45.
Sports Illustrated, May 16, 1988, pp. 64–68; May 7, 1990, pp. 38–42; August 8, 1994, pp. 24–31.
USA Today, May 7, 2008.

Online

"Box Score: Play-by-Play," SI.com, June 25, 2006, http://sportsillustrated.cnn.com/baseball/mlb/recaps/2006/06/25/12839_recap.html (accessed January 27, 2009).
Donovan, John, "Stars for Sale: Griffey Headlines Top-10 Players on the Trade Block," SI.com, July 19, 2007, http://sportsillustrated.cnn.com/2007/writers/john_donovan/07/19/griffey.reds/index.html (accessed January 27, 2009).
Heyman, John, "Reds, ChiSox Agree to Griffey Deal," SI.com, July 31, 2008, http://sportsillustrated.cnn.com/2008/baseball/mlb/07/31/griffey.whitesox/index.html (accessed January 27, 2009).
"Welcome Back: Griffey, Giambi Named Comeback Players of the Year," SI.com, October 6, 2005, http://sportsillustrated.cnn.com/2005/baseball/mlb/10/06/bc.bbm.lgns.comebackplayersyear.r/index.html (accessed January 27, 2009).
Wilkinson, Jack, "Junior's Dignified 600th Stroll," SI.com, June 10, 2008, http://sportsillustrated.cnn.com/2008/writers/jack_wilkinson/06/09/griffey.600/index.html (accessed January 27, 2009).

—Mark Kram and Melissa Doak

Danai Gurira

1978(?)—

Actor, playwright

Gurira, Danai, photograph. Ariel Ramerez/Landov.

Danai Gurira scored a resounding hit in 2005 with her debut work for the stage, *In the Continuum.* The actor and playwright cowrote the play with her classmate from New York University's graduate theater program, Nikkole Salter, and both women also starred in the heart-wrenching drama about two HIV-positive women on opposite ends of the globe. Gurira took the role of an affluent television journalist in Zimbabwe who learns that she has been infected with the virus by her unfaithful husband. Salter's character is a young woman from a rough area of Los Angeles who also learns she is HIV-positive on the same day her pregnancy test is confirmed by a medical professional. "The way that Africans and African-Americans are portrayed in the media can allow audiences to feel there is an us and a them," Gurira told Elizabeth Tannen in the alumni magazine *Macalester Today* about her and Salter's shared motivation in writing *In the Continuum.* "That's why this play requires our all because we have to live as much as we can in our humanity so that is translated regardless of their color: so that distance is lessened, so we realize that these people are the same, we're the same flesh and blood!"

Gurira was born in Iowa to Zimbabwean parents who had come to the United States to attend college and stayed on for a number of years. In the late 1970s her father was teaching chemistry to students of Grinnell College in Iowa, where Gurira spent the first five years of her life. The family returned to Zimbabwe around the time she was set to enter the first grade. Gurira described herself as outspoken, even as a child, which she viewed as a legacy of her American roots and her parents' embracing of certain aspects of American culture. "Even the way I was raised in Zimbabwe was not typical," she recounted in the interview with Tannen for *Macalester Today.* "To have a loudmouth daughter is unusual in a Zimbabwean home and my parents had loudmouth daughters! If they'd never spent time here, I don't know if I would have come out this way or if I'd have had the nerve to write this play."

Inspired by South African Artists

Gurira spent her formative years in Harare, Zimbabwe's capital, but returned to the United States for her college education. She graduated from Macalester Col-

At a Glance . . .

Born Danai Jekesai Gurira in 1978(?) in Grinnell, IA; daughter of Roger (a chemistry instructor) and Josephine Gurira. *Education:* Macalester College, BA, psychology, 2001; New York University, MFA, 2004.

Career: Made television debut as an actor on an episode of *Law & Order: Criminal Intent,* 2004; first play as a playwright and actor, *In the Continuum,* made its off-Broadway debut at Primary Stages, New York City, September 2005; made feature-film debut as an actor in *The Visitor,* 2007; signed deal with the Oxygen cable network to develop television projects.

Awards: Global Tolerance Award, United Nations, 2005, for *In the Continuum;* special Obie Award for writing, 2006, for *In the Continuum.*

Addresses: *Office*—c/o Overture Films, 521 Fifth Ave., Ste. 1900, New York, NY 10175; c/o Oxygen Media LLC, 75 Ninth Ave., New York, NY 10011.

lege in St. Paul, Minnesota, in 2001 with a psychology degree, but devoted some of her time to the school's drama-department productions. Her decision to choose a career in the performing arts was the direct result of her college's study-abroad program in South Africa, where she encountered "these amazing artists who performed their art during apartheid to make a difference," she told Tannen, "and that's when it hit me to the core that I needed to fly without a net, and go into this very insecure field! I knew that's where my passion lay."

Gurira applied to and won a spot at New York University's well-regarded graduate drama program at its Tisch School of the Arts. She met fellow drama student Nikkole Salter there when a professor suggested they work together on monologue assignments that, unbeknownst to them, were similar in scope: Each was writing about a black woman who is HIV-positive. They began working on what would become *In the Continuum* in 2003, then refined it at a workshop run by the Ojai Playwrights Conference in California, and then took it back to New York, where it premiered at the Mud/Bone Collective, a South Bronx theater space. By then Gurira had earned her MFA from Tisch and made her television debut with a role in an episode of *Law & Order: Criminal Intent.*

A producer for Primary Stages, an off-Broadway venue, saw *In the Continuum* at the Mud/Bone Collective and brought it to his stage in September of 2005. In the two-person drama Gurira played Abigail, a middle-class Zimbabwean woman with a prestigious job as a television news announcer for the state-run broadcasting network. Married and with a small child, she discovers she is HIV-positive when she finds out she is expecting her second child. Salter's character was Nia, who grew up in foster homes in south-central Los Angeles. Her life seems to be on the right track, until she is fired from her job and discovers that she is HIV-positive and pregnant, too—both of which are the result of her relationship with a talented young basketball player on his way to a lucrative contract in the National Basketball Association. Both women struggle with the devastating news and share it with a few trusted intimates; these secondary characters were also played by Gurira and Salter.

Took Play to Africa

In the Continuum won terrific reviews. In the *Los Angeles Daily News,* critic Evan Henerson asserted that "watching Gurira and Salter also share the same stage, tracking 'Continuum's' parallel cross-continental journeys while never interacting with each other, beyond the play's first scene, is a feat of dramatic beauty." In *Variety* Mark Blankenship commended the pair's "raw, astonishing" performances and also noted that Gurira and Salter ably "create two continents' worth of memorable people, but it's as the leads that they truly reveal their gifts. Faces flickering with despair, anger and hope, they show so many sides of their characters' hearts that Nia and Abigail become both unforgettable individuals and symbols for the larger face of HIV."

Though Harare and Los Angeles may seem a world apart, in both places black women were among the leading victims of acquired immunodeficiency syndrome (AIDS). Sexual practices and intravenous drug use varied in each place, but the majority of women who tested positive for the human immunodeficiency virus (HIV) that leads to AIDS were infected by their male sexual partners. Gurira and Salter wanted to portray the communal tragedy that their respective characters faced with the news of their diagnosis. "As the two women search for help, the play lays out … exactly how unsatisfactory their options are," noted *New York Times* critic Sylviane Gold in 2007. "The problem is the same for both the girl in the 'hood and the married woman in Africa: if either tries to prevent her man from infecting others by revealing his HIV status, she risks destroying his willingness and his ability to see her through the illness."

In the Continuum proved such a success that it went on to a larger venue in New York City, the Perry Street Theatre, and then on to the Yale Repertory Theatre in New Haven, Connecticut. In April of 2006 Gurira and Salter performed it at the Harare International Festival for the Arts in Zimbabwe and then for audiences in Johannesburg, South Africa. They also won a special Obie Award in 2006 from the *Village Voice* in its annual roundup of the best off-Broadway plays of the season.

Received Good Reviews for Film Role

Gurira went on to appear in a small but well-received feature film, *The Visitor,* which premiered at the 2007 Toronto Film Festival. Written and directed by Tom McCarthy (*The Station Agent*), Gurira costarred with the American actor Richard Jenkins, who plays Walter, a professor of economics and lonely widower who returns to his New York City apartment to find it has been unlawfully rented out to a pair of illegal immigrants. Gurira played Zainab, a woman from Senegal who makes and sells jewelry on the streets of New York, and she lives in the apartment with her Syrian boyfriend, Tarek, played by Haaz Sleiman. The owner's shock at finding two unexpected guests in the home he shared with his recently deceased wife gives way to a touching friendship—with both the couple and Tarek's mother—that forms the basis of the movie's plot. Walter vacated the place temporarily to take a teaching job in Connecticut, and in a somewhat ironic twist his academic specialty is third world economies. "Walter ends up despairing of a faceless bureaucracy that has derived further justification from the 'war on terror,'" wrote Philip French in a review of *The Visitor* appearing in the London *Observer.* "At the same time, his friendship for these three strangers has renewed his sense of social responsibility and broadened his feeling of humanity."

Gurira and Salter were collaborating on a few other projects, including a possible story about women soldiers during Liberia's devastating civil war of the 1990s. Gurira was also cast in two other films scheduled for release in 2009: Wes Craven's horror movie *25/8* and *Three Backyards,* a tale of intertwined suburban lives. Her career has brought her to the United States to live permanently, but her visits back home to family in Harare continued to provide inspiration and insight. When she and Salter took *In the Continuum* to Harare and Johannesburg, she was surprised to find that audiences there were able to identify with Salter's character. Yet she also said that

New York City audiences expressed surprise that her own character, Abigail, consults a *nganga,* or traditional Shona healer, at one point in the play. As she told Trey Graham in a 2006 interview for *American Theatre* magazine, New Yorkers seemed confused that a professional woman would turn to a spirit medium, whereas audiences in Harare accepted visits to traditional healers as entirely normal. "I mean, psychics are on every corner, in New York, anyway," she reflected. "The difference isn't that large. But sometimes people want to look for large differences."

Selected works

Plays; as playwright and actor

In the Continuum, produced at Primary Stages, New York City, 2005.

Films; as actor

The Visitor, 2007.
25/8, 2009.
Three Backyards, 2009.

Sources

Periodicals

American Theatre, July–August 2006, p. 50.
Back Stage West, September 20, 2007, p. 10.
Los Angeles Daily News, November 24, 2006, p. U17.
New York Times, October 1, 2005, p. B9; May 20, 2006, p. B11; January 21, 2007.
Observer (London), July 6, 2008, p. 20.
Variety, October 10, 2005, p. 85.

Online

Tannen, Elizabeth, "Tale of Two Women," Macalester Today, http://www.macalester.edu/whatshappening/mactoday/2006winter/gurira.html (accessed November 16, 2008).

—Carol Brennan

Corey Harris

1969—

Blues musician

Harris, Corey, photograph. David Rae Morris/Reuters/Landov.

"Corey Harris wants to redefine the blues," noted Steve Inskeep of National Public Radio in 2002, which is exactly what Harris has done throughout his career. Traditional acoustic blues attracted a host of young performers beginning in the 1990s, but Harris set himself apart from the pack by looking both back to the African roots of the blues and forward to reggae, hip-hop, and Latin styles. For Harris, the blues represent not simply a musical style but a manifestation of musical ideas that African-descended peoples everywhere hold in common. Furthermore, he has a distinct ability to bring together a variety of black musical traditions. He could be compared to the well-known elder musician Taj Mahal, who was instrumental in exploring the roots and revitalizing the traditional sounds of African-American blues.

Harris was born in February of 1969 in Denver, Colorado. As a small child, he demonstrated his musical leanings by banging on pots and pans at home. Both of his parents were music lovers, so they encouraged the young musician to explore his talent. Early on, Harris heard the folk music of Odetta and the reggae of Bob Marley. He started taking trumpet lessons at age five, but after listening to his mother's collection of records by bluesman Lightnin' Hopkins, he decided at age twelve to switch to the guitar. During his high school years Harris honed his guitar playing in a rock band and his singing voice in church.

Studied, Taught, and Played

Harris attended Bates College in Lewiston, Maine, a small liberal arts institution, to study anthropology and linguistics. During his undergraduate years, he spent a year abroad in both France and the West African nation of Cameroon. In Cameroon his goal was to study pidgin—the simplified form of English that arose in Africa as a way of communicating along trade routes. African linguistic patterns would eventually have an impact on Harris's music, but at this point he was content simply to soak up the African traditions he encountered in Cameroon, fascinated by the links he heard between the juju music of Cameroon and Nigeria, and the African-American blues he knew back home.

After graduating from Bates in 1991, Harris decided to spend two years with Teach for America, a national

At a Glance . . .

Born on February 21, 1969, in Denver, CO. *Education:* Bates College, BA, anthropology, 1991.

Career: Teach for America (national corps of teachers), taught English and French at a school in rural Louisiana, 1991–93; performed in clubs, coffeehouses, and the streets in New Orleans, LA, 1993–94; professional musician, 1995—.

Awards: Watson Fellowship for study in Cameroon, 1990; Fellowship, John D. and Catherine T. MacArthur Foundation, 2007.

Addresses: *Office*—Telarc International Corporation, 23307 Commerce Park Rd., Cleveland, OH 44122. *Web*—http://www.myspace.com/coreyharrismusic.

teacher corps of recent college grads who work in rural and urban schools that need resources and support. He taught English and French in rural Louisiana. He had not yet thought of making his career in music, although he sometimes performed at clubs and coffeehouses in nearby New Orleans.

Eventually, Harris left teaching and began playing for tips on the streets of New Orleans and barnstorming around the South in his car, performing wherever he could. "I didn't have a record deal or an agent or anything," Harris told *Guitar Player.* "It was just me and my guitar, making enough money for gas and motels. There were sacrifices, but I was just crazy about playing." In 1994 Harris made a demo tape, and a year later he was signed to the blues-oriented Alligator label, awaiting the release of his debut album, *Between Midnight and Day.*

Began to Write Music

That album featured Harris and his guitar covering acoustic blues classics such as Charley Patton's "Pony Blues," Sleepy John Estes' "I Ain't Gonna Be Worried No More," and Mississippi Fred McDowell's "Keep Your Lamp Trimmed and Burning." Strong sales and positive reviews for *Between Midnight and Day* put Harris on the cover of *Living Blues* magazine and led to an offer to open for 10,000 Maniacs vocalist Natalie Merchant on her 1996 tour. *Down Beat* reviewer Robert Santelli, however, even as he praised Harris's "jagged, salt-of-the-earth voice" and "rough-'n'-tumble, wonderfully rhythmic guitar style," argued that "Harris needs his own songs to make a real splash."

Harris took this advice to heart on his second album, *Fish Ain't Bitin'* (1997), which featured New Orleans–style brass on several tracks and offered his own compositions, including "5-0 Blues," one of several Harris songs that would address the issue of police misconduct. That album again snared the attention of alternative rock artists. For example, Harris was asked to perform on the album *Mermaid Avenue* (1998), which featured completions of previously unfinished songs by folk legend Woody Guthrie.

On his third album, *Greens from the Garden* (1999), Harris gave full expression to the stylistic freedom that had been brewing in his career up to that point. He rejected the blues revivalist label. "That's really the nature of the media," he told the *Chicago Sun-Times.* "Anything they can sum up in one simple phrase, they'll do it." Harris produced the album himself, lending it the feeling of a relaxed live performance. Singing in both English and French, and accompanied by his band and various guest musicians, he delved into Cajun music, New Orleans funk, jazz, Cameroonian juju, Piedmont blues, and other styles. With pieces such as "Basehead," which depicted cocaine users as inheritors of a slave mentality, Harris grew as a songwriter.

Moved to Rounder Label, Then Telarc

Greens from the Garden drew critical raves and planted Harris firmly on the playlists of Americana-oriented radio stations—an increasingly common format in the nonprofit public radio sector. The album's only downside was that it strained his relationship with Alligator, which was mostly devoted to straight-ahead blues material. As a result, the label insisted on a professional remix of the material Harris delivered. Label head Bruce Iglauer, while supporting Harris's new creative freedom, told the *Chicago Sun-Times* that the album "got away from my personal tastes as a blues fan." Harris recorded one more album for Alligator, *Vu-Du Menz* (2000), a duo collaboration with pianist Henry Butler. He moved to the eclectic Rounder label, though, for his next release, *Downhome Sophisticate* (2002).

The album reprised "Keep Your Lamp Trimmed and Burning," this time in an explosive electric sermon-like arrangement. Acoustic tracks included "Capitaine," an evocation of a Niger River fish, and in several places the album benefited from a fresh infusion of African influences—Harris had traveled to Mali shortly before going into the studio. He addressed the theme of African-American mistrust of the police in "Santoro," which likened a police car to a frightful biblical beast on the prowl. He even incorporated Latin traditions into the album, many of whose song texts were cast in reggae-influenced or African-influenced speech patterns. In all, noted Robert L. Doerschuk on the allmusic Web site, "few artists reflect the breadth of black music as vividly as Corey Harris." Harris was well on his way to becoming the alchemist of black music, recombining its constituent elements into new and powerful substances.

In September of 2003 the seven-part Public Broadcasting System (PBS) film series *The Blues* debuted with "Feel Like Going Home," an episode that focused on the Delta blues. Directed by Martin Scorsese, this first part in the film series traced the blues from Africa to the Mississippi delta and included Harris and Otha Turner, a well-known fife player, performing "Lay My Burden Down."

Harris dedicated his next album, *Mississippi to Mali* (2003), to Turner, continuing the concept of a melding of African and American blues expression that was the foundation of the PBS performance. Turner was to have performed on the album, but he died not only before the release of the PBS series but before the recording of the album. As such, Shardé Thomas, his twelve-year-old granddaughter, performed a version of "Sitting on Top of the World" (called "Station Blues" on the album) in his place. She was accompanied by the Rising Star Fife and Drum Band, which was made up by friends and relatives of Turner. This album was also unique in that Harris collaborated with African musicians Souleyman Kane on African percussion instruments and Ali Farka Toure on the njarka, a one-string violin; these tracks were recorded live in Mali, whereas the other tracks were recorded live in the United States.

Harris's last album on the Rounder label was *Daily Bread* (2005). James Reed in the *Boston Globe* referred to the album as "pure, easygoing charm" and noted that Harris was "all over the place" with Malian, reggae, pop, soul, and bossa nova undertones.

Harris left the Rounder label for Telarc Records, which released his next album, *Zion Crossroads,* in 2007. Harris's original songs on this album were influenced by the late Jamaican musician, singer-songwriter, and Rastafarian Bob Marley. Reggae provided the musical rhythm, and English Caribbean patois provided the primary language—a shift from Harris's past work. Mike Joyce wrote in the *Washington Post* that "Harris brings his own gifts to the mix: a strong, soulful voice; a knack for conjuring vintage reggae grooves (with plenty of help from a tight, horn-powered ensemble); some incisive guitar work; and a spiritual thrust that's unmistakable." As Harris's career continues, there is no doubt that he will continue to redefine the blues in new, interesting, and unique ways.

Selected discography

Between Midnight and Day, Alligator, 1995.
Fish Ain't Bitin', Alligator, 1997.
Greens from the Garden, Alligator, 1999.
(With Henry Butler) *Vu-Du Menz,* Alligator, 2000.
Downhome Sophisticate, Rounder, 2002.
Mississippi to Mali, Rounder, 2003.
Daily Bread, Rounder, 2005.
Zion Crossroads, Telarc, 2007.

Sources

Periodicals

Albuquerque Journal, November 16, 2001, p. 2.
Boston Globe, June 10, 2005, p. C13.
Chicago Sun-Times, May 21, 1999, p. 9.
Down Beat, March 1996, p. 55; July 1997, p. 63.
Guitar Player, August 1999, p. 35.
Plain Dealer (Cleveland, OH), May 12, 1999, p. E1.
Seattle Times, January 20, 2000, p. G11.
Vancouver Province, August 13, 2002, p. B11.
Washington Post, May 29, 2002, p. C5; December 6, 2002, p. C4; August 17, 2007, p. WE11.

Online

Doerschuk, Robert L., "*Downhome Sophisticate:* Review," allmusic, http://www.allmusic.com/cg/amg.dll?p=amg&sql=10:gnfpxq90ldte (accessed December 3, 2008).

Huey, Steve, "Corey Harris: Biography," allmusic, http://www.allmusic.com/cg/amg.dll?p=amg&sql=11:jvfuxq8gldje (accessed December 3, 2008).

Inskeep, Steve, "Corey Harris," National Public Radio, May 17, 2002, http://www.npr.org/templates/story/story.php?storyId=1143505 (accessed December 3, 2008).

"MacArthur Fellows 2007: Corey Harris," John D. and Catherine T. MacArthur Foundation, September 2007, http://www.macfound.org/site/c.lkLXJ8MQKrH/b.2913825/apps/nl/content2.asp?content_id=%7B24D5862A-4523-4604-B59B-4F1EA9375558%7D&notoc=1 (accessed December 3, 2008).

—James M. Manheim and Sandra Alters

Isaac Hayes

1942–2008

Musician, composer, actor

Hayes, Isaac, photograph. Tom Hill/WireImage/Getty Images.

Musician Isaac Hayes's is best known as the creator of the iconic "Theme from Shaft" from the soundtrack of the blaxploitation police drama *Shaft* (1971). From the beginning of his music career during the 1960s, Hayes was an innovator. He pioneered a cool vocal style featuring a relaxed baritone that was conversational and romantic. The elaborate production and insistent four-beat of such recordings as "Theme from Shaft" prefigured the disco movement, and Hayes himself had some success during the disco era. Years before the word "rap" came to denote a musical style, Hayes was referring to the lengthy spoken interludes in his songs and performances as rapping. His music career flagged after its early momentum as a top seller for the Stax label during the early 1970s. Yet Hayes remained active, seeking out new career opportunities and charitable work. By the late 1990s Hayes had found celebrity yet again as the voice of Chef on the animated television show *South Park* and in his final years could be found playing music for patrons of his Memphis eatery.

Struggled Out of Poverty

Isaac Hayes was born into poverty on a sharecropper's farm in Covington, Tennessee, on August 20, 1942. His mother died when he was a baby, and he was raised by his grandparents, who moved to Memphis when Hayes was seven. During his youth Hayes worked at such menial jobs as picking cotton, pumping gas, and helping out at a junkyard. He cultivated an interest in music that began when his grandparents encouraged him to sing in church at age five and had grown through the influence of another family member: "I can remember my aunt had a juke joint, and anybody who walked in the door could sing as good as B. B. King, Sonny Boy Williamson, Lightnin' Hopkins, Muddy Waters, or Howlin' Wolf," Hayes told *Interview* magazine. By sheer force of will, he learned to play the piano.

While working as a meat packer, Hayes fronted several bands that played in Memphis clubs during the early 1960s. Music became an integral part of his life in 1964 when he met saxophonist Floyd Newman, a

At a Glance . . .

Born on August 20, 1942, in Covington, TN; died August 10, 2008, in Memphis, TN; son of Isaac and Eula Hayes; married and divorced three times; married Adowja Hayes; children: twelve. *Religion:* Scientology.

Career: Soul music vocalist, 1962–2008; Stax Records, staff musician and songwriter, 1964–67, recording artist, 1967–75; ABC, recording artist, 1975; Polydor, recording artist, 1977; Point Blank, recording artist, 1995. Actor, 1976–2008; South Park, voice of Chef, 1997–2006; Isaac Hayes Foundation, founder, 1999–2008; Isaac Hayes-Music-Food-Passion, restaurant owner, 2001–07.

Awards: Academy Award, Best Song from a Motion Picture, and Grammy Awards for Best Instrumental Arrangement and Best Original Score, 1971, all for music from *Shaft*; Grammy Award, Best Pop Instrumental Performance, 1972, for *Black Moses*; coronated honorary king, Ghana, Ada district, 1992, for humanitarian work; inductee, Rock and Roll Hall of Fame, 2002; BMI Icon, 2003; inductee, Songwriters Hall of Fame, 2005.

member of the Mar-Keys and an early mainstay of Memphis's soul-music record label, Stax. Hayes was asked to replace the legendary Stax keyboardist Booker T. Jones on a session date, and was soon finding regular work as a Stax session musician. Many of Otis Redding's classic soul recordings for Stax, including "Respect" and "I've Been Lovin' You Too Long" featured Hayes at the keyboard.

Hayes also began to work with a lyricist friend, David Porter, and the pair had several spectacular successes as a songwriting team, most notably with the two big hits scored by the duo of Sam & Dave, "Soul Man" and "Hold On, I'm Coming." In 1967 Stax vice president Al Bell invited Hayes to cut an album. The resulting work, *Presenting Isaac Hayes,* sold poorly, but Hayes continued to refine his skills. When he received another opportunity to record an album in 1969, he was ready.

Found Fame with Unique Sound

The record that ignited Hayes's career, *Hot Buttered Soul,* was a groundbreaking work that represented Stax's effort to respond to the musical experimentation pioneered by Motown during the late 1960s. Featuring elaborate arrangements with strings and backup vocals, the entire album contained only four songs, one of them an eighteen-minute, forty-second version of Jimmy Webb's country-pop hit, "By the Time I Get to Phoenix." Hayes extended songs through the use of introductory monologues, which he called "rapping," and by playing long instrumental interludes on the organ. The album sold more than one million copies and reached number eight on the pop charts. It also marked Stax's most successful effort to cross over to popular audiences.

Hot Buttered Soul launched Hayes's solo career, and he became one of the top-grossing concert acts of the early 1970s. Although he became extremely wealthy, he squandered most of his money and was forced to declare bankruptcy on two occasions. The speech-song mixtures from *Hot Buttered Soul* appeared in his famous *Shaft* theme, which featured a dialogue between Hayes and his ever-present female backup singers, and offered an unusual arrangement that included a flute and a rhythmic use of wah-wah guitar. "Shaft" reached number one on the pop charts and earned Hayes both Academy and Grammy awards. He also became the first African-American composer to be honored with an Academy award.

Even as his financial troubles mounted and the careers of his fellow Stax artists declined, Hayes forged ahead during the middle and late 1970s. Signing with the ABC label in 1975 and with Polydor in 1977, Hayes made a successful foray into disco with the 1976 album *Juicy Fruit* and its single "Juicy Fruit (Disco Freak)." He also recorded duet albums with Dionne Warwick (*A Man and a Woman,* 1977) and fellow proto-rapper Millie Jackson (*Royal Rappin's,* 1979). Hayes also realized his long-held dream of becoming an actor, appearing on the television program *Rockford Files* and taking roles in several films, including the science-fiction thriller *Escape from New York* and *I'm Gonna Git You Sucka,* the Keenen Ivory Wayans parody of the blaxploitation film genre. He played himself in the movie *Soul Men,* a history and celebration of Soul music, which was released two months after his death

Hayes released the albums *U-Turn* in 1986 and *Love Attack* in 1988, both on the Columbia label. In 1995 he issued both *Branded* and the instrumental *Raw and Refined* on the Point Blank label. In *Interview* writer Dimitri Ehrlich remarked that *Raw and Refined* found Hayes "burrowing into jazzy, syncopated grooves, gracefully reveling in heightened realms of musicality and mojo." Ehrlich estimated that Hayes's recordings had been sampled—digitally quoted—more that fifty times by rappers and producers in 1993 alone, and the "gangsta" rap image plainly owed much to Hayes's grandiose stage productions. In 2002 Hayes was inducted into the Rock and Roll Hall of Fame.

Reached New Audience as Voice Actor

Hayes had sought voiceover work for some time when his agent landed him an audition for a new animated show called South Park in the late 1990s. Hayes was cast as the voice of Chef, a school cook and "mentor" to the show's youthful main characters. Early on Hayes had his doubts that joining the show was a wise career move. "We started putting episodes in the can, and when the airdate was announced, I started thinking, 'I've ruined my career, man. I'm going to have to run out of town,'" Hayes remembered to the *San Francisco Chronicle* in 2005. "But when the thing aired, the ratings went through the roof." By the early 2000s Hayes had gained considerable popularity as the voice of Chef, finding that he would be greeted at record signings by music fans as well as a number of fans wanting him to sign Chef dolls. "That's when I realized my fan base had spread from 6 to 96," he related to the *San Francisco Chronicle*. After a decade as the voice of Chef, Hayes abruptly quit the series in the spring of 2006 after an episode that mocked his religion, Scientology. In a statement quoted in the *Chicago Defender,* Hayes explained his reasoning: "Religious beliefs are sacred to people, and at all times should be respected and honored. As a civil rights activist of the past 40 years, I cannot support a show that disrespects those beliefs and practices." Hayes's comments provoked skeptics to point out that Hayes had participated in many *South Park* episodes that mocked other religions over the years. After Hayes left the show, South Park aired an episode in which Chef met with a gruesome demise.

The split with *South Park* did not seem to bother Hayes as he turned his attentions to other aspects of his career. He remained committed to his music, and began work on a new album. He continued hosting a soul music radio program and was a morning host on New York's KISS-FM radio station between 1996 and 2001. He later hosted WRBO Soul Classics in Memphis. He reaped rewards from the popularity of his memoir/cookbook, *Cooking with Heart & Soul: Making Music in the Kitchen with Family and Friends* (2000) as it went into multiple printings, and he introduced a successful barbecue sauce to the retail market in 2000. He also held court on stage at his Isaac Hayes Music-Food-Passion restaurants in Memphis and Chicago.

Through the Isaac Hayes Foundation, which he set up in 1999, Hayes offered aid to people, especially children around the globe. His humanitarian work in Ghana, including the construction of an 8,000-square-foot school, led to his honorary crowning as a king of the Ada district in 1994. He served as an international spokesperson for the nonprofit organization World Literacy Crusade until his death in 2008. Hayes died on August 10, 2008, at home in Memphis, Tennessee. Ben Sisario wrote in the *New York Times* that Hayes's

"luxurious, strutting funk arrangements... defined the glories and excesses of soul music in the early 1970s." and Collin Stanback, a spokesperson for the Stax label, told the Associated Press, Hayes embodied "everything that's soul music. When you think of soul music you think of Isaac Hayes—the expression...the sound and the creativity that goes along with it."

Selected works

Books

Cooking with Heart & Soul: Making Music in the Kitchen with Family and Friends, Putnam, 2000.

Albums

Presenting Isaac Hayes, Stax, 1967.
Hot Buttered Soul, Stax, 1969.
Isaac Hayes Movement, Stax, 1970.
Black Moses, Stax, 1971.
Shaft (soundtrack), Stax, 1971.
Tough Guys (soundtrack), Stax, 1973.
Chocolate Chip, ABC, 1975.
Juicy Fruit, ABC, 1976.
(With Dionne Warwick) *A Man and a Woman,* Polydor, 1977.
(With Millie Jackson) *Royal Rappin's,* Polydor, 1979.
Enterprise—His Greatest Hits, Stax, 1980.
U-Turn, Polydor, 1986.
Branded, Point Blank, 1995.
Raw and Refined, Point Blank, 1995.
Ultimate Isaac Hayes: Can You Dig It?, Stax, 2005.

Films

Tough Guys, 1974.
Truck Turner, 1974.
It Seemed Like a Good Idea at the Time, 1975.
Escape from New York, 1981.
Dead Aim, 1987.
Medium Rare, 1987.
I'm Gonna Git You Sucka, 1988.
Guilty as Charged, 1991.
Prime Target, 1991.
Final Judgement, 1992.
CB4, 1993.
Deadly Exposure, 1993.
Posse, 1993.
Robin Hood: Men in Tights, 1993.
It Could Happen to You, 1994.
Oblivion, 1994.
Once Upon a Time... When We Were Colored, 1995.
Flipper, 1996.
Illtown, 1996.
Oblivion 2: Backlash, 1996.
Six Ways to Sunday, 1997.
Uncle Sam, 1997.
Blues Brothers 2000, 1998.
Ninth Street, 1999.

South Park: Bigger Longer & Uncut, 1999.
Dead Dog, 2000.
Reindeer Games, 2000.
Dr. Dolittle 2, 2001.
Dream Warrior, 2003.
Dodge City: A Spaghetto Western, 2004.
Hustle & Flow, 2005.
Soul Men, 2008.

Television

Rockford Files, 1976–77.
South Park, 1997–2006.
The Hughleys, 1999.
Girlfriends, 2003.
Stargate SG-1, 2005–06.

Sources

Books

Guralnick, Peter, *Sweet Soul Music,* Harper & Row, 1986.

Periodicals

Associated Press, August 10, 2008.
Billboard, March 25, 1995, p. 23.
Chicago Defender, March 15, 2006, p. 16.

Entertainment Weekly, June 9, 1995, p. 59.
Interview, May 1995, p. 24.
Newsweek, March 23, 1998; p. 60.
New York Times, August 10, 2008; November 7, 2008.
People, July 8, 1996, p. 101.
Rolling Stone, November 3, 2005, p. 1.
San Francisco Chronicle, December 4, 2005, p. 50.

Online

Hinckley, David, "Radio Colleagues Fondly Recall Isaac Hayes," *Daily News: Music,* August 12, 2008, http://www.nydailynews.com/entertainment/music sic/2008/08/12/2008-08-12_radio_colleagues_ fondly_recall_isaac_hay.html (accessed January 27, 2009).

Isaac Hayes (official Web site), http://www.isaachayes. com (accessed January 27, 2009).

"Isaac Hayes," Rock and Roll Hall of Fame and Museum, http://www.rockhall.com/inductee/isaac-hayes (accessed January 27, 2009).

"Soul Legend Isaac Hayes Dies," CNN.com, August 11, 2008, http://www.cnn.com/2008/SHOWBIZ/ Music/08/10/hayes.obit/index.html (accessed January 27, 2009).

—James M. Manheim, Sara Pendergast, and Melissa Doak

Arlene Holt Baker

1951—

Labor union executive

In 2007 Arlene Holt Baker became the first African American to hold an executive officer position within the American Federation of Labor and Congress of Industrial Organizations (AFL-CIO). As executive vice president, she oversaw several important initiatives for the AFL-CIO, one of the most powerful labor organizations in the United States. During her tenure, some ten million U.S. workers were affiliated with the AFL-CIO through their workplace unions.

Holt Baker was born Arlene Leslie in 1951 in Fort Worth, Texas, into a family of seven children. Her father, W. S., was a laborer and her mother, Louise, worked as a housekeeper for other families. As a teenager, Holt Baker's first job was with a program set up in Fort Worth as part of President Lyndon B. Johnson's War on Poverty campaign of the mid-1960s. Later she rose through the ranks of her own union, the American Federation of State, County, and Municipal Employees (AFSCME) to become an organizer in the late 1980s. She subsequently served as international union staff representative and then AFSCME area director for California.

Holt Baker's work as an organizer led to an offer from the American Federation of Labor and Congress of Industrial Organizations (AFL-CIO), which was formed from the merger in 1955 of two of the oldest labor groups in the United States. In 1998 she was hired as executive assistant to Linda Chavez-Thompson, its executive vice president, and a year later became executive assistant to AFL-CIO president John Sweeney. In addition to her support roles, both posi-

tions entailed considerable additional responsibility. For example, Holt Baker was in charge of the AFL-CIO's 1998 campaign in California to defeat Proposition 226, which would have hampered the political lobbying efforts of unions. Effective organizing by the AFL-CIO and other unions led voters to reject the proposition at the ballot box.

Holt Baker also led the AFL-CIO's Voice@Work campaign, and in 2002 worked to mobilize labor voters in state and national elections. One example of her work in a close contest was the successful gubernatorial campaign of Pennsylvania Democrat Ed Rendell. She also headed the Working America Alliance and Voices for Working Families, both of which consisted of more than 500 local groups that worked during the political campaign season and maintained a regular lobbying presence in state capitals and Washington. When Sweeney ran for reelection in 2005, Holt Baker served as his campaign manager.

One of Holt Baker's toughest challenges was heading the AFL-CIO's recovery efforts following Hurricane Katrina. She worked on-site in 2005 and 2006 to supervise the distribution of union-donated relief supplies and funds, and also to ensure that rebuilding jobs went to union members. This oversight was of particular importance to the union because Louisiana was a right-to-work state, meaning that a union could be formed in a workplace only if 50 percent plus one of the eligible workforce voted in favor of it; then, membership in the union was not compulsory. This law severely restricted the ability of workers to organize and

At a Glance . . .

Born Arlene Leslie in 1951, in Fort Worth, TX; daughter of W. S. (a laborer) and Louise (a domestic worker) Leslie. *Politics:* Democrat.

Career: AFSCME, organizer, late 1980s; international union staff representative for AFSCME; AFSCME area director for California; AFL-CIO, executive assistant to executive vice president Linda Chavez-Thompson, 1995–99; executive assistant to president John Sweeney, 1999–2007. After 2003, director of the AFL-CIO's Voice[&]commat;Work campaign; president of its Working America Alliance; president of Voices for Working Families. Appointed AFL-CIO executive vice president, September 2007. Delegate to the 1988 Democratic National Convention from California; elected first vice chairwoman of the Democratic Party of California, served until 1995.

Addresses: *Office*—AFL-CIO, 815 16th St. NW, Washington, DC 20006.

maintain their collective-bargaining power. In states where union influence was strong, the law specified that a union could be formed by vote of one half of the workers, and that union membership was then compulsory for all workers.

In June of 2006 the AFL-CIO announced that it would launch a New Orleans investment program for the city's rebuilding using $700 million from its members' pension funds. The plan included a program to train future building-trades workers. "Hopefully they look back one day and say this opportunity was given to me through a union," Holt Baker told Jaquetta White in the New Orleans *Times-Picayune*. "I was able to get this job. I was able to build this home. My children were able to go to college. It was all through an organized labor effort."

On September 11, 2007, Linda Chavez-Thompson announced her retirement as AFL-CIO vice president, and Sweeney appointed Holt Baker to fill the rest of Chavez-Thompson's term, which ran until 2009. With that, Holt Baker became the first African American to hold one of the AFL-CIO's top leadership posts. She was based in Washington, DC, but spent much of the next year working to ensure a strong labor presence at the polls for the 2008 elections. The AFL-CIO backed Illinois Senator Barack Obama, the presidential candidate of the Democratic Party, and in January of 2008 Holt Baker gave a speech to a Labor Leaders' Breakfast Forum sponsored by Cornell University's School of Industrial and Labor Relations (ILR). "We are organizing around three basic issues," she said, according to the ILR News Web site of Cornell University. "Turning our economy into one that works for working families ... reforming health care so it provides affordable, high quality care for all ... and restoring the freedom of every worker to join a union."

A few months later, Holt Baker wrote an editorial essay in the *Los Angeles Sentinel* commemorating the fortieth anniversary of the assassination of the civil rights leader Martin Luther King Jr. Reflecting that on the day he was shot, King was in Memphis, Tennessee, to speak to striking black sanitation workers, she noted that "good jobs are few and far between these days. Yet working people don't have the opportunity to improve their lives by joining unions, even though union workers earn 30 percent more than their nonunion counterparts.... Sixty million people say they would join a union today if they could. Too few get the chance because employers routinely violate workers' freedom to form unions. Corporate and establishment resistance today is even greater than what those sanitation workers faced 40 years ago."

Sources

Periodicals

Los Angeles Sentinel, January 24, 2008.
South Bend Tribune (South Bend, IN), October 2, 2008, p. C8.

Online

"Former AFSCME Leader Elected AFL-CIO Executive VP," AFSCME.org, http://www.afscme.org/publications/16585.cfm (accessed December 10, 2008).
Hall, Mike, "AFL-CIO Executive Council Elects Holt Baker, Approves Political Mobilization Plans," AFL-CIONowBlog, September 21, 2007, http://blog.aflcio.org/2007/09/21/afl-cio-executive-council-elects-holt-baker-approves-political-mobilization-plans / (accessed December 10, 2008).
"Top AFL-CIO Leader Invokes Martin Luther King's Message at ILR Forum," Cornell University, ILR News, January 18, 2008, http://www.ilr.cornell.edu/news/Arlene-Holt-Bakers-NYC-speech.html (accessed December 10, 2008).

—Carol Brennan

Mary Jackson

1945—

Fiber artist, basket maker

Unquestionably, artist Mary Jackson has done more than anyone else to revive and sustain the traditional African-American art of basket making. Using local, hand-picked materials and the skills passed down to her by her forebears, Jackson has produced hundreds of stunningly beautiful baskets, many of which have been placed in the permanent collections of major museums, including the Smithsonian American Art Museum and the Boston Museum of Fine Arts. After nearly three decades of quiet success as a full-time basket maker, Jackson was the focus of intense media attention in 2008, when she received a fellowship from the John D. and Catherine T. MacArthur Foundation.

Jackson was born in 1945 in the small town of Mount Pleasant, South Carolina. She learned basket making at the age of four from her mother and grandmother. "During the summer months," she recalled to Bernadette Finnerty in the *Crafts Report,* "there wasn't much to do other than sit with my grandmother and learn to make baskets. This is a rural area, there wasn't much else going on. Everyone made baskets." The techniques Jackson learned had originated in West Africa and were brought to North America by slaves, among them Jackson's ancestors, who soon found a native plant, sweetgrass, to replace the grasses they had used in Africa. The process is a complex and time-consuming one. Essentially, the sweetgrass is twisted into cords, which are tied with another material (Jackson has often used saw palmetto, bulrush, or pine needles) as they are tightly coiled into the basket's final shape. The coastal region of South Carolina had become a basket-making center well before the Civil

War, both because of the then-plentiful supplies of sweetgrass found there and because the baskets proved particularly well suited for carrying the cotton and rice that constituted the region's chief crops. "The baskets are practical," Jackson told the South Carolina African American History Calendar. "They were made to be used."

Despite the importance of basket making in Jackson's childhood, she found it impractical to continue when she moved to New York City after high school. In 1972, however, she returned to South Carolina. While working as a secretary in Charleston, she found she could earn some extra money making and selling baskets in her spare time. It was at this stage that Jackson began experimenting with the innovative shapes and designs for which she has become known. This innovation, which she described to Finnerty as "tak[ing] the sweetgrass basket making tradition to a whole new contemporary level," always remained respectful of the tradition. It is noteworthy that Jackson has never used artificial or commercially produced materials, restricting herself instead to material gathered in the wild by members of her own family. This reliance on family is also part of the tradition. As Jackson herself has noted, an unwritten rule has long prevented outsiders from learning the technique. This restriction has enabled the small community of basket makers in and around Charleston to survive amid the increasing commercialization of traditional handicraft. Even so, the decline has been steep. Finnerty noted that in the 1920s twenty-five hundred families in the area were making baskets regularly. By 2001 that

At a Glance . . .

Born in 1945 in Mount Pleasant, SC; married Stoney Jackson; children: Aaron, April.

Career: Worked as an executive secretary, 1970s–80; full-time basket maker, 1980—.

Memberships: Mount Pleasant Sweetgrass Basket Makers' Association, founding member and president.

Awards: Fellowship, John D. and Catherine T. MacArthur Foundation, 2008.

Addresses: *Office*—Sweetgrass Baskets, Box 12027, Charleston, SC 29422.

number had decreased to about two hundred, with the vast majority doing so only part time.

Jackson herself made the switch to full time only in 1980, after her son Aaron, then a toddler, was diagnosed with serious asthma. To give him the care he needed, she quit her job and began making baskets full time at home. Fortunately, the quality of her work was already well known, and she realized relatively quickly that she would be able to support her family solely as an artist. In the early 1980s her career received a boost when Kenneth Trapp, a former curator at the Smithsonian American Art Museum, acquired some of her baskets for the museum's permanent collection. A number of other major museums followed suit, including Boston's Museum of Fine Arts, New York City's Museum of Arts and Design, and Detroit's Museum of African-American History. As news of these acquisitions spread, commissions from individual collectors, and the demands on Jackson's time, increased as well. By the early 2000s it was not unusual for a single basket to command a price of $20,000 or more.

By 2008 Jackson had been a full-time artist for more than twenty-five years. Though she was well known and highly respected in the craft and museum communities, most of the public remained unfamiliar with her work until September of that year, when she received what is arguably the nation's most coveted prize: a fellowship from the John D. and Catherine T. MacArthur Foundation. According to the MacArthur Foundation, the annual award is given to "talented individu-

als who have shown extraordinary originality and dedication in their creative pursuits and a marked capacity for self-direction." Jackson was one of twenty-five fellows selected in 2008. Besides a cash award of $500,000, a MacArthur fellowship "is so high-profile that it bumps artists who may be known only to locals or experts to another level entirely," writer Patricia Cohen explained to John Stoehr in the *Charleston City Paper* on the occasion of Jackson's prize. "It gives them more visibility, a kind of authority, and a kind of imprimatur of excellence."

In an online summary of the work that brought her its recognition, the MacArthur Foundation noted Jackson's leadership of the Mount Pleasant Sweetgrass Basket Makers' Association, an organization she co-founded in large part "to protect the threatened wetland habitats of sweetgrass." As rapid development of the southeastern coast has already destroyed a vast majority of the wetlands where sweetgrass once grew, protecting the remaining supplies has become an increasingly important aspect of Jackson's work, and she has lectured frequently on the subject to schools and community organizations across the nation. She told the South Carolina African American History Calendar, "Sweetgrass Basketmaking is a tradition that I am very proud of and I won't let die."

Sources

Periodicals

Charleston City Paper (Charleston, SC), October 1, 2008.
Crafts Report, November 2001.

Online

"MacArthur Fellows Program," John D. and Catherine T. MacArthur Foundation, http://www.macfound. org/site/c.lkLXJ8MQKrH/b.4536879/ (accessed December 1, 2008).
"Mary Jackson," Craft in America, http://www.craftin america.org/artists_fiber/story_118.php? (accessed December 1, 2008).
"Mary Jackson," South Carolina African American History Calendar, January 1995, http://www.scafri canamerican.com/honorees/view/1995/1/.
"2008 MacArthur Fellows: Mary Jackson," John D. and Catherine T. MacArthur Foundation, September 2008, http://www.macfound.org/site/pp.aspx?c= lkLXJ8MQKrH&b=4537265&printmode=1 (accessed December 1, 2008).

—R. Anthony Kugler

Valerie Jarrett

1956—

Political adviser

Jarrett, Valerie, photograph. Zbigniew Bzdak/MCT/Landov.

Valerie Jarrett was a well-known figure in Chicago city politics for many years, but attained national fame thanks to her role as senior adviser to Barack Obama during his historic 2008 campaign for the White House. A friend of both Obama and his wife for nearly two decades, Jarrett moved to Washington, DC, with the First Family to serve as a White House senior adviser and head of President Obama's Office of Public Liaison. As journalist Jodi Kantor noted in a November 15, 2008, article for the *New York Times*, Jarrett "shares Mr. Obama's calm, deliberative style, and is widely described as one of the few people who can speak for [him] with accuracy and authority." During the heat of the presidential race, the Illinois senator and Democratic Party nominee spoke highly of Jarrett, who had once been his wife's boss at Chicago City Hall. "I trust her completely," Obama told Don Terry in the *Chicago Tribune*.

Jarrett hails from a family of high achievers: Her maternal great-grandfather was Robert Robinson Taylor, the first African-American graduate of the Massachusetts Institute of Technology and the architect who designed many of the buildings on the campus of Tuskegee University. His son, Jarrett's grandfather, was Robert Rochon Taylor, who in the 1940s became the first African American to serve as head of the Chicago Housing Authority. The once-immense high-rise public housing projects on the South Side of Chicago were named in his honor. Jarrett's mother was Barbara Taylor, a child psychologist who wed James Bowman, a physician and research scientist originally from Washington, DC. Jarrett's father was the first African American ever to be granted a residency slot at St. Luke's Hospital in Chicago, and went on to take his wife to Shiraz, Iran, after applying to a U.S. international-aid program that sent doctors abroad to train other medical professionals in developing nations.

Spent First Years Abroad

Jarrett was born on November 14, 1956, in the centuries-old artistic center of Shiraz in southwest Iran, and in particular at Nemazee Hospital, where her father was teaching. She spent the first five years of her life in the city, and recalled in the interview with Terry in the *Chicago Tribune*, "I remember how welcoming

At a Glance . . .

Born Valerie Bowman on November 14, 1956, in Shiraz, Iran; daughter of James (a physician and professor) and Barbara Taylor (a child psychologist) Bowman; married William Robert Jarrett (a physician), 1983 (divorced, 1988; died, 1993); children: Laura. *Politics:* Democrat. *Education:* Stanford University, AB, psychology, 1978; University of Michigan Law School, JD, 1981.

Career: Associate attorney with Pope Ballard Shepard & Fowle Ltd., and Sonnenschein, Carlin, Nath & Rosenthal, 1981(?)–83(?); Chicago Law Department, deputy corporation counsel for finance and development, 1983(?)–89(?); Office of Chicago Mayor Richard Daley, deputy chief of staff, after 1989; Chicago Department of Planning and Development, commissioner, 1992–95; Chicago Transit Board, chair, 1995–2003; Habitat Company, executive vice president, 1995–2007, chief executive officer, 2007–08. Finance committee chair of the Barack Obama for U.S. Senate campaign, 2004; senior adviser to the Barack Obama for President campaign, 2007–08; Obama White House transition team, cochair, November 2008–January 2009; White House senior adviser and assistant to the president for intergovernmental relations and public liaison, 2009—.

Memberships: Board of the Chicago Stock Exchange, 2000–07, chair, 2004–07; University of Chicago Medical Center, chair, Board of Trustees; Museum of Science and Industry, Chicago, trustee; Chicago 2016 Olympic Committee, vice chair.

Addresses: *Office*—Office of Public Liaison, Bureau of Public Affairs, U.S. Department of State, 2201 C St. NW, Rm. 2206, Washington, DC 20520-2204.

everyone was to the many Americans who were there. We were viewed by the Iranians as Americans—not black Americans—so I had no awareness of race until we returned to the United States." Her parents settled in Chicago, her mother's hometown, after a year in London. Having picked up a slight British accent, Jarrett was teased by her new classmates at the elementary school she attended in the Hyde Park area that surrounds the University of Chicago.

The family of Jarrett's mother had deep roots in the Hyde Park area, which was becoming a genuinely integrated community of professionals, students, and ordinary working families when Jarrett was growing up there in the 1960s. Her father took a teaching post with the University of Chicago's medical school. Her mother—a specialist in early childhood education—became a cofounder of the Erikson Institute, which had been established to train teachers for an innovative federally funded preschool program called Head Start, for children from low-income households. Jarrett was an only child and traveled extensively with her parents every summer on behalf of her father's research projects in population genetics. "One summer we went from Ghana to Nigeria to Ethiopia to Uganda to Egypt and then back to Iran," Jarrett recalled in an interview with Jonathan Van Meter in *Vogue*. "We would be out in the countryside visiting different tribes, and my father would draw blood and I would help get the syringes together."

Jarrett spent her adolescent years at the University of Chicago Laboratory School, but for her junior and senior years of high school attended a Massachusetts boarding school, Northfield Mount Hermon. She entered Stanford University in 1974, graduated with a degree in psychology four years later, and from there earned a place at the University of Michigan Law School. After receiving her law degree in 1981 she returned to Chicago to work in private practice for two top downtown firms, one of which was located in the 108-story Sears Tower, the world's tallest building at the time. She had a spectacular office on the seventy-ninth floor with a breathtaking view of Lake Michigan. She also had become a wife, marrying physician William Jarrett, the son of prominent Chicago journalist Vernon Jarrett—the first syndicated African-American columnist at the *Chicago Tribune*—and had given birth to a daughter. Despite reaching so many personal and professional milestones before she turned the age of thirty, Jarrett recalled that she felt desperately unhappy with her choice of career. "I would sit in that office and just cry," she told Van Meter in *Vogue*.

Became Top Mayoral Aide

In 1983 Chicago voters elected the first African-American mayor to lead the city, Harold Washington, and Jarrett sought out a job with his administration. Washington named her to a post with the city's Law Department as deputy corporation counsel for finance and development, and she remained there after Washington died after suffering a heart attack in his City Hall office in November of 1987. Mayor Richard M. Daley, who took office in 1989, made Jarrett his deputy chief of staff, and it was in that position one day in 1991 that Jarrett interviewed a recent Harvard Law School graduate named Michelle Robinson. Like Jarrett, Robinson had landed a well-paying job with a top law firm in the city, but was unhappy with the line of work and was seeking a more meaningful job in public service. Jarrett offered Robinson the job during the interview, but Robinson asked for a few days to think it over; she then called Jarrett to ask if she would meet with her fiancé, Barack Obama, whom she had met at Harvard Law School. Their dinner meeting resulted in Robinson taking the City Hall job, and also served as the starting point for a long friendship between Jarrett and the couple. Over the next few years, Jarrett introduced Barack Obama, who had taking a teaching post with the University of Chicago Law School, to many of the city's political and civic leaders, and those introductions helped him raise the funds and endorsements necessary for his win of a seat in the Illinois state senate in 1996.

Jarrett, meanwhile, had become commissioner of the Chicago Department of Planning and Development, which at the time made her the highest ranking African American in the Daley administration. After 1995 she served as chair of the Chicago Transit Board but also worked full time at the Habitat Company, one of the city's largest residential real-estate development and management firms. She joined as executive vice president and became chief executive officer in January of 2007. She was also involved in several other organizations, including the board of trustees of the University of Chicago and the Board of the Chicago Stock Exchange. In 2004 the latter entity elected her as the first African-American woman to serve as its chair.

Jarrett's close friendship with the Obamas continued, and she headed the finance committee for his 2004 U.S. Senate campaign. After Obama announced his bid for the Democratic Party nomination for president in early 2007, Jarrett became a senior adviser to the campaign, and was said to have worked with the chief fund-raiser, David Axelrod, and campaign manager, David Plouffe, who traveled to the resort of Martha's Vineyard with Obama in the summer of 2007 to strategize a turnaround when it seemed as if Obama's main rival, the New York senator Hillary Clinton, was gaining significant ground in the contest for the party nomination. After that point, "Jarrett took on two roles, one internal and the other external," wrote Kantor in the *New York Times* on November 24, 2008. "The Obama campaign has often been described as so harmonious that, as one blogger joked, its members e-mailed hug-o-grams to one another all day. In fact, the campaign had the usual share of conflict, but also the ability to resolve the tensions before they became public or disabling. Ms. Jarrett served as a kind of ombudsman."

Appointed to Key Post

Jarrett's behind-the-scenes work included meeting with such civil rights leaders as the Reverend Al Sharpton

and music and entertainment moguls such as Russell Simmons and Sean Combs to shore up their support for Obama's presidential campaign. Though she remained on the job at the Habitat Company, she attended major campaign events and she and the candidate—who locked up the nomination in June after the California Democratic Party primary—spoke daily. A month later Obama was asked by Terry, writing for the *Chicago Tribune,* about Jarrett's role as senior adviser. "She's always very insistent on me trusting my instincts," Obama replied. "One of the dangers in running for high office is you get so much chatter in your ear that you stop listening to yourself."

Ten days after Obama's historic win in November of 2008 to become the first African American ever elected president of the United States, Jarrett was named the White House senior adviser and assistant to the president for intergovernmental relations and public liaison. She had already been appointed to cochair his official transition team, whose members work with senior officials in the outgoing administration to ensure a smooth changeover in the weeks prior to the January inauguration, and resigned from the Habitat Company. Her experience in housing and urban affairs issues, some pundits have noted, was a signal that the Obama administration planned to focus on fixing some of the deeply rooted problems that plague America's largest cities and their predominantly minority populations. Furthermore, Jarrett's role as White House senior adviser and head of the president's Office of Public Liaison was viewed as a sign that the Obama White House was committed to a greater accessibility and transparency in government. "The level of the engagement in the campaign was tremendous," Jarrett told Kantor in the November 15, 2008, article for the *New York Times,* "and we want people to understand this will be their White House."

Sources

Periodicals

Chicago Tribune, July 27, 2008.
New York Times, November 15, 2008, p. A12; November 24, 2008, p. A1.
Vogue, October 2008, p. 336.

Other

Suarez, Ray, and Judy Woodruff, broadcast transcript of interview, "Obama Transition Team Focused on Review, Quality Recruitment," *Online NewsHour,* Public Broadcasting Service, November 12, 2008, http://www.pbs.org/newshour/bb/politics/july-dec08/jarrett_11-12.html.

—Carol Brennan

Cullen Jones

1984—

Athlete

As of 2009 Cullen Jones was one of three African-American swimmers to have won a spot on the U.S. Olympic team, and one of just two to have earned a gold medal in the sport. The twenty-four-year-old was a member of the four-person men's team that took first place in the 4 x 100-meter freestyle relay at the 2008 Summer Olympic Games in Beijing, China. Back at home in New Jersey, Jones worked to bring more diversity to the ranks of professional swimming, beginning with learn-to-swim programs in urban areas. "There is a mind-set and I am trying to break that barrier," he told John Goodbody in the London *Sunday Times.* "Swimming is not regarded as a way of making a living. However, Tiger Woods broke the barrier and more and more people play golf now, thanks to seeing Woods play golf."

Jones was born on February 29, Leap Day of 1984, in New York City. His parents moved to the Irvington, New Jersey, area, and when Jones was about kindergarten age, the family visited a water park in Allentown, Pennsylvania. Jones did not yet know how to swim, but persuaded his parents to let him try a water slide that propelled inner-tube riders into the water. He

Jones, Cullen, photograph. AP Images.

loved the ride, but the inner-tube flipped over in the pool, and he nearly drowned. Revived by lifeguards using cardio-pulmonary resuscitation, Jones was not fazed, he recalled in an interview with John Henderson in the *Denver Post.* "When I came to," he recalled, "the next thing I said was, 'What's the next ride I'm getting on?'" Within a few days, his mother signed him up for swim lessons.

Jones's father, Ronald Jones, had been a standout college basketball player, and encouraged his son to make hoops, not swimming, his sport of choice. However, the elder Jones was won over once his son began winning races. Ronald Jones died of lung cancer when Cullen Jones was sixteen, by which time the son had amassed an impressive collection of trophies and state honors for both his Jersey Gators Swim Club and the team at Saint Benedict's Preparatory School. As in most so-called "country-club" sports like tennis and golf, it was rare to see a swimmer of color. "I used to hear all the time, 'What's with the black kid on the starting blocks?' But growing up, I was on a team that was mostly blacks and Latin[o]s," he told Kevin Manahan of the Newark, New Jersey, *Star-Ledger.* "I was 15 by the time I was the only black swimmer on a

At a Glance . . .

Born on February 29, 1984, in New York, NY; son of Ronald and Debra Jones. *Education:* North Carolina State University, BA, 2006.

Career: Professional swimmer, 2006—; endorsement deal with Nike, 2006; spokesperson for USA Swimming's Make a Splash program; member, U.S. men's Olympic swim team, 2008.

Awards: Gold medal, Olympic Games, 2008, for men's 4 x 100-meter freestyle relay.

Addresses: *Office*—c/o USA Swimming, One Olympic Plaza, Colorado Springs, CO 80909.

team. By that time, I was old enough to just say, 'Whatever.'"

After graduating from Saint Benedict's, Jones won a scholarship to North Carolina State University in Raleigh, where he majored in English. He was a top swimmer in college, and was predicted to do well in the 2004 Summer Olympics in Athens, Greece, but instead did poorly at the U.S. Olympic trials. "I froze," he told Manahan. "I felt like I was swimming with an anvil. When I finally touched the wall, I thought, 'I want to go home.'" In 2006, the same year he graduated from North Carolina State, he proved himself at the Pan Pacific Championships in Victoria, British Columbia, as a member of the U.S. men's team that set a new world record in the 4 x 100-meter freestyle relay. The win made Jones the first African-American swimmer to hold a world record, either solo or as part of a relay team, in swimming.

Jones also turned professional in the summer of 2006 when he signed a $2-million deal with Nike. A little over a year later, his pre-Olympic hopes were dashed again by a poor performance in the 50-yard freestyle sprint at the U.S. Short Course National Championships in Atlanta, Georgia. He came in last place after his eye goggles flipped up when he hit the water, which meant that he was unable to see the wall; he then dropped out of the 100-meter freestyle sprint. Critics claimed that Jones's career had ended before it had even begun because of the Nike deal and the ongoing filming of a documentary about his quest for Olympic gold. Both were distractions, according to his detractors, but Jones believed that the documentary was a valuable public service to promote diversity in the sport. Entitled *Parting the Waters,* the film followed his story, that of the more established swimmer Maritza Correia—a Puerto Rican-born member of the 2004 U.S. women's team—and the fortunes of a group of young black and Hispanic swimmers at a Massachusetts club.

Jones earned a spot on the U.S. Olympic team for the 2008 Beijing Games, which made him one of three African-American swimmers in Olympic history to swim for his country. His predecessors were Anthony Ervin, who won a gold medal at the 2000 Sydney Games, and Correia. At the 2008 Olympic swimming trials, Jones set a new U.S. record in the 50-meter freestyle (it stood for one day). In Beijing that August, Jones and teammates Michael Phelps, Jason Lezak, and Garrett Weber-Gale took the gold in the 4 x 100-meter freestyle relay.

Jones was the spokesperson for the Make a Splash program funded by USA Swimming, the national governing body for the sport. Of USA Swimming's 250,000-plus members, just 2 percent were African American—a reflection of the fact that an alarming number of African-American and Hispanic children did not know how to swim. Correspondingly, drowning fatalities for African-American children were three times higher than those of white children. "I know there's a big stigma—in the U.S. black people don't swim," Jones told Mike Celizic on the NBC *Today* Web site. "But if you go to the Caribbean, it's unheard of for people not to know how to swim. If you go to Africa, black people do know how to swim. But it's just a big stereotype here. And that's one thing that I want to work and change."

Jones promoted Make a Splash through public appearances to kick off learn-to-swim programs at local recreation centers in urban areas which featured free or reasonably priced lessons for kids. He also worked to encourage physical education teachers to use their local aquatic facilities to teach required swimming classes. "The kids are so excited," he told Henderson in the *Denver Post.* "You ask any kid, do they want to get in the water, and most of them, if they haven't had a traumatic incident already, they're ready and rarin' to go. They have no fear. That's the greatest asset to us."

Sources

Periodicals

Atlanta Journal-Constitution, June 30, 2008, p. C1.
Denver Post, May 4, 2008, p. C18.
New York Times, August 13, 2008, p. D6.
Star-Ledger (Newark, NJ), June 27, 2008, p. 1; October 22, 2008, p. 25.
Sunday Times (London), February 17, 2008, p. 26.
USA Today, August 12, 2008, p. D2.

Online

Celizic, Mike, "Cullen Jones Helps Minorities Swim Out of Deep End," TODAYshow.com, http://today. msnbc.msn.com/id/25064136/ (accessed December 10, 2008).

—Carol Brennan

Seu Jorge

1970—

Musician, actor

Musician and actor Seu Jorge is one of Brazil's most exciting exports in a long list of accomplished musical talents who came before him. Jorge has issued a string of solo records that offer a modern version of Brazil's traditional samba style, but has also forged a career as an actor with an international following. In 2002 he starred in *City of God* (*Cidade de Deus*), a wrenching tale of the poverty and violence that plague the poorest quarters of Rio de Janeiro, and then American filmmaker Wes Anderson cast him in *The Life Aquatic with Steve Zissou* (2005), in which Jorge both acted and performed cover versions of classic David Bowie songs from the 1970s. "When I was a boy, I couldn't have imagined I would end up being an actor," he told the British newspaper the *Independent on Sunday*. "Brazilian culture doesn't really permit us to dream…. So to have any kind of success as a black person, it's a huge honour. Not just for me, but for everyone in my community."

The musician and actor uses "Seu Jorge" (pronounced SAY-oo ZHOR-zhee) as his professional name, which roughly translates into "Mr. Jorge" in Brazilian Portu-

Jorge, Seu, photograph. AP Images.

guese. He was born Jorge Mário da Silva in 1970 in the city of Belford Roxo, which is part of the larger metropolitan area of Rio de Janeiro, Brazil's most famous city and focal point of its unique culture. Like many black Brazilians, however, Jorge grew up in poverty in one of the numerous favelas, or shantytowns, that ring Rio de Janeiro and are home to the poorest of the urban area's thirteen million people. He was from the favela known as Gogó da Ema, which means "Adam's apple." The favelas—settled generations ago by freed slaves—are generally not part of the formal municipal structure, and therefore often lack basic services such as electricity and sewers. Health problems and water contamination are issues that pale in comparison with the sense of lawlessness that pervades such areas, however. "People always ask me if the favelas were really that bad," Jorge told John Lewis writing for London's *Guardian* newspaper. "I always say they were much, much worse."

Raised in Musical Family

As a child, Jorge worked to help support his family with

At a Glance . . .

Born Jorge Mário da Silva on June 8, 1970, in Belford Roxo, Rio de Janeiro, Brazil; son of a musician; married Fernanda (divorced); married Mariana (a photographer); children: (with Fernanda) Maria Aimee; (with Mariana) Flor de Maria, Luz Bella.

Career: Active in Tuerj (Teatro da Universidade do Estado do Rio de Janeiro), a community theater group, after 1993; cofounder of Farofa Carioca (a musical group), 1993(?); released first solo LP, *Samba Esporte Fino*, 2001; made feature-film debut in *City of God*, 2002.

Awards: Latin Grammy award, Best MPB (Musica Popular Brasileira) Album, 2008.

Addresses: *Web*—http://www.seujorge.com. *Record label*—Wrasse Records, Wrasse House, Tyrrells Wood, Leatherhead KT22 8QW, United Kingdom.

a job repairing tires in a local junkyard. His parents were divorced by then, but his father remained a part of his life and encouraged his musical ambitions. "The main difference between me and other people was my dad," he told Lewis in the *Guardian*. "Most of my friends, they never had a father figure." He went on to explain that his father worked as "a percussionist, a sambista—he played the surdo bass drum and the pandeiro. My maternal grandfather, he was also a musician—he played accordion—but he was a bad guy, a hard man. But it meant that I grew up surrounded by music." In another interview, however, he noted that despite the prominent place music has in Brazilian life, his father "wasn't considered a professional then; a samba musician was seen as somebody who didn't want to work—poor and black, and beaten up by the police," he told Maya Jaggi in the *Sunday Times*.

Jorge was also fortunate to attend a private high school on a scholarship, which was a not-uncommon favor arranged by local politicians eager for votes from their favela constituents. He began playing the acoustic guitar as a teen, and then began a compulsory stint in Brazil's armed forces, where he played cornet in military band. Not long after his discharge, his sixteen-year-old brother was killed in a robbery. The tragedy forced Jorge to cut his community ties for a time, he explained to Ben Ratliff in the *New York Times*. "I had to be a role model to my other younger brothers, and we couldn't go back to where we were living, or I would

be put in the role of having to seek vengeance for the death of my brother."

Jorge moved in with an uncle, and during this period of his life studied acting with the theater company attached to the university for the state of Rio de Janeiro; he was also homeless for a time, living on the streets of the Zona Norte section of Rio, busking on the street for spare change, or staying at the theater space when it was available. Around 1993 he formed his first band with Gabriel Moura, the nephew of the prominent clarinetist Paulo Moura, which they called Farofa Carioca. They released their first album, *Moro no Brasil* (Live in Brazil), in 1998, and caught a lucky break when a filmmaker from Finland used footage of Jorge as Farofa Carioca's lead singer and gave the documentary about Brazil's exciting musical scene the same name as the album—*Moro no Brasil*.

Released Solo Debut

Jorge released his first solo record, *Samba Esporte Fino*, in 2001, but it was retitled *Carolina* for international release two years later. In between, Jorge made his film-acting debut in *City of God* (2002), from director Fernando Meirelles, which painted a bleak portrait of life for Brazilian blacks in the favelas of Rio de Janeiro. Jorge was cast as Mané Galinha, or "Knockout Ned," a recently discharged soldier who returns home and finds a job driving a bus, but is caught up in deadly gang war. The foreign-language film won a stunning four nominations for Academy Awards, including Best Director and Best Screenplay. Jorge was pleased with the warm reception *City of God* earned on the international circuit, but was briefly torn between his two careers before deciding "it was better not to be one thing or the other," he said in the *Independent on Sunday* interview. "It's better to be like an old Hollywood star, like Fred Astaire or Frank Sinatra, who danced, sang, acted. You shouldn't have limitations."

In 2005 Jorge released his second solo album, *Cru* (Raw), and also appeared in a movie from quirky independent filmmaker Wes Anderson (director of *The Royal Tenenbaums*). *The Life Aquatic with Steve Zissou* was a comedy about an oceanographer (Bill Murray) determined to find a killer "jaguar shark," and Jorge was cast as Pelé, a crew member aboard the research ship who entertains his shipmates with Portuguese versions of David Bowie songs, including "Rebel, Rebel" and "Space Oddity." This aspect of the film proved such a hit with audiences that Jorge released them as *The Life Aquatic Studio Sessions*, with the blessing of the formidable Mr. Bowie, who retains tight control over his back catalog and song-copyright issues. "Had Seu Jorge not recorded my songs acoustically in Portuguese," Bowie noted in the liner notes on the album, "I would never have heard this new level of beauty which he has imbued them with."

In 2005 Jorge appeared in *House of Sand* (*Casa de Areia*), another acclaimed example of Brazil's emerging cinema that did well on the international film-festival circuit. In 2008 he costarred in *The Escapist*, a gritty British ensemble drama, along with Joseph Fiennes and Brian Cox. The movie was filmed in London and Dublin and follows the exploits of a group of prisoners who undertake a daring jailbreak. In between both films, Jorge also released a new album of his music, *América Brasil* (2009), and began working on new cover songs, which he planned to sing in the original English. Like the Bowie tracks, however, he was still mining some unusual sources, including Kraftwerk, the pioneering German electronic act from the 1970s. "In English it's much harder for me to express myself," he said of this new experiment in the interview with Lewis for the *Guardian*. "I become a different person. I am less confident, more shy, more frightened. In a way it is more honest. I cannot act."

Remarried after a divorce from his first wife, Jorge was the father of three daughters, of whom the younger two lived in São Paulo with him and his second wife, Mariana. Though his acting roles and promotional tours took him far from home, he vowed never to leave his homeland. "It's very difficult to leave and immerse yourself in a different culture," he told the *Independent on Sunday*. "Plus, Brazil is still the greatest country in the world. In the future, you're all going to want to live here."

Selected works

Albums

(With Farofa Carioca) *Moro no Brasil,* 1997.
Samba Esporte Fino, Mr. Bongo Records, 2001.
Cru, Sony Japan, 2005.
The Life Aquatic Studio Sessions, Hollywood Records, 2005.
Live at Montreaux 2005, Eagle Rock, 2007.
América Brasil, EMI Music Brazil/Javali Valente Records, 2007.

Films

City of God (*Cidade de Deus*), 2002.
(Also composer) *The Life Aquatic with Steve Zissou,* 2004.
House of Sand (*Casa de Areia*), 2005.
The Escapist, 2008.

Sources

Periodicals

Guardian (London), October 3, 2008, p. 13.
Independent on Sunday (London), May 18, 2008, p. 24.
New York Times, October 30, 2005, p. AR34.
Sunday Times (London), November 5, 2006, p. 30.
Times (London), June 2, 2006, p. 13.

—Carol Brennan

John Keene

1965—

Poet, fiction writer

John Keene is a poet and fiction writer whose works challenge the traditional boundaries between genres by offering a bold hybrid form that blends prose, poetry, and even artwork. His 1995 debut work, *Annotations,* was hailed by literary critics as representing an exciting new direction in American—and, indeed, African-American—literature, and earned him the prestigious Whiting Writers' Award. He pursued further innovations in his 2006 collaborative work *Seismosis,* a dialogue of text and drawings.

Keene was born on June 18, 1965, in St. Louis, Missouri, the son of John and JoAnn Keene. Growing up, he was a shy, bookish child who displayed an early passion for literature. Encouraged by his mother, who valued all forms of self-expression, Keene wrote poems and stories at a furious pace as a child. However, he did not consider writing as a serious pursuit until high school, when, after submitting several poems to a literary contest and receiving rejection notices, he began to devote himself to the study of literature and poetry. He devoured the poetry of canonical poets such as William Blake, John Donne, T. S. Eliot, John Keats, William Wordsworth, and William Butler Yeats, as well as the African-American writers Amiri Baraka, Gwendolyn Brooks, Nikki Giovanni, and Langston Hughes.

Keene attended Harvard University, where he continued his literary studies. There, reading the writings of authors outside the United States, he gained a deeper appreciation for the "importance and beauty" of American literature, particularly the work of African-American writers. By the end of his four years at Harvard, Keene had determined his career path: "I knew that I was being called to write."

After graduating from Harvard, Keene joined the Dark Room Collective, a group founded in 1987 by the poets Thomas Sayers Ellis and Sharan Strange, then undergraduates at Harvard, to provide a forum for poets of color in the Cambridge, Massachusetts, area. The collective, which held readings in the living room of an old Victorian house, brought together emerging writers such as Keene with leading black authors of the day, including Derek Walcott and Alice Walker. The supportive atmosphere of the Dark Room Collective provided an ideal environment for Keene to develop his talent and distinctive literary voice. "I was always a shy person," Keene told Tom Mullaney in *Chicago Magazine,* "but with the collective, I gained more confidence."

Keene pursued a master of fine arts degree at New York University, receiving a fellowship from the New York Times Foundation, and from 1998 to 2001, he was a graduate fellow of Cave Canem, a community of African-American poets formed to cultivate new voices and to provide a forum for critiquing and supporting one another's work.

In 1995 Keene published *Annotations,* which he described in the book as "a series of mere life-notes aspiring to the condition of annotations." A semi-autobiographical novel comprising eighteen short chapters, *Annotations* traces the coming of age of an

At a Glance . . .

Born John R. Keene Jr. on June 18, 1965; son of John R. and JoAnn E. Keene. *Education:* Harvard University, BA, 1987; New York University, MFA.

Career: Massachusetts Institute of Technology, Laboratory for Manufacturing and Productivity Collegium, librarian, 1991–93, assistant to the director of the laboratory, 1991–93, assistant director of collegium affairs, 1992–93; University of Virginia at Charlottesville, lecturer in English, managing editor of *Callaloo,* and member of board of directors, Global Studies for Teachers Program, 1993–95; East Side Community High School, New York City, creative writing teacher, 1995–96; Brown University, creative writing faculty, 2001; Northwestern University, faculty in English and African-American studies, 2001—.

Memberships: Dark Room Collective.

Awards: Fiction Fellowship, Artists Foundation of Massachusetts and Massachusetts Cultural Council, 1990; Critics Choice Award, *San Francisco Review of Books,* 1995, for *Annotations;* Top 25 Fiction Book award, *Publishers Weekly,* 1995, for *Annotations;* Cave Canem Graduate Fellowship, 1998, 1999, 2001; Fellowship in Poetry, New Jersey State Council on the Arts, 2003; Award in Fiction and Poetry, Mrs. Giles Whiting Foundation, 2005; E. Leroy Award for Excellence in Undergraduate Teaching, Northwestern University, 2006.

Addresses: *Office*—Northwestern University, Department of English, University Hall, Room 413, 1897 Sheridan Rd., Evanston, IL 60208.

unnamed narrator—a middle-class black boy from St. Louis—from his birth in 1965 through "the swirl of adolescence," up to his acceptance at Harvard. The book's stream-of-consciousness style defies traditional conceptions of form, blurring the lines between prose and poetry, between history and fiction.

The novel was praised by such critics as Philip Gambone who wrote in the *New York Times* that Keene's "narrative is inventive, an amalgam of lyric, oratorical, sociopolitical and comic voices." A reviewer in *Publishers Weekly* declared, "*Annotations* is a work that should not be ignored and is worthy of the highest recommendation. It is an experimental work that pinpoints a new direction for literary fiction in the 21st century." *Annotations* was named one of the top twenty-five books of 1995 by *Publishers Weekly* and received the Critics Choice Award from the *San Francisco Review of Books.*

Keene's second book, *Seismosis,* was released in 2006 by the Ohio independent publisher 1913 Press. A collaboration with Brooklyn-based visual artist Christopher Stackhouse, the chapbook mixes Keene's poetry and Stackhouse's drawings, seeking to create a dialogue between the two and to break down the boundary between the verbal and the visual. The themes are abstract, focusing on concepts such as linearity, form, and chaos. In the newsletter of the Poetry Project, Frances Richard praised Keene and Stackhouse's work, noting, "*Seismosis* is a folded map, a two-handed graph of quakes that shake belief in bedrock individuality or medium specificity." Likewise, John Casteen of the *New Orleans Review* noted that "the premise of *Seismosis*…is immediately appealing in that it's out of the ordinary, and full of potential, and laden with risk."

Keene's poetry, fiction, essays, and translations (he speaks five languages) have appeared in such journals as the *African-American Review, AGNI, Bay Windows, Gay and Lesbian Review, Hambone, Kenyon Review, New American Writing,* and *Ploughshares.* In addition, his work has been widely anthologized, included in works such as *Brother to Brother: New Writings by Black Gay Men* (1991), *In the Tradition: An Anthology of Young Black Writers* (1993), *Ancestral House* (1995), *Seeking St. Louis: Voice from a River City* (2000), and *110 Stories: New York Writes after September 11* (2002).

In 2005 Keene earned the prestigious Whiting Writers' Award for fiction and poetry, which recognizes emerging authors who demonstrate exceptional talent and promise. The selection committee noted the "dense poetic prose" of Keene's *Annotations,* comparing the novel to Jean Toomer's *Cane,* and ventured that Keene did not "sound like anyone else" in contemporary literature. He has received fellowships from the Artists Foundation of Massachusetts and Massachusetts Cultural Council, the Bread Loaf Writers' Conference, the New Jersey Council on the Arts, the New York Times Foundation, and the Yaddo artist colony. Keene has served on the faculties of the University of Virginia, Brown University, and Northwestern University.

Selected writings

Annotations, New Directions, 1995.
(With Christopher Stackhouse) *Seismosis,* 1913 Press, 2006.

Sources

Periodicals

Chicago Magazine, May 2006.
New Orleans Review, December 2007.
The New Yorker, June 24, 1996.
New York Times, December 17, 1995; October 28, 2005.
Poetry Project Newsletter, April–June 2008.

Online

Hospodka, John, "Three Questions for John Keene, Author and Professor," Gapers Block, June 28, 2006, http://www.gapersblock.com/airbags/archives/john_keene_author_professor/ (accessed January 19, 2009).

Keller, Allie, "Office Hours: An Interview with Professor John Keene," North by Northwestern, April 22, 2008, http://www.northbynorthwestern.com/2008/04/9231/office-hours/ (accessed January 19, 2009).

Mrs. Giles Whiting Foundation, "2005 Whiting Writers' Award Recipients," http://www.whitingfoundation.org/whiting_2005_bios.html (accessed January 19, 2009).

—Deborah A. Ring

Jakaya Mrisho Kikwete

1950—

Politician

Kikwete, Jakaya Mrisho, photograph. AP Images.

In 2005 Jakaya Mrisho Kikwete was elected president of the United Republic of Tanzania, the East African nation that includes mainland Tanzania and the island archipelago of Zanzibar. Much of his career has been spent as an official of the leading political party, Chama Cha Mapinduzi (Party of the Revolution), and in cabinet positions of previous administrations. Praised for his unblemished record of public service and commitment to improving Tanzania's struggling economy, Kikwete became known for his dedication to the job. As president, he permitted himself just two weeks of vacation annually, staying in Tanzania to participate in a traditional safari hunt. "My staff groan, but the animals take my mind off work," he told a reporter from the *Economist*.

Kikwete was born in 1950 in Msoga, a village located in Bagamoyo District. At the time of his birth, Tanzania was known as Tanganyika and was a colony of Britain, which won control of what was formerly called German East Africa just after World War I. Tanganyika became Tanzania and merged with the Zanzibar archipelago in the years immediately following its independence from Britain in 1961. Kikwete's father was a district commissioner in the new government, and because of this the family moved frequently, but Kikwete also spent time with his grandfather, a respected local chief.

Emerged as Student Leader

In the first years of independence, Tanzania attempted to become a model of African socialism under its first democratically elected president, Julius Nyerere. Farms were collectivized under the principle of *ujamaa,* or familyhood, and foreign investment was spurned in favor of a doctrine of self-sufficiency. The country's economy suffered, however, and Tanzanians' standard of living sank precipitously. Nyerere remained in office for more than two decades, and the two leaders who succeeded him began to reverse many of the failed economic policies in the late 1980s.

During these earlier years of political and social upheaval, Kikwete was a studious and serious-minded teen and young adult. He served as student council president at both the Kibaha Secondary School and at the University of Dar es Salaam, where he studied economics. He was also active in the youth branch of the Tanzania African National Union (TANU) Party,

At a Glance . . .

Born on October 7, 1950, in Msoga, Bagamoyo District, Tanzania; married; wife's name, Salma; children: eight. *Military service:* Tanzanian Army, commissioned a lieutenant, 1976; retired as lieutenant colonel, 1992. *Politics:* Chama Cha Mapinduzi party of Tanzania. *Religion:* Muslim. *Education:* University of Dar es Salaam, bachelor's degree, economics, 1975; Tanzania Military Academy, officers' training course; completed company commanders' course, 1983.

Career: Began career with the Tanzania African National Union party, and later its successor, the Chama Cha Mapinduzi (CCM); held regional posts in the CCM in Zanzibar island, Tabora Region, Nachingwea, and Masasi District, 1977–88; became member of the CCM national executive committee, 1982, and member of its central committee, 1997; elected CCM chair, 2007; Tanzania Military Academy, chief political instructor and political commissar, 1984–86; member of the Bunge, or parliament of Tanzania, 1988–2005; minister for energy, minerals, and water, 1988–90; minister for finance, 1994–95; minister for foreign affairs and cooperation, 1995–2005; elected president of Tanzania, 2005; African Union, chair, 2008–09.

Addresses: *Office*—State House, Magogoni Rd., PO Box 9120, Dar es Salaam, Tanzania.

which had been founded by Nyerere, and went on to work for the main party after earning his degree in 1975. In 1977 TANU merged with Zanzibar's Afro-Shirazi Party to become Chama Cha Mapinduzi (CCM), or Party of the Revolution. He was assigned to Zanzibar to establish a CCM branch office there and subsequently went on to hold party posts in several regional offices.

Kikwete also trained with Tanzanian military forces during the 1970s and 1980s. He finished an officers' course at the Tanzania Military Academy and later became the school's chief political instructor and political commissar. Already part of a new generation of leaders in the CCM, he was named to the party's national executive committee in 1982 and was appointed by Nyerere's successor, Ali Hassan Mwinyi, to a seat in the Bunge, or parliament of Tanzania, in 1988. Mwinyi also named him to a cabinet post as the minister for energy, minerals, and water. In 1992

Kikwete retired his army commission at the rank of lieutenant colonel after Tanzania's election laws were reformed to disbar members of the armed forces from holding office. In 1994 Mwinyi named him as Tanzania's newest minister for finance. Mwinyi was succeeded in 1995 by Benjamin William Mkapa, who appointed Kikwete as minister for foreign affairs and cooperation. During Kikwete's decade-long stint in that cabinet post, he played a significant role as peacemaker for the region, especially in quelling tensions in nearby Burundi and the Democratic Republic of the Congo.

Won by Landslide

Tanzania's constitution limits its presidents to two consecutive terms, and Mkapa was therefore ineligible to run in the 2005 presidential contest. Kikwete beat several other contenders in a May of 2005 primary to become the CCM candidate. He campaigned on an anticorruption and reform platform, and also pledged to improve health care and education in the nation of thirty-nine million with a per capita income of just $330. "If I win the election, I will naturally be happy," he told Wilson Kaigarula in one of Tanzania's leading newspapers, the *Sunday Observer.* "But my bigger joy would spring from having Tanzanians happier at the end of my tenure, than when they were at its beginning."

Kikwete won the December balloting with a stunning 80 percent of the vote, and was sworn into office on December 21, 2005, as the fourth president of Tanzania. One of his first major initiatives involved the removal of corrupt government officials from previous administrations, and he then began seeking out foreign investment opportunities to bring more jobs to the languishing economy. After two years in office, Kikwete earned high marks from the electorate and international officials alike for vastly reducing corruption and overseeing a period of surprising economic growth.

As president, Kikwete spent time in Dar es Salaam, Tanzania's largest city, and in Dodoma, the city that serves as the seat of government. He also traveled extensively in the countryside, where in some rural areas he held public meetings at which thousands turned out to hear him speak and answer their questions. Ordinary Tanzanians were also able to send the president text messages on his mobile phone. "Even in Bukombe, with its streets of dust and brothels lit with kerosene lamps, the presidential phone, set on silent, lights up like a firefly with text messages, several of which he reads out at random," wrote a journalist from the *Economist* who accompanied Kikwete on one such rural jaunt in 2007. One message was from a medical professional concerned about the conditions in a rural hospital, "a message Mr. Kikwete forwards straight to his health minister. Another is from a whistle-blower who accuses a Pakistani-owned textile business of illegally bringing in family members from Pakistan in place of local workers. Mr. Kikwete forwards this to immigration officials. 'Sometimes,' he says, 'I think I'm nothing more than a post officer.'"

Moved to Halt AIDS

Kikwete also won praise from global health officials working to slow the spread of acquired immunodeficiency syndrome (AIDS) in Africa. In the summer of 2007 his government announced a new voluntary testing program for the human immunodeficiency virus (HIV) that causes AIDS, which is the leading killer in sub-Saharan Africa. Kikwete and his wife volunteered to become the first persons tested in the new program, but the president had previously distinguished himself from other African leaders by speaking out in support of safe-sex practices, including the use of condoms. The new HIV-testing program was part of a plan "to raise awareness among the public," a July of 2007 report from the BBC quoted him as saying, "and to assure those already affected that we will support them and protect them from abuses."

Later in 2007 Kikwete acted swiftly after a corruption scandal emerged involving his prime minister, Edward Lowassa, who promptly resigned over a questionable development deal with a U.S. energy company that had promised to provide backup power for Tanzania's meager electrical grid. Kikwete wound up dismissing his entire cabinet, and he consolidated the number of ministers from forty-seven to thirty-six. On the international front he won praise for mediating a two-month-old and violence-plagued conflict over elections in Kenya in early 2008 after other African leaders elected him to chair the African Union for a one-year term.

Sources

Periodicals

African Business, February 2006, p. 12; February 2008, p. 54; April 2008, p. 74.
Economist, September 1, 2007, p. 45.
Financial Times, December 14, 2005, p. 10.
New York Times, February 18, 2008, p. A7.

Online

Kaigarula, Wilson, "Kikwete: My Goal Is to Make Tanzanians Happier," *Sunday Observer* (Dar es Salaam, Tanzania), December 11, 2005, http://www.ippmedia.com/ipp/observer/2005/12/11/55696.html (accessed November 20, 2008).
Ngahyoma, John, "Profile: Tanzania's Friendly Politician," BBC News, May 9, 2005, http://news.bbc.co.uk/1/hi/world/africa/4529627.stm (accessed November 20, 2008).
"Tanzanian Leader Takes Aids Test," BBC News, July 14, 2007, http://news.bbc.co.uk/2/hi/africa/6899134.stm (accessed November 20, 2008).

—Carol Brennan

Wendo Kolosoy

1925–2008

Musician

Wendo Kolosoy was a Congolese singer and guitarist who did much to popularize his nation's distinctive rumba music. Though his career was interrupted by a politically motivated hiatus of nearly three decades, he found his popularity intact when he returned to the spotlight at the age of sixty-seven. Known throughout Africa as "Papa Wendo," his records are distinguished by his lilting, slightly high-pitched voice, his innovative adaptations of traditional melodies, and his dexterity on the guitar.

The son of a hunter, Antoine Wendo Kolosoy was born in April of 1925 in Mushie, a small village in Bandundu Province, a vast region in the western part of what was then known as the Belgian Congo. Orphaned at the age of nine, he was placed in the custody of Belgian priests, who gave him food, clothes, and a basic education. While grateful for their aid, the young boy quickly came to resent the strict controls they placed on his activities, particularly on music, which he had grown to love under the influence of his mother, a gifted vocalist in the local tradition. At the age of twelve or thirteen, he ran away from the priests and began to work as a crewman and mechanic on boats traveling up and down the Congo River. This occupation would sustain him off and on for decades. It would also provide him with a wealth of musical material, as he picked up new songs and even new languages on his travels. After adding Swahili and Lingala to Kikongo, his native tongue, he would become one of the relatively few vocalists worldwide able to perform in three languages.

To augment his meager earnings as a teenage boatman, Kolosoy began to sing and box for small crowds on the docks. For a period in the early 1940s, he concentrated on boxing, entering professional matches as far away as Dakar, Senegal, more than twenty-five hundred miles to the northwest. After retiring from that sport in 1946, he returned to music and the Congo River. When docked in the city then called Léopoldville (now Kinshasa), he came to the attention of Nicolas Jermonidis, a Greek expatriate who had recently founded a recording company. Kolosoy's first recording, a haunting melody called "Marie Louise," followed in 1948.

"Marie Louise" was a sensation. In a 2002 interview with Banning Eyre of Afropop Worldwide, a friend of Kolosoy's recalled "the priests believed that this record was starting to wake up dead people. This is why they arrested Papa Wendo." While this statement is difficult to verify, it is not implausible. The administration of the Belgian Congo was notoriously harsh, and its authorities rarely hesitated to imprison Africans they judged too popular or influential. Whatever the precise circumstances may have been, there is no doubt that Kolosoy was arrested after the release of what became his signature song. His imprisonment was a brief one, however, and he emerged to find the experience had only enhanced his popularity. With a full band known as Victoria Kin, he toured throughout his homeland and was heard frequently on the radio.

The style that Kolosoy established with "Marie Louise" would influence musicians across Africa. Like many of his peers, Kolosoy mixed the melodies of traditional song with styles borrowed from Cuba, notably the rumba, which is characterized by guitars, heavy percussion, and a fast, danceable beat. What set Kolosoy's performances apart from those of his rivals was the distinctive character of his singing voice. Often described as a high-pitched yodel, it inspired many imitators. "Lots of people were after me to know how to do that," Kolosoy told Eyre. "They would ask me in the street. 'Wendo, Wendo. How do you do that?'"

Kolosoy's enormous popularity in the 1950s and early 1960s coincided with one of the most hopeful periods in Congolese history. Optimism was high across Africa, as the repressive and exploitative colonial era came to an end in nation after nation. The prospects of an independent Congo seemed particularly bright, given the country's wealth of natural resources. The Belgians ceded control in a peaceful transition of power in 1960, and an anticolonial activist named Patrice Lumumba became the independent nation's first prime minister. Lumumba and Kolosoy were friends, though the latter would later insist that they never discussed politics. Whatever the basis of their friendship, it would have a major impact on the course of the singer's career. Less than three months after becoming prime minister, Lumumba was deposed and arrested amid steadily worsening political conditions; he was murdered in January of 1961. As the crisis deteriorated into civil war, a general named Mobutu Sese Seko grew steadily more powerful, eventually establishing a military dictatorship in June of 1965. Given his association with Lumumba and his own prominence, Kolosoy quickly realized that he was in danger of death or imprisonment himself. He therefore stopped perform-

ing, withdrew from public life, and went back to his life on the river. He would remain there for nearly thirty years. When Mobutu's power began to wane in the early 1990s, Kolosoy returned to the recording studio, but he would not feel fully at ease until the dictator's ouster and death in 1997.

Laurent Kabila, Mobutu's successor, strongly encouraged Kolosoy's return to music. Kabila's assistance, and the explosion of worldwide interest in Congolese music during the years of Kolosoy's absence, together sparked a major comeback for the singer in the late 1990s and into the 2000s. He went on several international tours, performing as far away as London, and recorded a number of new albums. In a review of one of these, 2003's *Amba,* Tom Orr in Rootsworld wrote that Kolosoy "still sings with more style, grace and emotive distinction than many a younger man." Several months after the release of his last album, 2007's *Banaya Papa Wendo,* the health of the man often called the father of the Congolese rumba began to deteriorate. He died in Kinshasa, Democratic Republic of the Congo, on July 28, 2008, at the age of eighty-three.

Selected discography

"Marie Louise" (single), 1948.
Marie Louise, Indigo, 2000.
Amba, World Village, 2003.
Banaya Papa Wendo, IglooMondo, 2007.
On the Rumba River, Marabi, 2007.

Sources

Periodicals

Economist, August 14, 2008.
Guardian (London), August 1, 2008.
Village Voice, June 3, 2008.

Online

Eyre, Banning, "Wendo Kolosoy, 2002," Afropop Worldwide, 2002, http://www.afropop.org/multi/interview/ID/27/Wendo Kolosoy (accessed December 2, 2008).

Orr, Tom, "Wendo Kolosoy: *Amba,*" Rootsworld, 2003, http://www.rootsworld.com/reviews/kolosoy-amba.shtml (accessed December 2, 2008).

—R. Anthony Kugler

K-Swift

1978–2008

Radio host, DJ

K-Swift was the self-appointed queen of Baltimore's club music scene. The city's only female hip-hop DJ, K-Swift hosted the popular "Off the Hook Radio" program on 92Q Jams, becoming its top on-air personality, and she regularly spun live at Baltimore's hottest nightclubs and private parties. She helped introduce the genre of music known as "Baltimore club" to a younger audience of fans and exported the city's trademark sound to cities up and down the East Coast. K-Swift's accidental death in the summer of 2008, just as she was reaching the height of her career, stunned the city and silenced one of its most beloved local celebrities.

K-Swift was born Khia Danielle Edgerton on October 19, 1978, in Baltimore, Maryland, one of two daughters of Joseph and Juanita Edgerton. She grew up in the predominantly black suburb of Randallstown and began spinning records at age eleven, practicing her mixing techniques with a turntable and a tape deck in the basement of her family home.

After graduating from Randallstown High School in 1996, K-Swift attended community college for a time, but soon dropped out to pursue a career as a DJ. She landed a job as an intern at WERQ-FM 92.3, known as 92Q Jams, the city's hip-hop and R&B radio station, and started spinning records in local clubs such as the Twilight Zone. Initially, K-Swift's parents hoped her interest in DJing was a passing fancy, urging her instead to finish college and pursue a more practical career as a sound engineer. However, they soon saw their daughter's passion for music and drive to succeed as a DJ, and they supported her wholeheartedly.

At 92Q, K-Swift started out as an intern in the programming department, but before long she was producing shows for the station, such as the "Mark Young Show" and the "Neke @ Night Show." Her talent and hard work earned her a regular gig on 92Q in 1998, when she began DJing for "Ladies Night," a hit program that she produced with on-air personality Neke. Soon K-Swift was mixing club music live with cohost Reggie Reg and spinning records for the station's "Big Phat Morning Show," becoming 92Q's first female DJ.

K-Swift's big break came in 2003, when she began hosting "Off the Hook Radio," which aired nightly from 6:00 to 10:00 pm. The first three-and-a-half hours of the show were devoted to standard hip-hop and R&B fare, but at the end of each show, K-Swift would spin Baltimore club for devoted listeners. She became the station's most popular on-air personality and boasted a quarter-hour audience of 28,000—an impressive number for a local radio station. In its Best of Baltimore Awards, the *City Paper* named K-Swift Best DJ in 2001 and Best Club DJ three years running, in 2004, 2005, and 2006.

On air and in local dance venues such as Club Fantasy, Paradox, Sonar, and Hammerjacks, K-Swift mixed a genre of house and dance music known as "Baltimore club," helping to popularize the sound among the young listeners who made up her fan base. Aggressive, harsh, and quick-paced—tempos top 130 beats per minute—Baltimore club is characterized by heavy beats, suggestive lyrics, repeated call-and-response

At a Glance . . .

Born Khia Danielle Edgerton on October 19, 1978, in Baltimore, MD; died July 21, 2008, in Baltimore, MD; daughter of Joseph and Juanita Edgerton. *Education:* Attended Community College of Baltimore County at Catonsville.

Career: WERQ-FM 92.3, intern, producer, on-air personality, 1998–2008.

Memberships: Violator All-Star DJ Coalition.

Awards: Best DJ, 2001, Best Club DJ, 2004–06, *City Paper,* Best of Baltimore Awards.

chants, and infectious hooks that are sampled from other songs or, most often, television shows. Baltimore record store owner Jason Urick described the music to S. H. Fernando Jr. in *Spin*: "It's just raw and heavy, and I wouldn't say primitive, but it kinda is. When you hear that beat, it's hard not to dance to it." K-Swift's skill in mixing Baltimore club was unparalleled. Fernando noted, "The music is all about the buildup and the release, and K-Swift is one of the finest at controlling the flow."

As K-Swift's local following began to grow, radio stations and clubs in other cities began to pick up on the Baltimore sound, which had long been an underground phenomenon. Soon, K-Swift was traveling to cities along the East Coast, most often Philadelphia and New York, to DJ at clubs and parties. She released numerous mix CDs, including the fourteen-volume series *Jumpoff*, produced by Baltimore-based Unruly Records; a two-disc collection called *K-Swift: Strictly for the Kids,* featuring cleaned-up versions of popular mixes; and *Club Queen,* a five-disc series. Available at Baltimore music stores and the retail clothing chain Downtown Locker Room, her albums often outsold nationally known hip-hop artists. Also an entrepreneur, K-Swift owned Club Queen Entertainment, a graphics and production management company, and served as the city's only female record pool director (a record pool is a group of DJs who test new recordings on audiences and provide feedback to record companies).

On the evening of July 20, 2008, K-Swift hosted a party at her northeast Baltimore home. Sometime after midnight, she jumped into a shallow aboveground pool. When she did not resurface after several minutes, friends in the pool pulled K-Swift onto an adjacent deck, calling 911. Paramedics were unable to revive K-Swift and transported her to Good Samaritan Hospital, where she was pronounced dead. According to

the medical examiner's report, K-Swift died of a fractured neck sustained when she dove into the pool. She was just months shy of her thirtieth birthday.

As news of K-Swift's death spread the next morning, a vigil organized via her MySpace page formed in the 92Q parking lot. The station suspended its regular programming, instead asking listeners to call in with their memories of K-Swift. By the end of the day, the station had received thousands of phone calls, e-mail messages, and posts on its Web site. "People like K-Swift are the true celebrities of Baltimore," one caller said, according to the *Baltimore Sun*. "When you say Baltimore, you say her name." Days later, thousands of grief-stricken fans attended K-Swift's funeral, held in the auditorium at Morgan State University. Baltimore mayor Sheila Dixon joined K-Swift's family at the wake and paid tribute to the DJ on 92Q. Maryland governor Martin O'Malley, who attended the funeral, issued a proclamation in K-Swift's honor.

Just days before her death, K-Swift headlined Baltimore's Artscape Festival, and she was on the verge of signing a national distribution deal that would place her CDs in record stores across the country. The deal went through the day after her death. "She had an enormous following and meant a lot to the people of Baltimore," 92Q general manager Howard Mazer told the *Baltimore Sun*. "People just gravitated to her.... When she threw parties, thousands of people would come." Reflecting on K-Swift's short life, her cousin Ronnissa Bailey said, "Her life shows the world that anything is possible with discipline and believing in yourself."

Selected discography

The Jumpoff, Vols. 1–14, Unruly Records, 2004–08.
K-Swift: Strictly for the Kids, Parts 1–2, Unruly Records, 2006.
The Club Queen, Vols. 1–5, Unruly Records, 2008.

Sources

Periodicals

Baltimore Sun, July 22, 2008; July 23, 2008; July 27, 2008.
City Paper (Baltimore, MD), July 30, 2008.
Spin, December 3, 2005.

Online

Club Queen DJ K-Swift, Official MySpace, http://profile.myspace.com/index.cfm?fuseaction=user.viewprofile&friendid=59133081 (accessed January 16, 2009).
"DJ K-Swift's Death in Pool Investigated," WJZ-TV, http://wjz.com/local/Khia.Edgerton.KSWIFT.2.775885.html (accessed January 16, 2009).

—Deborah A. Ring

Ledisi

197(?)—

Singer, songwriter

Ledisi, photograph. Michael Germana/Landov.

For years, the rhythm-and-blues (R&B) and jazz singer who goes by the professional name Ledisi toiled in obscurity, known only around her San Francisco Bay Area hometown and to pockets of devoted fans elsewhere. She released two albums on her own label before the legendary Verve Records signed her to a deal. The result was 2007's *Lost & Found,* which was nominated for a pair of Grammy awards. "We do what we do not only to make a living, but also to inspire people to do what they do," Ledisi told Joshunda Sanders in the *San Francisco Chronicle* about her vocation. "People are counting on the music to build them up. That's why people aren't buying as much music anymore, because it's not doing that. They don't want to talk about booty; they want depth."

Had Family Musical Roots

Ledisi (pronounced LED-duh-see) is evasive about her date of birth, but one 2008 article described her as being in her thirties. She was born Ledisi Anibade Young to Nyra Dynese, a singer with an R&B New Orleans band called Carnova. Her father was the singer and guitarist Larry Sanders, sometimes referred to as "the Prophet of Soul" for his work in the 1960s and 1970s. He wrote the classic "Blues Time in Birmingham," and his circle of acquaintances included Marvin Gaye, Curtis Mayfield, and even Angela Davis, a well-known radical figure and scholar active in the black power movement. Ledisi never knew her paternal grandfather, a well-known blues singer named Johnny Ace, who died in one of the more bizarre fatalities in music history: On Christmas Day of 1954, Ace shot himself after unwisely playing a game of Russian roulette with a weapon he apparently did not realize was loaded. The event happened backstage at a Houston venue where he was on the same bill as Big Mama Thornton, who witnessed the incident.

Ledisi was given a Yoruba first name that means "to bring forth" or "to come here," and she seemed to have inherited the musical gifts present on both sides of her lineage. She made her singing debut with the New Orleans Symphony Orchestra at the age of eight, and two years later the family moved to Oakland, California, where she won a spot in the Young Musicians Program at the University of California at Berkeley.

She studied opera and piano for five years and began working professionally after graduating from Oakland's Skyline High School. Her first steady work came as a regular in *Beach Blanket Babylon,* a San Francisco cabaret act and a fixture in the city's irreverent pop-culture scene since the early 1970s.

As a vocalist, Ledisi sang with an acid-jazz ensemble called Slide 5 and formed a group called Anibade in the early 1990s. The latter she formed with Sundra Manning, a keyboardist and songwriter who would become Ledisi's prime musical collaborator. Their group also included guitarist Cedricke Dennis, Nelson Braxton on bass, saxophonist Wayne Braxton, and Tommy Bradford on drums. Anibade quickly gained a devoted following in the Bay Area for their live performances. Their first album, *Soulsinger,* was released independently in 2000. Writing in the *San Francisco Chronicle,* Joshunda Sanders asserted that the work "showcases Ledisi's technical range as a vocalist, as well as her feisty but playful persona. One moment sad and sweet, loud and fierce the next, her music is part down-home lovin' and good advice."

Founded Music Label

Ledisi and Manning founded LeSun Music, their own label, which had released *Soulsinger.* It also issued Ledisi's second record, *Feeling Orange but Sometimes Blue,* in 2002, which demonstrated a more jazz-inspired new direction. Again, the record sold well in the Bay Area, but it failed to get picked up for national distribution. At that point Ledisi decided to move to New York City and create some new opportunities for herself. "I was just tired," she said of this time of her life in an August of 2007 interview with Gail Mitchell in *Billboard.* "I'd played every nook and cranny. All these people [were] seeing my shows. But it seemed like nobody wanted to help push me further."

Ledisi became involved in a revival of the musical *Hair* that ran for a special one-night performance in 2004, and was a standby performer for the Tony Kushner musical *Caroline, or Change* that same year. She also composed some of the music for *The Color Purple,* the Oprah Winfrey–produced musical of Alice Walker's acclaimed novel. Finally, she was signed to Verve Records in 2004, but as she was working on new material the legendary jazz label underwent some financial difficulties, and her first major-label release did not appear until 2007.

Lost & Found proved an immediate hit with critics. Dan Ouellette, writing in *Billboard* in September of 2007, commended the collection of fifteen original songs that demonstrate "her prowess as a powerhouse vocalist as well as her songwriting maturity." A few of the tracks did respectably well, including "Alright," which reached No. 45 on the Billboard "Hot R&B" chart, and the album itself peaked in the No. 10 spot on the "R&B/Hip-Hop" album chart. A writer for the *Seattle Times,* Andrew Gilbert, described the artist as "a supremely versatile singer" able to draw "from the entire spectrum of African-American music, infusing soul melisma into standards and jazz improvisation into smooth R&B grooves. She can scat Charlie Parker's blues 'Now's the Time' with the harmonic sophistication of a bebop saxophonist and deliver Billie Holiday's 'God Bless the Child' with keen emotional insight."

Received Grammy Nominations

In December of 2007, when the nominations for the Grammy awards were announced, a few mainstream media sources expressed surprise at Ledisi's name, which was included in the Best New Artist category, while *Lost & Found* was nominated in the Best R&B Album category. Ledisi lost the first honor to British soul singer Amy Winehouse, and the latter award went to Chaka Khan's *Funk This,* but Ledisi was as surprised as everyone else when she received the call notifying her about the nominations. In an interview with Joey Guerra for the *Houston Chronicle,* she explained that she was still asleep when the first calls began coming in to her phone, which she repeatedly had to shut off. "I was like, 'Let me wake up,'" she recalled, still unaware of the news. "I checked my voicemail, and the first message I got was, 'Led, you've just been nominated for best new artist.' I dropped the phone. Then someone called again and said, 'You're nominated again for R&B album.' It took a whole day of phone calls for me to get it."

Ledisi's Grammy nominations expanded her already-devoted fan base. A few months later she appeared as a blues singer in the 1920s-set football film/romantic comedy from George Clooney, *Leatherheads,* and she appeared on *The Tonight Show with Jay Leno* in July of 2008. A holiday-themed album, *It's Christmas,* appeared later that year. After years of struggle the singer was still stunned at the audience turnouts that were the result of her Grammy nods. "At the shows, I'm always expecting three people or so to be there," she told Melissa Ruggieri in the *Richmond Times-Dispatch,* "and then it's massive, with over 4,000 people, and I'm like, are they serious? And they know the words!"

Selected works

Albums

(With the group Anibade) *Soulsinger,* LeSun, 2000.
Feeling Orange but Sometimes Blue, LeSun, 2002.
(Contributor) *Forever, for Always, for Luther,* GRP, 2004.
Lost & Found (includes "Alright"), Verve Forecast, 2007.
(Contributor) *We All Love Ella: Celebrating the First Lady of Song,* Verve, 2007.
It's Christmas, Verve Forecast, 2008.

Films

Leatherheads, 2008.

Sources

Periodicals

Billboard, August 18, 2007, p. 43; September 1, 2007, p. 55.
Colorlines, March–April 2008, p. 58.
Houston Chronicle, February 10, 2008, p. 16.
Richmond Times-Dispatch, August 14, 2008.
San Francisco Chronicle, July 7, 2002, p. 43.
Seattle Times, October 3, 2008, p. H5.
USA Today, January 22, 2008, p. 3D.

—Carol Brennan

Lisa Leslie

1972—

Professional basketball player, model

Leslie, Lisa, photograph. Sergio Perez/Reuters/Landov.

Lisa Leslie would seem to have it all: beauty and poise, athletic talent that earned her four Olympic gold medals, a high-profile contract to play professional basketball within the Women's National Basketball Association for the Los Angeles Sparks, a modeling career that has landed her in the pages of *Vogue,* and an acting career in which she has appeared on various television shows and commercials. The six-foot-five-inch Leslie has been one of the biggest names in women's basketball since joining the U.S. national team for the 1996 Olympics. With her success—and her refusal to conform to any stereotype—she has helped popularize basketball as a sport any woman can play without sacrificing femininity or flair.

Played Basketball in Middle School

Leslie was born in July of 1972 in Los Angeles, California. Her father, who had played semi-pro basketball, deserted the family while she was very young. Her mother, Christine Leslie, had three daughters to raise and needed a livelihood that would bring in a dependable income. "We had no money and we could've gone on welfare, but my mom wanted to do something she was proud of," Leslie recalled in the book *Venus to the Hoop: A Gold-Medal Year in Women's Basketball* by Sara Corbett. "She sat us down and said, 'This is what I've got to do. I'm going to buy a truck and learn how to drive it. It's going to take time for me to pay it off and get a local route. I need you kids to give me five years.'"

Leslie's mother went to work as a long-haul trucker, crisscrossing the country in her rig while her daughters grew up in Los Angeles and were cared for by a live-in housekeeper and her aunt. Christine Leslie was often away for weeks at a time and then home for only a few days, but she still managed to keep her daughters close and self-sufficient. Young Lisa had yet another cross to bear: She was the tallest child ever to pass through her elementary school. By second grade she stood five-foot-two and was taller than her teacher. Not surprisingly, she was teased about her height. "They called me Olive Oyl, they called me all sorts of things," she remembered in *Venus to the Hoop.* "The grown-ups

At a Glance . . .

Born Lisa Deshaun Leslie on July 7, 1972, in Los Angeles, CA; daughter of Christine Leslie (a truck driver); married Michael Lockwood (a commercial pilot and former U.S. Air Force basketball player), November of 2005; daughter: Lauren Jolie Lockwood. *Education:* Attended University of Southern California, 1990–94.

Career: Member of Italian professional league, 1994–95; professional model, 1996—; U.S. Olympic women's basketball team, member, 1996, 2000, 2004, and 2008; Los Angeles Sparks, founding member, 1996—; has worked as an actress.

Memberships: Women's National Basketball Association.

Awards: Dial Award for outstanding female scholar-athlete, 1989; Pac-10 Freshman of the Year, 1992; All-American, 1992, 1993, and 1994; Female Athlete of the Year, USA Basketball, 1993; National College Player of the Year, U.S. Basketball Writers Association, 1994; Naismith Award, AT&T, 1994; Most Valuable Player, Women's National Basketball Association (WNBA), 2001, 2002, and 2006; WNBA Western Conference All-Star Team, 2006; WNBA All-Decade Team, 2006.

Addresses: *Office*—Los Angeles Sparks, 888 S. Figueroa St., Ste. 2010, Los Angeles, CA 90017.

Recognized as Outstanding High School Player

Leslie became more serious about basketball during her freshman year in high school. That year she moved in with an aunt and began playing ball with an older male cousin who served as a mentor and private coach. Honing her skills on teams that were otherwise all male, she became a very skilled player.

Leslie's mother finally got the local trucking route that she had coveted, and the family moved to Inglewood, California. Leslie attended Morningside High School in Inglewood, where she quickly established herself as a commanding force on the basketball team.

It was a Morningside High tradition that, in the last regular season game of the year, all the basketball players would give the ball to a chosen senior just to see how many points that senior could score. In 1990 that senior was Lisa Leslie, and the game in question was not the final one of the season, but the next to the last, against a hopelessly overmatched team from South Torrance. In one 16-minute flurry, Leslie scored 101 points—just 4 points short of the national scoring record for an entire game. Her performance so humiliated the opposing team that their coach forfeited the game at halftime, denying Leslie the opportunity to break the record.

Leslie's feat against South Torrance was covered by local and national television news crews and *Sports Illustrated*. This one performance served to overshadow what was otherwise a notable high school career: She had averaged 27.3 points and 15 rebounds per game as a senior, had been a member of the U.S. junior Olympic team, and had received the Dial Award as outstanding female scholar-athlete of 1989. *Sports Illustrated* called her "the best high school player in the nation."

Played College Ball at USC

Many colleges tended to agree with the *Sports Illustrated* opinion. Leslie received so many recruiting letters that she had to put them in boxes under her bed. She finally decided to attend the University of Southern California (USC), beginning in the fall of 1990. Even as a college freshman she was hailed by *Sports Illustrated* as "not just a star but the kind of superstar who can elevate the women's game to the next level in national popularity." Leslie, who was voted Pac-10 Freshman of the Year, realized that she was serving as a role model and an inspiration to other athletes. "I think we do need that one star that even people who aren't familiar with the game can recognize," she admitted in *Sports Illustrated*. "It not only gets the attention of the public, it gets the attention of the kids who will grow up to be the next superstars."

mostly thought my height was beautiful, but the kids gave me a hard time." Leslie's mother, who was herself six-foot-three, encouraged her daughter to keep her chin up and be proud of her height. It was valuable advice for someone who would one day turn her height into a valuable asset.

One question that Leslie heard constantly was: "Do you play basketball?" As a young teenager, she could not understand why people expected her to play hoops just because she was tall. She might never have tried the game if the other girls in her middle school had not begged her to come and join the school team. Even after making the team she was less than enthusiastic about the game. Nevertheless, her middle school team was undefeated that year.

Leslie left USC in 1994 with a wealth of basketball experience. She was a three-time All-American and was named National College Player of the Year by the U.S. Basketball Writers Association in 1994. She wanted more than anything to play for the U.S. Olympic team, but she realized that she would need some professional experience first. Because the United States did not have pro basketball leagues for women, Leslie had to take her talents abroad to Italy. She signed a contract with an Italian league and began playing there, but being abroad was not easy for her. She played one season in Italy before trying out for—and winning a place on—the U.S. national basketball team.

In preparation for the 1996 Olympics, the women's national basketball team began training in 1995 and embarked on an ambitious world tour in which they competed against the best international teams as well as top U.S. college teams. Led by coach Tara VanDerveer—and featuring the statuesque Lisa Leslie at center—the U.S. women's team went undefeated throughout their entire international tour.

Joined the WNBA after the Olympics

The performance of the U.S. women's basketball team was one of the highlights of the 1996 Summer Olympics. The U.S. women's team defeated Brazil in the gold medal game and—while the world watched—celebrated the triumphant end to a long year of hard work and high expectations.

For Leslie, as for the other Olympic gold medalists in women's basketball, the victory in Atlanta provided many exciting opportunities. Leslie originally thought she would go straight from the Olympics into a new women's professional league, the American Basketball League. She decided, however, that she needed a break from basketball. She signed a contract with Wilhelmina Models, one of the nation's top modeling agencies, and continued her association with Nike shoes.

Her hiatus from basketball was cut short when, in December of 1996, she was one of the first chosen to play in the fledgling Women's National Basketball Association (WNBA), a women's league financed and promoted by the National Basketball Association.

Signed with the Los Angeles Sparks

The WNBA proved to be a good fit for Leslie. She was signed to a team in Los Angeles, her hometown. As a founding member of the Los Angeles Sparks, Leslie made her American pro debut in June of 1997, after having spent the off-season modeling sportswear in the pages of *Vogue, TV Guide,* and *Shape.*

Again, Leslie emerged as the star of the team. Coach Michael Cooper, who played for the Los Angeles Lakers, likened her to one of his former teammates. "Lisa is smooth like Kareem [Abdul-Jabbar]," he once told *Sports Illustrated.* Leslie led the Sparks to two WNBA championships, in 2001 and 2002, and was named Most Valuable Player of the finals both times. In the summer of 2002 she scored one giant leap for womankind when, on July 30, she became the first woman to slam dunk in a professional game. She also returned to the Olympics in 2000 and 2004, winning two more gold medals with the U.S. women's basketball team.

In November of 2005 Leslie married former U.S. Air Force basketball player Michael Lockwood. The following year she was named to the WNBA Western Conference All-Star Team and won the WNBA Most Valuable Player award for the third time. She was also named to the WNBA All-Decade Team.

Earned Fourth Olympic Gold Medal

Leslie sat out the 2007 WNBA season on maternity leave. She returned to basketball for the 2008 WNBA season, which began in May of that year. Leslie also resumed play with the U.S. women's basketball team, traveling with them to Beijing for the summer Olympics. By the end of August, Leslie had her fourth Olympic gold medal but suggested that it would be her last Olympic competition.

In the fall of 2008 Leslie was still at the top of her game, as noted by Donna Orender, president of the WNBA, to Debbie Arrington in the *Sacramento Bee.* "Lisa Leslie continues to establish benchmarks of performance 12 seasons into it," Orender remarked. She viewed Leslie as a veteran basketball player who, along with many outstanding basketball veterans, had "stepped up their game" even after many years of play.

When her basketball career ends, Leslie has said that she would like to focus on acting and broadcasting. She would also like to become a new type of role model for women: an athlete who is proud to be feminine. If she has any message for youngsters, she concluded in *Women's Sports and Fitness,* it's this: "You can be whatever you want to be." Women don't have to fulfill the stereotype of looking "like men with their clothes hanging off them just because they play basketball."

Selected writings

(With Larry Burnett) *Don't Let the Lipstick Fool You: The Making of a Champion,* Dafina Books, 2008.

Sources

Books

Corbett, Sara, *Venus to the Hoop: A Gold-Medal Year in Women's Basketball,* Doubleday, 1997.

World Almanac and Book of Facts, World Almanac Books, 2002, p. 1026.

Periodicals

Associated Press, December 13, 2007.
Ebony, October 2001, p. 60.
Essence, January 1997, p. 80.
New York Times, July 17, 1996, p. B11; January 23, 1997, p. B14.
Newsweek, August 12, 2002, p. 11.
People, June 30, 1997, p. 109; November 21, 2005, p. 108.

Sacramento Bee, September 20, 2008.
San Diego Union-Tribune, August 24, 2008, p. D1.
Sports Illustrated, February 19, 1990, p. 30; November 25, 1991, p. 78; May 26, 1997, p. 36; August 20, 2001, p. 70; September 9, 2002, p. 56.
Sports Illustrated for Kids, March 1997, p. 62; June 1997, p. 28.
Women's Sports and Fitness, November 21, 1996, pp. 12, 50.

—Anne Janette Johnson and Sandra Alters

Nancy Hicks Maynard

1946–2008

Journalist, publisher

Maynard, Nancy Hicks, photograph. AP Images.

Nancy Hicks Maynard, a pioneering journalist and longtime champion of diversity in American newsrooms, never let the barriers of race or gender get in the way of her professional ambitions. During the late 1960s she was one of the first African-American women to report for the venerable *New York Times,* but that was only the beginning of her accomplishments. Maynard, together with her husband, would go on to become publisher of the *Oakland Tribune,* the only metropolitan daily ever to be owned by an African American, and the couple would found the Institute for Journalism Education, dedicated to broadening minority representation in journalism. In her career of more than forty years, Maynard succeeded in breaking the color and gender barriers and paved the way for thousands of minority journalists who have followed in her footsteps.

Born Nancy Alene Hall in New York City on November 1, 1946, Maynard was the daughter of Alfred Hall, a black jazz musician, and Eve Keller, a white nurse. Keller had a keen interest in journalism, and she steered her daughter's attention in that direction, encouraging her to work on the newspaper at her junior high school. As a teenager, Maynard had her first taste

of the power of the press—an experience that would determine her career path early on. When her former elementary school in Harlem burned down, Maynard was so outraged by the negative and inaccurate press coverage of her neighborhood that she determined to become a journalist and change the way reporting was done.

True to her word, Maynard began her career in the newspaper business at age twenty, landing a job as a copy clerk at the *New York Post* while studying journalism at Long Island University. When she completed her degree in 1967, she became a full-time reporter for the *Post*—one of the youngest on staff and one of only a few women. At the *Post,* Maynard soon attracted the attention of legendary reporter Ted Poston, one the first African Americans to be employed full-time by a white daily newspaper. Poston acted as a mentor to the young journalist and helped develop her talent.

In 1968 Maynard submitted a request to her editor at the *Post* to cover the sanitation workers' strike in Memphis, Tennessee, where union representatives from New York were headed. Dr. Martin Luther King, a supporter of the union, was slated to speak at a rally for the workers there. The editor refused, citing a lack of travel funds; on the evening of the rally, King was assassinated at the Lorraine Motel in Memphis. Maynard called the episode the "lone low point of her career" in a 2001 interview with the Center for Integration and Improvement of Journalism.

In September of 1968 Maynard took a job with the *New York Times,* making history as the youngest reporter in the newsroom and the first African-American woman on the paper's metropolitan staff. For the *Times,* she covered race riots, school desegregation, student takeovers at Columbia and Cornell universities, and a memorial for slain Senator Robert F. Kennedy. Later, she wrote on science and health topics for the *Times,* reporting on Medicare and the Apollo

space mission, as well as traveling to China to learn about that country's medical system.

Still with the *Times,* she transferred to its Washington bureau in 1975, and soon married Robert C. Maynard, a columnist for the *Washington Post.* (Her first husband, Daniel D. Hicks, died in 1974.) The dynamic and stylish couple were among an elite group of talented African-American reporters who had advanced to significant positions in American journalism.

Two years later, in 1977, the couple quit their newspaper jobs and moved to Berkeley, California, where they teamed up with seven colleagues—a mixed group of white, black, Asian, and Latino journalists—to establish the nonprofit Institute for Journalism Education (later renamed the Robert C. Maynard Institute for Journalism Education). The institute's program was designed to train minority reporters and to push newsrooms "to reflect the diversity of thought, lifestyle and heritage in our culture," as Maynard expressed in an interview on the institute's Web site. Nancy Maynard, the institute's first president, was known as a tough instructor, emphasizing the most rigorous standards of accuracy in reporting. Dorothy Gilliam, a cofounder of the institute, recalled Maynard telling students, "If your mother tells you she loves you, check it out."

In 1979 Robert Maynard was hired by Gannett newspapers to edit the *Oakland Tribune;* four years later, the couple bought the financially struggling paper, making it the only metropolitan daily in the country to be owned by African Americans, a distinction that stands to this day. Under the Maynards' able leadership, the *Tribune* won a Pulitzer Prize for its photographs of the 1990 Loma Prieta earthquake and garnered more than 150 journalism awards. Eric Newton, the paper's managing editor during this time, called Nancy Maynard "a mighty force in the reconstruction of the *Tribune,*" according to a editorial published in the paper in 2008. Declining revenues, however, forced the Maynards to sell the paper in 1992; Robert Maynard died the following year.

Following her husband's death, Maynard continued to work as a writer and a consultant, founding the firm Maynard Partners. In 1996 she was appointed chair of the Freedom Forum Media Studies Center at Columbia University, and she continued to serve on the board of directors of the Institute for Journalism Education until 2002. In addition, she was a member of the boards of directors of the Tribune Company, the Public Broadcasting Corporation, and the New York Stock Exchange, among other organizations. In 2000 she published the book *Mega Media: How Market Forces Are Transforming the News.* For her accomplishments in journalism, the National Association of Black Journalists honored Maynard with its Lifetime Achievement Award in 1998.

Maynard died of organ failure in Los Angeles on September 21, 2008. Upon her death, Steve Montiel, a former president of the Institute for Journalism

Education, wrote on the organization's Web site, "She was a fearless, astute champion of diversity in news media, and an early advocate of new business models...always pushing to be proactive. We've lost a leader who made a difference."

Selected writings

Mega Media: How Market Forces Are Transforming the News, Trafford, 2000.

Sources

Periodicals

New York Times, September 23, 2008.
Oakland Tribune, September 22, 2008.
San Francisco Chronicle, September 22, 2008.
Washington Post, September 22, 2008, p. B6.

Online

"Nancy Maynard: Maynard Was the Only Black Woman Covering News in NYC in '68," Robert C. Maynard Institute for Journalism Education, 2008, http://www.mije.org/black_journalists_movement/nancy_maynard (accessed January 19, 2009).

"News Watch Interviews Nancy Maynard," Center for Integration and Improvement of Journalism, February 1, 2001, http://www.ciij.org/newswatch?id=105 (accessed January 19, 2009).

—Deborah A. Ring

Thabo Mbeki

1942—

Activist, politician

Thabo Mbeki has spent his life working for civil rights within an apartheid (segregationist) regime that, until 1994, ruled the country of his birth. In 2008 Mbeki stepped down as president of South Africa after a lifetime of service, knowing that he helped the development of a black middle class in South Africa and feeling gratified at his country's tremendous economic growth during his years of service. Although allegations of corruption and political influence arose late in his career, Mbeki's most serious affront to the South African people was his mishandling of the HIV/AIDS crisis.

Mbeki, Thabo, photograph. AP Images.

Grew Up in an Activist Family

Mbeki was born in June of 1942 in Queenstown, South Africa. His father, Govan Mbeki, had become a civil rights activist after his first encounter with the South African Police Force in 1929. He was in Johannesburg visiting some friends when he witnessed a raid by the police. While city dwellers of all colors were so accustomed to these maneuvers that they could have recited the usual procedure to him without thinking, Govan Mbeki was outraged by the humiliation to which

he was subjected, from the moment the police banged on his host's door in the middle of the night through the routine inspection of the "pass," or travel document assessing his right to be in the city. The whole incident was a nightmare that galvanized him into joining the African National Congress (ANC), which had been trying since its founding in 1912 to stamp out such indignities.

An industrious man who was well focused on the common black goal of South African civil rights, Govan Mbeki worked first as a schoolteacher, then as an editor of the liberal paper *New Age*. He also found time to document the history of the struggle in the book *Time Longer Than Rope*, which was published in London.

Thabo Mbeki was just six years old in 1948, when white Afrikaner Nationalists took over governmental power in South Africa. The government implemented strict laws that upheld the principles of apartheid. There was population registration to sort every ethnic group into its proper designation of "white," "colored," "Indian," or "Bantu." Pass laws were tightened to ensure that no blacks were allowed in cities during evening hours. Also, the so-called scandal of biracial

At a Glance . . .

Born Thabo Mvuyelwa Mbeki on June 18, 1942, in Queenstown, South Africa; son of Govan (a schoolteacher, civil rights activist, and author) and Epainette (a schoolteacher and civil rights activist) Mbeki; married Zanele Dlamini, 1974; children: Monwabisi Kwanda (son; with Olive Mpahlwa). *Education:* University of London, external student in economics, 1961–62; University of Sussex, ME, 1966.

Career: African National Congress (ANC), London, England, member, 1967–70; ANC, Revolutionary Council, Lusaka, Zambia, assistant secretary, 1971; ANC, National Executive Committee (NEC), member, 1975; ANC, Office of the President, political secretary, 1978; ANC, Department of Information and Publicity, director, 1984–89; ANC, chairman, 1993; ANC, deputy president, 1994; deputy president of South Africa, 1994–99; ANC, president, 1997–2007; president of South Africa, 1999–2008.

Memberships: African National Congress Youth League; African National Congress, 1967—.

Awards: Five honorary doctorates, 1994, 1995, 1999, 2000, and 2004; Good Governance Award, Corporate Council on Africa, 1997; Oliver Tambo/Johnny Makatini Freedom Award, 2000; Honorary Knight Grand Cross of the Order of the Bath, Britain, 2001; Peace and Reconciliation Award, Institute for Justice and Reconciliation, 2003; Good Brother Award, National Congress of Black Women, 2004; Insignia of Honor, Sudan, 2005; Champion of the Earth Award, United Nations, 2005; Rotterdamse Jongeren Raad Antidiscrimination Award, the Netherlands, 2005; Presidential Award, South African Chambers of Commerce and Industry, 2006.

Addresses: *Office*—c/o African National Congress, 54 Sauer St., Johannesburg 2001, South Africa.

marriages was outlawed. In 1950 the Group Areas Act was enacted. This act allowed the government to uproot blacks from designated white areas and resettle them in "bantustans" or designated homelands, which were frequently rural areas without electricity, roads, or sewage facilities.

Became an Activist in High School

Bantustan life was a fate that Mbeki luckily escaped. He was permitted to attend high school at the Lovedale Institute in Alice, Eastern Cape, and at age fourteen, Mbeki joined a nearby ANC Youth League. He quickly became active in student politics, even going so far as to participate in a strike that got him expelled from high school in 1959. Undaunted, he simply used his home as a base for both his studies and his antiapartheid activities. The following year a tragedy would strike black South Africans.

The date March 21, 1960, was one that no South African would ever forget. It began with an anti-pass rally in Sharpeville, Transvaal, and it ended in clouds of teargas, bullets fired by police, and the urgent shriek of ambulances removing the bodies of 69 murdered demonstrators and 187 injured, most of whom had been shot in the back as they tried to run away.

Almost before the teargas had cleared, the government banned all political organizations and forbade all public political demonstrations. Like his fellow ANC Youth League members, Mbeki was forced to hide his political activities from the world. In 1961 he quietly began to mobilize students for a stay-at-home protest after the South African government announced its decision to leave the British Commonwealth and become a republic. His father opted for a more dangerous way to intensify the antiapartheid struggle while still living under the vigilant eye of the security police. Working alongside ANC leader Nelson Mandela, Govan Mbeki helped found a militant new ANC wing in December of 1961 known as Umkhonto we Sizwe (Spear of the Nation).

Attended the University of Sussex

In 1962 the ANC ordered Thabo Mbeki to leave the country, possibly to attend military training in Algeria or to avoid implication in the bombings and sabotage planned by Umkhonto we Sizwe. Regardless of the motive, Thabo Mbeki fared better than his father. In 1963 Govan Mbeki was arrested in a highly publicized police raid on the Rivonia, Transvaal, headquarters of Umkhonto we Sizwe. Along with Mandela, Govan Mbeki was sentenced to twenty-seven years at the notorious Robben Island, a maximum security prison near Cape Town.

If Algeria was indeed Thabo Mbeki's intended destination, he never made it there. Following a supposedly secret route specified by the ANC, Mbeki went through Bechuanaland (later Botswana) into Southern Rhodesia (later Zimbabwe) only to be captured by the police and jailed for six weeks. Following his release, he traveled to Tanzania, where he was granted political asylum by President Julius Nyerere, and then went on to England.

Upon his arrival in England, Mbeki resumed his education at the University of Sussex, where he majored in economics. At the same time, he worked at the ANC's London headquarters to mobilize black South African students for the liberation struggle. Mbeki graduated in 1966 and traveled on ANC business for several years. After receiving military training in the Soviet Union, he was sent to Zambia, where he served as assistant secretary to the ANC's Revolutionary Council. He was then stationed in Botswana, where his duties centered on the consolidation and mobilization of activists for the ANC's underground groups in neighboring South Africa. He also negotiated with the Botswana government concerning the establishment of an ANC office in the country.

Rose through the ANC Hierarchy

During the 1970s Mbeki continued to rise through the ranks of the ANC. He became an acting representative in Swaziland in 1974 and was soon honored with membership in the multiracial ninety-one-member National Executive Committee. This honor led to a new assignment in Nigeria, where a large share of his time was spent helping exiled South African students adjust to their new surroundings.

Back in South Africa, the government continued to strengthen the apartheid system, and the ANC stepped up its policy of protests and civil disobedience throughout the country to break the stranglehold of apartheid. By the 1980s Mbeki had risen to prominence in the ANC as director of the Department of Information and Publicity. It was a position that would allow Mbeki to serve an influential role in the gradual dismantling of apartheid.

In 1986 Mbeki traveled to New York City for a Ford Foundation conference. At the conference Mbeki met Pieter de Lange, who was both the president of Rand Afrikaans University in Johannesburg and a well-entrenched chairman of the pro-apartheid Broederbond. One evening, the two men talked about the situation in South Africa for several hours, and de Lange invited Mbeki to join him and his wife for lunch the next day.

It was a groundbreaking invitation. As veteran South African journalist Allister Sparks notes in his book *Tomorrow Is Another Country: The Inside Story of South Africa's Road to Change,* de Lange went home from this luncheon with Mbeki determined to resign from Rand Afrikaans University to devote himself to promoting interracial harmony by holding private talks with his fellow Broederbond members. This remarkable meeting between Mbeki and de Lange was enough to foster the start of other top secret talks, with sympathetic white Afrikaners acting as liaisons between the government and the ANC.

Between 1987 and early 1990 a series of meetings between the ANC and South African government officials were held in the remote English village of Mells. Mbeki was charged with presenting the ANC's positions. The talks centered on the immediate release of political prisoners, including Mandela, leader of the ANC; the possible suspension of the armed struggle by the ANC; equal rights for all minorities; and replacement of the Nationalist-dominated government with a multiracial interim ruling body.

In 1989 pro-apartheid South African president P. W. Botha was forced to resign. He was replaced by F. W. de Klerk, a moderate who sought dialog with the ANC and the eventual creation of a multiracial democratic government. On February 2, 1990, President de Klerk announced in a speech that the ANC, the Umkhonto we Sizwe, and the Communist Party were no longer banned. He also called for continued meetings between government representatives and ANC negotiators led by Mbeki. Owing to the delicate issues surrounding the release of Mandela, and the fact that many of the ANC diplomats were still officially persona non grata in South Africa, the arrangements for the meetings soon took on the melodramatic aura of an international espionage novel. Switzerland was eventually chosen as the meeting site because it was one of the few countries that South Africans could enter freely due to international sanctions. South African government representatives were given false passports and ANC delegates were kept under close surveillance.

Elected Deputy President of South Africa

The diplomatic negotiations soon bore fruit. After twenty-seven years in captivity, Mandela triumphantly emerged from Robben Island prison in February of 1990. In August of 1990 a pact called the Pretoria Minute announced the end of the ANC's thirty-year-long armed struggle. Negotiations continued for several years as the apartheid system was gradually dismantled. The culmination of all diplomatic negotiations occurred on April 27, 1994, when South Africa held the first democratic elections in which all South Africans, black and white, were allowed to participate. Mandela was elected president of South Africa, and Mbeki was elected deputy president.

By 1996 Mbeki began, in effect, running the government by taking over many of the day-to-day duties from an aging and tired Mandela. With his economic background, he was also working to rebuild the nation's economy. Mbeki supported the privatization of businesses, including the postal system, water utilities, and roadway construction. By late 1997 part of the telephone industry was privatized, as were some radio stations and an airline. Besides adapting to a new government and new economic structures, South Africans also faced a reconceptualization of their society. As Mbeki stated to Suzanne Daley in the *New York Times,* "Apartheid was inherently corrupt, immoral.

And it left behind a disrespect for legitimacy. There is a lack of sense of social ethics. This is something that has to be dealt with, and it's not a legislative thing. We must change the mood of a country and set new values."

By the time Mbeki was elected president of the ANC in December of 1997, it was a sure sign that he had been tapped to be the next South African leader. Mandela admitted that he was mainly a ceremonial president by this point, but still, he was a familiar father figure and living legend that his countrymen admired. It made it all the harder for people to accept Mbeki, who, due to his many years behind the scenes in the ANC, was shrouded in mystery. In addition, even though the nation was experiencing a new stability in government, exhilarating freedoms, and a jump in the quality of life for many, South Africa was sagging under a startling epidemic of HIV/AIDS, an unemployment rate of about 30 percent, a rapidly deteriorating educational system, and an alarming jump in violent crime, with a poor record of prosecutions.

Elected President of South Africa

Regardless of the problems facing the country, on June 4, 1999, South Africans reelected the ANC with 65.7 percent of the votes, which was three percentage points more than the 62.6 percent it garnered in 1994. Because Mbeki was the president of the ANC, he was inaugurated as president of South Africa on June 16.

After his inauguration, Mbeki promised to promote economic growth and foreign investment and to reduce poverty by relaxing restrictive labor laws. He also planned to step up the pace of privatization and cut unneeded governmental spending. Nonetheless, Mbeki was unable to avert an economic slowdown in his country in 2001, largely because it was tied to an international economic slowdown. By mid-2002 the South African rand was worth about half of what it had been worth in 1999 when compared with the U.S. dollar.

Not only did South Africa face serious economic troubles at this time but also it faced an enormous health crisis with the HIV/AIDS epidemic. Mbeki worsened the situation because he advocated unorthodox theories about AIDS. Questioning the medical basis of the disease, Mbeki argued that antiretroviral drugs were poison. In an address to the ANC's parliamentary caucus in 2001, Mbeki claimed that the Central Intelligence Agency and large pharmaceutical companies were opposing him because he stood in the way of plans to introduce expensive AIDS drugs into South Africa. Even Mandela split with Mbeki over the AIDS issue and said publicly that he would have preferred antiapartheid politician Cyril Ramaphosa to Mbeki as his successor as president.

On July 9, 2003, U.S. president George W. Bush made a plea to Mbeki to reconsider the implications of the controversial AIDS issue. Bush pledged greater funding for fighting the disease in South Africa. On September 25 Mbeki relented and rationalized governmental delays in the distribution of anti-AIDS drugs, which indicated that an insufficient number of properly trained public health care workers had been available to distribute the medications.

Experienced Turmoil, Criticism during Second Term

After two decades of democracy in South Africa, the ruling ANC secured 70 percent majority of the vote during the national elections held on April 14, 2004, thus ensuring Mbeki's continued administration as president. He was sworn in for his second term on April 27, and on April 28 he announced the names of his new cabinet, which included half of his previous ministers. Among those retained were the respected finance minister Trevor Manuel and the health minister Manto Tshabalala-Msimang. Once established in his second administration, Mbeki made an attempt to broker a peace in the Ivory Coast on November 9, 2004, in the wake of several days of rioting and protests there over the presence of French peacekeepers. Also in 2004 he helped prevent a coup in Equatorial Guinea, having reversed a similar situation in São Tomé and Principe Island in 2003. During the first three weeks of January of 2005, he attended peace talks in Kenya, Sudan, Congo, Gabon, and the Ivory Coast.

South African politics, however, were plunged into turmoil in June of 2005, when Mbeki fired his deputy president, Jacob Zuma, who had been considered likely to succeed him as president. A court had convicted Zuma's financial adviser of giving Zuma $178,000 and attempting to arrange bribes for Zuma from a French arms dealer. The firing fractured the ANC, as supporters of Zuma, who was popular with trade unions, many youth, and the Communist Party, launched furious protests. Zuma was also accused of rape. In 2006, however, the courts found Zuma not guilty of the rape charges and dismissed the corruption charges.

In the fall of 2006, responding to the repeated international criticism of its AIDS policies, the Mbeki government signaled a change. The new deputy president, Phumzile Mlambo-Ngcuka, was placed in charge of the government's AIDS response, pushing aside a health minister who had suggested that changes in diet could fight AIDS. Mbeki's new deputy president repeatedly acknowledged that HIV definitely causes AIDS and that antiretroviral drugs are key to fighting the disease. The government was also increasing programs to deliver the drugs to HIV/AIDS patients, though not enough to reach all South Africans who needed them.

While campaigning in support of ANC candidates in local elections in early 2006, Mbeki promised to bring clean water and sanitation to all homes in South Africa by 2010 and to cut poverty and unemployment in half by 2014. He also announced that he would not run for president again when his term ended in 2009. Throughout the year Mbeki faced increased criticism of his presidency. Some of it came from unions and the Communist Party, who charged that the country was drifting toward dictatorship, a claim mostly based on what they said was the government's leaking of information to influence court cases and press coverage. Furthermore, Desmond Tutu, a hero of the antiapartheid movement, also criticized Mbeki for his response to the AIDS crisis and supportive relationship with Robert Mugabe, the dictator of neighboring Zimbabwe.

Resigned from Office

In December of 2007 the ANC ousted Mbeki, voting in Zuma as its new leader during a national conference. Mbeki's popularity was low because many ANC members saw him as too dictatorial and not focusing enough on the working poor, which made up a huge proportion of the South African population. Even though Zuma had strong support in the ANC, he did not provide a clear and strong message as to how he would help the South African people. In addition, corruption investigations continued to follow Zuma. Nevertheless, he was becoming favored as Mbeki's successor to the presidency.

By August of 2008 Zuma was not the only political leader with allegations of corruption aimed at him. South Africa's *Times* newspaper suggested that a German firm had paid Mbeki millions over an arms deal, which included the guarantee of a submarine contract. Mbeki denied the allegations and no evidence was put forth to support them. After a judge implied, however, that the Mbeki government had tried to influence the outcome of Zuma's corruption case, the ANC requested that Mbeki resign before the end of his term. According to the *Times,* Mbeki accepted the ANC's decision, stating in his resignation speech, "I have been a loyal member of the African National Congress for 52 years. I remain a member of the ANC and therefore respect its decisions." He stepped down on September 21, 2008; many South Africans were stunned at the sudden turn of events and shocked at Mbeki's ouster.

The legacy of Mbeki's service to South Africa is mixed. A serious stain on his record is that he hindered appropriate health care for those with HIV/AIDS during his tenure and, as a result, has been blamed for 330,000 deaths. On the positive side, he helped his country make many significant strides in its development, including moving the country forward economically, making progress toward many of the United Nations Development Program's Millennium Development Goals (which include poverty reduction, education, maternal health, and gender equality), and empowering women. Mbeki received many awards during his years of government service, including five honorary doctorates at institutions of higher learning around the world, the prestigious Good Governance Award bestowed by the Corporate Council on Africa in 1997 for helping to strengthen commercial relationships between the United States and the African continent, the Oliver Tambo/Johnny Makatini Freedom Award in 2000 for his commitment to democracy, the Peace and Reconciliation Award in 2003 for enabling people from diverse backgrounds to learn to live together in the pursuit of the common good, and the Presidential Award in 2006 from the South African Chambers of Commerce and Industry for his promotion of economic growth and investor confidence in South Africa and Africa.

Sources

Books

Holland, Heidi, *The Struggle: A History of the African National Congress,* G. Braziller, 1990.

Malan, Rian, *My Traitor's Heart: A South African Exile Returns to Face His Country, His Tribe, and His Conscience,* Atlantic Monthly Press, 1990.

Norval, Morgan, *Inside the ANC: The Evolution of a Terrorist Organization,* Selous Foundation Press, 1990.

Saunders, Christopher, *Historical Dictionary of South Africa,* Scarecrow Press, 1983.

Sparks, Allister, *The Mind of South Africa,* Knopf, 1990.

Sparks, Allister, *Tomorrow Is Another Country: The Inside Story of South Africa's Road to Change,* Hill and Wang, 1995.

Periodicals

Africa Report, March–April 1989, p. 34; May–June 1993, p.5.

Associated Press, September 22, 2008.

BBC News, January 8, 2006; February 9, 2006; August 4, 2008; November 7, 2008.

Chicago Tribune, November 30, 1995, p.1; March 8, 1996, p. 11.

Christian Science Monitor, April 10, 1996, p. 19.

Economist, May 1, 2004, p. 48; January 22, 2005, p. 26.

Newsweek International, March 4, 2002 p. 32.

New York Times, May 12, 1995, p. A5; May 14, 1996, p. A4; July 23, 1996, p. A1; July 10, 2003; September 29, 2003; January 5, 2004; December 19, 2007.

Reuters, September 21, 2008.

Times (Johannesburg, South Africa), August 4, 2008.

Washington Post, May 27, 2006, p. A14; June 15, 2006, p. A14; October 9, 2006; October 27, 2006, p. A1; January 9, 2007, p. A10.

Online

"Mbeki Resignation Speech: The Full Text," *Times* (Johannesburg, South Africa), September 21, 2008, http://blogs.thetimes.co.za/hartley/2008/09/21/ mbeki-resignation-speech-the-full-text/ (accessed December 4, 2008).

—Gillian Wolf and Sandra Alters

Chi McBride

1961—

Actor

Chi McBride is a successful film and television actor best known for his role as principal Steven Harper in the popular Fox television drama *Boston Public* from 2000 to 2004. McBride's success in Hollywood is particularly notable as he never took an acting class and did not even step in front of a camera for the first time until he was thirty years old. Despite the late start, McBride—a hulk of a man at 6 feet, 5 inches tall, recognizable by his trademark bald dome—has become one of Hollywood's most prolific actors, with more than two dozen feature films to his credit. In comedies and dramas, on the big and the small screen, McBride has proven himself to be a versatile character actor who can take on any role—from a wisecracking janitor to a snarky private investigator—and make it his own.

He was born Kenneth McBride in Chicago, Illinois, in 1961 and grew up on the city's west side. His parents, of Caribbean descent, were active members of the Seventh-Day Adventist Church, and McBride attended the religious Shiloh Academy, graduating from high school at age sixteen. With hopes of a future career in music, he learned to play a number of instruments and

McBride, Chi, photograph. AP Images.

sang with gospel choirs in the Chicago area. In 1986 McBride relocated to Atlanta, where he found work handling customer service calls for the telephone giant MCI. "If you were living in the Southeastern region of the United States and you had a problem with your phone, chances are you might have talked to me. But only for a little while, because I put everyone on hold until it drove them crazy enough to hang up," McBride joked in an interview with Jenelle Riley in *Back Stage.*

Still harboring musical ambitions, McBride wrote and recorded the song "He's the Champ," which parodied the marriage of boxer Mike Tyson and actress Robin Givens. Though the song was not a chart topper, it attracted enough attention that McBride was signed to Esquire Records, and he joined the R&B group Covert, which released their only album, *For Your Bootay Only,* in 1991. The same year, McBride went to Los Angeles to shoot a music video for "He's the Champ." The video's producer, Sam Mayhew, arranged McBride's first Hollywood audition, for a part in the third installment of the film *Revenge of the Nerds.* In 1992 McBride—now billing himself as Chi (pro-

At a Glance . . .

Born Kenneth McBride on September 23, 1961, in Chicago, IL.

Career: MCI, customer service representative, 1980s; R&B singer with Covert, 1991; television and film actor, 1992—.

Awards: Best Actor in a Television Series, Golden Satellite Awards, 2002, for *Boston Public*.

Addresses: *Office*—c/o ABC, 500 South Buena Vista St., Burbank, CA 91521-4551.

nounced "shy"), a nod to his hometown of Chicago—made his screen debut in the *Nerds* television movie. In addition, he made guest appearances on Fox's *In Living Color* and NBC's *The Fresh Prince of Bel Air*.

Within a year of moving to Los Angeles, McBride landed his first television series, appearing in the role of Heavy Gene, a surly, wisecracking janitor on the NBC sitcom *The John Larroquette Show,* for four seasons (1993–96). He also had minor roles in several feature films, including *The Distinguished Gentleman* (1992) with Eddie Murphy, the Oscar-winning *What's Love Got to Do with It* (1993) with Angela Bassett, and Peter Jackson's *The Frighteners* (1996) with Michael J. Fox. McBride's first major film role came in 1998, when he appeared in *Mercury Rising* opposite Bruce Willis.

The year 1998 also saw McBride in the controversial UPN sitcom *The Secret Diary of Desmond Pfeiffer*. In the title role, McBride portrayed an English nobleman who is sold into slavery and sent to America to work as the butler of U.S. president Abraham Lincoln. Derided for its breezy take on American slavery, the show set off a storm of criticism before it ever aired, prompting protests from the NAACP. Cancelled after only a month, *Desmond* easily could have spelled the end of McBride's career. Undeterred, however, he returned to the big screen once again, appearing in four feature films in 2000: *Gone in Sixty Seconds,* Disney's *The Kid, Magicians,* and *Dancing in September.*

With the *Desmond* debacle behind him, McBride landed the role for which he is best known. In the acclaimed Fox drama *Boston Public,* written by David E. Kelley, creator of such hit series as *L.A. Law, Ally McBeal,* and *The Practice,* McBride played Steven Harper, the beleaguered principal of an inner-city high school. In an interview with Lori Blackman on CNN. com, McBride described the character as "a guy who has a piano on top of his head all of the time, and he is juggling a refrigerator, a chain saw and a broken bottle." Caryn James in the *New York Times* praised McBride's "strong, engaging performance," while the *Fort-Worth Star Telegram* called him the "force at the center" of the show. In 2001 McBride was nominated for the American Film Institute's Actor of the Year award for a dramatic television series, and in 2002 he was chosen for a Golden Satellite award for his performance.

Simultaneous with his four seasons on *Boston Public,* McBride landed roles in a number of motion pictures, including the comedy *Undercover Brother* (2002), the thriller *Cradle 2 the Grave* (2003), Stephen Spielberg's *The Terminal* (2004), and the sci-fi picture *I, Robot* (2004) with Will Smith. He made a five-episode appearance on the Fox drama *House* in 2005, playing tycoon Edward Vogler, and had stints on the Fox series *Killer Instinct* (2005–06) and ABC's *The Nine* (2006–07).

McBride signed on to a new hit show in 2007, playing private investigator Emerson Cod on ABC's *Pushing Daisies*. On the quirky series, described as a "forensic fairy tale," McBride's character befriends Ned Lee (Lee Pace), a man who can bring the dead back to life—but only for one minute. Cod and Lee team up to revive murder victims and identify their killers. Critics praised *Pushing Daisies* in its first season: *New York Magazine* called the show "funny, imaginative, and smart," while Rick Kissell in *Variety* hailed it as "the most buzzed-about drama" of the year. However, after only nine episodes, production of the show was interrupted by a writers strike. Despite winning three Emmy Awards, when the series resumed in the fall of 2008 it failed to retain its previous momentum and was cancelled in December of that year. Discussing his role in the show, McBride told BuzzSugar.com, "Comedy's something that I started with and got away from for a long time.... So I was really glad to come back to comedy, but it had to be something good. No 'You gettin' on my last nerve! Pow!' I didn't want to do that."

Selected works

Films

The Distinguished Gentleman, 1992.
What's Love Got to Do with It, 1993.
The Frighteners, 1996.
Hoodlum, 1997.
Mercury Rising, 1998.
Dancing in September, 2000.
Gone in Sixty Seconds, 2000.
The Kid, 2000.
Magicians, 2000.
Narc, 2002.
Paid in Full, 2002.
Undercover Brother, 2002.
Cradle 2 the Grave, 2003.

Delusion, 2003.
I, Robot, 2004.
The Terminal, 2004.
Roll Bounce, 2005.
Waiting, 2005.
Annapolis, 2006.
Let's Go to Prison, 2006.
The Brothers Solomon, 2007.
American Son, 2008.
First Sunday, 2008.
Who Do You Love, 2008.
Driving Lessons, 2009.

Television

Revenge of the Nerds III: The Next Generation (television movie), 1992.
The John Larroquette Show, 1993–96.
The Secret Diary of Desmond Pfeiffer, 1998.
Boston Public, 2000–04.
Max Steel, 2001.
House, 2005.
Killer Instinct, 2005–06.
The Nine, 2006–07.
Pushing Daisies, 2007–08.

Sources

Periodicals

Back Stage, October 17, 2008.
Fort Worth Star-Telegram, February 22, 2002.
New York Magazine, May 24, 2007.
New York Times, October 23, 2000.
Variety, May 25, 2007.

Online

Blackman, Lori, "Showbiz Today Star of Tomorrow: Chi McBride of 'Boston Public,'" CNN.com, April 10, 2001, http://archives.cnn.com/2001/SHOWBIZ/TV/04/10/sbtst.mcbride/ (accessed January 20, 2009).
"Interview: Chi McBride Talks Comedy and Knitting," BuzzSugar.com, October 7, 2008, http://www.buzzsugar.com/2283448 (accessed January 24, 2009).
"Chi McBride Biography," Variety.com, http://www.variety.com/profiles/people/Biography/34722/Chi +McBride.html?dataSet=1 (accessed January 20, 2009).
Pushing Daisies, ABC.com, http://abc.go.com/primetime/pushingdaisies/index?pn=index (accessed January 24, 2009).

—Deborah A. Ring

Jaunel McKenzie

1986—

Fashion model

Jamaica's Jaunel McKenzie is one of a handful of black models who work in the upper echelons of the fashion business. Discovered as a teenager when she entered a model search contest in 2002, McKenzie appeared on the runways of some of the world's top designers, including Giorgio Armani and Oscar de La Renta. She also appeared in advertising campaigns for Victoria's Secret and Tommy Hilfiger, among other leading brands. Her high-powered career, she told Polly Vernon in the London *Guardian,* was responsible for "broadening my own horizons, knowing myself more, understanding how to express myself as a person."

McKenzie, Jaunel, photograph. Thomas Concordia/WireImage/ Getty Images.

McKenzie was born in 1986 and grew up in the Nannyville Gardens section of Kingston, Jamaica's capital and largest city. She graduated from Excelsior High School at the age of sixteen, and planned to enroll in a local college to study finance and accounting, but on a whim entered a contest staged by Pulse Models, a Kingston-based modeling agency. She won the inaugural Caribbean Model Search, and agents Romae Gordon and Kingsley Cooper sent photo-

graphs of her to a top modeling agency in Paris, which signed her immediately and began booking her for shows. In this rarified world, McKenzie became the first Caribbean model since fellow Jamaican Lois Samuels to achieve such prominence. In 1997 Samuels had become the first Caribbean model of color to appear on the cover of an international edition of *Vogue.*

McKenzie introduced sportswear designer Tommy Hilfiger's 2004–05 Tommy Women collection in a seven-page layout that appeared in a premium front slot in all the major fashion magazines. In 2005 *Vibe* magazine named her to its annual "Hot List," which also included actor/singer Queen Latifah, rapper Kanye West, media mogul Sean "P. Diddy" Combs, and Illinois Senator Barack Obama. According to a report in the *Jamaica Gleaner, Vibe*'s founder, record producer Quincy Jones, asserted that McKenzie "has corporate clout, is fabulous, has super sex appeal, is elevating the game, and is undoubtedly sparking a major movement in world fashion." Anna Wintour, the editor of the American edition of *Vogue,* is another admirer of McKen-

At a Glance . . .

Born in 1986, in Kingston, Jamaica.

Career: Signed to Pulse Models, and began appearing in runway shows in Paris, 2002.

Addresses: *Office*—c/o Pulse Investments Ltd., 38A Trafalgar Rd., Kingston 10, Jamaica.

zie's, and by 2008 McKenzie had been booked for thirteen editorial layouts, a record for a model from the Caribbean.

Despite the prominence McKenzie attained in the fashion world, designers and magazine editors remained targets of criticism for the lack of women of color on runways and covers. In July of 2008 Italian *Vogue* ran a special "All-Black" issue as a statement (though McKenzie did not appear in it). In reply fashion journalist Constance C.R. White wrote an article in the September issue of *Ebony* entitled "Black Out: What Has Happened to the Black Models?" In it, White noted that "top American designers staged more than 100 presentations in New York in February at the biannual ready-to-wear shows and many were, shall we say, color-free. It was not unusual to watch a show and not see one woman (or man, for that matter) of color. In the European fashion capitals of Milan and Paris, the situation was far worse."

Citing a long and illustrious legacy of top black models, from Naomi Sims and Iman in the 1970s to Veronica Webb and Naomi Campbell later on, White wondered why, besides McKenzie, Liya Kebede, and Chanel Iman, there were so few black models at the top of the heap. "Eastern Europeans have flooded the market and become the beauty standard-bearers," White theorized. "The pace has quickened with disposable fashion worn by disposable models who all look alike. Celebrities have replaced supermodels. Add to the mix that Asian designers and Asian consumers preferred more Asians on the runway while the Black presence decreased." McKenzie discussed the topic during an interview in the *Jamaica Gleaner*, agreeing that among black models like herself, "there is not a shortage on the international scene but on the runway. They are there, but they are not getting the career-boosting hot jobs ... There are a lot of reasons that figure into it. I'm not sure why, though, because they are all skinny, beautiful, but I guess they are just not what they are going for."

Realizing that her peak years as a model would be relatively short ones, McKenzie planned for a second career by taking acting classes, and considering a college degree in business, which would be helpful if she ever launched her own clothing line. She noted that her industry holds signal perils for its teenaged stars, including eating disorders and substance abuse. "It is easy to be overwhelmed by the temptations of the industry and those temptations can easily lead to your downfall," she told Kimberly Stephenson in the *Jamaica Observer*.

Sources

Periodicals

America's Intelligence Wire, October 22, 2004.
Ebony, September 2008, p. 98.
Guardian (London), March 10, 2004.
Jamaica Gleaner, September 16, 2005; September 28, 2008.

Online

Stephenson, Kimberly, "Supermodel Jaunel McKenzie's Not So Steep Climb up the Success Ladder," *Jamaica Observer*, August 3, 2004, http://www.jamaicaobserver.com/magazines/TeenAge/html/20040802T200000-0500_63863_OBS_SUPERMODEL_JAUNEL_MCKENZIE_S_.asp (accessed December 10, 2008).

—Carol Brennan

Breno Mello

1931–2008

Actor

Actor Breno Mello burst onto the international scene in 1959 as the lead in the influential and critically acclaimed French-Brazilian movie *Orfeu Negro* (*Black Orpheus*). Set amid the music and pageantry of Carnival, an annual celebration in the Brazilian city of Rio de Janeiro, the movie superimposes the classic tale of Orpheus and Eurydice onto the realities of modern Brazilian life. As Orpheus, a musician striving to rescue his beloved from the clutches of death, Mello, in his debut role, displayed the physical grace he had perfected as a professional soccer player. His subsequent roles were disappointments, however, so he returned to private life. *Orfeu Negro,* in contrast, has retained its prominence. As of early 2009 the production that made Mello a star remained one of the most frequently shown films of the 1950s.

Few details of Mello's early life are available. He was born in September of 1931 in the Brazilian city of Porto Alegre, on the coast south of Rio. A gifted athlete, he was making his living as a professional soccer player by the time he was twenty years old. He played for some of the strongest and most popular franchises in the county, including Santos, Fluminense, and Gremio. In about 1958, at the height of his soccer career, he was spotted on a Rio beach by Marcel Camus, a French filmmaker who was in town to make a movie based on Brazilian playwright Vinicius de Moraes's retelling of the ancient Greek myth of Orpheus and Eurydice. Struck by Mello's good looks and physical grace, Camus immediately offered him a starring role. Within months, that chance encounter on the beach had propelled the local soccer star into the international spotlight.

In the ancient version of the story, Orpheus is a young musician whose songs are so beautiful that birds, animals, and the gods themselves are entranced. When his beloved, a young woman named Eurydice, dies suddenly, he travels to the underworld in an unsuccessful effort to bring her back to life. The tale had already inspired a number of films—including the first two installments in French director Jean Cocteau's so-called Orphic Trilogy—when Camus discovered Vinicius's 1956 play *Orfeu da Concei¸ão,* which reimagines the ancient lyre player as a guitarist at Carnival. Transferring Vinicius's vision to the screen presented a host of logistical problems for Camus and his cinematographer, the highly regarded Jean Bourgoin. Principal among these was the question of atmosphere. Should the tone be the ethereal, unworldly one of myth or the vibrant, sometimes disturbing one of life in Rio? Camus' achievement, according to critics, was to combine the two. Thus, at some moments the camera lingers on the hillside slums (known as *favelas*) where much of Rio's population lives and through which Mello, a tram driver, accompanies the country girl Eurydice, played by African-American dancer Marpessa Dawn. In other scenes the mythic element predominates, as when Orpheus, having found Eurydice in the city morgue, holds her lifeless body in his arms as he leaps from one of the cliffs that ring the city. Crucial to both the mythic and realistic scenes is the movie's soundtrack, which was assembled and performed by the internationally acclaimed Brazilian musicians Luiz

At a Glance . . .

Born on September 7, 1931, in Porto Alegre, Rio Grande do Sul, Brazil; died on July 14, 2008, in Porto Alegre; married twice; children: five.

Career: Professional soccer player, late 1940s–60s; star of six feature films, 1959–88, and a documentary, 2004.

Bonfá and Antonio Carlos Jobim. The soundtrack would later be credited with helping to launch a worldwide craze for Brazilian music in the 1960s.

Completed in 1958 and released the following year, *Orfeu Negro* was a sensation, with critics praising, above all, the soundtrack and Bourgoin's cinematography. Reaction to Mello's performance was more muted. While nearly all reviewers noted his grace and physical attractiveness, some were less impressed with his abilities as an actor. Film critic Bosley Crowther came close to expressing the critical consensus when he wrote in the *New York Times*, "Breno Mello makes a handsome, virile Orpheus who glistens when covered with sweat, but he performs the role more as a dancer than as an actor trying to show a man in love." As Crowther himself acknowledged, however, the film's "focus of interest" was not acting but "the music, the movement, the storm of color that go into the two-day festival." These he praised highly, as did critics and audiences worldwide. Among other honors, *Orfeu Negro* won the Palme D'Or at the Cannes Film Festival in 1959 and the Academy Award for best foreign film the following year.

After such an auspicious debut, Mello seemed poised for a long and successful movie career. Black leading men, while still rare at the time, were increasingly prominent, with Sidney Poitier and Harry Belafonte, for example, then at the height of their fame. For a native Portuguese speaker like Mello, however, the language barrier was a formidable obstacle to Hollywood, and the local Brazilian film industry was not yet sufficiently developed to offer Mello the kinds of roles and films he wanted. As a result, he appeared in only five more feature films in a twenty-five-year period between 1963 and 1988. Most of them were local Brazilian productions, and all of them failed to become critical or commercial successes.

To make ends meet in the years following *Orfeu Negro*, Mello resumed playing professional soccer and

later sold advertising in his hometown. He returned unexpectedly to public notice in 2004 with the release of the French documentary *À la recherche d'Orfeu Negro* (*In Search of Black Orpheus*). Directed by René Letzgus and Bernard Tournois, the film explored the impact of the original movie on the development of Brazilian music and on the personal lives of its stars. Letzgus and Tournois found Mello living in Porto Alegre and convinced him to appear once more on camera, not, of course, as Orpheus, but simply as a private citizen whose life was transformed by a celebrated film forty-five years earlier.

Though Mello was twice married and had five children, he was apparently alone in his home in Porto Alegre when he died of natural causes on July 14, 2008, at the age of seventy-six. His death was not widely noticed in the English-speaking world until the *New York Times* published an obituary nearly two months later.

Selected films

Orfeu Negro (*Black Orpheus*), 1959.
Os Vencidos, 1963.
Rata de puerto, 1963.
O Santo Módico, 1964.
O Negrinho do Pastoreio, 1973.
Prisoner of Rio, 1988.
À la recherche d'Orfeu Negro, 2004.

Sources

Periodicals

Guardian (London), November 4, 2005.
Los Angeles Times, March 6, 1960.
New York Times, December 22, 1959; September 6, 2008.
Times (London), May 30, 1960.

Online

"*Black Orpheus,*" moviediva, October 2004, http://www.moviediva.com/MD_root/reviewpages/MD-BlackOrpheus.htm (accessed December 2, 2008).
Buening, Michael, "*Black Orpheus:* Review," allmovie, http://www.allmovie.com/cg/avg.dll?p=avg&sql=1:5910˜T1 (accessed December 2, 2008).
Gerhard, Susan, "The Breno Mello of 'Black Orpheus,'" San Francisco Film Society, January 3, 2007, http://www.sf360.org/features/the-breno-mello-of-black-orpheus (accessed December 2, 2008).

—R. Anthony Kugler

Russ Mitchell

1960—

Broadcast journalist

As early as his junior year in high school, Russ Mitchell knew that he wanted to be a journalist. From his humble beginnings as a night switchboard operator at an ABC affiliate in St. Louis, Missouri, Mitchell climbed to prominence as an anchor on CBS television newscasts, news magazines, and talk shows. By 2008 Mitchell was concurrently anchoring a variety of morning and evening broadcasts and had been frequently honored for his achievements as a journalist. At that time he told an interviewer from the Missouri School of Journal-

Mitchell, Russ, photograph. Craig Blankenhorn/CBS/Landov.

ism: "The best thing about my job is that I am not chained to a desk. I experience the best of both worlds. I get to do things I like, such as anchor three newscasts,… and to go out into the field to report. Every day is different. If I were carve out my ideal job, this would be it."

Mitchell was born in St. Louis in March of 1960 and moved with his family to suburban Rock Hill, Missouri, when he was about six years old. Energized by a journalism course he took during his junior year of high school, Mitchell enrolled in a two-week journalism workshop for minorities the following summer at the main campus of the University of Missouri in Columbia.

During the workshop, he prepared stories for television and newspapers, and even appeared on a Columbia television station. Mitchell's experiences at the workshop convinced him to pursue long-term career opportunities in television journalism.

Started as Operator at ABC Affiliate

When Mitchell returned to the St. Louis area for his senior year of high school, his cousin told him about a job opening for a night switchboard operator at St. Louis's ABC affiliate, KTVI-TV. Mitchell applied for and landed the job. As Mitchell remarked in an interview with *Contemporary Black Biography* (*CBB*), "I thought I would be doing that for a week and then anchoring their newscast! I was seventeen years old. I didn't know anything!" Mitchell remained on the job for a year, answering phones in the newsroom on weekends and getting a bird's-eye view of the daily activities in a television station.

Mitchell left KTVI-TV in 1978 to begin his freshman year at the University of Missouri, Columbia, where he pursued a degree in broadcast journalism. During his

At a Glance . . .

Born Russell Edward Mitchell on March 25, 1960, in St. Louis, MO; son of Lowell E. Mitchell and Julia J. Mitchell; married Erica (divorced); married Karina Mahtani, 2006; children: (first marriage) Ashley. *Education:* University of Missouri, Bachelor of Journalism, 1982.

Career: KMBC-TV, reporter trainee, 1982; WFAA-TV, reporter, anchor, 1983–85; KTVI-TV, reporter, 1985–87; KMOV-TV, reporter, weekend news anchor, 1987–92; CBS News *Up to the Minute,* coanchor, 1992–93; CBS News *Eye to Eye,* correspondent, 1993–95; *CBS Sunday Night News,* Washington correspondent, anchor, 1995–97; *CBS News Saturday Morning/The Saturday Early Show,* coanchor, 1997–2007; *CBS Evening News* (Saturday edition), anchor, 1999—; *CBS News Sunday Morning,* correspondent, 2002—; *CBS Evening News* (Sunday edition), rotating anchor, 2006—; *CBS News Early Show,* news anchor and primary substitute anchor, 2007—.

Memberships: National Association of Black Journalists.

Awards: Two Emmy awards, St. Louis chapter, National Academy of Television Arts and Sciences; Best Reporter, Missouri United Press International, 1989; News award, National Association of Black Journalists, 1995; National Emmy award, 1997; Sigma Delta Chi Award, Society of Professional Journalists, 2001; New York Association of Black Journalists Award, 2005; National Journalism Achievement Award, Press Club of Metropolitan St. Louis, 2006.

Addresses: *Office*—CBS Television, 51 West 52nd St., New York, NY 10019.

junior year of college Mitchell made his on-air debut as a five-minute "cut-in" during the *Today Show* in New York City. "It was the scariest thing in my life," Mitchell recalled in an interview with *CBB.* "It was terrible, a horrible experience." After his television appearance, he began the long drive home to St. Louis. Mitchell mentally reviewed his performance as he drove, and with each passing mile his opinion of the cut-in improved. "By the time I got home, I thought I was ready for the network," he told *CBB.* Mitchell's family had

also watched his performance, and when he arrived home he found a note from his younger brother. As Mitchell related to *CBB,* the note read: "We watched you this morning. You were real bad."

Undeterred by such criticism, Mitchell continued his studies in the Missouri School of Journalism and served as a reporter and weekend anchor on the university's television station during his senior year. Although the station was run by the University of Missouri, it was an affiliate of NBC. Therefore, Mitchell was able to perfect his anchoring and reporting skills before a sizeable viewing audience.

Began Professional Journalism Career

Mitchell graduated from the University of Missouri in 1982 and landed a broadcasting job at KMBC-TV in Kansas City. He began working at the ABC affiliate as a reporter trainee, which meant that he covered stories in much the same way as a full-time reporter, but for much less compensation. Despite the low pay, Mitchell learned how to quickly assemble news stories, a skill that would serve him well as his career continued.

In 1983 Mitchell left Kansas City for a job at WFAA-TV in Dallas, Texas. For the next two years he served as an education and general assignment reporter and then as an anchor for *Daybreak,* the local ABC morning news talk show that preceded *Good Morning America.*

By 1985 Mitchell decided to return home to St. Louis. Eight years after his experience at KTVI-TV as a night switchboard operator, Mitchell was hired there as a full-time reporter. He spent the next two years at the ABC affiliate and during that time produced a highly acclaimed series about the violent street gangs that were plaguing the neighboring city of East St. Louis, Illinois. The series earned Mitchell several awards and, as he remarked to *CBB,* "put my name on the map in St. Louis." Mitchell transferred to the CBS affiliate KMOV-TV in St. Louis in 1987, where he worked as a weekend news anchor and daily reporter for the next five years. In 1989 he was honored by the Missouri United Press International with their "Best Reporter" award.

In 1992 Mitchell relocated to New York City and took a job with CBS News. His first position at CBS was as coanchor of the overnight news broadcast *Up to the Minute.* In 1993 he served as a correspondent for *Eye to Eye,* a news magazine show, in which he reported from such remote locations as Chile, France, Indonesia, and Russia. When *Eye to Eye* went off the air in 1995, Mitchell was reassigned to the CBS bureau in Washington, DC. As a Washington correspondent and anchor of the *CBS Sunday Night News,* he covered the 1996 presidential race and contributed a regular feature on the *CBS Evening News with Dan Rather* entitled "In Touch with America." Mitchell also covered the 1996 Republican National Convention in San Diego and reported from House Speaker Newt Gingrich's headquarters in Atlanta on election night. One of his most important reports that year was on the midair explosion and subsequent crash of TWA Flight 800 off the coast of New York. Mitchell received an Emmy for his outstanding work on reporting this tragedy to the American public.

Anchored CBS News Programs

In July of 1997 Mitchell was named coanchor of *CBS News Saturday Morning* (later known as the *Saturday Early Show*). He held this assignment through 2007. From 1999 on, along with coanchoring the *Saturday Early Show,* Mitchell was given top news spots. He was made the primary anchor for the Saturday edition of the *CBS Evening News* in 1999, and in 2002 he began working as a correspondent for *CBS News Sunday Morning*. In 2006 Mitchell earned a rotating anchor position on the Sunday edition of *CBS Evening News,* and in 2007 became news anchor and primary substitute anchor for the *Early Show*. During this period Mitchell also traveled extensively as a reporter for the CBS news programs *Eye on America* and *48 Hours.*

Mitchell was honored many times for his accomplishments in television news. In 2001 he received the Sigma Delta Chi Award from his peers in the Society of Professional Journalists for his coverage of the heart-wrenching Elián González story, which involved the custody and immigration status of a young Cuban boy. In 2005 the New York Association of Black Journalists honored Mitchell with an award for "best documentary" for his report on Stax Records for the *Sunday Morning* news magazine. Founded in Memphis, Tennessee, in 1957, Stax was instrumental in the creation of soul music during the 1960s and '70s. In December of 2006 Mitchell became the first person to receive the National Journalism Achievement Award from the Press Club of St. Louis. His *Sunday Morning* report on human memory, "Try to Remember," was awarded an Emmy in 2008 as the Outstanding Feature Story in a Regularly Scheduled Newscast.

After decades in broadcast journalism, Mitchell remained passionate about his work. "I can't imagine having a 'real' job," he remarked to *CBB*. "I get to meet interesting people, go places I would never go otherwise, and I get to have incredible experiences. Every day there is something new, you never know what's going to happen…. That's the beauty of it. It's unpredictable. It can be fast-paced, it can be a pain, but there are days it doesn't even seem like work." As Mitchell recounted to *CBB,* his career is guided by the sound advice he once received from his grandfather: "It's the biggest pain in the world to go to a job that you hate and know that you have to go to it, but to have something that you really like is indescribable."

Sources

Periodicals

Broadcasting and Cable, April 15, 1996, pp. 40–41.
Entertainment Weekly, June 18, 1993, p. 35.
New York Times, December 3, 2006.

Online

"Profiles in Success: Russ Mitchell '82," Missouri School of Journalism, October 24, 2008, http://www.journalism.missouri.edu/alumni/russ-mitchell-82.html (accessed February 4, 2009).
"Russ Mitchell Biography," The History Makers, March 20, 2007, http://thehistorymakers.com/biography/biography.asp?bioindex=1662&category=Media Makers&occupation=Journalist&name=Russ%20Mitchell (accessed February 4, 2009).
"Russ Mitchell," CBS News, 2005, http://www.cbsnews.com/stories/2002/02/25/earlyshow/saturday/printable502031.shtml (accessed February 4, 2009).

Other

Additional information for this profile was obtained from Mitchell's CBS News Biography and from an interview with Mitchell by Lisa S. Weitzman on February 2, 1999.

—Lisa S. Weitzman and Sandra Alters

Art Monk

1957—

Football player, businessman

Professional Football Hall of Famer Art Monk succeeded in large part because of his commitment to a grueling training schedule and his unsurpassed work ethic. While many NFL wide receivers rely on sheer speed and innate athletic ability, Monk made his mark through persistence and a disciplined training regimen at every stage of his football career. An NFL record that Monk set in the early 1990s testified to his approach to the game: he caught at least one pass in each of 183 consecutive regular-season contests. The consummate team player, Monk was a leader of the dominant Washington Redskins during the height of his career in the 1980s.

Monk, Art, photograph. AP Images.

Played College Football at Syracuse

A second-cousin to jazz piano great Thelonious Monk, James Arthur Monk was born in suburban White Plains, New York, on December 5, 1957. His father, Arthur, a welder, and his mother, Lela, a maid in a Westchester County mansion, instilled in him a strong desire to excel. Attending public schools in White Plains, Monk for a time seemed likely to follow in the footsteps of his jazz-playing cousin: he played the tuba and the electric guitar well, and his teachers urged him to pursue a college music scholarship.

However, Monk's performance on the football field in high school led him down a different path. He started out as a lineman (both offensive and defensive), but he had always admired several pro football wide receivers, so Monk set out to transform himself into an end. He joined the White Plains High School track team and trained for such grueling events as the decathlon and the 330-yard hurdles race. On the football team, Monk was moved to the position of tight end during his junior year. Although he was far from being a star during high school—he caught only a dozen passes over his whole high school career—Monk impressed his coaches with his good grades, positive attitude, and growing talent. On their recommendation he won a football scholarship to Syracuse University.

During his four years at Syracuse, Monk never missed a game or a practice. As he had in high school, Monk started slowly. In his freshman year he notched only two pass receptions. Determined to prove that he was worth the scholarship he had been given, however,

Monk embarked on an intense training program of daily ball drills and running. His hard work paid off: by the time he graduated from Syracuse in 1980, Monk had set school records with 102 receptions for 1,644 yards gained, 1,140 rushing yards gained (as a running back for several years), and 1,105 yards in return yardage.

Drafted by the Washington Redskins

Monk's speed on punt returns attracted the attention of Washington Redskins' scout Charley Taylor, a former professional wide receiver who had been one of Monk's heroes during his high school days. Monk was picked seventeenth in the first round of the 1980 pro draft by the Redskins, who had not had a first-round pick since 1968. "Being drafted was a surprise to me," Monk later recalled in the *Washington Post*. "I knew I had some abilities, but I didn't know I could compete on this level."

As he had in college, Monk started slowly as an NFL player. The *Washington Post* observed that he was "as confused and tentative as a high school student trying to solve his first algebra problem." Yet once again Monk buckled down and applied himself, training hard with hill running, sprints, weightlifting, and racquetball, and he also sought guidance from Redskins veterans. Midway through the season his hard work began to pay off.

By late October of 1980, Redskins coach Jack Pardee could tell the *Washington Post* that "cornerbacks are going to wish he had never come into the league." Even Pardee could not have known how right he was. Monk was named to the NFL All-Rookie Team after the 1980 season. He was a consistent performer in the early 1980s, learning to maneuver his six-foot three-inch, 209-pound bulk around defenders (he was one of the NFL's biggest wide receivers and one of its most physically powerful) and honing his already impressive ability, acquired as a former running back, to avoid fumbles.

In interviews Monk spoke of hard work and down-played expectations for his own career, but in 1984 everything came together and he exceeded his own expectations along with everyone else's. With 106 pass receptions, he set a new NFL record for a single season, and his 1,372 yards gained marked the first of five seasons in which he exceeded 1,000 yards (along with 1985, 1986, 1989, and 1991). Monk was named to the 1985 NFL Pro Bowl squad and received a host of other honors at the season's end. Coach Joe Gibbs said of Monk, "He's big, he's strong, he's intelligent, he has everything."

Set Records for NFL Pass Receptions

A local celebrity in Washington and a record-setter on the field, Monk seemed to lack only one thing: a star performance in a Super Bowl game. The Redskins were perennial Super Bowl contenders through much of the 1980s, but Monk sat out the 1982 Super Bowl with a foot injury, and caught only one pass en route to a losing Redskins effort in the 1983 game. In 1987 when the Redskins defeated the Denver Broncos by a 42–10 score, Monk notched only one reception.

By the 1990 season Monk and the rest of the Redskins' squad were struggling. Monk had emerged as an unofficial but crucial team leader who set the tone for NFL play, and he unexpectedly called the team together late in the 1990 season and declared that they all, himself included, could play with more effort and determination. The Redskins rallied to make the playoffs that year, and the following season the team went all the way to the Super Bowl, where they defeated the Buffalo Bills 37 to 24. In that game Monk caught seven passes for 113 yards.

In October of 1992 Monk broke the all-time NFL record for pass receptions, but the following spring was marked by disappointment and controversy. Monk, whose reception total had dropped to 46 the previous year, was benched by the Redskins at the start of the 1993 season. He ended up spending a good deal of time as a backup, and subsequently the thirty-seven-year-old Monk signed with the New York Jets for the 1994 season. Many Redskins fans and members of the organization thought that the team had treated him shabbily, and felt vindicated when they watched Monk, in a Jets uniform, break Steve Largent's record of 177 consecutive games with at least one pass reception, on the way to his eventual 183. At the end of that year he set the record for career receptions, 940, although Jerry Rice broke his record the following year. The Redskins' record that year was a dismal six wins and ten losses.

Elected to Hall of Fame

Monk played for the Philadelphia Eagles in 1995. He was re-signed by the Redskins so that he could remain with the organization where he had spent most of his professional life and officially retired in 1997. With 12,721 career yards gained, Monk was fourth on the NFL's all-time list, in addition to logging other record-breaking feats.

In retirement, Monk opened an advertising agency, Cactus Advertising Associates, in Chantilly, Virginia. He also founded Alliant Merchant Services, an electronic payment services company in Vienna, Virginia, where he continued to work in 2009. With his teammates Charles Mann, Tim Johnson, and Earnest Byner he established the Good Samaritan Foundation in Washington, DC, a nonprofit organization providing job- and leadership-training for youth, and served as secretary of that organization. He also invested in other businesses around the Washington area. In 2006 he was elected to the Syracuse University Board of Trustees.

Monk was elected to the Professional Football Hall of Fame in 2008, after being a finalist for the honor for eight years in a row. Discussing why he had supported Monk's election to the Hall of Fame, selection committee member Bernie Miklasz wrote on STLtoday.com that "Monk was a highly effective blocker who willingly and capably took on linebackers and safeties. His blocking skills were a real plus for the Redskins' power running game…. [He] happily sacrificed TD opportunities if it meant getting a TD for someone else. Monk was a great teammate. A winner. And a total football player." In accepting the honor, Monk said, "From the time I first picked up a football I fell in love with this game. It's all I ever wanted to do. From playing tackle

in the streets of White Plains to playing in the stadiums in the NFL, I never ever imagined it would take me this far. It's taken a lot of hard work and sacrifice and the belief from people and times when I didn't believe in myself. I've experienced some exciting moments. I've met some extraordinary people and I have a lot of great memories that I will never forget."

Sources

Periodicals

Houston Chronicle, June 27, 1993, p. Sports-14.
Jet, July 7, 1997, p. 46.
New York Times, December 16, 1984, p. E3; December 4, 1994, p. H5.
St. Petersburg Times, January 27, 1988, p. C3.
Washington Post, April 30, 1980, p. D1; October 24, 1980, p. E1; July 29, 1992, p. D1; December 4, 1994, p. D1; February 3, 2008, p. D1.

Online

"Art Monk Elected to Syracuse Board of Trustees," Syracuse University Athletics, December 11, 2006, http://www.suathletics.com/news/Football/2006/12/11/monk2006_trustees.asp?path=Football?path= (accessed January 28, 2009).
"Art Monk," Pro Football Hall of Fame, 2008, http://www.profootballhof.com/hof/member.jsp?PLAYER_ID=248 (accessed January 28, 2009).
"Art Monk's Enshrinement Speech Transcript," Pro Football Hall of Fame, August 2, 2008, http://www.profootballhof.com/history/release.jsp?release_id=2798 (accessed January 28, 2009).
"Ex-NFL Great Monk Joins Syracuse Board of Trustees," ESPN.com, December 12, 2006, http://sports.espn.go.com/ncf/news/story?id=2694872 (accessed January 28, 2009).
King, Peter, "'It's a Redskin Day': Monk, Green Top List of Deserving Canton Inductees," SI.com, February 2, 2008, http://sportsillustrated.cnn.com/2008/writers/peter_king/02/02/king.hall.of.fame/index.html (accessed January 28, 2009).
Miklasz, Bernie, "Welcome, Art Monk: Pro Football Hall of Fame, 2008," STLtoday.com, February 2, 2008, http://www.stltoday.com/blogzone/bernies-extra-points/bernies-extra-points/2008/02/welcome-art-monk-pro-football-hall-of-fame-2008/comment-page-2/ (accessed January 28, 2009).
"Profiles of the Founders," Good Samaritan Foundation, http://www.gsf-dc.org/about_profiles.html (accessed January 28, 2009).

—James M. Manheim and Melissa Doak

Otto Neals

1930—

Artist

Otto Neals is an artist whose works depict subjects drawn from his African heritage and African-American life. Largely self-taught in the arts, Neals has worked in several media, among them painting, sculpture, collage, and printmaking. He spent nearly four decades working for the U.S. Postal Service in New York City, creating signs and sculptures for several local branches. "My talent as an artist, I believe, comes directly from my ancestors," he told the Web site MojoPortfolio. com. "I am merely a receiver, an instrument for receiving some of those energies that permeate our entire universe, and I give thanks for having been chosen to absorb those artistic forces."

Neals was born in Lake City, South Carolina, in 1930, to Gus and Dell Neals. When the Great Depression and its soaring unemployment rates made it impossible for his father to find work, his mother headed north to New York City, where the family had relatives and she knew she would be able to find work as a domestic. The rest of the Neals family followed, living initially with relatives in Brooklyn, where Neals was fascinated by his older cousin's drawing abilities.

The Neals family moved several times, and as a youngster Neals experienced firsthand the differing levels of education offered by schools that served primarily white communities and schools in African-American or minority neighborhoods. When it came time to choose a high school, "I heard about the High School of Music and Art," Neal recalled in an interview with Richard Walkes in the e-journal *Ijele.* "It was supposed to be the school of Art. I put it down as my first choice. Then I put down Herron High School. They had industrial design. The last choice was Brooklyn High School for specialty trades. They had a commercial art program. It turned out that I got my third choice. I found out later that the school for specialty trades was more the school for hoodlums." "There were a lot of Italian and Irish gangs: the Red Rover Boys, the Garfield Boys," he told Walkes. "They would come to school with their German Lugers, and .45s. Everyone portrayed the Blacks and Puerto Ricans as the bad ones. It was incredible."

Neals graduated from high school in 1949 and for a time worked in a factory that made ironing boards. He was drafted into the U.S. Army during the Korean War in the early 1950s, and went through basic training at Fort Bragg, North Carolina, where he belonged to one of the first fully integrated units in the U.S. military. He rose to the rank of sergeant of an integrated platoon, but encountered discrimination after a white officer claimed the credit for training a unit under Neals's direction. After his military discharge, Neals married Vera Brandis, a woman of African-Caribbean ancestry, and traveled to Guyana and Barbados to meet her extended family—a trip he described as a major awakening for him. "I loved it," he said told Walkes. "It was the first foreign country I ever visited. It was so wonderful. I came in contact with so many people who behaved the way you expect people to behave. They were nice and normal as opposed to people here, who are crude and rude. It was nice being at a place where you had fresh air and good food."

Neals took the U.S. civil service exam and was hired by the Brooklyn post office for an entry-level position. He

At a Glance . . .

Born in 1930, in Lake City, SC; son of Gus and Dell Neals; married Vera Brandis, 1955. *Military service:* Served in the U.S. Army, early 1950s; rose to rank of sergeant. *Education:* Studied painting at the Brooklyn Museum School and printmaking at the Printmaking Workshop, New York City.

Career: Worked for the U.S. Postal Service, 1954(?)–90; began as clerk, became head illustrator for several New York City branches. Involved with the black artists' collectives Fulton Art Fair after 1958, the 20th Century Creators after 1963, and Weusi Gallery after 1967. Instructor in printmaking at the Printmaking Workshop, New York City and the Association of Caribbean American Artists (ACAA); gallery director, ACAA. Illustrator for *The African Heritage Cookbook* and *We Are the Children of the Great Ancient Africans.* Works are in the permanent collections of the Ghana National Museum, Columbia Museum of South Carolina, Smithsonian Institution, and U.S. Library of Congress.

Awards: Winner of New York City Arts Commission Award for excellence in design, 1992(?).

Addresses: *Gallery*—Dorsey's Gallery, 553 Rogers Ave., Brooklyn, NY 11225. *E-mail*—ottoneals[&]commat;aol.com.

eventually became head illustrator for the Brooklyn, Manhattan, and Long Island City branches, making signs and illustrations for their lobbies and counters. His side career as a serious artist began in 1958 when he became associated with the Fulton Art Fair, a coalition of local artists who wanted to bring a positive force to the Bedford-Stuyvesant neighborhood in Brooklyn. Among its other members were the painters Ernest Crichlow and Jacob Lawrence. A few years later, Neals became involved with another group, the 20th Century Creators, which staged its first group exhibition—Black Art for Black People—in 1963 at the Harlem NAACP headquarters. That group of artists disbanded a few years later after disagreements over the future of the coalition, and Neals and a few others went on to form the Weusi Gallery in Harlem in 1967. Taking its name

from the Swahili word for "blackness," the Weusi showcased the art of both African-American and African artists at its space on 132nd Street.

Neals had little formal training in art except for his commercial courses in high school, but took painting courses at the Brooklyn Museum School and learned printmaking techniques at Robert Blackburn's well-regarded Printmaking Workshop in New York City. Both Ernest Crichlow and the sculptor Vivian Schuyler Key served as mentors to him, and it was Key who encouraged him to work in three dimensions. The two shared a studio space at a building on Hanson Place in Brooklyn, and Key gave him his first stonecutting tools. For his earliest efforts, Neals scavenged rocks, wood, and other materials from buildings that had been recently demolished.

Neals's associates from the Weusi group gave him invaluable resources when he made his first trip to Africa in 1974, staying at the homes of contacts who treated him generously. After he retired from the Postal Service in the early 1990s, he was able to spend more time on his art, and won some important commissions. One was a twenty-foot mural at Kings County Hospital in Brooklyn, another a series of bronze plaques for the Harlem Walk of Fame along West 135th Street. One of his most beloved pieces was a bronze statue of a little boy and his dog located inside the Imagination Playground at Brooklyn's Prospect Park. The work is based on the 1964 children's book *Whistle for Willie,* by Ezra Jack Keats. Though Keats was white, he was among the first children's book writers to use a multicultural, urban setting in his works. Set in New York City, the book's main character, six-year-old Peter, was introduced in *The Snowy Day,* (1962) and went on to appear in six more titles, often with his pet dachshund, Willie. Neals's sculpture was entirely accessible to visitors and served as the meeting point for a weekly storytelling hour.

Sources

Periodicals

American Visions, August-Sept 1994, p. 20.

Online

"Otto Neals," MojoPortfolio.com, http://www.mojoportfolio.com/artist_search/african_american/neals.html (accessed December 10, 2008).

Walkes, Richard, "Otto Neals: Artist and Teacher," *Ijele: Art eJournal of the African World,* http://www.africaresource.com/ijele/vol1.2/walkes.html (accessed December 10, 2008).

—Carol Brennan

Lorraine O'Grady

1934—

Artist, writer

Lorraine O'Grady is a provocative artist whose works combine performance art and photo installation. As much a cultural critic as she is an artist, O'Grady uses her art to make powerful statements about the role of race and gender in American culture. When she burst onto the art scene in 1980 with her startling performance persona "Mlle Bourgeoise Noire" (Miss Black Middle Class) she dared black artists to be more forceful in their expression of racial themes. Such performances have gained O'Grady many admirers, including critic Holland Cotter, who hailed her in the *New York Times* as "one of the most interesting conceptualists around."

Raised in Multicultural Social Setting

Lorraine O'Grady was born in 1934 in Boston, Massachusetts, the youngest daughter of Jamaican immigrant parents of mixed African, Caribbean, and Irish heritage. She grew up in a well-to-do household, raised among Boston's black elite and educated at the prestigious Girls' Latin Academy, where she studied the classics and ancient history. From an early age, O'Grady was acutely aware of the contrast between her own privileged upbringing and that of her neighbors in Boston's African-American and Irish working-class communities, and she chafed under what she later described in "The Space Between" as the "middle- and upper-class British colonial values" imparted by her parents. From her multicultural upbringing, however, O'Grady learned to straddle racial, social, and class boundaries.

O'Grady did not set out to become an artist; rather, her career path was diverse and winding, taking her on many different journeys before depositing her in the art world in her forties. She attended Wellesley College, first studying Spanish literature, but after an early marriage and the birth of a child, she switched to a more practical major in economics, which she believed would open up better job prospects. Upon graduating from Wellesley in 1955, she took the entrance exam for the federal government's Management Intern Program. One of only 200 applicants out of 20,000 to gain acceptance, she took a job as a research economist in the federal Bureau of Labor Statistics, followed by a position in the State Department. After five years, uninspired by government work, O'Grady traveled to Europe, hoping to write a novel. However, when she did not find the inspiration she sought, she returned to the United States and enrolled in the respected writing program at the University of Iowa.

During the 1970s O'Grady bounded without a clear direction, marrying a second time and moving to Chicago, where she worked as a translator. Later she moved to New York and became a rock critic for the *Village Voice* and *Rolling Stone*. In 1973 she began teaching an English class at the School of Visual Arts in Manhattan. Inspired by energy of her students, she embarked on a program of self-education in the visual arts, reading voraciously about contemporary artists. Finally she experienced a moment of realization: "I can do *that!*" By the end of the decade, in 1979, she had written a screenplay, called *Dual Soul,* featuring a black woman who becomes a performance artist. The

At a Glance . . .

Born in 1934, in Boston, MA. *Education:* Wellesley College, BA, economics, 1955; University of Iowa Writers' Workshop.

Career: U.S. Bureau of Labor Statistics, research economist, 1956–61; U.S. State Department, analyst, 1960s; translator, 1970s; rock music critic, *Rolling Stone* and *Village Voice,* 1970s; School of Visual Arts, English instructor, 1970s; performance and installation artist, 1980—.

Awards: Emerging Artist Fellowship, National Endowment for the Arts, 1983; Bunting Fellowship in Visual Art, Harvard University, 1995–96; Vera List Senior Fellowship in Art and Politics, New School for Social Research, 1997–99; funded residencies at the Yaddo, MacDowell, and Millay artist colonies.

Addresses: *Gallery*—Alexander Gray Associates, 526 West 26 St., Ste. 1019, New York, NY 10001. *Web*—http://www.lorraineogrady.com.

work presaged O'Grady's next career, which would become her life's focus.

"Burst" onto the Art Scene

In early 1980 O'Grady attended the opening of Afro-American Abstraction, an exhibition at P.S. 1 that included works by such African-American artists as Houston Conwill, David Hammons, Maren Hassinger, Senga Nengudi, and Howardena Pindell. Though she was pleased to see such a display of black art, and so many black patrons, she found the work too timid. "I felt that the art on exhibit…had been too cautious…that it had been art 'with white gloves on,'" critic Judith Wilson quoted O'Grady. That disappointment inspired O'Grady's first, and most enduring, work of art.

Later that year, at the opening of an exhibition called Outlaw Aesthetics at the Just Above Midtown Gallery, an avant-garde space for black artists, O'Grady burst into the room wearing a rhinestone tiara, a full-length gown fashioned from 180 pairs of white gloves, and a beauty pageant sash proclaiming her "Mlle Bourgeoise Noire." She circulated the room on the arm of a tuxedoed male escort, distributing chrysanthemums to the crowd, and then began to whip herself with a cat-o-nine-tails, reciting for the stunned onlookers the following bit of verse: THAT'S ENOUGH! / No more boot licking… / No more ass-kissing… / No more pos…turing… / of super ass…imilates… / BLACK ART MUST TAKE MORE RISKS!!!

The following year O'Grady repeated her "guerilla invasion" at the New Museum for Contemporary Art's exhibition Persona, which included only white artists, warning gallery patrons, "Now is the time for an INVASION!" Intended as both a performance persona (a term O'Grady prefers over "performance art") and an act of cultural criticism, the piece was borne out of O'Grady's frustration with the exclusion of African-Americans from the art establishment and with what she perceived as black artists' self-oppression. *Mlle Bourgeoise Noire* would make O'Grady's name on the art scene, and it remains her best-known work. In 2007 it was included as an entry point to Wack! Art and the Feminist Revolution at the Museum of Contemporary Art in Los Angeles.

Juxtaposed Personal and Historical Subjects

Months after the debut of *Mlle Bourgeoise Noire,* O'Grady mounted a second performance—this one a commissioned work—called *Nefertiti/Devonia Evangeline,* which opened at the Just Above Midtown Gallery on October 31, 1980. The work featured images of the artist's late sister, Devonia Evangeline, and her children, juxtaposed with images of the Egyptian queen Nefertiti and her children, accompanied by an account of the two women's lives recorded by O'Grady. In front of this installation, O'Grady performed a ritual detailed in the Egyptian Book of the Dead. The work represented in visual form O'Grady's attempts to come to terms with the loss of her older sister, who had died suddenly at age thirty-eight, and to put to rest their troubled relationship. O'Grady retired the work in 1988 following its presentation in the exhibition Art as a Verb at the Maryland Art Institute.

O'Grady later distilled the images used in *Nefertiti/Devonia Evangeline* to create *Miscegenated Family Album,* which she has described as her "most complete and satisfying work," in 1994. The piece is a photo installation of sixteen diptychs that display images of ancient Egyptian sculpture alongside contemporary photographs of the artist and her family. The image pairs, which bear a striking resemblance to one another, are intended to draw together the women's narratives in a way that unites the personal with the historical. The work has been exhibited at the Davis Museum and Cultural Center at Wellesley College (1994), the Wadsworth Atheneum in Hartford, Connecticut (1995), and the galley of Alexander Gray Associates (2008); in May of 2008, the Art Institute of Chicago purchased the full installation, slated to open in 2009.

O'Grady's other notable works include the performance piece *Rivers, First Draft,* staged in Central Park in 1982; *Flowers of Evil and Good,* a study of French poet Charles Baudelaire and his common law wife Jeanne Duval, mounted at the Thomas Erben Gallery in New York in 1998; and *Persistent,* her first video installation, created during a residency at Artspace in San Antonio, Texas, in 2007. O'Grady has received much institutional support for her work, including grants from the National Endowment for the Arts and the New York Council on the Arts; fellowships from the Marie Walsh Sharpe Art Foundation, the Bunting Institute at Harvard University, and the Vera List Center for Art and Politics at the New School for Social Research; as well as funded residencies at the Yaddo, MacDowell, and Millay artist colonies.

In addition to her work as an artist, O'Grady has also contributed works of criticism to such publications as *Artforum* and *Afterimages.* Her essay "Olympia's Maid: Reclaiming Black Female Subjectivity" has been widely anthologized.

Selected works

Solo exhibitions

Critical Interventions: Photomontages, INTAR Gallery, New York, 1991.

Photo Images, 1980–91,Thomas Erben Gallery, New York, 1993.

Lorraine O'Grady/Matrix 127, Wadsworth Atheneum, Hartford, CT, 1995.

Lorraine O'Grady/The Secret History, Bunting Institute of Radcliffe College, Harvard University, Cambridge, MA, 1996.

Studies for Flowers of Evil and Good, Thomas Erben Gallery, New York, 1998.

Lorraine O'Grady/New Histories, Galerie Fotohof, Salzburg, Austria, 1999.

New Works: 07.2, Artspace, San Antonio, TX, 2007.

Miscegenated Family Album, Alexander Gray Associates, New York, 2008.

Performances

Mlle Bourgeoise Noire, Just Above Midtown Gallery, New York, 1980; New Museum for Contemporary Art, New York, 1981.

Nefertiti/Devonia Evangeline, Just Above Midtown Gallery, New York, 1980.

Rivers, First Draft, Central Park, New York, 1982.

Fly by Night, Franklin Furnace, New York, 1983.

Art Is, Afro-American Day Parade, Harlem, 1983.

Sources

Books

Jones, Amelia, ed., *The Feminism and Visual Culture Reader,* Routledge, 2002.

Periodicals

Hartford Advocate, June 29, 2005.

New York Times, March 24, 2006; March 9, 2007; September 25, 2008.

Online

Lorraine O'Grady, http://lorraineogrady.com (accessed January 21, 2009).

Other

"Lorraine O'Grady," exhibition catalog for Wack! Art and the Feminist Revolution, Museum of Contemporary Art, 2007.

Miller-Keller, Andrea, "Lorraine O'Grady: The Space Between," brochure article written for the exhibition Lorraine O'Grady/Matrix 127, Wadsworth Atheneum, May 21–August 20, 1995.

Wilson, Judith, "Lorraine O'Grady: Critical Interventions," exhibition catalog for Critical Interventions: Photomontages, INTAR Gallery, January 21–February 22, 1991.

—Deborah A. Ring

Jackie Ormes

1911–1985

Cartoonist, journalist

Jackie Ormes is believed to be the first African-American woman to have earned a living as a professional cartoonist. From the 1930s to the 1950s, her comics ran in the *Pittsburgh Courier,* the *Chicago Defender,* and other leading black newspapers. Her work won a devoted following for its spirited social criticism and its portrayal of clever, successful heroines. Ormes ended her cartooning career in the mid-1950s, and her accomplishment was not repeated until 1989, when Barbara Brandon-Croft's "Where I'm Coming From" series began its syndicated run in major U.S. newspapers. Brandon-Croft noted in an interview on National Public Radio that Ormes's presentation of accomplished, articulate heroines was particularly significant because at the time Ormes was active the popular culture presented many negative stereotypes of African-American women. "Black women were always fat, had bandanas on their heads, had large lips, were always porters," Brandon-Croft said on *All Things Considered.* "They were servants. Kids were pickaninnies. You know, we were maids."

Ormes was born in 1911 in Pittsburgh, Pennsylvania, but about 1917 her newly widowed mother moved the family to nearby Monongahela. A talented artist from an early age, Ormes sought work from the publisher of the *Pittsburgh Courier,* the city's leading black newspaper, while still a student at Monongahela High School. He gave her an assignment to cover a local boxing match, which she did with the paper's sportswriter serving as her chaperone. She returned to Pittsburgh and worked full time at the *Courier* after graduating from high school in 1930. Her first regular cartoon strip was "Torchy Brown: From Dixie to Harlem," which began appearing regularly in the paper in 1937. She gained many fans thanks to the *Courier*'s national readership and syndication arm. The poet Langston Hughes was among the many admirers of Ormes's attractive, intelligent heroine.

As the title of Ormes's strip indicates, Torchy leaves her home in the South to find work in New York City. Along the way she encounters the various forms of racism that were still legal at the time, and once she arrives in the big city she resourcefully recognizes and avoids a few predators. She winds up as a performer at Harlem's legendary Cotton Club, returns home for a visit, and embarks on other adventures, including an airplane trip. There were fifty-three of the original "Torchy" strips in all, running from May of 1937 to April of 1938, and they were groundbreaking for their portrayal of a successful African-American woman. Decades later, Torchy Brown would be the subject of a lengthy essay by Edward Brunner in the scholarly journal *MELUS.* Brunner described Ormes's strip as "a version of a great migration narrative…. For blacks in the South, Ormes's comic strip insisted that the right attitude is necessary if one is to escape to the North; zeal counts for a great deal, if only as a protective barrier against the inevitable rejection. For blacks in the North, Ormes's feature recalls their own or their family's early experiences in the new urban setting, including erroneous assumptions and necessary adjustments, all of which dramatically reveal just how far they have come."

At a Glance . . .

Born Zelda Mavin Jackson on August 1, 1911, in Pittsburgh, PA; died on December 26, 1985, in Chicago, IL; daughter of an entrepreneur and a homemaker; married Earl Clark Ormes (a banker), 1933(?); children: Jacqueline (deceased).

Career: *Pittsburgh Courier,* reporter after 1930; *Chicago Defender,* reporter after 1942; creator of the cartoon series "Torchy Brown: From Dixie to Harlem," 1937–38, "Patty-Jo 'n' Ginger," 1945–56, and "Torchy in Heartbeats," 1950–54, which ran in the *Pittsburgh Courier,* the *Chicago Defender,* and other syndicated newspapers.

Alongside the professional success of this period of her career, Ormes experienced a tremendous personal tragedy when her three-year-old, daughter Jacqueline, died of a brain tumor. For a time, she and her husband—banker Earl Clark Ormes, whom she wed in the early 1930s—moved to his hometown of Ohio, but she was unhappy in a small town, and the pair resettled in Chicago in 1942. There she went to work as a reporter at the *Defender,* the city's influential African-American newspaper. In 1945 she returned to cartooning with a single-panel feature called "Patty-Jo 'n' Ginger." It had an eleven-year run and once again appeared in several other black newspapers of the era through syndication arrangements. "In the cartoons, Patty-Jo, one of the best-dressed little girls to appear in any cartoon, expounds on injustices while her big sister, Ginger, tries on clothes or pretends to be shocked," wrote Meisha Rosenberg in a review that appeared on the Web site of the Wellesley Centers for Women. "Ginger, in the style of 'mute' cartoon figures of the time, never speaks, instead acting as a 'straight' foil."

Ormes also revived the much-loved Torchy at the request of the Smith-Mann syndicate in 1950, and "Torchy in Heartbeats" ran in a new color cartoon insert in several black newspapers for the next four years. "To today's readers, Ormes's cartoons seem remarkably radical," wrote Rosenberg. "In one revelatory episode ... Torchy helps a black doctor expose environmental pollution perpetrated on a black community. In another, Torchy fends off a potential rapist on board a freighter ship. This was bold, even protofeminist stuff for 1952." A side feature was "Torchy Togs," a paper doll whose glamorous outfits were hugely popular with young girls of the era. Ormes also created a "Patty-Jo" doll, sold in department stores in the late 1940s and believed to be the first high-end black doll for children that was widely sold. It was produced by a doll company for only a few years, and became a rare collectible among toy aficionados and those interested in African-American ephemera of the mid-twentieth century.

Ormes's career as a cartoonist ended in 1955, when the *Defender* and *Courier* came under the same ownership and began to focus on such serious issues as the civil rights movement in earnest. In Chicago, Ormes's husband managed the DuSable Hotel in Bronzeville, the city's African-American quarter, and the prestige of the job introduced the couple to many notable performers, writers, and other artists who stayed there while on tour. They became lifelong friends with such prominent figures as the jazz singers Sarah Vaughan and Lena Horne. A muralist and fine artist in her later years, Ormes was also active in the community through the Chicago Urban League, the South Side Community Art Center, and other organizations, but her creative work ceased when she was debilitated by rheumatoid arthritis. Her husband died in 1978, and she died seven years later at the age of seventy-four. Interest in her pioneering work was sparked in 2008 with Nancy Goldstein's biography, *Jackie Ormes: The First African American Woman Cartoonist,* published by the University of Michigan Press. Interviewed on National Public Radio's *All Things Considered,* Goldstein described Ormes's heroines as significant role models for a generation of young readers. "Here's Ginger. She's just graduated from college. I can do that, too," Goldstein said. "Here's Torchy. She's challenging the racism and the status quo of the era, and I can do that, too. And so she was giving voice to what was in the hearts and minds of so many people to move forward and make progress."

Sources

Periodicals

MELUS, Fall 2007, p, 23.

Online

Green, Karen, "Black and White and Color," Comixology.com, August 1, 2008, http://www.comixology.com/articles/96/Black-and-White-and-Color (accessed December 10, 2008).

Rosenberg, Meisha, "Drawing Pride," Wellesley Centers for Women.com, http://www.wcwonline.org/content/view/1804/38/ (accessed December 10, 2008).

Other

Norris, Kyle, "Comics Crusader: Remembering Jackie Ormes," *All Things Considered,* NPR.org, July 31, 2008.

—Carol Brennan

Joseph C. Phillips

1962—

Actor, political commentator

Phillips, Joseph C., photograph. John Sciulli/WireImage/Getty Images.

Joseph C. Phillips is a conservative political commentator and actor best known for his role as Lisa Bonet's television husband on the NBC hit comedy series *The Cosby Show* in its final seasons. Phillips's book, *He Talk Like a White Boy: Reflections on Faith, Family, Politics, and Authenticity* (2006), featured a range of personal essays about his family life, acting career, and social activism. "The values of family, faith, freedom I don't believe are conservative or liberal, Republican or Democrat," he told journalist Dwayne Campbell in the *Philadelphia Inquirer.* "These are old-school values that made black America strong and dynamic."

The son of a pediatrician and a schoolteacher, Phillips was born in 1962 in Denver, Colorado, where a classroom incident at Place Junior High School eventually inspired the title of his book. "I don't remember what the class discussion was about," wrote Phillips, "but after an undoubtedly brilliant and insightful observation on my part, a black girl from across the room raised her hand and announced to the class, 'He talk like a white boy!'" He elaborated on the incident further in an interview with columnist David Harsanyi in the

Denver Post. "Every moment after that was different from the moments before. I had no idea what she was talking about. I had never been called an Uncle Tom before that time. I had always been encouraged to raise my hand and answer questions. After that, I discovered that I was 'acting white.'"

Phillips had a different kind of tough time at George Washington High School after his parents moved into what his friends derided as "Honkyville," in the southeast section of Denver. "If we weren't the first black family in the neighborhood, we were the second," he told Harsanyi. After graduating in 1979, Phillips enrolled at the University of the Pacific in Stockton, California, but later transferred to the theater program at New York University, from which he earned an undergraduate fine arts degree in 1983. He spent several years searching for a breakout acting role, which came in 1989 when he was cast in a PBS production of Lorraine Hansberry's acclaimed play about African-American life, *A Raisin in the Sun,* starring veteran actors Danny Glover and Esther Rolle.

That same year Phillips appeared on *A Different World,* a spin-off of *The Cosby Show,* which starred

At a Glance . . .

Born Joseph Connor Phillips on January 17, 1962, in Denver, CO; son of Clarence Phillips (a pediatrician); his mother was a teacher; married Nicole, 1994; children: Connor, Ellis, Sam. *Politics:* Republican. *Education:* Attended University of the Pacific; New York University, BFA, 1983.

Career: Actor, political commentator, and syndicated newspaper columnist. Author of the weekly column "The Way I See It." Teacher of acting workshops at the National Black Theatre Festival, College of William and Mary, California State University Long Beach, Louisiana State University, and Delta State College, among others. Board member, California African American Museum, and the African American Advisory Board of the Republican National Committee.

Memberships: Screen Actors Guild, American Federation of Television and Radio Artists, Actors Equity Association, Academy of Television Arts and Sciences, Alpha Phi Alpha.

Addresses: *Agent*—Julia Buchwald, 6500 Wilshire Blvd., 22nd Fl., Los Angeles, CA 90048.

booza Lomboo, which premiered at the Minneapolis/St. Paul Fringe Festival and also had a run at the National Black Theatre Festival in Winston-Salem, North Carolina. In the play Phillips discussed his political outlook, which had become more focused after the bitterly contested 2000 national elections.

Phillips's first piece of mainstream media commentary appeared in the April 8, 2002, issue of *Newsweek.* In it he criticized some in the African-American community who had scorned the wave of patriotism that the September 11, 2001, terror attacks had prompted in the country. "It's true that the flag represents a nation that once enslaved and denied rights to a segment of its population," he wrote, "but it also stands for the revolutionary idea that every individual has God-given and inalienable rights. Focusing on the fact that this country hasn't always lived up to its ideals misses the point: it is the very existence of those ideals that allowed Americans, both black and white, to fight slavery and segregation."

Phillips began writing a weekly column, "The Way I See It," which was syndicated in dozens of U.S. newspapers, and became a featured guest commentator on Tavis Smiley's show for National Public Radio. It was Smiley who suggested that Phillips write a book, and the result was *He Talk Like a White Boy,* published in 2006. Phillips revealed in the book that once he began trying to win roles in Hollywood he was often asked to try to read parts with what producers considered a more urban cadence. He also discussed the lingering effects of his mother's suicide, which occurred when he was in his twenties, and his role as a husband and father of three. "The question of authenticity and what it means to be black in America has been addressed many times before," wrote Denise Simon in *Black Issues Book Review,* "but Phillips makes it personal, using the successes and failures of his own life to speak to larger issues."

Writing in "Is U.S. Obama-Ready?" in the Los Angeles *Daily News* during the presidential campaign of U.S. Senator Barack Obama, Phillips confessed that he was rooting for the Democratic Party hopeful instead of the candidate of his own Republican Party. "This is more than just a flashback to 1984, when I stood in a union hall in New York City chanting 'run, Jesse, run!'" he wrote, referring to the earlier candidacy of the Reverend Jesse Jackson. "Even in the naivete of my youth, I never really believed Jesse could win. Obama, however, is something different. The country is different."

Selected works

Television, as actor

A Raisin in the Sun, PBS, 1989.
The Cosby Show, NBC, 1989–92.
General Hospital, ABC, 1994–98.

comedian Bill Cosby as New York City physician, husband, and father Cliff Huxtable. The spin-off was set at a fictional black college in the South, where the second-eldest Huxtable daughter, Denise (Lisa Bonet), began college. Then Denise disappeared from both shows for a time, and *A Different World* carried on with its own cast of characters. When Bonet returned, her absence was explained by a sojourn in Africa and marriage to U.S. Navy Lieutenant Martin Kendall, played by Phillips. Martin and Denise seem an unlikely pair, but viewers were won over by the divorced dad's adorable TV daughter, Olivia (Raven-Symoné), who joined the Huxtable household when Denise and Martin return to the United States. Phillips remained with *The Cosby Show* until its 1992 finale.

Phillips went on to the role of Justin Ward on the top-rated ABC daytime drama *General Hospital* from 1994 to 1998. He also appeared in guest roles on *Living Single, The Parkers, The King of Queens,* and *Bones.* His feature film credits included *Strictly Business,* a 1991 romantic comedy that also starred Halle Berry and Tommy Davidson. In the summer of 2001 he starred in his own one-act play, *Professor Lom-*

Films, as actor

Strictly Business, 1991.
Let's Talk about Sex, 1998.
Midnight Blue, 2000.

Writings

Professor Lombooza Lomboo (one-act play), Minneapolis/St. Paul Fringe Festival, 2001.
He Talk Like a White Boy: Reflections on Faith, Family, Politics, and Authenticity (nonfiction), Running Press, 2006.

Sources

Periodicals

Black Issues Book Review, May-June 2006, p. 44.
Booklist, May 15, 2006, p. 10.
Daily News (Los Angeles), February 10, 2008, p. V3.
Denver Post, September 25, 2006, p. B1.
Newsweek, April 8, 2002, p. 12.
Philadelphia Inquirer, May 17, 2006.
Star Tribune (Minneapolis, MN), June 24, 2001, p. B4.

—Carol Brennan

Run

1964—

Hip-hop musician, religious leader, author, television personality

Run has been a prominent figure in American entertainment since the 1980s. As a founder of the early hip-hop group Run-DMC, he helped to popularize the heavy drumbeats, sound samples, and witty lyrics characteristic of that genre. Though the group disbanded in 2002, Run remained in the spotlight, forging a new career as an ordained minister, self-help author, and television personality.

Run was born Joseph Ward Simmons on November 14, 1964, in Hollis, a middle-class neighborhood in the New York City borough of Queens. As a young boy, he showed a remarkable talent in the impromptu rhyming contests that had been a standard feature of African-American street life for decades. By the time Run was in high school, many young people in Hollis and throughout New York had begun to experiment with setting these rhymes to music. This was the birth of hip-hop, and Run was one of the new genre's earliest practitioners.

Run's partners in these sonic experiments were two friends from school, Jason Mizell, better known as "Jam Master Jay," and Darryl McDaniels, whose initials formed "DMC." Run and McDaniels would trade rhymes, while Mizell, as the trio's DJ would manipulate the turntables, mixers, and drum machines that produced early hip-hop's distinctive sound. While the three achieved some local success even before the end of high school, it was by no means clear then that they would be able to make a career in popular music. Run, in fact, entered LaGuardia Community College to prepare himself for a more conventional career. En-

couraged, however, by his brother Russell, the co-founder of the influential Def Jam record label, Run and his partners continued to work on their music, and in 1983, under the name Run-DMC, they recorded and released their first single, "It's Like That/Sucker MCs." The song was a sensation, eventually selling more than 250,000 copies. When subsequent singles, including "Hard Times/Jam Master Jay," proved equally successful, the group issued its first full-length album, titled simply *Run-DMC,* in 1984.

Run-DMC and its successors, notably *King of Rock* (1985) and *Raising Hell* (1986), did much to establish hip-hop as a major force in popular music. The group's innovative use of rock-music motifs, particularly the electric-guitar riffs that punctuated many of their songs, drew the attention of rock fans and radio executives across the country. *Raising Hell* was the first rap or hip-hop album to reach number one on *Billboard* magazine's R&B chart and to be certified platinum by the Recording Industry Association of America; the latter is a distinction granted only to albums selling more than one million copies. Though *Raising Hell* contained at least four significant hits, the most successful track was undoubtedly "Walk This Way," a remake of a 1975 hit by the hard-rock group Aerosmith. Rather than simply redoing the song themselves, Run and his band mates convinced Steven Tyler and Joe Perry of Aerosmith to join them in the recording studio. The decision to collaborate proved a wise one, as "Walk This Way" became one of the first hip-hop singles to achieve crossover success on *Billboard's* pop chart, where it eventually reached number four.

At a Glance . . .

Born Joseph Ward Simmons in Queens, NY, on November 14, 1964; married Valerie Vaughn, 1983 (divorced); married Justine Jones, 1994; children: (first marriage) Vanessa, Angela, Joseph; (second marriage) Daniel, Russell, Victoria (deceased), Miley (adopted). *Religion:* Christian. *Education:* Attended LaGuardia Community College, early 1980s.

Career: Run-DMC, musician, 1983–2002; Zoe Ministries, ordained minister, 1994; Run Athletics, Inc., cofounder, 2003; *Run's House,* television performer, 2005—.

Awards: Outstanding Reality Series, NAACP Image Awards, 2008, for *Run's House;* inductee, Rock and Roll Hall of Fame, 2009.

Addresses: *Office*—c/o MTV Networks, Inc., 1515 Broadway, New York, NY 10036.

Though Run-DMC continued to release albums over the next decade and a half, most of these, with the exception of 1988's *Tougher Than Leather,* did not receive the attention that its earlier work had attracted. This was due, at least in part, to the explosive growth of the rap and hip-hop genres. The group nevertheless continued to fill concert halls and to maintain its reputation as the epitome of "old-school" hip-hop. Though Run and the other members were focusing increasingly on solo projects, business interests, and their families by the beginning of the 2000s, the group remained intact until the brutal shooting death of Mizell in a recording studio in October of 2002. Run and McDaniels disbanded Run-DMC shortly thereafter, and the murder remained unsolved as of 2009.

As he recounted in his 2000 memoir, *It's Like That,* Run began in the 1990s to explore issues of faith and to apply what he discovered to his own life. This process led him to Zoe Ministries, an evangelical Christian organization headed by Bishop E. Bernard Jordan. Following his ordination by Jordan in 1994, Run distributed most of his work under the name "Rev Run." He also became involved in several major business ventures after the 1980s, notably Phat Farm, a hip-hop-themed fashion company founded in 1992 by his brother Russell Simmons, and Run Athletics, a sneaker company he cofounded with Simmons in 2003.

Though Run continued to record music periodically, much of his prominence after the demise of Run-DMC

was attributable to *Run's House,* a popular reality series on the cable network MTV. The show, which debuted in October of 2005 and completed its fifth season in 2008, was an in-depth, essentially unscripted look at life in Run' New Jersey household. Much of the show's appeal, according to critic Ned Martel in the-*New York Times,* came from watching Run interact with his second wife, the former Justine Jones, and the couple's six children. In a review of the show shortly after its premiere, Martel wrote that Run "demonstrates how a respected dad can still sound like a cool brother."

Audiences responded enthusiastically to *Run's House,* and the program, which received an NAACP Image Award for Outstanding Reality Series in 2008, was frequently among MTV's highest-rated offerings. While Run revealed few of his plans for the future, it seemed likely, as of 2009, that *Run's House* and several associated projects would remain his focus for the foreseeable future. The most prominent of the subsidiary projects was a series of books capitalizing on Run' screen persona as a tough but loving father. The first volume, *Words of Wisdom: Daily Affirmations of Faith from Run's House to Yours* (2006), is a collection of the aphorisms with which Run concluded each episode. A longer, slightly more structured sequel, *Take Back Your Family: A Challenge to America's Parents,* went to press in 2008. Run explained to Jeannine Amber in *Essence,* "I'm here to do something special besides what I did with Run-DMC. I'm here to show the conduct of the Black American family, how we should be. This isn't arrogance; this is the gift God gave me to give the world."

Selected works

Singles; with Run-DMC

"It's Like That/Sucker MCs," 1983.
"Hard Times/Jam Master Jay," 1983.
"Rock Box," 1984.
"30 Days," 1984.
(With Aerosmith) "Walk This Way," 1986.

Albums; with Run-DMC

Run-DMC, Profile, 1984.
King of Rock, Profile, 1985.
Raising Hell, Profile, 1986.
Tougher Than Leather, Profile, 1988.
Back from Hell, Profile, 1990.
Together Forever (greatest hits), Profile, 1991.
Down with the King, Profile, 1993.
Crown Royal, Arista, 1999.

Solo Albums

(As Rev Run) *Distortion,* Def Jam, 2005.

Books

(As Reverend Run; with Curtis L. Taylor) *It's Like That: A Spiritual Memoir,* St. Martin's Press, 2000.

(As Rev Run) *Words of Wisdom: Daily Affirmations of Faith from Run's House to Yours,* Amistad, 2006.

(As Rev Run; with Justine Simmons and Chris Morrow) *Take Back Your Family: A Challenge to America's Parents,* Gotham, 2008.

Films

Krush Groove, 1985.
Tougher Than Leather, 1988.

Television

Run's House, 2005—.

Sources

Periodicals

Essence, May 2007.
Jet, July 28, 2008.
New York Times, October 27, 2005.

Online

Moody, Nekesa Mumbi, "Run DMC, Metallica Inducted into Rock Hall of Fame," Time.com, January 14, 2009, http://www.time.com/time/arts/article/0,8599,1871810,00.html?cnn=yes (accessed January 29, 2009).

"*Run's House*: Cast Bios," MTV.com, http://www.mtv.com/ontv/dyn/runs_house/cast.jhtml (accessed January 29, 2009).

—R. Anthony Kugler

Nikkole Salter

1979(?)—

Actor, playwright

Nikkole Salter is an actor and playwright who teamed with a fellow New York University student to write the award-winning play *In the Continuum.* Their two-person drama became an international sensation after its 2005 debut for its dual chronicle of the lives of two women—one African, the other African American—who discover they are infected with the virus that causes acquired immunodeficiency syndrome (AIDS). Salter and her coauthor, Danai Gurira, also starred in the off-Broadway work, which won a special Obie Award from the *Village Voice* and a commendation from the United Nations, and was listed as one of the ten best plays of 2005 by the *New York Times.* Writing in *Variety,* Mark Blankenship commended the pair's "raw, astonishing" performances, noting that they each "create two continents' worth of memorable people, but it's as the leads that they truly reveal their gifts. Faces flickering with despair, anger and hope, they show so many sides of their characters' hearts that Nia and Abigail become both unforgettable individuals and symbols for the larger face of HIV."

Like her character Nia from *In the Continuum,* Salter grew up in Los Angeles. Unlike Nia's dispiriting experiences in the foster-care system, however, Salter was raised by a single mother who proved to be an impressive role model. "My mother was a construction worker," Salter recalled in a 2006 interview with Libby Motika for the *Pacific Palisades Post.* "She was an anomaly because she did typical male jobs. She drove trucks, poured concrete, and has a black belt in karate. Although she never found what she was good at and wanted to pursue, she instilled in me that you must

follow your passion. If you're going to be broke, you may as well do what you want."

Salter's love of the theater was sparked at the age of eight when she attended her first play. Within a few years she was spending summers at special theater camps, and during the school year took classes at the Crossroads Arts Academy of Leimert Park and the Amazing Grace Conservatory in Los Angeles's Crenshaw neighborhood. She graduated from Palisades High School in 1997 and went on to Howard University in Washington, DC, one of the most prestigious historically black schools and universities in the United States. After earning a bachelor of fine arts in theater from Howard, she entered New York University's Tisch School of the Arts for its graduate theater program.

It was at Tisch that Salter met Gurira when a professor realized they were both working on monologues with a similar theme—women who had tested positive for the human immunodeficiency virus (HIV) that causes AIDS—and suggested they combine their talents into a single work. Salter had originally been inspired by reading a news article about the disproportionate number of African-American women who were HIV-positive or dying from AIDS. "Who were these women?" Salter recalled thinking to herself, as she told Felicia R. Lee in the *New York Times* in 2005. "Where were these stories?"

Gurira was equally moved by the plight of women with AIDS. Born in the United States, she returned with her

At a Glance . . .

Born in 1979(?) in Los Angeles, CA; daughter of a construction worker. *Education:* Howard University, BFA, 2001; New York University, MFA, 2004; also earned certificate from the British American Drama Academy, Oxford University.

Career: Made television debut as an actor in an episode of *Moesha*, 1996; cowrote first play, *In the Continuum,* with Danai Gurira; has appeared in numerous New York City stage productions; made feature-film debut in *The Architect,* 2006.

Awards: Global Tolerance Award, United Nations, 2005; special Obie Award for Writing, 2006.

Addresses: *Agent*—Annette Paparella, Artists Entertainment Agency, 165 W. 46th St., Ste. 1114, New York, NY 10036-2508. *Web*—http://www.nikkolesalter.com.

parents to their native Zimbabwe as a child, but she graduated from a college in Minnesota. She knew that in Zimbabwe and other parts of sub-Saharan Africa, about 57 percent of AIDS victims were women, and the fatal disease had even affected members of her own family. Gurira was also pursuing a graduate degree in theater at New York University when she was introduced to Salter. Their joint effort, *In the Continuum,* premiered at a South Bronx venue and then moved to an off-Broadway playhouse called Primary Stages in September of 2005. Salter played Nia, a young woman from Los Angeles who hopes that her unexpected pregnancy will bring a marriage proposal from her boyfriend, a talented athlete on his way to a pro basketball career, but she is stunned to learn she is also HIV-positive during her first prenatal doctor's visit. Abigail, Gurira's character, is a married ' journalist in Harare, Zimbabwe's capital, who also discovers she has tested positive for HIV when she visits a doctor to confirm a pregnancy. Though their lives could not be more different, Nia and Abigail's experiences demonstrate that the virus is devastatingly egalitarian as both struggle to come to terms with what amounts to a death sentence. Reviewing the play for the *Los Angeles Daily News,* Evan Henerson wrote that the "earlier braggadocio" of Salter's character "is all but dissipated, and the girl is shredding her last $5 bill on a park bench, talking to her unborn child about mansions in Malibu and making up verses. Salter's handling of this scene will stay with this critic for weeks."

The play proved an auspicious launch for Salter's career in the performing arts. It won a Global Tolerance Award from the United Nations and was hailed as one of the top ten plays of the season by the *New York Times.* She and Gurira also performed it in Harare and Johannesburg, South Africa, where it was equally well received by critics and audiences alike. "The success ... of 'In the Continuum' is in its humble, microcosmic tack," wrote Peter Marks in the *Washington Post,* who said that both actor-playwrights "are incisive observers of the cultures they bring to the stage: The vignettes at times radiate documentary immediacy. Plus they're both marvelous mimics, deftly shuffling accent and countenance to create a memorable gallery of characters, virtually all of them women." Marks also singled out one of Salter's scenes as Nia in particular, as she is "contemplating the leave-him-alone check she's accepted from Darnell's mother. If Salter were any more tenderly convincing, the check would be real, too."

The success of *In the Continuum* led to a deal with the Oxygen cable network to develop some television projects, and Salter and Gurira were working on a story about woman soldiers who fought in Liberia's civil conflict of the late 1990s. On the performing front, Salter won a supporting role in *The Architect,* a 2006 film starring Anthony LaPaglia as the callous designer of a notorious public housing project who becomes the target of its resident-activists. She was also cast in *Pride and Glory,* a 2008 cop-family saga that also starred Edward Norton, Jon Voight, and Colin Farrell. In between these projects she was developing another play with the help of the Studio Museum in Harlem, tentatively titled *Repairing a Nation,* and dealing with the movement for federal-government reparations for the enslavement of African Americans in previous centuries. Being able to develop her own material after the success of *In the Continuum* was an immensely fortunate position to be in, Salter related in a 2006 interview. "As an African-American actress, I complain often about the roles that are available even to audition for," she told Trey Graham in the interview, which appeared in *American Theatre,* "and how few of the meaty good ones there actually are, and how hard it is for an unknown to be considered—so to be a part of creating opportunities, that's a thing I want to do."

Selected works

Plays; as playwright and actor

In the Continuum, produced at Primary Stages, New York City, 2005.

Films; as actor

The Architect, 2006.
Pride and Glory, 2008.

Sources

Periodicals

American Theatre, July–August 2006, p. 50.
Connecticut Post, January 18, 2007.
Los Angeles Daily News, November 24, 2006, p. U17.
New York Times, October 1, 2005, p. B9; May 20, 2006, p. B11; January 21, 2007.
Observer (London), July 6, 2008, p. 20.
Pacific Palisades Post, December 6, 2006.

Variety, October 10, 2005, p. 85.
Washington Post, September 5, 2006, p. C1.

Online

"Biography," http://www.nikkolesalter.com/BIOGRAPHY.htm (accessed November 20, 2008).

Other

Lunden, Jeff, "Two Women, One Story," *Weekend Edition,* National Public Radio, February 12, 2006, http://www.npr.org/templates/story/story.php?storyId=5202209 (accessed November 20, 2008).

—Carol Brennan

Kimbo Slice

1974—

Mixed martial arts fighter

Slice, Kimbo, photograph. John Pyle/CSM/Landov.

Kimbo Slice is a mixed martial arts fighter who made his name brawling in underground street fights and is famous for knocking down opponents with a single brutal punch. At 6 feet, 2 inches tall and 250 pounds—almost all muscle—Slice became an Internet sensation almost overnight when video of his street fights started turning up on YouTube. Web surfers could not get enough of Slice's beatdowns, prompting *Rolling Stone* magazine to brand him the "undisputed online king of the underground bare-knuckle world" in 2006. The following year Slice became a star attraction of the professional mixed martial arts circuit, racking up three crushing wins before going down, for only the second time in his career, in 2008. Following the loss, fans were left wondering whether Slice could live up to his fearsome reputation.

Kimbo Slice was born Kevin Ferguson in Nassau, Bahamas, on February 8, 1974, the oldest son in a family of eleven children. Raised by single mother Rosemary Clarke in Cutler Ridge, Florida, south of Miami, Ferguson attended Palmetto High School, where he was a star middle linebacker with hopes of playing college ball. However, in August of 1992,

Ferguson's senior year, Hurricane Andrew devastated southern Florida. As the Category 5 storm barreled through the Miami area, Ferguson huddled under a mattress in his mother's home to shield himself from the falling debris. The hurricane cut off Palmetto's football season and, with it, Ferguson's hopes of winning a scholarship.

Ferguson enrolled at Bethune-Cookman University in Daytona Beach as a criminal justice major, planning on a career as a police officer, but he flunked out after two semesters. By early 1994, with no college degree and no job prospects, Ferguson was on the streets, living out of his 1987 Nissan Pathfinder. He first found work as a bouncer at a strip club, and then, with help from high school friend (and future manager) Mike "IceyMike" Ember, he took a job as a limousine driver and bodyguard for RK Netmedia, an online adult entertainment company. His earnings were enough to get him off the street and into an apartment.

Ferguson found that he could earn even more money by competing in street fights in alleys, parking lots, and backyards, netting $300 to $500 or more for each brawl. "At first, it was to make a couple bucks—I'd

At a Glance . . .

Born Kevin Ferguson on February 8, 1974, in Nassau, Bahamas; son of Rosemary Clarke; engaged to Antoinette Ray; children: Kevin Jr., Kevin II, Kevlar, Kassandra, Kiandra, Kevina. *Education:* Attended Bethune-Cookman University.

Career: ProElite, mixed martial arts fighter, 2007—.

Addresses: *Office*—Team Kimbo, 1031 North Miami Beach Blvd., North Miami Beach, FL 33162. *Web*—http://www.kimbo305.com/home.htm.

rather fight than steal—but it came natural," Ferguson told the *Miami Herald.* A friend got the idea to film the fights, and soon the crude videos were appearing on the Internet, attracting millions of blood-thirsty watchers. In twenty fights, he lost only one, to Boston cop Sean Gannon in 2003. Ditching the name Kevin Ferguson, he became known as Kimbo Slice: "Kimbo" was a nickname he'd had since childhood, while "Slice" was a moniker given to him by Internet fans after he tore a large gash in the side of an opponent's face.

As the legend of Kimbo Slice grew, promoters of mixed martial arts sought to draw him into the professional arena. Popularized in the 1990s, mixed martial arts is a full-contact sport that combines elements of boxing, wrestling, striking, and grappling with martial arts techniques from karate, judo, and jiu-jitsu. Bouts are organized by professional MMA organizations such as the Ultimate Fighting Championship (UFC) and ProElite. With fewer rules than professional boxing or wrestling, the sport tends toward extreme violence—so much so that until 2008, network television would not air MMA match-ups, despite their soaring popularity.

Slice, who had no formal training in martial arts, began working with retired MMA champion Bas Rutten and boxing instructor Randy Khatami in Thousand Oaks, California. However, MMA insiders doubted that Slice, a mere street fighter, could compete on the professional level. Dana White, president of the UFC, told ESPN that Slice "wouldn't last two minutes in the Octagon," referring to the octagonal cage that MMA fighters spar in, while Ricco Rodriguez, a UFC heavyweight champ, told a radio station, "Kimbo is a tomato can. What has he done to prove himself? He hasn't fought anybody. He's a nobody. Kimbo Slice is just a clown," according to ESPN.

Slice made his sanctioned MMA debut in an exhibition match against former boxer Ray Mercer on June 23, 2007, in Atlantic City. He defeated Mercer with a guillotine choke seventy-two seconds into the first round. The following November, in his first professional bout, Slice put down cage fighting veteran Bo Cantrell only nineteen seconds into the first round by submission due to strikes. Then, in February of 2008, Slice pummeled David "Tank" Abbott, winning by knockout in forty-three seconds. In the first MMA event to be shown live on network television, on May 31, 2008, Slice went three rounds against James "The Colossus" Thompson. In the third round, he ruptured Thompson's ear and threw three unanswered punches, prompting the referee to stop the bout. The win brought Slice's pro record to 3–0.

In his most anticipated contest yet, Slice was scheduled to fight forty-four-year-old Ken Shamrock, known as "The World's Most Dangerous Man," on October 4, 2008, during a live broadcast on the CBS network's *Saturday Night Fights.* At the last minute, however, Shamrock was declared ineligible because of a cut on his eye, and fight officials chose Seth Petruzelli as his stand-in. In a stunning upset, Petruzelli defeated Slice by technical knockout just fourteen seconds into the first round. In the aftermath of the fight, some fans and sports writers cheered the loss, happy to see Slice get his come-uppance. One headline on Yahoo! Sports declared, "Final Curtain for the Kimbo Show." In October of 2008, ProElite, the organizer of the fight, filed for bankruptcy, a move that was widely attributed to Slice's loss to Petruzelli.

Slice's imposing demeanor and choice of profession belie a softer side to the fighter, who is the father of six children and engaged to longtime girlfriend Antoinette Ray. Outside the ring, friends and family describe him as a gentle man. "People look at him as a big, bad beast, but he's a gentle, kind, easygoing guy, always sharing with his family," Slice's mother, who regularly attends his fights, told the *Miami Herald.* "He's just a lovable person."

Sources

Periodicals

ESPN: The Magazine, May 20, 2008.
Miami Herald, October 2, 2008.
Rolling Stone, July 28, 2006.
Ventura County Star, May 10, 2008.

Online

"Kimbo Slice," ProElite.com, http://kimboslice.proelite.com/ (accessed January 21, 2009).
Kimbo Slice: The Official Website, http://www.kimbo305.com/ (accessed January 21, 2009).
Wetzel, Dan, "Final Curtain for the Kimbo Show," Yahoo! Sports, http://sports.yahoo.com/mma/news?slug=dw-kimbo100508&prov=yhoo&type=lgns (accessed January 21, 2009).

—Deborah A. Ring

Tasha Smith

1971—

Actress

Actress Tasha Smith is a former stripper and drug user who turned her life around in dramatic fashion to build a successful television and film career. In her roles as Jennifer, the conniving ex-wife in Tyler Perry's *Daddy's Little Girls,* and as the sassy, straight-talking Angela in *Why Did I Get Married?,* Smith delivered some of the best lines in the movies and gained a reputation as a scene-stealer. Since achieving celebrity status, she has embarked on a second career as a mentor and motivational speaker, hoping to act as a role model for young people. Smith told Gayle King on Oprah & Friends radio, "I don't want to be a celebrity—I want to be an influence."

Smith, Tasha, photograph. Roger Walsh/Landov.

Tasha Smith was born, along with her twin sister Sidra, on February 28, 1971, in Camden, New Jersey. Her single mother, who was only fifteen when the twins were born, struggled with drug addition for many years. As a teenager, Smith sold marijuana, used drugs, and often got into fights. By the time she was fourteen years old, she was working behind the bar at a strip club. "I was the kid you did not want your kids to hang with," she explained to King. Still, Smith had bigger hopes for her future: "I always had a dream—I knew I was going

to go to Hollywood," she told Maureen Harrington in *People.*

Friends living on the West Coast gave Smith the opening she needed: They sent her a plane ticket, and soon she dropped out of high school and headed for Los Angeles. After seeing Martin Lawrence perform stand-up at the Comedy Act Theater, Smith decided to pursue a career as a comedian. She developed a raunchy routine and toured with well-known comics such as Dave Chappelle. When comedy did not pay the bills, however, she turned to stripping.

Smith also used drugs, a painful six-year addition that she has talked about openly. In an interview on Essence.com, she admitted to smoking two packs of cigarettes per day, using marijuana daily, and snorting cocaine at least three times per week. The turning point came at age twenty-five, when she hit rock bottom: "When you're so high that you think your soul is being ripped out of your body and you're hallucinating and crazy, you just need to stop," she said. Smith went cold turkey and conquered her addition, attributing her turnaround to the "grace of God." Once an avowed atheist, Smith experienced a powerful religious

---

At a Glance . . .

Born February 28, 1971, in Camden, NJ.

Career: Television and film actress, 1994—.

Addresses: *Publicist*—Perspective PR, 233 North Maclay Ave., Ste. 109, San Fernando, CA 91340.

---

conversion: "I was going through this major transition in life...and God really showed up and met me where I was," she recalled in an interview with Mona Austin on EURWeb.com. She became a devoted Christian and remained committed to her religious faith.

Smith began acting in 1994, when she and Sidra appeared in the movie *Twin Sitters,* followed the next year by a small part in the film *Let It Be Me.* In 1996 she landed her first television role, playing Tasha King on the NBC sitcom *Boston Common* for two seasons, then appearing as Tanya Cole on the WB's *The Tom Show* with Tom Arnold in 1997–98. Over the next several years she made guest appearances on such series as *Chicago Hope, The Steve Harvey Show, The Parkers, Without a Trace, Nip/Tuck,* and *Girlfriends,* in addition to a four-episode stint on the award-winning HBO crime drama *The Corner* in 2000.

Film roles began to come Smith's way as well. She delivered memorable performances in supporting roles in the features *Playas Ball* and *The Whole Ten Yards* with Bruce Willis, both in 2003. In 2006 she appeared in *ATL* and *You, Me, and Dupree* with Owen Wilson and Kate Hudson, and the following year worked with director Steven Ayromlooi in *Love...and Other Four-Letter Words.*

Smith's breakout role came in 2007, when she was cast in the film *Daddy's Little Girls,* written and directed by Tyler Perry, whom she met through their mutual friend Tyra Banks. "Tasha brings all her pain to her roles," Perry told Harrington. "She has taken her rough past and made it her art." In the movie Tasha played the role of Jennifer, a shrewish, vindictive woman who is embroiled in a bitter custody battle with her ex-husband over their three daughters. Speaking to BlackStarNews.com, Smith described her character: "Jennifer is what I call the devil of the script. Anytime there's a God, there has to be a devil. And anytime there's good, there has to be evil. And sometimes the evil is the best!"

Later the same year, Smith landed a plum role in another Tyler Perry vehicle, the romantic comedy *Why Did I Get Married?* Working alongside singers Janet Jackson and Jill Scott, Smith portrayed Angela, a headstrong woman who goes on a mountain retreat with her husband and three other couples. Smith, who received divorce papers ending her two-and-a-half-year marriage during the shooting of the film, had much personal experience to bring to her character. In the *New York Times* reviewer Jeannette Catsoulis praised Smith's performance: "Tasha Smith gives her aggrieved character a smart, tart spin: she's a welcome splash of acid among the sugar." The film topped the box office on its opening weekend, earning more than $20 million, and made Smith a bona fide star.

Her career bolstered by the success of *Why Did I Get Married?,* Smith appeared in *The Longshots* with Ice Cube in 2008 and was cast in a starring role in *Red Soil,* a drama dealing with child slavery in the cocoa fields of West Africa.

Off screen, Smith saw herself as a role model. She founded her own acting school, the Tasha Smith Acting Workshop, where she coached up-and-coming actors, and toured the country as a motivational speaker, advocating abstinence and celibacy among young people. "Tasha Smith is someone trying to pursue her purpose in life," she told Austin. "I believe I'm doing that between my acting, the school, going around speaking and trying to help plant the seeds and build foundations in young people."

Selected works

Films

Twin Sitters, 1994.
Playas Ball, 2003.
The Whole Ten Yards, 2003.
ATL, 2006.
You, Me, and Dupree, 2006.
Love... and Other Four-Letter Words, 2007.
Daddy's Little Girls, 2007.
Why Did I Get Married?, 2007.
The Longshots, 2008.
Couples Retreat, 2009.
Something Like a Business, 2009.
Red Soil, 2009.

Television

Boston Common, 1996–97.
The Tom Show, 1997–98.
The Corner, 2000.

Sources

Periodicals

Ebony, November 2007.
Jet, November 5, 2007.
New York Times, October 13, 2007.
People, November 5, 2007.

Online

"Actress Tasha Smith," Oprah & Friends Radio, 2008, http://www.oprah.com/article/oprahandfriends/gking/gking_20071114 (accessed January 22, 2009).

Austin, Mona, "Tasha Smith's Testimony: 'Why Did I Get Married' Co-Star Discusses Her Conversion from Atheism, Being a Transparent Christian in Hollywood and Her Passion for the Arts," EURWeb.com, October 15, 2007, http://www.eurweb.com/story/eur37634.cfm (accessed January 22, 2009).

Byrd, Kenya N., "Tasha Smith: Survival of the Fittest," Essence.com, October 9, 2007, http://www.essence.com/news_entertainment/entertainment/articles/tashasmithsurvivalofthefittest/ (accessed January 22, 2009).

Cane, Clay, "Out of the Box Office: Tasha Smith," Vibe.com, October 10, 2007, http://www.vibe.com/news/news_headlines/2007/10/tasha_smith/ (accessed January 22, 2009).

Williams, Kam, "Interview: Tasha Smith," BlackStar News.com, February 13, 2007, http://www.blackstarnews.com/?c=135&a=3004 (accessed January 22, 2009).

—Deborah A. Ring

Michael Steele

1958—

Lawyer, politician

Steele, Michael, photograph. Harry E. Walker/MCT/Landov.

Republican lawyer Michael Steele was the first African-American candidate to win the Maryland lieutenant governor's office and later became the first African American to lead the Republican Party. He became lieutenant governor in 2002 when his running mate, Bob Ehrlich, triumphed over Democratic opponent Kathleen Kennedy Townsend in a state that traditionally elected Democratic candidates. Steele hoped to further his political career and ran for the Senate in 2006. However, when his bid for that office was unsuccessful he returned to private law practice. In January of 2009 Steele was elected chairman of the powerful Republican National Committee (RNC). Stating that he wanted to take the Republican Party in a new direction, he said, "Our party needs new leadership, not just new management.... We must become a movement that seeks nothing less than transformation. It will take new ideas ... and a new structure that involves members and grassroots in a meaningful way."

Earned Law Degree at Georgetown

Michael Steele was born on October 19, 1958, and was adopted by William and Maebell Steele. William Steele died from complications of alcoholism when Steele was four years old. Maebell Steele remarried and raised Steele and his sister, Monica, with her second husband, John Turner, in the Petworth neighborhood of Washington, DC. Steele's mother worked as a laundress, and Turner drove an airport taxi. Although the family struggled financially, Steele's mother refused to go on public assistance, a lesson that young Steele never forgot. As he told Stephen Goode in *Insight on the News,* "She had been encouraged by family members and by our parish priest to go on welfare—'to take a government check,'as she put it.... She said, 'You know, I thought about it and I decided I didn't want the government to raise my son.'"

Steele entered Johns Hopkins University in Baltimore and earned a bachelor's degree in international relations in 1981. After graduating from Johns Hopkins, Steele was invited to join the university's Board of Trustees, a position he held until 1985. Raised as a Roman Catholic, Steele studied for two years at the Augustinian Friars Seminary at Villanova University after college. Although he ultimately decided not to

At a Glance . . .

Born Michael S. Steele on October 19, 1958, at Andrews Air Force Base in Prince George's County, Maryland; adopted by Maebell and William Steele; married Andrea (Derritt) Steele, 1985; children: Michael II, Drew. *Politics:* Republican. *Religion:* Roman Catholic. *Education:* Johns Hopkins University, BA, international relations, 1981; studied at Augustinian Friars Seminary at Villanova University; Georgetown University Law School, JD, 1991.

Career: Cleary, Gottlieb, Steen, and Hamilton, lawyer, 1991–97; Steele Group, founder and CEO, 1998—; Maryland Republican Party, chair, 2000–02; Maryland lieutenant governor, 2003–07; Dewey & LeBoeuf, partner, 2007—; Republican National Committee, chairman, 2009—.

Memberships: Maryland State Minority Outreach Task Force, chair, 1995–97; Archdiocese of Washington, member of Pastoral Council, 1996–99; East Baltimore Development, Inc., member of board of directors, 2003–07; HarVest Bank of Maryland, member of board of directors, 2007—; Edmund Burke Institute, member of Board of Governors, 2007—; Maryland Catholic Conference, member of administrative board, 2007—.

Awards: Man of the Year, Maryland State Republican Party, 1995; Community Leadership award, Thurgood Marshall Scholarship Fund, 2003; President's Award, Johns Hopkins Society of Black Alumni, 2003; Parren J. Mitchell Award, National Black Chamber of Commerce, 2004; Children's National Medical Center Chairman's Special Award, 2004; Bethune-DuBois Institute Award, 2005; James Cardinal Hickey National Figure Award, Archdiocese of Washington, 2005; Rodel Fellowship in Public Leadership, Aspen Institute, 2005–07; honorary doctorates, including Morgan State University and University of Mount St. Mary's.

Addresses: *Office*—Dewey & LeBoeuf, 1101 New York Ave. NW, Washington, DC 20005-4213.

enter the priesthood, Catholicism remained an important force in his life.

After working as a paralegal in Washington, DC, in the mid-1980s, Steele entered Georgetown University Law School and earned a JD in 1991. His sister also flourished academically; after studying at the University of Virginia, Monica Turner became a medical doctor. On the Maryland Republican Party's Web site, Steele spoke of his family's success in overcoming economic hardship as the basis of his identification with the Republican Party. "We are examples of what can happen when people are given opportunities, not handouts." According to the same Web site, during the 2002 gubernatorial campaign Steele declared: "Our opponents will never understand that working parents and their children need only a chance to learn, to save, to succeed. Every child in this great state deserves an opportunity just like the ones Bob [Ehrlich] and I were given."

Rose to Leadership Positions in GOP

In 1991 Steele joined the Washington, DC, law firm of Cleary, Gottlieb, Steen, and Hamilton. He remained with the firm until 1997 and specialized in corporate and financial law. Steele worked not only with Wall Street clients but also in Japan and in the United Kingdom. In 1997 Steele left the law firm to work for the Mills Corporation, a real estate development company based in Virginia, and in the following year he founded the Steele Group, a consulting and lobbying agency based in Largo, Maryland. By that time he had already taken his first run for statewide elective office, in a bid for Comptroller that ended unsuccessfully.

Always interested in politics, Steele once served as student body president while attending Johns Hopkins University. Inspired by the presidency of Ronald Reagan in the 1980s, Steele became active in Republican Party politics during that decade. In 1994 Steele was appointed the chair of the Republican Central Committee for Prince George's County, Maryland, a suburban area adjacent to the nation's capital that was home to thousands of upwardly mobile African Americans. Steele also served on several other Republican Party committees in Maryland, and in 1995 was named Maryland State Republican Man of the Year. Although his 1998 run for the state comptroller's office was unsuccessful, Steele advanced to the position of chair of the Maryland State Republican Party two years later. In gaining the office he became the first African American to head a state Republican Party organization. In 2000 Steele attended the Republican National Convention as a delegate from Maryland.

As he became a more prominent figure in Maryland's Republican Party, Steele also became a target of criticism by his opponents. When Steele noted that he had taken a major pay cut to open up his own consulting and lobbying agency, Democrats pointed out the $5,000 monthly salary that Steele drew from the Republican Party. A more pointed controversy arose in 2001 when Steele championed Republican proposals for redistricting legislative districts in Maryland. In response to Steele's position, State Senate leader Thomas Miller, a Democrat, called his opponent an "Uncle Tom," a phrase that implied that Steele had sold out the interests of African Americans in deference to the Republican Party. In a rebuttal released through the Maryland Republican Party's Web site, Steele declared, "As an African-American, I find Senator Miller's remarks, and his plantation mentality, both offensive and beneath the dignity of his office.... African-Americans and all concerned citizens of our state should be aware of what his true colors are, and should know that he will attempt to preserve his own power without regard for the voters who put him in office."

Entered 2002 Race for Lieutenant Governor

A frequently mentioned candidate for statewide office, Steele was asked in July of 2002 to join the ticket as the candidate for lieutenant governor with Republican Bob Ehrlich, who was running for governor. Early in the election the Republicans were not given much chance of winning the election as they faced a respected and well-financed opponent in incumbent lieutenant governor Kathleen Kennedy Townsend. Townsend also had a significant national profile as a member of the politically prominent Kennedy family.

The Townsend campaign was plagued by a number of missteps throughout the fall of 2002, including allegations that its supporters had distributed Oreo cookies at the candidates' debate at Morgan State University in September of 2002 in order to question Steele's pride in his racial identity. Ehrlich and Steele stuck to their major theme of fiscal responsibility in the campaign, however, and predicted that Townsend would raise taxes if elected. Helped by a visit from President George Bush, who raised $1.8 million in a record-setting fundraising appearance for the Republicans, Ehrlich and Steele emerged victorious in the election. Although their victory was part of a national trend toward Republican candidates in 2002, the outcome was nonetheless surprising in a state that had not sent Republicans to the two top offices since 1968.

In becoming lieutenant governor, Steele occupied the highest-level office that an African American had ever held in Maryland's history. Remarking on his feat, Steele told WBAL-TV reporter Mindy Basara on election night, "Every Black child in this state—every child in this state—can picture themselves standing in my shoes tonight. That's what opportunity is all about." In 2004 Steele first entered the national scene with a speech to the Republican National Convention.

Elected Chairman of the Republican Party

After Senator Paul Sarbanes announced he would not run for reelection in 2006, Steele announced his candidacy for the seat. He overcame a serious political misstep in February of 2006 when he compared embryonic stem-cell research to Nazi medical experiments at a speech to a Baltimore Jewish group and won the primary the following September. However, Steele was defeated in the general election by Benjamin L. Cardin in November. After his loss, Steele became chairman of the political action committee GOPAC in February 2007. He joined the law firm of Dewey & LeBoeuf in April of the same year and became a partner in the law firm's Washington, DC, office.

Following the election of Democrat Barack Obama to the presidency in November of 2008 and major losses by Republicans in House and Senate races around the country, the Washington Times reported that Mike Duncan's job as RNC chairman was in jeopardy, and Steele's name was in the mix to replace him. A few days later Steele confirmed that he was seeking the chairmanship. In an interview with Jon Ward and Ralph Z. Hallow in the Washington Times, Steele scolded the leadership of the party for having a "country club" mentality, saying, "Let's just be very frank about it. What the party's got to do is get its head out of the clouds and out of the sand and recognize that the dynamics politically and otherwise around them have changed."

His message resonated with Republicans who sought to rejuvenate the party. In January of 2009 the Republican Party elected Steele its leader, installing him as chairman of the RNC. With President Obama leading the Democrats, many observers noted the historic significance of Steele's election since it meant that for the first time in history African Americans headed both of the major U.S. political parties. Accepting the position, Steele told Republicans, "We're going to bring this party to every corner, every boardroom, every neighborhood, every community. And we're going to say to friend and foe alike, we want you to be part of us. We want you to work with us. And for those of you who wish to obstruct, get ready to get knocked over." Later, in an interview with Sean Hannity on Fox News, he said, "It is an incredible honor right now to stand with my friends around the country as we help to grow this party and make it a viable political entity out here. We have got a lot of work to do but today is a good day."

Sources

Periodicals

Baltimore Sun, November 6, 2002.
Congress Daily, July 1, 2002, p. 13.
Human Events, October 21, 2002, p. 17.
Insight on the News, November 26, 2002, p. 36.
Washington Post, October 31, 2002, p. B1.
Washington Times, November 11, 2008; November 19, 2008.

Online

"Congratulations, Michael Steele, New RNC Chairman," Republican National Committee, 2009, http://www.rnc.org/ (accessed February 3, 2009).

"Michael S. Steele," Dewey & LeBoeuf, 2008, http://www.deweyleboeuf.com/michael_steele/ (accessed January 29, 2009).

"Michael Steele Gives First Interview as RNC Chairman," FoxNews.com, February 2, 2009, http://www.foxnews.com/story/0,2933,486585,00.html (accessed February 3, 2009).

"Steele Apologizes for Jewish Council Remarks," WBAL-TV Baltimore, February 10, 2006, http://www.wbaltv.com/news/6901748/detail.html

Steele for RNC Chairman, 2009, http://www.steeleforchairman.com/ (accessed January 29, 2009).

—Timothy Borden and Melissa Doak

Charles R. Stith

1949—

Minister, former ambassador

Charles R. Stith made his name known as a Methodist minister and a U.S. ambassador to Tanzania, but his long record in public services includes several other notable achievements. In 1985 he founded the Organization for a New Equality (ONE), a nonprofit group that has worked to ensure fair credit and lending practices in low-income communities across the United States. Since 2002 he has taught at Boston University and directed its African Presidential Archives and Research Center.

A native of St. Louis, Missouri, Stith was born on August 26, 1949, and grew up in its predominantly African-American neighborhood of Ville. In an interview with Tim O'Neil for the *St. Louis Post-Dispatch,* Stith described the close-knit community "as very nourishing, where people expected the best of you. We saw teachers and people in our churches who were models of success. It was a strong sense of community that encouraged us to succeed." During his senior year at Soldan High School in 1966–67, he served as student council president. He went on to Baker University, a Methodist-affiliated school in Baldwin City, Kansas, and graduated in 1973. He trained for the ministry at the Interdenominational Theological Center in Atlanta, Georgia, from which he earned his master's degree in divinity in 1975. Two years later he earned a second master's degree, this one in theology, from Harvard University.

Stith's first post at the pulpit was at Atlanta's Central United Methodist Church, and in 1977 he became a minister at the Wesley United Methodist Church in Boston. Two years later he was invited to become senior pastor at the Union United Methodist Church, which was founded in 1796 and is Boston's oldest African-American United Methodist congregation. He continued to serve as pastor at Union United after he founded the ONE in 1985. This national nonprofit civil rights organization rallied public support and pressured lawmakers to enact new federal and state regulations to ensure fair banking and loan practices in urban communities, and also organized such projects as Campaign for Economic Literacy, which offered free classes in churches and community centers to educate consumers about mortgages and other forms of credit.

In 1994 Stith was invited to be part of the U.S special delegation sent to South Africa as observers of the first democratic elections in that country's history. A year later he published a book, *Political Religion: A Liberal Answers the Question, "Should Politics and Religion Mix?"* In the summer of 1998 U.S. President Bill Clinton appointed him to become the next U.S. ambassador to the East African nation of Tanzania. The appointment was confirmed by Senate vote in late June, and Stith and his family were scheduled to move there in August. On August 7, 1998, the U.S. embassy in Tanzania's capital, Dar es Salaam, was bombed, and ten people died. That same day, the U.S. embassy in Nairobi, Kenya, was also decimated by an explosive device that killed 247 U.S. State Department employees, American military personnel, and Kenyan civilians. It was a somewhat fearful start to this new era of Stith's career, and he noted that "the staff will be coming out of crisis mode by the time I get there," he qualification standards for Heavily-Indebted Poor Countries Initiative, which provides special assistance from the International Monetary Fund and the World Bank.

Stith served as ambassador until the end of the Clinton administration in early 2001. Returning to the Boston area, he took up adjunct teaching positions at Harvard University and Boston College, and at the latter he founded the African Presidential Archives and Research Center, which serves as a policy center to devise solutions to aid the nations and people of sub-Saharan Africa. Stith's wide range of expertise in community service and foreign affairs also led to a side career as an editorial writer for newspapers. At the onset of the U.S. invasion of Iraq in 2003, for example, he commented on widespread antiwar demonstrations in many U.S. cities, which echoed those in other nations, as he wrote in a *Denver Post* guest commentary. "Countries need to know why the position we're taking in response to a particular set of circumstances is in their best interest as well as ours," he wrote, adding that he had just spent several weeks in a half-dozen African countries, where "there was much consternation and concern about what the U.S. was preparing to do in Iraq. Our lack of engagement with those governments on this significant move gives the impression that we believe they have nothing to lose."

Stith has also written about the majestic beauty of Africa for *Ebony,* noting that too often "Western media outlets most often portray Africa, at best, as the land of the exotic or, at worst, a place defined by extreme conditions of disease and natural disasters." Stith cited several nations—among them South Africa, Cape Verde, and the Indian Ocean island of Zanzibar that is part of his former home, Tanzania—and pointed out "these are all places where democratic traditions are being fostered and economic progress is a sign of the times." He also admitted that during his stint as ambassador, "one of the places I loved to take special guests was Zanzibar. The narrow streets and Afro-Arab architecture reminded me of the set of a James Bond movie."

In 1975 Stith married Deborah Prothrow, a physician affiliated with the Harvard University School of Public Health. They had met when he was studying for the ministry at the Interdenominational Theology Center and she was a Spelman College student. They have raised three children: Percy, Mary Mildred, and a nephew, Trey. Many years ago, when all three children were quite young, Stith and his wife were interviewed for a lengthy *New York Times Magazine* article about how professional middle-class African-American families discussed racism and the civil rights movement with their children. "I tell the boys they are as good as anybody else," Stith told writer Thomas Morgan in 1985. "They have a responsibility to help those who do not have the opportunities and options that they have, and that they really have to deal with people on the basis of their humanity, and that includes white people."

told O'Neil in the *St. Louis Post-Dispatch* interview. "They will need time to grieve. I'm going to have to employ a few pastoral skills as I move into the situation and start work."

Stith's duties as U.S. ambassador included arranging the first Open Skies Agreement between an African country and the United States. These treaties provide a freer flow of passenger and cargo for airlines that operate between the two nations. Stith also played a key role in the visit of the Tanzanian president Benjamin Mkapa to the United States, and sought to expand trade relations between Tanzanian companies and those in England and South Africa. Stith's previous experience in the financial sector also proved a bonus to the Tanzanian government when it attained the

Selected works

Books

Political Religion: A Liberal Answers the Question, "Should Politics and Religion Mix?," Abingdon Press, 1995.

Periodicals

"Recovering the Art of Diplomacy," *Denver Post,* March 30, 2003, p. E5.
"Let's Hope Old Attitudes Pass along with Helms," *Atlanta Journal-Constitution,* July 10, 2008, p. A11.
"The Best of Africa," *Ebony,* October 2008, p. 124.

Sources

Periodicals

Jet, October 5, 1998, p. 34.
New York Times Magazine, October 27, 1985, p. 32.
St. Louis Post-Dispatch, August 27, 1998, p. B1.

Other

"Interview: Charles Stith Discusses Why Many African Presidents Find It Difficult to Step Down," *All Things Considered,* National Public Radio, August 11, 2003.

—Carol Brennan

Carl Stokes

1927–1996

Lawyer, politician, broadcaster, judge, diplomat

Stokes, Carl, photograph. R. Gates/Getty Images.

Carl Stokes gained national recognition in November of 1967, when he was elected mayor of Cleveland, Ohio, becoming the first African American elected to lead a major American city. After serving two terms as mayor, Stokes became a television news correspondent and anchorman in New York City. He returned to Cleveland and served for many years as a judge in the city's municipal court before being appointed U.S. ambassador to the Republic of the Seychelles. He resigned that post in 1995 for medical reasons and died on April 3, 1996, of cancer of the esophagus.

Experienced Childhood of Poverty

Stokes was born in 1927 in Central, a poor, predominantly African-American neighborhood in Cleveland, Ohio. His father, Louis, a laundry worker, died two years later. Carl and his younger brother, Louis, were raised by their mother, Louise, on her small earnings as a cleaning woman and supplemental welfare aid. "Study, so you'll be somebody," she constantly exhorted her children, according to *Time*.

The struggling family lived in the first floor of a rickety old two-story house and covered the house's many rat holes with the tops of tin cans. A coal stove in the living room provided the only heat. All three shared one bed, wrapping heated bricks or a flatiron in flannel to keep them warm while sleeping in the winter.

Cleveland was the first city in the country to accept federal funds to construct housing for the poor. In 1938, when Stokes was eleven years old, the family moved into a new housing project. For the first time they had hot and cold running water, a washing machine, refrigerator, central heat, and two bedrooms. One block away from their new home was the project's recreation center, complete with swimming pool, boxing ring, ping pong tables, and art classes. Stokes took full advantage of the facilities, learning to box and play ping pong.

Entered College after Military Service

Once Stokes reached high school, his formerly good grades began to deteriorate. "Reading was against the

Basic training at Fort McClellan, Alabama, was an eye-opening experience for this African-American ghetto youth. In his autobiography, *Promises of Power,* Stokes recalled it as the time when he learned to hate white people. So fearful was he of being racially humiliated by the local southern townsfolk that he never left the shelter of the base throughout his training. Sent to U.S.-occupied Germany, Stokes continued boxing and won the table-tennis championship among U.S. servicemen in Europe. His two years in the army convinced him of the wisdom of his mother's advice about scholarship; discharged in 1946, he returned to Cleveland and completed his high school diploma.

The next year he enrolled at West Virginia State College (now West Virginia State University), a historically African-American college. After one year, Stokes transferred to Western Reserve University in Cleveland. While in school, he began to work with John Holly, the chief political organizer of Cleveland's African-American community. Holly became Stokes's mentor, securing for him an after-school job at one of the Ohio Department of Liquor control stores. Stokes left school in 1950 to take a full-time position as a state liquor enforcement agent. His first posting was in Canton, Ohio. His assignment there was to close down illegal bootleg operations in the town's African-American neighborhood. Before long, he had the second-highest arrest record among the department's eighty-five inspectors.

Prepared for Law Career

Transferred to Dayton, Stokes met and married Edith Smith, a girl from a middle-class African-American family, in 1951. Toledo was his next posting—until a shoot-out in a bar forced a career reassessment. Setting his sights higher, Stokes decided that becoming a lawyer would be his next step. In 1952 he enrolled in the University of Minnesota's undergraduate law program.

It took Stokes two years to get his bachelor's degree. During this time his marriage broke up. He worked weekends as a waiter on the Rock Island Rocket passenger train to Dallas to make ends meet. After graduating in 1954, he returned to Cleveland, moved back in with his mother, enrolled in the Cleveland-Marshall School of Law, and began working as a probation officer for the Cleveland Municipal Court. Two years later he had his law degree. The day he passed the bar in June of 1957, he quit his probation job and entered into a law practice with his brother. That year he also joined the Young Democrats and began to get involved in local politics. He became the campaign manager for an African-American candidate working to defeat a white incumbent in an African-American city council district. That campaign proved a success.

mores," he later told *Time.* "All of us looked on boxing as a way of life. You had to fight." He began hanging around pool halls instead of the recreation center. At age seventeen he dropped out of school and went to work in a local foundry. Shortly after his eighteenth birthday, Stokes joined the army.

Stokes quickly became acquainted with the leaders of Cleveland's African-American community. Following their advice, he started working with many of the city's civic and civil rights groups, including the Boy Scouts, National Association for the Advancement of Colored People, Urban League, and African-American churches. He volunteered his time to help with events, campaigns, and fund drives. He was learning the art of politics—working with people—and establishing valuable contacts for the future.

Elected to Ohio House of Representatives

By 1958 Stokes was spending too much time on these activities to concentrate on building his law practice. His old mentor, John Holly, helped him receive an appointment as assistant city police prosecutor. From this secure post, Stokes made unsuccessful runs in Democratic primaries as a candidate for the Ohio State Senate in 1958, and the state legislature in 1960. Two years later, however, the results were different: Stokes won his party's nomination and the general election to the Ohio House of Representatives, becoming the first African-American Democrat ever to sit in this body. He believed this victory was due to his ability to appeal to both African-American and white voters.

Stokes proved a hardworking legislator and a political moderate, strongly supporting civil rights and welfare bills—he helped draft legislation establishing a state department of urban affairs, wrote a new mental-health services act, promoted gun control and tougher air-pollution control—while also sponsoring a bill giving the governor power to send the national guard into a city in advance of a potential riot. Re-elected twice, Stokes traveled 125,000 miles throughout the country during his legislative years calling for increased African-American political action. He was about to begin practicing what he preached.

Cleveland was the nation's tenth-largest city, with a proud and prosperous history, a diversified economy, and renowned cultural institutions. Like many industrial cities along the Great Lakes, it was composed of numerous ingrown ethnic neighborhoods, home to a diverse population descended from many European nationalities, as well as African Americans who had moved north following the Civil War and in the first half of the twentieth century. By the mid-1960s, however, its economy had slowed and middle-class whites were fleeing to the suburbs in large numbers, taking their tax dollars with them—thereby choking off future development of the central city. Unemployment climbed, particularly among African Americans, leading to racial unrest.

Between 1960 and 1965, median family income in Hough, Cleveland's poorest African-American neighborhood, declined by 16 percent, while the number of families headed by women rose from 23 percent to 32 percent. Blocks of old homes, mostly in African-American inner-city areas, were bulldozed for urban renewal, but few new homes were built for former residents. City government under Mayor Ralph Locher made no attempt to alleviate these mounting problems. Inertia ruled city hall, while the police held a growing, increasingly angry minority populace in line.

Built Coalition of Voters in Cleveland

In 1965, in this climate, Stokes decided to run for mayor. The United Freedom Movement, an association of civil rights groups, gathered enough signatures for him to be put on the ballot as an independent candidate. Mayor Locher and his Republican challenger split the white vote and Stokes came in second in a close election, losing by just over 2,000 votes.

Instead of being discouraged, Stokes immediately began campaigning for the 1967 mayoral election and decided to run in the 1967 Democratic primary against Mayor Locher. His strategy was simple: register and organize African Americans into a solid voting block behind him by demanding change, while stressing his record as a political moderate to whites. The local Congress of Racial Equality (CORE) used a Ford Foundation grant to finance a voter registration drive in the African-American community, helped by Dr. Martin Luther King's periodic visits on the organization's behalf. Militants passed the word around Cleveland's black neighborhoods to "cool it for Carl" and keep calm during the summer, so as not to spoil his chances at election.

Frustrated with Locher, the business community, led by the *Cleveland Plain Dealer,* the city's leading newspaper, endorsed Stokes in hopes that he could unite their troubled city. The candidate also used his considerable personal charm to his advantage, impressing white society women with his affability and long-range plans, as well as African-American ghetto denizens with his call for change. His strategy worked; Stokes received approximately 93,000 African-American votes, 96 percent of those cast, and 17,000 white votes to beat Locher by nearly 20,000 votes and take control of the local Democratic machine.

In the general election Stokes's opponent was Seth Taft, a blue-blooded Republican who was the grandson of President William Howard Taft, son of a former mayor of Cincinnati, nephew of Senator Robert A. Taft, and cousin of Congressman Robert Taft Jr. Unlike his more famous relatives, though, this Taft was a liberal with a set of specific ideas to reform Cleveland. However, Cleveland was a staunchly Democratic city that had not elected a Republican mayor in twenty-six years. In addition, Taft was stigmatized among the city's large working class by the anti-labor Taft-Hartley

Act sponsored by his uncle. To his credit, Taft refused to make race a campaign issue.

Stokes realized that he had to win the votes of more than just Cleveland's 300,000 African-American citizens, 38 percent of the population, to be elected mayor. He concentrated his efforts in the city's white ethnic wards. By making as many campaign appearances as possible before white groups, he helped convince some that, except for skin color, he was much like them.

Elected First Big-City Black Mayor

Even with the overwhelming support of the African-American community, most white liberals, some leading businessmen, and the continued endorsement of the city's two newspapers, the election was close; Stokes won by only 1,644 votes, a plurality of just 0.6 percent. Taft was gracious in defeat, calling Cleveland "the least bigoted city in America," according to *Time*.

Stokes's election brought more national attention to Cleveland. Though not the first African-American elected as mayor, Stokes was the first African-American elected as mayor of a metropolitan city without a majority African-American population. "This is not a Carl Stokes victory," he told an election night crowd, as quoted in *Time*, "not a vote for a man but a vote for a program, for a visionary dream of what our city can become."

Stokes began his administration with the high hopes of most of Cleveland behind him. He appointed talented people to key positions and convinced the business community to raise $4 million to back CLEVELAND NOW, a project to support city programs that could not be financed by federal funds. He also used his friendship with Vice President Hubert Humphrey to restore a cancelled $10 million HUD grant.

Nevertheless, by the summer of 1968 the tensions besetting Cleveland had brought the city's temperature back to the boiling point. A riot ensued, which shook the confidence of whites who assumed that electing Stokes had guaranteed racial peace and harmony. Even more damaging was the arrest of Fred (Ahmed) Evans, an African-American militant who had bought guns for himself and others using funds from CLEVELAND NOW. This signaled the end for that organization and much of the mayor's support from the white community.

Left Politics for TV News

Despite these setbacks, Stokes won re-election in 1969 by 4,500 votes, a greater margin than had defined his first victory. However, his troubles continued into his second term. He broke with his police chief, antagonized the city council president, and granted wage increases for city workers without securing adequate funds to make the increases a reality. Voters refused a tax increase, city workers had to be laid off, a sewage pump broke and released millions of gallons of raw sewage into Lake Erie, and the city was all but shut down by a devastating snowstorm. An unimproved economy led to the demise of several major downtown businesses, and crime continued to rise.

Realizing he had lost the support of the business community, the newspapers, and many African Americans, Stokes announced that he would not run for re-election in 1971. Instead, he supported Arnold Pickney, the African-American president of the school board, who ran as an independent candidate. Pickney ran second to Ralph Perk in the mayoral election, the Republican capturing the great majority of Cleveland's white ethnic voters.

Pickney's defeat marked the end of Stokes's political power in Cleveland. He left the city in 1972 to become a television anchorman and reporter with WNBC-TV in New York City. The following year he divorced his second wife, Shirley, whom he had married in 1958. In 1980 he returned to Cleveland, becoming a senior partner in a firm specializing in labor law.

Served as Ambassador to Seychelles

Three years later Stokes was elected a presiding administrative judge on Cleveland's municipal court. In 1986 he became that court's chief judge, holding the position until 1994, when he was appointed by President Bill Clinton to be U.S. ambassador to the Republic of Seychelles, an island nation off the coast of Africa. "Seychelles will be quite a change for me after a long career in public service," Stokes told *Jet* magazine. "I have looked all around home in Cleveland and in Ohio and there was just not anything that was challenging for me. I have been interested in the foreign service for a long while."

In 1995 Stokes left his ambassadorship for medical reasons, having been diagnosed with esophageal cancer. He underwent chemotherapy and radiation treatment at the Cleveland Clinic, expecting to recover and resume his post in Seychelles. While undergoing treatment in January of 1996, Stokes remarried Raija Kostadinov, whom he had divorced in 1993. Stokes died on April 3, 1996, at the age of sixty-eight. He is buried in Cleveland at the city's Lake View cemetery.

During his tenure as the mayor of Cleveland, Stokes garnered many awards, including the prestigious Chubb award, in which dignitaries are asked to live in residence at Yale University for a short time, give talks, and answer questions for students. His many awards also included the Equal Opportunity Award from the National Urban League in 1970 and the Outstanding

Achievement Award given by the University of Minnesota Law School in 1971. Stokes also received numerous honorary degrees from U.S. universities and colleges, including a posthumous honorary Doctor of Laws degree in 2008 from his alma mater, the Cleveland-Marshall College of Law at Cleveland State University.

Selected works

Books

Quality of the Environment, University of Oregon Press, 1968.
Promises of Power: A Political Autobiography, Simon & Shuster, 1973.

Sources

Books

Moore, Leonard N., *Carl B. Stokes and the Rise of Black Political Power,* University of Illinois Press, 2002.
Porter, Philip Wiley, *Cleveland: Confused City on a Seesaw,* Ohio State University Press, 1976.

Weinberg, Kenneth G., *African-American Victory: Carl Stokes and the Winning of Cleveland,* Quadrangle Books, 1968.
Zannes, Estelle, *Checkmate in Cleveland: The Rhetoric of Confrontation during the Stokes Years,* Press of Case Western Reserve University, 1972.

Periodicals

Ebony, January 1968, p. 24.
Jet, April 25, 1994, p. 33; September 19, 1994, p. 4; January 22, 1996.
New York Times Magazine, November 5, 1967, p. 30; February 25, 1968, p. 26.
Time, November 17, 1967, pp. 23–27.

Online

"Former Congressman Louis Stokes to Speak at Cleveland-Marshall College of Law Graduation on May 17th," Cleveland State University, News Release, April 29, 2008, http://www.csuohio.edu/news/releases/2008/04/14495.html (accessed February 5, 2009).

—James J. Podesta and Sandra Alters

T-Pain

1985—

Musician

T-Pain, photograph. Jeff Siner/MCT/Landov.

Rapper T-Pain scored a string of hits that made him one of the hottest new acts in the genre in 2007. His featured performances included Kanye West's "Good Life," which earned West the 2008 Grammy award for Best Rap Song, and so many of T-Pain's own hits have become best-selling ring tones that *Billboard* magazine dubbed him "The Ring King." The basic elements of writing and production are at the core of his success, he told writer Sonia Murray in the *Atlanta Journal-Constitution*. "Everybody is so busy concentrating on a song, trying to be different or abstract," he reflected, "instead of just being a basic, beautiful picture."

T-Pain takes the *T* in his stage name from his hometown of Tallahassee, Florida, where he was born Faheem Rasheed Najm on September 30, 1985. He was raised in a Muslim household, but his father, Shasheem, was a working rhythm-and-blues (R&B) musician, and T-Pain was exposed to the music business at an early age because of it. At the age of ten he set up a makeshift recording studio in his bedroom, where he began laying down mixed tapes of his own compositions. In his teens he attended Cuyahoga Val-

ley Christian Academy in Cuyahoga Falls, Ohio, but returned to Tallahassee and joined a local rap act called Nappy Headz. They had some local success with the singles "F.L.A." and "Oops," which found fans across the Atlantic, but as T-Pain recalled in a 2006 interview with writer Steve Jones in *USA Today*, "we even had callers from London saying they wanted us to perform over there, but we couldn't go there because nobody had passports."

As a solo artist, T-Pain scored his first hit after reworking an as-yet-to-be-released track from Senegalese-American rapper Akon. The original song was titled "Locked Up," but T-Pain refashioned it into "I'm [Messed] Up" after obtaining an advance promotional copy of the song before it was officially released to radio in early 2005. "I jacked his beat, basically," he admitted to Jones in the *USA Today* interview. "I made my own song and my own video and everything. It started to get so big that people thought when 'Locked Up' came out, he stole it from me. It was crazy." The song came to the attention of Akon, who tried to contact the upstart, but T-Pain initially thought it was a prank call. Instead the African-born musician invited him to sign with his own label, called Konvict Muzik, but "I'm

[Messed] Up" had also attracted the attention of a major label, Interscope, whose executives also began to court T-Pain. At the time, his father was his manager, and "my dad was really looking at the money rather than the artistic situation," T-Pain recalled in a 2008 interview with Hillary Crosley in *Billboard.* "He wanted me to sign with Interscope because they were throwing out the most money. But the day I had a meeting with Interscope, I ran away from home."

T-Pain released his debut on Akon's Konvict Muzik—a subsidiary of Jive Records—in 2005. Its title, *Rappa Ternt Sanga,* was a slangy turn on the phrase "rapper turned singer," and its eighteen tracks were autobiographical and dealt in frank terms with certain aspects of his private life. The album yielded a pair of Billboard top ten hits: "I'm Sprung" and "I'm N Luv (Wit a Stripper)"; moreover, both songs were released as downloadable ring tones and became massive hits in that particular sales territory. The first racked up sales of nearly two million, while "I'm N Luv (Wit a Stripper)" hit the five-million ring tone mark. That feat earned him some respect from Jive executives, who had until then been uninterested in providing any marketing or promotional money for Akon's new protégé. "I had people at Jive tell me they didn't believe in my product and let me know that they didn't too much care," Antony Bruno in *Billboard* quoted T-Pain as saying in 2007. "But selling 6.7 million ringtones … changed their minds." He also noted in another interview that the tale about the exotic dancer came when he and friend took a third pal, whom they dubbed "Choir Boy," to an adult-entertainment establishment. On a more serious note, however, he told *Blender* magazine's Ryan Dombal that "I've been to a lot of strip clubs and I've heard a lot of life stories. It's saddening. This one girl showed me a bunch of pictures of her kids and told me how she really wanted to be with them but

she couldn't because she can only strip out of town because everyone in her city knows her."

T-Pain's second album was *Epiphany,* and it debuted at the No. 1 spot on the Billboard R&B chart in June of 2007. Its first single, "Buy U a Drank (Shawty Snappin')" featuring Atlanta rapper Yung Joc, became the top-selling ring tone of the year. *Epiphany* also featured guest spots from Akon on the track "Bartender," reached platinum-status million sales, and climbed to the top of the Billboard "Top 200" album charts as well. The sudden fame made T-Pain an in-demand guest vocalist on tracks by others, including "The Boss" from Rick Ross, "Kiss Kiss" from Chris Brown, and Kanye West's "Good Life," which won West the Grammy award for Best Rap Song of 2007.

Known for his songwriting and production skills as well as his songwriting talents, T-Pain founded his own label, Nappy Boy Entertainment, in 2007 and began working with a number of up-and-coming artists, including Jay Lyriq, Tay Dizm, and Sophia Fresh. The label also released his third album, *Thr33 Ringz,* in late 2008, which kicked off with an advance single, "Can't Believe It," featuring rapper Lil Wayne; both appeared as musical guests on NBC's *Saturday Night Live* later that November. The second single from *Thr33 Ringz* was "Chopped N Skrewed," which featured Ludacris, and the Chris Brown–featured "Freeze" was the third track. T-Pain told the *Tampa Tribune* that despite the circus-themed promotional efforts used to sell *Thr33 Ringz,* it was a more mature record for him. "I think it takes everyone two albums to find themselves," he told reporter Curtis Ross. "It took me that long."

T-Pain is known for the top hats that cover his dreadlocks and has a collection of more than three hundred of them, many of them custom made. The only downside to fame, he admitted, was the arduous tours. "It's too demanding," he told Bruno in *Billboard.* "You got tour rules. You can't be you and they stop you from doing stuff and you can't do what you want to do onstage." In his former hometown of Tallahassee, however, he holds an annual concert event, "T-Pain and Friends," with the proceeds donated to local charities. He lives in Duluth, a suburb of Atlanta, with his wife and three children, and made his film-acting debut in the fourth installment, scheduled for release in 2009, of the successful car-racing *Fast and Furious* franchise. Some of his income is spent on unusual rides, including a pricey Lamborghini sports car and an orange-colored hearse. "I'm still having fun," he told Ross in the *Tampa Tribune.* "It's like being an old teenager."

Selected discography

Singles; as featured artist

(Also co-songwriter; with E-40) "U and Dat," Warner Bros./BME/Sick Wid It Records, 2006.

(Also co-songwriter; with R. Kelly) "I'm a Flirt (Remix)," Jive Records, 2007.

(With Bow Wow) "Outta My System," Columbia Records, 2007.

(Also co-songwriter; with Kanye West) "Good Life," Good Music/Island Def Jam, 2007.

(Also co-songwriter; with Baby Bash) "Cyclone," Arista Records, 2007.

(With Chris Brown) "Kiss Kiss," Jive/Zomba, 2007.

(Also co-songwriter; with Flo Rida) "Low," Atlantic, 2007.

(Also songwriter; with Lil Mama) "Shawty Get Loose," Jive Records, 2008.

(Also co-songwriter; with Lil Wayne) "Got Money," Cash Money/Young Money/Universal, 2008.

Albums

Rappa Ternt Sanga (includes "I'm Sprung" and "I'm N Luv (Wit a Stripper)"), Konvict Muzik/Jive Records, 2005.

Epiphany (includes "Buy U a Drank (Shawty Snappin')" and "Bartender"), Konvict Muzik/Jive Records, 2007.

Thr33 Ringz (includes "Can't Believe It," "Chopped N Skrewed," and "Freeze"), Nappy Boy Entertainment, 2008.

Sources

Periodicals

Atlanta Journal-Constitution, November 11, 2008, p. E1.

Billboard, October 27, 2007, p. 28; October 18, 2008, p. 22.

Tampa Tribune, November 7, 2008, p. 14.

USA Today, March 31, 2006, p. 5E; November 11, 2008, p. 4D.

Online

Dombal, Ryan, "Interview: T-Pain's Stripper Secrets," Blender.com, May 30, 2008, http://www.blender.com/InterviewTPainsStripperSecrets/Blender-Blog/blogs/1168/25980.aspx (accessed November 22, 2008).

Reid, Shaheem, "T-Pain Celebrates First #1 Album," MTV.com, June 13, 2007, http://www.mtv.com/news/articles/1562434/20070613/t_pain.jhtml (accessed November 22, 2008).

—Carol Brennan

Richard Wesley

1945—

Playwright, screenwriter, educator

Richard Wesley rose to prominence in the early 1970s as a playwright known for his uncompromising examination of the contemporary African-American experience. The decades that followed revealed his versatility, as he moved increasingly from playwriting to screenwriting for films and television. In all of these media Wesley has tried, in the words of Megan Rosenfeld in the *Washington Post,* "to lead audiences to make their own choices."

Wesley was born in July of 1945 in Newark, New Jersey, and was raised there in a comfortable, middle-class household. While his father, George Richard Wesley, worked primarily as a laborer, both of his grandfathers were highly educated ministers, so education was one of the family's central values. As Wesley himself has noted, it was education that saved him from the deteriorating social conditions that distinguished life in Newark's African-American neighborhoods in the 1950s and 1960s. "In order to function on the street," he told Samuel G. Freedman in the *New York Times,* "you had to have a sense there are no possibilities for you. I always saw long-term payoffs. That's why I wasn't a gang member; that's why I wasn't a great athlete. I had alternatives."

After high school Wesley entered Howard University, one of the nation's leading African-American institutions. Within weeks of him graduating from there in 1967, Newark exploded in rioting that lasted for six days and left several dozen people dead. While the causes of the riot were complex, a major factor was the frustration felt by many in the city's African-American community over issues such as substandard housing and police brutality. The contrast between conditions in his native city and the relatively idyllic Howard campus prompted Wesley to reflect on economic and social divisions within the African-American community. Those divisions have been a prominent theme throughout his work.

Even as an undergraduate, Wesley was devoted to the theater and playwriting. At Howard he studied under Owen Dodson, a well-known playwright who had a major role in creating the atmosphere of militant activism that dominated African-American theater in the 1960s and early 1970s. Wesley's first play, an experimental drama entitled *Put My Dignity on 307,* was produced at Howard during his senior year. Following graduation he took a job as a passenger service agent for United Airlines, a position he held for two years. Throughout this period he continued to work on his writing and to make connections in the theater world, most notably with Ed Bullins, a leading figure in an influential Harlem program known as the Black Playwrights Workshop. Wesley left United in 1969 to become managing editor of *Black Theatre* magazine, where he remained until 1973. It was during his tenure there that his first major play, *The Black Terror,* appeared on stage.

A probing study of the uncompromising militancy embraced by many African-American radicals at the time, *The Black Terror* was produced in 1971 at the prestigious New York Shakespeare Festival. Under the clear influence of Dodson and Bullins, Wesley focused

At a Glance . . .

Born Richard Errol Wesley on July 11, 1945, in Newark, NJ; son of George Richard (a laborer) and Gertrude (maiden name, Thomas) Wesley; married Valerie Wilson, 1972; children: four. *Education:* Howard University, BFA, 1967.

Career: Playwright, 1967—; United Airlines, passenger service agent, 1967–69; *Black Theatre* magazine, managing editor, 1969–73; Manhattanville College, adjunct professor, 1973–74; Wesleyan University, adjunct professor, 1973–74; screenwriter, 1974—; Manhattan Community College, adjunct professor, 1980–83; Rutgers University, adjunct professor, 1984; New York University, associate professor, 1995—.

Memberships: Frank Silvera Writers' Workshop, founding member, 1973, board of directors, 1976–80; Theatre of Universal Images, board of directors, 1979–82; Library of Congress, National Film Preservation Board; Newark Museum Black Film Festival, Selection Committee.

Awards: Drama Desk Award for most promising playwright, 1971–72, for *The Black Terror;* Rockefeller Foundation grant, 1973; NAACP Image Award, 1974, for *Uptown Saturday Night,* and 1975, for *Let's Do It Again;* Audelco Award, 1974, 1977, and 1989 (six categories) for *The Talented Tenth.*

Addresses: *Office*—c/o Department of Dramatic Writing, Tisch School of the Arts, New York University, 721 Broadway, Seventh Fl., New York, NY 10003.

on feeling and character, rather than on plot. The play's central figure is a Vietnam veteran named Keusi, who gradually comes to question his involvement in an armed revolutionary movement. *The Black Terror* received warm reviews and brought Wesley a 1971–72 Drama Desk Award as one of seven playwrights judged most promising. In its use of dramatic monologues and the vivid, sometimes off-color language of the street, the play foreshadowed much of Wesley's subsequent work.

The mid-1970s proved to be a particularly fertile period for Wesley. After receiving a grant from the Rockefeller Foundation in 1973, he produced a number of well-received dramas, including *The Mighty Gents* (1974), a powerful study of aging gang members

in Newark. A revised version of the play appeared on Broadway in 1978. In his review of that production, Richard Eder wrote in the *New York Times,* "The play's brief scenes and recitations are like sardonic ballads in a street opera about hopelessness."

Despite the prominence of that Broadway production, Wesley's best-known play is probably *The Talented Tenth,* which was first produced in 1989. The title is taken from a comment made by W. E. B. Du Bois in 1903 about the community responsibilities of the most successful African Americans. Wesley's play focuses on six members of that elite, all of them Howard University graduates, who react in differing ways to the plight of the African-American underclass. Despite some mixed reviews, the play has become a staple of repertory companies around the nation.

Though Wesley's work as a playwright did not cease with the completion of *The Talented Tenth,* his focus has moved steadily toward screenwriting. His involvement with Hollywood began in 1974, when he provided the screenplay for *Uptown Saturday Night,* a comedy starring Bill Cosby and Sidney Poitier. The movie proved successful, and a sequel called *Let's Do It Again,* also written by Wesley, was made the following year. Both films brought him an Image Award from the National Association for the Advancement of Colored People. He continued working off and on for Hollywood throughout the 1980s, providing scripts for films such as *Fast Forward* (1985), a musical drama directed by Poitier, and *Native Son* (1986), an adaptation of the Richard Wright novel of the same name. Since the 1990s Wesley's focus has shifted increasingly toward television. His best-known work in that medium remains *Mandela and De Klerk,* a 1997 drama about the end of apartheid in South Africa.

In 1995 Wesley became an associate professor of playwriting and screenwriting at New York University's Tisch School of the Arts. His involvement in teaching had begun more than two decades earlier, with adjunct appointments at Manhattanville College and Wesleyan University in 1973. Over the years, he would hold similar positions at a variety of institutions in the New York City area, including Manhattan Community College and Rutgers University. As of early 2009 he remained at Tisch, serving as chair of the Department of Dramatic Writing and teaching a variety of courses, including screenwriting, developing the screenplay, and film script analysis.

Selected writings

Plays

Put My Dignity on 307, 1967.
The Black Terror, 1971.
Strike Heaven on the Face, 1973.
The Mighty Gents, 1974, revised, 1977–78.
The Past Is the Past, 1974.

The Sirens, 1974.
The Talented Tenth, 1989.

Screenplays—film

Uptown Saturday Night, 1974.
Let's Do It Again, 1975.
Fast Forward, 1985.
Native Son, 1986.

Screenplays—television

Murder without Motive: The Edmund Perry Story, 1992.
Mandela and De Klerk, 1997.
Bojangles, 2000.

Sources

Periodicals

Chicago Tribune, March 24, 2008.
New York Times, April 17, 1978; October 29, 1989; May 31, 1992.
Washington Post, November 16, 1982, p. C1.

Online

"Faculty Directory: Richard Wesley," Tisch School of the Arts, New York University, http://ddw.tisch.nyu.edu/object/WesleyR.html (accessed December 2, 2008).

—R. Anthony Kugler

Norman Whitfield

1940–2008

Songwriter, record producer

As a songwriter and producer, Norman Whitfield helped to shape the sound of legendary Motown Records as it matured into one of the most successful music labels of the twentieth century. After joining the company in its infancy, Whitfield rose quickly to a position of influence and crafted some of the most enduring songs of the late 1960s and early '70s for Marvin Gaye, the Temptations, and other top-selling Motown acts. "Much of what is now regarded as classic soul owes a large debt to Whitfield, who persuaded skeptical Motown founder Berry Gordy to let him stray from a wildly successful formula," wrote Steve Jones in *USA Today,* referring to the early three-minute pop tunes that gave way to a "psychedelic funk/soul sound that featured sinister keys, reverberating guitars, moaning horns and haunting strings." When the two-time Grammy Award winner died in 2008 at the age of sixty-eight, the London *Times* wrote that "it is not an exaggeration to describe Norman Whitfield as black music's answer to Phil Spector. In the mid-1960s both men transformed a simple musical form and took it to previously unimagined heights of sophistication and ambition."

Whitfield, Norman, photograph. M. Von Holden/FilmMagic/Getty Images.

Whitfield was born in 1940 and grew up in New York City's Harlem neighborhood. In the late 1950s his family moved to Detroit, where he finished his education at the city's Northwestern High School. He spent most of his teen years frequenting pool halls in both cities, and eventually drifted into the music business. "I don't have any formal musical training," he once admitted, according to an obituary in the London *Independent.* "It was done basically by a desire. When I saw Smokey Robinson driving in a Cadillac, to be absolutely point-blank, that's what inspired me. I actually ran up behind him and asked him: 'How do you get started?'"

Whitfield became a percussionist for an act called Popcorn and the Mohawks. The group had a minor local hit with Tamla Records, the predecessor to the Motown label. Both were launched in 1959 by Berry Gordy Jr., a Detroit autoworker, who hired Whitfield full time in 1962 to sift through the dozens of songs brought weekly to Motown's "Hitsville U.S.A." offices and recording studio. Whitfield's job was to weed out the potential hits. Motown's earliest chart successes came from such acts as the Miracles, whom Smokey Robinson originally fronted, Martha and the Vandellas,

At a Glance . . .

Born Norman Jesse Whitfield on May 12, 1940, in New York, NY; died of complications from diabetes on September 16, 2008, in Los Angeles, CA; children: Irasha, Norman, Michael, Johnnie, Roland.

Career: Motown Records, began in quality control, became songwriter and producer, until 1973; founded Whitfield Records, 1973.

Awards: Grammy Award for Best Rhythm & Blues Song, National Academy of Recording Arts and Sciences, 1972, for "Papa Was a Rollin' Stone" (with Barrett Strong); Grammy Award for Album of Best Original Score Written for a Motion Picture or Television Special, 1976, for *Car Wash.*

and the Supremes. The majority of the enduring, snappy three-minute hits were crafted by the songwriting team known as Holland/Dozier/Holland, named for brothers Brian and Eddie Holland and Lamont Dozier.

Whitfield cowrote his first Motown track with singer Marvin Gaye and songwriter William Stevenson. Recorded by Gaye in 1963, "Pride & Joy" became a minor hit. Subsequent songs that Whitfield wrote with lyricist Eddie Holland went on to success, and those sales figures gained him much-needed traction in the highly competitive company, which Gordy ruled in a high-handed style. Whitfield accrued an even better track record by producing the songs he wrote. The first of these, which came after a long stand-off with Robinson over songwriting and producing opportunities, was "Ain't Too Proud to Beg," which shot a relatively new Motown act called the Temptations to stardom in 1966. Whitfield became the main producer for the Tempts, as the quintet was known.

Sensing a shift in the pop-culture winds, Whitfield began writing longer, more serious songs with another Motown songwriter, Barrett Strong. The first of these was "I Wish It Would Rain," which gave the Temptations another No. 1 hit on the R&B charts in 1967. The duo also wrote "I Heard It Through the Grapevine," which was rumored to hint at the ongoing rivalry the two men had involving various female stars on the label. The song became a hit for Gladys Knight & the Pips in 1967 and an even bigger one for Marvin Gaye the following year.

In 1968 the Temptations' lead singer, David Ruffin, departed and was replaced by Dennis Edwards. Taking advantage of the change in line-up, Whitfield began

crafting a new sound which was soon dubbed "psychedelic soul." The first of these songs was "Cloud Nine," which earned the Motown label its first Grammy Award for Best Rhythm & Blues Group Performance, Vocal or Instrumental, in early 1969. Whitfield subsequently wrote and produced such hits for the Temptations as "Runaway Child, Running Wild," "Ball of Confusion (That's What the World Is Today)," and "Papa Was a Rollin' Stone," which earned another Grammy for the act. These and the rest of Whitfield's songs from this period were the first for the label to touch upon issues of social unrest. His biggest hit came after convincing Gordy to let Edwin Starr re-record a minor Temptations' song, "War," with a darker backing track. The Vietnam War protest song went to No. 1 on the U.S. singles chart after its release at the end of 1970.

Whitfield parted ways with Motown in 1973, a year after he and the label permanently relocated to Los Angeles. In 1976 he launched his own company, Whitfield Records, and had his biggest post-Motown hit with the song "Car Wash" in that same year. The song, which was issued on MCA Records, was recorded by a group called Rose Royce, who had originally been the backing band for Starr. It served as the theme song to the 1976 movie of the same name, which won the Grammy Award for Best Score Soundtrack Album in 1977. Whitfield reconnected with Motown during the early 1980s, working with the Temptations once again on their 1983 comeback LP, *Back to Basics.*

Little was heard from Whitfield for several years, when his name appeared in news reports in early 2005. He was convicted of failing to report royalty income to the Internal Revenue Service for a four-year period in 1990s. The amount was estimated at $2 million, but because Whitfield's health was already in decline, the judge sentenced him to six months of house arrest with a $25,000 fine. He lived in Toluca Lake, California, and died at the age of sixty-eight on September 16, 2008, at Cedars-Sinai Medical Center in Los Angeles. Speaking of the legacy of the hundreds of song credits he accrued both with the Motown label and on his own, Whitfield once reflected, according to the *Independent,* "Melodies and good lyrics are forever. The people make the songs what they are. As writers, we only do what we do and then we have to give it to the public. They're the ones who determine if you're a genius or a failure."

Selected discography

As songwriter

(With Marvin Gaye and William Stevenson) "Pride & Joy" (recorded by Marvin Gaye), 1963.
(With Eddie Holland) "Too Many Fish in the Sea" (recorded by the Marvelettes), 1964.
(With Holland) "Ain't Too Proud to Beg" (recorded by the Temptations), 1966.
(With Holland and Cornelius Grant) "(I Know) I'm Losing You" (recorded by the Temptations), 1966.

(With Barrett Strong) "I Heard It Through the Grapevine" (recorded by Gladys Knight & the Pips, Marvin Gaye, Creedence Clearwater Revival), 1967.

(With Strong and Roger Penzabene) "I Wish It Would Rain" (recorded by the Temptations), 1967.

(With Strong) "Cloud Nine" (recorded by the Temptations), 1968.

(With Sylvia Moy) "Ain't No Sun Since You've Been Gone" (recorded by Diana Ross & the Supremes), 1968.

(With Strong) "Runaway Child, Running Wild" (recorded by the Temptations), 1969.

(With Strong) "I Can't Get Next to You" (recorded by the Temptations), 1969.

(With Strong) "Ball of Confusion (That's What the World Is Today)" (recorded by the Temptations), 1970.

(With Strong) "War" (recorded by Edwin Starr), 1970.

(With Strong) "Just My Imagination (Running Away with Me)" (recorded by the Temptations), 1971.

(With Strong) "Papa Was a Rollin' Stone" (recorded by the Temptations), 1972.

"Car Wash" (recorded by Rose Royce), 1976.

As composer

Car Wash (film score), 1976.

Sources

Periodicals

Billboard, September 27, 2008, p. 10.
Detroit Free Press, September 18, 2008.
Independent (London), September 18, 2008, p. 36.
New York Times, September 18, 2008, p. B8.
Times (London), September 19, 2008, p. 83.
USA Today, September 18, 2008, p. D2.

—Carol Brennan

Michelle Williams

1980—

Singer, actor

Williams, Michelle, photograph. Yui Mok/PA Photos/Landov.

Michelle Williams became famous overnight when the unknown singer was hired to replace two of the original members of Destiny's Child, the immensely successful rhythm-and-blues (R&B) group that scored a string of hits in the 1990s. Williams joined what would go on to become the top-selling all-female R&B act of all time in early 2000 after internal discord within Destiny's Child resulted in the replacement of founding members LeToya Luckett and LaTavia Roberson. With the group's founding members, Beyoncé Knowles and Kelly Rowland, Williams helped Destiny's Child surpass the initial success of their first album, and all of the women subsequently went on to successful solo careers. "The best thing I take away is that I've gained two sisters who have my back," she told Gail Mitchell in *Billboard* in 2006 after the group had officially disbanded. "I learned about love and loyalty through good and bad, thick and thin."

Born Tenitra Michelle Williams on July 23, 1980, in Rockford, Illinois, Williams began singing as a child in the youth choir of her church, St. Paul Church of God in Christ. In her teens she performed as a duo with her sister Cameron in a group they called United Har-

mony. After graduating from Rockford's Auburn High School, Williams spent two years at Illinois State University as a criminal justice major before winning a slot as a backup singer for Monica, who had a hit with "The Boy Is Mine" with fellow R&B singer Brandy in 1998. Williams first met the members of Destiny's Child in the lobby of an Atlanta hotel when both groups were on tour. At the time, Destiny's Child was a quartet that had scored a massive hit with their debut single, "No, No, No," in 1997.

Won Grammy Award

The second Destiny's Child album, *The Writing's on the Wall,* was released in the summer of 1999 and went on to spend nearly two years on the Billboard 200 album chart. The flurry of hit singles that came out of it turned the four members into superstars, but Luckett and Roberson objected to some of the decisions made by their manager, who was also Knowles's father. When the video for the album's third single, "Say My Name," debuted in February of 2000, fans were stunned to see that Luckett and Roberson had been replaced by two new singers—Williams and Farrah

At a Glance . . .

Born Tenitra Michelle Williams on July 23, 1980, in Rockford, IL; daughter of Dennis (a financial company manager) and Anita (a missionary) Williams. *Education:* Attended Illinois State University, 1998(?)–2000(?).

Career: Backup singer for Monica, 1999(?); joined Destiny's Child, 2000; released first solo album, *Heart to Yours,* 2002; shareholder in the Chicago Sky, the Women's National Basketball Association franchise, since 2006.

Awards: Grammy Award (with Destiny's Child), best rhythm & blues performance by a duo or group with vocals, 2002.

Addresses: *Office*—c/o Music World Entertainment, 1384 Broadway, 22nd Fl., New York, NY 10018-0494.

Franklin. Franklin would leave the group a few months later, and Destiny's Child remained a trio from that point onward. "It was hard for me to come in," Williams recalled in the *Billboard* interview with Mitchell. "I was coming into an organization already in existence. I couldn't show myself weak, but it's hard when you know God has given you a talent and you want everybody to accept it. It turns out you can be stronger than what you think you are."

Once the turmoil and the rumors faded away, Destiny's Child went on to achieve even more impressive chart success. *Survivor,* the third album, was the first in which Williams played a full role as a vocalist on all of the tracks. "Everybody can basically hold their own," she told writer Margena A. Christian in *Jet* in 2001. "We're able to sing a cappella. We're able to do tricky harmonies and chords that before the group couldn't do.... With the three of us in the group there is no envy and no jealousy about who is going to sing lead and who is going to sing what. We support one another. We know who sounds the best at doing what." The debut single from *Survivor,* "Independent Women Part I," spent eleven weeks at the No. 1 spot on the Billboard Hot 100, while the album itself became one of the top-selling releases of 2001. Of the pointed lyrics on *Survivor*'s title track, Williams admitted in the *Jet* interview that they were indeed directed "at everybody who's ever said we wouldn't survive and that this group is going to self-destruct. That means even if it applies to everyone who was in the group who thought we

wouldn't make it without them. But, like Beyoncé wrote, we're still here." The song "Survivor" won Williams and her singing partners the 2001 Grammy Award for best R&B performance by a duo or group with vocals.

Following that intense period of success, the members of Destiny's Child took a break to work on some solo material. Williams's debut, *Heart to Yours,* came first in the spring of 2002, and it became the best-selling gospel album of the year, peaking at No. 1 on the Billboard gospel album chart. In 2003 she replaced Toni Braxton in the Broadway musical *Aida,* an updating of the Verdi opera with music and lyrics by Elton John and Tim Rice. A year later her second solo release, *Do You Know,* failed to repeat the chart success she had with her first gospel record, but a year later it was rereleased with a new marketing strategy. Williams believed that some of her more conservative fans may have been wary of her earlier R&B records and the content of some lyrics in them. "Some of my favorite Christian bookstores would not carry my record because of my association with Destiny's Child," she explained to writer Deborah Evans Price in *Billboard* in 2005. "The crazy thing is when I first came out, even with my second album, I was just wearing myself out trying to prove to the world that I really love God.... I know it's about protecting the integrity of gospel music, but I have integrity."

Began Acting Career

Williams reunited with Knowles and Rowland for another album, *Destiny Fulfilled,* which was released in 2004. Some music writers and fans perceived the title as the harbinger of the end for the group, and on the European leg of their world tour in 2005 they made it official. After a farewell performance in late 2005 the group officially disbanded. Williams moved on to an acting career, appearing on the UPN series *Half & Half* and taking over as Shug Avery in the Oprah Winfrey–produced Broadway musical adaptation of *The Color Purple* in 2007. She won excellent reviews, from Winfrey and from the trade journal *Variety,* in which critic Steven Oxman commended "a genuinely revelatory performance.... Shug tends to get overshadowed by the admirable Sofia, but not in this case. Williams brings an authentic glamour to the role, making it instantly believable that all the men in town would drop everything—including their families—to spend time just looking at her. And Williams' version of the songs—she goes straight from the sweet 'Too Beautiful for Words' to the burlesque 'Push Da Button'—stands out as contemporary and unique."

In the fall of 2008 Williams released another solo record, *Unexpected.* It was her first without a strong gospel or Christian theme, and its debut single, "We Break the Dawn," reached No. 1 on the Billboard dance chart. Williams told one interviewer that the album's title summed up her entire career to date. "The past nine years have taken some wonderful, unexpected twists and turns," she told Alisha Cowan in *Ebony*. "I want people to continue on that journey with me, so we're going to keep the party going with the album."

In 2008 Williams served as a judge on *Top Pop Group*, a reality talent-search contest on MTV. She was also a regular fixture courtside at Chicago Sky games as a part-owner of the Women's National Basketball Association franchise. Her future plans might include a return to school to finish her criminal justice degree, she told *Jet* in 2006. "I'm a 'Law & Order' chick, 'CSI' and '24.' My channel stays on A&E or TNT ... I love forensics and all that stuff. When I'm having a lazy day, that's what I do."

Selected works

Albums; with Destiny's Child

Survivor (includes "Independent Women Part I,"), Columbia, 2001.
8 Days of Christmas, Sony, 2001.
Destiny Fulfilled, Sony Urban Music/Columbia, 2004.

Albums; solo

Heart to Yours, Music World/Columbia, 2002.

Do You Know, Sony Urban/Music World/Columbia, 2004.
Unexpected (includes "We Break the Dawn"), Music World/Columbia, 2008.

Stage

Elton John and Tim Rice's Aida, Palace Theatre, New York City, 2003–04.
The Color Purple, Cadillac Palace Theatre, Chicago, 2007.

Sources

Periodicals

Billboard, April 9, 2005, p. 16; January 14, 2006, p. 29.
Ebony, September 2008, p. 34.
Jet, May 14, 2001, p. 56; May 29, 2006, p. 47; May 28, 2007, p. 34.
New York Times, August 1, 2005, p. E1.
Variety, May 14, 2007, p. 58.
W, October 2005.

—Carol Brennan

Serena Williams

1981—

Tennis player, clothing designer, actor

Williams, Serena, photograph. AP Images.

Serena Williams is a top-ranked tennis player who has been one of the sport's most exciting and closely watched players since her professional debut in 1995. With her older sister Venus, she formed half of a tennis-prodigy pair that began making headlines at an early age. As an African American in a historically white- and European-dominated sport, she found herself in the spotlight and under scrutiny. Serena and Venus Williams were coached by their father, Richard, an unorthodox career-builder whose methods stirred comment and controversy. Beyond all these reasons Serena Williams caught the attention of tennis fans simply because she was a player of extraordinary ability and dynamism. She rose to the top of her game achieving the number one ranking among female tennis players in the world and winning ten Grand Slam events by 2009.

Serena Williams was born in Saginaw, Michigan, on September 26, 1981, but she and her sister were raised in the economically depressed and often violence-riddled Los Angeles suburb of Compton. Her father, Richard Williams, ran a private security firm, and her mother Oracene (also called Brandy) was a nurse. A fan of televised tennis, Richard Williams dreamed of the opportunities that might await his offspring-to-be: "I went to my wife and said, 'Let's have kids and make them tennis players,'" he told Newsweek. Venus, born in 1980, and Serena, the youngest of the Williamses' five daughters, both showed promise from the start. "Venus and Serena took to tennis as soon as rackets were put in their hands," their older sister Lyndrea told Sport magazine.

Coached from Childhood by Her Father

The sisters' early training took place on public tennis courts in and around Compton, where they later remembered having to duck gunfire. Despite this difficult beginning, their skills developed rapidly. Williams entered her first tournament at age four, and over the next five years, her father has claimed, she won forty-six of forty-nine tournaments she entered. She succeeded Venus as the number-one player in the Southern California rankings for players under twelve years old, and well before reaching adolescence both sisters had attracted national attention in the form of

At a Glance . . .

Born on September 26, 1981, in Saginaw, MI; daughter of Richard (a security agency owner and tennis coach) and Oracene Williams (a nurse and tennis coach). *Religion:* Jehovah's Witness. *Education:* Attended the Art Institute of Fort Lauderdale.

Career: Professional tennis player, 1995—; actress, 2002—; clothing designer, 2003—.

Memberships: Women's Tennis Association.

Awards: Wimbledon Championships, mixed doubles, 1998, women's doubles, 2000, 2002, 2008, singles, 2002, 2003; U.S. Open Championships, mixed doubles, 1998, women's doubles, 1999; singles, 1999, 2002, 2008; French Open Championships, women's doubles, 1999, singles, 2002; Australian Open Championships, women's doubles, 2001, 2003, 2009, singles, 2003, 2005, 2007, 2009; Olympic gold medal, women's doubles tennis, 2000, 2008; Women's Tennis Association singles champion, 2001; Female Athlete of the Year, Associated Press, 2003; ESPY awards, 2003, for female tennis player of the year and female athlete of the year; Sportswoman of the Year, Laureus World Sports Academy, 2003.

Addresses: *Office*—Aneres, 4199 Maya Cay, Jupiter, FL 33458.

invitations to prestigious tennis camps, promises of lucrative product-endorsement deals, and glowing newspaper reportage.

In 1991 Richard Williams, who managed and coached his daughters, made the first of several unorthodox moves in regard to their career: he decided that they should enter no more tournaments on the national junior circuit. Junior tournaments are the usual path to stardom for young tennis players, so Williams's development as a player took place to some degree in isolation from her peers. Richard Williams has said that he hoped to avoid subjecting his daughters to competitive pressures, including an undertone of racial hostility. Serena and Venus were sent to the Florida tennis academy of teaching pro Ric Macci, who had also worked with teenage standouts Jennifer Capriati and Mary Pierce, and thanks to a clothing endorsement deal, the family was able to move to a rambling estate in Palm Beach Gardens, Florida. In 1993 both Williams

girls left school and continued their education at home.

After raising eyebrows by pulling his daughters out of the junior circuit, Richard Williams once again stirred talk in the tennis world by allowing them to turn professional at the age of fourteen. Banned from Women's Tennis Association (WTA) events at that age, Williams made her professional debut in October of 1995 at the non-WTA Bell Challenge in Vanier, Quebec, Canada, losing in less than an hour to a virtual unknown. However, her father, who has defenders as well as critics on the tennis circuit, offered constant encouragement, and the play of both sisters improved dramatically. "Nobody knows those girls better than their parents—the road they've gone on couldn't have been better selected," legendary coach Nick Bollettieri told *Newsweek.* Williams took 1996 off from tournament play but continued to train.

Rose in WTA Rankings

Williams's first professional match in the WTA was in Moscow in 1997, in which she was taken out in the first round by a highly ranked player. Many critics claimed that she did not have the talent of her older sister, who was climbing the ranks of the WTA, but that perception was soon to change. Williams qualified for an Ameritech-sponsored tournament in Chicago, where she was slated to face Pierce in the second round. At that time, Pierce was ranked number seven in the world. Williams staged a stunning upset over Pierce, beating her in only two sets. This advanced Williams to the quarterfinals, where she faced an even more difficult opponent, fourth-ranked Monica Seles. At first it seemed that Williams had given her all in the match against Pierce as she dropped the first set to Seles. Then, in a shocking turn of events, Williams rallied and won the next two sets, defeating Seles. Critics who had said that she showed little promise only a few weeks before, now spoke of her as the next rising WTA star. This perception of Williams's talent was reflected in her ranking, which jumped from 304 to 102 after the tournament. She finished 1997—her first full season with the WTA—as the ninety-ninth ranked player in the world.

By the following year Williams's world ranking had risen to twenty-one, and both Williams and her sister Venus were bona-fide celebrities. She served notice that her time had come when she advanced to the semifinals of a tournament in Sydney, Australia, by beating the third-ranked woman in the world, Lindsay Davenport. Williams was expected to do well in her first Grand Slam tournament, the Australian Open. (Grand Slam events are the four most important tournaments in tennis: the Australian Open [January-February], the French Open [May-June], Wimbledon [June-July], and the U.S. Open [August-September].) However, Williams had the bad luck of having to face her sister in the second round after ousting ninth-ranked Irina Spirlea in the first round.

Venus emerged victorious, and *Essence* magazine reported that she was heard to say, "I'm sorry I had to take you out, Serena," as the two sisters walked off the court. This was the first time that the public caught a glimpse of the relationship between the two sisters and how they worked not only to be the best for themselves, but also to motivate each other. "They haven't admitted to it, but there's definitely a competitiveness between Serena and Venus," former U.S. Open finalist Pam Shriver told *Sport*. "They motivate each other and feed off each other's successes. Venus's jump to a number ten ranking has definitely inspired Serena to improve her ranking," she continued. The sisters met again that year at the Italian Open, this time in the quarterfinals, where once again Venus took the victory.

Won First Grand Slam Title

Nineteen-ninety-eight continued to be an excellent year for Williams as she realized success beyond expectations. She began doubles play and won two doubles titles that year with Venus in Oklahoma City and Zurich. Her victory in Oklahoma City became Williams's first pro title in doubles, but it would not be her last. She also went on to win two mixed double titles (a man and a woman as a team) at Wimbledon and the U.S. Open with partner Max Mirnyi.

Nineteen-ninety-nine was a watershed year for Williams because she won her first singles title as well as a Grand Slam tournament. Ranked twenty-first in the world at the beginning of the year, Williams won her first singles title in February at the Paris Indoor tournament, defeating Amélie Mauresmo in three sets. From there Williams went on to win Indian Wells where she plowed through Davenport, Pierce, and number-seven ranked Steffi Graf to gain the victory. Williams was on a sixteen-match winning streak when she went against Venus again in the finals of a tournament in Miami, having defeated Seles, Amanda Coetzer, and number-one ranked Martina Hingis without losing a set. Despite losing to her sister again, Williams cracked the top ten in the rankings for the first time, becoming the ninth-best player in the world.

Williams's biggest match of the year, however, came when she entered the U.S. Open in August. Her road to the finals took her through fourth-ranked Seles and second-ranked Davenport. Once she had defeated them, she had to face number-one-ranked Hingis, and when the final match was over, Williams had won her first Grand Slam tournament in record-setting fashion. She became the lowest-ranked player to ever win the U.S. Open and only the second African-American woman to win a Grand Slam title. (The first was Althea Gibson in 1956.) The only thing Williams had not done yet was to beat her sister Venus, and that happened later in the year when the sisters met in the finals of the Grand Slam Cup, a tournament to which the best Grand Slam players of that year were invited. It seemed that nothing could stop Williams and that she was poised to take over the world of women's tennis.

Plagued by Injuries and Illness

Williams was forced to slow down at the end of 1999 when she began to have health issues that took her out of numerous matches. She withdrew from a tournament in Hilton Head, South Carolina, with inflammation of a tendon in her right knee and also left the quarterfinals at the German Open with a strained right elbow. Perhaps the most crushing moment for Williams came when she was forced to withdraw from Wimbledon with severe influenza and from the season-ending championship (which she had qualified to play in that year for the first time) with a back injury sustained in practice. Regardless of her inability to compete, Williams still ended the season ranked number four in the world and was prepared to rise even higher in 2000.

Williams's play during the 2000 season, however, was also affected by injury and health problems. While she was able to defend her Los Angeles title by defeating Hingis and Davenport and also won a title at Hanover, Germany, Williams suffered a ligament injury to her right knee that many suspect led to her defeat at the Paris Indoor tournament.

By June of 2000 Williams was healthier then she had been the entire season, and she qualified for Wimbledon. She quickly showed that she was back on track by advancing to the semifinals round and losing only thirteen games in five matches, the least number of games lost since Chris Evert in 1976. (Tennis matches are composed of sets, and sets are composed of games.) In the semifinals round however, Williams once again had to face her sister Venus. The *Star-Ledger* called the match "the event of the year in tennis and a watershed event for a sport that has spent more than a decade in the doldrums." The match ended up being a letdown to many—Venus won in two sets 6-2, 7-6—but it proved to Serena Williams that while she had won a Grand Slam title in the past, she still had room to improve on her game. She entered the Canadian Open in August and was dominating in a match against Hingis, but was forced to retire when one of the small bones in the base of her left foot became inflamed. This would be her most serious injury all season and would result in her withdrawal from the U.S. Open doubles competition during the semifinals round and completely from the championship. Even though Williams felt that she was not at the top of her game, she emerged from the 2000 season with two important wins: the doubles title at Wimbledon and the doubles gold medal at the Summer Olympics in Australia, both with her sister Venus as her partner.

Defeated Sister Venus in Wimbledon Final

The 2001 season started slowly for Williams when she lost twice to Hingis, once in Sydney and once at the Australian Open. She did, however, find victory again in the doubles tournament of the Australian Open with

Venus. As doubles partners, the Williams sisters seemed undefeatable. Yet while Venus continued to succeed early in the season, Williams continued down the familiar path she had traveled in 1999 and 2000, and she withdrew from the Paris Indoor tournament with fatigue and from the Scottsdale tournament with the flu. She won a title at Indian Wells over Kim Clijsters, but she fell to Capriati in the quarterfinals of the Miami tournament and withdrew from tournaments in Charleston, Madrid, and Rome because of knee injuries.

Williams bounced back to win the Canadian Open over third-ranked Capriati who had knocked her out of Wimbledon that year. Then Williams dominated the U.S. Open, defeating Davenport and Hingis on her way to the finals where she once again was matched up against her sister Venus. It was the first time that the sisters had ever met in a Grand Slam final and while the match-up proved to be much more exciting than their semifinal round in Wimbledon the previous year, Williams still walked away defeated by her older sister. Williams took the loss hard, but by the end of the season she was in peak form and—for the first time—was healthy enough to compete in the WTA Tour Championship, a tournament played by the top-ranking players at the end of each season. She advanced to the finals where she faced Davenport, but the match was never played because Davenport withdrew with a knee injury. Williams said she would have rather played the match to prove that she was the best player that year, but she still walked away with a major win, her first since the U.S. Open in 1999.

Finally, in 2002 Williams hit her stride and began to accumulate victories. She started off slowly with an ankle injury in the Australian Open, but went on to win the Miami Masters tournament, where she beat the three top players in the world (Hingis, Venus Williams, and Capriati) on the way to the title. From there Williams took the Italian Open victory from Capriati and then captured the French Open title, beating Venus for the first time in a Grand Slam competition and rising to number two in the world rankings, bested only by her sister. The siblings got a chance at a rematch later that year when they met in the final at Wimbledon, where Williams defeated Venus to take the title. To Williams, this was the most important win of her career to date, because, as she told the Sunday *Mercury,* "it has so much prestige and so much history." As in past years, Williams also competed with Venus in the doubles competition at Wimbledon and came away with another title, their fifth Grand Slam victory as a team.

Ranked as World #1 Tennis Player

After Wimbledon, Williams quickly snatched the number one ranking away from Venus and for the next year

held on to it with amazing play on the courts. She defeated Venus at the 2002 U.S. Open, for a third Grand Slam victory that year. She also won numerous other tournaments both in singles and doubles play including the Princess Cup in Tokyo and the Leipzig tournament, but ended up losing the WTA Tour Championship to Clijsters in two sets.

She started off strong in 2003 by winning her fourth straight Grand Slam event, once again beating Venus in the finals at the Australian Open, and becoming one of only five women to have ever held all four Grand Slam titles at one time. The Williams sisters took the doubles title as well at the Australian Open. Williams went on to win the Paris Indoor tournament and the Miami Masters tournament before losing in the Charleston tournament finals to Justine Henin-Hardenne (also known as Justine Henin), ending a twenty-one-match winning streak.

Williams reigned supreme in 2002 and early 2003. In the spring of 2003 Williams was named the Sportswoman of the Year by the Laureus World Sports Academy for her outstanding performance in tennis. Nonetheless, the early summer of 2003 was a roller coaster of failure and success. The first major setback came at the French Open in early June when Williams lost a rematch with Henin-Hardenne in the semifinal round. Williams made seventy-five unforced errors (that is, mistakes of her own and not those "forced" by the aggressive play of her opponent) and lost the match in three sets. Even worse for Williams, however, was the partisan crowd reaction that included heckling Williams when she challenged calls, or starting chants in favor of Henin-Hardenne, a European favorite. The heckling got so bad that it drove Williams to tears by the end of the match.

Pursued Interests outside of Tennis

Many people wondered if the French Open was the beginning of a downturn in Williams's play, but they were proved wrong a month later when Williams stormed back to win her second straight Wimbledon title, again facing Venus in the final. Shortly after her Wimbledon victory in July of 2003, Williams won two ESPY Awards, including Best Female Tennis Player and Best Female Athlete. She signed a five-year endorsement deal with Nike—rumored as high as $40 million—late in 2003. Although Williams won at Wimbledon, she reinjured her knee during doubles play and withdrew from other competitions that summer, including the Los Angeles tournament, the Canadian Open, and the U.S. Open.

To the dismay of some observers, Williams did not focus solely on her tennis career, but sought to diversify her life by pursuing side careers as a fashion designer and actress. She believed it was prudent to create a well-rounded life that could sustain her as she got older and eventually retired from professional tennis, particularly if her ability to compete was going to be compromised by injuries. As she told the *Los Angeles Times,* "I've never considered tennis as my only outlet. I've always liked doing different things when I was younger. I just never really liked focusing on tennis. I do see myself as a crossover." Williams's ventures outside of tennis included attending the Art Institute of Fort Lauderdale, designing clothing for her signature line, Aneres, with her sponsor Nike, and doing guest spots on television talk shows. She also acted on a variety of television shows, including *ER, Higglytown Heroes, Law and Order: SVU, My Wife and Kids, Avatar: The Last Airbender, Loonatics Unleashed,* and *The Division.* She appeared in the 2004 movie *Hair Show* as Agent Ross.

Williams was filming an episode of the television series *Street Time* when she learned of the death of her sister Yetunde Price in September of 2003. Price and a companion had been driving on a street in Compton, California, when she was shot. Reports indicated Price was caught in the crossfire of two gangs. Price was a divorced mother of three children, whom Williams and her sister Venus vowed to help raise.

Overcame Injuries to Win Major Tournaments

Following minor knee surgery, Williams returned to WTA play in 2004, claiming a third consecutive title at the Miami Masters tournament and winning the China Open. In 2005 she added a seventh Grand Slam singles title to her resume by defeating Davenport at the Australian Open. During the U.S. Open in September, however, Williams continued to have problems with her knee and played poorly. She lost to her sister, although Venus was ranked below Williams going into the match.

During the next eight months Williams played just four matches, with her only tournament being the Australian Open. She lost in the third round. By May of 2006 Williams's chronic knee injury caused her to withdraw from the French Open and from Wimbledon. She sank to 108th in the WTA Tour rankings.

In January of 2007 Williams believed she was healed and ready for the Australian Open. The tennis world was not expecting much from her, ranked eighty-first in the world when the tournament began. Nevertheless, Williams won this major tournament, pummeling Russian Maria Sharapova in the final, and giving Williams an eighth Grand Slam singles victory. In spite of her spectacular play in the Australian Open, Williams had difficulty overcoming Henin in the finals match at the Miami Masters tournament in March of that year. She did, however, and the win added a fourth Miami Masters title to her resumé. It was nearly a year before

Williams won her next titles in March of 2008, defeating Patty Schnyder in the Bangalore Open final and defeating Jelena Jankovic in the Miami Masters final. Williams won her third title of the year the following month in Charleston, defeating Vera Zvonareva in the Family Circle Cup final.

Dominated Pro Tennis with Sister Venus

In spite of Williams's strong play, Venus overpowered her at the 2008 Wimbledon final to win her fifth Wimbledon title. A few hours after the conclusion of their singles final, the Williams sisters teamed up in the women's doubles final, defeating Lisa Raymond of the United States and Samantha Stosur of Australia. At the 2008 Olympic games in Beijing, China the following month, the Williamses captured another doubles victory, winning the gold as they had done eight years prior in Sydney, Australia. In the final match of the Beijing competition, the Williams sisters beat the Spanish team of Anabel Medina Garrigues and Virginia Ruano Pascual.

In September of 2008 Serena Williams again became the top-ranked female tennis player in the world. She achieved this ranking, rising from number three, by winning her third U.S. Open title, beating Jankovic in the championship match. Williams told Karen Crouse in the *New York Times* "I feel like I have a new career, like I feel so young and I feel so energized to play every week and to play every tournament. I feel like there's just so much that I can do in my career yet."

She succeeded at the following Grand Slam event, the Australian Open in January-February 2009, winning both the doubles championship with Venus and the singles championship. With her $1.3 million prize money for the singles tournament, Williams had earned an estimated $23.5 million and was ranked as the top-grossing female athlete of all time. She used some of her earnings to fund charity works, and in 2008 sponsored a secondary school in the Maukena district of Kenya, which opened in 2009 and was named in her honor. The dominance of the Williams sisters was seen as a good thing for women's tennis. Former tennis champion Billie Jean King commented in *USA Today,* "Every day that they are active and visible in tennis the sport is stronger. They have the 'it' factor, and people want to see that and will always support it."

Sources

Periodicals

Arizona Republic, September 5, 1998, C2.

Associated Press, April 21, 2008.

Courier-Mail (Brisbane, Australia), July 18, 2003, p. 8.

Daily News (New York), January 28, 2007, p. 60.

Daily Telegraph (London), May 27, 2002, p. 14.

Essence, August 1998, p. 78.

Jet, September 21, 1998, p. 49.

Knight Ridder/Tribune News Service, July 7, 2000; June 8, 2002; June 5, 2003; June 23, 2003; July 20, 2003.

Los Angeles Times, October 30, 2002, p. E1; August 18, 2008, p. S5.

News of the World (London), August 3, 2003, p. 73.

Newsweek, August 24, 1998, p. 44.

New York Post, September 18, 2003, p. 27.

New York Times, March 16, 1997; September 5, 2005; September 8, 2008.

Rocky Mountain News (Denver, CO), September 29, 2000, p. 4Q.

Sport, July 1998, p. 70.

Sports Illustrated, June 13, 1994, p. 10.

Star-Ledger (Newark, NJ), July 6, 2000, p. 33; June 14, 2003, p. 30; July 25, 2003, p. 52.

St. Louis Post-Dispatch, February 9, 2001, p. E1.

Sun (London), September 19, 2003, p. 13.

Sunday Mercury (Birmingham, England), July 7, 2002, pp. 4-5.

Times (London), May 21, 2003, p. 41.

Wall Street Journal, August 31, 1998, p. A17.

Washington Times, November 1, 1995, p. B3.

Online

Serena Williams Official MySpace, January 19, 2009, http://www.myspace.com/serenawilliams (accessed February 8, 2009).

Serena Williams Official Site, 2009, http://serena williams.com/ (accessed February 8, 2009).

"Serena Williams Stats, News, Photos, Record," ESPN, February 2009, http://sports.espn.go.com/sports/tennis/players/profile?playerId=394 (accessed February 8, 2009).

"Serena Williams (USA)," Sony Ericsson WTA Tour, February 2, 2009, http://www.sonyericssonwtatour.com/2/players/playerprofiles/PlayerBio.asp?PlayerID=230234 (accessed February 8, 2009).

—James M. Manheim, Ralph G. Zerbonia, and Sandra Alters

Maury Wills

1932—

Professional baseball player, baseball coach, sports commentator

Wills, Maury, photograph. Robbie Rogers/MLB Photos via Getty Images.

Widely considered to have been one of the best base-stealers in the history of baseball, Maury Wills spent fourteen seasons in the major leagues, most of them with the Los Angeles Dodgers. Though best known for breaking Ty Cobb's long-standing record for the most stolen bases in a season, Wills also excelled on defense, winning several awards for his prowess at the crucial position of shortstop. He has had mixed success in his subsequent career, but he has remained one of the nation's most prominent and popular sports personalities.

The seventh of thirteen children born to a Baptist minister and his wife, Maurice Morning Wills was born in October of 1932 in Washington, DC. After attending public schools in that city, he signed his first minor-league contract in 1949, when he was only seventeen years old. A decade later he made his major league debut as a shortstop with the Los Angeles Dodgers in June of 1959. In eighty-three games that season, which ended with a victory for the Dodgers in the World Series, Wills had a respectable batting average of .260 but stole only seven bases. His performance improved markedly the following year, with a batting average of .295 and fifty stolen bases. While his record on offense declined slightly in 1961, with thirty-five stolen bases and an average of .282, that season brought him the first of his Gold Gloves, an annual award sponsored by the Rawlings sporting-goods company. While Gold Gloves are awarded for each of the nine defensive positions, competition for the honor is particularly intense among shortstops, whose fielding abilities are a critical and highly visible component of any effective defense.

Wills's career peaked in 1962. Besides winning a second Gold Glove, he had an impressive .299 batting average. It was his achievement as a base runner, however, that drew national attention and earned him the title of Most Valuable Player in the National League. The legendary Ty Cobb's record of 96 stolen bases in a season had stood for almost half a century when Wills broke it toward the end of the 1962 season; he ended the year with 104. Even though that record was broken by Lou Brock in 1974, Wills's accomplishment is still widely remembered, largely because Cobb's record had been considered nearly unbreakable.

At a Glance . . .

Born Maurice Morning Wills on October 2, 1932, in Washington, DC; son of a Baptist minister.

Career: Variety of minor-league teams, shortstop, 1949–58; Los Angeles Dodgers, shortstop, 1959–66, 1969–72; Pittsburgh Pirates, shortstop, 1967–68; Montreal Expos, shortstop, 1969; variety of teams, base-running coach, 1970s–2008; National Broadcasting Company, baseball commentator, 1973–77; Seattle Mariners, manager, 1980–81; freelance career as a celebrity spokesperson and endorser, 1960s—.

Awards: Most Valuable Player, National League, 1962; Gold Glove Award, Rawlings Group, 1961 and 1962; Council of the District of Columbia, declaration of Maury Wills Day in the District of Columbia, April 4, 2004.

Addresses: *Office*—c/o M&R Sports Marketing LLP, 5 Dalton Valley Dr., St. Peters, MO 63376. *Web*—http://www.maurywills.com.

Wills remained with the Dodgers through the end of the 1966 season. His performance there never again reached the level of 1962, but he played a major role in two more World Series victories (1963 and 1965). He was then traded to the Pittsburgh Pirates, where he played for two seasons before being selected in an expansion draft by the Montreal Expos. After playing forty-seven games for the Expos in 1969, their first season, he was traded back to the Dodgers, for whom he played until his retirement at the end of the 1972 season. He would finish his career with 2,134 hits, 1,067 runs, and 586 stolen bases. In an interview with Dave Anderson in the *New York Times,* Joe Morgan, an outstanding second baseman who often played against Wills, offered an assessment of Wills's impact on the sport. "Maury brought back the stolen base," Morgan said. "He changed the dynamics of the game…. When Maury was on first base, you had to pay attention to him *every* pitch."

Despite his retirement, Wills remained closely connected to professional baseball. For example, from 1973 to 1977 he served as a color commentator and analyst on NBC's *Game of the Week,* which was then one of the nation's premier baseball broadcasts. He also worked extensively as a base-running coach. Because these assignments were often on a temporary, freelance basis, he was able to work with no less than fifteen professional teams in the United States and Japan between the 1970s and 2008. Despite his considerable success as a coach, Wills often expressed the desire to work as a manager. He was given a chance to do so in 1980, when, with the Seattle Mariners, he became only the third African-American manager in major league history. His brief stay in Seattle was not a success, and he was roundly criticized in the media before being fired the following year. As his defenders have often pointed out, however, the Mariners were already one of the weakest teams in the league when Wills took charge.

In the wake of his dismissal from the Mariners, Wills turned increasingly to drugs and alcohol. By his own account, his addictions grew steadily worse until he was arrested in Los Angeles for cocaine possession in 1983. Though the charges were eventually dropped, the incident did considerable, if largely temporary, damage to his public persona. Wills subsequently completed a rehabilitation program and, with the help of Mike Celizic, published the memoir *On the Run: The Never Dull and Often Shocking Life of Maury Wills* (1991), which focused on his experiences with addiction and recovery. According to his Web site, he has since devoted considerable time to drug and alcohol education, notably through his involvement with the national program called Red Ribbon Week.

Since 2002, the thirtieth anniversary of Wills's retirement, there has been considerable speculation in the media regarding his chances for induction into the National Baseball Hall of Fame in Cooperstown, New York. The selection process is a complicated one, with ballots cast by both the Baseball Writers' Association of America and living hall of famers. A candidate must be selected by 75 percent of the ballots to win induction. Though Wills's career statistics are comparable with many players already in the Hall of Fame, as of early 2009 he had not yet won enough votes. Among fans and baseball professionals, however, there seemed to be a strong consensus that his induction was only a matter of time. For example, in June of 2008 Morgan, himself a hall of famer, told Gordon Wittenmyer in the *Chicago Sun-Times* that Wills's eventual induction was a "no-brainer."

Selected works

(With Mike Celizic) *On the Run: The Never Dull and Often Shocking Life of Maury Wills,* Carroll and Graf, 1991.

Sources

Periodicals

Chicago Sun-Times, June 24, 2008.
New York Times, August 11, 1980; April 7, 1991; March 13, 2002.

Online

Hill, Justice B., "Cooperstown Case for Wills Far More Than Just Stolen Bases," National Baseball Hall of Fame, February 25, 2007, http://web.archive.org/web/20070423154219/http://www.baseballhalloffame.org/news/2007/election/vc/wills.htm (accessed December 2, 2008).

"Maury Wills," Baseball-Reference.com, October 30, 2008, http://www.baseball-reference.com/w/willsma01.shtml (accessed December 2, 2008).

"Maury Wills Biography," Maury Wills Web site, http://maurywills.com/MW/Bio.aspx (accessed December 2, 2008).

—R. Anthony Kugler

Cumulative Nationality Index

Volume numbers appear in **bold**

American

Aaliyah **30**
Aaron, Hank **5**
Abbott, Robert Sengstacke **27**
Abdul-Jabbar, Kareem **8**
Abdur-Rahim, Shareef **28**
Abele, Julian **55**
Abernathy, Ralph David **1**
Aberra, Amsale **67**
Abu-Jamal, Mumia **15**
Ace, Johnny **36**
Adams, Eula L. **39**
Adams, Floyd, Jr. **12**
Adams, Jenoyne **60**
Adams, Johnny **39**
Adams, Leslie **39**
Adams, Oleta **18**
Adams, Osceola Macarthy **31**
Adams, Sheila J. **25**
Adams, Yolanda **17, 67**
Adams-Campbell, Lucille L. **60**
Adams Earley, Charity **13, 34**
Adams-Ender, Clara **40**
Adderley, Julian "Cannonball" **30**
Adderley, Nat **29**
Adkins, Rod **41**
Adkins, Rutherford H. **21**
Adu, Freddy **67**
Agyeman, Jaramogi Abebe **10, 63**
Ailey, Alvin **8**
Akil, Mara Brock **60**
Akon **68**
Al-Amin, Jamil Abdullah **6**
Albright, Gerald **23**
Alcorn, George Edward, Jr. **59**
Alert, Kool DJ Red **33**
Alexander, Archie Alphonso **14**
Alexander, Clifford **26**
Alexander, Joyce London **18**
Alexander, Khandi **43**
Alexander, Margaret Walker **22**
Alexander, Sadie Tanner Mossell **22**
Alexander, Shaun **58**
Ali, Hana Yasmeen **52**
Ali, Laila **27, 63**
Ali, Muhammad **2, 16, 52**
Ali, Tatyana **73**
Allain, Stephanie **49**
Allen, Byron **3, 24**
Allen, Claude **68**
Allen, Debbie **13, 42**
Allen, Ethel D. **13**
Allen, Marcus **20**

Allen, Robert L. **38**
Allen, Samuel W. **38**
Allen, Tina **22**
Allen-Buillard, Melba **55**
Alston, Charles **33**
Amaker, Norman **63**
Amaker, Tommy **62**
Amerie **52**
Ames, Wilmer **27**
Amos, Emma **63**
Amos, John **8, 62**
Amos, Wally **9**
Anderson, Anthony **51**
Anderson, Carl **48**
Anderson, Charles Edward **37**
Anderson, Eddie "Rochester" **30**
Anderson, Elmer **25**
Anderson, Jamal **22**
Anderson, Lauren **72**
Anderson, Marian **2, 33**
Anderson, Michael P. **40**
Anderson, Mike **63**
Anderson, Norman B. **45**
Anderson, William G(ilchrist), D.O. **57**
Andrews, Benny **22, 59**
Andrews, Bert **13**
Andrews, Raymond **4**
Angelou, Maya **1, 15**
Ansa, Tina McElroy **14**
Anthony, Carmelo **46**
Anthony, Wendell **25**
Appiah, Kwame Anthony **67**
Archer, Dennis **7, 36**
Archie-Hudson, Marguerite **44**
Ardoin, Alphonse **65**
Arkadie, Kevin **17**
Armstrong, Louis **2**
Armstrong, Robb **15**
Armstrong, Vanessa Bell **24**
Arnez J **53**
Arnold, Tichina **63**
Arnwine, Barbara **28**
Arrington, Richard **24**
Arroyo, Martina **30**
Artest, Ron **52**
Asante, Molefi Kete **3**
Ashanti **37**
Ashe, Arthur **1, 18**
Ashford, Emmett **22**
Ashford, Evelyn **63**
Ashford, Nickolas **21**
Ashley-Ward, Amelia **23**
Asim, Jabari **71**

Atkins, Cholly **40**
Atkins, Erica **34**
Atkins, Juan **50**
Atkins, Russell **45**
Atkins, Tina **34**
Aubert, Alvin **41**
Auguste, Donna **29**
Austin, Gloria **63**
Austin, Jim **63**
Austin, Junius C. **44**
Austin, Lovie **40**
Austin, Patti **24**
Autrey, Wesley **68**
Avant, Clarence **19**
Avery, Byllye Y. **66**
Ayers, Roy **16**
Babatunde, Obba **35**
Bacon-Bercey, June **38**
Badu, Erykah **22**
Bahati, Wambui **60**
Bailey, Buster **38**
Bailey, Chauncey **68**
Bailey, Clyde **45**
Bailey, DeFord **33**
Bailey, Philip **63**
Bailey, Radcliffe **19**
Bailey, Xenobia **11**
Baines, Harold **32**
Baiocchi, Regina Harris **41**
Baisden, Michael **25, 66**
Baker, Anita **21, 48**
Baker, Augusta **38**
Baker, Dusty **8, 43, 72**
Baker, Ella **5**
Baker, Gwendolyn Calvert **9**
Baker, Houston A., Jr. **6**
Baker, Josephine **3**
Baker, LaVern **26**
Baker, Maxine B. **28**
Baker, Thurbert **22**
Baker, Vernon Joseph **65**
Baldwin, James **1**
Ballance, Frank W. **41**
Ballard, Allen Butler, Jr. **40**
Ballard, Hank **41**
Baltimore, Richard Lewis, III **71**
Bambaataa, Afrika **34**
Bambara, Toni Cade **10**
Bandele, Asha **36**
Banks, Ernie **33**
Banks, Jeffrey **17**
Banks, Michelle **59**
Banks, Paula A. **68**
Banks, Tyra **11, 50**

Banks, William **11**
Banner, David **55**
Baquet, Dean **63**
Baraka, Amiri **1, 38**
Barbee, Lloyd Augustus **71**
Barber, Ronde **41**
Barber, Tiki **57**
Barboza, Anthony **10**
Barclay, Paris **37**
Barden, Don H. **9, 20**
Barker, Danny **32**
Barkley, Charles **5, 66**
Barlow, Roosevelt **49**
Barnes, Roosevelt "Booba" **33**
Barnes, Steven **54**
Barnett, Amy Du Bois **46**
Barnett, Etta Moten **56**
Barnett, Marguerite **46**
Barney, Lem **26**
Barnhill, David **30**
Barrax, Gerald William **45**
Barrett, Andrew C. **12**
Barrett, Jacquelyn **28**
Barrino, Fantasia **53**
Barry, Marion S(hepilov, Jr.) **7, 44**
Barthe, Richmond **15**
Basie, Count **23**
Basquiat, Jean-Michel **5**
Bass, Charlotta Spears **40**
Bass, Karen **70**
Bassett, Angela **6, 23, 62**
Bates, Daisy **13**
Bates, Karen Grigsby **40**
Bates, Peg Leg **14**
Bath, Patricia E. **37**
Batiste, Alvin **66**
Battle, Kathleen **70**
Baugh, David **23**
Baylor, Don **6**
Baylor, Helen **36**
Beach, Michael **26**
Beal, Bernard B. **46**
Beals, Jennifer **12**
Beals, Melba Patillo **15**
Bearden, Romare **2, 50**
Beasley, Jamar **29**
Beasley, Phoebe **34**
Beatty, Talley **35**
Bechet, Sidney **18**
Beckford, Tyson **11, 68**
Beckham, Barry **41**
Belafonte, Harry **4, 65**
Bell, Derrick **6**
Bell, James "Cool Papa" **36**

Bell, James A. **50**
Bell, James Madison **40**
Bell, Michael **40**
Bell, Robert Mack **22**
Bellamy, Bill **12**
Bellamy, Terry **58**
Belle, Albert **10**
Belle, Regina **1, 51**
Belton, Sharon Sayles **9, 16**
Benberry, Cuesta **65**
Benét, Eric **28**
Ben-Israel, Ben Ami **11**
Benjamin, Andre **45**
Benjamin, Regina **20**
Benjamin, Tritobia Hayes **53**
Bennett, George Harold "Hal" **45**
Bennett, Gwendolyn B. **59**
Bennett, Lerone, Jr. **5**
Benson, Angela **34**
Bentley, Lamont **53**
Berry, Halle **4, 19, 57**
Berry, Bertice **8, 55**
Berry, Chuck **29**
Berry, Fred "Rerun" **48**
Berry, Mary Frances **7**
Berry, Theodore **31**
Berrysmith, Don Reginald **49**
Bethune, Mary McLeod **4**
Betsch, MaVynee **28**
Bettis, Jerome **64**
Beverly, Frankie **25**
Beyoncé **39, 70**
Bibb, Eric **49**
Bibb, Henry and Mary **54**
Bickerstaff, Bernie **21**
Biggers, John **20, 33**
Biggers, Sanford **62**
Bing, Dave **3, 59**
Birch, Glynn R. **61**
Bishop, Sanford D., Jr. **24**
Bivins, Michael **72**
Black, Albert **51**
Black, Barry C. **47**
Black, Keith Lanier **18**
Black Thought **63**
Blackburn, Robert **28**
Blackmon, Brenda **58**
Blackshear, Leonard **52**
Blackwell, Kenneth, Sr. **61**
Blackwell, Robert D., Sr. **52**
Blackwell, Unita **17**
Blacque, Taurean **58**
Blair, Jayson **50**
Blair, Paul **36**
Blake, Asha **26**
Blake, Eubie **29**
Blake, James **43**
Blakey, Art **37**
Blanchard, Terence **43**
Bland, Bobby "Blue" **36**
Bland, Eleanor Taylor **39**
Blanks, Billy **22**
Blanks, Deborah K. **69**
Blanton, Dain **29**
Blassingame, John Wesley **40**
Blayton, Jesse B., Sr. **55**
Bleu, Corbin **65**
Blige, Mary J. **20, 34, 60**
Blockson, Charles L. **42**
Blow, Charles M. **73**
Blow, Kurtis **31**
Bluford, Guy **2, 35**
Bluitt, Juliann S. **14**

Bobo, Lawrence **60**
Bogle, Donald **34**
Bogues, Tyrone "Muggsy" **56**
Bolden, Buddy **39**
Bolden, Charles F., Jr. **7**
Bolden, Frank E. **44**
Bolden, Tonya **32**
Bolin, Jane **22, 59**
Bolton, Terrell D. **25**
Bolton-Holifield, Ruthie **28**
Bond, Beverly **53**
Bond, Julian **2, 35**
Bonds, Barry **6, 34, 63**
Bonds, Bobby **43**
Bonds, Margaret **39**
Bonet, Lisa **58**
Bontemps, Arna **8**
Booker, Cory Anthony **68**
Booker, Simeon **23**
Borders, James **9**
Bosley, Freeman, Jr. **7**
Boston, Kelvin E. **25**
Boston, Lloyd **24**
Bow Wow **35**
Bowe, Riddick **6**
Bowman, Bertie **71**
Bowser, Yvette Lee **17**
Boyd, Edward **70**
Boyd, Gerald M. **32, 59**
Boyd, Gwendolyn **49**
Boyd, John W., Jr. **20, 72**
Boyd, T. B., III **6**
Boykin, Keith **14**
Bradley, David Henry, Jr. **39**
Bradley, Ed **2, 59**
Bradley, J. Robert **65**
Bradley, Jennette B. **40**
Bradley, Thomas **2, 20**
Brady, Wayne **32, 71**
Brae, C. Michael **61**
Braithwaite, William Stanley **52**
Branch, William Blackwell **39**
Brand, Elton **31**
Brandon, Barbara **3**
Brandon, Terrell **16**
Brandy **14, 34, 72**
Branham, George, III **50**
Brashear, Carl **29**
Brashear, Donald **39**
Braugher, Andre **13, 58**
Braun, Carol Moseley **4, 42**
Brawley, Benjamin **44**
Braxton, Toni **15, 61**
Brazile, Donna **25, 70**
Bridges, Sheila **36**
Bridges, Todd **37**
Bridgewater, Dee Dee **32**
Bridgforth, Glinda **36**
Brimmer, Andrew F. **2, 48**
Briscoe, Connie **15**
Briscoe, Marlin **37**
Britt, Donna **28**
Broadbent, Hydeia **36**
Brock, Lou **18**
Bronner, Nathaniel H., Sr. **32**
Brooke, Edward **8**
Brooks, Tyrone **59**
Brooks, Aaron **33**
Brooks, Avery **9**
Brooks, Derrick **43**
Brooks, Golden **62**
Brooks, Gwendolyn **1, 28**
Brooks, Hadda **40**

Brooks, Mehcad **62**
Brower, William **49**
Brown, Angela M. **54**
Brown, Anthony G. **72**
Brown, Bobby **58**
Brown, Byrd **49**
Brown, Byron W. **72**
Brown, Cecil M. **46**
Brown, Charles **23**
Brown, Clarence Gatemouth **59**
Brown, Claude **38**
Brown, Cora **33**
Brown, Corrine **24**
Brown, Cupcake **63**
Brown, Donald **19**
Brown, Eddie C. **35**
Brown, Elaine **8**
Brown, Erroll M. **23**
Brown, Foxy **25**
Brown, George Leslie **62**
Brown, Homer S. **47**
Brown, James **15, 60**
Brown, James **22**
Brown, Janice Rogers **43**
Brown, Jesse **6, 41**
Brown, Jesse Leroy **31**
Brown, Jim **11**
Brown, Joe **29**
Brown, Joyce F. **25**
Brown, Lee Patrick **1, 24**
Brown, Les **5**
Brown, Lloyd Louis **42**
Brown, Marie Dutton **12**
Brown, Nappy **73**
Brown, Oscar, Jr. **53**
Brown, Patrick "Sleepy" **50**
Brown, Robert **65**
Brown, Ron **5**
Brown, Sterling Allen **10, 64**
Brown, Tony **3**
Brown, Uzee **42**
Brown, Vivian **27**
Brown, Warren **61**
Brown, Wesley **23**
Brown, Willa **40**
Brown, Willard **36**
Brown, Willie L., Jr. **7**
Brown, Zora Kramer **12**
Browne, Roscoe Lee **66**
Broyard, Anatole **68**
Broyard, Bliss **68**
Bruce, Blanche Kelso **33**
Bruce, Bruce **56**
Bruce, Isaac **26**
Brunson, Dorothy **1**
Bryan, Ashley F. **41**
Bryant, John **26**
Bryant, John R. **45**
Bryant, Kobe **15, 31, 71**
Bryant, Wayne R. **6**
Bryant, William Benson **61**
Buchanan, Ray **32**
Buckley, Gail Lumet **39**
Buckley, Victoria (Vikki) **24**
Bullard, Eugene **12**
Bullins, Ed **25**
Bullock, Steve **22**
Bully-Cummings, Ella **48**
Bumbry, Grace **5**
Bunche, Ralph J. **5**
Bunkley, Anita Richmond **39**
Burgess, John **46**
Burgess, Marjorie L. **55**

Burke, Selma **16**
Burke, Solomon **31**
Burke, Yvonne Braithwaite **42**
Burks, Mary Fair **40**
Burleigh, Henry Thacker **56**
Burnett, Charles **16, 68**
Burnim, Mickey L. **48**
Burns, Eddie **44**
Burns, Ursula **60**
Burnside, R.L. **56**
Burrell, Tom **21, 51**
Burris, Chuck **21**
Burris, Roland W. **25**
Burroughs, Margaret Taylor **9**
Burrows, Stephen **31**
Burrus, William Henry "Bill" **45**
Burt-Murray, Angela **59**
Burton, LeVar **8**
Busby, Jheryl **3**
Bush, Reggie **59**
Butler, George, Jr. **70**
Butler, Jerry **26**
Butler, Leroy, III **17**
Butler, Louis **70**
Butler, Octavia **8, 43, 58**
Butler, Paul D. **17**
Butts, Calvin O., III **9**
Bynoe, Peter C.B. **40**
Bynum, Juanita **31, 71**
Byrd, Donald **10**
Byrd, Eugene **64**
Byrd, Michelle **19**
Byrd, Robert **11**
Cadoria, Sherian Grace **14**
Caesar, Shirley **19**
Cage, Byron **53**
Cain, Herman **15**
Caldwell, Benjamin **46**
Caldwell, Earl **60**
Caldwell, Kirbyjon **55**
Callender, Clive O. **3**
Calloway, Cab **14**
Camp, Kimberly **19**
Campanella, Roy **25**
Campbell, Bebe Moore **6, 24, 59**
Campbell, Bill **9**
Campbell, Donald J. **66**
Campbell, E. Simms **13**
Campbell, Mary Schmidt **43**
Campbell-Martin, Tisha **8, 42**
Canada, Geoffrey **23**
Canady, Alexa **28**
Cannon, Katie **10**
Cannon, Nick **47, 73**
Cannon, Reuben **50**
Carr, Johnnie **69**
Cardozo, Francis L. **33**
Carew, Rod **20**
Carey, Mariah **32, 53, 69**
Cargill, Victoria A. **43**
Carr, Kurt **56**
Carr, Leroy **49**
Carroll, Diahann **9**
Carroll, L. Natalie **44**
Carruthers, George R. **40**
Carson, André **69**
Carson, Benjamin **1, 35**
Carson, Julia **23, 69**
Carson, Lisa Nicole **21**
Carter, Anson **24**
Carter, Benny **46**
Carter, Betty **19**
Carter, Butch **27**

Carter, Cris 21
Carter, Joe 30
Carter, Joye Maureen 41
Carter, Kenneth 53
Carter, Mandy 11
Carter, Nell 39
Carter, Pamela Lynn 67
Carter, Regina 23
Carter, Robert L. 51
Carter, Rubin 26
Carter, Stephen L. 4
Carter, Vince 26
Carter, Warrick L. 27
Cartey, Wilfred 1992 47
Cartiér, Xam Wilson 41
Carver, George Washington 4
Cary, Lorene 3
Cary, Mary Ann Shadd 30
Cash, Rosalind 28
Cash, Swin 59
Cashin, Sheryll 63
CasSelle, Malcolm 11
Catchings, Tamika 43
Catlett, Elizabeth 2
Cayton, Horace 26
Cedric the Entertainer 29, 60
Cee-Lo 70
Chadiha, Jeffri 57
Chamberlain, Wilt 18, 47
Chambers, Julius 3
Chaney, John 67
Chapman, Nathan A., Jr. 21
Chapman, Tracy 26
Chappell, Emma 18
Chappelle, Dave 50
Charles, Ray 16, 48
Charleston, Oscar 39
Chase, Debra Martin 49
Chase, Leah 57
Chase-Riboud, Barbara 20, 46
Chatard, Peter 44
Chavis, Benjamin 6
Cheadle, Don 19, 52
Checker, Chubby 28
Cheeks, Maurice 47
Chenault, John 40
Chenault, Kenneth I. 4, 36
Cherry, Deron 40
Chesnutt, Charles 29
Chestnut, J. L., Jr. 73
Chestnut, Morris 31
Chideya, Farai 14, 61
Childress, Alice 15
Chinn, May Edward 26
Chisholm, Samuel 32
Chisholm, Shirley 2, 50
Christian, Barbara T. 44
Christian, Spencer 15
Christian-Green, Donna M. 17
Christie, Angella 36
Chuck D 9
Ciara 56
Ciara, Barbara 69
Clack, Zoanne 73
Claiborne, Loretta 34
Clark, Celeste 15
Clark, Joe 1
Clark, Kenneth B. 5, 52
Clark, Mattie Moss 61
Clark, Patrick 14
Clark, Septima 7
Clark-Cole, Dorinda 66
Clarke, Cheryl 32

Clarke, Hope 14
Clarke, John Henrik 20
Clarke, Kenny 27
Clark-Sheard, Karen 22
Clash, Kevin 14
Clay, Bryan Ezra 57
Clay, William Lacy 8
Clayton, Constance 1
Clayton, Eva M. 20
Clayton, Mayme Agnew 62
Clayton, Xernona 3, 45
Claytor, Helen 14, 52
Cleage, Pearl 17, 64
Cleaver, Eldridge 5
Cleaver, Emanuel 4, 45, 68
Cleaver, Kathleen 29
Clements, George 2
Clemmons, Reginal G. 41
Clemons, Clarence 41
Clemons, Michael "Pinball" 64
Clendenon, Donn 26, 56
Cleveland, James 19
Cliff, Michelle 42
Clifton, Lucille 14, 64
Clifton, Nathaniel "Sweetwater" 47
Clinton, George 9
Clyburn, James E. 21, 71
Coachman, Alice 18
Cobb, Jewel Plummer 42
Cobb, W. Montague 39
Cobb, William Jelani 59
Cobbs, Price M. 9
Cochran, Johnnie 11, 39, 52
Cohen, Anthony 15
Colbert, Virgis William 17
Cole, Johnnetta B. 5, 43
Cole, Keyshia 63
Cole, Lorraine 48
Cole, Nat King 17
Cole, Natalie 17, 60
Cole, Rebecca 38
Coleman, Bessie 9
Coleman, Donald 24, 62
Coleman, Gary 35
Coleman, Ken 57
Coleman, Leonard S., Jr. 12
Coleman, Mary 46
Coleman, Michael B. 28
Coleman, Ornette 39, 69
Coleman, Wanda 48
Coleman, William F., III 61
Colemon, Johnnie 11
Colescott, Robert 69
Collins, Albert 12
Collins, Barbara-Rose 7
Collins, Bootsy 31
Collins, Cardiss 10
Collins, Janet 33, 64
Collins, Lyn 53
Collins, Marva 3, 71
Collins, Patricia Hill 67
Collins, Paul 61
Colston, Hal 72
Colter, Cyrus J. 36
Coltrane, Alice 70
Coltrane, John 19
Coltrane, Ravi 71
Combs, Sean "Puffy" 17, 43
Comer, James P. 6
Common 31, 63
Cone, James H. 3
Coney, PonJola 48
Connerly, Ward 14

Conyers, John, Jr. 4
Conyers, Nathan G. 24, 45
Cook, (Will) Mercer 40
Cook, Charles "Doc" 44
Cook, Samuel DuBois 14
Cook, Suzan D. Johnson 22
Cook, Toni 23
Cook, Will Marion 40
Cooke, Marcia 60
Cooke, Marvel 31
Cooper, Andrew W. 36
Cooper, Andy "Lefty" 63
Cooper, Anna Julia 20
Cooper, Barry 33
Cooper, Charles "Chuck" 47
Cooper, Cynthia 17
Cooper, Edward S. 6
Cooper, Evern 40
Cooper, J. California 12
Cooper, Lisa 73
Cooper, Margaret J. 46
Cooper, Michael 31
Cooper Cafritz, Peggy 43
Copeland, Michael 47
Corbi, Lana 42
Corley, Tony 62
Cornelius, Don 4
Cornish, Sam 50
Cornwell, Edward E., III 70
Cortez, Jayne 43
Corthron, Kia 43
Cortor, Eldzier 42
Cosby, Bill 7, 26, 59
Cosby, Camille 14
Cose, Ellis 5, 50
Cotter, Joseph Seamon, Sr. 40
Cottrell, Comer 11
Cowans, Adger W. 20
Cowboy Troy 54
Cox, Ida 42
Cox, Joseph Mason Andrew 51
Cox, Renée 67
Cox, William E. 68
Craig, Carl 31, 71
Craig-Jones, Ellen Walker 44
Crawford, Randy 19
Cray, Robert 30
Creagh, Milton 27
Crennel, Romeo 54
Crew, Rudolph F. 16
Crew, Spencer R. 55
Crite, Alan Rohan 29
Crocker, Frankie 29
Crockett, George W., Jr. 10, 64
Croom, Sylvester 50
Cross, Dolores E. 23
Crothers, Scatman 19
Crouch, Andraé 27
Crouch, Stanley 11
Crowder, Henry 16
Cruse, Harold 54
Crutchfield, James N. 55
Cullen, Countee 8
Cullers, Vincent T. 49
Culpepper, Daunte 32
Cummings, Elijah E. 24
Cuney, William Waring 44
Cunningham, Evelyn 23
Cunningham, Randall 23
Currie, Betty 21
Currie, Ulysses 73
Curry, George E. 23
Curry, Mark 17

Curtis, Christopher Paul 26
Curtis-Hall, Vondie 17
Daemyon, Jerald 64
Daly, Marie Maynard 37
Dandridge, Dorothy 3
Dandridge, Ray 36
Dandridge, Raymond Garfield 45
D'Angelo 27
Daniels, Lee Louis 36
Daniels-Carter, Valerie 23
Danner, Margaret Esse 49
Dantley, Adrian 72
Dara, Olu 35
Darden, Calvin 38
Darden, Christopher 13
Dash, Damon 31
Dash, Julie 4
Dash, Leon 47
Datcher, Michael 60
David, Keith 27
Davidson, Jaye 5
Davidson, Tommy 21
Davis, Allison 12
Davis, Angela 5
Davis, Anthony 11
Davis, Arthur Paul 41
Davis, Artur 41
Davis, Belva 61
Davis, Benjamin O., Jr. 2, 43
Davis, Benjamin O., Sr. 4
Davis, Charles T. 48
Davis, Chuck 33
Davis, Danny K. 24
Davis, Ed 24
Davis, Eisa 68
Davis, Ernie 48
Davis, Erroll B., Jr. 57
Davis, Frank Marshall 47
Davis, Gary 41
Davis, George 36
Davis, Guy 36
Davis, James E. 50
Davis, Mike 41
Davis, Miles 4
Davis, Nolan 45
Davis, Ossie 5, 50
Davis, Piper 19
Davis, Ruth 37
Davis, Shani 58
Davis, Terrell 20
Davis, Thulani 61
Davis, Tyrone 54
Davis, Viola 34
Dawes, Dominique 11
Dawkins, Wayne 20
Dawson, Matel "Mat," Jr. 39
Dawson, Michael C. 63
Dawson, Rosario 72
Dawson, William Levi 39
Day, Leon 39
Days, Drew S., III 10
de Passe, Suzanne 25
De Shields, André 72
De Veaux, Alexis 44
De' Alexander, Quinton 57
Dean, Mark E. 35
DeBaptiste, George 32
DeCarava, Roy 42
Deconge-Watson, Lovenia 55
Dee, Merri 55
Dee, Ruby 8, 50, 68
Deezer D 53
DeFrantz, Anita 37

Deggans, Eric 71
Delaney, Beauford 19
Delaney, Joseph 30
Delany, Bessie 12
Delany, Martin R. 27
Delany, Sadie 12
Delany, Samuel R., Jr. 9
Delco, Wilhemina 33
DeLille, Henriette 30
Dellums, Ronald 2
DeLoach, Nora 30
Delsarte, Louis 34
Demby, William 51
Dennard, Brazeal 37
Dent, Thomas C. 50
DePriest, James 37
DeVard, Jerri 61
Devers, Gail 7
Devine, Loretta 24
Dickens, Helen Octavia 14, 64
Dickenson, Vic 38
Dickerson, Debra J. 60
Dickerson, Eric 27
Dickerson, Ernest R. 6, 17
Dickey, Eric Jerome 21, 56
Diddley, Bo 39, 72
Diesel, Vin 29
Diggs, Charles C. 21
Diggs, Taye 25, 63
Diggs-Taylor, Anna 20
Dillard, Godfrey J. 45
Dinkins, David 4
Divine, Father 7
Dixon, Dean 68
Dixon, Ivan 69
Dixon, Julian C. 24
Dixon, Margaret 14
Dixon, Sharon Pratt 1
Dixon, Sheila 68
Dixon, Willie 4
DMX 28, 64
Dobbs, Mattiwilda 34
Doby, Lawrence Eugene, Sr. 16, 41
Dodson, Howard, Jr. 7, 52
Dodson, Owen Vincent 38
Doley, Harold, Jr. 26
Domino, Fats 20
Donald, Arnold Wayne 36
Donaldson, Jeff 46
Donegan, Dorothy 19
Dorrell, Karl 52
Dorsey, Lee 65
Dorsey, Thomas 15
Dortch, Thomas W., Jr. 45
Dougherty, Mary Pearl 47
Douglas, Aaron 7
Dourdan, Gary 37
Dove, Rita 6
Dove, Ulysses 5
Downing, Will 19
Draper, Sharon Mills 16, 43
Dre, Dr. 10, 14, 30
Drew, Alvin, Jr. 67
Drew, Charles Richard 7
Drexler, Clyde 4, 61
Driskell, David C. 7
Driver, David E. 11
Drummond, William J. 40
Du Bois, David Graham 45
DuBois, Shirley Graham 21
DuBois, W. E. B. 3
Ducksworth, Marilyn 12
Dudley, Edward R. 58

Due, Tananarive 30
Duggins, George 64
Duke, Bill 3
Duke, George 21
Dukes, Hazel Nell 56
Dumars, Joe 16, 65
Dumas, Henry 41
Dunbar, Paul Laurence 8
Dunbar-Nelson, Alice Ruth Moore 44
Duncan, Michael Clarke 26
Duncan, Tim 20
Dungey, Merrin 62
Dungy, Tony 17, 42, 59
Dunham, Katherine 4, 59
Dunlap, Ericka 55
Dunn, Jerry 27
Dunner, Leslie B. 45
Dunnigan, Alice Allison 41
Dunston, Georgia Mae 48
Duplechan, Larry 55
Dupri, Jermaine 13, 46
Durham, Bobby 73
Dutton, Charles S. 4, 22
Dworkin, Aaron P. 52
Dwight, Edward 65
Dye, Jermaine 58
Dyson, Michael Eric 11, 40
Early, Gerald 15
Earthquake 55
Easley, Annie J. 61
Ebanks, Michelle 60
Eckstine, Billy 28
Edelin, Ramona Hoage 19
Edelman, Marian Wright 5, 42
Edley, Christopher 2, 48
Edley, Christopher F., Jr. 48
Edmonds, Kenneth "Babyface" 10, 31
Edmonds, Terry 17
Edmonds, Tracey 16, 64
Edmunds, Gladys 48
Edwards, Esther Gordy 43
Edwards, Harry 2
Edwards, Herman 51
Edwards, Melvin 22
Edwards, Teresa 14
Edwards, Willarda V. 59
El Wilson, Barbara 35
Elder, Larry 25
Elder, Lee 6
Elder, Lonne, III 38
Elders, Joycelyn 6
Eldridge, Roy 37
Elise, Kimberly 32
Ellerbe, Brian 22
Ellington, Duke 5
Ellington, E. David 11
Ellington, Mercedes 34
Elliott, Missy "Misdemeanor" 31
Elliott, Sean 26
Ellis, Clarence A. 38
Ellis, Jimmy 44
Ellison, Keith 59
Ellison, Ralph 7
Elmore, Ronn 21
Emanuel, James A. 46
Emeagwali, Dale 31
Ephriam, Mablean 29
Epperson, Sharon 54
Epps, Archie C., III 45
Epps, Mike 60
Epps, Omar 23, 59

Ericsson-Jackson, Aprille 28
Ervin, Anthony 66
Erving, Julius 18, 47
Escobar, Damien 56
Escobar, Tourie 56
Esposito, Giancarlo 9
Espy, Mike 6
Estes, Rufus 29
Estes, Simon 28
Estes, Sleepy John 33
Eubanks, Kevin 15
Eugene-Richard, Margie 63
Europe, James Reese 10
Evans, Darryl 22
Evans, Etu 55
Evans, Faith 22
Evans, Harry 25
Evans, Mari 26
Eve 29
Everett, Francine 23
Evers, Medgar 3
Evers, Myrlie 8
Ewing, Patrick 17, 73
Fabio, Sarah Webster 48
Fabre, Shelton 71
Fair, Ronald L. 47
Faison, Donald 50
Faison, Frankie 55
Faison, George 16
Falana, Lola 42
Falconer, Etta Zuber 59
Fargas, Antonio 50
Farley, Christopher John 54
Farmer, Art 38
Farmer, Forest J. 1
Farmer, James 2, 64
Farmer-Paellmann, Deadria 43
Farr, Mel 24
Farrakhan, Louis 2, 15
Farris, Isaac Newton, Jr. 63
Fattah, Chaka 11, 70
Faulk, Marshall 35
Fauntroy, Walter E. 11
Fauset, Jessie 7
Favors, Steve 23
Fax, Elton 48
Feelings, Muriel 44
Feelings, Tom 11, 47
Felix, Allyson 48
Felix, Larry R. 64
Feemster, Herbert 72
Fennoy, Ilene 72
Fenty, Adrian 60
Ferguson, Roger W. 25
Ferrell, Rachelle 29
Fetchit, Stepin 32
Fiasco, Lupe 64
Fielder, Cecil 2
Fielder, Prince Semien 68
Fields, C. Virginia 25
Fields, Cleo 13
Fields, Evelyn J. 27
Fields, Felicia P. 60
Fields, Julia 45
Fields, Kim 36
Files, Lolita 35
Fine, Sam 60
Finner-Williams, Paris Michele 62
Fishburne, Laurence 4, 22, 70
Fisher, Antwone 40
Fitzgerald, Ella 1, 18
Flack, Roberta 19
Flanagan, Tommy 69

Flavor Flav 67
Fleming, Raymond 48
Fletcher, Arthur A. 63
Fletcher, Bill, Jr. 41
Flowers, Sylester 50
Flowers, Vonetta 35
Floyd, Elson S. 41
Forbes, Calvin 46
Forbes, James A., Jr. 71
Ford, Cheryl 45
Ford, Clyde W. 40
Ford, Harold E(ugene) 42
Ford, Harold E(ugene), Jr. 16, 70
Ford, Jack 39
Ford, Johnny 70
Ford, Nick Aaron 44
Ford, Wallace 58
Forman, James 7, 51
Forrest, Leon 44
Forrest, Vernon 40
Forte, Linda Diane 54
Foster, Ezola 28
Foster, George "Pops" 40
Foster, Henry W., Jr. 26
Foster, Jylla Moore 45
Foster, Marie 48
Fowler, Reggie 51
Fox, Vivica A. 15, 53
Foxx, Jamie 15, 48
Francis, Norman (C.) 60
Franklin, Aretha 11, 44
Franklin, C. L. 68
Franklin, J. E. 44
Franklin, Kirk 15, 49
Franklin, Shirley 34
Frazer, Jendayi 68
Frazier, E. Franklin 10
Frazier, Joe 19
Frazier, Kevin 58
Frazier, Oscar 58
Frazier-Lyde, Jacqui 31
Freelon, Nnenna 32
Freeman, Aaron 52
Freeman, Al, Jr. 11
Freeman, Charles 19
Freeman, Harold P. 23
Freeman, Leonard 27
Freeman, Marianna 23
Freeman, Morgan 2, 20, 62
Freeman, Paul 39
Freeman, Yvette 27
French, Albert 18
Friday, Jeff 24
Fryer, Roland G. 56
Fudge, Ann (Marie) 11, 55
Fulani, Lenora 11
Fuller, A. Oveta 43
Fuller, Arthur 27
Fuller, Charles 8
Fuller, Howard L. 37
Fuller, Hoyt 44
Fuller, Meta Vaux Warrick 27
Fuller, S.B. 13
Fuller, Solomon Carter, Jr. 15
Fuller, Vivian 33
Funderburg, I. Owen 38
Funnye, Capers C., Jr. 73
Fuqua, Antoine 35
Futch, Eddie 33
Gaines, Brenda 41
Gaines, Clarence E., Sr. 55
Gaines, Ernest J. 7
Gaines, Grady 38

Gaither, Alonzo Smith (Jake) 14
Gaither, Israel L. 65
Gantt, Harvey 1
Gardner, Chris 65
Gardner, Edward G. 45
Garnett, Kevin 14, 70
Garrett, Joyce Finley 59
Garrison, Zina 2
Gary, Willie E. 12
Gaskins, Eric 64
Gaston, Arthur George 3, 38, 59
Gaston, Cito 71
Gaston, Marilyn Hughes 60
Gates, Henry Louis, Jr. 3, 38, 67
Gates, Sylvester James, Jr. 15
Gaye, Marvin 2
Gaye, Nona 56
Gayle, Addison, Jr. 41
Gayle, Helene D. 3, 46
Gaynor, Gloria 36
Gentry, Alvin 23
George, Nelson 12
George, Zelma Watson 42
Gibson, Althea 8, 43
Gibson, Bob 33
Gibson, Donald Bernard 40
Gibson, Johnnie Mae 23
Gibson, Josh 22
Gibson, Kenneth Allen 6
Gibson, Ted 66
Gibson, Truman K., Jr. 60
Gibson, Tyrese 27, 62
Gibson, William F. 6
Giddings, Paula 11
Gidron, Richard D. 68
Gilbert, Christopher 50
Flanagan, Tommy 69
Gill, Johnny 51
Gilles, Ralph 61
Gillespie, Dizzy 1
Gilliam, Frank 23
Gilliam, Joe 31
Gilliam, Sam 16
Gilliard, Steve 69
Gilmore, Marshall 46
Ginuwine 35
Giovanni, Nikki 9, 39
Gist, Carole 1
Givens, Adele 62
Givens, Robin 4, 25, 58
Givhan, Robin Deneen 72
Glover, Corey 34
Glover, Danny 1, 24
Glover, Nathaniel, Jr. 12
Glover, Savion 14
Goapele 55
Goines, Donald 19
Goings, Russell 59
Goldberg, Whoopi 4, 33, 69
Golden, Marita 19
Golden, Thelma 10, 55
Goldsberry, Ronald 18
Golson, Benny 37
Golston, Allan C. 55
Gomes, Peter J. 15
Gomez, Jewelle 30
Gomez-Preston, Cheryl 9
Goode, Mal 13
Goode, W. Wilson 4
Gooden, Dwight 20
Gooding, Cuba, Jr. 16, 62
Goodnight, Paul 32
Gorden, W. C. 71

Gordon, Bruce S. 41, 53
Gordon, Dexter 25
Gordon, Ed 10, 53
Gordone, Charles 15
Gordy, Berry, Jr. 1
Goss, Carol A. 55
Goss, Tom 23
Gossett, Louis, Jr. 7
Gotti, Irv 39
Gourdine, Meredith 33
Gourdine, Simon 11
Grace, George H. 48
Graham, Lawrence Otis 12
Graham, Lorenz 48
Graham, Stedman 13
Granderson, Curtis 66
Grant, Augustus O. 71
Grant, Bernie 57
Grant, Gwendolyn Goldsby 28
Granville, Evelyn Boyd 36
Gravely, Samuel L., Jr. 5, 49
Graves, Denyce Antoinette 19, 57
Graves, Earl G. 1, 35
Gray, Darius 69
Gray, F. Gary 14, 49
Gray, Farrah 59
Gray, Fred 37
Gray, Ida 41
Gray, Macy 29
Gray, William H., III 3
Gray, Willie 46
Gray, Yeshimbra "Shimmy" 55
Greaves, William 38
Greely, M. Gasby 27
Green, A. C. 32
Green, Al 13, 47
Green, Darrell 39
Green, Dennis 5, 45
Green, Grant 56
Green, Jonathan 54
Greene, Joe 10
Greene, Maurice 27
Greene, Petey 65
Greene, Richard Thaddeus, Sr. 67
Greenfield, Eloise 9
Greenhouse, Bunnatine "Bunny" 57
Greenlee, Sam 48
Greenwood, Monique 38
Gregory, Ann 63
Gregory, Dick 1, 54
Gregory, Frederick 8, 51
Gregory, Wilton 37
Grier, David Alan 28
Grier, Mike 43
Grier, Pam 9, 31
Grier, Roosevelt 13
Griffey, Ken, Jr. 12, 73
Griffin, Anthony 71
Griffin, Bessie Blout 43
Griffin, Johnny 71
Griffin, LaShell 51
Griffith, Mark Winston 8
Griffith, Yolanda 25
Griffith-Joyner, Florence 28
Grimké, Archibald H. 9
Grooms, Henry R(andall) 50
Guillaume, Robert 3, 48
Guinier, Lani 7, 30
Gumbel, Bryant 14
Gumbel, Greg 8
Gunn, Moses 10
Gurira, Danai 73
Guy, George "Buddy" 31

Guy, Jasmine 2
Guy, Rosa 5
Guy-Sheftall, Beverly 13
Guyton, Tyree 9
Gwynn, Tony 18
Haddon, Dietrick 55
Hageman, Hans 36
Hageman, Ivan 36
Hailey, JoJo 22
Hailey, K-Ci 22
Hale, Clara 16
Hale, Lorraine 8
Haley, Alex 4
Haley, George Williford Boyce 21
Hall, Aaron 57
Hall, Arsenio 58
Hall, Arthur 39
Hall, Elliott S. 24
Hall, Juanita 62
Hall, Kevan 61
Hall, Lloyd A. 8
Halliburton, Warren J. 49
Ham, Cynthia Parker 58
Hamblin, Ken 10
Hamer, Fannie Lou 6
Hamilton, Anthony 61
Hamilton, Samuel C. 47
Hamilton, Lisa Gay 71
Hamilton, Virginia 10
Hamlin, Larry Leon 49, 62
Hammer, M. C. 20
Hammond, Fred 23
Hammonds, Evelynn 69
Hammons, David 69
Hampton, Fred 18
Hampton, Henry 6
Hampton, Lionel 17, 41
Hancock, Herbie 20, 67
Handy, W. C. 8
Hannah, Marc 10
Hansberry, Lorraine 6
Hansberry, William Leo 11
Hardaway, Anfernee (Penny) 13
Hardaway, Tim 35
Hardin Armstrong, Lil 39
Harding, Vincent 67
Hardison, Bethann 12
Hardison, Kadeem 22
Hare, Nathan 44
Harkless, Necia Desiree 19
Harmon, Clarence 26
Harold, Erika 54
Harper, Ben 34, 62
Harper, Frances Ellen Watkins 11
Harper, Hill 32, 65
Harper, Michael S. 34
Harrell, Andre 9, 30
Harrington, Oliver W. 9
Harris, Alice 7
Harris, Barbara 12
Harris, Barry 68
Harris, Bill 72
Harris, Carla A. 67
Harris, Corey 39, 73
Harris, E. Lynn 12, 33
Harris, Eddy L. 18
Harris, Jay T. 19
Harris, Kamala D. 64
Harris, Leslie 6
Harris, Marcelite Jordon 16
Harris, Mary Styles 31
Harris, Monica 18
Harris, Patricia Roberts 2

Harris, Richard E. 61
Harris, Robin 7
Harris, Sylvia 70
Harrison, Alvin 28
Harrison, Calvin 28
Harrison, Charles 72
Harsh, Vivian Gordon 14
Hart, Alvin Youngblood 61
Harvard, Beverly 11
Harvey, Steve 18, 58
Harvey, William R. 42
Haskins, Clem 23
Haskins, James 36, 54
Hassell, Leroy Rountree, Sr. 41
Hastie, William H. 8
Hastings, Alcee L. 16
Hatcher, Richard G. 55
Hatchett, Glenda 32
Hathaway, Donny 18
Hathaway, Isaac Scott 33
Hathaway, Lalah 57
Hawkins, Augustus F. 68
Hawkins, Coleman 9
Hawkins, Erskine 14
Hawkins, La-Van 17, 54
Hawkins, Screamin' Jay 30
Hawkins, Steven 14
Hawkins, Tramaine 16
Hayden, Carla D. 47
Hayden, Palmer 13
Hayden, Robert 12
Hayes, Cecil N. 46
Hayes, Dennis 54
Hayes, Isaac 20, 58, 73
Hayes, James C. 10
Hayes, Roland 4
Hayes, Teddy 40
Haynes, George Edmund 8
Haynes, Marques 22
Haynes, Trudy 44
Haysbert, Dennis 42
Haywood, Gar Anthony 43
Haywood, Jimmy 58
Haywood, Margaret A. 24
Hazel, Darryl B. 50
Healy, James Augustine 30
Heard, Gar 25
Heard, Nathan C. 45
Hearns, Thomas 29
Hedgeman, Anna Arnold 22
Height, Dorothy I. 2, 23
Hemphill, Essex 10
Hemphill, Jessie Mae 33, 59
Hemsley, Sherman 19
Henderson, Cornelius Langston 26
Henderson, David 53
Henderson, Fletcher 32
Henderson, Gordon 5
Henderson, Jeff 72
Henderson, Rickey 28
Henderson, Stephen E. 45
Henderson, Thelton E. 68
Henderson, Wade J. 14
Henderson, Zelma 71
Hendrix, Jimi 10
Hendryx, Nona 56
Hendy, Francis 47
Henries, A. Doris Banks 44
Henry, Aaron 19
Henry, Clarence "Frogman" 46
Henson, Darrin 33
Henson, Matthew 2
Henson, Taraji 58

Herbert, Bob **63**
Hercules, Frank **44**
Herenton, Willie W. **24**
Herman, Alexis M. **15**
Hernandez, Aileen Clarke **13**
Hernton, Calvin C. **51**
Hickman, Fred **11**
Higginbotham, A. Leon, Jr. **13, 25**
Higginbotham, Jay C. **37**
Higginsen, Vy **65**
Hightower, Dennis F. **13**
Hill, Andrew **66**
Hill, Anita **5, 65**
Hill, Bonnie Guiton **20**
Hill, Calvin **19**
Hill, Donna **32**
Hill, Dulé **29**
Hill, Grant **13**
Hill, Janet **19**
Hill, Jesse, Jr. **13**
Hill, Lauryn **20, 53**
Hill, Leslie Pinckney **44**
Hill, Oliver W. **24, 63**
Hillard, Terry **25**
Hillary, Barbara **65**
Hilliard, Asa Grant, III **66**
Hilliard, David **7**
Hilliard, Earl F. **24**
Hilliard, Wendy **53**
Himes, Chester **8**
Hinderas, Natalie **5**
Hine, Darlene Clark **24**
Hines, Earl "Fatha" **39**
Hines, Garrett **35**
Hines, Gregory **1, 42**
Hinton, Milt **30**
Hinton, William Augustus **8**
Hoagland, Everett H. **45**
Hobson, Julius W. **44**
Hobson, Mellody **40**
Hogan, Beverly Wade **50**
Holder, Eric H., Jr. **9**
Holder, Laurence **34**
Holdsclaw, Chamique **24**
Holiday, Billie **1**
Holland, Endesha Ida Mae **3, 57**
Holland, Kimberly N. **62**
Holland, Robert, Jr. **11**
Holland-Dozier-Holland **36**
Holloway, Brenda **65**
Hollowell, Donald L. **57**
Holmes, Amy **69**
Holmes, Clint **57**
Holmes, Larry **20, 68**
Holmes, Shannon **70**
Holt, Lester **66**
Holt, Nora **38**
Holt Baker, Arlene **73**
Holton, Hugh, Jr. **39**
Holyfield, Evander **6**
Honeywood, Varnette P. **54**
Honoré, Russel L. **64**
Hooker, John Lee **30**
hooks, bell **5**
Hooks, Benjamin L. **2**
Hope, John **8**
Hopkins, Bernard **35, 69**
Horn, Shirley **32, 56**
Horne, Frank **44**
Horne, Lena **5**
Horton, Andre **33**
Horton, James Oliver **58**
Horton, Suki **33**

House, Son **8**
Houston, Charles Hamilton **4**
Houston, Cissy **20**
Houston, Whitney **7, 28**
Howard, Ayanna **65**
Howard, Desmond **16, 58**
Howard, Juwan **15**
Howard, M. William, Jr. **26**
Howard, Michelle **28**
Howard, Ryan **65**
Howard, Sherri **36**
Howard, Terrence Dashon **59**
Howlin' Wolf **9**
Howroyd, Janice Bryant **42**
Hoyte, Lenon **50**
Hrabowski, Freeman A., III **22**
Hubbard, Arnette Rhinehart **38**
Hudlin, Reginald **9**
Hudlin, Warrington **9**
Hudson, Cheryl **15**
Hudson, Ernie **72**
Hudson, Jennifer **63**
Hudson, Wade **15**
Huggins, Edie **71**
Huggins, Larry **21**
Huggins, Nathan Irvin **52**
Hughes, Albert **7**
Hughes, Allen **7**
Hughes, Cathy **27**
Hughes, Ebony **57**
Hughes, Langston **4**
Hughley, D. L. **23**
Hull, Akasha Gloria **45**
Humphrey, Bobbi **20**
Humphries, Frederick **20**
Hunt, Richard **6**
Hunter, Alberta **42**
Hunter, Clementine **45**
Hunter, Torii **43**
Hunter-Gault, Charlayne **6, 31**
Hurston, Zora Neale **3**
Hurt, Byron **61**
Hurtt, Harold **46**
Hutch, Willie **62**
Hutcherson, Hilda Yvonne **54**
Hutchinson, Earl Ofari **24**
Hutson, Jean Blackwell **16**
Hyde, Cowan F. "Bubba" **47**
Hyman, Earle **25**
Hyman, Phyllis **19**
Ice Cube **8, 30, 60**
Iceberg Slim **11**
Ice-T **6, 31**
Iman, Chanel **66**
Ifill, Gwen **28**
Imes, Elmer Samuel **39**
India.Arie **34**
Ingram, Rex **5**
Innis, Roy **5**
Irvin, Michael **64**
Irvin, Monford Merrill **31**
Irvin, Vernon **65**
Irving, Larry, Jr. **12**
Irvis, K. Leroy **67**
Isley, Ronald **25, 56**
Iverson, Allen **24, 46**
Ivey, Phil **72**
Ja Rule **35**
Jackson, Alexine Clement **22**
Jackson, Alphonso R. **48**
Jackson, Earl **31**
Jackson, Edison O. **67**
Jackson, Fred James **25**

Jackson, George **14**
Jackson, George **19**
Jackson, Hal **41**
Jackson, Isaiah **3**
Jackson, Jamea **64**
Jackson, Janet **6, 30, 68**
Jackson, Jesse **1, 27, 72**
Jackson, Jesse, Jr. **14, 45**
Jackson, John **36**
Jackson, Judith D. **57**
Jackson, Mae **57**
Jackson, Mahalia **5**
Jackson, Mannie **14**
Jackson, Mary **73**
Jackson, Maynard **2, 41**
Jackson, Michael **19, 53**
Jackson, Millie **25**
Jackson, Milt **26**
Jackson, Randy **40**
Jackson, Reggie **15**
Jackson, Samuel **8, 63**
Jackson, Sheneska **18**
Jackson, Shirley Ann **12**
Jackson, Tom **70**
Jackson, Vera **40**
Jackson Lee, Sheila **20**
Jacob, John E. **2**
Jacobs, Regina **38**
Jacquet, Illinois **49**
Jaheim **58**
Jakes, Thomas "T.D." **17, 43**
Jamal, Ahmad **69**
Jamerson, James **59**
James, Charles H., III **62**
James, Daniel, Jr. **16**
James, Donna A. **51**
James, Etta **13, 52**
James, Juanita **13**
James, LeBron **46**
James, Rick **19**
James, Sharpe **23, 69**
James, Skip **38**
Jamison, Judith **7, 67**
Jarreau, Al **21, 65**
Jarrett, Valerie **73**
Jarrett, Vernon D. **42**
Jarvis, Charlene Drew **21**
Jarvis, Erich **67**
Jasper, Kenji **39**
Jay-Z **27, 69**
Jazzy Jeff **32**
Jealous, Benjamin **70**
Jefferson, William J. **25, 72**
Jeffries, Leonard **8**
Jemison, Mae C. **1, 35**
Jemison, Major L. **48**
Jenifer, Franklyn G. **2**
Jenkins, Beverly **14**
Jenkins, Ella **15**
Jennings, Lyfe **56, 69**
Jerkins, Rodney **31**
Jeter, Derek **27**
Jimmy Jam **13**
Joe, Yolanda **21**
John, Daymond **23**
Johns, Vernon **38**
Johnson, Angela **52**
Johnson, Avery **62**
Johnson, Beverly **2**
Johnson, Buddy **36**
Johnson, Charles **1**
Johnson, Charles S. **12**
Johnson, Clifford "Connie" **52**

Johnson, Earvin "Magic" **3, 39**
Johnson, Eddie Bernice **8**
Johnson, George E. **29**
Johnson, Georgia Douglas **41**
Johnson, Harry E. **57**
Johnson, Harvey, Jr. **24**
Johnson, J. J. **37**
Johnson, Jack **8**
Johnson, James Weldon **5**
Johnson, Je'Caryous **63**
Johnson, Jeh Vincent **44**
Johnson, John H. **3, 54**
Johnson, Johnnie **56**
Johnson, Katherine (Coleman Goble) **61**
Johnson, Kevin **70**
Johnson, Larry **28**
Johnson, Levi **48**
Johnson, Lonnie **32**
Johnson, Mamie "Peanut" **40**
Johnson, Mat **31**
Johnson, Michael **13**
Johnson, Norma L. Holloway **17**
Johnson, R. M. **36**
Johnson, Rafer **33**
Johnson, Robert **2**
Johnson, Robert L. **3, 39**
Johnson, Robert T. **17**
Johnson, Rodney Van **28**
Johnson, Sheila Crump **48**
Johnson, Shoshana **47**
Johnson, Virginia **9**
Johnson, William Henry **3**
Jolley, Willie **28**
Jones, Absalom **52**
Jones, Alex **64**
Jones, Bill T. **1, 46**
Jones, Bobby **20**
Jones, Carl **7**
Jones, Caroline **29**
Jones, Clara Stanton **51**
Jones, Cobi N'Gai **18**
Jones, Cullen **73**
Jones, Donell **29**
Jones, Doris W. **62**
Jones, E. Edward, Sr. **45**
Jones, Ed "Too Tall" **46**
Jones, Edith Mae Irby **65**
Jones, Edward P. **43, 67**
Jones, Elaine R. **7, 45**
Jones, Elvin **14, 68**
Jones, Etta **35**
Jones, Frederick McKinley **68**
Jones, Gayl **37**
Jones, Hank **57**
Jones, Ingrid Saunders **18**
Jones, James Earl **3, 49**
Jones, Jonah **39**
Jones, Lois Mailou **13**
Jones, Lou **64**
Jones, Marion **21, 66**
Jones, Merlakia **34**
Jones, Orlando **30**
Jones, Quincy **8, 30**
Jones, Randy **35**
Jones, Sarah **39**
Jones, Thad **68**
Jones, Thomas W. **41**
Jones, Van **70**
Jones, Wayne **53**
Jones, William A., Jr. **61**
Joplin, Scott **6**
Jordan, Barbara **4**

Jordan, June **7, 35**
Jordan, Michael **6, 21**
Jordan, Montell **23**
Jordan, Vernon E. **3, 35**
Joseph, Kathie-Ann **56**
Josey, E. J. **10**
Joyner, Marjorie Stewart **26**
Joyner, Matilda Sissieretta **15**
Joyner, Tom **19**
Joyner-Kersee, Jackie **5**
Julian, Percy Lavon **6**
July, William **27**
Just, Ernest Everett **3**
Justice, David **18**
Kaigler, Denise **63**
Kaiser, Cecil **42**
Kani, Karl **10**
Karenga, Maulana **10, 71**
Karim, Benjamin **61**
Kaufman, Monica **66**
Kay, Ulysses **37**
Kearney, Janis **54**
Kearse, Amalya Lyle **12**
Kee, John P. **43**
Keene, John **73**
Keflezighi, Meb **49**
Keith, Damon J. **16**
Keith, Floyd A. **61**
Kelis **58**
Kelley, Elijah **65**
Kelley, Malcolm David **59**
Kellogg, Clark **64**
Kelly, Patrick **3**
Kelly, R. **18, 44, 71**
Kem **47**
Kendrick, Erika **57**
Kendricks, Eddie **22**
Kennedy, Adrienne **11**
Kennedy, Florynce **12, 33**
Kennedy, Randall **40**
Kennedy-Overton, Jayne Harris **46**
Kenney, John A., Jr. **48**
Kenoly, Ron **45**
Kenyatta, Robin **54**
Kerry, Leon G. **46**
Keyes, Alan L. **11**
Keys, Alicia **32, 68**
Khan, Chaka **12, 50**
Khanga, Yelena **6**
Kidd, Mae Street **39**
Killens, John O. **54**
Killings, Debra **57**
Killingsworth, Cleve, Jr. **54**
Kilpatrick, Carolyn Cheeks **16**
Kilpatrick, Kwame **34, 71**
Kimbro, Dennis **10**
Kimbro, Henry A. **25**
Kincaid, Bernard **28**
Kincaid, Jamaica **4**
King, Alonzo **38**
King, B. B. **7**
King, Barbara **22**
King, Bernice **4**
King, Colbert I. **69**
King, Coretta Scott **3, 57**
King, Dexter **10**
King, Don **14**
King, Gayle **19**
King, Martin Luther, III **20**
King, Martin Luther, Jr. **1**
King, Preston **28**
King, Reatha Clark **65**
King, Regina **22, 45**

King, Robert Arthur **58**
King, Woodie, Jr. **27**
King, Yolanda **6**
Kirby, George **14**
Kirk, Ron **11**
Kitt, Eartha **16**
Kitt, Sandra **23**
Kittles, Rick **51**
Klugh, Earl **59**
Knight, Etheridge **37**
Knight, Gladys **16, 66**
Knight, Suge **11, 30**
Knowles, Tina **61**
Knowling, Robert E., Jr. **38**
Knox, Simmie **49**
Knuckles, Frankie **42**
Komunyakaa, Yusef **9**
Kong, B. Waine **50**
Kool Moe Dee **37**
Kotto, Yaphet **7**
Kountz, Samuel L. **10**
Kravitz, Lenny **10, 34**
KRS-One **34**
K-Swift **73**
Kunjufu, Jawanza **3, 50**
La Salle, Eriq **12**
LaBelle, Patti **13, 30**
Lacy, Sam **30, 46**
Ladd, Ernie **64**
Ladner, Joyce A. **42**
Lafontant, Jewel Stradford **3, 51**
Lampkin, Daisy **19**
Lampley, Oni Faida **43, 71**
Lane, Charles **3**
Lane, Vincent **5**
Langhart Cohen, Janet **19, 60**
Lanier, Bob **47**
Lanier, Willie **33**
Lankford, Ray **23**
Larkin, Barry **24**
Larrieux, Amel **63**
Lars, Byron **32**
Larsen, Nella **10**
Laryea, Thomas Davies, III **67**
Lashley, Bobby **63**
Lassiter, Roy **24**
Lathan, Sanaa **27**
Latimer, Lewis H. **4**
Lattimore, Kenny **35**
Lavizzo-Mourey, Risa **48**
Lawless, Theodore K. **8**
Lawrence, Jacob **4, 28**
Lawrence, Martin **6, 27**
Lawrence, Robert H., Jr. **16**
Lawrence-Lightfoot, Sara **10**
Lawson, Jennifer **1, 50**
Leary, Kathryn D. **10**
Leavell, Dorothy R. **17**
Ledisi **73**
Lee, Annie Frances **22**
Lee, Barbara **25**
Lee, Canada **8**
Lee, Debra L. **62**
Lee, Joe A. **45**
Lee, Joie **1**
Lee, Spike **5, 19**
Lee, Bertram M., Sr. **46**
Lee-Smith, Hughie **5, 22**
Leevy, Carrol M. **42**
Leffall, Lasalle, Jr. **3, 64**
Legend, John **67**
Leggs, Kingsley **62**
Leland, Mickey **2**

Lemmons, Kasi **20**
Lennox, Betty **31**
LeNoire, Rosetta **37**
Lenox, Adriane **59**
Leon, Kenny **10**
Leonard, Buck **67**
Leonard, Sugar Ray **15**
Leslie, Lisa **16, 73**
Lester, Bill **42**
Lester, Julius **9**
Lesure, James **64**
LeTang, Henry **66**
Letson, Al **39**
Levert, Eddie **70**
Levert, Gerald **22, 59**
Lewellyn, J. Bruce **13**
Lewis, Ananda **28**
Lewis, Aylwin **51**
Lewis, Butch **71**
Lewis, Byron E. **13**
Lewis, Carl **4**
Lewis, David Levering **9**
Lewis, Delano **7**
Lewis, Edmonia **10**
Lewis, Edward T. **21**
Lewis, Emmanuel **36**
Lewis, Henry **38**
Lewis, John **2, 46**
Lewis, Marvin **51**
Lewis, Norman **39**
Lewis, Oliver **56**
Lewis, Ramsey **35, 70**
Lewis, Ray **33**
Lewis, Reginald F. **6**
Lewis, Samella **25**
Lewis, Shirley A. R. **14**
Lewis, Terry **13**
Lewis, Thomas **19**
Lewis, William M., Jr. **40**
Lewis-Thornton, Rae **32**
Ligging, Alfred, III **43**
Lil' Kim **28**
Lil Wayne **66**
Liles, Kevin **42**
Lincoln, Abbey **3**
Lincoln, C. Eric **38**
Lindsey, Tommie **51**
Lipscomb, Mance **49**
LisaRaye **27**
Lister, Marquita **65**
Liston, Sonny **33**
Little Milton **36, 54**
Little Richard **15**
Little Walter **36**
Little, Benilde **21**
Little, Robert L. **2**
Littlepage, Craig **35**
LL Cool J **16, 49**
Lloyd, Earl **26**
Lloyd, John Henry "Pop" **30**
Lloyd, Reginald **64**
Locke, Alain **10**
Locke, Eddie **44**
Lofton, James **42**
Lofton, Kenny **12**
Logan, Onnie Lee **14**
Logan, Rayford W. **40**
Lomax, Michael L. **58**
Long, Eddie L. **29**
Long, Loretta **58**
Long, Nia **17**
Long, Richard Alexander **65**
Lopes, Lisa "Left Eye" **36**

Lorde, Audre **6**
Lott, Ronnie **9**
Louis, Errol T. **8**
Louis, Joe **5**
Loury, Glenn **36**
Love, Darlene **23**
Love, Ed **58**
Love, Laura **50**
Love, Nat **9**
Lover, Ed **10**
Loving, Alvin, Jr. **35, 53**
Loving, Mildred **69**
Lowe, Herbert **57**
Lowe, Sidney **64**
Lowery, Joseph **2**
Lowry, A. Leon **60**
Lucas, John **7**
Lucien, Jon **66**
Luckett, Letoya **61**
Lucy, William **50**
Lucy Foster, Autherine **35**
Ludacris **37, 60**
Luke, Derek **61**
Lumbly, Carl **47**
Lyles, Lester Lawrence **31**
Lymon, Frankie **22**
Lynch, Shola **61**
Lyons, Henry **12**
Lyttle, Hulda Margaret **14**
Mabley, Moms **15**
Mabrey, Vicki **26**
Mabry, Marcus **70**
Mac, Bernie **29, 61, 72**
Madhubuti, Haki R. **7**
Madison, Joseph E. **17**
Madison, Paula **37**
Madison, Romell **45**
Mahal, Taj **39**
Mahorn, Rick **60**
Majette, Denise **41**
Major, Clarence **9**
Majors, Jeff **41**
Malco, Romany **71**
Mallett, Conrad, Jr. **16**
Mallory, Mark **62**
Malone Jones, Vivian **59**
Malone, Annie **13**
Malone, Karl **18, 51**
Malone, Maurice **32**
Malveaux, Floyd **54**
Malveaux, Julianne **32, 70**
Manigault, Earl "The Goat" **15**
Manigault-Stallworth, Omarosa **69**
Manley, Audrey Forbes **16**
Marable, Manning **10**
March, William Carrington **56**
Mariner, Jonathan **41**
Marino, Eugene Antonio **30**
Mario **71**
Marrow, Queen Esther **24**
Marsalis, Branford **34**
Marsalis, Delfeayo **41**
Marsalis, Wynton **16**
Marsh, Henry, III **32**
Marshall, Bella **22**
Marshall, Kerry James **59**
Marshall, Paule **7**
Marshall, Thurgood **1, 44**
Martin, Darnell **43**
Martin, Helen **31**
Martin, Jesse L. **31**
Martin, Louis E. **16**
Martin, Roberta **58**

Martin, Roland S. **49**
Martin, Ruby Grant **49**
Martin, Sara **38**
Mase **24**
Mason, Felicia **31**
Mason, Ronald **27**
Massaquoi, Hans J. **30**
Massenburg, Kedar **23**
Massey, Brandon **40**
Massey, Walter E. **5, 45**
Massie, Samuel Proctor, Jr. **29**
Master P **21**
Mathis, Greg **26**
Mathis, Johnny **20**
Matthews, Mark **59**
Matthews Shatteen, Westina **51**
Maxey, Randall **46**
Maxis, Theresa **62**
Maxwell **20**
May, Derrick **41**
Mayfield, Curtis **2, 43**
Mayhew, Richard **39**
Maynard, Nancy Hicks **73**
Maynard, Robert C. **7**
Maynor, Dorothy **19**
Mayo, Whitman **32**
Mays, Benjamin E. **7**
Mays, Leslie A. **41**
Mays, William G. **34**
Mays, Willie **3**
Mayweather, Floyd, Jr. **57**
MC Lyte **34**
McAnulty, William E., Jr. **66**
McBride, Bryant **18**
McBride, Chi **73**
McBride, James C. **35**
McCabe, Jewell Jackson **10**
McCall, H. Carl **27**
McCall, Nathan **8**
McCann, Renetta **44**
McCarthy, Sandy **64**
McCarty, Osceola **16**
McClendon, Lisa **61**
McClurkin, Donnie **25**
McCoo, Marilyn **53**
McCoy, Elijah **8**
McCrary Anthony, Crystal **70**
McCray, Nikki **18**
McCullough, Geraldine **58**
McDaniel, Hattie **5**
McDonald, Audra **20, 62**
McDonald, Erroll **1**
McDonald, Gabrielle Kirk **20**
McDougall, Gay J. **11, 43**
McDuffie, Dwayne **62**
McEwen, Mark **5**
McFadden, Bernice L. **39**
McFarlan, Tyron **60**
McFarland, Roland **49**
McFerrin, Bobby **68**
McGee, Charles **10**
McGee, James Madison **46**
McGlowan, Angela **64**
McGriff, Fred **24**
McGriff, Jimmy **72**
McGruder, Aaron **28, 56**
McGruder, Robert **22, 35**
McGuire, Raymond J. **57**
McKay, Claude **6**
McKay, Nellie Yvonne **17, 57**
Mckee, Lonette **12**
McKenzie, Vashti M. **29**
McKinney, Cynthia Ann **11, 52**

McKinney, Nina Mae **40**
McKinney-Whetstone, Diane **27**
McKinnon, Isaiah **9**
McKissick, Floyd B. **3**
McKnight, Brian **18, 34**
McLeod, Gus **27**
McMillan, Rosaylnn A. **36**
McMillan, Terry **4, 17, 53**
McMurray, Georgia L. **36**
McNabb, Donovan **29**
McNair, Ronald **3, 58**
McNair, Steve **22, 47**
McNeil, Lori **1**
McPhail, Sharon **2**
McPherson, David **32**
McPherson, James Alan **70**
McQueen, Butterfly **6, 54**
McWhorter, John **35**
Meadows, Tim **30**
Meek, Carrie **6, 36**
Meek, Kendrick **41**
Meeks, Gregory **25**
Mell, Patricia **49**
Memphis Minnie **33**
Mengestu, Dinaw **66**
Mercado-Valdes, Frank **43**
Meredith, James H. **11**
Merkerson, S. Epatha **47**
Metcalfe, Ralph **26**
Mfume, Kweisi **6, 41**
Micheaux, Oscar **7**
Michele, Michael **31**
Mickelbury, Penny **28**
Miles, Buddy **69**
Millender-McDonald, Juanita **21, 61**
Miller, Bebe **3**
Miller, Cheryl **10**
Miller, Dorie **29**
Miller, Larry G. **72**
Miller, Reggie **33**
Miller, Warren F., Jr. **53**
Miller-Travis, Vernice **64**
Millines Dziko, Trish **28**
Mills, Florence **22**
Mills, Joseph C. **51**
Mills, Sam **33**
Mills, Stephanie **36**
Mills, Steve **47**
Milner, Ron **39**
Milton, DeLisha **31**
Mingo, Frank **32**
Mingus, Charles **15**
Minor, DeWayne **32**
Mitchell, Arthur **2, 47**
Mitchell, Brian Stokes **21**
Mitchell, Corinne **8**
Mitchell, Elvis **67**
Mitchell, Kel **66**
Mitchell, Leona **42**
Mitchell, Loften **31**
Mitchell, Nicole **66**
Mitchell, Parren J. **42, 66**
Mitchell, Russ **21, 73**
Mitchell, Stephanie **36**
Mo', Keb' **36**
Mohammed, Nazr **64**
Mohammed, W. Deen **27**
Monica **21**
Mo'Nique **35**
Monk, Art **38, 73**
Monk, Thelonious **1**
Monroe, Bryan **71**
Monroe, Mary **35**

Montgomery, Tim **41**
Moon, Warren **8, 66**
Mooney, Paul **37**
Moore, Barbara C. **49**
Moore, Chante **26**
Moore, Dorothy Rudd **46**
Moore, Gwendolynne S. **55**
Moore, Harry T. **29**
Moore, Jessica Care **30**
Moore, Johnny B. **38**
Moore, LeRoi **72**
Moore, Melba **21**
Moore, Minyon **45**
Moore, Shemar **21**
Moore, Undine Smith **28**
Moorer, Michael **19**
Moose, Charles **40**
Morgan, Garrett **1**
Morgan, Gertrude **63**
Morgan, Irene **65**
Morgan, Joe Leonard **9**
Morgan, Rose **11**
Morgan, Tracy **61**
Morial, Ernest "Dutch" **26**
Morial, Marc H. **20, 51**
Morris, Garrett **31**
Morris, Greg **28**
Morrison, Sam **50**
Morrison, Toni **2, 15**
Morton, Azie Taylor **48**
Morton, Jelly Roll **29**
Morton, Joe **18**
Mos Def **30**
Moses, Edwin **8**
Moses, Gilbert **12**
Moses, Robert Parris **11**
Mosley, Shane **32**
Mosley, Walter **5, 25, 68**
Moss, Carlton **17**
Moss, J. **64**
Moss, Otis, Jr. **72**
Moss, Otis, III **72**
Moss, Preacher **63**
Moss, Randy **23**
Mossell, Gertrude Bustill **40**
Moten, Etta **18**
Motley, Archibald, Jr. **30**
Motley, Constance Baker **10, 55**
Motley, Marion **26**
Mourning, Alonzo **17, 44**
Moutoussamy-Ashe, Jeanne **7**
Mowry, Jess **7**
Moyo, Karega Kofi **36**
Moyo, Yvette Jackson **36**
Muhammad, Ava **31**
Muhammad, Elijah **4**
Muhammad, Jabir Herbert **72**
Muhammad, Khallid Abdul **10, 31**
Mullen, Harryette **34**
Mullen, Nicole C. **45**
Murphy, Eddie **4, 20, 61**
Murphy, John H. **42**
Murphy, Laura M. **43**
Murray, Albert L. **33**
Murray, Cecil **12, 47**
Murray, Eddie **12**
Murray, Lenda **10**
Murray, Pauli **38**
Murray, Tai **47**
Murrell, Sylvia Marilyn **49**
Muse, Clarence Edouard **21**
Musiq **37**
Mya **35**

Myers, Walter Dean **8, 70**
Myles, Kim **69**
Nabrit, Samuel Milton **47**
Nagin, C. Ray **42, 57**
Nance, Cynthia **71**
Nanula, Richard D. **20**
Napoleon, Benny N. **23**
Nas **33**
Nash, Diane **72**
Nash, Joe **55**
Nash, Johnny **40**
Nash, Niecy **66**
Naylor, Gloria **10, 42**
Ndegéocello, Me'Shell **15**
Ne-Yo **65**
Neal, Elise **29**
Neal, Larry **38**
Neal, Raful **44**
Neals, Otto **73**
Nelly **32**
Nelson, Jill **6, 54**
Nelson Meigs, Andrea **48**
Neville, Aaron **21**
Neville, Arthel **53**
Newcombe, Don **24**
Newkirk, Pamela **69**
Newman, Lester C. **51**
Newsome, Ozzie **26**
Newton, Huey **2**
Nicholas, Fayard **20, 57**
Nicholas, Harold **20**
Nichols, Nichelle **11**
Nissel, Angela **42**
Nix, Robert N. C., Jr. **51**
N'Namdi, George R. **17**
Noble, Ronald **46**
Norman, Christina **47**
Norman, Jessye **5**
Norman, Maidie **20**
Norman, Pat **10**
Norton, Eleanor Holmes **7**
Norton, Meredith **72**
Notorious B.I.G. **20**
Nottage, Lynn **66**
Nugent, Richard Bruce **39**
Nunn, Annetta **43**
Nutter, Michael **69**
Obama, Barack **49**
Obama, Michelle **61**
Odetta **37**
Oglesby, Zena **12**
Ogletree, Charles, Jr. **12, 47**
O'Grady, Lorraine **73**
Ojikutu, Bayo **66**
Ojikutu, Bisola **65**
Ol' Dirty Bastard **52**
Olden, Georg(e) **44**
O'Leary, Hazel **6**
Oliver, Jerry **37**
Oliver, Joe "King" **42**
Oliver, John J., Jr. **48**
Oliver, Kimberly **60**
Oliver, Pam **54**
O'Neal, Ron **46**
O'Neal, Shaquille **8, 30**
O'Neal, Stanley **38, 67**
O'Neil, Buck **19, 59**
Onyewu, Oguchi **60**
Orlandersmith, Dael **42**
Orman, Roscoe **55**
Ormes, Jackie **73**
Osborne, Jeffrey **26**
Osborne, Na'taki **54**

Otis, Clarence, Jr. 55
Otis, Clyde 67
Owens, Helen 48
Owens, Jack 38
Owens, Jesse 2
Owens, Major 6
Owens, Terrell 53
P.M. Dawn 54
Pace, Betty 59
Pace, Orlando 21
Packer, Daniel 56
Packer, Will 71
Packer, Z. Z. 64
Page, Alan 7
Page, Clarence 4
Paige, Rod 29
Paige, Satchel 7
Painter, Nell Irvin 24
Palmer, Keke 68
Palmer, Rissi 65
Palmer, Violet 59
Parham, Marjorie B. 71
Parish, Robert 43
Parker, Charlie 20
Parker, Jim 64
Parker, Kellis E. 30
Parker, Maceo 72
Parker, Nicole Ari 52
Parker, Pat 19
Parker, Star 70
Parks, Bernard C. 17
Parks, Gordon 1, 35, 58
Parks, Rosa 1, 35, 56
Parks, Suzan-Lori 34
Parr, Russ 51
Parsons, James 14
Parsons, Richard Dean 11, 33
Paterson, Basil A. 69
Paterson, David A. 59
Patrick, Deval 12, 61
Patterson, Floyd 19, 58
Patterson, Frederick Douglass 12
Patterson, Gilbert Earl 41
Patterson, Louise 25
Patterson, Mary Jane 54
Patton, Antwan 45
Patton, Paula 62
Payne, Allen 13
Payne, Donald M. 2, 57
Payne, Ethel L. 28
Payne, Freda 58
Payne, Ulice 42
Payne, William D. 60
Payton, Benjamin F. 23
Payton, John 48
Payton, Walter 11, 25
Peck, Carolyn 23
Peete, Calvin 11
Peete, Holly Robinson 20
Peete, Rodney 60
Pena, Paul 58
Pendergrass, Teddy 22
Peoples, Dottie 22
Perez, Anna 1
Perkins, Edward 5
Perkins, James, Jr. 55
Perkins, Marion 38
Perkins, Pinetop 70
Perkins, Tony 24
Perren, Freddie 60
Perrineau, Harold, Jr. 51
Perrot, Kim 23
Perry, Laval 64

Perry, Lowell 30
Perry, Tyler 40, 54
Perry, Warren 56
Person, Waverly 9, 51
Peters, Margaret 43
Peters, Matilda 43
Petersen, Frank E. 31
Peterson, James 38
Peterson, Marvin "Hannibal" 27
Petry, Ann 19
Phifer, Mekhi 25
Phillips, Charles E., Jr. 57
Phillips, Helen L. 63
Phillips, Joseph C. 73
Phillips, Teresa L. 42
Phipps, Wintley 59
Pickens, James, Jr. 59
Pickett, Bill 11
Pickett, Cecil 39
Pierce, Paul 71
Pierre, Percy Anthony 46
Pincham, R. Eugene, Sr. 69
Pinchback, P. B. S. 9
Pinckney, Bill 42
Pinckney, Sandra 56
Pindell, Howardena 55
Pinderhughes, John 47
Pinkett Smith, Jada 10, 41
Pinkett, Randal 61
Pinkney, Jerry 15
Pinkston, W. Randall 24
Pinn, Vivian Winona 49
Piper, Adrian 71
Pippen, Scottie 15
Pippin, Horace 9
Pitts, Byron 71
Pitts, Leonard, Jr. 54
Player, Willa B. 43
Pleasant, Mary Ellen 9
Plessy, Homer Adolph 31
Poitier, Sidney 11, 36
Poitier, Sydney Tamiia 65
Pollard, Fritz 53
Pope.L, William 72
Porter, James A. 11
Potter, Myrtle 40
Pough, Terrell 58
Pounder, CCH 72
Poussaint, Alvin F. 5, 67
Powell, Adam Clayton, Jr. 3
Powell, Bud 24
Powell, Colin 1, 28
Powell, Debra A. 23
Powell, Kevin 31
Powell, Maxine 8
Powell, Michael 32
Powell, Mike 7
Powell, Renee 34
Pratt, Awadagin 31
Pratt, Geronimo 18
Pratt, Kyla 57
Premice, Josephine 41
Pressley, Condace L. 41
Preston, Billy 39, 59
Price, Florence 37
Price, Frederick K.C. 21
Price, Glenda 22
Price, Hugh B. 9, 54
Price, Kelly 23
Price, Leontyne 1
Price, Richard 51
Pride, Charley 26
Primus, Pearl 6

Prince 18, 65
Prince, Richard E. 71
Prince, Ron 64
Prince, Tayshaun 68
Prince-Bythewood, Gina 31
Pritchard, Robert Starling 21
Procope, Ernesta 23
Procope, John Levy 56
Prophet, Nancy Elizabeth 42
Prothrow-Stith, Deborah 10
Pryor, Rain 65
Pryor, Richard 3, 24, 56
Puckett, Kirby 4, 58
Purnell, Silas 59
Puryear, Martin 42
Quarles, Benjamin Arthur 18
Quarles, Norma 25
Quarterman, Lloyd Albert 4
Queen Latifah 1, 16, 58
Quigless, Helen G. 49
Quince, Peggy A. 69
Quivers, Robin 61
Rabb, Maurice F., Jr. 58
Rahman, Aishah 37
Raines, Franklin Delano 14
Rainey, Ma 33
Ralph, Sheryl Lee 18
Ramsey, Charles H. 21, 69
Rand, A. Barry 6
Randall, Alice 38
Randall, Dudley 8, 55
Randle, Theresa 16
Randolph, A. Philip 3
Randolph, Linda A. 52
Randolph, Willie 53
Rangel, Charles 3, 52
Raoul, Kwame 55
Rashad, Ahmad 18
Rashad, Phylicia 21
Raspberry, William 2
Raven 44
Rawls, Lou 17, 57
Ray, Charlotte E. 60
Ray, Gene Anthony 47
Razaf, Andy 19
Reagon, Bernice Johnson 7
Reason, J. Paul 19
Record, Eugene 60
Reddick, Lance 52
Reddick, Lawrence Dunbar 20
Redding, J. Saunders 26
Redding, Louis L. 26
Redding, Otis 16
Redman, Joshua 30
Redmond, Eugene 23
Reed, A. C. 36
Reed, Ishmael 8
Reed, Jimmy 38
Reems, Ernestine Cleveland 27
Reese, Della 6, 20
Reese, Milous J., Jr. 51
Reese, Pokey 28
Reese, Tracy 54
Reeves, Dianne 32
Reeves, Gregory 49
Reeves, Rachel J. 23
Reeves, Triette Lipsey 27
Reid, Antonio "L.A." 28
Reid, Irvin D. 20
Reid, Senghor 55
Reid, Tim 56
Reid, Vernon 34
Reynolds, Star Jones 10, 27, 61

Rhames, Ving 14, 50
Rhimes, Shonda Lynn 67
Rhoden, Dwight 40
Rhoden, William C. 67
Rhodes, Ray 14
Rhone, Sylvia 2
Rhymes, Busta 31
Ribbs, Willy T. 2
Ribeau, Sidney 70
Ribeiro, Alfonso 17
Rice, Condoleezza 3, 28, 72
Rice, Constance LaMay 60
Rice, Jerry 5, 55
Rice, Linda Johnson 9, 41
Rice, Louise Allen 54
Rice, Norm 8
Richards, Beah 30
Richards, Hilda 49
Richards, Sanya 66
Richardson, Desmond 39
Richardson, Donna 39
Richardson, LaTanya 71
Richardson, Nolan 9
Richardson, Rupert 67
Richardson, Salli 68
Richie, Leroy C. 18
Richie, Lionel 27, 65
Richmond, Mitch 19
Rideau, Iris 46
Ridley, John 69
Riggs, Marlon 5, 44
Riley, Helen Caldwell Day 13
Riley, Rochelle 50
Ringgold, Faith 4
Riperton, Minnie 32
Rivers, Glenn "Doc" 25
Roach, Max 21, 63
Roberts, Darryl 70
Roberts, Deborah 35
Roberts, Kimberly Rivers 72
Roberts, Marcus 19
Roberts, Mike 57
Roberts, Robin 16, 54
Roberts, Roy S. 14
Robertson, Oscar 26
Robeson, Eslanda Goode 13
Robeson, Paul 2
Robinson, Aminah 50
Robinson, Bill "Bojangles" 11
Robinson, Bishop L. 66
Robinson, Cleo Parker 38
Robinson, David 24
Robinson, Eddie G. 10
Robinson, Fatima 34
Robinson, Fenton 38
Robinson, Frank 9
Robinson, Jackie 6
Robinson, LaVaughn 69
Robinson, Malcolm S. 44
Robinson, Matt 69
Robinson, Max 3
Robinson, Patrick 19, 71
Robinson, Rachel 16
Robinson, Randall 7, 46
Robinson, Reginald R. 53
Robinson, Sharon 22
Robinson, Shaun 36
Robinson, Smokey 3, 49
Robinson, Spottswood W., III 22
Robinson, Sugar Ray 18
Robinson, Will 51, 69
Roble, Abdi 71
Roche, Joyce M. 17

Rochon, Lela 16
Rock, Chris 3, 22, 66
Rock, The 29, 66
Rodgers, Johnathan 6, 51
Rodgers, Rod 36
Rodman, Dennis 12, 44
Rodriguez, Jimmy 47
Rodriguez, Cheryl 64
Rogers, Alan G. 72
Rogers, Jimmy 38
Rogers, Joe 27
Rogers, Joel Augustus 30
Rogers, John W., Jr. 5, 52
Roker, Al 12, 49
Roker, Roxie 68
Rolle, Esther 13, 21
Rollins, Charlemae Hill 27
Rollins, Howard E., Jr. 16
Rollins, Jimmy 70
Rollins, Sonny 37
Rose, Anika Noni 70
Ross, Charles 27
Ross, Diana 8, 27
Ross, Don 27
Ross, Isaiah "Doc" 40
Ross, Tracee Ellis 35
Ross-Lee, Barbara 67
Roundtree, Richard 27
Rowan, Carl T. 1, 30
Rowell, Victoria 13, 68
Roxanne Shante 33
Roy, Kenny 51
Rubin, Chanda 37
Rucker, Darius 34
Rudolph, Maya 46
Rudolph, Wilma 4
Ruley, Ellis 38
Run 31, 73
Rupaul 17
Rush, Bobby 26
Rush, Otis 38
Rushen, Patrice 12
Rushing, Jimmy 37
Russell, Bill 8
Russell, Brenda 52
Russell, Herman Jerome 17
Russell, Nipsey 66
Russell-McCloud, Patricia A. 17
Rustin, Bayard 4
Saar, Alison 16
St. Jacques, Raymond 8
Saint James, Synthia 12
St. John, Kristoff 25
St. Julien, Marlon 29
St. Patrick, Mathew 48
Saldana, Zoe 72
Sallee, Charles 38
Salter, Nikkole 73
Salters, Lisa 71
Samara, Noah 15
Sample, Joe 51
Sampson, Charles 13
Sanchez, Sonia 17, 51
Sanders, Barry 1, 53
Sanders, Bob 72
Sanders, Deion 4, 31
Sanders, Joseph R., Jr. 11
Sanders, Malika 48
Sanders, Pharoah 64
Sanford, Isabel 53
Sapp, Warren 38
Sapphire 14
Satcher, David 7, 57

Savage, Augusta 12
Sayers, Gale 28
Sayles Belton, Sharon 9, 16
Scantlebury-White, Velma 64
Schmoke, Kurt 1, 48
Schuyler, George Samuel 40
Schuyler, Philippa 50
Scott, C(ornelius) A(dolphus) 29
Scott, David 41
Scott, George 55
Scott, Harold Russell, Jr. 61
Scott, Hazel 66
Scott, Jill 29
Scott, John T. 65
Scott, "Little" Jimmy 48
Scott, Milton 51
Scott, Robert C. 23
Scott, Stuart 34
Scott, Wendell Oliver, Sr. 19
Scurry, Briana 27
Seals, Son 56
Sears, Stephanie 53
Sebree, Charles 40
Seele, Pernessa 46
Sengstacke, John 18
Serrano, Andres 3
Shabazz, Attallah 6
Shabazz, Betty 7, 26
Shabazz, Ilyasah 36
Shakur, Afeni 67
Shakur, Assata 6
Shakur, Tupac 14
Shange, Ntozake 8
Sharper, Darren 32
Sharpton, Al 21
Shavers, Cheryl 31
Shaw, Bernard 2, 28
Shaw, William J. 30
Sheard, Kierra "Kiki 61
Sheffield, Gary 16
Shell, Art 1, 66
Shepherd, Sherri 55
Sherrod, Clayton 17
Shinhoster, Earl 32
Shipp, E. R. 15
Shippen, John 43
Shirley, George 33
Short, Bobby 52
Showers, Reggie 30
Shropshire, Thomas B. 49
Shuttlesworth, Fred 47
Sifford, Charlie 4, 49
Sigur, Wanda 44
Silas, Paul 24
Silver, Horace 26
Simmons, Bob 29
Simmons, Gary 58
Simmons, Henry 55
Simmons, Jamal 72
Simmons, Kimora Lee 51
Simmons, Russell 1, 30
Simmons, Ruth J. 13, 38
Simone, Nina 15, 41
Simpson, Carole 6, 30
Simpson, Lorna 4, 36
Simpson, O. J. 15
Simpson, Valerie 21
Simpson-Hoffman, N'kenge 52
Sims, Howard "Sandman" 48
Sims, Lowery Stokes 27
Sims, Naomi 29
Sinbad 1, 16
Singletary, Mike 4

Singleton, John 2, 30
Sinkford, Jeanne C. 13
Sisqo 30
Sissle, Noble 29
Sister Souljah 11
Sizemore, Barbara A. 26
Skinner, Kiron K. 65
Sklarek, Norma Merrick 25
Slater, Rodney E. 15
Slaughter, John Brooks 53
Sledge, Percy 39
Sleet, Moneta, Jr. 5
Slice, Kimbo 73
Slocumb, Jonathan 52
Slyde, Jimmy 70
Smaltz, Audrey 12
Smiley, Rickey 59
Smiley, Tavis 20, 68
Smith, Anna Deavere 6, 44
Smith, B(arbara) 11
Smith, Barbara 28
Smith, Bessie 3
Smith, Bruce W. 53
Smith, Cladys "Jabbo" 32
Smith, Clarence O. 21
Smith, Damu 54
Smith, Danyel 40
Smith, Dr. Lonnie 49
Smith, Emmitt 7
Smith, Greg 28
Smith, Hilton 29
Smith, Ian 62
Smith, Jane E. 24
Smith, Jessie Carney 35
Smith, John L. 22
Smith, Joshua 10
Smith, Kemba 70
Smith, Lonnie Liston 49
Smith, Lovie 66
Smith, Mamie 32
Smith, Marie F. 70
Smith, Marvin 46
Smith, Mary Carter 26
Smith, Morgan 46
Smith, Nate 49
Smith, Rick 72
Smith, Roger Guenveur 12
Smith, Stephen A. 69
Smith, Stuff 37
Smith, Tasha 73
Smith, Trixie 34
Smith, Tubby 18
Smith, Vincent D. 48
Smith, Will 8, 18, 53
Smith, Willi 8
Smythe Haith, Mabel 61
Sneed, Paula A. 18
Snipes, Wesley 3, 24, 67
Snoop Dogg 35
Snow, Samuel 71
Snowden, Frank M., Jr. 67
Solomon, Jimmie Lee 38
Sommore 61
Southern, Eileen 56
Southgate, Martha 58
Sowell, Thomas 2
Sparks, Jordin 66
Spaulding, Charles Clinton 9
Spears, Warren 52
Spencer, Anne 27
Spikes, Dolores 18
Spiller, Bill 64
Sprewell, Latrell 23

Spriggs, William 67
Stackhouse, Jerry 30
Staley, Dawn 57
Stallings, George A., Jr. 6
Stampley, Micah 54
Stanford, John 20
Stanford, Olivia Lee Dilworth 49
Stanton, Robert 20
Staples, "Pops" 32
Staples, Brent 8
Staples, Mavis 50
Stargell, Willie 29
Staton, Candi 27
Staton, Dakota 62
Staupers, Mabel K. 7
Stearnes, Norman "Turkey" 31
Steave-Dickerson, Kia 57
Steele, Claude Mason 13
Steele, Lawrence 28
Steele, Michael 38, 73
Steele, Shelby 13
Steinberg, Martha Jean "The Queen" 28
Stephens, Charlotte Andrews 14
Stew 69
Steward, David L. 36
Steward, Emanuel 18
Stewart, Alison 13
Stewart, Ella 39
Stewart, James "Bubba," Jr. 60
Stewart, Kordell 21
Stewart, Maria W. Miller 19
Stewart, Paul Wilbur 12
Still, William Grant 37
Stingley, Darryl 69
Stinson, Denise L. 59
Stith, Charles R. 73
Stokes, Carl 10, 73
Stokes, Louis 3
Stone, Angie 31
Stone, Chuck 9
Stone, Toni 15
Stoney, Michael 50
Stoudemire, Amaré 59
Stout, Juanita Kidd 24
Stout, Renee 63
Stoute, Steve 38
Strahan, Michael 35
Strawberry, Darryl 22
Strayhorn, Billy 31
Street, John F. 24
Streeter, Sarah 45
Stringer, C. Vivian 13, 66
Stringer, Korey 35
Stringer, Vickie 58
Studdard, Ruben 46
Sudarkasa, Niara 4
Sudduth, Jimmy Lee 65
Sullivan, Leon H. 3, 30
Sullivan, Louis 8
Sullivan, Maxine 37
Summer, Donna 25
Sun Ra 60
Sundiata, Sekou 66
Sutton, Percy E. 42
Swann, Lynn 28
Sweat, Keith 19
Sweet, Ossian 68
Swoopes, Sheryl 12, 56
Swygert, H. Patrick 22
Sykes, Roosevelt 20
Sykes, Wanda 48
Syler, Rene 53

Tademy, Lalita 36
Tait, Michael 57
Talbert, David 34
Talley, André Leon 56
Tamar-kali 63
Tamia 24, 55
Tampa Red 63
Tancil, Gladys Quander 59
Tanksley, Ann 37
Tanner, Henry Ossawa 1
Tate, Eleanora E. 20, 55
Tate, Larenz 15
Tatum, Art 28
Tatum, Beverly Daniel 42
Taulbert, Clifton Lemoure 19
Taylor, Billy 23
Taylor, Bo 72
Taylor, Cecil 70
Taylor, Charles 20
Taylor, Ephren W., II 61
Taylor, Helen (Lavon Hollingshed) 30
Taylor, Jason 70
Taylor, Jermain 60
Taylor, Koko 40
Taylor, Kristin Clark 8
Taylor, Lawrence 25
Taylor, Marshall Walter "Major" 62
Taylor, Meshach 4
Taylor, Mildred D. 26
Taylor, Natalie 47
Taylor, Regina 9, 46
Taylor, Ron 35
Taylor, Susan C. 62
Taylor, Susan L. 10
Taylor, Susie King 13
Terrell, Dorothy A. 24
Terrell, Mary Church 9
Terrell, Tammi 32
Terry, Clark 39
Tharpe, Rosetta 65
Thigpen, Lynne 17, 41
Thomas, Alma 14
Thomas, Arthur Ray 52
Thomas, Clarence 2, 39, 65
Thomas, Claudia Lynn 64
Thomas, Debi 26
Thomas, Derrick 25
Thomas, Emmitt 71
Thomas, Frank 12, 51
Thomas, Franklin A. 5, 49
Thomas, Irma 29
Thomas, Isiah 7, 26, 65
Thomas, Michael 69
Thomas, Mickalene 61
Thomas, Rozonda "Chilli" 34
Thomas, Rufus 20
Thomas, Sean Patrick 35
Thomas, Trisha R. 65
Thomas, Vivien 9
Thomas-Graham, Pamela 29
Thompson, Bennie G. 26
Thompson, Cynthia Bramlett 50
Thompson, Don 56
Thompson, John W. 26
Thompson, Kenan 52
Thompson, Larry D. 39
Thompson, Tazewell 13
Thompson, Tina 25
Thompson, William C. 35
Thoms, Tracie 61
Thornton, Big Mama 33
Thornton, Yvonne S. 69

Thrash, Dox 35
Thrower, Willie 35
Thurman, Howard 3
Thurman, Wallace 16
Thurston, Stephen J. 49
Till, Emmett 7
Tillard, Conrad 47
Tillis, Frederick 40
Tillman, George, Jr. 20
Timbaland 32
Tinsley, Boyd 50
Tirico, Mike 68
Tisdale, Wayman 50
Todman, Terence A. 55
Tolliver, Mose 60
Tolliver, William 9
Tolson, Melvin 37
Tolton, Augustine 62
Tomlinson, LaDainian 65
Tonex 54
Tooks, Lance 62
Toomer, Jean 6
Toote, Gloria E.A. 64
Torres, Gina 52
Torry, Guy 31
Touré, Askia (Muhammad Abu Bakr el) 47
Touré, Faya Ora Rose 56
Toussaint, Allen 60
Towns, Edolphus 19
Townsend, Robert 4, 23
T-Pain 73
Tresvant, Ralph 57
Tribble, Israel, Jr. 8
Trotter, Donne E. 28
Trotter, Lloyd G. 56
Trotter, Monroe 9
Trueheart, William E. 49
Tubbs Jones, Stephanie 24, 72
Tubman, Harriet 9
Tucker, C. Delores 12, 56
Tucker, Chris 13, 23, 62
Tucker, Cynthia 15, 61
Tucker, Rosina 14
Tuckson, Reed V. 71
Tunie, Tamara 63
Tunnell, Emlen 54
Turnbull, Charles Wesley 62
Turnbull, Walter 13, 60
Turner, Henry McNeal 5
Turner, Ike 68
Turner, Tina 6, 27
Tyler, Aisha N. 36
Tyree, Omar Rashad 21
Tyson, Andre 40
Tyson, Asha 39
Tyson, Cicely 7, 51
Tyson, Mike 28, 44
Tyson, Neil deGrasse 15, 65
Uggams, Leslie 23
Underwood, Blair 7, 27
Union, Gabrielle 31
Unseld, Wes 23
Upshaw, Gene 18, 47, 72
Usher 23, 56
Usry, James L. 23
Ussery, Terdema, II 29
Utendahl, John 23
Valentino, Bobby 62
Van Lierop, Robert 53
Van Peebles, Mario 2, 51
Van Peebles, Melvin 7
Vance, Courtney B. 15, 60

VanDerZee, James 6
Vandross, Luther 13, 48, 59
Vanzant, Iyanla 17, 47
Vaughan, Sarah 13
Vaughn, Countess 53
Vaughn, Gladys Gary 47
Vaughn, Mo 16
Vaughn, Viola 70
Vaughns, Cleopatra 46
Vega, Marta Moreno 61
Velez-Rodriguez, Argelia 56
Verdelle, A. J. 26
Vereen, Ben 4
Verrett, Shirley 66
Vick, Michael 39, 65
Vincent, Marjorie Judith 2
Von Lipsey, Roderick K. 11
Waddles, Charleszetta "Mother" 10, 49
Wade, Dwyane 61
Wade-Gayles, Gloria Jean 41
Wagner, Annice 22
Wainwright, Joscelyn 46
Walker, A'lelia 14
Walker, Albertina 10, 58
Walker, Alice 1, 43
Walker, Bernita Ruth 53
Walker, Cedric "Ricky" 19
Walker, Cora T. 68
Walker, Dianne 57
Walker, George 37
Walker, Herschel 1, 69
Walker, Hezekiah 34
Walker, John T. 50
Walker, Madame C. J. 7
Walker, Maggie Lena 17
Walker, Margaret 29
Walker, Rebecca 50
Walker, T. J. 7
Wallace, Ben 54
Wallace, Joaquin 49
Wallace, Michele Faith 13
Wallace, Perry E. 47
Wallace, Phyllis A. 9
Wallace, Rasheed 56
Wallace, Sippie 1
Waller, Fats 29
Ward, Andre 62
Ward, Benjamin 68
Ward, Douglas Turner 42
Ward, Lloyd 21, 46
Ware, Andre 37
Ware, Carl H. 30
Warfield, Marsha 2
Warner, Malcolm-Jamal 22, 36
Warren, Michael 27
Warwick, Dionne 18
Washington, Alonzo 29
Washington, Booker T. 4
Washington, Denzel 1, 16
Washington, Dinah 22
Washington, Fredi 10
Washington, Gene 63
Washington, Grover, Jr. 17, 44
Washington, Harold 6
Washington, Harriet A. 69
Washington, Isaiah 62
Washington, James, Jr. 38
Washington, James Melvin 50
Washington, Kenny 50
Washington, Kerry 46
Washington, Laura S. 18
Washington, MaliVai 8

Washington, Mary T. 57
Washington, Patrice Clarke 12
Washington, Regynald G. 44
Washington, Val 12
Washington, Walter 45
Wasow, Omar 15
Waters, Benny 26
Waters, Ethel 7
Waters, Maxine 3, 67
Waters, Muddy 34
Watkins, Donald 35
Watkins, Levi, Jr. 9
Watkins, Perry 12
Watkins, Shirley R. 17
Watkins, Tionne "T-Boz" 34
Watkins, Walter C. 24
Watley, Jody 54
Watson, Bob 25
Watson, Carlos 50
Watson, Diane 41
Watson, Johnny "Guitar" 18
Watt, Melvin 26
Wattleton, Faye 9
Watts, J. C., Jr. 14, 38
Watts, Reggie 52
Watts, Rolonda 9
Wayans, Damon 8, 41
Wayans, Keenen Ivory 18
Wayans, Marlon 29
Wayans, Shawn 29
Weathers, Carl 10
Weaver, Afaa Michael 37
Weaver, Robert C. 8, 46
Webb, Veronica 10
Webb, Wellington 3
Webber, Chris 15, 30, 59
Webster, Katie 54
Wedgeworth, Robert W. 42
Weeks, Thomas, III 70
Weems, Carrie Mae 63
Weems, Renita J. 44
Wein, Joyce 62
Welburn, Edward T. 50
Welch, Elisabeth 52
Wells, Henrietta Bell 69
Wells, James Lesesne 10
Wells, Mary 28
Wells-Barnett, Ida B. 8
Welsing, Frances Cress 5
Wesley, Dorothy Porter 19
Wesley, Richard 73
Wesley, Valerie Wilson 18
West, Cornel 5, 33
West, Dorothy 12, 54
West, Kanye 52
West, Togo D., Jr. 16
Westbrook, Kelvin 50
Westbrook, Peter 20
Westbrooks, Bobby 51
Whack, Rita Coburn 36
Whalum, Kirk 37, 64
Wharton, Clifton R., Jr. 7
Wharton, Clifton Reginald, Sr. 36
Wheat, Alan 14
Whitaker, Forest 2, 49, 67
Whitaker, Mark 21, 47
Whitaker, Pernell 10
White, Barry 13, 41
White, Bill 1, 48
White, Charles 39
White, Dondi 34
White, Jesse 22
White, John H. 27

White, Josh, Jr. 52
White, Linda M. 45
White, Lois Jean 20
White, Maurice 29
White, Michael Jai 71
White, Michael R. 5
White, Reggie 6, 50
White, Walter F. 4
White, Willye 67
White-Hammond, Gloria 61
Whitfield, Fred 23
Whitfield, Lynn 18
Whitfield, Mal 60
Whitfield, Norman 73
Whitfield, Van 34
Wideman, John Edgar 5
Wilbekin, Emil 63
Wilbon, Michael 68
Wilder, L. Douglas 3, 48
Wiley, Kehinde 62
Wiley, Ralph 8
Wilkens, J. Ernest, Jr. 43
Wilkens, Lenny 11
Wilkerson, Isabel 71
Wilkins, Ray 47
Wilkins, Roger 2
Wilkins, Roy 4
Wilkins, Thomas Alphonso 71
will.i.am 64
Williams, Anthony 21
Williams, Armstrong 29
Williams, Bert 18
Williams, Billy Dee 8
Williams, Clarence 33
Williams, Clarence 70
Williams, Clarence, III 26
Williams, Daniel Hale 2
Williams, David Rudyard 50
Williams, Deniece 36
Williams, Doug 22
Williams, Dudley 60
Williams, Eddie N. 44
Williams, Evelyn 10
Williams, Fannie Barrier 27
Williams, Frederick (B.) 63
Williams, George Washington 18
Williams, Gregory 11
Williams, Hosea Lorenzo 15, 31
Williams, Joe 5, 25
Williams, John A. 27
Williams, Ken 68
Williams, Lauryn 58
Williams, Maggie 7, 71
Williams, Malinda 57
Williams, Marco 53
Williams, Mary Lou 15
Williams, Michelle 73
Williams, Montel 4, 57
Williams, Natalie 31
Williams, O. S. 13
Williams, Patricia 11, 54
Williams, Paul R. 9
Williams, Pharrell 47
Williams, Preston Warren, II 64
Williams, Robert F. 11
Williams, Ronald A. 57
Williams, Russell, II 70
Williams, Samm-Art 21
Williams, Saul 31
Williams, Serena 20, 41, 73
Williams, Sherley Anne 25
Williams, Stanley "Tookie" 29, 57
Williams, Stevie 71

Williams, Terrie M. 35
Williams, Tony 67
Williams, Vanessa A. 32, 66
Williams, Vanessa L. 4, 17
Williams, Venus 17, 34, 62
Williams, Walter E. 4
Williams, Wendy 62
Williams, William T. 11
Williams, Willie L. 4
Williamson, Fred 67
Williamson, Mykelti 22
Willie, Louis, Jr. 68
Willingham, Tyrone 43
Willis, Bill 68
Willis, Dontrelle 55
Wills, Maury 73
Wilson, August 7, 33, 55
Wilson, Cassandra 16
Wilson, Chandra 57
Wilson, Charlie 31
Wilson, Debra 38
Wilson, Dorien 55
Wilson, Ellis 39
Wilson, Flip 21
Wilson, Gerald 49
Wilson, Jackie 60
Wilson, Jimmy 45
Wilson, Mary 28
Wilson, Nancy 10
Wilson, Natalie 38
Wilson, Phill 9
Wilson, Stephanie 72
Wilson, Sunnie 7, 55
Wilson, William Julius 20
Winans, Angie 36
Winans, BeBe 14
Winans, CeCe 14, 43
Winans, Debbie 36
Winans, Marvin L. 17
Winans, Ronald 54
Winans, Vickie 24
Winfield, Dave 5
Winfield, Paul 2, 45
Winfrey, Oprah 2, 15, 61
Winkfield, Jimmy 42
Wisdom, Kimberlydawn 57
Withers, Bill 61
Withers, Ernest C. 68
Withers-Mendes, Elisabeth 64
Witherspoon, John 38
Witt, Edwin T. 26
Wolfe, George C. 6, 43
Womack, Bobby 60
Wonder, Stevie 11, 53
Woodard, Alfre 9
Woodruff, Hale 9
Woodruff, John 68
Woods, Georgie 57
Woods, Granville T. 5
Woods, Jacqueline 52
Woods, Mattiebelle 63
Woods, Scott 55
Woods, Sylvia 34
Woods, Teri 69
Woods, Tiger 14, 31
Woodson, Carter G. 2
Woodson, Robert L. 10
Woodward, Lynette 67
Worrill, Conrad 12
Worthy, James 49
Wright, Antoinette 60
Wright, Bruce McMarion 3, 52
Wright, Charles H. 35

Wright, Deborah C. 25
Wright, Jeffrey 54
Wright, Jeremiah A., Jr. 45, 69
Wright, Lewin 43
Wright, Louis Tompkins 4
Wright, Nathan, Jr. 56
Wright, Rayfield 70
Wright, Richard 5
Wyatt, Addie L. 56
Wynn, Albert R. 25
X, Malcolm 1
X, Marvin 45
Xuma, Madie Hall 59
Yancy, Dorothy Cowser 42
Yarbrough, Camille 40
Yarbrough, Cedric 51
Yette, Samuel F. 63
Yoba, Malik 11
York, Dwight D. 71
York, Vincent 40
Young Jeezy 63
Young, Andrew 3, 48
Young, Coleman 1, 20
Young, Donald, Jr. 57
Young, Jean Childs 14
Young, Jimmy 54
Young, Lee 72
Young, Lester 37
Young, Roger Arliner 29
Young, Whitney M., Jr. 4
Youngblood, Johnny Ray 8
Youngblood, Shay 32
Zane 71
Zollar, Alfred 40
Zollar, Jawole Willa Jo 28
Zook, Kristal Brent 62

Angolan
Bonga, Kuenda 13
dos Santos, José Eduardo 43
Neto, António Agostinho 43
Roberto, Holden 65
Savimbi, Jonas 2, 34

Antiguan
Spencer, Winston Baldwin 68
Williams, Denise 40

Aruban
Williams, David Rudyard 50

Australian
Freeman, Cathy 29
Mundine, Anthony 56
Rose, Lionel 56

Austrian
Kodjoe, Boris 34

Bahamian
Christie, Perry Gladstone 53
Ingraham, Hubert A. 19
Spence, Joseph 49

Barbadian
Arthur, Owen 33
Brathwaite, Kamau 36
Clarke, Austin C. 32
Foster, Cecil 32
Grandmaster Flash 33, 60
Kamau, Kwadwo Agymah 28
Lamming, George 35

Rihanna 65

Belizean
Barrow, Dean 69
Jones, Marion 21, 66

Beninese
Gantin, Bernardin 70
Hounsou, Djimon 19, 45
Joachim, Paulin 34
Kerekou, Ahmed (Mathieu) 1
Kidjo, Anjelique 50
Mogae, Festus Gontebanye 19
Soglo, Nicéphore 15

Bermudian
Cameron, Earl 44
Gordon, Pamela 17
Smith, Jennifer 21

Botswana
Masire, Quett 5

Brazilian
Caymmi, Dorival 72
da Silva, Benedita 5
dos Santos, Manuel Francisco 65
Gil, Gilberto 53
Jorge, Seu 73
Mello, Breno 73
Nascimento, Milton 2, 64
Pelé 7
Pitta, Celso 17
Ronaldinho 69

British
Abbott, Diane 9
Adjaye, David 38
Akinnuoye-Agbaje, Adewale 56
Akomfrah, John 37
Amos, Valerie 41
Anderson, Ho Che 54
Anthony, Trey 63
Appiah, Kwame Anthony 67
Armatrading, Joan 32
Barnes, John 53
Bassey, Shirley 25
Berry, James 41
Blackwood, Maureen 37
Boateng, Ozwald 35
Boateng, Paul Yaw 56
Breeze, Jean "Binta" 37
Brown, Melanie 73
Campbell, Naomi 1, 31
Carby, Hazel 27
Christie, Linford 8
Crooks, Garth 53
D'Aguiar, Fred 50
David, Craig 31, 53
Davidson, Jaye 5
Edwards, Trevor 54
Ejiofor, Chiwetel 67
Elba, Idris 49
Emmanuel, Alphonsia 38
Evans, Diana 72
Garrett, Sean 57
Gladwell, Malcolm 62
Hamilton, Lewis 66
Harewood, David 52
Harris, Naomie 55
Henriques, Julian 37
Henry, Lenny 9, 52
Holmes, Kelly 47
Ibrahim, Mo 67
Jamelia 51

Jean-Baptiste, Marianne 17, 46
Jordan, Ronny 26
Julien, Isaac 3
Kay, Jackie 37
King, Oona 27
Lester, Adrian 46
Lewis, Denise 33
Lewis, Lennox 27
Lindo, Delroy 18, 45
Markham, E. A. 37
McGrath, Pat 72
McKinney Hammond, Michelle 51
Morris, William "Bill" 51
Newton, Thandie 26
Okonedo, Sophie 67
Pitt, David Thomas 10
Regis, Cyrille 51
Scantlebury, Janna 47
Seacole, Mary 54
Seal 14
Siji 56
Smith, Anjela Lauren 44
Smith, Richard 51
Smith, Zadie 51
Taylor, John (David Beckett) 16
Thomason, Marsha 47
Walker, Eamonn 37

Burkinabé
Somé, Malidoma Patrice 10

Burundian
Ndadaye, Melchior 7
Ntaryamira, Cyprien 8

Cameroonian
Bebey, Francis 45
Beti, Mongo 36
Biya, Paul 28
Eto'o, Samuel 73
Kotto, Yaphet 7
Milla, Roger 2
Oyono, Ferdinand 38

Canadian
Auguste, Arnold A. 47
Augustine, Jean 53
Bell, Ralph S. 5
Boyd, Suzanne 52
Brand, Dionne 32
Brathwaite, Fred 35
Brown, Rosemary 62
Brown, Sean 52
Carnegie, Herbert 25
Chanté, Keshia 50
Chong, Rae Dawn 62
Clarke, Austin 32
Clarke, George 32
Cools, Anne 64
Cooper, Afua 53
Cox, Deborah 28
Curling, Alvin 34
Dixon, George 52
Doig, Jason 45
Elliot, Lorris 37
Foster, Cecil 32
Fox, Rick 27
Fuhr, Grant 1, 49
Grand-Pierre, Jean-Luc 46
Hammond, Lenn 34
Harris, Claire 34
Iginla, Jarome 35
Isaac, Julius 34
Jean, Michaëlle; 70

Jenkins, Fergie 46
Johnson, Ben 1
Laraque, Georges 48
Lewis, Daurene 72
Mayers, Jamal 39
McKegney, Tony 3
Mollel, Tololwa 38
Neale, Haydain 52
O'Ree, Willie 5
Peterson, Oscar 52
Philip, Marlene Nourbese 32
Reuben, Gloria 15
Richards, Lloyd 2
Rodrigues, Percy 68
Sadlier, Rosemary 62
Salvador, Bryce 51
Scarlett, Millicent 49
Senior, Olive 37
Sparks, Corinne Etta 53
Vanity 67
Verna, Gelsy 70
Weekes, Kevin 67
Williams, Denise 40

Cape Verdean
Evora, Cesaria 12
Pereira, Aristides 30

Caymanian
Ebanks, Selita 67

Chadian
Déby, Idriss 30
Habré, Hissène 6

Colombian
Pomare, Eleo 72

Congolese
Kabila, Joseph 30
Kintaudi, Leon 62
Kolosoy, Wendo 73
Lumumba, Patrice 33
Mudimbe, V. Y. 61

Costa Rican
McDonald, Erroll 1

Cuban
Ferrer, Ibrahim 41
Güines, Tata 69
León, Tania 13
Portuondo, Omara 53
Quirot, Ana 13
Velez-Rodriguez, Argelia 56

Dominican (from Dominica)
Charles, Mary Eugenia 10, 55
Charles, Pierre 52
Skerrit, Roosevelt 72

Dominican (from Dominican Republic)
Ortiz, David 52
Sosa, Sammy 21, 44
Virgil, Ozzie 48

Dutch
Liberia-Peters, Maria Philomena 12

Eritrean
Keflezighi, Meb 49

Ethiopian
Aberra, Amsale 67
Dibaba, Tirunesh 73

Gabre-Medhin, Tsegaye 64
Gebrselassie, Haile 70
Gerima, Haile 38
Haile Selassie 7
Kebede, Liya 59
Meles Zenawi 3
Mengistu, Haile Mariam 65
Samuelsson, Marcus 53

French
Baker, Josephine 3
Baldwin, James 1
Bebey, Francis 45
Bonaly, Surya 7
Chase-Riboud, Barbara 20, 46
Dieudonné 67
Fanon, Frantz 44
Henry, Thierry 66
Kanouté, Fred 68
Noah, Yannick 4, 60
Tanner, Henry Ossawa 1

Gabonese
Bongo, Omar 1

Gambian
Jammeh, Yahya 23
Peters, Lenrie 43

German
Massaquoi, Hans J. 30
Watts, Andre 42

Ghanaian
Adu, Freddy 67
Aidoo, Ama Ata 38
Ali, Mohammed Naseehu 60
Annan, Kofi Atta 15, 48
Appiah, Kwame Anthony 67
Armah, Ayi Kwei 49
Awoonor, Kofi 37
DuBois, Shirley Graham 21
Jawara, Dawda Kairaba 11
Kufuor, John Agyekum 54
Mensah, Thomas 48
Nkrumah, Kwame 3
Rawlings, Jerry 9
Rawlings, Nana Konadu Agyeman 13
Yeboah, Emmanuel Ofosu 53

Grenadian
Bishop, Maurice 39
Isaac, Julius 34

Guinea-Bissauan
Vieira, Joao 14

Guinean
Conté, Lansana 7
Diallo, Amadou 27
Niane, Katoucha 70
Touré, Sekou 6

Guyanese
Amos, Valerie 41
Beaton, Norman 14
Burnham, Forbes 66
Carter, Martin 49
Dabydeen, David 48
D'Aguiar, Fred 50
Damas, Léon-Gontran 46
Dathorne, O. R. 52
Griffith, Patrick A. 64
Jagan, Cheddi 16
Lefel, Edith 41

van Sertima, Ivan 25

Haitian
Aristide, Jean-Bertrand 6, 45
Auguste, Rose-Anne 13
Beauvais, Garcelle 29
Charlemagne, Manno 11
Christophe, Henri 9
Danticat, Edwidge 15, 68
Delice, Ronald 48
Delice, Rony 48
Jean, Wyclef 20
Laferriere, Dany 33
Laraque, Paul 67
Magloire, Paul Eugène 68
Pascal-Trouillot, Ertha 3
Peck, Raoul 32
Pierre, Andre 17
Siméus, Dumas M. 25
Verna, Gelsy 70

Irish
Mumba, Samantha 29

Italian
Esposito, Giancarlo 9

Ivorian
Bedie, Henri Konan 21
Blondy, Alpha 30
Dadié, Bernard 34
Gbagbo, Laurent 43
Guéï, Robert 66
Houphouët-Boigny, Félix 4, 64
Ouattara 43

Jamaican
Ashley, Maurice 15, 47
Barnes, John 53
Barrett, Lindsay 43
Beenie Man 32
Belafonte, Harry 4
Bennett, Louise 69
Berry, James 41
Bolt, Usain 73
Channer, Colin 36
Cliff, Jimmy 28
Cliff, Michelle 42
Cooper, Afua 53
Cox, Renée 67
Curling, Alvin 34
Dunbar, Sly 34
Ewing, Patrick 17, 73
Fagan, Garth 18
50 Cent 46
Figueroa, John J. 40
Garvey, Marcus 1
Goodison, Lorna 71
Griffiths, Marcia 29
Hammond, Lenn 34
Hearne, John Edgar Caulwell 45
Heavy, D 58
Johnson, Ben 1
Johnson, Linton Kwesi 37
Joseph, Kathie-Ann 56
Kong, B. Waine 50
Manley, Edna 26
Manley, Ruth 34
Marley, Bob 5
Marley, Rita 32, 70
Marley, Ziggy 41
McKay, Claude 6
McKenzie, Jaunel 73
Moody, Ronald 30

Morrison, Keith 13
Mowatt, Judy 38
Palmer, Everard 37
Patterson, Orlando 4
Patterson, P. J. 6, 20
Perry, Ruth 19
Reece, E. Albert 63
Rhoden, Wayne 70
Rogers, Joel Augustus 30
Senior, Olive 37
Shaggy 31
Shakespeare, Robbie 34
Simpson-Miller, Portia 62
Taylor, Karin 34
Tosh, Peter 9
White, Willard 53

Kenyan
Cheruiyot, Robert 69
Juma, Calestous 57
Kariuki, J. M. 67
Kenyatta, Jomo 5
Kibaki, Mwai 60
Kobia, Samuel 43
Loroupe, Tegla 59
Maathai, Wangari 43
Mazrui, Ali A. 12
Moi, Daniel Arap 1, 35
Mutu, Wangechi 44
Mwangi, Meja 40
Ngilu, Charity 58
Ngugi wa Thiong'o 29, 61
Odinga, Raila 67
Otunga, Maurice Michael 55
Tergat, Paul 59
Wambugu, Florence 42

Lesothoian
Mofolo, Thomas 37

Liberian
Conneh, Sekou Damate, Jr. 51
Cooper, Lisa 73
Fuller, Solomon Carter, Jr. 15
Keith, Rachel Boone 63
Perry, Ruth 15
Sawyer, Amos 2
Sirleaf, Ellen Johnson 71
Taylor, Charles 20
Weah, George 58

Malawian
Banda, Hastings Kamuzu 6, 54
Kayira, Legson 40
Muluzi, Bakili 14

Malian
Touré, Amadou Toumani 18

Martinican
Césaire, Aimé 48, 69

Mozambican
Chissano, Joaquim 7, 55, 67
Couto, Mia 45
Diogo, Luisa Dias 63
Machel, Graca Simbine 16
Machel, Samora Moises 8
Mutola, Maria 12

Namibian
Mbuende, Kaire 12
Nujoma, Samuel 10

Nigerian
Abacha, Sani 11, 70
Abiola, Moshood 70

Abubakar, Abdulsalami 66
Achebe, Chinua 6
Ade, King Sunny 41
Adichie, Chimamanda Ngozi 64
Ake, Claude 30
Akinola, Peter Jasper 65
Akpan, Uwem 70
Akunyili, Dora Nkem 58
Amadi, Elechi 40
Arinze, Francis Cardinal 19
Azikiwe, Nnamdi 13
Babangida, Ibrahim 4
Bandele, Biyi 68
Clark-Bekedermo, J. P. 44
Darego, Agbani 52
Ekwensi, Cyprian 37
Emeagwali, Philip 30
Emecheta, Buchi 30
Fela 1, 42
Kuti, Femi 47
Lawal, Kase L. 45
Obasanjo, Olusegun 5, 22
Obasanjo, Stella 32, 56
Ogunlesi, Adebayo O. 37
Okara, Gabriel 37
Okosuns, Sonny 71
Olajuwon, Hakeem 2, 72
Olatunji, Babatunde 36
Olojede, Dele 59
Olopade, Olufunmilayo Falusi 58
Onwueme, Tess Osonye 23
Onwurah, Ngozi 38
Rotimi, Ola 1
Sade 15
Saro-Wiwa, Kenule 39
Siji 56
Sowande, Fela 39
Soyinka, Wole 4
Tutuola, Amos 30
Wiwa, Ken 67
Yar'adua, Umaru 69

Nigerien
Mamadou, Tandja 33

Panamanian
Bailey, Preston 64
Williams, Juan 35

Puerto Rican
Schomburg, Arthur Alfonso 9

Rhodesian
Brutus, Dennis 38

Russian
Khanga, Yelena 6

Rwandan
Bizimungu, Pasteur 19
Habyarimana, Juvenal 8
Ilibagiza, Immaculée 66
Kagame, Paul 54
Rusesabagina, Paul 60

St. Kitts and Nevis
Douglas, Denzil Llewellyn 53

Saint Lucian
Compton, John 65

Senegalese
Acogny, Germaine 55
Akon 68
Ba, Mariama 30

Boye, Madior 30
Diop, Birago 53
Diop, Cheikh Anta 4
Diouf, Abdou 3
Maal, Baaba 66
Mbaye, Mariétou 31
Mboup, Souleymane 10
N'Dour, Youssou 1, 53
Sané, Pierre Gabriel 21
Sembène, Ousmane 13, 62
Senghor, Augustin Diamancoune 66
Senghor, Léopold Sédar 12, 66
Sy, Oumou 65
Wade, Abdoulaye 66

Sierra Leonean
Beah, Ishmael 69
Cheney-Coker, Syl 43
Jones, Monty 66
Kabbah, Ahmad Tejan 23

Somalian
Ali, Ayaan Hirsi 58
Ali Mahdi Mohamed 5
Dirie, Waris 56
Farah, Nuruddin 27
Iman 4, 33
Roble, Abdi 71

South African
Abrahams, Peter 39
Adams, Paul 50
Biko, Steven 4
Brutus, Dennis 38
Buthelezi, Mangosuthu Gatsha 9
Butler, Jonathan 28
Chweneyagae, Presley 63
Grae, Jean 51
Hani, Chris 6
Head, Bessie 28
Ka Dinizulu, Mcwayizeni 29
Kente, Gibson 52
Khumalo, Leleti 51
Kuzwayo, Ellen 68
LaGuma, Alex 30
Luthuli, Albert 13
Mabuza, Lindiwe 18
Mabuza-Suttle, Felicia 43
Mahlasela, Vusi 65
Makeba, Miriam 2, 50
Mandela, Nelson 1, 14
Mandela, Winnie 2, 35
Masekela, Barbara 18
Masekela, Hugh 1
Mathabane, Mark 5
Mbeki, Thabo 14, 73
Mhlaba, Raymond 55
Mphalele, Es'kia (Ezekiel) 40
Naki, Hamilton 63
Ngubane, Ben 33
Nkoli, Simon 60
Nkosi, Lewis 46
Ntshona, Winston 52
Nyanda, Siphiwe 21
Nzo, Alfred 15
Ramaphosa, Cyril 3
Ramphele, Mamphela 29
Sisulu, Albertina 57
Sisulu, Sheila Violet Makate 24
Sisulu, Walter 47
Thugwane, Josia 21
Tutu, Desmond (Mpilo) 6, 44
Tutu, Nontombi Naomi 57
Zuma, Jacob 33

Zuma, Nkosazana Dlamini 34

Spanish
Eto'o, Samuel 73

Sudanese
Bashir, Halima 73
Bol, Manute 1
Nour, Nawal M. 56
Salih, Al-Tayyib 37
Wek, Alek 18, 63

Swazi
Mswati III 56

Swedish
Hendricks, Barbara 3, 67

Tanzanian
Kikwete, Jakaya Mrisho 73
Mkapa, Benjamin 16
Mollel, Tololwa 38
Mongella, Gertrude 11
Mwinyi, Ali Hassan 1
Nyerere, Julius 5
Rugambwa, Laurean 20

Togolese
Eyadéma, Gnassingbé 7, 52
Gnassingbé, Faure 67
Soglo, Nicéphore 15

Trinidadian
Anthony, Michael 29
Auguste, Arnold A. 47
Brand, Dionne 32
Carmichael, Stokely 5, 26
Cartey, Wilfred 1992 47
Dymally, Mervyn 42
Guy, Rosa 5
Harris, Claire 34
Hendy, Francis 47
Hercules, Frank 44
Hill, Errol 40
Lushington, Augustus Nathaniel 56
Nakhid, David 25
Nunez, Elizabeth 62
Primus, Pearl 6
Shorty, Ras, I 47
Toussaint, Lorraine 32
Williams, Eric Eustace 65

Tunisian
Memmi, Albert 37

Ugandan
Amin, Idi 42
Arac de Nyeko, Monica 66
Atim, Julian 66
Atyam, Angelina 55
Museveni, Yoweri 4
Mutebi, Ronald 25
Obote, Milton 63
Okaalet, Peter 58
Sentamu, John 58

Upper Voltan
Sankara, Thomas 17

West Indian
Césaire, Aimé 48, 69
Coombs, Orde M. 44
Innis, Roy 5
Kincaid, Jamaica 4

Knight, Gwendolyn **63**
Rojas, Don **33**
Staupers, Mabel K. **7**
Pitt, David Thomas **10**
Taylor, Susan L. **10**
Walcott, Derek **5**

Zairean
Kabila, Laurent **20**
Mobutu Sese Seko **1, 56**
Mutombo, Dikembe **7**
Ongala, Remmy **9**

Zambian
Kaunda, Kenneth **2**
Mwanawasa, Levy **72**
Zulu, Princess Kasune **54**

Zimbabwean
Chideya, Farai **14**
Chiluba, Frederick Jacob Titus **56**
Marechera, Dambudzo **39**
Mugabe, Robert **10, 71**
Nkomo, Joshua **4, 65**
Tsvangirai, Morgan **26, 72**
Vera, Yvonne **32**

Cumulative Occupation Index

*Volume numbers appear in **bold***

Art and design

Abele, Julian **55**
Aberra, Amsale **67**
Adjaye, David **38**
Allen, Tina **22**
Alston, Charles **33**
Amos, Emma **63**
Anderson, Ho Che **54**
Andrews, Benny **22, 59**
Andrews, Bert **13**
Armstrong, Robb **15**
Bailey, Preston **64**
Bailey, Radcliffe **19**
Bailey, Xenobia **11**
Barboza, Anthony **10**
Barnes, Ernie **16**
Barthe, Richmond **15**
Basquiat, Jean-Michel **5**
Bearden, Romare **2, 50**
Beasley, Phoebe **34**
Benberry, Cuesta **65**
Benjamin, Tritobia Hayes **53**
Biggers, John **20, 33**
Biggers, Sanford **62**
Blackburn, Robert **28**
Brandon, Barbara **3**
Brown, Donald **19**
Brown, Robert **65**
Burke, Selma **16**
Burroughs, Margaret Taylor **9**
Camp, Kimberly **19**
Campbell, E. Simms **13**
Campbell, Mary Schmidt **43**
Catlett, Elizabeth **2**
Chase-Riboud, Barbara **20, 46**
Colescott, Robert **69**
Collins, Paul **61**
Cortor, Eldzier **42**
Cowans, Adger W. **20**
Cox, Renée **67**
Crite, Alan Rohan **29**
De Veaux, Alexis **44**
DeCarava, Roy **42**
Delaney, Beauford **19**
Delaney, Joseph **30**
Delsarte, Louis **34**
Donaldson, Jeff **46**
Douglas, Aaron **7**
Driskell, David C. **7**
Dwight, Edward **65**
Edwards, Melvin **22**
El Wilson, Barbara **35**
Ewing, Patrick **17, 73**

Fax, Elton **48**
Feelings, Tom **11, 47**
Fine, Sam **60**
Freeman, Leonard **27**
Fuller, Meta Vaux Warrick **27**
Gantt, Harvey **1**
Gilles, Ralph **61**
Gilliam, Sam **16**
Golden, Thelma **10, 55**
Goodnight, Paul **32**
Green, Jonathan **54**
Guyton, Tyree **9**
Hammons, David **69**
Harkless, Necia Desiree **19**
Harrington, Oliver W. **9**
Harrison, Charles **72**
Hathaway, Isaac Scott **33**
Hayden, Palmer **13**
Hayes, Cecil N. **46**
Honeywood, Varnette P. **54**
Hope, John **8**
Hudson, Cheryl **15**
Hudson, Wade **15**
Hunt, Richard **6**
Hunter, Clementine **45**
Hutson, Jean Blackwell **16**
Jackson, Earl **31**
Jackson, Mary **73**
Jackson, Vera **40**
John, Daymond **23**
Johnson, Jeh Vincent **44**
Johnson, William Henry **3**
Jones, Lois Mailou **13**
King, Robert Arthur **58**
Kitt, Sandra **23**
Knight, Gwendolyn **63**
Knox, Simmie **49**
Lawrence, Jacob **4, 28**
Lee, Annie Frances **22**
Lee-Smith, Hughie **5, 22**
Lewis, Edmonia **10**
Lewis, Norman **39**
Lewis, Samella **25**
Loving, Alvin, Jr., **35, 53**
Manley, Edna **26**
Marshall, Kerry James **59**
Mayhew, Richard **39**
McCullough, Geraldine **58**
McDuffie, Dwayne **62**
McGee, Charles **10**
McGruder, Aaron **28, 56**
Mitchell, Corinne **8**
Moody, Ronald **30**
Morrison, Keith **13**

Motley, Archibald, Jr. **30**
Moutoussamy-Ashe, Jeanne **7**
Mutu, Wangechi **44**
Myles, Kim **69**
Neals, Otto **73**
N'Namdi, George R. **17**
Nugent, Richard Bruce **39**
O'Grady, Lorraine **73**
Olden, Georg(e) **44**
Ormes, Jackie **73**
Ouattara **43**
Perkins, Marion **38**
Pierre, Andre **17**
Pindell, Howardena **55**
Pinderhughes, John **47**
Pinkney, Jerry **15**
Piper, Adrian **71**
Pippin, Horace **9**
Pope.L, William **72**
Porter, James A. **11**
Prophet, Nancy Elizabeth **42**
Puryear, Martin **42**
Reid, Senghor **55**
Ringgold, Faith **4**
Roble, Abdi **71**
Ruley, Ellis **38**
Saar, Alison **16**
Saint James, Synthia **12**
Sallee, Charles **38**
Sanders, Joseph R., Jr. **11**
Savage, Augusta **12**
Scott, John T. **65**
Sebree, Charles **40**
Serrano, Andres **3**
Shabazz, Attallah **6**
Shonibare, Yinka **58**
Simmons, Gary **58**
Simpson, Lorna **4, 36**
Sims, Lowery Stokes **27**
Sklarek, Norma Merrick **25**
Sleet, Moneta, Jr. **5**
Smith, Bruce W. **53**
Smith, Marvin **46**
Smith, Morgan **46**
Smith, Vincent D. **48**
Steave-Dickerson, Kia **57**
Stout, Renee **63**
Sudduth, Jimmy Lee **65**
Tanksley, Ann **37**
Tanner, Henry Ossawa **1**
Thomas, Alma **14**
Thrash, Dox **35**
Tolliver, Mose **60**
Tolliver, William **9**

Tooks, Lance **62**
VanDerZee, James **6**
Verna, Gelsy **70**
Wainwright, Joscelyn **46**
Walker, A'lelia **14**
Walker, Kara **16**
Washington, Alonzo **29**
Washington, James, Jr. **38**
Weems, Carrie Mae **63**
Wells, James Lesesne **10**
White, Charles **39**
White, Dondi **34**
White, John H. **27**
Wiley, Kehinde **62**
Williams, Billy Dee **8**
Williams, Clarence **70**
Williams, O. S. **13**
Williams, Paul R. **9**
Williams, William T. **11**
Wilson, Ellis **39**
Withers, Ernest C. **68**
Woodruff, Hale **9**

Business

Abbot, Robert Sengstacke **27**
Abdul-Jabbar, Kareem **8**
Abiola, Moshood **70**
Adams, Eula L. **39**
Adams, Jenoyne **60**
Adkins, Rod **41**
Ailey, Alvin **8**
Akil, Mara Brock **60**
Al-Amin, Jamil Abdullah **6**
Alexander, Archie Alphonso **14**
Allen, Byron **24**
Allen-Buillard, Melba **55**
Ames, Wilmer **27**
Amos, Wally **9**
Auguste, Donna **29**
Austin, Gloria **63**
Austin, Jim **63**
Avant, Clarence **19**
Baker, Dusty **8, 43, 72**
Baker, Ella **5**
Baker, Gwendolyn Calvert **9**
Baker, Maxine **28**
Banks, Jeffrey **17**
Banks, Paula A. **68**
Banks, William **11**
Barden, Don H. **9, 20**
Barrett, Andrew C. **12**
Beal, Bernard B. **46**
Beamon, Bob **30**
Beasley, Phoebe **34**

Bell, James A. **50**
Bennett, Lerone, Jr. **5**
Bing, Dave **3, 59**
Blackshear, Leonard **52**
Blackwell, Robert D., Sr. **52**
Blayton, Jesse B., Sr. **55**
Bolden, Frank E. **44**
Borders, James **9**
Boston, Kelvin E. **25**
Boston, Lloyd **24**
Boyd, Edward **70**
Boyd, Gwendolyn **49**
Boyd, John W., Jr. **20, 72**
Boyd, T. B., III **6**
Bradley, Jennette B. **40**
Brae, C. Michael **61**
Bridges, Shelia **36**
Bridgforth, Glinda **36**
Brimmer, Andrew F. **2, 48**
Bronner, Nathaniel H., Sr. **32**
Brown, Eddie C. **35**
Brown, Les **5**
Brown, Marie Dutton **12**
Brunson, Dorothy **1**
Bryant, John **26**
Burgess, Marjorie L. **55**
Burns, Ursula **60**
Burrell, Tom **21, 51**
Burroughs, Margaret Taylor **9**
Burrus, William Henry "Bill" **45**
Burt-Murray, Angela **59**
Busby, Jheryl **3**
Butler, George, Jr. **70**
Cain, Herman **15**
Caldwell, Earl **60**
Carter, Pamela Lynn **67**
CasSelle, Malcolm **11**
Chamberlain, Wilt **18, 47**
Chapman, Nathan A., Jr. **21**
Chappell, Emma **18**
Chase, Debra Martin **49**
Chase, Leah **57**
Chenault, Kenneth I. **4, 36**
Cherry, Deron **40**
Chisholm, Samuel J. **32**
Clark, Celeste **15**
Clark, Patrick **14**
Clay, William Lacy **8**
Clayton, Xernona **3, 45**
Cobbs, Price M. **9**
Colbert, Virgis William **17**
Coleman, Donald **24, 62**
Coleman, Ken **57**
Combs, Sean "Puffy" **17, 43**
Connerly, Ward **14**
Conyers, Nathan G. **24**
Cooper, Barry **33**
Cooper, Evern **40**
Corbi, Lana **42**
Cornelius, Don **4**
Cottrell, Comer **11**
Cox, William E. **68**
Creagh, Milton **27**
Cullers, Vincent T. **49**
Daniels-Carter, Valerie **23**
Darden, Calvin **38**
Dash, Darien **29**
Davis, Belva **61**
Davis, Ed **24**
Davis, Erroll B., Jr. **57**
Dawson, Matel "Mat," Jr. **39**
de Passe, Suzanne **25**
Dean, Mark **35**

Dee, Merri **55**
Delany, Bessie **12**
Delany, Martin R. **27**
Delany, Sadie **12**
DeVard, Jerri **61**
Diallo, Amadou **27**
Divine, Father **7**
Doley, Harold, Jr. **26**
Donald, Arnold Wayne **36**
Dre, Dr. **10, 14, 30**
Driver, David E. **11**
Ducksworth, Marilyn **12**
Easley, Annie J. **61**
Ebanks, Michelle **60**
Edelin, Ramona Hoage **19**
Edmonds, Tracey **16, 64**
Edmunds, Gladys **48**
Edwards, Trevor **54**
El Wilson, Barbara **35**
Elder, Lee **6**
Ellington, E. David **11**
Evans, Darryl **22**
Evers, Myrlie **8**
Farmer, Forest J. **1**
Farr, Mel **24**
Farrakhan, Louis **15**
Fauntroy, Walter E. **11**
Fletcher, Alphonse, Jr. **16**
Flowers, Sylester **50**
Ford, Harold E(ugene), Jr. **16, 70**
Forte, Linda Diane **54**
Foster, Jylla Moore **45**
Fowler, Reggie **51**
Franklin, Hardy R. **9**
Friday, Jeff **24**
Fryer, Roland G. **56**
Fudge, Ann **11, 55**
Fuller, S. B. **13**
Funderburg, I. Owen **38**
Gaines, Brenda **41**
Gardner, Chris **65**
Gardner, Edward G. **45**
Gaston, Arthur George **3, 38, 59**
Gibson, Kenneth Allen **6**
Gibson, Ted **66**
Gidron, Richard D. **68**
Gilles, Ralph **61**
Goings, Russell **59**
Goldsberry, Ronald **18**
Golston, Allan C. **55**
Gordon, Bruce S. **41, 53**
Gordon, Pamela **17**
Gordy, Berry, Jr. **1**
Goss, Carol A. **55**
Goss, Tom **23**
Grace, George H. **48**
Graham, Stedman **13**
Graves, Earl G. **1, 35**
Gray, Farrah **59**
Greely, M. Gasby **27**
Greene, Richard Thaddeus, Sr. **67**
Greenwood, Monique **38**
Griffith, Mark Winston **8**
Grooms, Henry R(andall) **50**
Hale, Lorraine **8**
Ham, Cynthia Parker **58**
Hamer, Fannie Lou **6**
Hamilton, Samuel C. **47**
Hammer, M. C. **20**
Handy, W. C. **8**
Hannah, Marc **10**
Hardison, Bethann **12**
Harrell, Andre **9, 30**

Harris, Alice **7**
Harris, Carla A. **67**
Harris, E. Lynn **12, 33**
Harris, Monica **18**
Harris, Richard E. **61**
Harvey, Steve **18, 58**
Harvey, William R. **42**
Hawkins, La-Van **17, 54**
Hayden, Carla D. **47**
Hazel, Darryl B. **50**
Henderson, Gordon **5**
Henry, Lenny **9, 52**
Hightower, Dennis F. **13**
Hill, Bonnie Guiton **20**
Hill, Calvin **19**
Hill, Janet **19**
Hill, Jesse, Jr. **13**
Hobson, Mellody **40**
Holland, Kimberly N. **62**
Holland, Robert, Jr. **11**
Holmes, Larry **20, 68**
Houston, Whitney **7**
Howroyd, Janice Bryant **42**
Hudlin, Reginald **9**
Hudlin, Warrington **9**
Hudson, Cheryl **15**
Hudson, Wade **15**
Huggins, Larry **21**
Hughes, Cathy **27**
Ibrahim, Mo **67**
Ice Cube **8, 30, 60**
Irvin, Vernon **65**
Jackson, George **19**
Jackson, Mannie **14**
Jackson, Michael **19, 53**
Jakes, Thomas "T. D." **17, 43**
James, Charles H., III **62**
James, Donna A. **51**
James, Juanita **13**
John, Daymond **23**
Johnson, Earvin "Magic" **3, 39**
Johnson, Eddie Bernice **8**
Johnson, George E. **29**
Johnson, John H. **3, 54**
Johnson, Kevin **70**
Johnson, Robert L. **3, 39**
Johnson, Sheila Crump **48**
Jolley, Willie **28**
Jones, Bobby **20**
Jones, Carl **7**
Jones, Caroline **29**
Jones, Ingrid Saunders **18**
Jones, Quincy **8, 30**
Jones, Thomas W. **41**
Jones, Wayne **53**
Jordan, Michael **6, 21**
Jordan, Montell **23**
Joyner, Marjorie Stewart **26**
Julian, Percy Lavon **6**
Kaigler, Denise **63**
Keith, Floyd A. **61**
Kelly, Patrick **3**
Kendrick, Erika **57**
Kidd, Mae Street **39**
Killingsworth, Cleve, Jr. **54**
Kimbro, Dennis **10**
King, Dexter **10**
King, Don **14**
Knight, Suge **11, 30**
Knowles, Tina **61**
Knowling, Robert E., Jr. **38**
Lane, Vincent **5**
Langhart Cohen, Janet **19, 60**

Lanier, Willie **33**
Laryea, Thomas Davies, III **67**
Lawal, Kase L. **45**
Lawless, Theodore K. **8**
Lawson, Jennifer **1, 50**
Leary, Kathryn D. **10**
Leavell, Dorothy R. **17**
Lee, Annie Frances **22**
Lee, Bertram M., Sr. **46**
Lee, Debra L. **62**
Leonard, Sugar Ray **15**
Lewellyn, J. Bruce **13**
Lewis, Aylwin **51**
Lewis, Byron E. **13**
Lewis, Delano **7**
Lewis, Edward T. **21**
Lewis, Reginald F. **6**
Lewis, William M., Jr. **40**
Ligging, Alfred, III **43**
Long, Eddie L. **29**
Lott, Ronnie **9**
Louis, Errol T. **8**
Lucas, John **7**
Lucy, William **50**
Madhubuti, Haki R. **7**
Madison, Paula **37**
Malone, Annie **13**
March, William Carrington **56**
Marshall, Bella **22**
Massenburg, Kedar **23**
Master P **21**
Matthews Shatteen, Westina **51**
Maynard, Robert C. **7**
Mays, Leslie A. **41**
Mays, William G. **34**
McCabe, Jewell Jackson **10**
McCann, Renetta **44**
McCoy, Elijah **8**
McDonald, Erroll **1**
McGee, James Madison **46**
McGuire, Raymond J. **57**
McLeod, Gus **27**
McPherson, David **32**
Micheaux, Oscar **7**
Miller, Larry G. **72**
Millines Dziko, Trish **28**
Mills, Steve **47**
Mingo, Frank **32**
Monk, Art **38, 73**
Monroe, Bryan **71**
Morgan, Garrett **1**
Morgan, Joe Leonard **9**
Morgan, Rose **11**
Morris, William "Bill" **51**
Morrison, Sam **50**
Moyo, Karega Kofi **36**
Moyo, Yvette Jackson **36**
Muhammad, Jabir Herbert **72**
Nanula, Richard D. **20**
Nash, Diane **72**
Nelson Meigs, Andrea **48**
Nichols, Nichelle **11**
Norman, Christina **47**
Ogunlesi, Adebayo O. **37**
Olojede, Dele **59**
O'Neal, Stanley **38, 67**
Otis, Clarence, Jr. **55**
Packer, Daniel **56**
Parham, Marjorie B. **71**
Parks, Gordon **1, 35, 58**
Parsons, Richard Dean **11, 33**
Payton, Walter **11, 25**
Peck, Carolyn **23**

Perez, Anna **1**
Perkins, James, Jr. **55**
Perry, Laval **64**
Perry, Lowell **30**
Phillips, Charles E., Jr. **57**
Pinckney, Bill **42**
Pinkett, Randal **61**
Pleasant, Mary Ellen **9**
Potter, Myrtle **40**
Powell, Maxine **8**
Price, Frederick K. C. **21**
Price, Hugh B. **9, 54**
Procope, Ernesta **23**
Procope, John Levy **56**
Queen Latifah **1, 16, 58**
Quivers, Robin **61**
Ralph, Sheryl Lee **18**
Rand, A. Barry **6**
Reeves, Rachel J. **23**
Reid, Antonio "L.A." **28**
Rhone, Sylvia **2**
Rice, Linda Johnson **9, 41**
Rice, Norm **8**
Richardson, Donna **39**
Richie, Leroy C. **18**
Rideau, Iris **46**
Roberts, Mike **57**
Roberts, Roy S. **14**
Robertson, Oscar **26**
Robeson, Eslanda Goode **13**
Robinson, Jackie **6**
Robinson, Rachel **16**
Robinson, Randall **7, 46**
Roche, Joyce M. **17**
Rodgers, Johnathan **6, 51**
Rodriguez, Jimmy **47**
Rogers, John W., Jr. **5, 52**
Rojas, Don **33**
Ross, Charles **27**
Ross, Diana **8, 27**
Russell, Bill **8**
Russell, Herman Jerome **17**
Russell-McCloud, Patricia **17**
Saint James, Synthia **12**
Samara, Noah **15**
Samuelsson, Marcus **53**
Sanders, Dori **8**
Scott, C. A. **29**
Scott, Milton **51**
Sengstacke, John **18**
Shakur, Afeni **67**
Shropshire, Thomas B. **49**
Siméus, Dumas M. **25**
Simmons, Kimora Lee **51**
Simmons, Russell **1, 30**
Sims, Naomi **29**
Sinbad **1, 16**
Smith, B(arbara) **11**
Smith, Clarence O. **21**
Smith, Jane E. **24**
Smith, Joshua **10**
Smith, Willi **8**
Sneed, Paula A. **18**
Spaulding, Charles Clinton **9**
Staley, Dawn **57**
Stanford, Olivia Lee Dilworth **49**
Steinberg, Martha Jean "The
    Queen" **28**
Steward, David L. **36**
Stewart, Ella **39**
Stewart, Paul Wilbur **12**
Stinson, Denise L. **59**
Stringer, Vickie **58**

Sullivan, Leon H. **3, 30**
Sutton, Percy E. **42**
Taylor, Ephren W., II **61**
Taylor, Karin **34**
Taylor, Kristin Clark **8**
Taylor, Natalie **47**
Taylor, Susan L. **10**
Terrell, Dorothy A. **24**
Thomas, Franklin A. **5, 49**
Thomas, Isiah **7, 26, 65**
Thomas-Graham, Pamela **29**
Thompson, Cynthia Bramlett **50**
Thompson, Don **56**
Thompson, John W. **26**
Tribble, Israel, Jr. **8**
Trotter, Lloyd G. **56**
Trotter, Monroe **9**
Tuckson, Reed V. **71**
Tyson, Asha **39**
Ussery, Terdema, II **29**
Utendahl, John **23**
Van Peebles, Melvin **7**
VanDerZee, James **6**
Vaughn, Gladys Gary **47**
Vaughns, Cleopatra **46**
Walker, A'lelia **14**
Walker, Cedric "Ricky" **19**
Walker, Madame C. J. **7**
Walker, Maggie Lena **17**
Walker, T. J. **7**
Ward, Lloyd **21, 46**
Ware, Carl H. **30**
Washington, Alonzo **29**
Washington, Mary T. **57**
Washington, Regynald G. **44**
Washington, Val **12**
Wasow, Omar **15**
Watkins, Donald **35**
Watkins, Walter C., Jr. **24**
Wattleton, Faye **9**
Wein, Joyce **62**
Wek, Alek **18, 63**
Welburn, Edward T. **50**
Wells-Barnett, Ida B. **8**
Westbrook, Kelvin **50**
Wharton, Clifton R., Jr. **7**
White, Linda M. **45**
White, Walter F. **4**
Wiley, Ralph **8**
Wilkins, Ray **47**
Williams, Armstrong **29**
Williams, O. S. **13**
Williams, Paul R. **9**
Williams, Ronald A. **57**
Williams, Terrie **35**
Williams, Walter E. **4**
Williams, Wendy **62**
Willie, Louis, Jr. **68**
Wilson, Phill **9**
Wilson, Sunnie **7, 55**
Winfrey, Oprah **2, 15, 61**
Woods, Jacqueline **52**
Woods, Sylvia **34**
Woodson, Robert L. **10**
Wright, Antoinette **60**
Wright, Charles H. **35**
Wright, Deborah C. **25**
Wright, Rayfield **70**
Yoba, Malik **11**
Zollar, Alfred **40**

Dance
Acogny, Germaine **55**
Adams, Jenoyne **60**
Ailey, Alvin **8**
Alexander, Khandi **43**
Allen, Debbie **13, 42**
Anderson, Lauren **72**
Atkins, Cholly **40**
Babatunde, Obba **35**
Baker, Josephine **3**
Bates, Peg Leg **14**
Beals, Jennifer **12**
Beatty, Talley **35**
Byrd, Donald **10**
Clarke, Hope **14**
Collins, Janet **33, 64**
Davis, Chuck **33**
Davis, Sammy, Jr. **18**
Diggs, Taye **25, 63**
Dove, Ulysses **5**
Dunham, Katherine **4, 59**
Ellington, Mercedes **34**
Fagan, Garth **18**
Falana, Lola **42**
Glover, Savion **14**
Guy, Jasmine **2**
Hall, Arthur **39**
Hammer, M. C. **20**
Henson, Darrin **33**
Hines, Gregory **1, 42**
Horne, Lena **5**
Jackson, Michael **19, 53**
Jamison, Judith **7, 67**
Johnson, Virginia **9**
Jones, Bill T. **1, 46**
Jones, Doris W. **62**
King, Alonzo **38**
LeTang, Henry **66**
McQueen, Butterfly **6, 54**
Miller, Bebe **3**
Mills, Florence **22**
Mitchell, Arthur **2, 47**
Moten, Etta **18**
Muse, Clarence Edouard **21**
Nash, Joe **55**
Nicholas, Fayard **20, 57**
Nicholas, Harold **20**
Nichols, Nichelle **11**
Pomare, Eleo **72**
Powell, Maxine **8**
Premice, Josephine **41**
Primus, Pearl **6**
Ray, Gene Anthony **47**
Rhoden, Dwight **40**
Ribeiro, Alfonso **17**
Richardson, Desmond **39**
Robinson, Bill "Bojangles" **11**
Robinson, Cleo Parker **38**
Robinson, Fatima **34**
Robinson, LaVaughn **69**
Rodgers, Rod **36**
Rolle, Esther **13, 21**
Sims, Howard "Sandman" **48**
Slyde, Jimmy **70**
Spears, Warren **52**
Tyson, Andre **40**
Vereen, Ben **4**
Walker, Cedric "Ricky" **19**
Walker, Dianne **57**
Washington, Fredi **10**
Williams, Dudley **60**
Williams, Vanessa L. **4, 17**

Zollar, Jawole Willa Jo **28**

Education
Achebe, Chinua **6**
Adams, Leslie **39**
Adams-Ender, Clara **40**
Adkins, Rutherford H. **21**
Aidoo, Ama Ata **38**
Ake, Claude **30**
Alexander, Margaret Walker **22**
Allen, Robert L. **38**
Allen, Samuel W. **38**
Allen-Buillard, Melba **55**
Alston, Charles **33**
Amadi, Elechi **40**
Anderson, Charles Edward **37**
Appiah, Kwame Anthony **67**
Archer, Dennis **7**
Archie-Hudson, Marguerite **44**
Aristide, Jean-Bertrand **6, 45**
Asante, Molefi Kete **3**
Aubert, Alvin **41**
Awoonor, Kofi **37**
Bacon-Bercey, June **38**
Bahati, Wambui **60**
Baiocchi, Regina Harris **41**
Baker, Augusta **38**
Baker, Gwendolyn Calvert **9**
Baker, Houston A., Jr. **6**
Ballard, Allen Butler, Jr. **40**
Bambara, Toni Cade **10**
Baraka, Amiri **1, 38**
Barbee, Lloyd Augustus **71**
Barboza, Anthony **10**
Barnett, Marguerite **46**
Bath, Patricia E. **37**
Batiste, Alvin **66**
Beckham, Barry **41**
Bell, Derrick **6**
Benberry, Cuesta **65**
Benjamin, Tritobia Hayes **53**
Berry, Bertice **8, 55**
Berry, Mary Frances **7**
Bethune, Mary McLeod **4**
Biggers, John **20, 33**
Black, Albert **51**
Black, Keith Lanier **18**
Blassingame, John Wesley **40**
Blockson, Charles L. **42**
Bluitt, Juliann S. **14**
Bobo, Lawrence **60**
Bogle, Donald **34**
Bolden, Tonya **32**
Bosley, Freeman, Jr. **7**
Boyd, T. B., III **6**
Bradley, David Henry, Jr. **39**
Branch, William Blackwell **39**
Brathwaite, Kamau **36**
Braun, Carol Moseley **4, 42**
Briscoe, Marlin **37**
Brooks, Avery **9**
Brown, Claude **38**
Brown, Joyce F. **25**
Brown, Sterling Allen **10, 64**
Brown, Uzee **42**
Brown, Wesley **23**
Brown, Willa **40**
Bruce, Blanche Kelso **33**
Brutus, Dennis **38**
Bryan, Ashley F. **41**
Burke, Selma **16**
Burke, Yvonne Braithwaite **42**
Burks, Mary Fair **40**

Burnim, Mickey L. 48
Burroughs, Margaret Taylor 9
Burton, LeVar 8
Butler, Paul D. 17
Callender, Clive O. 3
Campbell, Bebe Moore 6, 24, 59
Campbell, Mary Schmidt 43
Cannon, Katie 10
Carby, Hazel 27
Cardozo, Francis L. 33
Carnegie, Herbert 25
Carruthers, George R. 40
Carter, Joye Maureen 41
Carter, Kenneth 53
Carter, Warrick L. 27
Cartey, Wilfred 47
Carver, George Washington 4
Cary, Lorene 3
Cary, Mary Ann Shadd 30
Catlett, Elizabeth 2
Cayton, Horace 26
Chaney, John 67
Cheney-Coker, Syl 43
Clark, Joe 1
Clark, Kenneth B. 5, 52
Clark, Septima 7
Clarke, Cheryl 32
Clarke, George 32
Clarke, John Henrik 20
Clayton, Constance 1
Cleaver, Kathleen Neal 29
Clements, George 2
Clemmons, Reginal G. 41
Clifton, Lucille 14, 64
Cobb, Jewel Plummer 42
Cobb, W. Montague 39
Cobb, William Jelani 59
Cobbs, Price M. 9
Cohen, Anthony 15
Cole, Johnnetta B. 5, 43
Coleman, William F., III 61
Colescott, Robert 69
Collins, Janet 33, 64
Collins, Marva 3, 71
Collins, Patricia Hill 67
Comer, James P. 6
Cone, James H. 3
Coney, PonJola 48
Cook, Mercer 40
Cook, Samuel DuBois 14
Cook, Toni 23
Cooper, Afua 53
Cooper, Anna Julia 20
Cooper, Edward S. 6
Cooper Cafritz, Peggy 43
Copeland, Michael 47
Cortez, Jayne 43
Cosby, Bill 7, 26, 59
Cotter, Joseph Seamon, Sr. 40
Cottrell, Comer 11
Cox, Joseph Mason Andrew 51
Cox, William E. 68
Creagh, Milton 27
Crew, Rudolph F. 16
Crew, Spencer R. 55
Cross, Dolores E. 23
Crouch, Stanley 11
Cruse, Harold 54
Cullen, Countee 8
Daly, Marie Maynard 37
Dathorne, O. R. 52
Davis, Allison 12
Davis, Angela 5

Davis, Arthur P. 41
Davis, Charles T. 48
Davis, Erroll B., Jr. 57
Davis, George 36
Dawson, William Levi 39
Days, Drew S., III 10
Deconge-Watson, Lovenia 55
Delany, Sadie 12
Delany, Samuel R., Jr. 9
Delco, Wilhemina R. 33
Delsarte, Louis 34
Dennard, Brazeal 37
DePriest, James 37
Dickens, Helen Octavia 14, 64
Diop, Cheikh Anta 4
Dixon, Margaret 14
Dodson, Howard, Jr. 7, 52
Dodson, Owen Vincent 38
Donaldson, Jeff 46
Douglas, Aaron 7
Dove, Rita 6
Dove, Ulysses 5
Draper, Sharon Mills 16, 43
Driskell, David C. 7
Drummond, William J. 40
Du Bois, David Graham 45
Dumas, Henry 41
Dunbar-Nelson, Alice Ruth Moore 44
Dunnigan, Alice Allison 41
Dunston, Georgia Mae 48
Dymally, Mervyn 42
Dyson, Michael Eric 11, 40
Early, Gerald 15
Edelin, Ramona Hoage 19
Edelman, Marian Wright 5, 42
Edley, Christopher 2, 48
Edley, Christopher F., Jr. 48
Edwards, Harry 2
Elders, Joycelyn 6
Elliot, Lorris 37
Ellis, Clarence A. 38
Ellison, Ralph 7
Epps, Archie C., III 45
Evans, Mari 26
Falconer, Etta Zuber 59
Fauset, Jessie 7
Favors, Steve 23
Feelings, Muriel 44
Figueroa, John J. 40
Fleming, Raymond 48
Fletcher, Bill, Jr. 41
Floyd, Elson S. 41
Ford, Jack 39
Foster, Ezola 28
Foster, Henry W., Jr. 26
Francis, Norman (C.) 60
Franklin, John Hope 5
Franklin, Robert M. 13
Frazier, E. Franklin 10
Freeman, Al, Jr. 11
Fryer, Roland G. 56
Fuller, A. Oveta 43
Fuller, Arthur 27
Fuller, Howard L. 37
Fuller, Solomon Carter, Jr. 15
Futrell, Mary Hatwood 33
Gaines, Ernest J. 7
Gates, Henry Louis, Jr. 3, 38, 67
Gates, Sylvester James, Jr. 15
Gayle, Addison, Jr. 41
George, Zelma Watson 42
Gerima, Haile 38

Gibson, Donald Bernard 40
Giddings, Paula 11
Gill, Gerald 69
Giovanni, Nikki 9, 39
Golden, Marita 19
Gomes, Peter J. 15
Gomez, Jewelle 30
Goodison, Lorna 71
Granville, Evelyn Boyd 36
Greenfield, Eloise 9
Guinier, Lani 7, 30
Guy-Sheftall, Beverly 13
Hageman, Hans and Ivan 36
Hale, Lorraine 8
Halliburton, Warren J. 49
Hammonds, Evelynn 69
Handy, W. C. 8
Hansberry, William Leo 11
Harding, Vincent 67
Harkless, Necia Desiree 19
Harper, Michael S. 34
Harris, Alice 7
Harris, Barry 68
Harris, Bill 72
Harris, Jay T. 19
Harris, Patricia Roberts 2
Harsh, Vivian Gordon 14
Harvey, William R. 42
Haskins, James 36, 54
Hathaway, Isaac Scott 33
Hayden, Carla D. 47
Hayden, Robert 12
Haynes, George Edmund 8
Henderson, Stephen E. 45
Henries, A. Doris Banks 44
Herenton, Willie W. 24
Hill, Andrew 66
Hill, Anita 5, 65
Hill, Bonnie Guiton 20
Hill, Errol 40
Hill, Leslie Pinckney 44
Hilliard, Asa Grant, III 66
Hine, Darlene Clark 24
Hinton, William Augustus 8
Hoagland, Everett H. 45
Hogan, Beverly Wade 50
Holland, Endesha Ida Mae 3, 57
Holt, Nora 8
hooks, Bell 5
Hope, John 8
Horton, James Oliver 58
Houston, Charles Hamilton 4
Hoyte, Lenon 50
Hrabowski, Freeman A., III 22
Huggins, Nathan Irvin 52
Hughes, Ebony 57
Hull, Akasha Gloria 45
Humphries, Frederick 20
Hunt, Richard 6
Hutcherson, Hilda Yvonne 54
Hutson, Jean Blackwell 16
Imes, Elmer Samuel 39
Jackson, Edison O. 67
Jackson, Fred James 25
Jackson, Vera 40
Jarrett, Vernon D. 42
Jarvis, Charlene Drew 21
Jarvis, Erich 67
Jeffries, Leonard 8
Jenifer, Franklyn G. 2
Jenkins, Ella 15
Johns, Vernon 38
Johnson, Hazel 22

Johnson, James Weldon 5
Johnson, Katherine (Coleman Goble) 61
Jones, Bobby 20
Jones, Clara Stanton 51
Jones, Edward P. 43, 67
Jones, Gayl 37
Jones, Ingrid Saunders 18
Jones, Lois Mailou 13
Joplin, Scott 6
Jordan, Barbara 4
Jordan, June 7, 35
Josey, E. J. 10
Just, Ernest Everett 3
Karenga, Maulana 10, 71
Kay, Ulysses 37
Keith, Damon J. 16
Kennedy, Florynce 12, 33
Kennedy, Randall 40
Kilpatrick, Carolyn Cheeks 16
Kimbro, Dennis 10
King, Preston 28
King, Reatha Clark 65
Kittles, Rick 51
Komunyakaa, Yusef 9
Kunjufu, Jawanza 3, 50
Ladner, Joyce A. 42
Lawrence, Jacob 4, 28
Lawrence-Lightfoot, Sara 10
Lee, Annie Frances 22
Lee, Joe A. 45
Leevy, Carrol M. 42
Leffall, Lasalle 3, 64
Lester, Julius 9
Lewis, David Levering 9
Lewis, Norman 39
Lewis, Samella 25
Lewis, Shirley A. R. 14
Lewis, Thomas 19
Liberia-Peters, Maria Philomena 12
Lincoln, C. Eric 38
Lindsey, Tommie 51
Locke, Alain 10
Logan, Rayford W. 40
Lomax, Michael L. 58
Long, Loretta 58
Long, Richard Alexander 65
Lorde, Audre 6
Loury, Glenn 36
Loving, Alvin, Jr. 35, 53
Lowry, A. Leon 60
Lucy Foster, Autherine 35
Lyttle, Hulda Margaret 14
Madhubuti, Haki R. 7
Major, Clarence 9
Malveaux, Floyd 54
Manley, Audrey Forbes 16
Marable, Manning 10
Markham, E. A. 37
Marsalis, Wynton 16
Marshall, Paule 7
Masekela, Barbara 18
Mason, Ronald 27
Massey, Walter E. 5, 45
Massie, Samuel P., Jr. 29
Mayhew, Richard 39
Maynard, Robert C. 7
Maynor, Dorothy 19
Mayo, Whitman 32
Mays, Benjamin E. 7
McCarty, Osceola 16
McCullough, Geraldine 58
McKay, Nellie Yvonne 17, 57

McMillan, Terry **4, 17, 53**
McMurray, Georgia L. **36**
McPherson, James Alan **70**
McWhorter, John **35**
Meek, Carrie **6**
Mell, Patricia **49**
Memmi, Albert **37**
Meredith, James H. **11**
Millender-McDonald, Juanita **21, 61**
Mitchell, Corinne **8**
Mitchell, Nicole **66**
Mitchell, Sharon **36**
Mofolo, Thomas Mokopu **37**
Mollel, Tololwa **38**
Mongella, Gertrude **11**
Mooney, Paul **37**
Moore, Barbara C. **49**
Moore, Harry T. **29**
Moore, Melba **21**
Morrison, Keith **13**
Morrison, Toni **15**
Moses, Robert Parris **11**
Mphalele, Es'kia (Ezekiel) **40**
Mudimbe, V.Y. **61**
Mullen, Harryette **34**
Murray, Pauli **38**
Nabrit, Samuel Milton **47**
Nance, Cynthia **71**
Naylor, Gloria **10, 42**
Neal, Larry **38**
Newkirk, Pamela **69**
Newman, Lester C. **51**
N'Namdi, George R. **17**
Norman, Maidie **20**
Norton, Eleanor Holmes **7**
Nour, Nawal M. **56**
Ogletree, Charles, Jr. **12, 47**
Ojikutu, Bisola **65**
Oliver, Kimberly **60**
Onwueme, Tess Osonye **23**
Onwurah, Ngozi **38**
Owens, Helen **48**
Owens, Major **6**
Page, Alan **7**
Paige, Rod **29**
Painter, Nell Irvin **24**
Palmer, Everard **37**
Parker, Kellis E. **30**
Parks, Suzan-Lori **34**
Patterson, Frederick Douglass **12**
Patterson, Mary Jane **54**
Patterson, Orlando **4**
Payton, Benjamin F. **23**
Perry, Warren **56**
Peters, Margaret **43**
Peters, Matilda **43**
Pickett, Cecil **39**
Pinckney, Bill **42**
Pindell, Howardena **55**
Piper, Adrian **71**
Player, Willa B. **43**
Porter, James A. **11**
Poussaint, Alvin F. **5, 67**
Price, Florence **37**
Price, Glenda **22**
Price, Richard **51**
Primus, Pearl **6**
Prophet, Nancy Elizabeth **42**
Purnell, Silas **59**
Puryear, Martin **42**
Quarles, Benjamin Arthur **18**
Quigless, Helen G. **49**
Rahman, Aishah **37**

Ramphele, Mamphela **29**
Reagon, Bernice Johnson **7**
Reddick, Lawrence Dunbar **20**
Redding, J. Saunders **26**
Redmond, Eugene **23**
Reid, Irvin D. **20**
Ribeau, Sidney **70**
Rice, Condoleezza **3, 28, 72**
Rice, Louise Allen **54**
Richards, Hilda **49**
Ringgold, Faith **4**
Robinson, Sharon **22**
Robinson, Spottswood W., III **22**
Rodriguez, Cheryl **64**
Rogers, Joel Augustus **30**
Rollins, Charlemae Hill **27**
Ross-Lee, Barbara **24**
Russell-McCloud, Patricia **17**
Salih, Al-Tayyib **37**
Sallee, Charles Louis, Jr. **38**
Satcher, David **7, 57**
Schomburg, Arthur Alfonso **9**
Sears, Stephanie **53**
Senior, Olive **37**
Shabazz, Betty **7, 26**
Shange, Ntozake **8**
Shipp, E. R. **15**
Shirley, George **33**
Simmons, Ruth J. **13, 38**
Sinkford, Jeanne C. **13**
Sisulu, Sheila Violet Makate **24**
Sizemore, Barbara A. **26**
Smith, Anna Deavere **6**
Smith, Barbara **28**
Smith, Jessie Carney **35**
Smith, John L. **22**
Smith, Mary Carter **26**
Smith, Tubby **18**
Snowden, Frank M., Jr. **67**
Southern, Eileen **56**
Sowande, Fela **39**
Soyinka, Wole **4**
Spears, Warren **52**
Spikes, Dolores **18**
Spriggs, William **67**
Stanford, John **20**
Steele, Claude Mason **13**
Steele, Shelby **13**
Stephens, Charlotte Andrews **14**
Stewart, Maria W. Miller **19**
Stone, Chuck **9**
Sudarkasa, Niara **4**
Sullivan, Louis **8**
Swygert, H. Patrick **22**
Tancil, Gladys Quander **59**
Tanksley, Ann **37**
Tatum, Beverly Daniel **42**
Taylor, Helen (Lavon Hollingshed) **30**
Taylor, Susie King **13**
Terrell, Mary Church **9**
Thomas, Alma **14**
Thomas, Michael **69**
Thurman, Howard **3**
Tillis, Frederick **40**
Tolson, Melvin **37**
Tribble, Israel, Jr. **8**
Trueheart, William E. **49**
Tucker, Rosina **14**
Turnbull, Charles Wesley **62**
Turnbull, Walter **13, 60**
Tutu, Desmond **6**
Tutu, Nontombi Naomi **57**

Tutuola, Amos **30**
Tyson, Andre **40**
Tyson, Asha **39**
Tyson, Neil deGrasse **15, 65**
Usry, James L. **23**
van Sertima, Ivan **25**
Vaughn, Viola **70**
Vega, Marta Moreno **61**
Velez-Rodriguez, Argelia **56**
Verna, Gelsy **70**
Wade-Gayles, Gloria Jean **41**
Walcott, Derek **5**
Walker, George **37**
Wallace, Michele Faith **13**
Wallace, Perry E. **47**
Wallace, Phyllis A. **9**
Washington, Booker T. **4**
Watkins, Shirley R. **17**
Wattleton, Faye **9**
Weaver, Afaa Michael **37**
Wedgeworth, Robert W. **42**
Wells, Henrietta Bell **69**
Wells, James Lesesne **10**
Wells-Barnett, Ida B. **8**
Welsing, Frances Cress **5**
Wesley, Dorothy Porter **19**
Wesley, Richard **73**
West, Cornel **5, 33**
Wharton, Clifton R., Jr. **7**
White, Charles **39**
White, Lois Jean **20**
Wilkens, J. Ernest, Jr. **43**
Wilkins, Roger **2**
Williams, David Rudyard **50**
Williams, Fannie Barrier **27**
Williams, Gregory **11**
Williams, Patricia **11, 54**
Williams, Sherley Anne **25**
Williams, Walter E. **4**
Wilson, William Julius **22**
Woodruff, Hale **9**
Woodson, Carter G. **2**
Worrill, Conrad **12**
Wright, Antoinette **60**
Xuma, Madie Hall **59**
Yancy, Dorothy Cowser **42**
Young, Jean Childs **14**
Zook, Kristal Brent **62**

Fashion
Aberra, Amsale **67**
Bailey, Xenobia **11**
Banks, Jeffrey **17**
Banks, Tyra **11, 50**
Barboza, Anthony **10**
Beals, Jennifer **12**
Beckford, Tyson **11, 68**
Boateng, Ozwald **35**
Bond, Beverly **53**
Boyd, Suzanne **52**
Bridges, Sheila **36**
Brown, Joyce F. **25**
Burrows, Stephen **31**
Campbell, Naomi **1, 31**
Common **31, 63**
Darego, Agbani **52**
Dash, Damon **31**
Davidson, Jaye **5**
De' Alexander, Quinton **57**
Delice, Ronald **48**
Delice, Rony **48**
Dirie, Waris **56**
Ebanks, Selita **67**

Evans, Etu **55**
Gaskins, Eric **64**
Gibson, Ted **66**
Givhan, Robin Deneen **72**
Hall, Kevan **61**
Harold, Erika **54**
Henderson, Gordon **5**
Hendy, Francis **47**
Iman **4, 33**
Iman, Chanel **66**
John, Daymond **23**
Johnson, Beverly **2**
Jones, Carl **7**
Kani, Karl **10**
Kebede, Liya **59**
Kelly, Patrick **3**
Kodjoe, Boris **34**
Lars, Byron **32**
Malone, Maurice **32**
McGrath, Pat **72**
McKenzie, Jaunel **73**
Michele, Michael **31**
Niane, Katoucha **70**
Onwurah, Ngozi **38**
Powell, Maxine **8**
Reese, Tracy **54**
Rhymes, Busta **31**
Robinson, Patrick **19, 71**
Rochon, Lela **16**
Rowell, Victoria **13, 68**
Sims, Naomi **29**
Smaltz, Audrey **12**
Smith, B(arbara) **11**
Smith, Willi **8**
Smythe Haith, Mabel **61**
Steele, Lawrence **28**
Stoney, Michael **50**
Sy, Oumou **65**
Talley, André Leon **56**
Taylor, Karin **34**
Walker, T. J. **7**
Webb, Veronica **10**
Wek, Alek **18, 63**
Williams, Serena **20, 41, 73**

Film
Aaliyah **30**
Akinnuoye-Agbaje, Adewale **56**
Akomfrah, John **37**
Alexander, Khandi **43**
Ali, Tatyana **73**
Allain, Stephanie **49**
Allen, Debbie **13, 42**
Amos, John **8, 62**
Anderson, Anthony **51**
Anderson, Eddie "Rochester" **30**
Awoonor, Kofi **37**
Babatunde, Obba **35**
Baker, Josephine **3**
Banks, Michelle **59**
Banks, Tyra **11, 50**
Barclay, Paris **37**
Barnett, Etta Moten **56**
Bassett, Angela **6, 23, 62**
Beach, Michael **26**
Beals, Jennifer **12**
Beckford, Tyson **11, 68**
Belafonte, Harry **4, 65**
Bellamy, Bill **12**
Bennett, Louise **69**
Bentley, Lamont **53**
Berry, Fred "Rerun" **48**
Berry, Halle **4, 19, 57**

Beyoncé **39, 70**
Bivins, Michael **72**
Blackwood, Maureen **37**
Blacque, Taurean **58**
Bleu, Corbin **65**
Bogle, Donald **34**
Bonet, Lisa **58**
Brady, Wayne **32, 71**
Brandy **14, 34, 72**
Braugher, Andre **13, 58**
Breeze, Jean "Binta" **37**
Brooks, Golden **62**
Brooks, Hadda **40**
Brown, Jim **11**
Brown, Tony **3**
Browne, Roscoe Lee **66**
Burnett, Charles **16, 68**
Byrd, Michelle **19**
Byrd, Robert **11**
Calloway, Cab **14**
Campbell, Naomi **1, 31**
Campbell-Martin, Tisha **8, 42**
Cannon, Nick **47, 73**
Cannon, Reuben **50**
Carroll, Diahann **9**
Carson, Lisa Nicole **21**
Cash, Rosalind **28**
Cedric the Entertainer **29, 60**
Chase, Debra Martin **49**
Cheadle, Don **19, 52**
Chestnut, Morris **31**
Chong, Rae Dawn **62**
Chweneyagae, Presley **63**
Clash, Kevin **14**
Cliff, Jimmy **28**
Combs, Sean "Puffy" **17, 43**
Cortez, Jayne **43**
Cosby, Bill **7, 26, 59**
Crothers, Scatman **19**
Curry, Mark **17**
Curtis-Hall, Vondie **17**
Dandridge, Dorothy **3**
Daniels, Lee Louis **36**
Dash, Julie **4**
David, Keith **27**
Davidson, Jaye **5**
Davidson, Tommy **21**
Davis, Eisa **68**
Davis, Guy **36**
Davis, Ossie **5, 50**
Davis, Sammy, Jr. **18**
Dawson, Rosario **72**
de Passe, Suzanne **25**
De Shields, André **72**
Dee, Ruby **8, 50, 68**
Devine, Loretta **24**
Dickerson, Ernest **6, 17**
Diesel, Vin **29**
Dieudonné **67**
Diggs, Taye **25, 63**
Dixon, Ivan **69**
DMX **28, 64**
Dourdan, Gary **37**
Driskell, David C. **7**
Duke, Bill **3**
Duncan, Michael Clarke **26**
Dunham, Katherine **4, 59**
Dutton, Charles S. **4, 22**
Earthquake **55**
Edmonds, Kenneth "Babyface" **10, 31**
Ejiofor, Chiwetel **67**
Elder, Lonne, III **38**

Elise, Kimberly **32**
Emmanuel, Alphonsia **38**
Epps, Omar **23, 59**
Esposito, Giancarlo **9**
Evans, Darryl **22**
Everett, Francine **23**
Faison, Donald **50**
Faison, Frankie **55**
Fetchit, Stepin **32**
Fishburne, Laurence **4, 22, 70**
Fisher, Antwone **40**
Fox, Rick **27**
Fox, Vivica A. **15, 53**
Foxx, Jamie **15, 48**
Foxx, Redd **2**
Franklin, Carl **11**
Freeman, Al, Jr. **11**
Freeman, Morgan **2, 20, 62**
Freeman, Yvette **27**
Friday, Jeff **24**
Fuller, Charles **8**
Fuqua, Antoine **35**
Gaye, Nona **56**
George, Nelson **12**
Gerima, Haile **38**
Gibson, Tyrese **27, 62**
Givens, Adele **62**
Givens, Robin **4, 25, 58**
Glover, Danny **1, 24**
Glover, Savion **14**
Goldberg, Whoopi **4, 33, 69**
Gooding, Cuba, Jr. **16, 62**
Gordon, Dexter **25**
Gordy, Berry, Jr. **1**
Gossett, Louis, Jr. **7**
Gray, F. Gary **14, 49**
Greaves, William **38**
Grier, David Alan **28**
Grier, Pam **9, 31**
Guillaume, Robert **3, 48**
Gunn, Moses **10**
Gurira, Danai **73**
Guy, Jasmine **2**
Hall, Arsenio **58**
Hall, Juanita **62**
Hamilton, Lisa Gay **71**
Hampton, Henry **6**
Hardison, Kadeem **22**
Harewood, David **52**
Harper, Hill **32, 65**
Harris, Leslie **6**
Harris, Naomie **55**
Harris, Robin **7**
Hawkins, Screamin' Jay **30**
Hayes, Isaac **20, 58, 73**
Hayes, Teddy **40**
Haysbert, Dennis **42**
Hemsley, Sherman **19**
Henriques, Julian **37**
Henry, Lenny **9, 52**
Henson, Darrin **33**
Henson, Taraji **58**
Hill, Dulé **29**
Hill, Lauryn **20, 53**
Hines, Gregory **1, 42**
Horne, Lena **5**
Hounsou, Djimon **19, 45**
Houston, Whitney **7, 28**
Howard, Sherri **36**
Howard, Terrence **59**
Hudlin, Reginald **9**
Hudlin, Warrington **9**
Hudson, Ernie **72**

Hudson, Jennifer **63**
Hughes, Albert **7**
Hughes, Allen **7**
Hurt, Byron **61**
Ice Cube **8, 30, 60**
Ice-T **6, 31**
Iman **4, 33**
Ingram, Rex **5**
Jackson, George **19**
Jackson, Janet **6, 30, 68**
Jackson, Samuel **8, 19, 63**
Jean, Michaëlle; **70**
Jean-Baptiste, Marianne **17, 46**
Johnson, Beverly **2**
Jones, James Earl **3, 49**
Jones, Orlando **30**
Jones, Quincy **8, 30**
Jorge, Seu **73**
Julien, Isaac **3**
Kelley, Elijah **65**
Keys, Alicia **32, 68**
Khumalo, Leleti **51**
King, Regina **22, 45**
King, Woodie, Jr. **27**
Kirby, George **14**
Kitt, Eartha **16**
Kool Moe Dee **37**
Kotto, Yaphet **7**
Kunjufu, Jawanza **3, 50**
La Salle, Eriq **12**
LaBelle, Patti **13, 30**
Lane, Charles **3**
Lathan, Sanaa **27**
Lawrence, Martin **6, 27, 60**
Lee, Joie **1**
Lee, Spike **5, 19**
Lemmons, Kasi **20**
LeNoire, Rosetta **37**
Lester, Adrian **46**
Lewis, Samella **25**
Lil' Kim **28**
Lincoln, Abbey **3**
Lindo, Delroy **18, 45**
LisaRaye **27**
LL Cool J **16, 49**
Long, Nia **17**
Love, Darlene **23**
Lover, Ed **10**
Luke, Derek **61**
Lynch, Shola **61**
Mabley, Jackie "Moms" **15**
Mac, Bernie **29, 61, 72**
Malco, Romany **71**
Marsalis, Branford **34**
Martin, Darnell **43**
Martin, Helen **31**
Master P **21**
McBride, Chi **73**
McDaniel, Hattie **5**
McKee, Lonette **12**
McKinney, Nina Mae **40**
McQueen, Butterfly **6, 54**
Meadows, Tim **30**
Mello, Breno **73**
Micheaux, Oscar **7**
Michele, Michael **31**
Mitchell, Elvis **67**
Mitchell, Kel **66**
Mo'Nique **35**
Mooney, Paul **37**
Moore, Chante **26**
Moore, Melba **21**
Moore, Shemar **21**

Morris, Garrett **31**
Morris, Greg **28**
Morton, Joe **18**
Mos Def **30**
Moses, Gilbert **12**
Moss, Carlton **17**
Murphy, Eddie **4, 20, 61**
Muse, Clarence Edouard **21**
Nas **33**
Nash, Johnny **40**
Nash, Niecy **66**
Neal, Elise **29**
Newton, Thandie **26**
Nicholas, Fayard **20, 57**
Nicholas, Harold **20**
Nichols, Nichelle **11**
Norman, Maidie **20**
Odetta **37**
Okonedo, Sophie **67**
O'Neal, Ron **46**
Onwurah, Ngozi **38**
Packer, Will **71**
Palmer, Keke **68**
Parker, Nicole Ari **52**
Parks, Gordon **1, 35, 58**
Patton, Paula **62**
Payne, Allen **13**
Peck, Raoul **32**
Perrineau, Harold, Jr. **51**
Perry, Tyler **54**
Phifer, Mekhi **25**
Pinkett Smith, Jada **10, 41**
Poitier, Sidney **11, 36**
Poitier, Sydney Tamiia **65**
Pounder, CCH **72**
Pratt, Kyla **57**
Prince **18, 65**
Prince-Bythewood, Gina **31**
Pryor, Richard **3, 24, 56**
Queen Latifah **1, 16, 58**
Ralph, Sheryl Lee **18**
Randle, Theresa **16**
Reddick, Lance **52**
Reese, Della **6, 20**
Reid, Tim **56**
Reuben, Gloria **15**
Rhames, Ving **14, 50**
Rhimes, Shonda Lynn **67**
Rhymes, Busta **31**
Richards, Beah **30**
Richardson, LaTanya **71**
Richardson, Salli **68**
Ridley, John **69**
Riggs, Marlon **5, 44**
Roberts, Darryl **70**
Roberts, Kimberly Rivers **72**
Robinson, Matt **69**
Robinson, Shaun **36**
Rochon, Lela **16**
Rock, Chris **3, 22, 66**
Rock, The **29, 66**
Rodrigues, Percy **68**
Rolle, Esther **13, 21**
Rollins, Howard E., Jr. **16**
Rose, Anika Noni **70**
Ross, Diana **8, 27**
Roundtree, Richard **27**
Rowell, Victoria **13, 68**
Rupaul **17**
Russell, Nipsey **66**
St. Jacques, Raymond **8**
St. John, Kristoff **25**
Saldana, Zoe **72**

Salter, Nikkole **73**
Schultz, Michael A. **6**
Scott, Hazel **66**
Seal **14**
Sembène, Ousmane **13, 62**
Shakur, Tupac **14**
Shepherd, Sherri **55**
Simmons, Henry **55**
Simpson, O. J. **15**
Sinbad **1, 16**
Singleton, John **2, 30**
Sisqo **30**
Smith, Anjela Lauren **44**
Smith, Anna Deavere **6, 44**
Smith, Roger Guenveur **12**
Smith, Tasha **73**
Smith, Will **8, 18, 53**
Snipes, Wesley **3, 24, 67**
Sullivan, Maxine **37**
Tate, Larenz **15**
Taylor, Meshach **4**
Taylor, Regina **9, 46**
Thigpen, Lynne **17, 41**
Thomas, Sean Patrick **35**
Thompson, Kenan **52**
Thurman, Wallace **16**
Tillman, George, Jr. **20**
Torres, Gina **52**
Torry, Guy **31**
Toussaint, Lorraine **32**
Townsend, Robert **4, 23**
Tucker, Chris **13, 23, 62**
Tunie, Tamara **63**
Turner, Tina **6, 27**
Tyler, Aisha N. **36**
Tyson, Cicely **7, 51**
Uggams, Leslie **23**
Underwood, Blair **7, 27**
Union, Gabrielle **31**
Usher **23, 56**
Van Lierop, Robert **53**
Van Peebles, Mario **2, 51**
Van Peebles, Melvin **7**
Vance, Courtney B. **15, 60**
Vanity **67**
Vereen, Ben **4**
Walker, Eamonn **37**
Ward, Douglas Turner **42**
Warfield, Marsha **2**
Warner, Malcolm-Jamal **22, 36**
Warren, Michael **27**
Warwick, Dionne **18**
Washington, Denzel **1, 16**
Washington, Fredi **10**
Washington, Kerry **46**
Waters, Ethel **7**
Wayans, Damon **8, 41**
Wayans, Keenen Ivory **18**
Wayans, Marlon **29**
Wayans, Shawn **29**
Weathers, Carl **10**
Webb, Veronica **10**
Wesley, Richard **73**
Whitaker, Forest **2, 49, 67**
White, Michael Jai **71**
Whitfield, Lynn **18**
Williams, Billy Dee **8**
Williams, Clarence, III **26**
Williams, Marco **53**
Williams, Russell, II **70**
Williams, Samm-Art **21**
Williams, Vanessa A. **32, 66**

Williams, Vanessa L. **4, 17**
Williamson, Fred **67**
Williamson, Mykelti **22**
Wilson, Debra **38**
Wilson, Dorien **55**
Winfield, Paul **2, 45**
Winfrey, Oprah **2, 15, 61**
Witherspoon, John **38**
Woodard, Alfre **9**
Wright, Jeffrey **54**
Yarbrough, Cedric **51**
Yoba, Malik **11**

Government and politics--international

Abacha, Sani **11, 70**
Abbott, Diane **9**
Abiola, Moshood **70**
Abubakar, Abdulsalami **66**
Achebe, Chinua **6**
Akunyili, Dora Nkem**58**
Ali, Ayaan Hirsi **58**
Ali Mahdi Mohamed **5**
Amadi, Elechi **40**
Amin, Idi **42**
Amos, Valerie **41**
Annan, Kofi Atta **15, 48**
Aristide, Jean-Bertrand **6, 45**
Arthur, Owen **33**
Augustine, Jean **53**
Awoonor, Kofi **37**
Azikiwe, Nnamdi **13**
Babangida, Ibrahim **4**
Baker, Gwendolyn Calvert **9**
Banda, Hastings Kamuzu **6, 54**
Barrow, Dean **69**
Bedie, Henri Konan **21**
Berry, Mary Frances **7**
Biko, Steven **4**
Bishop, Maurice **39**
Biya, Paul **28**
Bizimungu, Pasteur **19**
Boateng, Paul Yaw **56**
Bongo, Omar **1**
Boye, Madior **30**
Brown, Rosemary **62**
Bunche, Ralph J. **5**
Burnham, Forbes **66**
Buthelezi, Mangosuthu Gatsha **9**
Césaire, Aimé **48, 69**
Charlemagne, Manno **11**
Charles, Mary Eugenia **10, 55**
Charles, Pierre **52**
Chiluba, Frederick Jacob Titus **56**
Chissano, Joaquim **7, 55, 67**
Christie, Perry Gladstone **53**
Christophe, Henri **9**
Compton, John **65**
Conneh, Sekou Damate, Jr. **51**
Conté, Lansana **7**
Cools, Anne **64**
Curling, Alvin **34**
da Silva, Benedita **5**
Dadié, Bernard **34**
Davis, Ruth **37**
Déby, Idriss **30**
Diogo, Luisa Dias **63**
Diop, Cheikh Anta **4**
Diouf, Abdou **3**
dos Santos, José Eduardo **43**
Douglas, Denzil Llewellyn **53**
Ekwensi, Cyprian **37**
Eyadéma, Gnassingbé **7, 52**

Fela **1, 42**
Frazer, Jendayi **68**
Gbagbo, Laurent **43**
Gnassingbé, Faure **67**
Gordon, Pamela **17**
Grant, Bernie **57**
Habré, Hissène **6**
Habyarimana, Juvenal **8**
Haile Selassie **7**
Haley, George Williford Boyce **21**
Hani, Chris **6**
Houphouët-Boigny, Félix **4, 64**
Ifill, Gwen **28**
Ingraham, Hubert A. **19**
Isaac, Julius **34**
Jagan, Cheddi **16**
Jammeh, Yahya **23**
Jawara, Dawda Kairaba **11**
Jean, Michaëlle; **70**
Ka Dinizulu, Mcwayizeni **29**
Kabbah, Ahmad Tejan **23**
Kabila, Joseph **30**
Kabila, Laurent **20**
Kabunda, Kenneth **2**
Kagame, Paul **54**
Kariuki, J. M. **67**
Kenyatta, Jomo **5**
Kerekou, Ahmed (Mathieu) **1**
Kibaki, Mwai **60**
Kikwete, Jakaya Mrisho **73**
King, Oona **27**
Kufuor, John Agyekum **54**
Laraque, Paul **67**
Lewis, Daurene **72**
Liberia-Peters, Maria Philomena **12**
Lumumba, Patrice **33**
Luthuli, Albert **13**
Maathai, Wangari **43**
Mabuza, Lindiwe **18**
Machel, Samora Moises **8**
Magloire, Paul Eugène **68**
Mamadou, Tandja **33**
Mandela, Nelson **1, 14**
Mandela, Winnie **2, 35**
Masekela, Barbara **18**
Masire, Quett **5**
Mbeki, Thabo **14, 73**
Mbuende, Kaire **12**
Meles Zenawi **3**
Mengistu, Haile Mariam **65**
Mhlaba, Raymond **55**
Mkapa, Benjamin **16**
Mobutu Sese Seko **1, 56**
Mogae, Festus Gontebanye **19**
Moi, Daniel Arap **1, 35**
Mongella, Gertrude **11**
Mswati III **56**
Mugabe, Robert **10, 71**
Muluzi, Bakili **14**
Museveni, Yoweri **4**
Mutebi, Ronald **25**
Mwanawasa, Levy **72**
Mwinyi, Ali Hassan **1**
Ndadaye, Melchior **7**
Neto, António Agostinho **43**
Ngilu, Charity **58**
Ngubane, Ben **33**
Nkoli, Simon **60**
Nkomo, Joshua **4, 65**
Nkrumah, Kwame **3**
Ntaryamira, Cyprien **8**
Nujoma, Samuel **10**
Nyanda, Siphiwe **21**

Nyerere, Julius **5**
Nzo, Alfred **15**
Obasanjo, Olusegun **5, 22**
Obasanjo, Stella **32, 56**
Obote, Milton **63**
Odinga, Raila **67**
Okara, Gabriel **37**
Oyono, Ferdinand **38**
Pascal-Trouillot, Ertha **3**
Patterson, P. J. **6, 20**
Pereira, Aristides **30**
Perkins, Edward **5**
Perry, Ruth **15**
Pitt, David Thomas **10**
Pitta, Celso **17**
Poitier, Sidney **11, 36**
Ramaphosa, Cyril **3**
Rawlings, Jerry **9**
Rawlings, Nana Konadu Agyeman **13**
Roberto, Holden **65**
Robinson, Randall **7, 46**
Sampson, Edith S. **4**
Sankara, Thomas **17**
Savimbi, Jonas **2, 34**
Sawyer, Amos **2**
Senghor, Augustin Diamacoune **66**
Senghor, Léopold Sédar **12, 66**
Simpson-Miller, Portia **62**
Sirleaf, Ellen Johnson **71**
Sisulu, Walter **47**
Skerrit, Roosevelt **72**
Skinner, Kiron K. **65**
Smith, Jennifer **21**
Soglo, Nicephore **15**
Soyinka, Wole **4**
Spencer, Winston Baldwin **68**
Taylor, Charles **20**
Taylor, John (David Beckett) **16**
Todman, Terence A. **55**
Touré, Amadou Toumani **18**
Touré, Sekou **6**
Tsvangirai, Morgan **26, 72**
Tutu, Desmond (Mpilo) **6, 44**
Van Lierop, Robert **53**
Vieira, Joao **16**
Wade, Abdoulaye **66**
Weah, George **58**
Wharton, Clifton R., Jr. **7**
Wharton, Clifton Reginald, Sr. **36**
Williams, Eric Eustace **65**
Wiwa, Ken **67**
Yar'adua, Umaru **69**
Zuma, Jacob G. **33**
Zuma, Nkosazana Dlamini **34**

Government and politics--U.S.

Adams, Floyd, Jr. **12**
Alexander, Archie Alphonso **14**
Alexander, Clifford **26**
Allen, Claude **68**
Allen, Ethel D. **13**
Archer, Dennis **7, 36**
Arrington, Richard **24**
Avant, Clarence **19**
Baker, Thurbert **22**
Ballance, Frank W. **41**
Baltimore, Richard Lewis, III **71**
Barbee, Lloyd Augustus **71**
Barden, Don H. **9, 20**
Barrett, Andrew C. **12**
Barrett, Jacqueline **28**
Barry, Marion S(hepilov, Jr.) **7, 44**

Bass, Karen 70
Bell, Michael 40
Bellamy, Terry 58
Belton, Sharon Sayles 9, 16
Berry, Mary Frances 7
Berry, Theodore M. 31
Bethune, Mary McLeod 4
Blackwell, Kenneth, Sr. 61
Blackwell, Unita 17
Bond, Julian 2, 35
Booker, Cory Anthony 68
Bosley, Freeman, Jr. 7
Bowman, Bertie 71
Boykin, Keith 14
Bradley, Jennette B. 40
Bradley, Thomas 2
Braun, Carol Moseley 4, 42
Brazile, Donna 25, 70
Brimmer, Andrew F. 2, 48
Brooke, Edward 8
Brooks, Tyrone 59
Brown, Anthony G. 72
Brown, Byrd 49
Brown, Byron W. 72
Brown, Cora 33
Brown, Corrine 24
Brown, Elaine 8
Brown, George Leslie 62
Brown, Jesse 6, 41
Brown, Lee Patrick 24
Brown, Les 5
Brown, Ron 5
Brown, Willie L., Jr. 7
Bruce, Blanche K. 33
Bryant, Wayne R. 6
Buckley, Victoria (Vicki) 24
Bunche, Ralph J. 5
Burke, Yvonne Braithwaite 42
Burris, Chuck 21
Burris, Roland W. 25
Butler, Jerry 26
Caesar, Shirley 19
Campbell, Bill 9
Cardozo, Francis L. 33
Carson, André 69
Carson, Julia 23, 69
Carter, Pamela Lynn 67
Carter, Robert L. 51
Chavis, Benjamin 6
Chisholm, Shirley 2, 50
Christian-Green, Donna M. 17
Clay, William Lacy 8
Clayton, Eva M. 20
Cleaver, Eldridge 5
Cleaver, Emanuel 4, 45, 68
Clyburn, James E. 21, 71
Coleman, Mary 46
Coleman, Michael B. 28
Collins, Barbara-Rose 7
Collins, Cardiss 10
Colter, Cyrus J. 36
Connerly, Ward 14
Conyers, John, Jr. 4, 45
Cook, Mercer 40
Cose, Ellis 5, 50
Craig-Jones, Ellen Walker 44
Crockett, George W., Jr. 10, 64
Cummings, Elijah E. 24
Cunningham, Evelyn 23
Currie, Betty 21
Currie, Ulysses 73
Davis, Angela 5
Davis, Artur 41

Davis, Benjamin O., Jr. 2, 43
Davis, Benjamin O., Sr. 4
Davis, Danny K. 24
Davis, James E. 50
Days, Drew S., III 10
Delany, Martin R. 27
Delco, Wilhemina R. 33
Dellums, Ronald 2
Diggs, Charles R. 21
Dinkins, David 4
Dixon, Julian C. 24
Dixon, Sharon Pratt 1
Dixon, Sheila 68
Dougherty, Mary Pearl 47
Du Bois, W. E. B. 3
Dudley, Edward R. 58
Dukes, Hazel Nell 56
Dunbar-Nelson, Alice Ruth Moore
   44
Dymally, Mervyn 42
Easley, Annie J. 61
Edmonds, Terry 17
Elders, Joycelyn 6
Ellison, Keith 59
Espy, Mike 6
Farmer, James 2, 64
Farrakhan, Louis 2
Fattah, Chaka 11, 70
Fauntroy, Walter E. 11
Felix, Larry R. 64
Fenty, Adrian 60
Ferguson, Roger W. 25
Fields, C. Virginia 25
Fields, Cleo 13
Flake, Floyd H. 18
Fletcher, Arthur A. 63
Flipper, Henry O. 3
Ford, Harold E(ugene) 42
Ford, Harold E(ugene), Jr. 16, 70
Ford, Jack 39
Ford, Johnny 70
Fortune, T. Thomas 6
Foster, Ezola 28
Franklin, Shirley 34
Franks, Gary 2
Frazer, Jendayi 68
Fulani, Lenora 11
Gantt, Harvey 1
Garrett, Joyce Finley 59
Garvey, Marcus 1
Gibson, Johnnie Mae 23
Gibson, Kenneth Allen 6
Gibson, William F. 6
Goode, W. Wilson 4
Gravely, Samuel L., Jr. 5, 49
Gray, William H., III 3
Grimké, Archibald H. 9
Guinier, Lani 7, 30
Haley, George Williford Boyce 21
Hamer, Fannie Lou 6
Harmon, Clarence 26
Harris, Alice 7
Harris, Patricia Roberts 2
Harvard, Beverly 11
Hastie, William H. 8
Hastings, Alcee L. 16
Hatcher, Richard G. 55
Hawkins, Augustus F. 68
Hayes, James C. 10
Henderson, Thelton E. 68
Henry, Aaron 19
Herenton, Willie W. 24
Herman, Alexis M. 15

Hernandez, Aileen Clarke 13
Hill, Bonnie Guiton 20
Hilliard, Earl F. 24
Hobson, Julius W. 44
Holder, Eric H., Jr. 9
Holmes, Amy 69
Holt Baker, Arlene 73
Ifill, Gwen 28
Irving, Larry, Jr. 12
Irvis, K. Leroy 67
Jackson, Alphonso R. 48
Jackson, George 14
Jackson, Jesse 1, 27, 72
Jackson, Jesse, Jr. 14, 45
Jackson, Mae 57
Jackson, Maynard 2, 41
Jackson, Shirley Ann 12
Jackson Lee, Sheila 20
Jacob, John E. 2
James, Sharpe 23, 69
Jarrett, Valerie 73
Jarvis, Charlene Drew 21
Jefferson, William J. 25, 72
Johnson, Eddie Bernice 8
Johnson, Harvey, Jr. 24
Johnson, James Weldon 5
Johnson, Katherine (Coleman
   Goble) 61
Johnson, Kevin 70
Johnson, Norma L. Holloway 17
Johnson, Robert T. 17
Jones, Elaine R. 7, 45
Jordan, Barbara 4
Jordan, Vernon 3, 35
Kennard, William Earl 18
Keyes, Alan L. 11
Kidd, Mae Street 39
Kilpatrick, Carolyn Cheeks 16
Kilpatrick, Kwame 34, 71
Kincaid, Bernard 28
King, Martin Luther, III 20
Kirk, Ron 11
Lafontant, Jewel Stradford 3, 51
Lee, Barbara 25
Leland, Mickey 2
Lewis, Delano 7
Lewis, John 2, 46
Majette, Denise 41
Mallett, Conrad, Jr. 16
Mallory, Mark 62
Marsh, Henry, III 32
Marshall, Bella 22
Marshall, Thurgood 1, 44
Martin, Louis E. 16
Martin, Ruby Grant 49
McCall, H. Carl 27
McGee, James Madison 46
McKinney, Cynthia Ann 11, 52
McKissick, Floyd B. 3
Meek, Carrie 6, 36
Meek, Kendrick 41
Meeks, Gregory 25
Meredith, James H. 11
Metcalfe, Ralph 26
Mfume, Kweisi 6, 41
Millender-McDonald, Juanita 21, 61
Mitchell, Parren J. 42, 66
Moore, Gwendolynne S. 55
Moore, Minyon 45
Morial, Ernest "Dutch" 26
Morial, Marc H. 20, 51
Morton, Azie Taylor 48
Moses, Robert Parris 11

Murrell, Sylvia Marilyn 49
Nagin, C. Ray 42, 57
Nix, Robert N.C., Jr. 51
Norton, Eleanor Holmes 7
Nutter, Michael 69
Obama, Barack 49
O'Leary, Hazel 6
Owens, Major 6
Page, Alan 7
Paige, Rod 29
Paterson, Basil A. 69
Paterson, David A. 59
Patrick, Deval 12, 61
Patterson, Louise 25
Payne, Donald M. 2, 57
Payne, William D. 60
Perez, Anna 1
Perkins, Edward 5
Perkins, James, Jr. 55
Perry, Lowell 30
Pinchback, P. B. S. 9
Powell, Adam Clayton, Jr. 3
Powell, Colin 1, 28
Powell, Debra A. 23
Powell, Michael 32
Raines, Franklin Delano 14
Randolph, A. Philip 3
Rangel, Charles 3, 52
Raoul, Kwame 55
Reeves, Gregory 49
Reeves, Triette Lipsey 27
Rice, Condoleezza 3, 28, 72
Rice, Norm 8
Richardson, Rupert 67
Robinson, Bishop L. 66
Robinson, Randall 7, 46
Rogers, Joe 27
Ross, Don 27
Rush, Bobby 26
Rustin, Bayard 4
Sampson, Edith S. 4
Sanders, Malika 48
Satcher, David 7, 57
Sayles Belton, Sharon 9
Schmoke, Kurt 1, 48
Scott, David 41
Scott, Robert C. 23
Sears-Collins, Leah J. 5
Shakur, Assata 6
Sharpton, Al 21
Shavers, Cheryl 31
Simmons, Jamal 72
Simpson, Carole 6, 30
Sisulu, Sheila Violet Makate 24
Smith, Nate 49
Smythe Haith, Mabel 61
Slater, Rodney E. 15
Stanton, Robert 20
Staupers, Mabel K. 7
Steele, Michael 38, 73
Stokes, Carl 10, 73
Stokes, Louis 3
Stone, Chuck 9
Street, John F. 24
Sullivan, Louis 8
Sutton, Percy E. 42
Terry, Clark 39
Thomas, Clarence 2, 39, 65
Thompson, Bennie G. 26
Thompson, Larry D. 39
Thompson, William C. 35
Todman, Terence A. 55
Toote, Gloria E.A. 64

Towns, Edolphus **19**
Tribble, Israel, Jr. **8**
Trotter, Donne E. **28**
Tubbs Jones, Stephanie **24, 72**
Tucker, C. Delores **12, 56**
Turnbull, Charles Wesley **62**
Turner, Henry McNeal **5**
Usry, James L. **23**
Vaughn, Gladys Gary **47**
Von Lipsey, Roderick K. **11**
Wallace, Phyllis A. **9**
Washington, Harold **6**
Washington, Val **12**
Washington, Walter **45**
Waters, Maxine **3, 67**
Watkins, Shirley R. **17**
Watson, Diane **41**
Watt, Melvin **26**
Watts, J. C., Jr. **14, 38**
Weaver, Robert C. **8, 46**
Webb, Wellington **3**
Wharton, Clifton R., Jr. **7**
Wharton, Clifton Reginald, Sr. **36**
Wheat, Alan **14**
White, Jesse **22**
White, Michael R. **5**
Wilder, L. Douglas **3, 48**
Wilkins, Roger **2**
Williams, Anthony **21**
Williams, Eddie N. **44**
Williams, George Washington **18**
Williams, Hosea Lorenzo **15, 31**
Williams, Maggie **7, 71**
Wilson, Sunnie **7, 55**
Wynn, Albert **25**
Young, Andrew **3, 48**

Law

Alexander, Clifford **26**
Alexander, Joyce London **18**
Alexander, Sadie Tanner Mossell **22**
Allen, Samuel W. **38**
Amaker, Norman **63**
Archer, Dennis **7, 36**
Arnwine, Barbara **28**
Bailey, Clyde **45**
Banks, William **11**
Barbee, Lloyd Augustus **71**
Barrett, Andrew C. **12**
Barrett, Jacqueline **28**
Baugh, David **23**
Bell, Derrick **6**
Berry, Mary Frances **7**
Berry, Theodore M. **31**
Bishop, Sanford D., Jr. **24**
Bolin, Jane **22, 59**
Bolton, Terrell D. **25**
Booker, Cory Anthony **68**
Bosley, Freeman, Jr. **7**
Boykin, Keith **14**
Bradley, Thomas **2**
Braun, Carol Moseley **4, 42**
Brooke, Edward **8**
Brown, Byrd **49**
Brown, Cora **33**
Brown, Cupcake **63**
Brown, Homer S. **47**
Brown, Janice Rogers **43**
Brown, Joe **29**
Brown, Lee Patrick **1, 24**
Brown, Ron **5**
Brown, Willie L., Jr. **7**

Bryant, Wayne R. **6**
Bryant, William Benson **61**
Bully-Cummings, Ella **48**
Burke, Yvonne Braithwaite **42**
Burris, Roland W. **25**
Butler, Louis **70**
Butler, Paul D. **17**
Bynoe, Peter C. B. **40**
Campbell, Bill **9**
Carter, Pamela Lynn **67**
Carter, Robert L. **51**
Carter, Stephen L. **4**
Cashin, Sheryll **63**
Chambers, Julius **3**
Chestnut, J. L., Jr. **73**
Cleaver, Kathleen Neal **29**
Clendenon, Donn **26, 56**
Cochran, Johnnie **11, 39, 52**
Colter, Cyrus J. **36**
Conyers, John, Jr. **4, 45**
Crockett, George W., Jr. **10, 64**
Darden, Christopher **13**
Davis, Artur **41**
Days, Drew S., III **10**
DeFrantz, Anita **37**
Diggs-Taylor, Anna **20**
Dillard, Godfrey J. **45**
Dinkins, David **4**
Dixon, Sharon Pratt **1**
Edelman, Marian Wright **5, 42**
Edley, Christopher **2, 48**
Edley, Christopher F., Jr. **48**
Ellington, E. David **11**
Ephriam, Mablean **29**
Espy, Mike **6**
Farmer-Paellmann, Deadria **43**
Feemster, Herbert **72**
Fields, Cleo **13**
Finner-Williams, Paris Michele **62**
Ford, Wallace **58**
Frazier-Lyde, Jacqui **31**
Freeman, Charles **19**
Gary, Willie E. **12**
Gibson, Johnnie Mae **23**
Glover, Nathaniel, Jr. **12**
Gomez-Preston, Cheryl **9**
Graham, Lawrence Otis **12**
Gray, Fred **37**
Gray, Willie **14**
Greenhouse, Bunnatine "Bunny" **57**
Grimké, Archibald H. **9**
Guinier, Lani **7, 30**
Haley, George Williford Boyce **21**
Hall, Elliott S. **24**
Harris, Kamala D. **64**
Harris, Patricia Roberts **2**
Harvard, Beverly **11**
Hassell, Leroy Rountree, Sr. **41**
Hastie, William H. **8**
Hastings, Alcee L. **16**
Hatcher, Richard G. **55**
Hatchett, Glenda **32**
Hawkins, Augustus F. **68**
Hawkins, Steven **14**
Hayes, Dennis **54**
Haywood, Margaret A. **24**
Henderson, Thelton E. **68**
Higginbotham, A. Leon, Jr. **13, 25**
Hill, Anita **5, 65**
Hillard, Terry **25**
Hills, Oliver W. **24**
Holder, Eric H., Jr. **9**
Hollowell, Donald L. **57**

Holton, Hugh, Jr. **39**
Hooks, Benjamin L. **2**
Houston, Charles Hamilton **4**
Hubbard, Arnette Rhinehart **38**
Hunter, Billy **22**
Hurtt, Harold **46**
Isaac, Julius **34**
Jackson, Maynard **2, 41**
Jackson Lee, Sheila **20**
Johnson, Harry E. **57**
Johnson, James Weldon **5**
Johnson, Norma L. Holloway **17**
Jones, Elaine R. **7, 45**
Jones, Van **70**
Jordan, Vernon E. **3, 35**
Kearse, Amalya Lyle **12**
Keith, Damon J. **16**
Kennard, William Earl **18**
Kennedy, Florynce **12, 33**
Kennedy, Randall **40**
Kibaki, Mwai **60**
King, Bernice **4**
Kirk, Ron **11**
Lafontant, Jewel Stradford **3, 51**
Lewis, Delano **7**
Lewis, Reginald F. **6**
Lloyd, Reginald **64**
Majette, Denise **41**
Mallett, Conrad, Jr. **16**
Mandela, Nelson **1, 14**
Marsh, Henry, III **32**
Marshall, Thurgood **1, 44**
Mathis, Greg **26**
McAnulty, William E., Jr. **66**
McCrary Anthony, Crystal **70**
McDonald, Gabrielle Kirk **20**
McDougall, Gay J. **11, 43**
McKinnon, Isaiah **9**
McKissick, Floyd B. **3**
McPhail, Sharon **2**
Meek, Kendrick **41**
Meeks, Gregory **25**
Moose, Charles **40**
Morial, Ernest "Dutch" **26**
Motley, Constance Baker **10, 55**
Muhammad, Ava **31**
Murray, Pauli **38**
Nance, Cynthia **71**
Napoleon, Benny N. **23**
Nix, Robert N.C., Jr. **51**
Noble, Ronald **46**
Norton, Eleanor Holmes **7**
Nunn, Annetta **43**
Obama, Barack **49**
Obama, Michelle **61**
Ogletree, Charles, Jr. **12, 47**
Ogunlesi, Adebayo O. **37**
O'Leary, Hazel **6**
Oliver, Jerry **37**
Page, Alan **7**
Parker, Kellis E. **30**
Parks, Bernard C. **17**
Parsons, James **14**
Parsons, Richard Dean **11, 33**
Pascal-Trouillot, Ertha **3**
Paterson, Basil A. **69**
Patrick, Deval **12**
Payne, Ulice **42**
Payton, John **48**
Perry, Lowell **30**
Philip, Marlene Nourbese **32**
Pincham, R. Eugene, Sr. **69**
Powell, Michael **32**

Quince, Peggy A. **69**
Ramsey, Charles H. **21, 69**
Raoul, Kwame **55**
Ray, Charlotte E. **60**
Redding, Louis L. **26**
Reynolds, Star Jones **10, 27, 61**
Rice, Constance LaMay **60**
Richie, Leroy C. **18**
Robinson, Bishop L. **66**
Robinson, Malcolm S. **44**
Robinson, Randall **7, 46**
Russell-McCloud, Patricia **17**
Sampson, Edith S. **4**
Schmoke, Kurt **1, 48**
Sears-Collins, Leah J. **5**
Solomon, Jimmie Lee **38**
Sparks, Corinne Etta **53**
Steele, Michael **38, 73**
Stokes, Carl **10, 73**
Stokes, Louis **3**
Stout, Juanita Kidd **24**
Sutton, Percy E. **42**
Taylor, John (David Beckett) **16**
Thomas, Arthur Ray **52**
Thomas, Clarence **2, 39, 65**
Thomas, Franklin A. **5, 49**
Thompson, Larry D. **39**
Touré, Faya Ora Rose **56**
Tubbs Jones, Stephanie **24, 72**
Van Lierop, Robert **53**
Vanzant, Iyanla **17, 47**
Wagner, Annice **22**
Wainwright, Joscelyn **46**
Walker, Cora T. **68**
Wallace, Perry E. **47**
Ward, Benjamin **68**
Washington, Harold **6**
Watkins, Donald **35**
Watt, Melvin **26**
Wharton, Clifton Reginald, Sr. **36**
Wilder, L. Douglas **3, 48**
Wilkins, Roger **2**
Williams, Evelyn **10**
Williams, Gregory **11**
Williams, Patricia **11, 54**
Williams, Willie L. **4**
Wilson, Jimmy **45**
Wright, Bruce McMarion **3, 52**
Wynn, Albert **25**

Military

Abacha, Sani **11, 70**
Adams Early, Charity **13, 34**
Adams-Ender, Clara **40**
Alexander, Margaret Walker **22**
Amin, Idi **42**
Babangida, Ibrahim **4**
Baker, Vernon Joseph **65**
Black, Barry C. **47**
Bolden, Charles F., Jr. **7**
Brashear, Carl **29**
Brown, Anthony G. **72**
Brown, Erroll M. **23**
Brown, Jesse **6, 41**
Brown, Jesse Leroy **31**
Brown, Willa **40**
Bullard, Eugene **12**
Cadoria, Sherian Grace **14**
Chissano, Joaquim **7, 55, 67**
Christophe, Henri **9**
Clemmons, Reginal G. **41**
Conté, Lansana **7**
Cooke, Marcia **60**

Davis, Benjamin O., Jr. **2, 43**
Davis, Benjamin O., Sr. **4**
Drew, Alvin, Jr. **67**
Duggins, George **64**
Europe, James Reese **10**
Eyadéma, Gnassingbé **7, 52**
Fields, Evelyn J. **27**
Flipper, Henry O. **3**
Gravely, Samuel L., Jr. **5, 49**
Gregory, Frederick **8, 51**
Guéï, Robert **66**
Habré, Hissène **6**
Habyarimana, Juvenal **8**
Harris, Marcelite Jordan **16**
Honoré, Russel L. **64**
Howard, Michelle **28**
Jackson, Fred James **25**
James, Daniel, Jr. **16**
Johnson, Hazel **22**
Johnson, Shoshana **47**
Kagame, Paul **54**
Kerekou, Ahmed (Mathieu) **1**
Laraque, Paul **67**
Lawrence, Robert H., Jr. **16**
Lyles, Lester **31**
Magloire, Paul Eugène **68**
Matthews, Mark **59**
Miller, Dorie **29**
Nyanda, Siphiwe **21**
Obasanjo, Olusegun **5, 22**
Petersen, Frank E. **31**
Powell, Colin **1, 28**
Pratt, Geronimo **18**
Rawlings, Jerry **9**
Reason, J. Paul **19**
Rogers, Alan G. **72**
Scantlebury, Janna **47**
Snow, Samuel **71**
Stanford, John **20**
Staupers, Mabel K. **7**
Stokes, Louis **3**
Touré, Amadou Toumani **18**
Vieira, Joao **14**
Von Lipsey, Roderick K. **11**
Watkins, Perry **12**
West, Togo, D., Jr. **16**
Wilson, Jimmy **45**
Wright, Lewin **43**

Music
Aaliyah **30**
Ace, Johnny **36**
Adams, Johnny **39**
Adams, Leslie **39**
Adams, Oleta **18**
Adams, Yolanda **17, 67**
Adderley, Julian "Cannonball" **30**
Adderley, Nat **29**
Ade, King Sunny **41**
Akon **68**
Albright, Gerald **23**
Alert, Kool DJ **33**
Amerie **52**
Anderson, Carl **48**
Anderson, Marian **2, 33**
Ardoin, Alphonse **65**
Armatrading, Joan **32**
Armstrong, Louis **2**
Armstrong, Vanessa Bell **24**
Arroyo, Marina **30**
Ashanti **37**
Ashford, Nickolas **21**
Atkins, Juan **50**

Austin, Lovie **40**
Austin, Patti **24**
Avant, Clarence **19**
Ayers, Roy **16**
Badu, Erykah **22**
Bailey, Buster **38**
Bailey, DeFord **33**
Bailey, Philip **63**
Baiocchi, Regina Harris **41**
Baker, Anita **21, 48**
Baker, Josephine **3**
Baker, LaVern **26**
Ballard, Hank **41**
Bambaataa, Afrika **34**
Banner, David **55**
Barker, Danny **32**
Barnes, Roosevelt "Booba" **33**
Barrino, Fantasia **53**
Basie, Count **23**
Bassey, Shirley **25**
Batiste, Alvin **66**
Battle, Kathleen **70**
Baylor, Helen **36**
Bebey, Francis **45**
Bechet, Sidney **18**
Beenie Man **32**
Belafonte, Harry **4, 65**
Belle, Regina **1, 51**
Benét, Eric **28**
Benjamin, Andre **45**
Bentley, Lamont **53**
Berry, Chuck **29**
Beverly, Frankie **25**
Beyoncé **39, 70**
Bibb, Eric **49**
Bivins, Michael **72**
Black Thought **63**
Blake, Eubie **29**
Blakey, Art **37**
Blanchard, Terence **43**
Bland, Bobby "Blue" **36**
Bleu, Corbin **65**
Blige, Mary J. **20, 34, 60**
Blondy, Alpha **30**
Blow, Kurtis **31**
Bolden, Buddy **39**
Bond, Beverly **53**
Bonds, Margaret **39**
Bonga, Kuenda **13**
Bow Wow **35**
Bradley, J. Robert **65**
Brae, C. Michael **61**
Brandy **14, 34, 72**
Braxton, Toni **15, 61**
Bridgewater, Dee Dee **32**
Brooks, Avery **9**
Brooks, Hadda **40**
Brown, Angela M. **54**
Brown, Bobby **58**
Brown, Charles **23**
Brown, Clarence Gatemouth **59**
Brown, Foxy **25**
Brown, James **15, 60**
Brown, Melanie **73**
Brown, Nappy **73**
Brown, Oscar, Jr. **53**
Brown, Patrick "Sleepy" **50**
Brown, Uzee **42**
Bumbry, Grace **5**
Burke, Solomon **31**
Burleigh, Henry Thacker **56**
Burns, Eddie **44**
Burnside, R.L. **56**

Busby, Jheryl **3**
Butler, George, Jr. **70**
Butler, Jerry **26**
Butler, Jonathan **28**
Caesar, Shirley **19**
Cage, Byron **53**
Calloway, Cab **1**
Campbell-Martin, Tisha **8, 42**
Cannon, Nick **47, 73**
Carey, Mariah **32, 53, 69**
Carr, Kurt **56**
Carr, Leroy **49**
Carroll, Diahann **9**
Carter, Benny **46**
Carter, Betty **19**
Carter, Nell **39**
Carter, Regina **23**
Carter, Warrick L. **27**
Cartiér, Xam Wilson **41**
Caymmi, Dorival **72**
Cee-Lo **70**
Chanté, Keshia **50**
Chapman, Tracy **26**
Charlemagne, Manno **11**
Charles, Ray **16, 48**
Cheatham, Doc **17**
Checker, Chubby **28**
Chenault, John **40**
Christie, Angella **36**
Chuck D **9**
Ciara **56**
Clark, Mattie Moss **61**
Clark-Cole, Dorinda **66**
Clarke, Kenny **27**
Clark-Sheard, Karen **22**
Clemons, Clarence **41**
Cleveland, James **19**
Cliff, Jimmy **28**
Clinton, George **9**
Cole, Keyshia **63**
Cole, Nat King **17**
Cole, Natalie **17, 60**
Coleman, Ornette **39, 69**
Collins, Albert **12**
Collins, Bootsy **31**
Collins, Lyn **53**
Coltrane, Alice **70**
Coltrane, John **19**
Coltrane, Ravi **71**
Combs, Sean "Puffy" **17, 43**
Common **31, 63**
Cook, Charles "Doc" **44**
Cook, Will Marion **40**
Cooke, Sam **17**
Cortez, Jayne **43**
Count Basie **23**
Cowboy Troy **54**
Cox, Deborah **28**
Cox, Ida **42**
Craig, Carl **31, 71**
Crawford, Randy **19**
Cray, Robert **30**
Creagh, Milton **27**
Crocker, Frankie **29**
Crothers, Scatman **19**
Crouch, Andraé **27**
Crouch, Stanley **11**
Crowder, Henry **16**
Daemyon, Jerald **64**
D'Angelo **27**
Dara, Olu **35**
Dash, Damon **31**
Dash, Darien **29**

David, Craig **31, 53**
Davis, Anthony **11**
Davis, Gary **41**
Davis, Guy **36**
Davis, Miles **4**
Davis, Sammy, Jr. **18**
Davis, Tyrone **54**
Dawson, William Levi **39**
de Passe, Suzanne **25**
Deezer D **53**
Dennard, Brazeal **37**
Dickenson, Vic **38**
Diddley, Bo **39, 72**
Dixon, Dean **68**
Dixon, Willie **4**
DJ Jazzy Jeff **32**
DMX **28, 64**
Dobbs, Mattiwilda **34**
Domino, Fats **20**
Donegan, Dorothy **19**
Dorsey, Lee **65**
Dorsey, Thomas **15**
Downing, Will **19**
Dre, Dr. **10, 14, 30**
Duke, George **21**
Dumas, Henry **41**
Dunner, Leslie B. **45**
Duplechan, Larry **55**
Dupri, Jermaine **13, 46**
Durham, Bobby **73**
Dworkin, Aaron P. **52**
Earthquake **55**
Eckstine, Billy **28**
Edmonds, Kenneth "Babyface" **10, 31**
Edmonds, Tracey **16, 64**
Edwards, Esther Gordy **43**
Eldridge, Roy **37**
Ellington, Duke **5**
Elliott, Missy "Misdemeanor" **31**
Escobar, Damien **56**
Escobar, Tourie **56**
Estes, Simon **28**
Estes, Sleepy John **33**
Eubanks, Kevin **15**
Europe, James Reese **10**
Evans, Faith **22**
Eve **29**
Evora, Cesaria **12**
Falana, Lola **42**
Farmer, Art **38**
Feemster, Herbert **72**
Fela **1, 42**
Ferrell, Rachelle **29**
Ferrer, Ibrahim **41**
Fiasco, Lupe **64**
50 Cent **46**
Fitzgerald, Ella **8, 18**
Flack, Roberta **19**
Flanagan, Tommy **69**
Flavor Flav **67**
Foster, George "Pops" **40**
Foxx, Jamie **15, 48**
Franklin, Aretha **11, 44**
Franklin, Kirk **15, 49**
Freelon, Nnenna **32**
Freeman, Paul **39**
Freeman, Yvette **27**
Fuqua, Antoine **35**
Gaines, Grady **38**
Garrett, Sean **57**
Gaye, Marvin **2**
Gaye, Nona **56**

Gaynor, Gloria 36
George, Zelma Watson 42
Gibson, Althea 8, 43
Gibson, Tyrese 27, 62
Gil, Gilberto 53
Gill, Johnny 51
Gillespie, Dizzy 1
Ginuwine 35
Glover, Corey 34
Goapele 55
Golson, Benny 37
Gordon, Dexter 25
Gordy, Berry, Jr. 1
Gotti, Irv 39
Grae, Jean 51
Grandmaster Flash 33, 60
Graves, Denyce Antoinette 19, 57
Gray, F. Gary 14, 49
Gray, Macy 29
Greaves, William 38
Greely, M. Gasby 27
Green, Al 13, 47
Green, Grant 56
Griffin, Johnny 71
Griffin, LaShell 51
Griffiths, Marcia 29
Güines, Tata 69
Guy, Buddy 31
Haddon, Dietrick 55
Hailey, JoJo 22
Hailey, K-Ci 22
Hall, Aaron 57
Hall, Juanita 62
Hamilton, Anthony 61
Hammer, M. C. 20
Hammond, Fred 23
Hammond, Lenn 34
Hampton, Lionel 17, 41
Hancock, Herbie 20, 67
Handy, W. C. 8
Hardin Armstrong, Lil 39
Harper, Ben 34, 62
Harrell, Andre 9, 30
Harris, Barry 68
Harris, Corey 39, 73
Hart, Alvin Youngblood 61
Hathaway, Donny 18
Hathaway, Lalah 57
Hawkins, Coleman 9
Hawkins, Erskine 14
Hawkins, Screamin' Jay 30
Hawkins, Tramaine 16
Hayes, Isaac 20, 58, 73
Hayes, Roland 4
Hayes, Teddy 40
Heavy, D 58
Hemphill, Jessie Mae 33, 59
Henderson, Fletcher 32
Hendricks, Barbara 3, 67
Hendrix, Jimi 10
Hendryx, Nona 56
Henry, Clarence "Frogman" 46
Higginbotham, J. C. 37
Higginsen, Vy 65
Hill, Andrew 66
Hill, Lauryn 20, 53
Hinderas, Natalie 5
Hines, Earl "Fatha" 39
Hinton, Milt 30
Holiday, Billie 1
Holland-Dozier-Holland 36
Holloway, Brenda 65
Holmes, Clint 57

Holt, Nora 38
Hooker, John Lee 30
Horn, Shirley 32, 56
Horne, Lena 5
House, Son 8
Houston, Cissy 20
Houston, Whitney 7, 28
Howlin' Wolf 9
Hudson, Jennifer 63
Humphrey, Bobbi 20
Hunter, Alberta 42
Hutch, Willie 62
Hyman, Phyllis 19
Ice Cube 8, 30, 60
Ice-T 6, 31
India.Arie 34
Isley, Ronald 25, 56
Ja Rule 35
Jackson, Fred James 25
Jackson, George 19
Jackson, Hal 41
Jackson, Isaiah 3
Jackson, Janet 6, 30, 68
Jackson, John 36
Jackson, Mahalia 5
Jackson, Michael 19, 53
Jackson, Millie 25
Jackson, Milt 26
Jackson, Randy 40
Jacquet, Illinois 49
Jaheim 58
Jamal, Ahmad 69
Jamelia 51
Jamerson, James 59
James, Etta 13, 52
James, Rick 17
James, Skip 38
Jarreau, Al 21, 65
Jay-Z 27, 69
Jean, Wyclef 20
Jean-Baptiste, Marianne 17, 46
Jenkins, Ella 15
Jennings, Lyfe 56, 69
Jerkins, Rodney 31
Jimmy Jam 13
Johnson, Beverly 2
Johnson, Buddy 36
Johnson, J. J. 37
Johnson, James Weldon 5
Johnson, Johnnie 56
Johnson, Robert 2
Jones, Bobby 20
Jones, Donell 29
Jones, Elvin 14, 68
Jones, Etta 35
Jones, Hank 57
Jones, Jonah 39
Jones, Quincy 8, 30
Jones, Thad 68
Joplin, Scott 6
Jordan, Montell 23
Jordan, Ronny 26
Jorge, Seu 73
Joyner, Matilda Sissieretta 15
Joyner, Tom 19
Kay, Ulysses 37
Kee, John P. 43
Kelis 58
Kelley, Elijah 65
Kelly, R. 18, 44, 71
Kem 47
Kendricks, Eddie 22
Kenoly, Ron 45

Kenyatta, Robin 54
Keys, Alicia 32, 68
Khan, Chaka 12, 50
Kidjo, Anjelique 50
Killings, Debra 57
King, B. B. 7
King, Coretta Scott 3, 57
Kitt, Eartha 16
Klugh, Earl 59
Knight, Gladys 16, 66
Knight, Suge 11, 30
Knowles, Tina 61
Knuckles, Frankie 42
Kolosoy, Wendo 73
Kool Moe Dee 37
Kravitz, Lenny 10, 34
KRS-One 34
K-Swift 73
Kuti, Femi 47
LaBelle, Patti 13, 30
Larrieux, Amel 63
Lattimore, Kenny 35
Ledisi 73
Lefel, Edith 41
Legend, John 67
León, Tania 13
Lester, Julius 9
Levert, Eddie 70
Levert, Gerald 22, 59
Lewis, Ananda 28
Lewis, Butch 71
Lewis, Henry 38
Lewis, Ramsey 35, 70
Lewis, Terry 13
Lil' Kim 28
Lil Wayne 66
Liles, Kevin 42
Lincoln, Abbey 3
Lipscomb, Mance 49
Lister, Marquita 65
Little Milton 36, 54
Little Richard 15
Little Walter 36
LL Cool J 16, 49
Locke, Eddie 44
Lopes, Lisa "Left Eye" 36
Love, Darlene 23
Love, Ed 58
Love, Laura 50
Lover, Ed 10
Lucien, Jon 66
Luckett, Letoya 61
Ludacris 37, 60
Lymon, Frankie 22
Maal, Baaba 66
Madhubuti, Haki R. 7
Mahal, Taj 39
Mahlasela, Vusi 65
Majors, Jeff 41
Makeba, Miriam 2, 50
Mario 71
Marley, Bob 5
Marley, Rita 32, 70
Marley, Ziggy 41
Marrow, Queen Esther 24
Marsalis, Branford 34
Marsalis, Delfeayo 41
Marsalis, Wynton 16
Martin, Roberta 58
Martin, Sara 38
Mary Mary 34
Mase 24
Masekela, Hugh 1

Massenburg, Kedar 23
Master P 21
Mathis, Johnny 20
Maxwell 20
May, Derrick 41
Mayfield, Curtis 2, 43
Maynor, Dorothy 19
MC Lyte 34
McBride, James 35
McClendon, Lisa 61
McClurkin, Donnie 25
McCoo, Marilyn 53
McDaniel, Hattie 5
McFerrin, Bobby 68
McGriff, Jimmy 72
McKee, Lonette 12
McKinney, Nina Mae 40
McKnight, Brian 18, 34
McPherson, David 32
Memphis Minnie 33
Miles, Buddy 69
Mills, Stephanie 36
Mingus, Charles 15
Mitchell, Leona 42
Mitchell, Nicole 66
Mo', Keb' 36
Monica 21
Monk, Thelonious 1
Moore, Chante 26
Moore, Dorothy Rudd 46
Moore, Johnny B. 38
Moore, LeRoi 72
Moore, Melba 21
Moore, Undine Smith 28
Morton, Jelly Roll 29
Mos Def 30
Moses, Gilbert 12
Moss, J 64
Moten, Etta 18
Mowatt, Judy 38
Mullen, Nicole C. 45
Mumba, Samantha 29
Murphy, Eddie 4, 20, 61
Murray, Tai 47
Muse, Clarence Edouard 21
Musiq 37
Mya 35
Nas 33
Nascimento, Milton 2, 64
Nash, Johnny 40
Ndegéocello, Me'Shell 15
N'Dour, Youssou 1, 53
Neal, Raful 44
Neale, Haydain 52
Nelly 32
Neville, Aaron 21
Ne-Yo 65
Nicholas, Fayard 20, 57
Nicholas, Harold 20
Noah, Yannick 4, 60
Norman, Jessye 5
Notorious B.I.G. 20
Odetta 37
Okosuns, Sonny 71
Ol' Dirty Bastard 52
Olatunji, Babatunde 36
Oliver, Joe "King" 42
O'Neal, Shaquille 8, 30
Ongala, Remmy 9
Osborne, Jeffrey 26
Otis, Clyde 67
OutKast 35
Owens, Jack 38

P.M. Dawn 54
Palmer, Keke 68
Palmer, Rissi 65
Parker, Charlie 20
Parker, Maceo 72
Parks, Gordon 1, 35, 58
Patton, Antwan 45
Payne, Freda 58
Pena, Paul 58
Pendergrass, Teddy 22
Peoples, Dottie 22
Perkins, Pinetop 70
Perren, Freddie 60
Perry, Ruth 19
Peterson, James 38
Peterson, Marvin "Hannibal" 27
Peterson, Oscar 52
Phillips, Helen L. 63
Phipps, Wintley 59
Portuondo, Omara 53
Pounder, CCH 72
Powell, Bud 24
Powell, Maxine 8
Pratt, Awadagin 31
Premice, Josephine 41
Preston, Billy 39, 59
Price, Florence 37
Price, Kelly 23
Price, Leontyne 1
Pride, Charley 26
Prince 18, 65
Pritchard, Robert Starling 21
Pryor, Rain 65
Queen Latifah 1, 16, 58
Rainey, Ma 33
Ralph, Sheryl Lee 18
Randall, Alice 38
Rawls, Lou 17, 57
Razaf, Andy 19
Reagon, Bernice Johnson 7
Record, Eugene 60
Redman, Joshua 30
Reed, A. C. 36
Reed, Jimmy 38
Reese, Della 6, 20
Reeves, Dianne 32
Reid, Antonio "L.A." 28
Reid, Vernon 34
Rhoden, Wayne 70
Rhone, Sylvia 2
Rhymes, Busta 31
Richie, Lionel 27, 65
Rihanna 65
Riperton, Minnie 32
Roach, Max 21, 63
Roberts, Kimberly Rivers 72
Roberts, Marcus 19
Robeson, Paul 2
Robinson, Fenton 38
Robinson, Reginald R. 53
Robinson, Smokey 3, 49
Rogers, Jimmy 38
Rollins, Sonny 37
Ross, Diana 8, 27
Ross, Isaiah "Doc" 40
Roxanne Shante 33
Rucker, Darius 34
Run 31, 73
Run-DMC 31
Rupaul 17
Rush, Otis 38
Rushen, Patrice 12
Rushing, Jimmy 37

Russell, Brenda 52
Sade 15
Sample, Joe 51
Sanders, Pharoah 64
Sangare, Oumou 18
Scarlett, Millicent 49
Schuyler, Philippa 50
Scott, George 55
Scott, Hazel 66
Scott, Jill 29
Scott, "Little" Jimmy 48
Seal 14
Seals, Son 56
Shaggy 31
Shakur, Afeni 67
Shakur, Tupac 14
Sheard, Kierra "Kiki" 61
Shirley, George 33
Short, Bobby 52
Shorty, Ras, I 47
Siji 56
Silver, Horace 26
Simmons, Russell 1, 30
Simone, Nina 15, 41
Simpson, Valerie 21
Simpson-Hoffman, N'kenge 52
Sisqo 30
Sissle, Noble 29
Sister Souljah 11
Sledge, Percy 39
Sly & Robbie 34
Smith, Bessie 3
Smith, Cladys "Jabbo" 32
Smith, Dr. Lonnie 49
Smith, Lonnie Liston 49
Smith, Mamie 32
Smith, Stuff 37
Smith, Trixie 34
Smith, Will 8, 18, 53
Snoop Dogg 35
Southern, Eileen 56
Sowande, Fela 39
Sparks, Jordin 66
Spence, Joseph 49
Stampley, Micah 54
Stanford, Olivia Lee Dilworth 49
Staples, Mavis 50
Staples, "Pops" 32
Staton, Candi 27
Staton, Dakota 62
Steinberg, Martha Jean "The
 Queen" 28
Stew 69
Still, William Grant 37
Stone, Angie 31
Stoute, Steve 38
Strayhorn, Billy 31
Streeter, Sarah 45
Studdard, Ruben 46
Sullivan, Maxine 37
Summer, Donna 25
Sun Ra 60
Sundiata, Sekou 66
Supremes, The 33
Sweat, Keith 19
Sykes, Roosevelt 20
Tait, Michael 57
Tamar-kali 63
Tamia 24, 55
Tampa Red 63
Tatum, Art 28
Taylor, Billy 23
Taylor, Cecil 70

Taylor, Koko 40
Tempations, The 33
Terrell, Tammi 32
Terry, Clark 39
Tharpe, Rosetta 65
Thomas, Irma 29
Thomas, Rufus 20
Thornton, Big Mama 33
Three Mo' Tenors 35
Thurston, Stephen J. 49
Tillis, Frederick 40
Timbaland 32
Tinsley, Boyd 50
Tisdale, Wayman 50
TLC 34
Tonex 54
Tosh, Peter 9
Toussaint, Allen 60
T-Pain 73
Tresvant, Ralph 57
Turnbull, Walter 13, 60
Turner, Ike 68
Turner, Tina 6, 27
Uggams, Leslie 23
Usher 23, 56
Valentino, Bobby 62
Vandross, Luther 13, 48, 59
Vanity 67
Vaughan, Sarah 13
Vereen, Ben 4
Verrett, Shirley 66
Walker, Albertina 10, 58
Walker, Cedric "Ricky" 19
Walker, George 37
Walker, Hezekiah 34
Wallace, Sippie 1
Waller, Fats 29
Warwick, Dionne 18
Washington, Dinah 22
Washington, Grover, Jr. 17, 44
Waters, Benny 26
Waters, Ethel 7
Waters, Muddy 34
Watley, Jody 54
Watson, Johnny "Guitar" 18
Watts, Andre 42
Watts, Reggie 52
Webster, Katie 29
Wein, Joyce 62
Welch, Elisabeth 52
Wells, Mary 28
West, Kanye 52
Whalum, Kirk 37, 64
White, Barry 13, 41
White, Josh, Jr. 52
White, Maurice 29
White, Willard 53
Whitfield, Norman 73
Wilkins, Thomas Alphonso 71
will.i.am 64
Williams, Bert 18
Williams, Clarence 33
Williams, Deniece 36
Williams, Denise 40
Williams, Joe 5, 25
Williams, Mary Lou 15
Williams, Michelle 73
Williams, Pharrell 47
Williams, Saul 31
Williams, Tony 67
Williams, Vanessa L. 4, 17
Wilson, Cassandra 16
Wilson, Charlie 31

Wilson, Gerald 49
Wilson, Jackie 60
Wilson, Mary 28
Wilson, Nancy 10
Wilson, Natalie 38
Wilson, Sunnie 7, 55
Winans, Angie 36
Winans, BeBe 14
Winans, CeCe 14, 43
Winans, Debbie 36
Winans, Marvin L. 17
Winans, Ronald 54
Winans, Vickie 24
Withers, Bill 61
Withers-Mendes, Elisabeth 64
Womack, Bobby 60
Wonder, Stevie 11, 53
Woods, Georgie 57
Woods, Scott 55
Yarbrough, Camille 40
Yoba, Malik 11
York, Vincent 40
Young, Lee 72
Young, Lester 37
Young Jeezy 63

Religion
Abernathy, Ralph David 1
Adams, Yolanda 17, 67
Agyeman, Jaramogi Abebe 10, 63
Akinola, Peter Jasper 65
Akpan, Uwem 70
Al-Amin, Jamil Abdullah 6
Anthony, Wendell 25
Arinze, Francis Cardinal 19
Aristide, Jean-Bertrand 6, 45
Armstrong, Vanessa Bell 24
Austin, Junius V. 44
Banks, William 11
Baylor, Helen 36
Bell, Ralph S. 5
Ben-Israel, Ben Ami 11
Black, Barry C. 47
Blanks, Deborah K. 69
Boyd, T. B., III 6
Bryant, John R. 45
Burgess, John 46
Butts, Calvin O., III 9
Bynum, Juanita 31, 71
Caesar, Shirley 19
Cage, Byron 53
Caldwell, Kirbyjon 55
Cannon, Katie 10
Cardozo, Francis L. 33
Carr, Kurt 56
Chavis, Benjamin 6
Cleaver, Emanuel 4, 45, 68
Clements, George 2
Cleveland, James 19
Colemon, Johnnie 11
Collins, Janet 33, 64
Coltrane, Alice 70
Cone, James H. 3
Cook, Suzan D. Johnson 22
Crouch, Andraé 27
DeLille, Henriette 30
Divine, Father 7
Dyson, Michael Eric 11, 40
Elmore, Ronn 21
Fabre, Shelton 71
Farrakhan, Louis 2, 15
Fauntroy, Walter E. 11
Flake, Floyd H. 18

Forbes, James A., Jr. 71
Foreman, George 15
Franklin, C. L. 68
Franklin, Kirk 15, 49
Franklin, Robert M. 13
Funnye, Capers C., Jr. 73
Gaither, Israel L. 65
Gantin, Bernardin 70
Gilmore, Marshall 46
Gomes, Peter J. 15
Gray, Darius 69
Gray, William H., III 3
Green, Al 13, 47
Gregory, Wilton 37
Grier, Roosevelt 13
Haddon, Dietrick 55
Haile Selassie 7
Harding, Vincent 67
Harris, Barbara 12
Hawkins, Tramaine 16
Hayes, James C. 10
Healy, James Augustine 30
Hooks, Benjamin L. 2
Howard, M. William, Jr. 26
Jackson, Jesse 1, 27, 72
Jakes, Thomas "T. D." 17, 43
Jemison, Major L. 48
Johns, Vernon 38
Jones, Absalom 52
Jones, Alex 64
Jones, Bobby 20
Jones, E. Edward, Sr. 45
Jones, William A., Jr. 61
Karim, Benjamin 61
Kelly, Leontine 33
King, Barbara 22
King, Bernice 4
King, Martin Luther, Jr. 1
Kobia, Samuel 43
Lester, Julius 9
Lewis-Thornton, Rae 32
Lincoln, C. Eric 38
Little Richard 15
Long, Eddie L. 29
Lowery, Joseph 2
Lowry, A. Leon 60
Lyons, Henry 12
Majors, Jeff 41
Marino, Eugene Antonio 30
Maxis, Theresa 62
Mays, Benjamin E. 7
McClurkin, Donnie 25
McKenzie, Vashti M. 29
Morgan, Gertrude 63
Moss, J 64
Moss, Otis, Jr. 72
Moss, Otis, III 72
Muhammad, Ava 31
Muhammad, Elijah 4
Muhammad, Jabir Herbert 72
Muhammad, Khallid Abdul 10, 31
Muhammed, W. Deen 27
Murray, Cecil 12, 47
Okaalet, Peter 58
Otunga, Maurice Michael 55
Patterson, Gilbert Earl 41
Phipps, Wintley 59
Pierre, Andre 17
Powell, Adam Clayton, Jr. 3
Price, Frederick K. C. 21
Reems, Ernestine Cleveland 27
Reese, Della 6, 20
Riley, Helen Caldwell Day 13

Rogers, Alan G. 72
Rugambwa, Laurean 20
Scott, George 55
Senghor, Augustin Diamancoune 66
Sentamu, John 58
Shabazz, Betty 7, 26
Sharpton, Al 21
Shaw, William J. 30
Shuttlesworth, Fred 47
Slocumb, Jonathan 52
Somé, Malidoma Patrice 10
Stallings, George A., Jr. 6
Stampley, Micah 54
Steinberg, Martha Jean "The Queen" 28
Stith, Charles R. 73
Sullivan, Leon H. 3, 30
Thurman, Howard 3
Tillard, Conrad 47
Tolton, Augustine 62
Tonex 54
Turner, Henry McNeal 5
Tutu, Desmond (Mpilo) 6, 44
Vanity 67
Vanzant, Iyanla 17, 47
Waddles, Charleszetta "Mother" 10, 49
Walker, Hezekiah 34
Walker, John T. 50
Washington, James Melvin 50
Waters, Ethel 7
Weeks, Thomas, III 70
Weems, Renita J. 44
West, Cornel 5, 33
White, Reggie 6, 50
White-Hammond, Gloria 61
Williams, Frederick (B.) 63
Williams, Hosea Lorenzo 15, 31
Williams, Preston Warren, II 64
Wilson, Natalie 38
Winans, BeBe 14
Winans, CeCe 14, 43
Winans, Marvin L. 17
Winans, Ronald 54
Wright, Jeremiah A., Jr. 45, 69
Wright, Nathan, Jr. 56
Wyatt, Addie L. 56
X, Malcolm 1
York, Dwight D. 71
Youngblood, Johnny Ray 8

Science and technology
Adams-Campbell, Lucille L. 60
Adkins, Rod 41
Adkins, Rutherford H. 21
Alcorn, George Edward, Jr. 59
Alexander, Archie Alphonso 14
Allen, Ethel D. 13
Anderson, Charles Edward 37
Anderson, Michael P. 40
Anderson, Norman B. 45
Anderson, William G(ilchrist) 57
Atim, Julian 66
Auguste, Donna 29
Auguste, Rose-Anne 13
Bacon-Bercey, June 38
Banda, Hastings Kamuzu 6, 54
Bashir, Halima 73
Bath, Patricia E. 37
Benjamin, Regina 20
Benson, Angela 34
Black, Keith Lanier 18
Bluford, Guy 2, 35

Bluitt, Juliann S. 14
Bolden, Charles F., Jr. 7
Brown, Vivian 27
Brown, Willa 40
Bullard, Eugene 12
Callender, Clive O. 3
Campbell, Donald J. 66
Canady, Alexa 28
Cargill, Victoria A. 43
Carroll, L. Natalie 44
Carruthers, George R. 40
Carson, Benjamin 1, 35
Carter, Joye Maureen 41
Carver, George Washington 4
CasSelle, Malcolm 11
Chatard, Peter 44
Chinn, May Edward 26
Christian, Spencer 15
Clack, Zoanne 73
Cobb, W. Montague 39
Cobbs, Price M. 9
Cole, Rebecca 38
Coleman, Bessie 9
Coleman, Ken 57
Comer, James P. 6
Coney, PonJola 48
Cooper, Edward S. 6
Cooper, Lisa 73
Cornwell, Edward E., III 70
Daly, Marie Maynard 37
Davis, Allison 12
Dean, Mark 35
Deconge-Watson, Lovenia 55
Delany, Bessie 12
Delany, Martin R. 27
Dickens, Helen Octavia 14, 64
Diop, Cheikh Anta 4
Drew, Alvin, Jr. 67
Drew, Charles Richard 7
Dunham, Katherine 4, 59
Dunston, Georgia Mae 48
Edwards, Willarda V. 59
Elders, Joycelyn 6
Ellington, E. David 11
Ellis, Clarence A. 38
Emeagwali, Dale 31
Emeagwali, Philip 30
Ericsson-Jackson, Aprille 28
Fennoy, Ilene 72
Fields, Evelyn J. 27
Fisher, Rudolph 17
Flipper, Henry O. 3
Flowers, Sylester 50
Foster, Henry W., Jr. 26
Freeman, Harold P. 23
Fulani, Lenora 11
Fuller, A. Oveta 43
Fuller, Arthur 27
Fuller, Solomon Carter, Jr. 15
Gaston, Marilyn Hughes 60
Gates, Sylvester James, Jr. 15
Gayle, Helene D. 3, 46
Gibson, Kenneth Allen 6
Gibson, William F. 6
Gilliard, Steve 69
Gourdine, Meredith 33
Grant, Augustus O. 71
Granville, Evelyn Boyd 36
Gray, Ida 41
Gregory, Frederick 8, 51
Griffin, Anthony 71
Griffin, Bessie Blout 43
Griffith, Patrick A. 64

Hall, Lloyd A. 8
Hammonds, Evelynn 69
Hannah, Marc 10
Harris, Mary Styles 31
Haywood, Jimmy 58
Henderson, Cornelius Langston 26
Henson, Matthew 2
Hillary, Barbara 65
Hinton, William Augustus 8
Howard, Ayanna 65
Hutcherson, Hilda Yvonne 54
Ibrahim, Mo 67
Imes, Elmer Samuel 39
Irving, Larry, Jr. 12
Jackson, Shirley Ann 12
Jarvis, Erich 67
Jawara, Dawda Kairaba 11
Jemison, Mae C. 1, 35
Jenifer, Franklyn G. 2
Johnson, Eddie Bernice 8
Johnson, Lonnie G. 32
Jones, Edith Mae Irby 65
Jones, Frederick McKinley 68
Jones, Monty 66
Jones, Randy 35
Jones, Wayne 53
Joseph, Kathie-Ann 56
Julian, Percy Lavon 6
Juma, Calestous 57
Just, Ernest Everett 3
Keith, Rachel Boone 63
Kenney, John A., Jr. 48
King, Reatha Clark 65
Kintaudi, Leon 62
Kittles, Rick 51
Knowling, Robert E., Jr. 38
Kong, B. Waine 50
Kountz, Samuel L. 10
Laryea, Thomas Davies, III 67
Latimer, Lewis H. 4
Lavizzo-Mourey, Risa 48
Lawless, Theodore K. 8
Lawrence, Robert H., Jr. 16
Leevy, Carrol M. 42
Leffall, Lasalle 3, 64
Lewis, Daurene 72
Lewis, Delano 7
Logan, Onnie Lee 14
Lushington, Augustus Nathaniel 56
Lyttle, Hulda Margaret 14
Madison, Romell 45
Malveaux, Floyd 54
Manley, Audrey Forbes 16
Massey, Walter E. 5, 45
Massie, Samuel P., Jr. 29
Maxey, Randall 46
Mays, William G. 34
Mboup, Souleymane 10
McCoy, Elijah 8
McNair, Ronald 3, 58
Mensah, Thomas 48
Miller, Warren F., Jr. 53
Millines Dziko, Trish 28
Mills, Joseph C. 51
Morgan, Garrett 1
Murray, Pauli 38
Nabrit, Samuel Milton 47
Naki, Hamilton 63
Neto, António Agostinho 43
Nour, Nawal M. 56
Ojikutu, Bisola 65
O'Leary, Hazel 6
Olopade, Olufunmilayo Falusi 58

Osborne, Na'taki 54
Pace, Betty 59
Perry, Warren 56
Person, Waverly 9, 51
Peters, Lenrie 43
Pickett, Cecil 39
Pierre, Percy Anthony 46
Pinn, Vivian Winona 49
Pitt, David Thomas 10
Poussaint, Alvin F. 5, 67
Price, Richard 51
Prothrow-Stith, Deborah 10
Quarterman, Lloyd Albert 4
Rabb, Maurice F., Jr. 58
Randolph, Linda A. 52
Reece, E. Albert 63
Reese, Milous J., Jr. 51
Riley, Helen Caldwell Day 13
Robeson, Eslanda Goode 13
Robinson, Rachel 16
Roker, Al 12, 49
Ross-Lee, Barbara 67
Samara, Noah 15
Satcher, David 7, 57
Seacole, Mary 54
Shabazz, Betty 7, 26
Shavers, Cheryl 31
Sigur, Wanda 44
Sinkford, Jeanne C. 13
Slaughter, John Brooks 53
Smith, Ian 62
Smith, Richard 51
Staples, Brent 8
Staupers, Mabel K. 7
Stewart, Ella 39
Sullivan, Louis 8
Sweet, Ossian 68
Taylor, Susan C. 62
Terrell, Dorothy A. 24
Thomas, Vivien 9
Thornton, Yvonne S. 69
Tuckson, Reed V. 71
Tyson, Neil deGrasse 15, 65
Wambugu, Florence 42
Washington, Patrice Clarke 12
Watkins, Levi, Jr. 9
Wein, Joyce 62
Welsing, Frances Cress 5
Westbrooks, Bobby 51
White-Hammond, Gloria 61
Wilkens, J. Ernest, Jr. 43
Williams, Daniel Hale 2
Williams, David Rudyard 50
Williams, O. S. 13
Wilson, Stephanie 72
Wisdom, Kimberlydawn 57
Witt, Edwin T. 26
Woods, Granville T. 5
Wright, Louis Tompkins 4
Young, Roger Arliner 29

Social issues

Aaron, Hank 5
Abbot, Robert Sengstacke 27
Abbott, Diane 9
Abdul-Jabbar, Kareem 8
Abernathy, Ralph David 1
Abu-Jamal, Mumia 15
Achebe, Chinua 6
Adams, Sheila J. 25
Agyeman, Jaramogi Abebe 10, 63
Ake, Claude 30
Al-Amin, Jamil Abdullah 6

Alexander, Clifford 26
Alexander, Sadie Tanner Mossell 22
Ali, Muhammad 2, 16, 52
Allen, Ethel D. 13
Amaker, Norman 63
Andrews, Benny 22, 59
Angelou, Maya 1, 15
Annan, Kofi Atta 15, 48
Anthony, Wendell 25
Appiah, Kwame Anthony 67
Arac de Nyeko, Monica 66
Archer, Dennis 7
Aristide, Jean-Bertrand 6, 45
Arnwine, Barbara 28
Asante, Molefi Kete 3
Ashe, Arthur I, 18
Atyam, Angelina 55
Auguste, Rose-Anne 13
Autrey, Wesley 68
Avery, Byllye Y. 66
Azikiwe, Nnamdi 13
Ba, Mariama 30
Baisden, Michael 25, 66
Baker, Ella 5
Baker, Gwendolyn Calvert 9
Baker, Houston A., Jr. 6
Baker, Josephine 3
Baker, Thurbert 22
Baldwin, James 1
Banks, Paula A. 68
Baraka, Amiri 1, 38
Barbee, Lloyd Augustus 71
Barlow, Roosevelt 49
Barnett, Etta Moten 56
Bass, Charlotta Spears 40
Bates, Daisy 13
Beals, Melba Patillo 15
Belafonte, Harry 4, 65
Bell, Derrick 6
Bell, Ralph S. 5
Bennett, Lerone, Jr. 5
Berry, Bertice 8, 55
Berry, Mary Frances 7
Berrysmith, Don Reginald 49
Bethune, Mary McLeod 4
Betsch, MaVynee 28
Bibb, Henry and Mary 54
Biko, Steven 4
Birch, Glynn R. 61
Black, Albert 51
Blackwell, Unita 17
Bobo, Lawrence 60
Bolin, Jane 22, 59
Bond, Julian 2, 35
Bonga, Kuenda 13
Booker, Cory Anthony 68
Bosley, Freeman, Jr. 7
Boyd, Gwendolyn 49
Boyd, John W., Jr. 20, 72
Boyd, T. B., III 6
Boykin, Keith 14
Bradley, David Henry, Jr. 39
Braun, Carol Moseley 4, 42
Broadbent, Hydeia 36
Brooke, Edward 8
Brown, Byrd 49
Brown, Cora 33
Brown, Eddie C. 35
Brown, Elaine 8
Brown, Homer S. 47
Brown, Jesse 6, 41
Brown, Jim 11

Brown, Lee P. 1
Brown, Les 5
Brown, Lloyd Louis 10 42
Brown, Oscar, Jr. 53
Brown, Tony 3
Brown, Willa 40
Brown, Zora Kramer 12
Brutus, Dennis 38
Bryant, Wayne R. 6
Bullock, Steve 22
Bunche, Ralph J. 5
Burks, Mary Fair 40
Burroughs, Margaret Taylor 9
Butler, Paul D. 17
Butts, Calvin O., III 9
Campbell, Bebe Moore 6, 24, 59
Canada, Geoffrey 23
Carby, Hazel 27
Carmichael, Stokely 5, 26
Carr, Johnnie 69
Carter, Mandy 11
Carter, Robert L. 51
Carter, Rubin 26
Carter, Stephen L. 4
Cary, Lorene 3
Cary, Mary Ann Shadd 30
Cayton, Horace 26
Chavis, Benjamin 6
Chestnut, J. L., Jr. 73
Chideya, Farai 14, 61
Childress, Alice 15
Chissano, Joaquim 7, 55, 67
Christophe, Henri 9
Chuck D 9
Clark, Joe 1
Clark, Kenneth B. 5, 52
Clark, Septima 7
Clay, William Lacy 8
Clayton, Mayme Agnew 62
Claytor, Helen 14, 52
Cleaver, Eldridge 5
Cleaver, Kathleen Neal 29
Clements, George 2
Cobbs, Price M. 9
Cole, Johnnetta B. 5, 43
Cole, Lorraine 48
Collins, Barbara-Rose 7
Collins, Patricia Hill 67
Colston, Hal 72
Comer, James P. 6
Cone, James H. 3
Connerly, Ward 14
Conté, Lansana 7
Conyers, John, Jr. 4, 45
Cook, Toni 23
Cooke, Marvel 31
Cooper, Anna Julia 20
Cooper, Edward S. 6
Cooper, Margaret J. 46
Cosby, Bill 7, 26, 59
Cosby, Camille 14
Cose, Ellis 5, 50
Creagh, Milton 27
Crew, Spencer R. 55
Crockett, George W., Jr. 10, 64
Crouch, Stanley 11
Cruse, Harold 54
Cummings, Elijah E. 24
Cunningham, Evelyn 23
da Silva, Benedita 5
Dash, Julie 4
Davis, Angela 5
Davis, Artur 41

Davis, Danny K. 24
Davis, Ossie 5, 50
Dawson, Matel "Mat," Jr. 39
Dawson, Michael C. 63
DeBaptiste, George 32
Dee, Ruby 8, 50, 68
Delany, Martin R. 27
Dellums, Ronald 2
Dent, Thomas C. 50
Diallo, Amadou 27
Dickerson, Ernest 6
Dieudonné 67
Diop, Cheikh Anta 4
Dirie, Waris 56
Dixon, Margaret 14
Dodson, Howard, Jr. 7, 52
Dortch, Thomas W., Jr. 45
Dove, Rita 6
Drew, Charles Richard 7
Du Bois, W. E. B. 3
DuBois, Shirley Graham 21
Duggins, George 64
Dukes, Hazel Nell 56
Dumas, Henry 41
Dunham, Katherine 4, 59
Early, Gerald 15
Edelin, Ramona Hoage 19
Edelman, Marian Wright 5, 42
Edley, Christopher 2, 48
Edwards, Harry 2
Elder, Larry 25
Elder, Lee 6
Elders, Joycelyn 6
Ellison, Ralph 7
Esposito, Giancarlo 9
Espy, Mike 6
Eugene-Richard, Margie 63
Europe, James Reese 10
Evers, Medgar 3
Evers, Myrlie 8
Farmer, James 2, 64
Farrakhan, Louis 15
Farris, Isaac Newton, Jr. 63
Fauntroy, Walter E. 11
Fauset, Jessie 7
Fela 1, 42
Fields, C. Virginia 25
Finner-Williams, Paris Michele 62
Flavor Flav 67
Fletcher, Bill, Jr. 41
Forbes, James A., Jr. 71
Foreman, George 15
Forman, James 7, 51
Fortune, T. Thomas 6
Foster, Marie 48
Franklin, C. L. 68
Franklin, Hardy R. 9
Franklin, John Hope 5
Franklin, Robert M. 13
Frazier, E. Franklin 10
Fulani, Lenora 11
Fuller, Arthur 27
Fuller, Charles 8
Gaines, Ernest J. 7
Gardner, Chris 65
Garvey, Marcus 1
Gates, Henry Louis, Jr. 3, 38, 67
Gayle, Helene D. 3
George, Zelma Watson 42
Gibson, Kenneth Allen 6
Gibson, William F. 6
Gilbert, Christopher 50

Gist, Carole **1**
Goldberg, Whoopi **4, 33, 69**
Golden, Marita **19**
Golston, Allan C. **55**
Gomez, Jewelle **30**
Gomez-Preston, Cheryl **9**
Goss, Carol A. **55**
Gossett, Louis, Jr. **7**
Graham, Lawrence Otis **12**
Gray, Fred **37**
Greene, Petey **65**
Gregory, Dick **1, 54**
Gregory, Wilton **37**
Grier, Roosevelt **13**
Griffith, Mark Winston **8**
Grimké, Archibald H. **9**
Guinier, Lani **7, 30**
Guy, Rosa **5**
Guy-Sheftall, Beverly **13**
Hale, Lorraine **8**
Haley, Alex **4**
Hall, Elliott S. **24**
Hamblin, Ken **10**
Hamer, Fannie Lou **6**
Hampton, Fred **18**
Hampton, Henry **6**
Hani, Chris **6**
Hansberry, Lorraine **6**
Hansberry, William Leo **11**
Harding, Vincent **67**
Harper, Frances Ellen Watkins **11**
Harrington, Oliver W. **9**
Harris, Alice **7**
Harris, Leslie **6**
Harris, Marcelite Jordan **16**
Harris, Patricia Roberts **2**
Hastings, Alcee L. **16**
Hawkins, Augustus F. **68**
Hawkins, Steven **14**
Hayes, Dennis **54**
Haynes, George Edmund **8**
Hedgeman, Anna Arnold **22**
Height, Dorothy I. **2, 23**
Henderson, Thelton E. **68**
Henderson, Wade J. **14**
Henderson, Zelma **71**
Henry, Aaron Edd **19**
Henry, Lenny **9, 52**
Hernandez, Aileen Clarke **13**
Hernton, Calvin C. **51**
Hill, Anita **5, 65**
Hill, Jesse, Jr. **13**
Hill, Lauryn **20, 53**
Hill, Oliver W. **24, 63**
Hilliard, Asa Grant, III **66**
Hilliard, David **7**
Holland, Endesha Ida Mae **3, 57**
Holt Baker, Arlene **73**
hooks, bell **5**
Hooks, Benjamin L. **2**
Horne, Lena **5**
Houston, Charles Hamilton **4**
Howard, M. William, Jr. **26**
Hoyte, Lenon **50**
Hubbard, Arnette Rhinehart **38**
Huggins, Nathan Irvin **52**
Hughes, Albert **7**
Hughes, Allen **7**
Hughes, Langston **4**
Hunter-Gault, Charlayne **6, 31**
Hutchinson, Earl Ofari **24**
Hutson, Jean Blackwell **16**
Ibrahim, Mo **67**

Iceberg Slim **11**
Ice-T **6, 31**
Iman **4, 33**
Ingram, Rex **5**
Innis, Roy **5**
Irvis, K. Leroy **67**
Jackson, Edison O. **67**
Jackson, Fred James **25**
Jackson, George **14**
Jackson, Janet **6, 30, 68**
Jackson, Jesse **1, 27, 72**
Jackson, Judith D. **57**
Jackson, Mahalia **5**
Jacob, John E. **2**
Jagan, Cheddi **16**
James, Daniel, Jr. **16**
Jealous, Benjamin **70**
Jean, Wyclef **20**
Jeffries, Leonard **8**
Johnson, Charles S. **12**
Johnson, Earvin "Magic" **3, 39**
Johnson, James Weldon **5**
Johnson, Kevin **70**
Jolley, Willie **28**
Jones, Cullen **73**
Jones, Elaine R. **7, 45**
Jones, Van **70**
Jones, William A., Jr. **61**
Jordan, Barbara **4**
Jordan, June **7, 35**
Jordan, Vernon E. **3, 35**
Joseph, Kathie-Ann **56**
Josey, E. J. **10**
Joyner, Marjorie Stewart **26**
Joyner, Tom **19**
Julian, Percy Lavon **6**
Karim, Benjamin **61**
Kaunda, Kenneth **2**
Keith, Damon J. **16**
Kennedy, Florynce **12, 33**
Khanga, Yelena **6**
Kidd, Mae Street **39**
King, B. B. **7**
King, Bernice **4**
King, Coretta Scott **3, 57**
King, Dexter **10**
King, Martin Luther, III **20**
King, Martin Luther, Jr. **1**
King, Preston **28**
King, Yolanda **6**
Kitt, Eartha **16**
Kuzwayo, Ellen **68**
Ladner, Joyce A. **42**
LaGuma, Alex **30**
Lampkin, Daisy **19**
Lane, Charles **3**
Lane, Vincent **5**
Laraque, Paul **67**
Lee, Canada **8**
Lee, Spike **5, 19**
Leland, Mickey **2**
Lester, Julius **9**
Lewis, Ananda **28**
Lewis, Delano **7**
Lewis, John **2, 46**
Lewis, Thomas **19**
Lewis-Thornton, Rae **32**
Little, Robert L. **2**
Logan, Rayford W. **40**
Long, Eddie L. **29**
Lorde, Audre **6**
Louis, Errol T. **8**
Loving, Mildred **69**

Lowery, Joseph **2**
Lowry, A. Leon **60**
Lucas, John **7**
Lucy, William **50**
Lucy Foster, Autherine **35**
Maathai, Wangari **43**
Mabuza-Suttle, Felicia **43**
Madhubuti, Haki R. **7**
Madison, Joseph E. **17**
Makeba, Miriam **2, 50**
Malone Jones, Vivian **59**
Malveaux, Julianne **32, 70**
Mandela, Nelson **1, 14**
Mandela, Winnie **2, 35**
Manley, Audrey Forbes **16**
Marable, Manning **10**
Marley, Bob **5**
Marshall, Paule **7**
Marshall, Thurgood **1, 44**
Martin, Louis E. **16**
Masekela, Barbara **18**
Masekela, Hugh **1**
Mason, Ronald **27**
Mathabane, Mark **5**
Maynard, Robert C. **7**
Mays, Benjamin E. **7**
Mbeki, Thabo **14, 73**
McCabe, Jewell Jackson **10**
McCarty, Osceola **16**
McDaniel, Hattie **5**
McDougall, Gay J. **11, 43**
McKay, Claude **6**
McKenzie, Vashti M. **29**
McKinney Hammond, Michelle **51**
McKissick, Floyd B. **3**
McMurray, Georgia L. **36**
McQueen, Butterfly **6, 54**
McWhorter, John **35**
Meek, Carrie **6, 36**
Meredith, James H. **11**
Mfume, Kweisi **6, 41**
Mhlaba, Raymond **55**
Micheaux, Oscar **7**
Millender-McDonald, Juanita **21, 61**
Miller-Travis, Vernice **64**
Millines Dziko, Trish **28**
Mkapa, Benjamin **16**
Mongella, Gertrude **11**
Moore, Gwendolynne S. **55**
Moore, Harry T. **29**
Morgan, Irene **65**
Morial, Ernest "Dutch" **26**
Morrison, Toni **2**
Moses, Robert Parris **11**
Mosley, Walter **5, 25, 68**
Moss, Otis, Jr. **72**
Mossell, Gertrude Bustill **40**
Motley, Constance Baker **10, 55**
Moutoussamy-Ashe, Jeanne **7**
Mowry, Jess **7**
Muhammad, Elijah **4**
Muhammad, Khallid Abdul **10, 31**
Murphy, Laura M. **43**
Murray, Pauli **38**
Nash, Diane **72**
Ndadaye, Melchior **7**
Nelson, Jill **6, 54**
Newton, Huey P. **2**
Niane, Katoucha **70**
Nkoli, Simon **60**
Nkrumah, Kwame **3**
Norman, Pat **10**
Norton, Eleanor Holmes **7**

Nour, Nawal M. **56**
Nzo, Alfred **15**
Obasanjo, Olusegun **5**
Oglesby, Zena **12**
Ojikutu, Bisola **65**
O'Leary, Hazel **6**
Ormes, Jackie **73**
Osborne, Na'taki **54**
Owens, Major **6**
Page, Alan **7**
Page, Clarence **4**
Paige, Satchel **7**
Parker, Kellis E. **30**
Parker, Pat **19**
Parks, Rosa **1, 35, 56**
Parr, Russ **51**
Patterson, Frederick Douglass **12**
Patterson, Louise **25**
Patterson, Orlando **4**
Patterson, P. J. **6, 20**
Perkins, Edward **5**
Pitt, David Thomas **10**
Pleasant, Mary Ellen **9**
Plessy, Homer Adolph **31**
Pough, Terrell **58**
Poussaint, Alvin F. **5, 67**
Powell, Adam Clayton, Jr. **3**
Powell, Kevin **31**
Pratt, Geronimo **18**
Pressley, Condace L. **41**
Price, Hugh B. **9, 54**
Primus, Pearl **6**
Pritchard, Robert Starling **21**
Prothrow-Stith, Deborah **10**
Quarles, Benjamin Arthur **18**
Quigless, Helen G. **49**
Ramaphosa, Cyril **3**
Ramphele, Mamphela **29**
Ramsey, Charles H. **21, 69**
Rand, A. Barry **6**
Randolph, A. Philip **3**
Randolph, Linda A. **52**
Rangel, Charles **3, 52**
Rawlings, Nana Konadu Agyeman **13**
Reagon, Bernice Johnson **7**
Reed, Ishmael **8**
Rice, Louise Allen **54**
Rice, Norm **8**
Richards, Hilda **49**
Richardson, Rupert **67**
Riggs, Marlon **5**
Riley, Helen Caldwell Day **13**
Ringgold, Faith **4**
Robeson, Eslanda Goode **13**
Robeson, Paul **2**
Robinson, Jackie **6**
Robinson, Rachel **16**
Robinson, Randall **7, 46**
Robinson, Sharon **22**
Robinson, Spottswood W., III **22**
Roble, Abdi **71**
Rodriguez, Cheryl **64**
Rowan, Carl T. **1, 30**
Rowell, Victoria **13, 68**
Rusesabagina, Paul **60**
Rustin, Bayard **4**
Sampson, Edith S. **4**
Sanders, Malika **48**
Sané, Pierre Gabriel **21**
Sapphire **14**
Saro-Wiwa, Kenule **39**
Satcher, David **7, 57**

Savimbi, Jonas **2, 34**
Sawyer, Amos **2**
Sayles Belton, Sharon **9, 16**
Scantlebury-White, Velma **64**
Schomburg, Arthur Alfonso **9**
Seacole, Mary **54**
Seale, Bobby **3**
Sears, Stephanie **53**
Seele, Pernessa **46**
Senghor, Léopold Sédar **12**
Shabazz, Attallah **6**
Shabazz, Betty **7, 26**
Shakur, Afeni **67**
Shakur, Assata **6**
Shinhoster, Earl **32**
Shuttlesworth, Fred **47**
Sifford, Charlie **4, 49**
Simone, Nina **15, 41**
Simpson, Carole **6, 30**
Sister Souljah **11**
Sisulu, Albertina **57**
Sisulu, Sheila Violet Makate **24**
Sleet, Moneta, Jr. **5**
Smith, Anna Deavere **6**
Smith, Barbara **28**
Smith, Damu **54**
Smith, Greg **28**
Smith, Kemba **70**
Smith, Marie F. **70**
Smith, Nate **49**
Snowden, Frank M., Jr. **67**
Soyinka, Wole **4**
Spriggs, William **67**
Stallings, George A., Jr. **6**
Staupers, Mabel K. **7**
Steele, Claude Mason **13**
Steele, Shelby **13**
Stewart, Alison **13**
Stewart, Ella **39**
Stewart, Maria W. Miller **19**
Stone, Chuck **9**
Sullivan, Leon H. **3, 30**
Sutton, Percy E. **42**
Sweet, Ossian **68**
Tate, Eleanora E. **20, 55**
Taulbert, Clifton Lemoure **19**
Taylor, Bo **72**
Taylor, Mildred D. **26**
Taylor, Susan L. **10**
Terrell, Mary Church **9**
Thomas, Arthur Ray **52**
Thomas, Franklin A. **5, 49**
Thomas, Isiah **7, 26, 65**
Thompson, Bennie G. **26**
Thompson, Cynthia Bramlett **50**
Thurman, Howard **3**
Thurman, Wallace **16**
Till, Emmett **7**
Toomer, Jean **6**
Tosh, Peter **9**
Touré, Askia (Muhammad Abu Bakr el) **47**
Touré, Faya Ora Rose **56**
Tribble, Israel, Jr. **8**
Trotter, Donne E. **28**
Trotter, Monroe **9**
Tsvangirai, Morgan **26, 72**
Tubman, Harriet **9**
Tucker, C. Delores **12, 56**
Tucker, Cynthia **15, 61**
Tucker, Rosina **14**
Tutu, Desmond **6**
Tyree, Omar Rashad **21**

Underwood, Blair **7, 27**
Van Peebles, Melvin **7**
Vanzant, Iyanla **17, 47**
Vaughn, Viola **70**
Vega, Marta Moreno **61**
Velez-Rodriguez, Argelia **56**
Vincent, Marjorie Judith **2**
Waddles, Charleszetta "Mother" **10, 49**
Walcott, Derek **5**
Walker, A'lelia **14**
Walker, Alice **1, 43**
Walker, Bernita Ruth **53**
Walker, Cedric "Ricky" **19**
Walker, Madame C. J. **7**
Wallace, Joaquin **49**
Wallace, Michele Faith **13**
Wallace, Phyllis A. **9**
Washington, Booker T. **4**
Washington, Fredi **10**
Washington, Harold **6**
Waters, Maxine **3, 67**
Wattleton, Faye **9**
Wells, Henrietta Bell **69**
Wells, James Lesesne **10**
Wells-Barnett, Ida B. **8**
Welsing, Frances Cress **5**
West, Cornel **5, 33**
White, Michael R. **5**
White, Reggie **6, 50**
White, Walter F. **4**
White, Willye **67**
White-Hammond, Gloria **61**
Wideman, John Edgar **5**
Wilkins, Roger **2**
Wilkins, Roy **4**
Williams, Armstrong **29**
Williams, Evelyn **10**
Williams, Fannie Barrier **27**
Williams, George Washington **18**
Williams, Hosea Lorenzo **15, 31**
Williams, Maggie **7, 71**
Williams, Montel **4, 57**
Williams, Patricia **11, 54**
Williams, Robert F. **11**
Williams, Stanley "Tookie" **29, 57**
Williams, Walter E. **4**
Williams, Willie L. **4**
Wilson, August **7, 33, 55**
Wilson, Phill **9**
Wilson, Sunnie **7, 55**
Wilson, William Julius **22**
Winfield, Paul **2, 45**
Winfrey, Oprah **2, 15, 61**
Withers, Ernest C. **68**
Wiwa, Ken **67**
Wolfe, George C. **6, 43**
Woodson, Robert L. **10**
Worrill, Conrad **12**
Wright, Charles H. **35**
Wright, Louis Tompkins **4**
Wright, Nathan, Jr. **56**
Wright, Richard **5**
Wyatt, Addie L. **56**
X, Malcolm **1**
Xuma, Madie Hall **59**
Yancy, Dorothy Cowser **42**
Yarbrough, Camille **40**
Yeboah, Emmanuel Ofosu **53**
Yoba, Malik **11**
Young, Andrew **3, 48**
Young, Jean Childs **14**
Young, Whitney M., Jr. **4**

Youngblood, Johnny Ray **8**
Zulu, Princess Kasune **54**

Sports

Aaron, Hank **5**
Abdul-Jabbar, Kareem **8**
Abdur-Rahim, Shareef **28**
Adams, Paul **50**
Adu, Freddy **67**
Alexander, Shaun **58**
Ali, Laila **27, 63**
Ali, Muhammad **2, 16, 52**
Allen, Marcus **20**
Amaker, Tommy **62**
Amos, John **8, 62**
Anderson, Elmer **25**
Anderson, Jamal **22**
Anderson, Mike **63**
Anderson, Viv **58**
Anthony, Carmelo **46**
Artest, Ron **52**
Ashe, Arthur **1, 18**
Ashford, Emmett **22**
Ashford, Evelyn **63**
Ashley, Maurice **15, 47**
Baines, Harold **32**
Baker, Dusty **8, 43, 72**
Banks, Ernie **33**
Barber, Ronde **41**
Barber, Tiki **57**
Barkley, Charles **5, 66**
Barnes, Ernie **16**
Barnes, John **53**
Barnes, Steven **54**
Barney, Lem **26**
Barnhill, David **30**
Baylor, Don **6**
Beamon, Bob **30**
Beasley, Jamar **29**
Bell, James "Cool Papa" **36**
Belle, Albert **10**
Bettis, Jerome **64**
Bickerstaff, Bernie **21**
Bing, Dave **3, 59**
Bivins, Michael **72**
Blair, Paul **36**
Blake, James **43**
Blanks, Billy **22**
Blanton, Dain **29**
Bogues, Tyrone "Muggsy" **56**
Bol, Manute **1**
Bolt, Usain **73**
Bolton-Holifield, Ruthie **28**
Bonaly, Surya **7**
Bonds, Barry **6, 34, 63**
Bonds, Bobby **43**
Bowe, Riddick **6**
Brand, Elton **31**
Brandon, Terrell **16**
Branham, George, III **50**
Brashear, Donald **39**
Brathwaite, Fred **35**
Briscoe, Marlin **37**
Brock, Lou **18**
Brooks, Aaron **33**
Brooks, Derrick **43**
Brown, James **22**
Brown, Jim **11**
Brown, Sean **52**
Brown, Willard **36**
Bruce, Isaac **26**
Bryant, Kobe **15, 31, 71**
Buchanan, Ray **32**

Bush, Reggie **59**
Butler, Leroy, III **17**
Bynoe, Peter C.B. **40**
Campanella, Roy **25**
Carew, Rod **20**
Carnegie, Herbert **25**
Carter, Anson **24**
Carter, Butch **27**
Carter, Cris **21**
Carter, Joe **30**
Carter, Kenneth **53**
Carter, Rubin **26**
Carter, Vince **26**
Cash, Swin **59**
Catchings, Tamika **43**
Chamberlain, Wilt **18, 47**
Chaney, John **67**
Charleston, Oscar **39**
Cheeks, Maurice **47**
Cherry, Deron **40**
Cheruiyot, Robert **69**
Christie, Linford **8**
Claiborne, Loretta **34**
Clay, Bryan Ezra **57**
Clemons, Michael "Pinball" **64**
Clendenon, Donn **26, 56**
Clifton, Nathaniel "Sweetwater" **47**
Coachman, Alice **18**
Coleman, Leonard S., Jr. **12**
Cooper, Andy "Lefty" **63**
Cooper, Charles "Chuck" **47**
Cooper, Cynthia **17**
Cooper, Michael **31**
Copeland, Michael **47**
Corley, Tony **62**
Cottrell, Comer **11**
Crennel, Romeo **54**
Crooks, Garth **53**
Croom, Sylvester **50**
Culpepper, Daunte **32**
Cunningham, Randall **23**
Dandridge, Ray **36**
Dantley, Adrian **72**
Davis, Ernie **48**
Davis, Mike **41**
Davis, Piper **19**
Davis, Shani **58**
Davis, Terrell **20**
Dawes, Dominique **11**
Day, Leon **39**
DeFrantz, Anita **37**
Devers, Gail **7**
Dibaba, Tirunesh **73**
Dickerson, Eric **27**
Dixon, George **52**
Doby, Lawrence Eugene, Sr. **16, 41**
Doig, Jason **45**
Dorrell, Karl **52**
dos Santos, Manuel Francisco **65**
Drew, Charles Richard **7**
Drexler, Clyde **4, 61**
Dumars, Joe **16, 65**
Duncan, Tim **20**
Dungy, Tony **17, 42, 59**
Dunn, Jerry **27**
Dye, Jermaine **58**
Edwards, Harry **2**
Edwards, Herman **51**
Edwards, Teresa **14**
Elder, Lee **6**
Ellerbe, Brian **22**
Elliott, Sean **26**
Ellis, Jimmy **44**

Ervin, Anthony 66
Erving, Julius 18, 47
Eto'o, Samuel 73
Ewing, Patrick 17, 73
Farr, Mel 24
Faulk, Marshall 35
Felix, Allyson 48
Fielder, Cecil 2
Fielder, Prince Semien 68
Flood, Curt 10
Flowers, Vonetta 35
Ford, Cheryl 45
Foreman, George 1, 15
Fowler, Reggie 51
Fox, Rick 27
Frazier, Joe 19
Frazier-Lyde, Jacqui 31
Freeman, Cathy 29
Freeman, Marianna 23
Fuhr, Grant 1, 49
Fuller, Vivian 33
Futch, Eddie 33
Gaines, Clarence E., Sr. 55
Gaither, Alonzo Smith (Jake) 14
Garnett, Kevin 14, 70
Garrison, Zina 2
Gaston, Cito 71
Gebrselassie, Haile 70
Gentry, Alvin 23
Gibson, Althea 8, 43
Gibson, Bob 33
Gibson, Josh 22
Gibson, Truman K., Jr. 60
Gilliam, Frank 23
Gilliam, Joe 31
Gooden, Dwight 20
Gorden, W. C. 71
Goss, Tom 23
Gourdine, Meredith 33
Gourdine, Simon 11
Granderson, Curtis 66
Grand-Pierre, Jean-Luc 46
Gray, Yeshimbra "Shimmy" 55
Green, A. C. 32
Green, Darrell 39
Green, Dennis 5, 45
Greene, Joe 10
Greene, Maurice 27
Gregg, Eric 16
Gregory, Ann 63
Grier, Mike 43
Grier, Roosevelt 1
Griffey, Ken, Jr. 12, 73
Griffith, Yolanda 25
Griffith-Joyner, Florence 28
Gumbel, Bryant 14
Gumbel, Greg 8
Gwynn, Tony 18
Hamilton, Lewis 66
Hardaway, Anfernee (Penny) 13
Hardaway, Tim 35
Harris, Sylvia 70
Harrison, Alvin 28
Harrison, Calvin 28
Haskins, Clem 23
Heard, Gar 25
Hearns, Thomas 29
Henderson, Rickey 28
Henry, Thierry 66
Hickman, Fred 11
Hill, Calvin 19
Hill, Grant 13
Hillary, Barbara 65

Hilliard, Wendy 53
Hines, Garrett 35
Holdsclaw, Chamique 24
Holland, Kimberly N. 62
Holmes, Kelly 47
Holmes, Larry 20, 68
Holyfield, Evander 6
Hopkins, Bernard 35, 69
Horton, Andre 33
Horton, Suki 33
Howard, Desmond 16, 58
Howard, Juwan 15
Howard, Ryan 65
Howard, Sherri 36
Hunter, Billy 22
Hunter, Torii 43
Hyde, Cowan F. "Bubba" 47
Iginla, Jarome 35
Irvin, Michael 64
Irvin, Monte 31
Iverson, Allen 24, 46
Ivey, Phil 72
Jackson, Jamea 64
Jackson, Mannie 14
Jackson, Reggie 15
Jackson, Tom 70
Jacobs, Regina 38
James, LeBron 46
Jenkins, Fergie 46
Jeter, Derek 27
Johnson, Avery 62
Johnson, Ben 1
Johnson, Clifford "Connie" 52
Johnson, Earvin "Magic" 3, 39
Johnson, Jack 8
Johnson, Kevin 70
Johnson, Larry 28
Johnson, Levi 48
Johnson, Mamie "Peanut" 40
Johnson, Michael 13
Johnson, Rafer 33
Johnson, Rodney Van 28
Jones, Cobi N'Gai 18
Jones, Cullen 73
Jones, Ed "Too Tall" 46
Jones, Lou 64
Jones, Marion 21, 66
Jones, Merlakia 34
Jones, Randy 35
Jones, Roy, Jr. 22
Jordan, Michael 6, 21
Joyner-Kersee, Jackie 5
Justice, David 18
Kaiser, Cecil 42
Kanouté, Fred 68
Keflezighi, Meb 49
Keith, Floyd A. 61
Kellogg, Clark 64
Kennedy-Overton, Jayne Harris 46
Kerry, Leon G. 46
Kimbro, Henry A. 25
King, Don 14
Lacy, Sam 30, 46
Ladd, Ernie 64
Lanier, Bob 47
Lanier, Willie 33
Lankford, Ray 23
Laraque, Georges 48
Larkin, Barry 24
Lashley, Bobby 63
Lassiter, Roy 24
Lee, Canada 8
Lennox, Betty 31

Leonard, Buck 67
Leonard, Sugar Ray 15
Leslie, Lisa 16, 73
Lester, Bill 42
Lewis, Butch 71
Lewis, Carl 4
Lewis, Denise 33
Lewis, Lennox 27
Lewis, Marvin 51
Lewis, Oliver 56
Lewis, Ray 33
Liston, Sonny 33
Littlepage, Craig 35
Lloyd, Earl 26
Lloyd, John Henry "Pop" 30
Lofton, James 42
Lofton, Kenny 12
Loroupe, Tegla 59
Lott, Ronnie 9
Louis, Joe 5
Love, Nat 9
Lowe, Sidney 64
Lucas, John 7
Mahorn, Rick 60
Malone, Karl 18, 51
Manigault, Earl "The Goat" 15
Mariner, Jonathan 41
Master P 21
Mayers, Jamal 39
Mays, Willie 3
Mayweather, Floyd, Jr. 57
McBride, Bryant 18
McCarthy, Sandy 64
McCray, Nikki 18
McGriff, Fred 24
McKegney, Tony 3
McNabb, Donovan 29
McNair, Steve 22, 47
McNeil, Lori 1
Mello, Breno 73
Metcalfe, Ralph 26
Milla, Roger 2
Miller, Cheryl 10
Miller, Larry G. 72
Miller, Reggie 33
Mills, Sam 33
Milton, DeLisha 31
Minor, DeWayne 32
Mohammed, Nazr 64
Monk, Art 38, 73
Montgomery, Tim 41
Moon, Warren 8, 66
Moorer, Michael 19
Morgan, Joe Leonard 9
Moses, Edwin 8
Mosley, Shane 32
Moss, Randy 23
Motley, Marion 26
Mourning, Alonzo 17, 44
Muhammad, Jabir Herbert 72
Mundine, Anthony 56
Murray, Eddie 12
Murray, Lenda 10
Mutola, Maria 12
Mutombo, Dikembe 7
Nakhid, David 25
Newcombe, Don 24
Newsome, Ozzie 26
Noah, Yannick 4, 60
Olajuwon, Hakeem 2, 72
Oliver, Pam 54
O'Neal, Shaquille 8, 30
O'Neil, Buck 19, 59

Onyewu, Oguchi 60
O'Ree, Willie 5
Ortiz, David 52
Owens, Jesse 2
Owens, Terrell 53
Pace, Orlando 21
Page, Alan 7
Paige, Satchel 7
Palmer, Violet 59
Parish, Robert 43
Parker, Jim 64
Patterson, Floyd 19, 58
Payne, Ulice 42
Payton, Walter 11, 25
Peck, Carolyn 23
Peete, Calvin 11
Peete, Rodney 60
Pelé 7
Perrot, Kim 23
Perry, Lowell 30
Peters, Margaret 43
Peters, Matilda 43
Phillips, Teresa L. 42
Pickett, Bill 11
Pierce, Paul 71
Pippen, Scottie 15
Pollard, Fritz 53
Powell, Mike 7
Powell, Renee 34
Pride, Charley 26
Prince, Ron 64
Prince, Tayshaun 68
Puckett, Kirby 4, 58
Quirot, Ana 13
Randolph, Willie 53
Rashad, Ahmad 18
Ready, Stephanie 33
Reese, Pokey 28
Regis, Cyrille 51
Rhoden, William C. 67
Rhodes, Ray 14
Ribbs, Willy T. 2
Rice, Jerry 5, 55
Richards, Sanya 66
Richardson, Donna 39
Richardson, Nolan 9
Richmond, Mitch 19
Rivers, Glenn "Doc" 25
Robertson, Oscar 26
Robinson, David 24
Robinson, Eddie G. 10, 61
Robinson, Frank 9
Robinson, Jackie 6
Robinson, Sugar Ray 18
Robinson, Will 51, 69
Rock, The 29, 66
Rodman, Dennis 12, 44
Rollins, Jimmy 70
Ronaldinho 69
Rose, Lionel 56
Rubin, Chanda 37
Rudolph, Wilma 4
Russell, Bill 8
St. Julien, Marlon 29
Salvador, Bryce 51
Sampson, Charles 13
Sanders, Barry 1, 53
Sanders, Bob 72
Sanders, Deion 4, 31
Sapp, Warren 38
Sayers, Gale 28
Scott, Stuart 34
Scott, Wendell Oliver, Sr. 19

Scurry, Briana **27**
Sharper, Darren **32**
Sheffield, Gary **16**
Shell, Art **1, 66**
Shippen, John **43**
Showers, Reggie **30**
Sifford, Charlie **4, 49**
Silas, Paul **24**
Simmons, Bob **29**
Simpson, O. J. **15**
Singletary, Mike **4**
Slice, Kimbo **73**
Smith, Emmitt **7**
Smith, Hilton **29**
Smith, Lovie **66**
Smith, Rick **72**
Smith, Stephen A. **69**
Smith, Tubby **18**
Solomon, Jimmie Lee **38**
Sosa, Sammy **21, 44**
Spiller, Bill **64**
Sprewell, Latrell **23**
Stackhouse, Jerry **30**
Staley, Dawn **57**
Stargell, Willie **29**
Stearns, Norman "Turkey" **31**
Steward, Emanuel **18**
Stewart, James "Bubba," Jr. **60**
Stewart, Kordell **21**
Stingley, Darryl **69**
Stone, Toni **15**
Stoudemire, Amaré **59**
Strahan, Michael **35**
Strawberry, Darryl **22**
Stringer, C. Vivian **13, 66**
Stringer, Korey **35**
Swann, Lynn **28**
Swoopes, Sheryl **12, 56**
Taylor, Jason **70**
Taylor, Jermain **60**
Taylor, Lawrence **25**
Taylor, Marshall Walter "Major" **62**
Tergat, Paul **59**
Thomas, Debi **26**
Thomas, Derrick **25**
Thomas, Emmitt **71**
Thomas, Frank **12, 51**
Thomas, Isiah **7, 26, 65**
Thompson, Tina **25**
Thrower, Willie **35**
Thugwane, Josia **21**
Tirico, Mike **68**
Tisdale, Wayman **50**
Tomlinson, LaDainian **65**
Tunnell, Emlen **54**
Tyson, Mike **28, 44**
Unseld, Wes **23**
Upshaw, Gene **18, 47, 72**
Ussery, Terdema, II **29**
Vick, Michael **39**
Virgil, Ozzie **48**
Wade, Dwyane **61**
Walker, Herschel **1, 69**
Wallace, Ben **54**
Wallace, Perry E. **47**
Wallace, Rasheed **56**
Ward, Andre **62**
Ware, Andre **37**
Washington, Gene **63**
Washington, Kenny **50**
Washington, MaliVai **8**
Watson, Bob **25**
Watts, J. C., Jr. **14, 38**

Weah, George **58**
Weathers, Carl **10**
Webber, Chris **15, 30, 59**
Weekes, Kevin **67**
Westbrook, Peter **20**
Whitaker, Pernell **10**
White, Bill **1, 48**
White, Jesse **22**
White, Reggie **6, 50**
White, Willye **67**
Whitfield, Fred **23**
Whitfield, Mal **60**
Wilbon, Michael **68**
Wilkens, Lenny **11**
Williams, Doug **22**
Williams, Ken **68**
Williams, Lauryn **58**
Williams, Natalie **31**
Williams, Serena **20, 41, 73**
Williams, Stevie **71**
Williams, Venus **17, 34, 62**
Williamson, Fred **67**
Willingham, Tyrone **43**
Willis, Bill **68**
Willis, Dontrelle **55**
Wills, Maury **73**
Wilson, Sunnie **7, 55**
Winfield, Dave **5**
Winkfield, Jimmy **42**
Woodruff, John **68**
Woods, Tiger **14, 31**
Woodward, Lynette **67**
Worthy, James **49**
Wright, Rayfield **70**
Yeboah, Emmanuel Ofosu **53**
Young, Donald, Jr. **57**
Young, Jimmy **54**

Television

Akil, Mara Brock **60**
Akinnuoye-Agbaje, Adewale **56**
Alexander, Khandi **43**
Ali, Tatyana **73**
Allen, Byron **3**
Allen, Debbie **13, 42**
Allen, Marcus **20**
Amos, John **8, 62**
Anderson, Anthony **51**
Anderson, Eddie "Rochester" **30**
Arkadie, Kevin **17**
Arnez J **53**
Arnold, Tichina **63**
Babatunde, Obba **35**
Banks, Michelle **59**
Banks, William **11**
Barclay, Paris **37**
Barden, Don H. **9**
Bassett, Angela **6, 23, 62**
Beach, Michael **26**
Beaton, Norman **14**
Beauvais, Garcelle **29**
Belafonte, Harry **4, 65**
Bellamy, Bill **12**
Bennett, Louise **69**
Bentley, Lamont **53**
Berry, Bertice **8, 55**
Berry, Fred "Rerun" **48**
Berry, Halle **4, 19, 57**
Blackmon, Brenda **58**
Blackwood, Maureen **37**
Blacque, Taurean **58**
Blake, Asha **26**
Bleu, Corbin **65**

Bonet, Lisa **58**
Boston, Kelvin E. **25**
Bowser, Yvette Lee **17**
Bradley, Ed **2, 59**
Brady, Wayne **32, 71**
Brandy **14, 34, 72**
Braugher, Andre **13, 58**
Bridges, Todd **37**
Brooks, Avery **9**
Brooks, Golden **62**
Brooks, Hadda **40**
Brooks, Mehcad **62**
Brown, James **22**
Brown, Joe **29**
Brown, Les **5**
Brown, Tony **3**
Brown, Vivian **27**
Brown, Warren **61**
Browne, Roscoe Lee **66**
Bruce, Bruce **56**
Burnett, Charles **16, 68**
Burton, LeVar **8**
Byrd, Eugene **64**
Byrd, Robert **11**
Caldwell, Benjamin **46**
Cameron, Earl **44**
Campbell, Naomi **1, 31**
Campbell-Martin, Tisha **8, 42**
Cannon, Nick **47, 73**
Cannon, Reuben **50**
Carroll, Diahann **9**
Carson, Lisa Nicole **21**
Carter, Nell **39**
Cash, Rosalind **28**
Cedric the Entertainer **29, 60**
Chappelle, Dave **50**
Cheadle, Don **19, 52**
Chestnut, Morris **31**
Chideya, Farai **14, 61**
Christian, Spencer **15**
Ciara, Barbara **69**
Clack, Zoanne **73**
Clash, Kevin **14**
Clayton, Xernona **3, 45**
Cole, Nat King **17**
Cole, Natalie **17, 60**
Coleman, Gary **35**
Corbi, Lana **42**
Cornelius, Don **4**
Cosby, Bill **7, 26, 59**
Crothers, Scatman **19**
Curry, Mark **17**
Curtis-Hall, Vondie **17**
Davidson, Tommy **21**
Davis, Eisa **68**
Davis, Ossie **5, 50**
Davis, Viola **34**
de Passe, Suzanne **25**
De Shields, André **72**
Dee, Ruby **8, 50, 68**
Deezer D **53**
Devine, Loretta **24**
Dickerson, Eric **27**
Dickerson, Ernest **6**
Diggs, Taye **25, 63**
Dixon, Ivan **69**
Dourdan, Gary **37**
Dre, Dr. **10**
Duke, Bill **3**
Dungey, Merrin **62**
Dutton, Charles S. **4, 22**
Earthquake **55**
Ejiofor, Chiwetel **67**

Elba, Idris **49**
Elder, Larry **25**
Elise, Kimberly **32**
Emmanuel, Alphonsia **38**
Ephriam, Mablean **29**
Epperson, Sharon **54**
Erving, Julius **18, 47**
Esposito, Giancarlo **9**
Eubanks, Kevin **15**
Evans, Harry **25**
Faison, Donald **50**
Faison, Frankie **55**
Falana, Lola **42**
Fargas, Antonio **50**
Fields, Kim **36**
Fishburne, Laurence **4, 22, 70**
Flavor Flav **67**
Fox, Rick **27**
Foxx, Jamie **15, 48**
Foxx, Redd **2**
Frazier, Kevin **58**
Freeman, Aaron **52**
Freeman, Al, Jr. **11**
Freeman, Morgan **2, 20, 62**
Freeman, Yvette **27**
Gaines, Ernest J. **7**
Gibson, Tyrese **27, 62**
Givens, Adele **62**
Givens, Robin **4, 25, 58**
Glover, Danny **3, 24**
Glover, Savion **14**
Goldberg, Whoopi **4, 33, 69**
Goode, Mal **13**
Gooding, Cuba, Jr. **16, 62**
Gordon, Ed **10, 53**
Gossett, Louis, Jr. **7**
Gray, Darius **69**
Greely, M. Gasby **27**
Greene, Petey **65**
Grier, David Alan **28**
Grier, Pam **9, 31**
Guillaume, Robert **3, 48**
Gumbel, Bryant **14**
Gumbel, Greg **8**
Gunn, Moses **10**
Gurira, Danai **73**
Guy, Jasmine **2**
Haley, Alex **4**
Hall, Arsenio **58**
Hamilton, Lisa Gay **71**
Hampton, Henry **6**
Hardison, Kadeem **22**
Harewood, David **52**
Harper, Hill **32, 65**
Harrell, Andre **9, 30**
Harris, Naomie **55**
Harris, Robin **7**
Harvey, Steve **18, 58**
Hatchett, Glenda **32**
Hayes, Isaac **20, 58, 73**
Haynes, Trudy **44**
Haysbert, Dennis **42**
Hemsley, Sherman **19**
Henderson, Jeff **72**
Henriques, Julian **37**
Henry, Lenny **9, 52**
Henson, Darrin **33**
Hickman, Fred **11**
Hill, Dulé **29**
Hill, Lauryn **20, 53**
Hinderas, Natalie **5**
Hines, Gregory **1, 42**
Holmes, Amy **69**

Holt, Lester **66**
Horne, Lena **5**
Hounsou, Djimon **19, 45**
Houston, Whitney **7, 28**
Howard, Sherri **36**
Howard, Terrence **59**
Hudson, Ernie **72**
Huggins, Edie **71**
Hughley, D. L. **23**
Hunter-Gault, Charlayne **6, 31**
Hyman, Earle **25**
Ice-T **6, 31**
Ifill, Gwen **28**
Iman **4, 33**
Ingram, Rex **5**
Jackson, George **19**
Jackson, Janet **6, 30, 68**
Jackson, Randy **40**
Jackson, Tom **70**
Jarrett, Vernon D. **42**
Joe, Yolanda **21**
Johnson, Beverly **2**
Johnson, Linton Kwesi **37**
Johnson, Robert L. **3, 39**
Johnson, Rodney Van **28**
Jones, Bobby **20**
Jones, James Earl **3, 49**
Jones, Orlando **30**
Jones, Quincy **8, 30**
Kaufman, Monica **66**
Kelley, Malcolm David **59**
Kennedy-Overton, Jayne Harris **46**
Keys, Alicia **32, 68**
King, Gayle **19**
King, Regina **22, 45**
King, Woodie, Jr. **27**
Kirby, George **14**
Kitt, Eartha **16**
Knight, Gladys **16, 66**
Kodjoe, Boris **34**
Kotto, Yaphet **7**
La Salle, Eriq **12**
LaBelle, Patti **13, 30**
Langhart Cohen, Janet **19, 60**
Lathan, Sanaa **27**
Lawrence, Martin **6, 27, 60**
Lawson, Jennifer **1, 50**
Lemmons, Kasi **20**
Lesure, James **64**
Lewis, Ananda **28**
Lewis, Byron E. **13**
Lewis, Emmanuel **36**
Lil' Kim **28**
Lindo, Delroy **18, 45**
LisaRaye **27**
LL Cool J **16, 49**
Lofton, James **42**
Long, Loretta **58**
Long, Nia **17**
Lover, Ed **10**
Luke, Derek **61**
Lumbly, Carl **47**
Mabrey, Vicki **26**
Mabuza-Suttle, Felicia **43**
Mac, Bernie **29, 61, 72**
Madison, Paula **37**
Malco, Romany **71**
Manigault-Stallworth, Omarosa **69**
Martin, Helen **31**
Martin, Jesse L. **31**
Mathis, Greg **26**
Mayo, Whitman **32**
McBride, Chi **73**

McCoo, Marilyn **53**
McCrary Anthony, Crystal **70**
McDaniel, Hattie **5**
McEwen, Mark **5**
McFarland, Roland **49**
McGlowan, Angela **64**
McKee, Lonette **12**
McKenzie, Vashti M. **29**
McKinney, Nina Mae **40**
McQueen, Butterfly **6, 54**
Meadows, Tim **30**
Mello, Breno **73**
Mercado-Valdes, Frank **43**
Merkerson, S. Epatha **47**
Michele, Michael **31**
Mickelbury, Penny **28**
Miller, Cheryl **10**
Mitchell, Brian Stokes **21**
Mitchell, Kel **66**
Mitchell, Russ **21, 73**
Mo'Nique **35**
Mooney, Paul **37**
Moore, Chante **26**
Moore, Melba **21**
Moore, Shemar **21**
Morgan, Joe Leonard **9**
Morgan, Tracy **61**
Morris, Garrett **31**
Morris, Greg **28**
Morton, Joe **18**
Mos Def **30**
Moses, Gilbert **12**
Moss, Carlton **17**
Murphy, Eddie **4, 20, 61**
Muse, Clarence Edouard **21**
Myles, Kim **69**
Nash, Johnny **40**
Nash, Niecy **66**
Neal, Elise **29**
Nichols, Nichelle **11**
Nissel, Angela **42**
Neville, Arthel **53**
Norman, Christina **47**
Norman, Maidie **20**
Odetta **37**
Okonedo, Sophie **67**
Oliver, Pam **54**
Onwurah, Ngozi **38**
Orman, Roscoe **55**
Palmer, Keke **68**
Parker, Nicole Ari **52**
Parr, Russ **51**
Payne, Allen **13**
Peete, Holly Robinson **20**
Peete, Rodney **60**
Perkins, Tony **24**
Perrineau, Harold, Jr. **51**
Perry, Lowell **30**
Perry, Tyler **40**
Phifer, Mekhi **25**
Phillips, Joseph C. **73**
Pickens, James, Jr. **59**
Pinckney, Sandra **56**
Pinkett Smith, Jada **10, 41**
Pinkston, W. Randall **24**
Pitts, Byron **71**
Poitier, Sydney Tamiia **65**
Pounder, CCH **72**
Price, Frederick K. C. **21**
Price, Hugh B. **9, 54**
Quarles, Norma **25**
Queen Latifah **1, 16, 58**
Quivers, Robin **61**

Ralph, Sheryl Lee **18**
Randle, Theresa **16**
Rashad, Ahmad **18**
Rashad, Phylicia **21**
Raven **44**
Ray, Gene Anthony **47**
Reddick, Lance **52**
Reese, Della **6, 20**
Reid, Tim **56**
Reuben, Gloria **15**
Reynolds, Star Jones **10, 27, 61**
Rhimes, Shonda Lynn **67**
Ribeiro, Alfonso **17**
Richards, Beah **30**
Richardson, Donna **39**
Richardson, LaTanya **71**
Richardson, Salli **68**
Ridley, John **69**
Roberts, Deborah **35**
Roberts, Robin **16, 54**
Robinson, Matt **69**
Robinson, Max **3**
Robinson, Shaun **36**
Rochon, Lela **16**
Rock, Chris **3, 22, 66**
Rock, The **29, 66**
Rodgers, Johnathan **6, 51**
Rodrigues, Percy **68**
Roker, Al **12, 49**
Roker, Roxie **68**
Rolle, Esther **13, 21**
Rollins, Howard E., Jr. **16**
Ross, Diana **8, 27**
Ross, Tracee Ellis **35**
Roundtree, Richard **27**
Rowan, Carl T. **1, 30**
Rowell, Victoria **13, 68**
Rudolph, Maya **46**
Run **31, 73**
Rupaul **17**
Russell, Bill **8**
Russell, Nipsey **66**
St. Jacques, Raymond **8**
St. John, Kristoff **25**
St. Patrick, Mathew **48**
Saldana, Zoe **72**
Salters, Lisa **71**
Sanford, Isabel **53**
Schultz, Michael A. **6**
Scott, Hazel **66**
Scott, Stuart **34**
Shaw, Bernard **2, 28**
Shepherd, Sherri **55**
Simmons, Henry **55**
Simmons, Jamal **72**
Simpson, Carole **6, 30**
Simpson, O. J. **15**
Sinbad **1, 16**
Smiley, Tavis **20, 68**
Smith, Anjela Lauren **44**
Smith, B(arbara) **11**
Smith, Ian **62**
Smith, Roger Guenveur **12**
Smith, Tasha **73**
Smith, Will **8, 18, 53**
Stewart, Alison **13**
Stokes, Carl **10, 73**
Stone, Chuck **9**
Sykes, Wanda **48**
Syler, Rene **53**
Swann, Lynn **28**
Tate, Larenz **15**
Taylor, Jason **70**

Taylor, Karin **34**
Taylor, Meshach **4**
Taylor, Regina **9, 46**
Thigpen, Lynne **17, 41**
Thomas-Graham, Pamela **29**
Thomason, Marsha **47**
Thompson, Kenan **52**
Thoms, Tracie **61**
Tirico, Mike **68**
Torres, Gina **52**
Torry, Guy **31**
Toussaint, Lorraine **32**
Townsend, Robert **4, 23**
Tucker, Chris **13, 23, 62**
Tunie, Tamara **63**
Tyler, Aisha N. **36**
Tyson, Cicely **7, 51**
Uggams, Leslie **23**
Underwood, Blair **7, 27**
Union, Gabrielle **31**
Usher **23, 56**
Van Peebles, Mario **2, 51**
Van Peebles, Melvin **7**
Vaughn, Countess **53**
Vereen, Ben **4**
Walker, Eamonn **37**
Ware, Andre **37**
Warfield, Marsha **2**
Warner, Malcolm-Jamal **22, 36**
Warren, Michael **27**
Warwick, Dionne **18**
Washington, Denzel **1, 16**
Washington, Isaiah **62**
Watson, Carlos **50**
Wattleton, Faye **9**
Watts, Rolonda **9**
Wayans, Damon **8, 41**
Wayans, Keenen Ivory **18**
Wayans, Marlon **29**
Wayans, Shawn **29**
Weathers, Carl **10**
Wesley, Richard **73**
Whack, Rita Coburn **36**
Whitfield, Lynn **1, 18**
Wilbon, Michael **68**
Wilkins, Roger **2**
Williams, Armstrong **29**
Williams, Billy Dee **8**
Williams, Clarence, III **26**
Williams, Juan **35**
Williams, Malinda **57**
Williams, Montel **4, 57**
Williams, Russell, II **70**
Williams, Samm-Art **21**
Williams, Vanessa A. **32, 66**
Williams, Vanessa L. **4, 17**
Williams, Wendy **62**
Williamson, Mykelti **22**
Wills, Maury **73**
Wilson, Chandra **57**
Wilson, Debra **38**
Wilson, Dorien **55**
Wilson, Flip **21**
Winfield, Paul **2, 45**
Winfrey, Oprah **2, 15, 61**
Witherspoon, John **38**
Wright, Jeffrey **54**
Yarbrough, Cedric **51**
Yoba, Malik **11**

Theater

Adams, Osceola Macarthy **31**
Ailey, Alvin **8**

Alexander, Khandi 43
Allen, Debbie 13, 42
Amos, John 8, 62
Anderson, Carl 48
Andrews, Bert 13
Angelou, Maya 1, 15
Anthony, Trey 63
Arkadie, Kevin 17
Armstrong, Vanessa Bell 24
Arnez J 53
Babatunde, Obba 35
Bandele, Biyi 68
Baraka, Amiri 1, 38
Barnett, Etta Moten 56
Barrett, Lindsay 43
Bassett, Angela 6, 23, 62
Beach, Michael 26
Beaton, Norman 14
Belafonte, Harry 4, 65
Bennett, Louise 69
Borders, James 9
Branch, William Blackwell 39
Brooks, Avery 9
Brown, Oscar, Jr. 53
Browne, Roscoe Lee 66
Bruce, Bruce 56
Caldwell, Benjamin 46
Calloway, Cab 14
Cameron, Earl 44
Campbell, Naomi 1
Carroll, Diahann 9
Carroll, Vinnette 29
Carter, Nell 39
Cash, Rosalind 28
Cheadle, Don 19, 52
Chenault, John 40
Childress, Alice 15
Clarke, Hope 14
Cleage, Pearl 17, 64
Cook, Will Marion 40
Corthron, Kia 43
Curtis-Hall, Vondie 17
Dadié, Bernard 34
David, Keith 27
Davis, Eisa 68
Davis, Ossie 5, 50
Davis, Sammy, Jr. 18
Davis, Viola 34
De Shields, André 72
Dee, Ruby 8, 50, 68
Devine, Loretta 24
Dieudonné 67
Diggs, Taye 25, 63
Dixon, Ivan 69
Dodson, Owen Vincent 38
Dourdan, Gary 37
Duke, Bill 3
Dunham, Katherine 4, 59
Dutton, Charles S. 4, 22
Ejiofor, Chiwetel 67
Elba, Idris 49
Elder, Lonne, III 38
Emmanuel, Alphonsia 38
Epps, Mike 60
Esposito, Giancarlo 9
Europe, James Reese 10
Faison, Frankie 55
Falana, Lola 42
Fargas, Antonio 50
Fields, Felicia P. 60
Fishburne, Laurence 4, 22, 70
Franklin, J. E. 44
Freeman, Aaron 52

Freeman, Al, Jr. 11
Freeman, Morgan 2, 20, 62
Freeman, Yvette 27
Fuller, Charles 8
Givens, Adele 62
Glover, Danny 1, 24
Glover, Savion 14
Goldberg, Whoopi 4, 33, 69
Gordone, Charles 15
Gossett, Louis, Jr. 7
Graves, Denyce Antoinette 19, 57
Greaves, William 38
Grier, Pam 9, 31
Guillaume, Robert 3, 48
Gunn, Moses 10
Gurira, Danai 73
Guy, Jasmine 2
Hall, Juanita 62
Hamilton, Lisa Gay 71
Hamlin, Larry Leon 49, 62
Hansberry, Lorraine 6
Harewood, David 52
Harris, Bill 72
Harris, Robin 7
Hayes, Teddy 40
Hemsley, Sherman 19
Higginsen, Vy 65
Hill, Dulé 29
Hill, Errol 40
Hines, Gregory 1, 42
Holder, Laurence 34
Holland, Endesha Ida Mae 3, 57
Horne, Lena 5
Hyman, Earle 25
Hyman, Phyllis 19
Ingram, Rex 5
Jackson, Millie 25
Jackson, Samuel 8, 19, 63
Jamison, Judith 7, 67
Jean-Baptiste, Marianne 17, 46
Johnson, Je'Caryous 63
Jones, James Earl 3, 49
Jones, Sarah 39
Joyner, Matilda Sissieretta 15
Kente, Gibson 52
Khumalo, Leleti 51
King, Woodie, Jr. 27
King, Yolanda 6
Kitt, Eartha 16
Kotto, Yaphet 7
La Salle, Eriq 12
Lampley, Oni Faida 43, 71
Lathan, Sanaa 27
Lee, Canada 8
Leggs, Kingsley 62
Lemmons, Kasi 20
LeNoire, Rosetta 37
Lenox, Adriane 59
Leon, Kenny 10
Lester, Adrian 46
Letson, Al 39
Lincoln, Abbey 3
Lindo, Delroy 18, 45
Lister, Marquita 65
Mabley, Jackie "Moms" 15
Marrow, Queen Esther 24
Martin, Helen 31
Martin, Jesse L. 31
McDaniel, Hattie 5
McDonald, Audra 20, 62
McFarlan, Tyron 60
McKee, Lonette 12
McQueen, Butterfly 6, 54

Mickelbury, Penny 28
Mills, Florence 22
Milner, Ron 39
Mitchell, Brian Stokes 21
Mollel, Tololwa 38
Moore, Melba 21
Morgan, Tracy 61
Moses, Gilbert 12
Moss, Carlton 17
Moss, Preacher 63
Moten, Etta 18
Muse, Clarence Edouard 21
Nicholas, Fayard 20, 57
Nicholas, Harold 20
Norman, Maidie 20
Nottage, Lynn 66
Ntshona, Winston 52
Okonedo, Sophie 67
Orlandersmith, Dael 42
Parks, Suzan-Lori 34
Payne, Allen 13
Perrineau, Harold, Jr. 51
Perry, Tyler 54
Pounder, CCH 72
Powell, Maxine 8
Premice, Josephine 41
Primus, Pearl 6
Pryor, Rain 65
Ralph, Sheryl Lee 18
Randle, Theresa 16
Rashad, Phylicia 21
Raven 44
Reese, Della 6, 20
Reid, Tim 56
Rhames, Ving 14, 50
Richards, Beah 30
Richards, Lloyd 2
Richardson, Desmond 39
Richardson, LaTanya 71
Robeson, Paul 2
Rolle, Esther 13, 21
Rollins, Howard E., Jr. 16
Rose, Anika Noni 70
Rotimi, Ola 1
St. Jacques, Raymond 8
Salter, Nikkole 73
Sanford, Isabel 53
Schultz, Michael A. 6
Scott, Harold Russell, Jr. 61
Shabazz, Attallah 6
Shange, Ntozake 8
Slocumb, Jonathan 52
Smiley, Rickey 59
Smith, Anjela Lauren 44
Smith, Anna Deavere 6, 44
Smith, Roger Guenveur 12
Snipes, Wesley 3, 24, 67
Sommore 61
Soyinka, Wole 4
Stew 69
Sundiata, Sekou 66
Talbert, David 34
Taylor, Meshach 4
Taylor, Regina 9, 46
Taylor, Ron 35
Thigpen, Lynne 17, 41
Thompson, Tazewell 13
Thurman, Wallace 16
Torres, Gina 52
Toussaint, Lorraine 32
Townsend, Robert 4, 23
Tyson, Cicely 7, 51
Uggams, Leslie 23

Underwood, Blair 7, 27
Van Peebles, Melvin 7
Vance, Courtney B. 15, 60
Vereen, Ben 4
Verrett, Shirley 66
Walcott, Derek 5
Walker, Eamonn 37
Ward, Douglas Turner 42
Washington, Denzel 1, 16
Washington, Fredi 10
Waters, Ethel 7
Watts, Reggie 52
Whitaker, Forest 2, 49, 67
White, Willard 53
Whitfield, Lynn 18
Williams, Bert 18
Williams, Billy Dee 8
Williams, Clarence, III 26
Williams, Michelle 73
Williams, Samm-Art 21
Williams, Vanessa L. 4, 17
Williamson, Mykelti 22
Wilson, August 7, 33, 55
Wilson, Dorien 55
Winfield, Paul 2, 45
Withers-Mendes, Elisabeth 64
Wolfe, George C. 6, 43
Woodard, Alfre 9
Wright, Jeffrey 54
Yarbrough, Cedric 51

Writing
Abrahams, Peter 39
Abu-Jamal, Mumia 15
Achebe, Chinua 6
Adams, Jenoyne 60
Adams-Ender, Clara 40
Adichie, Chimamanda Ngozi 64
Aidoo, Ama Ata 38
Ake, Claude 30
Akpan, Uwem 70
Al-Amin, Jamil Abdullah 6
Alexander, Margaret Walker 22
Ali, Hana Yasmeen 52
Ali, Mohammed Naseehu 60
Allen, Robert L. 38
Allen, Samuel W. 38
Amadi, Elechi 40
Ames, Wilmer 27
Anderson, Ho Che 54
Andrews, Raymond 4
Angelou, Maya 1, 15
Ansa, Tina McElroy 14
Anthony, Michael 29
Appiah, Kwame Anthony 67
Arac de Nyeko, Monica 66
Aristide, Jean-Bertrand 6, 45
Arkadie, Kevin 17
Armah, Ayi Kwei 49
Asante, Molefi Kete 3
Ashley-Ward, Amelia 23
Asim, Jabari 71
Atkins, Cholly 40
Atkins, Russell 45
Aubert, Alvin 41
Auguste, Arnold A. 47
Awoonor, Kofi 37
Azikiwe, Nnamdi 13
Ba, Mariama 30
Bahati, Wambui 60
Bailey, Chauncey 68
Baiocchi, Regina Harris 41
Baisden, Michael 25, 66

Baker, Augusta 38
Baker, Houston A., Jr. 6
Baldwin, James 1
Ballard, Allen Butler, Jr. 40
Bambara, Toni Cade 10
Bandele, Asha 36
Bandele, Biyi 68
Baquet, Dean 63
Baraka, Amiri 1, 38
Barnes, Steven 54
Barnett, Amy Du Bois 46
Barrax, Gerald William 45
Barrett, Lindsay 43
Bashir, Halima 73
Bass, Charlotta Spears 40
Bates, Karen Grigsby 40
Beah, Ishmael 69
Beals, Melba Patillo 15
Bebey, Francis 45
Beckham, Barry 41
Bell, Derrick 6
Bell, James Madison 40
Benberry, Cuesta 65
Bennett, George Harold "Hal" 45
Bennett, Gwendolyn B. 59
Bennett, Lerone, Jr. 5
Bennett, Louise 69
Benson, Angela 34
Berry, James 41
Berry, Mary Frances 7
Beti, Mongo 36
Bishop, Maurice 39
Blair, Jayson 50
Bland, Eleanor Taylor 39
Blassingame, John Wesley 40
Blockson, Charles L. 42
Blow, Charles M. 73
Bluitt, Juliann S. 14
Bolden, Tonya 32
Bontemps, Arna 8
Booker, Simeon 23
Borders, James 9
Boston, Lloyd 24
Boyd, Gerald M. 32, 59
Boyd, Suzanne 52
Bradley, David Henry, Jr. 39
Bradley, Ed 2, 59
Braithwaite, William Stanley 52
Branch, William Blackwell 39
Brand, Dionne 32
Brathwaite, Kamau 36
Brawley, Benjamin 44
Breeze, Jean "Binta" 37
Bridges, Sheila 36
Brimmer, Andrew F. 2, 48
Briscoe, Connie 15
Britt, Donna 28
Brooks, Gwendolyn 1, 28
Brower, William 49
Brown, Cecil M. 46
Brown, Claude 38
Brown, Elaine 8
Brown, Les 5
Brown, Lloyd Louis 10, 42
Brown, Marie Dutton 12
Brown, Sterling Allen 10, 64
Brown, Tony 3
Brown, Wesley 23
Browne, Roscoe Lee 66
Broyard, Anatole 68
Broyard, Bliss 68
Brutus, Dennis 38
Bryan, Ashley F. 41

Buckley, Gail Lumet 39
Bullins, Ed 25
Bunche, Ralph J. 5
Bunkley, Anita Richmond 39
Burgess, Marjorie L. 55
Burroughs, Margaret Taylor 9
Butler, Octavia 8, 43, 58
Bynum, Juanita 31, 71
Caldwell, Earl 60
Campbell, Bebe Moore 6, 24, 59
Carby, Hazel 27
Carmichael, Stokely 5, 26
Carroll, Vinnette 29
Carter, Joye Maureen 41
Carter, Martin 49
Carter, Stephen L. 4
Cartey, Wilfred 47
Cartiér, Xam Wilson 41
Cary, Lorene 3
Cary, Mary Ann Shadd 30
Cayton, Horace 26
Césaire, Aimé 48, 69
Chadiha, Jeffri 57
Channer, Colin 36
Chase-Riboud, Barbara 20, 46
Chenault, John 40
Cheney-Coker, Syl 43
Chesnutt, Charles 29
Chideya, Farai 14, 61
Childress, Alice 15
Christian, Barbara T. 44
Clack, Zoanne 73
Clark, Kenneth B. 5, 52
Clark, Septima 7
Clark-Bekedermo, J. P. 44
Clarke, Austin C. 32
Clarke, Cheryl 32
Clarke, George 32
Cleage, Pearl 17, 64
Cleaver, Eldridge 5
Cliff, Michelle 42
Clifton, Lucille 14, 64
Cobb, William Jelani 59
Cobbs, Price M. 9
Cohen, Anthony 15
Cole, Johnnetta B. 5, 43
Coleman, Wanda 48
Collins, Patricia Hill 67
Colter, Cyrus J. 36
Comer, James P. 6
Common 31, 63
Cone, James H. 3
Cook, Suzan D. Johnson 22
Cooke, Marvel 31
Coombs, Orde M. 44
Cooper, Afua 53
Cooper, Andrew W. 36
Cooper, Anna Julia 20
Cooper, J. California 12
Cornish, Sam 50
Cortez, Jayne 43
Cosby, Bill 7, 26, 59
Cosby, Camille 14
Cose, Ellis 5, 50
Cotter, Joseph Seamon, Sr. 40
Couto, Mia 45
Cox, Joseph Mason Andrew 51
Creagh, Milton 27
Crouch, Stanley 11
Cruse, Harold 54
Crutchfield, James N. 55
Cullen, Countee 8
Cuney, William Waring 44

Cunningham, Evelyn 23
Curry, George E. 23
Curtis, Christopher Paul 26
Curtis-Hall, Vondie 17
Dabydeen, David 48
Dadié, Bernard 34
D'Aguiar, Fred 50
Damas, Léon-Gontran 46
Dandridge, Raymond Garfield 45
Danner, Margaret Esse 49
Danticat, Edwidge 15, 68
Dash, Leon 47
Datcher, Michael 60
Dathorne, O.R. 52
Davis, Allison 12
Davis, Angela 5
Davis, Charles T. 48
Davis, Eisa 68
Davis, Frank Marshall 47
Davis, George 36
Davis, Nolan 45
Davis, Ossie 5, 50
Davis, Thulani 61
Dawkins, Wayne 20
de Passe, Suzanne 25
De Veaux, Alexis 44
Deggans, Eric 71
Delany, Martin R. 27
Delany, Samuel R., Jr. 9
DeLoach, Nora 30
Demby, William 51
Dent, Thomas C. 50
Dickerson, Debra J. 60
Dickey, Eric Jerome 21, 56
Diop, Birago 53
Diop, Cheikh Anta 4
Dodson, Howard, Jr. 7, 52
Dodson, Owen Vincent 38
Dove, Rita 6
Draper, Sharon Mills 16, 43
Driskell, David C. 7
Driver, David E. 11
Drummond, William J. 40
Du Bois, David Graham 45
Du Bois, W. E. B. 3
DuBois, Shirley Graham 21
Due, Tananarive 30
Dumas, Henry 41
Dunbar, Paul Laurence 8
Dunbar-Nelson, Alice Ruth Moore 44
Dunham, Katherine 4, 59
Dunnigan, Alice Allison 41
Duplechan, Larry 55
Dyson, Michael Eric 11, 40
Edmonds, Terry 17
Ekwensi, Cyprian 37
Elder, Lonne, III 38
Elliot, Lorris 37
Ellison, Ralph 7
Elmore, Ronn 21
Emanuel, James A. 46
Emecheta, Buchi 30
Estes, Rufus 29
Evans, Diana 72
Evans, Mari 26
Fabio, Sarah Webster 48
Fair, Ronald L. 47
Fanon, Frantz 44
Farah, Nuruddin 27
Farley, Christopher John 54
Farrakhan, Louis 15
Fauset, Jessie 7

Feelings, Muriel 44
Feelings, Tom 11, 47
Fields, Julia 45
Figueroa, John J. 40
Files, Lolita 35
Finner-Williams, Paris Michele 62
Fisher, Antwone 40
Fisher, Rudolph 17
Fleming, Raymond 48
Fletcher, Bill, Jr. 41
Forbes, Calvin 46
Ford, Clyde W. 40
Ford, Nick Aaron 44
Ford, Wallace 58
Forman, James 7, 51
Forrest, Leon 44
Fortune, T. Thomas 6
Foster, Cecil 32
Foster, Jylla Moore 45
Franklin, John Hope 5
Franklin, Robert M. 13
Frazier, E. Franklin 10
Frazier, Oscar 58
French, Albert 18
Fuller, Charles 8
Fuller, Hoyt 44
Gabre-Medhin, Tsegaye 64
Gaines, Ernest J. 7
Gardner, Chris 65
Gaston, Marilyn Hughes 60
Gates, Henry Louis, Jr. 3, 38, 67
Gayle, Addison, Jr. 41
George, Nelson 12
Gibson, Donald Bernard 40
Giddings, Paula 11
Gilbert, Christopher 50
Gilliard, Steve 69
Giovanni, Nikki 9, 39
Givhan, Robin Deneen 72
Gladwell, Malcolm 62
Goines, Donald 19
Golden, Marita 19
Gomez, Jewelle 30
Goodison, Lorna 71
Graham, Lawrence Otis 12
Graham, Lorenz 48
Grant, Gwendolyn Goldsby 28
Gray, Darius 69
Greaves, William 38
Greenfield, Eloise 9
Greenlee, Sam 48
Greenwood, Monique 38
Griffith, Mark Winston 8
Grimké, Archibald H. 9
Guinier, Lani 7, 30
Guy, Rosa 5
Guy-Sheftall, Beverly 13
Haley, Alex 4
Halliburton, Warren J. 49
Hamblin, Ken 10
Hamilton, Virginia 10
Hansberry, Lorraine 6
Harding, Vincent 67
Hare, Nathan 44
Harkless, Necia Desiree 19
Harper, Frances Ellen Watkins 11
Harper, Michael S. 34
Harrington, Oliver W. 9
Harris, Bill 72
Harris, Claire 34
Harris, Eddy L. 18
Harris, Jay 19
Harris, Leslie 6

Harris, Monica 18
Harrison, Alvin 28
Harrison, Calvin 28
Haskins, James 36, 54
Hayden, Robert 12
Hayes, Teddy 40
Haywood, Gar Anthony 43
Head, Bessie 28
Heard, Nathan C. 45
Hearne, John Edgar Caulwell 45
Hemphill, Essex 10
Henderson, David 53
Henderson, Stephen E. 45
Henries, A. Doris Banks 44
Henriques, Julian 37
Henry, Lenny 9, 52
Henson, Matthew 2
Herbert, Bob 63
Hercules, Frank 44
Hernton, Calvin C. 51
Hill, Donna 32
Hill, Errol 40
Hill, Leslie Pinckney 44
Hilliard, David 7
Hoagland, Everett H. 45
Hobson, Julius W. 44
Holland, Endesha Ida Mae 3, 57
Holmes, Shannon 70
Holt, Nora 38
Holton, Hugh, Jr. 39
hooks, bell 5
Horne, Frank 44
Hrabowski, Freeman A., III 22
Hudson, Cheryl 15
Hudson, Wade 15
Hughes, Langston 4
Hull, Akasha Gloria 45
Hunter-Gault, Charlayne 6, 31
Hurston, Zora Neale 3
Iceberg Slim 11
Ifill, Gwen 28
Ilibagiza, Immaculée 66
Jackson, Fred James 25
Jackson, George 14
Jackson, Sheneska 18
Jarrett, Vernon D. 42
Jasper, Kenji 39
Jenkins, Beverly 14
Joachim, Paulin 34
Joe, Yolanda 21
Johnson, Angela 52
Johnson, Charles 1
Johnson, Charles S. 12
Johnson, Georgia Douglas 41
Johnson, James Weldon 5
Johnson, John H. 3, 54
Johnson, Linton Kwesi 37
Johnson, Mat 31
Johnson, R. M. 36
Jolley, Willie 28
Jones, Edward P. 43, 67
Jones, Gayl 37
Jones, Orlando 30
Jones, Sarah 39
Jordan, June 7, 35
Josey, E. J. 10
July, William 27
Just, Ernest Everett 3
Kamau, Kwadwo Agymah 28
Karenga, Maulana 10, 71
Kariuki, J. M. 67
Kay, Jackie 37
Kayira, Legson 40

Kearney, Janis 54
Keene, John 73
Kendrick, Erika 57
Kennedy, Adrienne 11
Kennedy, Florynce 12, 33
Kennedy, Randall 40
Khanga, Yelena 6
Killens, John O. 54
Kimbro, Dennis 10
Kincaid, Jamaica 4
King, Colbert I. 69
King, Coretta Scott 3, 57
King, Preston 28
King, Woodie, Jr. 27
King, Yolanda 6
Kitt, Sandra 23
Knight, Etheridge 37
Kobia, Samuel 43
Komunyakaa, Yusef 9
Kunjufu, Jawanza 3, 50
Lacy, Sam 30, 46
Ladner, Joyce A. 42
Laferriere, Dany 33
LaGuma, Alex 30
Lamming, George 35
Lampley, Oni Faida 43, 71
Larsen, Nella 10
Lawrence, Martin 6, 27, 60
Lawrence-Lightfoot, Sara 10
Lemmons, Kasi 20
Lester, Julius 9
Letson, Al 39
Lewis, David Levering 9
Lewis, Samella 25
Lincoln, C. Eric 38
Little, Benilde 21
Locke, Alain 10
Lorde, Audre 6
Louis, Errol T. 8
Loury, Glenn 36
Lowe, Herbert 57
Mabry, Marcus 70
Mabuza-Suttle, Felicia 43
Madhubuti, Haki R. 7
Madison, Paula 37
Major, Clarence 9
Makeba, Miriam 2, 50
Malveaux, Julianne 32, 70
Manley, Ruth 34
Marechera, Dambudzo 39
Markham, E. A. 37
Marshall, Paule 7
Martin, Roland S. 49
Mason, Felicia 31
Massaquoi, Hans J. 30
Mathabane, Mark 5
Maynard, Nancy Hicks 73
Maynard, Robert C. 7
Mays, Benjamin E. 7
Mbaye, Mariétou 31
McBride, James 35
McCall, Nathan 8
McCrary Anthony, Crystal 70
McDuffie, Dwayne 62
McFadden, Bernice L. 39
McGruder, Robert 22, 35
McKay, Claude 6
McKinney Hammond, Michelle 51
McKinney-Whetstone, Diane 27
McMillan, Rosalynn A. 36
McMillan, Terry 4, 17, 53
McPherson, James Alan 70
Memmi, Albert 37

Mengestu, Dinaw 66
Meredith, James H. 11
Mfume, Kweisi 6, 41
Micheaux, Oscar 7
Mickelbury, Penny 28
Milner, Ron 39
Mitchell, Elvis 67
Mitchell, Loften 31
Mitchell, Russ 21, 73
Mitchell, Sharon 36
Mofolo, Thomas Mokopu 37
Mollel, Tololwa 38
Monroe, Bryan 71
Monroe, Mary 35
Moore, Jessica Care 30
Morrison, Toni 2, 15
Mosley, Walter 5, 25, 68
Moss, Carlton 17
Mossell, Gertrude Bustill 40
Moutoussamy-Ashe, Jeanne 7
Mowry, Jess 7
Mphalele, Es'kia (Ezekiel) 40
Mudimbe, V.Y. 61
Mugo, Micere Githae 32
Mullen, Harryette 34
Murphy, John H. 42
Murray, Albert L. 33
Murray, Pauli 38
Mwangi, Meja 40
Myers, Walter Dean 8, 70
Naylor, Gloria 10, 42
Neal, Larry 38
Nelson, Jill 6, 54
Neto, António Agostinho 43
Newkirk, Pamela 69
Newton, Huey 2
Ngugi wa Thiong'o 29, 61
Nissel, Angela 42
Nkosi, Lewis 46
Nkrumah, Kwame 3
Norton, Meredith 72
Nugent, Richard Bruce 39
Nunez, Elizabeth 62
Ojikutu, Bayo 66
Okara, Gabriel 37
Oliver, John J., Jr. 48
Onwueme, Tess Osonye 23
Orlandersmith, Dael 42
Owens, Major 6
Oyono, Ferdinand 38
Packer, Z. Z. 64
Page, Clarence 4
Painter, Nell Irvin 24
Palmer, Everard 37
Parker, Pat 19
Parker, Star 70
Parks, Suzan-Lori 34
Patterson, Orlando 4
Payne, Ethel L. 28
Peters, Lenrie 43
Petry, Ann 19
Philip, Marlene Nourbese 32
Phillips, Joseph C. 73
Piper, Adrian 71
Pitts, Leonard, Jr. 54
Poussaint, Alvin F. 5, 67
Powell, Adam Clayton, Jr. 3
Powell, Kevin 31
Pressley, Condace L. 41
Prince, Richard E. 71
Prince-Bythewood, Gina 31
Pryor, Rain 65
Pryor, Richard 3, 24, 56

Quarles, Benjamin Arthur 18
Rahman, Aishah 37
Randall, Alice 38
Randall, Dudley 8, 55
Raspberry, William 2
Reagon, Bernice Johnson 7
Reddick, Lawrence Dunbar 20
Redding, J. Saunders 26
Redmond, Eugene 23
Reed, Ishmael 8
Rhimes, Shonda Lynn 67
Rhoden, William C. 67
Richards, Beah 30
Ridley, John 69
Riggs, Marlon 5
Riley, Rochelle 50
Ringgold, Faith 4
Robeson, Eslanda Goode 13
Robinson, Aminah 50
Robinson, Matt 69
Rogers, Joel Augustus 30
Rotimi, Ola 1
Rowan, Carl T. 1, 30
Run 31, 73
Sadlier, Rosemary 62
Saint James, Synthia 12
St. John, Kristoff 25
Salih, Al-Tayyib 37
Sanchez, Sonia 17, 51
Sanders, Dori 8
Sapphire 14
Saro-Wiwa, Kenule 39
Schomburg, Arthur Alfonso 9
Schuyler, George Samuel 40
Seale, Bobby 3
Sembène, Ousmane 13, 62
Senghor, Léopold Sédar 12, 66
Sengstacke, John 18
Senior, Olive 9
Shabazz, Attallah 6
Shabazz, Ilyasah 36
Shakur, Assata 6
Shange, Ntozake 8
Shaw, Bernard 2, 28
Shipp, E. R. 15
Simone, Nina 15, 41
Simpson, Carole 6, 30
Singleton, John 2, 30
Sister Souljah 11
Skinner, Kiron K. 65
Smiley, Tavis 20, 68
Smith, Anna Deavere 6
Smith, B(arbara) 11
Smith, Barbara 28
Smith, Bruce W. 53
Smith, Danyel 40
Smith, Jessie Carney 35
Smith, Mary Carter 26
Smith, Stephen A. 69
Smith, Zadie 51
Snowden, Frank M., Jr. 67
Somé, Malidoma Patrice 10
Southgate, Martha 58
Sowell, Thomas 2
Soyinka, Wole 4
Spencer, Anne 27
Spriggs, William 67
Staples, Brent 8
Stewart, Alison 13
Stone, Chuck 9
Stringer, Vickie 58
Sundiata, Sekou 66
Tademy, Lalita 36

Talbert, David **34**
Talley, André Leon **56**
Tate, Eleanora E. **20, 55**
Taulbert, Clifton Lemoure **19**
Taylor, Kristin Clark **8**
Taylor, Mildred D. **26**
Taylor, Susan C. **62**
Taylor, Susan L. **10**
Thomas, Michael **69**
Thomas, Trisha R. **65**
Thomas-Graham, Pamela **29**
Thornton, Yvonne S. **69**
Thurman, Howard **3**
Tillis, Frederick **40**
Tolson, Melvin **37**
Toomer, Jean **6**
Touré, Askia (Muhammad Abu Bakr el) **47**
Townsend, Robert **4**
Trotter, Monroe **9**
Tucker, Cynthia **15, 61**
Turner, Henry McNeal **5**
Tutuola, Amos **30**
Tyree, Omar Rashad **21**

Tyson, Asha **39**
Tyson, Neil deGrasse **15, 65**
Van Peebles, Melvin **7**
van Sertima, Ivan **25**
Vega, Marta Moreno **61**
Vera, Yvonne **32**
Verdelle, A. J. **26**
Wade-Gayles, Gloria Jean **41**
Walcott, Derek **5**
Walker, Alice **1, 43**
Walker, Margaret **29**
Walker, Rebecca **50**
Wallace, Michele Faith **13**
Wallace, Phyllis A. **9**
Ward, Douglas Turner **42**
Washington, Booker T. **4**
Washington, Harriet A. **69**
Washington, James, Jr. **38**
Washington, Laura S. **18**
Wattleton, Faye **9**
Wayans, Damon **8, 41**
Weaver, Afaa Michael **37**
Webb, Veronica **10**
Weems, Renita J. **44**

Wells-Barnett, Ida B. **8**
Wesley, Dorothy Porter **19**
Wesley, Richard **73**
Wesley, Valerie Wilson **18**
West, Cornel **5, 33**
West, Dorothy **12, 54**
Whack, Rita Coburn **36**
Wharton, Clifton R., Jr. **7**
Whitaker, Mark **21, 47**
White, Walter F. **4**
Whitfield, Van **34**
Wideman, John Edgar **5**
Wilbekin, Emil **63**
Wiley, Ralph **8**
Wilkerson, Isabel **71**
Wilkins, Roger **2**
Wilkins, Roy **4**
Williams, Armstrong **29**
Williams, Fannie Barrier **27**
Williams, George Washington **18**
Williams, John A. **27**
Williams, Juan **35**
Williams, Patricia **11, 54**
Williams, Robert F. **11**

Williams, Samm-Art **21**
Williams, Saul **31**
Williams, Sherley Anne **25**
Williams, Stanley "Tookie" **29, 57**
Williams, Wendy **62**
Wilson, August **7, 33, 55**
Wilson, Mary **28**
Wilson, William Julius **22**
Winans, Marvin L. **17**
Wiwa, Ken **67**
Wolfe, George C. **6, 43**
Woods, Mattiebelle **63**
Woods, Scott **55**
Woods, Teri **69**
Woodson, Carter G. **2**
Worrill, Conrad **12**
Wright, Bruce McMarion **3, 52**
Wright, Richard **5**
X, Marvin **45**
Yarbrough, Camille **40**
Yette, Samuel F. **63**
Young, Whitney M., Jr., **4**
Youngblood, Shay **32**
Zane **71**
Zook, Kristal Brent **62**

Cumulative Subject Index

Volume numbers appear in **bold**

A Better Chance
Lewis, William M., Jr. **40**

AA
See Alcoholics Anonymous

AAAS
See American Association for the Advancement of Science

Aaron Gunner series
Haywood, Gar Anthony **43**

AARP
Dixon, Margaret **14**
Smith, Marie F. **70**

ABC
See American Broadcasting Company

Abstract expressionism
Lewis, Norman **39**

A. C. Green Youth Foundation
Green, A. C. **32**

Academy awards
Austin, Patti **24**
Freeman, Morgan **2, 20, 62**
Goldberg, Whoopi **4, 33, 69**
Gooding, Cuba, Jr. **16, 62**
Gossett, Louis, Jr. **7**
Jean-Baptiste, Marianne **17, 46**
McDaniel, Hattie **5**
Poitier, Sidney **11, 36**
Prince **18, 65**
Richie, Lionel **27, 65**
Washington, Denzel **1, 16**
Whitaker, Forest **2, 49, 67**
Williams, Russell, II **70**
Wonder, Stevie **11, 53**

Academy of Praise
Kenoly, Ron **45**

A cappella
Cooke, Sam **17**
Reagon, Bernice Johnson **7**

Access Hollywood
Robinson, Shaun **36**

ACDL
See Association for Constitutional Democracy in Liberia

ACLU
See American Civil Liberties Union

Acquired immune deficiency syndrome (AIDS)
Ashe, Arthur **1, 18**
Atim, Julian **66**
Broadbent, Hydeia **36**
Cargill, Victoria A. **43**
Gayle, Helene D. **3, 46**
Hale, Lorraine **8**
Johnson, Earvin "Magic" **3, 39**
Lewis-Thornton, Rae **32**
Mboup, Souleymane **10**
Moutoussamy-Ashe, Jeanne **7**
Norman, Pat **10**
Ojikutu, Bisola **65**
Okaalet, Peter **58**
Pickett, Cecil **39**
Riggs, Marlon **5, 44**
Satcher, David **7, 57**
Seele, Pernessa **46**
Wilson, Phill **9**
Zulu, Princess Kasune **54**

Act*1 Personnel Services
Howroyd, Janice Bryant **42**

ACT-SO
See Afro-Academic Cultural, Technological, and Scientific Olympics

Acting
Aaliyah **30**
Adams, Osceola Macarthy **31**
Ailey, Alvin **8**
Akinnuoye-Agbaje, Adewale **56**
Alexander, Khandi **43**
Ali, Tatyana **73**
Allen, Debbie **13, 42**
Amos, John **8, 62**
Anderson, Anthony **51**
Anderson, Carl **48**
Anderson, Eddie "Rochester" **30**
Angelou, Maya **1, 15**
Armstrong, Vanessa Bell **24**
Ashanti **37**
Babatunde, Obba **35**
Bahati, Wambui **60**
Baker, Josephine **3**
Banks, Michelle **59**
Banks, Tyra **11, 50**
Barnett, Etta Moten **56**
Bassett, Angela **6, 23, 62**
Beach, Michael **26**

Beals, Jennifer **12**
Beaton, Norman **14**
Beauvais, Garcelle **29**
Bennett, Louise **69**
Bentley, Lamont **53**
Berry, Fred "Rerun" **48**
Berry, Halle **4, 19, 57**
Beyoncé **39, 70**
Bivins, Michael **72**
Blacque, Taurean **58**
Blanks, Billy **22**
Blige, Mary J. **20, 34, 60**
Bonet, Lisa **58**
Borders, James **9**
Bow Wow **35**
Brady, Wayne **32, 71**
Branch, William Blackwell **39**
Braugher, Andre **13, 58**
Bridges, Todd **37**
Brooks, Avery **9**
Brooks, Golden **62**
Brooks, Mehcad **62**
Brown, Jim **11**
Browne, Roscoe Lee **66**
Byrd, Eugene **64**
Caesar, Shirley **19**
Calloway, Cab **14**
Cameron, Earl **44**
Campbell, Naomi **1, 31**
Campbell-Martin, Tisha **8, 42**
Cannon, Nick **47, 73**
Carroll, Diahann **9**
Carson, Lisa Nicole **21**
Carey, Mariah **32, 53, 69**
Cash, Rosalind **28**
Cedric the Entertainer **29, 60**
Cheadle, Don **19, 52**
Chestnut, Morris **31**
Childress, Alice **15**
Chong, Rae Dawn **62**
Chweneyagae, Presley **63**
Clarke, Hope **14**
Cliff, Jimmy **28**
Cole, Nat King **17**
Cole, Natalie **17, 60**
Coleman, Gary **35**
Combs, Sean "Puffy" **17, 43**
Cosby, Bill **7, 26, 59**
Crothers, Scatman **19**
Curry, Mark **17**
Curtis-Hall, Vondie **17**
Dandridge, Dorothy **3**
David, Keith **27**
Davidson, Jaye **5**

Davis, Eisa **68**
Davis, Guy **36**
Davis, Ossie **5, 50**
Davis, Sammy, Jr. **18**
Davis, Viola **34**
Dawson, Rosario **72**
De Shields, André **72**
Dee, Ruby **8, 50, 68**
Devine, Loretta **24**
Diesel, Vin **29**
Diggs, Taye **25, 63**
Dixon, Ivan **69**
DMX **28, 64**
Dourdan, Gary **37**
Duke, Bill **3**
Duncan, Michael Clarke **26**
Dungey, Merrin **62**
Dutton, Charles S. **4, 22**
Ejiofor, Chiwetel **67**
Elba, Idris **49**
Elise, Kimberly **32**
Emmanuel, Alphonsia **38**
Epps, Mike **60**
Epps, Omar **23, 59**
Esposito, Giancarlo **9**
Everett, Francine **23**
Faison, Donald **50**
Faison, Frankie **55**
Falana, Lola **42**
Fargas, Antonio **50**
Fields, Felicia P. **60**
Fields, Kim **36**
Fetchit, Stepin **32**
Fishburne, Laurence **4, 22, 70**
Fox, Rick **27**
Fox, Vivica A. **15, 53**
Foxx, Jamie **15, 48**
Foxx, Redd **2**
Freeman, Al, Jr. **11**
Freeman, Morgan **2, 20, 62**
Freeman, Yvette **27**
Gaye, Nona **56**
Gibson, Althea **8, 43**
Gibson, Tyrese **27, 62**
Ginuwine **35**
Givens, Adele **62**
Givens, Robin **4, 25, 58**
Glover, Danny **1, 24**
Goldberg, Whoopi **4, 33, 69**
Gooding, Cuba, Jr. **16, 62**
Gordon, Dexter **25**
Gossett, Louis, Jr. **7**
Greaves, William **38**
Grier, David Alan **28**

Grier, Pam **9, 31**
Guillaume, Robert **3, 48**
Gunn, Moses **10**
Gurira, Danai **73**
Guy, Jasmine **2**
Hall, Arsenio **58**
Hamilton, Lisa Gay **71**
Hamlin, Larry Leon **49, 62**
Hammer, M. C. **20**
Hammond, Fred **23**
Hardison, Kadeem **22**
Harewood, David **52**
Harper, Hill **32, 65**
Harris, Naomie **55**
Harris, Robin **7**
Harvey, Steve **18, 58**
Hawkins, Screamin' Jay **30**
Hayes, Isaac **20, 58, 73**
Haysbert, Dennis **42**
Hemsley, Sherman **19**
Henry, Lenny **9, 52**
Henson, Taraji **58**
Hill, Dulé **29**
Hill, Lauryn **20, 53**
Hines, Gregory **1, 42**
Horne, Lena **5**
Hounsou, Djimon **19, 45**
Houston, Whitney **7, 28**
Howard, Sherri **36**
Howard, Terrence **59**
Hudson, Ernie **72**
Hudson, Jennifer **63**
Hughley, D. L. **23**
Hyman, Earle **25**
Ice Cube **8, 30, 60**
Iman **4, 33**
Ingram, Rex **5**
Ja Rule **35**
Jackson, Janet **6, 30, 68**
Jackson, Michael **19, 53**
Jackson, Millie **25**
Jackson, Samuel **8, 19, 63**
Jean-Baptiste, Marianne **17, 46**
Johnson, Rafer **33**
Johnson, Rodney Van **28**
Jones, James Earl **3, 49**
Jones, Orlando **30**
Jorge, Seu **73**
Kelley, Elijah **65**
Kelley, Malcolm David **59**
Kennedy-Overton, Jayne Harris **46**
Khumalo, Leleti **51**
King, Regina **22, 45**
King, Woodie, Jr. **27**
Kirby, George **14**
Kitt, Eartha **16**
Knight, Gladys **16, 66**
Kodhoe, Boris **34**
Kotto, Yaphet **7**
La Salle, Eriq **12**
LaBelle, Patti **13, 30**
Lampley, Oni Faida **43, 71**
Lane, Charles **3**
Lassiter, Roy **24**
Lathan, Sanaa **27**
Lawrence, Martin **6, 27, 60**
Lee, Canada **8**
Lee, Joie **1**
Lee, Spike **5, 19**
Leggs, Kingsley **62**
Lemmons, Kasi **20**
LeNoire, Rosetta **37**
Lenox, Adriane **59**

Lester, Adrian **46**
Lesure, James **64**
Lewis, Emmanuel **36**
Lil' Kim **28**
Lincoln, Abbey **3**
Lindo, Delroy **18, 45**
LisaRaye **27**
LL Cool J **16, 49**
Love, Darlene **23**
Luke, Derek **61**
Lumbly, Carl **47**
Mabley, Jackie "Moms" **15**
Mac, Bernie **29, 61, 72**
Malco, Romany **71**
Mario **71**
Marrow, Queen Esther **24**
Martin, Helen **31**
Martin, Jesse L. **31**
Master P **21**
Mayo, Whitman **32**
McBride, Chi **73**
McDaniel, Hattie **5**
McDonald, Audra **20, 62**
McKee, Lonette **12**
McKinney, Nina Mae **40**
McQueen, Butterfly **6, 54**
Meadows, Tim **30**
Mello, Breno **73**
Merkerson, S. Epatha **47**
Michele, Michael **31**
Mitchell, Brian Stokes **21**
Mitchell, Kel **66**
Mo'Nique **35**
Moore, Chante **26**
Moore, Melba **21**
Moore, Shemar **21**
Morris, Garrett **31**
Morris, Greg **28**
Morton, Joe **18**
Mos Def **30**
Moten, Etta **18**
Murphy, Eddie **4, 20, 61**
Muse, Clarence Edouard **21**
Nash, Johnny **40**
Nash, Niecy **66**
Neal, Elise **29**
Newton, Thandie **26**
Nicholas, Fayard **20, 57**
Nicholas, Harold **20**
Nichols, Nichelle **11**
Norman, Maidie **20**
Notorious B.I.G. **20**
Ntshona, Winston **52**
Okonedo, Sophie **67**
O'Neal, Ron **46**
Orlandersmith, Dael **42**
Orman, Roscoe **55**
Parker, Nicole Ari **52**
Patton, Paula **62**
Payne, Allen **13**
Payne, Freda **58**
Peete, Holly Robinson **20**
Perrineau, Harold, Jr. **51**
Perry, Tyler **40, 54**
Phifer, Mekhi **25**
Phillips, Joseph C. **73**
Pickens, James, Jr. **59**
Pinkett Smith, Jada **10, 41**
Poitier, Sidney **11, 36**
Poitier, Sydney Tamiia **65**
Pounder, CCH **72**
Pratt, Kyla **57**
Premice, Josephine **41**

Prince **18, 65**
Pryor, Rain **65**
Pryor, Richard **3, 24, 56**
Queen Latifah **1, 16, 58**
Randle, Theresa **16**
Rashad, Phylicia **21**
Raven **44**
Ray, Gene Anthony **47**
Reddick, Lance **52**
Reese, Della **6, 20**
Reid, Tim **56**
Reuben, Gloria **15**
Rhames, Ving **14, 50**
Rhymes, Busta **31**
Ribeiro, Alfonso **17**
Richards, Beah **30**
Richards, Lloyd **2**
Richardson, LaTanya **71**
Richardson, Salli **68**
Robeson, Paul **2**
Robinson, Shaun **36**
Rock, Chris **3, 22, 66**
Rock, The **29 66**
Rodgers, Rod **36**
Rodrigues, Percy **68**
Roker, Roxie **68**
Rolle, Esther **13, 21**
Rose, Anika Noni **70**
Ross, Diana **8, 27**
Ross, Tracee Ellis **35**
Roundtree, Richard **27**
Rowell, Victoria **13, 68**
Rudolph, Maya **46**
Russell, Nipsey **66**
St. Jacques, Raymond **8**
St. John, Kristoff **25**
St. Patrick, Mathew **48**
Saldana, Zoe **72**
Salter, Nikkole **73**
Scott, Hazel **66**
Shakur, Tupac **14**
Simmons, Henry **55**
Sinbad **1, 16**
Sisqo **30**
Smith, Anjela Lauren **44**
Smith, Anna Deavere **6, 44**
Smith, B(arbara) **11**
Smith, Roger Guenveur **12**
Smith, Tasha **73**
Smith, Will **8, 18, 53**
Snipes, Wesley **3, 24, 67**
Snoop Dogg **35**
Sommore **61**
Tamia **24, 55**
Tate, Larenz **15**
Taylor, Meshach **4**
Taylor, Regina **9, 46**
Taylor, Ron **35**
Thomas, Sean Patrick **35**
Thomason, Marsha **47**
Thompson, Kenan **52**
Thompson, Tazewell **13**
Thoms, Tracie **61**
Torres, Gina **52**
Torry, Guy **31**
Toussaint, Lorraine **32**
Townsend, Robert **4, 23**
Tucker, Chris **13, 23, 62**
Tunie, Tamara **63**
Turner, Tina **6, 27**
Tyler, Aisha N. **36**
Tyson, Cicely **7, 51**
Uggams, Leslie **23**

Underwood, Blair **7, 27**
Union, Gabrielle **31**
Usher **23, 56**
Van Peebles, Mario **2, 51**
Van Peebles, Melvin **7**
Vance, Courtney B. **15, 60**
Vanity **67**
Vereen, Ben **4**
Walker, Eamonn **37**
Ward, Douglas Turner **42**
Warfield, Marsha **2**
Warner, Malcolm-Jamal **22, 36**
Warren, Michael **27**
Washington, Denzel **1, 16**
Washington, Fredi **10**
Washington, Isaiah **62**
Washington, Kerry **46**
Waters, Ethel **7**
Wayans, Damon **8, 41**
Wayans, Keenen Ivory **18**
Wayans, Marlon **29**
Wayans, Shawn **29**
Weathers, Carl **10**
Webb, Veronica **10**
Whitaker, Forest **2, 49, 67**
White, Michael Jai **71**
Whitfield, Lynn **18**
Williams, Bert **18**
Williams, Billy Dee **8**
Williams, Clarence, III **26**
Wilson, Chandra **57**
Wilson, Dorien **55**
Williams, Joe **5, 25**
Williams, Malinda **57**
Williams, Samm-Art **21**
Williams, Saul **31**
Williams, Vanessa A. **32, 66**
Williams, Vanessa L. **4, 17**
Williamson, Fred **67**
Williamson, Mykelti **22**
Wilson, Debra **38**
Wilson, Flip **21**
Winfield, Paul **2, 45**
Winfrey, Oprah **2, 15, 61**
Withers-Mendes, Elisabeth **64**
Witherspoon, John **38**
Woodard, Alfre **9**
Wright, Jeffrey **54**
Yarbrough, Cedric **51**
Yoba, Malik **11**

Active Ministers Engaged in Nurturance (AMEN)
King, Bernice **4**

Actors Equity Association
Lewis, Emmanuel **36**

Actuarial science
Hill, Jesse, Jr. **13**

ACT UP
See AIDS Coalition to Unleash Power

Acustar, Inc.
Farmer, Forest **1**

ADC
See Agricultural Development Council

Addiction Research and Treatment Corporation
Cooper, Andrew W. **36**

Adoption and foster care
Baker, Josephine **3**
Blacque, Taurean **58**
Clements, George **2**
Gossett, Louis, Jr. **7**
Hale, Clara **16**
Hale, Lorraine **8**
Oglesby, Zena **12**
Rowell, Victoria **13, 68**

Adventures in Movement (AIM)
Morgan, Joe Leonard **9**

Advertising
Barboza, Anthony **10**
Boyd, Edward **70**
Burrell, Tom **21, 51**
Campbell, E. Simms **13**
Chisholm, Samuel J. **32**
Coleman, Donald **24, 62**
Cullers, Vincent T. **49**
Johnson, Beverly **2**
Jones, Caroline R. **29**
Jordan, Montell **23**
Lewis, Byron E. **13**
McKinney Hammond, Michelle **51**
Mingo, Frank **32**
Olden, Georg(e) **44**
Pinderhughes, John **47**
Roche, Joyce M. **17**

Advocates Scene
Seale, Bobby **3**

Aetna
Williams, Ronald A. **57**

AFCEA
See Armed Forces Communications and Electronics Associations

Affirmative action
Arnwine, Barbara **28**
Berry, Mary Frances **7**
Carter, Stephen L. **4**
Edley, Christopher F., Jr. **48**
Higginbotham, A. Leon, Jr. **13, 25**
Maynard, Robert C. **7**
Norton, Eleanor Holmes **7**
Rand, A. Barry **6**
Thompson, Bennie G. **26**
Waters, Maxine **3, 67**

AFL-CIO
See American Federation of Labor and Congress of Industrial Organizations

Africa Harvest Biotech Foundation International
Wambugu, Florence **42**

African/African-American Summit
Sullivan, Leon H. **3, 30**

African American Catholic Congregation
Stallings, George A., Jr. **6**

African American Dance Ensemble
Davis, Chuck **33**

African American folklore
Bailey, Xenobia **11**
Brown, Sterling Allen **10, 64**

Driskell, David C. **7**
Ellison, Ralph **7**
Gaines, Ernest J. **7**
Hamilton, Virginia **10**
Hughes, Langston **4**
Hurston, Zora Neale **3**
Lester, Julius **9**
Morrison, Toni **2, 15**
Primus, Pearl **6**
Tillman, George, Jr. **20**
Williams, Bert **18**
Yarbrough, Camille **40**

African American folk music
Cuney, William Waring **44**
Handy, W. C. **8**
House, Son **8**
Johnson, James Weldon **5**
Lester, Julius **9**
Southern, Eileen **56**

African American history
Angelou, Maya **1, 15**
Appiah, Kwame Anthony **67**
Ashe, Arthur **1, 18**
Benberry, Cuesta **65**
Bennett, Lerone, Jr. **5**
Berry, Mary Frances **7**
Blackshear, Leonard **52**
Blockson, Charles L. **42**
Burroughs, Margaret Taylor **9**
Camp, Kimberly **19**
Chase-Riboud, Barbara **20, 46**
Cheadle, Don **19, 52**
Clarke, John Henrik **20**
Clayton, Mayme Agnew **62**
Cobb, William Jelani **59**
Coombs, Orde M. **44**
Cooper, Anna Julia **20**
Dodson, Howard, Jr. **7, 52**
Douglas, Aaron **7**
Du Bois, W. E. B. **3**
DuBois, Shirley Graham **21**
Dyson, Michael Eric **11, 40**
Feelings, Tom **11, 47**
Franklin, John Hope **5**
Gaines, Ernest J. **7**
Gates, Henry Louis, Jr. **3, 38, 67**
Gill, Gerald **69**
Haley, Alex **4**
Halliburton, Warren J. **49**
Harkless, Necia Desiree **19**
Harris, Richard E. **61**
Hine, Darlene Clark **24**
Hughes, Langston **4**
Johnson, James Weldon **5**
Jones, Edward P. **43, 67**
Lewis, David Levering **9**
Madhubuti, Haki R. **7**
Marable, Manning **10**
Morrison, Toni **2**
Painter, Nell Irvin **24**
Pritchard, Robert Starling **21**
Quarles, Benjamin Arthur **18**
Reagon, Bernice Johnson **7**
Ringgold, Faith **4**
Schomburg, Arthur Alfonso **9**
Southern, Eileen **56**
Tancil, Gladys Quander **59**
Wilson, August **7, 33, 55**
Woodson, Carter G. **2**

Yarbrough, Camille **40**

African American Images
Kunjufu, Jawanza **3, 50**

African American literature
Andrews, Raymond **4**
Angelou, Maya **1, 15**
Appiah, Kwame Anthony **67**
Baisden, Michael **25, 66**
Baker, Houston A., Jr. **6**
Baldwin, James **1**
Bambara, Toni Cade **1**
Baraka, Amiri **1, 38**
Bennett, George Harold "Hal" **45**
Bontemps, Arna **8**
Briscoe, Connie **15**
Brooks, Gwendolyn **1, 28**
Brown, Claude **38**
Brown, Wesley **23**
Burroughs, Margaret Taylor **9**
Campbell, Bebe Moore **6, 24, 59**
Cary, Lorene **3**
Childress, Alice **15**
Cleage, Pearl **17, 64**
Cullen, Countee **8**
Curtis, Christopher Paul **26**
Davis, Arthur P. **41**
Davis, Nolan **45**
Dickey, Eric Jerome **21, 56**
Dove, Rita **6**
Du Bois, W. E. B. **3**
Dunbar, Paul Laurence **8**
Ellison, Ralph **7**
Evans, Mari **26**
Fair, Ronald L. **47**
Fauset, Jessie **7**
Feelings, Tom **11, 47**
Fisher, Rudolph **17**
Ford, Nick Aaron **44**
Fuller, Charles **8**
Gaines, Ernest J. **7**
Gates, Henry Louis, Jr. **3, 38, 67**
Gayle, Addison, Jr. **41**
Gibson, Donald Bernard **40**
Giddings, Paula **11**
Giovanni, Nikki **9, 39**
Goines, Donald **19**
Golden, Marita **19**
Guy, Rosa **5**
Haley, Alex **4**
Hansberry, Lorraine **6**
Harper, Frances Ellen Watkins **11**
Heard, Nathan C. **45**
Himes, Chester **8**
Holland, Endesha Ida Mae **3, 57**
Holmes, Shannon **70**
Hughes, Langston **4**
Hull, Akasha Gloria **45**
Hurston, Zora Neale **3**
Iceberg Slim **11**
Joe, Yolanda **21**
Johnson, Charles **1**
Johnson, James Weldon **5**
Jones, Gayl **37**
Jordan, June **7, 35**
July, William **27**
Kitt, Sandra **23**
Larsen, Nella **10**
Lester, Julius **9**
Little, Benilde **21**
Lorde, Audre **6**
Madhubuti, Haki R. **7**

Major, Clarence **9**
Marshall, Paule **7**
McKay, Claude **6**
McKay, Nellie Yvonne **17, 57**
McKinney-Whetstone, Diane **27**
McMillan, Terry **4, 17, 53**
McPherson, James Alan **70**
Morrison, Toni **2, 15**
Mowry, Jess **7**
Myers, Walter Dean **8, 20**
Naylor, Gloria **10, 42**
Painter, Nell Irvin **24**
Petry, Ann **19**
Pinkney, Jerry **15**
Rahman, Aishah **37**
Randall, Dudley **8, 55**
Redding, J. Saunders **26**
Redmond, Eugene **23**
Reed, Ishmael **8**
Ringgold, Faith **4**
Sanchez, Sonia **17, 51**
Schomburg, Arthur Alfonso **9**
Schuyler, George Samuel **40**
Shange, Ntozake **8**
Smith, Mary Carter **26**
Taylor, Mildred D. **26**
Thomas, Trisha R. **65**
Thurman, Wallace **16**
Toomer, Jean **6**
Tyree, Omar Rashad **21**
Van Peebles, Melvin **7**
Verdelle, A. J. **26**
Walker, Alice **1, 43**
Wesley, Valerie Wilson **18**
Wideman, John Edgar **5**
Williams, John A. **27**
Williams, Sherley Anne **25**
Wilson, August **7, 33, 55**
Wolfe, George C. **6, 43**
Wright, Richard **5**
Yarbrough, Camille **40**

African American Research Library and Cultural Center
Morrison, Sam **50**

African American studies
Brawley, Benjamin **44**
Carby, Hazel **27**
Christian, Barbara T. **44**
De Veaux, Alexis **44**
Ford, Nick Aaron **44**
Hare, Nathan **44**
Henderson, Stephen E. **45**
Huggins, Nathan Irvin **52**
Long, Richard Alexander **65**

African Ancestry Inc.
Kittles, Rick **51**

African Burial Ground Project
Perry, Warren **56**

African Canadian literature
Elliott, Lorris **37**
Foster, Cecil **32**
Senior, Olive **37**

African Continental Telecommunications Ltd.
Sutton, Percy E. **42**

African dance
Acogny, Germaine **55**
Adams, Jenoyne **60**

Ailey, Alvin **8**
Davis, Chuck **33**
Fagan, Garth **18**
Primus, Pearl **6**

African Heritage Network
See The Heritage Network

African history
Appiah, Kwame Anthony **67**
Chase-Riboud, Barbara **20, 46**
Clarke, John Henrik **20**
Diop, Cheikh Anta **4**
Dodson, Howard, Jr. **7, 52**
DuBois, Shirley Graham **21**
Feelings, Muriel **44**
Halliburton, Warren J. **49**
Hansberry, William Leo **11**
Harkless, Necia Desiree **19**
Henries, A. Doris Banks **44**
Hilliard, Asa Grant, III **66**
Jawara, Dawda Kairaba **11**
Madhubuti, Haki R. **7**
Marshall, Paule **7**
van Sertima, Ivan **25**

African literature
Aidoo, Ama Ata **38**
Akpan, Uwem **70**
Appiah, Kwame Anthony **67**
Arac de Nyeko, Monica **66**
Armah, Ayi Kwei **49**
Awoonor, Kofi **37**
Bandele, Biyi **68**
Cartey, Wilfred **47**
Cheney-Coker, Syl **43**
Couto, Mia **45**
Dadié, Bernard **34**
Dathorne, O.R. **52**
Ekwensi, Cyprian **37**
Farah, Nuruddin **27**
Gabre-Medhin, Tsegaye **64**
Head, Bessie **28**
Kayira, Legson **40**
Memmi, Albert **37**
Mphalele, Es'kia **40**
Mwangi, Meja **40**
Oyono, Ferdinand **38**
Peters, Lenrie **43**
Salih, Al-Tayyib **37**

**African Methodist Episcopal
Church (AME)**
Blanks, Deborah K. **69**
Bryant, John R. **45**
Flake, Floyd H. **18**
McKenzie, Vashti M. **29**
Mudimbe, V.Y. **61**
Murray, Cecil **12, 47**
Shuttlesworth, Fred **47**
Turner, Henry McNeal **5**
Youngblood, Johnny Ray **8**

African music
Ade, King Sunny **41**
Fela **1, 42**
Kidjo, Anjelique **50**
Kolosoy, Wendo **73**
Kuti, Femi **47**
Maal, Baaba **66**
Mahlasela, Vusi **65**
Makeba, Miriam **2, 50**

Nascimento, Milton **2, 64**

**African National Congress
(ANC)**
Baker, Ella **5**
Hani, Chris **6**
Ka Dinizulu, Mcwayizeni **29**
Kaunda, Kenneth **2**
Kuzwayo, Ellen **68**
Luthuli, Albert **13**
Mandela, Nelson **1, 14**
Mandela, Winnie **2, 35**
Masekela, Barbara **18**
Mbeki, Thabo **14, 73**
Mhlaba, Raymond **55**
Nkomo, Joshua **4, 65**
Nyanda, Siphiwe **21**
Nzo, Alfred **15**
Ramaphosa, Cyril **3**
Sisulu, Albertina **57**
Sisulu, Walter **47**
Tutu, Desmond Mpilo **6, 44**
Weems, Renita J. **44**
Xuma, Madie Hall **59**
Zuma, Nkosazana Dlamini **34**

**African Party for the Indepen-
dence of Guinea and Cape
Verde**
Pereira, Aristides **30**

**African Women's Health Cen-
ter**
Nour, Nawal M. **56**

**Afro-Academic Cultural, Tech-
nological, and Scientific
Olympics**
Jarrett, Vernon D. **42**

**Afro-American Dance En-
semble**
Hall, Arthur **39**

Afro-American League
Fortune, T. Thomas **6**

**Afro-American Newspaper
Company**
Murphy, John H. **42**

Afro-Beat music
Fela **1, 42**

Afro-Brazilian music
Caymmi, Dorival **72**
Gil, Gilberto **53**
Jorge, Seu **73**

Afrocentricity
Asante, Molefi Kete **3**
Biggers, John **20, 33**
Diop, Cheikh Anta **4**
Hansberry, Lorraine **6**
Hansberry, William Leo **11**
Sanchez, Sonia **17, 51**
Turner, Henry McNeal **5**

Afro-Cuban music
Lefel, Edith **41**

Aftermath Entertainment
Dre, Dr. **10, 14, 30**

**Agency for International De-
velopment (AID)**
Gayle, Helene D. **3, 46**
Perkins, Edward **5**

Wilkins, Roger **2**

**A. G. Gaston Boys and Girls
Club**
Gaston, Arthur George **3, 38, 59**

**Agricultural Development
Council (ADC)**
Wharton, Clifton R., Jr. **7**

Agriculture
Boyd, John W., Jr. **20, 72**
Carver, George Washington **4**
Espy, Mike **6**
Hall, Lloyd A. **8**
Jones, Monty **66**
Masire, Quett **5**
Obasanjo, Olusegun **5**
Sanders, Dori **8**
Wambugu, Florence **42**

AHA
See American Heart Association

AID
See Agency for International Development

AIDS
See Acquired Immune Deficiency
Syndrome

**AIDS Coalition to Unleash
Power (ACT UP)**
Norman, Pat **10**

AIDS Health Care Foundation
Wilson, Phill **9**

AIDS Prevention Team
Wilson, Phill **9**

AIDS research
Mboup, Souleymane **10**
Ojikutu, Bisola **65**

AIM
See Adventures in Movement

Akron Beacon Journal
Crutchfield, James N. **55**

**Akwaaba Mansion Bed &
Breakfast**
Greenwood, Monique **38**

ALA
See American Library Association

Alabama state government
Davis, Artur **41**
Ford, Johnny **70**
Gray, Fred **37**

Alamerica Bank
Watkins, Donald **35**

Alcoholics Anonymous (AA)
Hilliard, David **7**
Lucas, John **7**

**All Afrikan People's Revolu-
tionary Party**
Carmichael, Stokely **5, 26**
Moses, Robert Parris **11**

Alliance for Children
McMurray, Georgia L. **36**

Alliance Theatre
Leon, Kenny **10**

Allied Arts Academy
Bonds, Margaret **39**

Alpha & Omega Ministry
White, Reggie **6, 50**

Alpha Kappa Alpha Sorority
White, Linda M. **45**

**Alvin Ailey American Dance
Theater**
Ailey, Alvin **8**
Clarke, Hope **14**
Dove, Ulysses **5**
Faison, George **16**
Jamison, Judith **7, 67**
Primus, Pearl **6**
Rhoden, Dwight **40**
Richardson, Desmond **39**
Spears, Warren **52**
Tyson, Andre **40**
Williams, Dudley **60**

**Alvin Ailey Repertory En-
semble**
Ailey, Alvin **8**
Miller, Bebe **3**

Amadou Diallo Foundation
Diallo, Amadou **27**

AMAS Repertory Theater
LeNoire, Rosetta **37**

Ambassadors
Braun, Carol Moseley **4, 42**
Cook, Mercer **40**
Dudley, Edward R. **58**
Dymally, Mervyn **42**
Frazer, Jendayi **68**
Stith, Charles R. **73**
Todman, Terence A. **55**
Watson, Diane **41**
Whitfield, Mal **60**

AME
See African Methodist Episcopal
Church

AMEN
See Active Ministers Engaged in
Nurturance

**American Academy of Arts
and Sciences**
Loury, Glenn **36**

American Art Award
Simpson, Lorna **4, 36**

**American Association for the
Advancement of Science
(AAAS)**
Cobb, W. Montague **39**
Massey, Walter E. **5, 45**
Pickett, Cecil **39**

**American Association of Uni-
versity Women**
Granville, Evelyn Boyd **36**

American Ballet Theatre
Dove, Ulysses **5**
Richardson, Desmond **39**

American Bar Association
Archer, Dennis 7, 36
Pincham, R. Eugene, Sr. 69
Thompson, Larry D. 39
Walker, Cora T. 68

American Basketball Association (ABA)
Chamberlain, Wilt 18, 47
Erving, Julius 18, 47

American Beach
Betsch, MaVynee 28

American Book Award
Baraka, Amiri 1, 38
Bates, Daisy 13
Bradley, David Henry, Jr. 39
Clark, Septima 7
Gates, Henry Louis, Jr. 3, 38, 67
Lorde, Audre 6
Loury, Glenn 36
Marshall, Paule 7
Sanchez, Sonia 17, 51
Walker, Alice 1, 43

American Broadcasting Company (ABC)
Christian, Spencer 15
Goode, Mal 13
Jackson, Michael 19, 53
Joyner, Tom 19
Mickebury, Penny 28
Reynolds, Star Jones 10, 27, 61
Roberts, Robin 16, 54
Robinson, Max 3
Simpson, Carole 6, 30
Winfrey, Oprah 2, 15, 61

American Cancer Society
Ashe, Arthur 1, 18
Leffall, Lasalle 3, 64
Riperton, Minnie 32
Thomas, Arthur Ray 52

American Choral Directors Association
Adams, Leslie 39

American Civil Liberties Union (ACLU)
Baugh, David 23
Murphy, Laura M. 43
Murray, Pauli 38
Norton, Eleanor Holmes 7
Pincham, R. Eugene, Sr. 69

American Communist Party
Patterson, Louise 25

American Community Housing Associates, Inc.
Lane, Vincent 5

American Composers Alliance
Tillis, Frederick 40

American Counseling Association
Mitchell, Sharon 36

American Dance Guild
Hall, Arthur 39

American Economic Association
Loury Glenn 36

American Enterprise Institute
Woodson, Robert L. 10

American Express Company
Adams, Eula L. 39
Chenault, Kenneth I. 4, 36

American Express Consumer Card Group, USA
Chenault, Kenneth I. 4, 36

American Federation of Labor and Congress of Industrial Organizations (AFL-CIO)
Fletcher, Bill, Jr. 41
Holt Baker, Arlene 73
Randolph, A. Philip 3

American Federation of Television and Radio Artists
Falana, Lola 42
Fields, Kim 36
Lewis, Emmanuel 36
Daniels, Lee Louis 36

American Guild of Organists
Adams, Leslie 39

American Heart Association (AHA)
Cooper, Edward S. 6
Grant, Augustus O. 71
Richardson, Donna 39

American Idol
Hudson, Jennifer 63
Jackson, Randy 40

American Institute for the Prevention of Blindness
Bath, Patricia E. 37

American Library Association (ALA)
Franklin, Hardy R. 9
Hayden, Carla D. 47
Jones, Clara Stanton 51
Josey, E. J. 10
McFadden, Bernice L. 39
Rollins, Charlamae Hill 27
Wedgeworth, Robert W. 42

American Management Association
Cooper, Andrew W. 36

American Negro Academy
Grimké, Archibald H. 9
Schomburg, Arthur Alfonso 9

American Negro Theater
Martin, Helen 31

American Nuclear Society
Wilkens, J. Ernest, Jr. 43

American Nurses' Association (ANA)
Kennedy, Adrienne 11
Staupers, Mabel K. 7

American Postal Worker's Union
Burrus, William Henry "Bill" 45

American Psychological Association
Anderson, Norman B. 45
Mitchell, Sharon 36

American Red Cross
Bullock, Steve 22
Drew, Charles Richard 7

American Society of Magazine Editors
Curry, George E. 23

American Tennis Association
Gibson, Althea 8, 43
Peters, Margaret and Matilda 43

American Writers Association
Schuyler, George Samuel 40

America's Promise
Powell, Colin 1, 28

Amistad Freedom Schooner
Pinckney, Bill 42

Amos Fraser Bernard Consultants
Amos, Valerie 41

Amsterdam News
Cooper, Andrew W. 36
Holt, Nora 38

ANA
See American Nurses' Association

ANC
See African National Congress

Angella Christie Sound Ministries
Christie, Angella 36

Anglican church hierarchy
Akinola, Peter Jasper 65
Tutu, Desmond Mpilo 6, 44

Angolan government
dos Santos, José Eduardo 43
Neto, António Agostinho 43

Anheuser-Busch distribution
Cherry, Deron 40

Anthropology
Asante, Molefi Kete 3
Bunche, Ralph J. 5
Cole, Johnnetta B. 5, 43
Davis, Allison 12
Diop, Cheikh Anta 4
Dunham, Katherine 4, 59
Hansberry, William Leo 11
Morrison, Toni 2, 15
Primus, Pearl 6
Robeson, Eslanda Goode 13
Rodriguez, Cheryl 64

Antoinette Perry awards
See Tony awards

APA
See American Psychological Association

Apartheid
Abrahams, Peter 39
Ashe, Arthur 18

Berry, Mary Frances 7
Biko, Steven 4
Brutus, Dennis 38
Butler, Jonathan 28
Howard, M. William, Jr. 26
Ka Dinizulu, Mcwayizeni 29
Kuzwayo, Ellen 68
LaGuma, Alex 30
Luthuli, Albert 13
Mahlasela, Vusi 65
Makeba, Miriam 2, 50
Mandela, Nelson 1, 14
Mandela, Winnie 2, 35
Masekela, Hugh 1
Mathabane, Mark 5
Mbeki, Thabo 14, 73
Mbuende, Kaire 12
McDougall, Gay J. 11, 43
Mhlaba, Raymond 55
Mphalele, Es'kia 40
Nkoli, Simon 60
Ntshona, Winston 52
Nyanda, Siphiwe 21
Nzo, Alfred 15
Ramaphosa, Cyril 3
Ramphele, Mamphela 29
Robinson, Randall 7, 46
Sisulu, Albertina 57
Sisulu, Walter 47
Sullivan, Leon H. 13, 30
Tutu, Desmond Mpilo 6, 44

Apollo Theater
Sims, Howard "Sandman" 48
Sutton, Percy E. 42

Apollo
Williams, O. S. 13

APWU
See American Postal Worker's Union

Arab-Israeli conflict
Bunche, Ralph J. 5

Architecture
Abele, Julian 55
Adjaye, David 38
Gantt, Harvey 1
Johnson, Jeh Vincent 44
King, Robert Arthur 58
Sklarek, Norma Merrick 25
Williams, Paul R. 9

Argonne National Laboratory
Massey, Walter E. 5, 45
Quarterman, Lloyd Albert 4
Massey, Walter E. 5, 45

Ariel Capital Management
Rogers, John W., Jr. 5, 52
Hobson, Mellody 40

Arista Records
Lattimore, Kenny 35
Reid, Antonio "L.A." 28

Arkansas Department of Health
Elders, Joycelyn 6

Armed Forces Communications and Electronics Associations (AFCEA)
Gravely, Samuel L., Jr. 5, 49

Art history
Benjamin, Tritobia Hayes **53**
Campbell, Mary Schmidt **43**

Arthur Andersen
Scott, Milton **51**

ASALH
See Association for the Study of
Afro-American Life and History

ASH
See Association for the Sexually
Harassed

**Asheville, North Carolina, city
government**
Bellamy, Terry **58**

**Association for Constitutional
Democracy in Liberia (ACDL)**
Sawyer, Amos **2**

**Association for the Sexually
Harassed (ASH)**
Gomez-Preston, Cheryl **9**

**Assocation of Tennis Profes-
sionals (ATP)**
Blake, James **43**

Astronauts
Anderson, Michael P. **40**
Bluford, Guy **2, 35**
Bolden, Charles F., Jr. **7**
Gregory, Frederick **8, 51**
Jemison, Mae C. **1, 35**
Lawrence, Robert H., Jr. **16**
McNair, Ronald **3, 58**
Wilson, Stephanie **72**

Astrophysics
Alcorn, George Edward, Jr. **59**
Carruthers, George R. **40**

Atco-EastWest
Rhone, Sylvia **2**

ATD Publishing
Tyson, Asha **39**

Athletic administration
Goss, Tom **23**
Littlepage, Craig **35**

**Atlanta Association of Black
Journalists**
Pressley, Condace L. **41**

Atlanta Baptist College
See Morehouse College

Atlanta Beat
Scurry, Briana **27**

Atlanta Board of Education
Mays, Benjamin E. **7**

Atlanta Braves baseball team
Aaron, Hank **5**
Baker, Dusty **8, 43, 72**
Justice, David **18**
McGriff, Fred **24**
Sanders, Deion **4, 31**

**Atlanta Chamber of Com-
merce**
Hill, Jesse, Jr. **13**

Atlanta city government
Campbell, Bill **9**
Franklin, Shirley **34**

Jackson, Maynard **2, 41**
Williams, Hosea Lorenzo **15, 31**
Young, Andrew **3, 48**

Atlanta Falcons football team
Anderson, Jamal **22**
Buchanan, Ray **32**
Sanders, Deion **4, 31**
Vick, Michael **39, 65**

**Atlanta Hawks basketball
team**
Silas, Paul **24**
Wilkens, Lenny **11**

**Atlanta Life Insurance Com-
pany**
Hill, Jesse, Jr. **13**

Atlanta Negro Voters League
Hill, Jesse, Jr. **13**

Atlanta Police Department
Brown, Lee Patrick **1, 24**
Harvard, Beverly **11**

Atlanta World
Scott, C. A. **29**

Atlantic City city government
Usry, James L. **23**

Atlantic Records
Franklin, Aretha **11, 44**
Lil' Kim **28**
Rhone, Sylvia **2**

ATP
See Association of Tennis Professionals

Audelco awards
Holder, Laurence **34**
Rodgers, Rod **36**
Wesley, Richard **73**

Aurelian Honor Society Award
Lewis, William M., Jr. **40**

Authors Guild
Davis, George **36**
Gayle, Addison, Jr. **41**
Schuyler, George Samuel **40**

Authors League of America
Abrahams, Peter **39**
Cotter, Joseph Seamon, Sr. **40**
Davis, George **36**
Gayle, Addison, Jr. **41**

Automobile dealership
Farr, Mel **24**
Gidron, Richard D. **68**
Parker, Jim **64**

**Avery Institute for Social
Change**
Avery, Byllye Y. **66**

Aviation
Brown, Jesse Leroy **31**
Brown, Willa **40**
Bullard, Eugene **12**
Coleman, Bessie **9**
McLeod, Gus **27**
Petersen, Frank E. **31**

Roy, Kenny **51**

Baby Phat
Simmons, Kimora Lee **51**

"Back to Africa" movement
Turner, Henry McNeal **5**

Bad Boy Entertainment
Combs, Sean "Puffy" **17, 43**
Harrell, Andre **9, 30**
Notorious B.I.G. **20**

Bahamian government
Christie, Perry Gladstone **53**

Ballet
Ailey, Alvin **8**
Allen, Debbie **13, 42**
Anderson, Lauren **72**
Collins, Janet **33, 64**
Dove, Ulysses **5**
Faison, George **16**
Jamison, Judith **7, 67**
Johnson, Virginia **9**
Jones, Doris W. **62**
Mitchell, Arthur **2, 47**
Nichols, Nichelle **11**
Parks, Gordon **1, 35, 58**
Rhoden, Dwight **40**
Richardson, Desmond **39**
Rowell, Victoria **13, 68**
Tyson, Andre **40**

Balm in Gilead, The
Seele, Pernessa **46**

**Baltimore Black Sox baseball
team**
Day, Leon **39**

Baltimore city government
Dixon, Sheila **68**
Robinson, Bishop L. **66**
Schmoke, Kurt **1, 48**

Baltimore Colts football team
Barnes, Ernie **16**
Parker, Jim **64**

**Baltimore Elite Giants base-
ball team**
Campanella, Roy **25**
Day, Leon **39**
Kimbro, Henry A. **25**

**Baltimore Orioles baseball
team**
Baylor, Don **6**
Blair, Paul **36**
Carter, Joe **30**
Jackson, Reggie **15**
Robinson, Frank **9**

Banking
Boyd, T. B., III **6**
Bradley, Jennette B. **40**
Bridgforth, Glinda **36**
Brimmer, Andrew F. **2, 48**
Bryant, John **26**
Chapman, Nathan A., Jr. **21**
Chappell, Emma **18**
Ferguson, Roger W. **25**
Forte, Linda Diane **54**
Funderburg, I. Owen **38**
Greene, Richard Thaddeus, Sr. **67**

Griffith, Mark Winston **8**
Harris, Carla A. **67**
Lawless, Theodore K. **8**
Louis, Errol T. **8**
March, William Carrington **56**
McGuire, Raymond J. **57**
Morgan, Rose **11**
Parsons, Richard Dean **11**
Utendahl, John **23**
Walker, Maggie Lena **17**
Watkins, Walter C. **24**
Willie, Louis, Jr. **68**
Wright, Deborah C. **25**

Baptist
Austin, Junius C. **44**
Bradley, J. Robert **65**
Davis, Gary **41**
Forbes, James A., Jr. **71**
Franklin, C. L. **68**
Gomes, Peter J. **15**
Jemison, Major L. **48**
Jones, E. Edward, Sr. **45**
Long, Eddie L. **29**
Meek, Carrie **6**
Meek, Kendrick **41**
Moss, Otis, Jr. **72**
Rogers, Alan G. **72**
Thurston, Stephen J. **49**

Barnett-Ader Gallery
Thomas, Alma **14**

Barnum and Bailey Circus
McFarlan, Tyron **60**

Baseball
Aaron, Hank **5**
Anderson, Elmer **25**
Ashford, Emmett **22**
Baines, Harold **32**
Baker, Dusty **8, 43, 72**
Banks, Ernie **33**
Barnhill, David **30**
Baylor, Don **6**
Bell, James "Cool Papa" **36**
Belle, Albert **10**
Blair, Paul **36**
Bonds, Barry **6, 34, 63**
Bonds, Bobby **43**
Brock, Lou **18**
Brown, Willard **36**
Campanella, Roy **25**
Carew, Rod **20**
Carter, Joe **30**
Charleston, Oscar **39**
Clendenon, Donn **26, 56**
Coleman, Leonard S., Jr. **12**
Cooper, Andy "Lefty" **63**
Cottrell, Comer **11**
Dandridge, Ray **36**
Davis, Piper **19**
Day, Leon **39**
Doby, Lawrence Eugene, Sr. **16**
Dye, Jermaine **58**
Edwards, Harry **2**
Fielder, Cecil **2**
Fielder, Prince Semien **68**
Flood, Curt **10**
Gaston, Cito **71**
Gibson, Bob **33**
Gibson, Josh **22**
Gooden, Dwight **20**
Granderson, Curtis **66**

Gregg, Eric **16**
Griffey, Ken, Jr. **12, 73**
Hammer, M. C. **20**
Henderson, Rickey **28**
Howard, Ryan **65**
Hunter, Torii **43**
Hyde, Cowan F. "Bubba" **47**
Irvin, Monte **31**
Jackson, Reggie **15**
Jenkins, Fergie **46**
Jeter, Derek **27**
Johnson, Clifford "Connie" **52**
Johnson, Mamie "Peanut" **40**
Justice, David **18**
Kaiser, Cecil **42**
Kimbro, Henry A. **25**
Lacy, Sam **30, 46**
Lankford, Ray **23**
Larkin, Barry **24**
Lloyd, John Henry "Pop" **30**
Lofton, Kenny **12**
Mariner, Jonathan **41**
Mays, Willie **3**
McGriff, Fred **24**
Morgan, Joe Leonard **9**
Murray, Eddie **12**
Newcombe, Don **24**
O'Neil, Buck **19, 59**
Ortiz, David **52**
Paige, Satchel **7**
Payne, Ulice **42**
Pride, Charley **26**
Puckett, Kirby **4, 58**
Randolph, Willie **53**
Reese, Pokey **28**
Robinson, Frank **9**
Robinson, Jackie **6**
Robinson, Sharon **22**
Rollins, Jimmy **70**
Sanders, Deion **4, 31**
Sheffield, Gary **16**
Smith, Hilton **29**
Sosa, Sammy **21, 44**
Stargell, Willie **29**
Stearnes, Norman "Turkey" **31**
Stone, Toni **15**
Strawberry, Darryl **22**
Thomas, Frank **12, 51**
Vaughn, Mo **16**
Virgil, Ozzie **48**
Watson, Bob **25**
White, Bill **1, 48**
Williams, Ken **68**
Willis, Dontrelle **55**
Wills, Maury **73**
Winfield, Dave **5**

Baseball Hall of Fame
Banks, Ernie **33**
Bell, James "Cool Papa" **36**
Brown, Willard **36**
Campanella, Roy **25**
Charleston, Oscar **39**
Dandridge, Ray **36**
Day, Leon **39**
Doby, Lawrence Eugene, Sr. **16, 41**
Gibson, Josh **22**
Irvin, Monte **31**
Leonard, Buck **67**
Lloyd, John Henry "Pop" **30**
Paige, Satchel **7**
Robinson, Jackie **6**
Smith, Hilton **29**

Stearnes, Norman "Turkey" **31**

Barbadian government
Arthur, Owen **33**

Basket making
Jackson, Mary **73**

Basketball
Abdul-Jabbar, Kareem **8**
Abdur-Rahim, Shareef **28**
Amaker, Tommy **62**
Anderson, Mike **63**
Anthony, Carmelo **46**
Artest, Ron **52**
Barkley, Charles **5, 66**
Bing, Dave **3, 59**
Bogues, Tyrone "Muggsy" **56**
Bol, Manute **1**
Bolton-Holifield, Ruthie **28**
Brand, Elton **31**
Brandon, Terrell **16**
Bryant, Kobe **15, 31, 71**
Carter, Butch **27**
Carter, Kenneth **53**
Carter, Vince **26**
Catchings, Tamika **43**
Chamberlain, Wilt **18, 47**
Chaney, John **67**
Cheeks, Maurice **47**
Clifton, Nathaniel "Sweetwater" **47**
Cooper, Charles "Chuck" **47**
Cooper, Cynthia **17**
Cooper, Michael **31**
Davis, Mike **41**
Drexler, Clyde **4, 61**
Dumars, Joe **16, 65**
Duncan, Tim **20**
Dunn, Jerry **27**
Edwards, Harry **2**
Edwards, Teresa **14**
Ellerbe, Brian **22**
Elliott, Sean **26**
Ewing, Patrick **17, 73**
Fox, Rick **27**
Freeman, Marianna **23**
Gaines, Clarence E., Sr. **55**
Garnett, Kevin **14, 70**
Gentry, Alvin **23**
Gossett, Louis, Jr. **7**
Gray, Yeshimbra "Shimmy" **55**
Green, A. C. **32**
Griffith, Yolanda **25**
Hardaway, Anfernee (Penny) **13**
Hardaway, Tim **35**
Haskins, Clem **23**
Haynes, Marques **22**
Heard, Gar **25**
Hill, Grant **13**
Holdsclaw, Chamique **24**
Howard, Juwan **15**
Hunter, Billy **22**
Iverson, Allen **24, 46**
James, LeBron **46**
Johnson, Avery **62**
Johnson, Earvin "Magic" **3, 39**
Johnson, Kevin **70**
Johnson, Larry **28**
Jones, Merlakia **34**
Jones, Roy, Jr. **22**
Jordan, Michael **6, 21**
Justice, David **18**
Kellogg, Clark **64**
Lanier, Bob **47**

Lennox, Betty **31**
Leslie, Lisa **16, 73**
Lloyd, Earl **26**
Lofton, Kenny **12**
Lowe, Sidney **64**
Lucas, John **7**
Mahorn, Rick **60**
Malone, Karl **18, 51**
Manigault, Earl "The Goat" **15**
Master P **21**
Miller, Cheryl **10**
Miton, DeLisha **31**
Mohammed, Nazr **64**
Mourning, Alonzo **17, 44**
Mutombo, Dikembe **7**
Olajuwon, Hakeem **2, 72**
O'Neal, Shaquille **8, 30**
Palmer, Violet **59**
Parish, Robert **43**
Peck, Carolyn **23**
Phillips, Teresa L. **42**
Pierce, Paul **71**
Pippen, Scottie **15**
Prince, Tayshaun **68**
Richardson, Nolan **9**
Richmond, Mitch **19**
Rivers, Glenn "Doc" **25**
Robertson, Oscar **26**
Robinson, David **24**
Robinson, Will **51, 69**
Russell, Bill **8**
Silas, Paul **24**
Smith, Stephen A. **69**
Smith, Tubby **18**
Sprewell, Latrell **23**
Stackhouse, Jerry **30**
Staley, Dawn **57**
Stoudemire, Amaré **59**
Stringer, C. Vivian **13, 66**
Swoopes, Sheryl **12, 56**
Thomas, Isiah **7, 26, 65**
Thompson, Tina **25**
Tisdale, Wayman **50**
Unseld, Wes **23**
Wallace, Ben **54**
Wallace, Perry E. **47**
Wallace, Rasheed **56**
Webber, Chris **15, 30, 59**
Wilkens, Lenny **11**
Williams, Natalie **31**
Woodward, Lynette **67**
Worthy, James **49**

Basketball Hall of Fame
Abdul-Jabbar, Kareem **8**
Barkley, Charles **5, 66**
Bing, Dave **3, 59**
Chamberlain, Wilt **18, 47**
Dantley, Adrian **72**
Olajuwon, Hakeem **2, 72**
Parish, Robert **43**

Bass
Foster, George "Pops" **40**
Jamerson, James **59**

BBC
See British Broadcasting Company

BCALA
See Black Caucus of the American
Library Association

BDP
See Botswana Democratic Party

Beale Streeters
Ace, Johnny **36**
Bland, Bobby "Blue" **36**
King, B.B. **7**

Bear, Stearns & Co.
Fletcher, Alphonso, Jr. **16**

Beatrice International
See TLC Beatrice International
Holdings, Inc.

Beauty Salons and Products
Fine, Sam **60**
Gibson, Ted **66**
Stanford, Olivia Lee Dilworth **49**

Bebop
Carter, Betty **19**
Clarke, Kenny **27**
Coltrane, John **19**
Davis, Miles **4**
Eckstine, Billy **28**
Fitzgerald, Ella **8, 18**
Gillespie, Dizzy **1**
Gordon, Dexter **25**
Hancock, Herbie **20, 67**
Harris, Barry **68**
Hawkins, Coleman **9**
Jackson, Milt **26**
Parker, Charlie **20**
Powell, Bud **24**
Roach, Max **21, 63**
Vaughan, Sarah **13**

**Bechuanaland Protectorate
Legislative Council**
Masire, Quett **5**

**Beckham Publications Group
Inc.**
Beckham, Barry **41**

Bell of Pennsylvania
Gordon, Bruce S. **41, 53**

**Ben & Jerry's Homemade Ice
Cream, Inc.**
Holland, Robert, Jr. **11**

Bennett College
Cole, Johnnetta B. **5, 43**
Player, Willa B. **43**

Bessie award
Richardson, Desmond **39**

BET
See Black Entertainment Television

Bethann Management, Inc.
Hardison, Bethann **12**

Bethune-Cookman College
Bethune, Mary McLeod **4**
Joyner, Marjorie Stewart **26**

BFF
See Black Filmmaker Foundation

BGLLF
See Black Gay and Lesbian Leadership Forum

Big Easy Award
Adams, Johnny **39**

Bill and Melinda Gates Foundation
Golston, Allan C. **55**

Billy Graham Evangelistic Association
Bell, Ralph S. **5**
Waters, Ethel **7**

Bing Group, The
Bing, Dave **3, 59**
Lloyd, Earl **26**

Biology
Cobb, Jewel Plummer **42**
Pickett, Cecil **39**
Emeagwali, Dale **31**
Jarvis, Erich **67**
Just, Ernest Everett **3**
Malveaux, Floyd **54**

Biotechnology
Juma, Calestous **57**
Wambugu, Florence **42**

Birmingham city government
Kincaid, Bernard **28**
Nunn, Annetta **43**

Birmingham (AL) Police Department
Nunn, Annetta **43**

Birth control
Elders, Joycelyn **6**
Williams, Maggie **7, 71**

Bishop College
Cottrell, Comer **11**

Bismark Bisons baseball team
Dandridge, Ray **36**

BLA
See Black Liberation Army

Black Aesthetic
Baker, Houston A., Jr. **6**

Black Academy of Arts & Letters
White, Charles **39**

Black Alliance for Educational Options
Fuller, Howard L. **37**

Black American West Museum
Stewart, Paul Wilbur **12**

Black Americans for Family Values
Foster, Ezola **28**

Black and White Minstrel Show
Henry, Lenny **9, 52**

Black arts movement
Barrett, Lindsay **43**
Caldwell, Benjamin **46**
Cornish, Sam **50**
Cortez, Jayne **43**
Cruse, Harold **54**
Dent, Thomas C. **50**

Donaldson, Jeff **46**
Dumas, Henry **41**
Gayle, Addison, Jr. **41**
Giovanni, Nikki **9, 39**
Henderson, David **53**
Hoagland, Everett H. **45**
Neal, Larry **38**
Pomare, Eleo **72**
Smith, Vincent D. **48**
Touré, Askia (Muhammad Abu Bakr el) **47**
X, Marvin **45**

Black Cabinet
Hastie, William H. **8**

Black Caucus of the American Library Association (BCALA)
Josey, E. J. **10**

Black Coaches Association (BCA)
Freeman, Marianna **23**
Keith, Floyd A. **61**

Black Consciousness movement
Biko, Steven **4**
Fanon, Frantz **44**
Fuller, Hoyt **44**
Muhammad, Elijah **4**
Ramaphosa, Cyril **3**
Ramphele, Mamphela **29**
Tutu, Desmond Mpilo **6, 44**

Black Economic Union (BEU)
Brown, Jim **11**

Black Enterprise magazine
Brimmer, Andrew F. **2, 48**
Graves, Earl G. **1, 35**
Wallace, Phyllis A. **9**

Black Enterprise Corporate Executive of the Year
Chenault, Kenneth I. **5, 36**
Steward, David L. **36**

Black Entertainment Television (BET)
Ames, Wilmer **27**
Gordon, Ed **10, 53**
Greely, M. Gasby **27**
Johnson, Robert L. **3, 39**
Johnson, Sheila Crump **48**
Jones, Bobby **20**
Lee, Debra L. **62**
McCrary Anthony, Crystal **70**
Smiley, Tavis **20, 68**

Black Filmmaker Foundation (BFF)
Hudlin, Reginald **9**
Hudlin, Warrington **9**
Jackson, George **19**
Williams, Terrie **35**

Black Filmmakers Hall of Fame
Browne, Roscoe Lee **66**
Dee, Ruby **8, 50, 68**
Dixon, Ivan **69**
McKinney, Nina Mae **40**

Black Gay and Lesbian Leadership Forum (BGLLF)
Wilson, Phill **9**

Black Guerrilla Family (BGF)
Jackson, George **14**

Black History Month
Woodson, Carter G. **2**

Black Horizons on the Hill
Wilson, August **7, 33, 55**

Black Liberation Army (BLA)
Shakur, Assata **6**
Williams, Evelyn **10**

Black literary theory
Gates, Henry Louis, Jr. **3, 38, 67**

Black Manifesto
Forman, James **7, 51**

Black Music Center
Moore, Undine Smith **28**

Black Muslims
Abdul-Jabbar, Kareem **8**
Ali, Muhammad **2, 16, 52**
Farrakhan, Louis **2**
Muhammad, Elijah **4**
Muhammed, W. Deen **27**
X, Malcolm **1**

Black nationalism
Baker, Houston A., Jr. **6**
Baraka, Amiri **1, 38**
Caldwell, Benjamin **46**
Carmichael, Stokely **5, 26**
Donaldson, Jeff **46**
Farrakhan, Louis **2**
Forman, James **7, 51**
Garvey, Marcus **1**
Heard, Nathan C. **45**
Innis, Roy **5**
Muhammad, Elijah **4**
Turner, Henry McNeal **5**
X, Malcolm **1**
York, Dwight D. **71**

Black Oscar Awards
Daniels, Lee Louis **36**

Black Panther Party (BPP)
Abu-Jamal, Mumia **15**
Al-Amin, Jamil Abdullah **6**
Brown, Elaine **8**
Carmichael, Stokely **5**
Cleaver, Eldridge **5**
Cleaver, Kathleen Neal **29**
Davis, Angela **5**
Forman, James **7, 51**
Hampton, Fred **18**
Hilliard, David **7**
Jackson, George **14**
Neal, Larry **38**
Newton, Huey **2**
Pratt, Geronimo **18**
Rush, Bobby **26**
Shakur, Afeni **67**
Seale, Bobby **3**
Shakur, Assata **6**

Black Power movement
Al-Amin, Jamil Abdullah **6**
Baker, Houston A., Jr. **6**

Brown, Elaine **8**
Carmichael, Stokely **5, 26**
Dodson, Howard, Jr. **7, 52**
Donaldson, Jeff **46**
Dumas, Henry **41**
Giovanni, Nikki **9, 39**
Hare, Nathan **44**
McKissick, Floyd B. **3**
Stone, Chuck **9**

Blackside, Inc.
Hampton, Henry **6**

Black theology
Cone, James H. **3**

Black Think Tank
Hare, Nathan **44**

Blackvoices.com
Cooper, Barry **33**

Blackwell Consulting Services
Blackwell, Robert D., Sr. **52**

Black World magazine
See *Negro Digest* magazine

Black Writers Conference
McMillan, Rosalynn A. **36**

Blessed Martin House
Riley, Helen Caldwell Day **13**

Blind Boys of Alabama
Scott, George **55**

"Blood for Britain"
Drew, Charles Richard **7**

Blood plasma research/preservation
Drew, Charles Richard **7**

Blues
Ace, Johnny **36**
Austin, Lovie **40**
Barnes, Roosevelt "Booba" **33**
Bibb, Eric **49**
Bland, Bobby "Blue" **36**
Brown, Charles **23**
Brown, Nappy **73**
Burns, Eddie **44**
Burnside, R. L. **56**
Carr, Leroy **49**
Clarke, Kenny **27**
Collins, Albert **12**
Cox, Ida **42**
Cray, Robert **30**
Davis, Gary **41**
Davis, Guy **36**
Davis, Tyrone **54**
Dixon, Willie **4**
Dorsey, Thomas **15**
Estes, Sleepy John **33**
Evora, Cesaria **12**
Freeman, Yvette **27**
Gaines, Grady **38**
Guy, Buddy **31**
Handy, W. C. **8**
Harris, Corey **39, 73**
Hemphill, Jessie Mae **33, 59**
Holiday, Billie **1**
Hooker, John Lee **30**
House, Son **8**
Howlin' Wolf **9**

Hunter, Alberta **42**
Jean-Baptiste, Marianne **17, 46**
Jackson, John **36**
James, Skip **38**
Johnson, Buddy **36**
King, B. B. **7**
Lipscomb, Mance **49**
Little Milton **36**
Little Walton **36**
Mahal, Taj **39**
Martin, Sara **38**
McGriff, Jimmy **72**
Mo', Keb' **36**
Moore, Johnny B. **38**
Muse, Clarence Edouard **21**
Neal, Raful **44**
Odetta **37**
Owens, Jack **38**
Parker, Charlie **20**
Pena, Paul **58**
Perkins, Pinetop **70**
Peterson, James **38**
Rawls, Lou **17, 57**
Reed, A. C. **36**
Reed, Jimmy **38**
Reese, Della **6, 20**
Robinson, Fenton **38**
Rogers, Jimmy **38**
Ross, Isaiah "Doc" **40**
Rush, Otis **38**
Seals, Son **56**
Smith, Bessie **3**
Smith, Mamie **32**
Smith, Trixie **34**
Staples, Mavis **50**
Staples, "Pops" **32**
Streeter, Sarah **45**
Sykes, Roosevelt **20**
Tampa Red **63**
Taylor, Koko **40**
Turner, Ike **68**
Wallace, Sippie **1**
Washington, Dinah **22**
Waters, Ethel **7**
Waters, Muddy **34**
Watson, Johnny "Guitar" **18**
Webster, Katie **29**
White, Josh, Jr. **52**
Williams, Joe **5, 25**
Wilson, August **7, 33, 55**

Blues Hall of Fame
Little Milton **36**

Blues Heaven Foundation
Dixon, Willie **4**

Blues vernacular
Baker, Houston A., Jr. **6**

Bobsledding
Flowers, Vonetta **35**
Hines, Garrett **35**
Jones, Randy **35**
Moses, Edwin **8**

Bodybuilding
Murray, Lenda **10**

Boeing Company, The
Bell, James A. **50**
Grooms, Henry R(andall) **50**

Mills, Joseph C. **51**

Bola Press
Cortez, Jayne **43**

Bolero music
Ferrer, Ibrahim **41**

Boogie music
Brooks, Hadda **40**

Booker T. Washington Business College
Gaston, Arthur George **3, 38, 59**

Booker T. Washington Insurance Company
Gaston, Arthur George **3, 38, 59**
Willie, Louis, Jr. **68**

The Boondocks
McGruder, Aaron **28, 56**

Boston Bruins hockey team
O'Ree, Willie **5**

Boston Celtics basketball team
Cooper, Charles "Chuck" **47**
Fox, Rick **27**
Garnett, Kevin **14, 70**
Parish, Robert **43**
Pierce, Paul **71**
Russell, Bill **8**
Silas, Paul **24**

Boston Red Sox baseball team
Baylor, Don **6**
Ortiz, David **52**
Vaughn, Mo **16**

Boston University
Loury, Glenn **36**
Mitchell, Sharon **36**

Botany
Carver, George Washington **4**

Botswana Democratic Party (BDP)
Masire, Quett **5**
Mogae, Festus Gontebanye **19**

Bountiful Blessings magazine
Patterson, Gilbert Earl **41**

Bowling
Branham, George, III **50**

Boxing
Ali, Laila **27, 63**
Ali, Muhammad **2, 16, 52**
Bowe, Riddick **6**
Carter, Rubin **26**
Dixon, George **52**
Ellis, Jimmy **44**
Foreman, George **1, 15**
Frazier, Joe **19**
Frazier-Lyde, Jacqui **31**
Futch, Eddie **33**
Gibson, Truman K., Jr. **60**
Hearns, Thomas **29**
Holmes, Larry **20, 68**
Holyfield, Evander **6**
Hopkins, Bernard **35, 69**
Johnson, Jack **8**

Jones, Roy, Jr. **22**
King, Don **14**
Lee, Canada **8**
Leonard, Sugar Ray **15**
Lewis, Butch **71**
Lewis, Lennox **27**
Louis, Joe **5**
Mayweather, Floyd, Jr. **57**
Moorer, Michael **19**
Mosley, Shane **32**
Muhammad, Jabir Herbert **72**
Mundine, Anthony **56**
Patterson, Floyd **19, 58**
Robinson, Sugar Ray **18**
Rose, Lionel **56**
Steward, Emanuel **18**
Taylor, Jermain **60**
Tyson, Mike **28, 44**
Ward, Andre **62**
Whitaker, Pernell **10**
Young, Jimmy **54**

Boys Choir of Harlem
Turnbull, Walter **13, 60**

BPP
See Black Panther Party

Brazeal Dennard Chorale
Dennard, Brazeal **37**

Brazilian Congress
da Silva, Benedita **5**

Breast cancer awareness
Brown, Zora Kramer **12**
Norton, Meredith **72**
Riperton, Minnie **32**

Bristol-Myers Squibb Inc.
Potter, Myrtle **40**

British Broadcasting Company (BBC)
Figueroa, John J. **40**

British Film Institute
Akomfrah, John **37**

British government
Abbott, Diane **9**
Amos, Valerie **41**
Boateng, Paul Yaw **56**
Grant, Bernie **57**
King, Oona **27**
Pitt, David Thomas **10**

British Open golf tournament
Woods, Tiger **14, 31**

British Parliament
See British government

Broadcasting
Allen, Byron **3, 24**
Ashley, Maurice **15, 47**
Banks, William **11**
Barden, Don H. **9, 20**
Bettis, Jerome **64**
Blackmon, Brenda **58**
Bradley, Ed **2, 59**
Branch, William Blackwell **39**
Brown, Les **5**
Brown, Tony **3**
Brown, Vivian **27**
Brunson, Dorothy **1**

Clayton, Xernona **3, 45**
Cornelius, Don **4**
Davis, Ossie **5, 50**
Dee, Merri **55**
Elder, Larry **25**
Evans, Harry **25**
Figueroa, John J. **40**
Freeman, Aaron **52**
Goode, Mal **13**
Gumbel, Bryant **14**
Gumbel, Greg **8**
Hamblin, Ken **10**
Hickman, Fred **11**
Holt, Lester **66**
Hunter-Gault, Charlayne **6, 31**
Jackson, Hal **41**
Johnson, Rafer **33**
Johnson, Robert L. **3, 39**
Jones, Bobby **20**
Joyner, Tom **19**
Kellogg, Clark **64**
Kennedy-Overton, Jayne Harris **46**
Langhart Cohen, Janet **19, 60**
Lawson, Jennifer **1, 50**
Lewis, Delano **7**
Lofton, James **42**
Long, Eddie L. **29**
Mabrey, Vicki **26**
Madison, Joseph E. **17**
Madison, Paula **37**
McEwen, Mark **5**
McFarland, Roland **49**
Mickelbury, Penny **28**
Miller, Cheryl **10**
Mitchell, Russ **21, 73**
Morgan, Joe Leonard **9**
Neville, Arthel **53**
Peete, Rodney **60**
Pinckney, Sandra **56**
Pinkston, W. Randall **24**
Quarles, Norma **25**
Reynolds, Star Jones **10, 27, 61**
Roberts, Deborah **35**
Roberts, Robin **16, 54**
Robinson, Max **3**
Rodgers, Johnathan **6, 51**
Russell, Bill **8**
Shaw, Bernard **2, 28**
Simmons, Jamal **72**
Simpson, Carole **6, 30**
Simpson, O. J. **15**
Smiley, Tavis **20, 68**
Stewart, Alison **13**
Swann, Lynn **28**
Syler, Rene **53**
Tirico, Mike **68**
Watts, Rolonda **9**
White, Bill **1, 48**
Williams, Armstrong **29**
Williams, Juan **35**
Williams, Montel **4, 57**
Winfrey, Oprah **2, 15, 61**

Broadside Press
Hoagland, Everett H. **45**
Randall, Dudley **8, 55**

Brookings Institute
Ladner, Joyce A. **42**

Brooklyn Academy of Music
Miller, Bebe **3**

Brooklyn Dodgers baseball team
Campanella, Roy 25
Newcombe, Don 24
Robinson, Jackie 6

Brooklyn Eagles baseball team
Day, Leon 39

Brotherhood of Sleeping Car Porters
Randolph, A. Philip 3
Tucker, Rosina 14

Brown Capital Management
Brown, Eddie C. 35

Brown University
Beckham, Barry 41
Gibson, Donald Bernard 40
Simmons, Ruth 13, 38

Brown v. Board of Education of Topeka
Bell, Derrick 6
Carter, Robert L. 51
Clark, Kenneth B. 5, 52
Franklin, John Hope 5
Henderson, Zelma 71
Hill, Oliver W. 24, 63
Houston, Charles Hamilton 4
Malone Jones, Vivian 59
Marshall, Thurgood 1, 44
Motley, Constance Baker 10, 55
Redding, Louis L. 26
Robinson, Spottswood W., III 22

Buena Vista Social Club
Ferrer, Ibrahim 41

Buffalo Bills football team
Lofton, James 42
Simpson, O. J. 15

Bull-riding
Sampson, Charles 13

Busing (anti-busing legislation)
Bosley, Freeman, Jr. 7

Cabinet
See U.S. Cabinet

Cable News Network (CNN)
Chideya, Farai 14, 61
Hickman, Fred 11
Quarles, Norma 25
Shaw, Bernard 2, 28
Watson, Carlos 50

Calabash International Literary Festival
Channer, Colin 36

Calgary Flames hockey team
Iginla, Jarome 35

California Angels baseball team
See Los Angeles Angels baseball team

California Eagle newspaper
Bass, Charlotta Spears 40
Jackson, Vera 40

California State Assembly
Bass, Karen 70
Brown, Willie L., Jr. 7
Dixon, Julian C. 24
Dymally, Mervyn 42
Hawkins, Augustus F. 68
Lee, Barbara 25
Millender-McDonald, Juanita 21, 61
Waters, Maxine 3, 67

California state government
Bass, Karen 70
Brown, Janice Rogers 43
Dymally, Mervyn 42
Watson, Diane 41

California State University
Cobb, Jewel Plummer 42
Granville, Evelyn Boyd 36
Karenga, Maulana 10, 71

California Supreme Court
Brown, Janice Rogers 43

Calypso
Belafonte, Harry 4, 65
Jean, Wyclef 20
Premice, Josephine 41
Rhoden, Wayne 70

Camac Holdings, Inc.
Lawal, Kase L. 45

Cameroonian government
Biya, Paul 28
Oyono, Ferdinand 38

Canadian Agricultural Chemistry Association
Donald, Arnold Wayne 36

Canadian Football League (CFL)
Clemons, Michael "Pinball" 64
Gilliam, Frank 23
Moon, Warren 8, 66
Thrower, Willie 35
Weathers, Carl 10

Canadian government
Augustine, Jean 53
Brown, Rosemary 62
Cools, Anne 64
Jean, Michaëlle; 70
Lewis, Daurene 72
Sparks, Corinne Etta 53

Canadian Provincial baseball league
Kaiser, Cecil 42

Cancer research
Adams-Campbell, Lucille L. 60
Chinn, May Edward 26
Clark, Celeste 15
Daly, Marie Maynard 37
Dunston, Georgia Mae 48
Freeman, Harold P. 23
Leffall, Lasalle 3, 64
Olopade, Olufunmilayo Falusi 58

Capital punishment
Hawkins, Steven 14

Cardiac research
Watkins, Levi, Jr. 9

CARE
Gossett, Louis, Jr. 7
Stone, Chuck 9

Caribbean Artists' Movement
Brathwaite, Kamau 36

Caribbean dance
Ailey, Alvin 8
Dunham, Katherine 4, 59
Fagan, Garth 18
Nichols, Nichelle 11
Primus, Pearl 6

Caribbean literature
Breeze, Jean "Binta" 37
Carter, Martin 49
Cartey, Wilfred 47
Dabydeen, David 48
Hearne, John Edgar Caulwell 45

Casamance, Senegal
Senghor, Augustin Dimacoune 66

Casting
Cannon, Reuben 50

Catalyst Award (American Express)
Chenault, Kenneth I. 5, 36

Cartoonists
Armstrong, Robb 15
Brandon, Barbara 3
Brown, Robert 65
Campbell, E. Simms 13
Fax, Elton 48
Harrington, Oliver W. 9
McDuffie, Dwayne 62
McGruder, Aaron 28, 56
Ormes, Jackie 73
Smith, Bruce W. 53

Catholicism
See Roman Catholic Church

CBC
See Congressional Black Caucus

CBEA
See Council for a Black Economic Agenda

CBS
See Columbia Broadcasting System

CBS Television Stations Division
Rodgers, Johnathan 6, 51

CDC
See Centers for Disease Control and Prevention

CDF
See Children's Defense Fund

CEDBA
See Council for the Economic Development of Black Americans

Celebrities for a Drug-Free America
Vereen, Ben 4

Censorship
Butts, Calvin O., III 9
Ice-T 6, 31

Centers for Disease Control and Prevention (CDC)
Gayle, Helene D. 3
Satcher, David 7, 57
Wisdom, Kimberlydawn 57

Central Intercollegiate Athletic Association (CIAA)
Kerry, Leon G. 46
Yancy, Dorothy Cowser 42

Certified Public Accountant
Jones, Thomas W. 41
Washington, Mary T. 57

CFL
See Canadian Football League

CHA
See Chicago Housing Authority

Chadian government
Habré, Hissène 6

Challenged Athletes Foundation
Yeboah, Emmanuel Ofosu 53

Challenger
McNair, Ronald 3, 58

Challenger Air Pilot's Association
Brown, Willa 40

Chama cha Mapinduzi (Tanzania; Revolutionary Party)
Kikwete, Jakaya Mrisho 73
Mkapa, Benjamin 16
Mongella, Gertrude 11
Nyerere, Julius 5

Chamber of Deputies (Brazil)
da Silva, Benedita 5

Chanteuses
Baker, Josephine 3
Dandridge, Dorothy 3
Horne, Lena 5
Kitt, Eartha 16
Lefel, Edith 41
Moore, Melba 21
Moten, Etta 18
Reese, Della 6, 20

Charles H. Wright Museum of African American History (CWMAAH)
Wright, Charles H. 35

Charles R. Drew University
Bath, Patricia E. 37

Charlotte Hornets basketball team
Bryant, Kobe 15, 31, 71
Parish, Robert 43

Charter Schools USA
Mariner, Jonathan 41

Che-Lumumba Club
Davis, Angela 5

Chemistry
Daly, Marie Maynard 37
Hall, Lloyd A. 8

Humphries, Frederick **20**
Julian, Percy Lavon **6**
King, Reatha Clark **65**
Massie, Samuel Proctor, Jr. **29**
Mays, William G. **34**
Mensah, Thomas **48**

Chemurgy
Carver, George Washington **4**

Chesapeake and Potomac Telephone Company
Lewis, Delano **7**

Chess
Ashley, Maurice **15, 47**

Chess Records
Taylor, Koko **40**

Chicago American Giants baseball team
Bell, James "Cool Papa" **36**
Charleston, Oscar **39**

Chicago Art League
Wilson, Ellis **39**

Chicago Bears football team
Page, Alan **7**
Payton, Walter **11, 25**
Sayers, Gale **28**
Singletary, Mike **4**
Thrower, Willie **35**

Chicago Black Arts Movement
Cortor, Eldzier **42**
Sebree, Charles **40**

Chicago Blaze basketball team
Catchings, Tamika **43**

Chicago Bulls basketball team
Brand, Elton **31**
Jordan, Michael **6, 21**
Parish, Robert **43**
Pippen, Scottie **15**
Rodman, Dennis **12, 44**

Chicago city government
Metcalfe, Ralph **26**
Washington, Harold **6**

Chicago Cubs baseball team
Baker, Dusty **8, 43, 72**
Banks, Ernie **33**
Bonds, Bobby **43**
Carter, Joe **30**
Sosa, Sammy **21, 44**

Chicago Defender
Abbott, Robert Sengstacke **27**
Holt, Nora **38**
Martin, Roland S. **49**
Ormes, Jackie **73**
Payne, Ethel L. **28**

Chicago Defender Charities
Joyner, Marjorie Stewart **26**

Chicago Eight
Seale, Bobby **3**

Chicago Housing Authority (CHA)
Lane, Vincent **5**

Chicago Library Board
Williams, Fannie Barrier **27**

Chicago Negro Chamber of Commerce
Fuller, S. B. **13**

Chicago Police Department
Hillard, Terry **25**
Holton, Hugh, Jr. **39**

Chicago Reporter
Washington, Laura S. **18**

Chicago Tribune
Page, Clarence **4**

Chicago White Sox baseball team
Baines, Harold **32**
Bonds, Bobby **43**
Doby, Lawrence Eugene, Sr. **16, 41**
Johnson, Clifford "Connie" **52**
Thomas, Frank **12, 51**
Williams, Ken **68**

Chicago Women's Club
Williams, Fannie Barrier **27**

Child Care Trust
Obasanjo, Stella **32, 56**

Child psychiatry
Comer, James P. **6**

Child psychology
Hale, Lorraine **8**

Child Welfare Administration
Little, Robert L. **2**

Children's Defense Fund (CDF)
Edelman, Marian Wright **5, 42**
Williams, Maggie **7, 71**

Children's literature
Asim, Jabari **71**
Berry, James **41**
Bryan, Ashley F. **41**
Common **31, 63**
De Veaux, Alexis **44**
Feelings, Muriel **44**
Graham, Lorenz **48**
Johnson, Angela **52**
Mollel, Tololwa **38**
Myers, Walter Dean **8, 20**
Okara, Gabriel **37**
Palmer, Everard **37**
Yarbrough, Camille **40**

Chi-Lites
Record, Eugene **60**

Chiropractics
Ford, Clyde W. **40**
Reese, Milous J., Jr. **51**
Westbrooks, Bobby **51**

Chisholm-Mingo Group, Inc.
Chisholm, Samuel J. **32**
Mingo, Frank **32**

Choreography
Acogny, Germaine **55**
Ailey, Alvin **8**
Alexander, Khandi **43**
Allen, Debbie **13, 42**

Atkins, Cholly **40**
Babatunde, Obba **35**
Beatty, Talley **35**
Brooks, Avery **9**
Byrd, Donald **10**
Campbell-Martin, Tisha **8, 42**
Collins, Janet **33, 64**
Davis, Chuck **33**
de Passe, Suzanne **25**
De Shields, André **72**
Dove, Ulysses **5**
Dunham, Katherine **4, 59**
Ellington, Mercedes **34**
Fagan, Garth **18**
Faison, George **16**
Glover, Savion **14**
Hall, Arthur **39**
Henson, Darrin **33**
Jamison, Judith **7, 67**
Johnson, Virginia **9**
Jones, Bill T. **1**
King, Alonzo **38**
LeTang, Henry **66**
Miller, Bebe **3**
Mitchell, Arthur **2, 47**
Nicholas, Fayard **20, 57**
Nicholas, Harold **20**
Pomare, Eleo **72**
Primus, Pearl **6**
Rhoden, Dwight **40**
Richardson, Desmond **39**
Robinson, Cleo Parker **38**
Robinson, Fatima **34**
Rodgers, Rod **36**
Spears, Warren **52**
Tyson, Andre **40**
Zollar, Jawole **28**

Christian Financial Ministries, Inc.
Ross, Charles **27**

Christian Science Monitor
Khanga, Yelena **6**

Chrysler Corporation
Colbert, Virgis William **17**
Farmer, Forest **1**
Gilles, Ralph **61**
Richie, Leroy C. **18**

Church of God in Christ
Franklin, Robert M. **13**
Hayes, James C. **10**
Patterson, Gilbert Earl **41**

CIAA
See Central Intercollegiate Athletic Association

Cincinnati city government
Berry, Theodore M. **31**
Mallory, Mark **62**

Cincinnati Reds baseball team
Baker, Dusty **8, 43, 72**
Blair, Paul **36**
Larkin, Barry **24**
Morgan, Joe Leonard **9**
Reese, Pokey **28**
Robinson, Frank **9**
Sanders, Deion **4, 31**

Cinematography
Dickerson, Ernest **6, 17**

Citadel Press
Achebe, Chinua **6**

Citigroup
Gaines, Brenda **41**
Jones, Thomas W. **41**
McGuire, Raymond J. **57**

Citizens Federal Savings and Loan Association
Gaston, Arthur George **3, 38, 59**
Willie, Louis, Jr. **68**

Citizens for Affirmative Action's Preservation
Dillard, Godfrey J. **45**

City Capital Corporation
Taylor, Ephren W., II **61**

City government--U.S.
Archer, Dennis **7, 36**
Barden, Don H. **9, 20**
Barry, Marion S. **7, 44**
Berry, Theodore M. **31**
Bosley, Freeman, Jr. **7**
Bradley, Thomas **2, 20**
Brown, Lee P. **1, 24**
Burris, Chuck **21**
Caesar, Shirley **19**
Campbell, Bill **9**
Clayton, Constance **1**
Cleaver, Emanuel **4, 45, 68**
Craig-Jones, Ellen Walker **44**
Dinkins, David **4**
Dixon, Sharon Pratt **1**
Evers, Myrlie **8**
Fauntroy, Walter E. **11**
Fields, C. Virginia **25**
Ford, Jack **39**
Ford, Johnny **70**
Gibson, Kenneth Allen **6**
Goode, W. Wilson **4**
Harmon, Clarence **26**
Hayes, James C. **10**
Jackson, Maynard **2, 41**
James, Sharpe **23, 69**
Jarvis, Charlene Drew **21**
Johnson, Eddie Bernice **8**
Johnson, Harvey, Jr. **24**
Kirk, Ron **11**
Mallett, Conrad, Jr. **16**
McPhail, Sharon **2**
Metcalfe, Ralph **26**
Millender-McDonald, Juanita **21, 61**
Morial, Ernest "Dutch" **26**
Morial, Marc H. **20, 51**
Murrell, Sylvia Marilyn **49**
Powell, Adam Clayton, Jr. **3**
Powell, Debra A. **23**
Rice, Norm **8**
Sayles Belton, Sharon **9, 16**
Schmoke, Kurt **1, 48**
Stokes, Carl **10, 73**
Street, John F. **24**
Usry, James L. **23**
Washington, Harold **6**
Webb, Wellington **3**
White, Michael R. **5**
Williams, Anthony **21**
Young, Andrew **3, 48**

Young, Coleman **1, 20**

City Sun newspaper
Cooper, Andrew W. **36**

City University of New York
Ballard, Allen Butler, Jr. **40**
Davis, George **36**
Gayle, Addison, Jr. **41**
Shabazz, Ilyasah **36**

Civil rights
Abbott, Diane **9**
Abernathy, Ralph **1**
Agyeman, Jaramogi Abebe **10, 63**
Al-Amin, Jamil Abdullah **6**
Alexander, Clifford **26**
Ali, Ayaan Hirsi **58**
Ali, Muhammad **2, 16, 52**
Amaker, Norman **63**
Angelou, Maya **1, 15**
Anthony, Wendell **25**
Aristide, Jean-Bertrand **6, 45**
Arnwine, Barbara **28**
Baker, Ella **5**
Baker, Houston A., Jr. **6**
Baker, Josephine **3**
Ballance, Frank W. **41**
Barbee, Lloyd Augustus **71**
Bashir, Halima **73**
Bass, Charlotta Spears **40**
Bates, Daisy **13**
Baugh, David **23**
Beals, Melba Patillo **15**
Belafonte, Harry **4, 65**
Bell, Derrick **6**
Bell, James Madison **40**
Bennett, Lerone, Jr. **5**
Berry, Mary Frances **7**
Berry, Theodore M. **31**
Biko, Steven **4**
Bishop, Sanford D., Jr. **24**
Bond, Julian **2, 35**
Booker, Simeon **23**
Boyd, John W., Jr. **20, 72**
Bradle, David Henry, Jr. **39**
Brooks, Tyrone **59**
Brown, Byrd **49**
Brown, Elaine **8**
Brown, Homer S. **47**
Brown, Tony **3**
Brown, Wesley **23**
Brown, Willa **40**
Burks, Mary Fair **40**
Caldwell, Earl **60**
Campbell, Bebe Moore **6, 24, 59**
Carmichael, Stokely **5, 26**
Carr, Johnnie **69**
Carter, Mandy **11**
Carter, Rubin **26**
Carter, Stephen L. **4**
Cary, Mary Ann Shadd **30**
Cayton, Horace **26**
Chambers, Julius **3**
Chavis, Benjamin **6**
Chestnut, J. L., Jr. **73**
Clark, Septima **7**
Clay, William Lacy **8**
Cleaver, Eldridge **5**
Cleaver, Kathleen Neal **29**
Clyburn, James E. **21, 71**
Cobb, W. Montague **39**
Cobbs, Price M. **9**
Cooper, Anna Julia **20**

Cosby, Bill **7, 26, 59**
Crockett, George W., Jr. **10, 64**
Cunningham, Evelyn **23**
Davis, Angela **5**
Davis, Artur **41**
Davis, James E. **50**
Days, Drew S., III **10**
Dee, Ruby **8, 50, 68**
Dent, Thomas C. **50**
Diallo, Amadou **27**
Diggs, Charles C. **21**
Diggs-Taylor, Anna **20**
Divine, Father **7**
Dodson, Howard, Jr. **7, 52**
Du Bois, W. E. B. **3**
Dudley, Edward R. **58**
Dukes, Hazel Nell **56**
Dumas, Henry **41**
Edelman, Marian Wright **5, 42**
Ellison, Ralph **7**
Evers, Medgar **3**
Evers, Myrlie **8**
Farmer, James **2, 64**
Farmer-Paellmann, Deadria **43**
Fauntroy, Walter E. **11**
Fletcher, Bill, Jr. **41**
Forman, James **7, 51**
Fortune, T. Thomas **6**
Foster, Marie **48**
Franklin, C. L. **68**
Franklin, John Hope **5**
Gaines, Ernest J. **7**
George, Zelma Watson **42**
Gibson, William F. **6**
Gray, Fred **37**
Gregory, Dick **1, 54**
Grimké, Archibald H. **9**
Guinier, Lani **7, 30**
Haley, Alex **4**
Haley, George Williford Boyce **21**
Hall, Elliott S. **24**
Hamer, Fannie Lou **6**
Hampton, Fred **18**
Hampton, Henry **6**
Hansberry, Lorraine **6**
Harding, Vincent **67**
Harper, Frances Ellen Watkins **11**
Harris, Patricia Roberts **2**
Hastie, William H. **8**
Hatcher, Richard G. **55**
Hawkins, Augustus F. **68**
Hawkins, Steven **14**
Hayes, Dennis **54**
Hedgeman, Anna Arnold **22**
Height, Dorothy I. **2, 23**
Henderson, Thelton E. **68**
Henderson, Wade J. **14**
Henry, Aaron **19**
Higginbotham, A. Leon, Jr. **13, 25**
Hill, Jesse, Jr. **13**
Hill, Oliver W. **24, 63**
Hilliard, David **7**
Hobson, Julius W. **44**
Holland, Endesha Ida Mae **3, 57**
Hollowell, Donald L. **57**
hooks, bell **5**
Hooks, Benjamin L. **2**
Horne, Lena **5**
Houston, Charles Hamilton **4**
Howard, M. William, Jr. **26**
Hughes, Langston **4**
Innis, Roy **5**
Irvis, K. Leroy **67**

Jackson, Alexine Clement **22**
Jackson, Jesse **1, 27, 72**
James, Daniel, Jr. **16**
Jarrett, Vernon D. **42**
Johns, Vernon **38**
Johnson, Eddie Bernice **8**
Johnson, Georgia Douglas **41**
Johnson, James Weldon **5**
Johnson, Norma L. Holloway **17**
Jones, Elaine R. **7, 45**
Jones, William A., Jr. **61**
Jordan, Barbara **4**
Jordan, June **7, 35**
Jordan, Vernon E. **3, 35**
Julian, Percy Lavon **6**
Karim, Benjamin **61**
Kennedy, Florynce **12, 33**
Kenyatta, Jomo **5**
Kidd, Mae Street **39**
King, Bernice **4**
King, Coretta Scott **3, 57**
King, Martin Luther, Jr. **1**
King, Martin Luther, III **20**
King, Preston **28**
King, Yolanda **6**
Ladner, Joyce A. **42**
Lampkin, Daisy **19**
Lee, Spike **5, 19**
Lester, Julius **9**
Lewis, John **2, 46**
Logan, Rayford W. **40**
Lorde, Audre **6**
Loving, Mildred **69**
Lowery, Joseph **2**
Lowry, A. Leon **60**
Lucy Foster, Autherine **35**
Makeba, Miriam **2, 50**
Malone Jones, Vivian **59**
Mandela, Nelson **1, 14**
Mandela, Winnie **2, 35**
Martin, Louis E. **16**
Martin, Ruby Grant **49**
Mayfield, Curtis **2, 43**
Mays, Benjamin E. **7**
Mbeki, Thabo **14, 73**
McDonald, Gabrielle Kirk **20**
McDougall, Gay J. **11, 43**
McKissick, Floyd B. **3**
Meek, Carrie **6**
Meredith, James H. **11**
Metcalfe, Ralph **26**
Morgan, Irene **65**
Moore, Barbara C. **49**
Moore, Harry T. **29**
Morial, Ernest "Dutch" **26**
Morrison, Toni **2, 15**
Moses, Robert Parris **11**
Moss, Otis, Jr. **72**
Motley, Constance Baker **10, 55**
Mowry, Jess **7**
Murphy, Laura M. **43**
Murray, Pauli **38**
Nash, Diane **72**
Ndadaye, Melchior **7**
Nelson, Jill **6, 54**
Newton, Huey **2**
Nkoli, Simon **60**
Nkomo, Joshua **4, 65**
Norman, Pat **10**
Norton, Eleanor Holmes **7**
Nunn, Annetta **43**
Nzo, Alfred **15**
Parker, Kellis E. **30**

Parks, Rosa **1, 35, 56**
Patrick, Deval **12, 61**
Patterson, Louise **25**
Patterson, Orlando **4**
Perkins, Edward **5**
Pincham, R. Eugene, Sr. **69**
Pinchback, P. B. S. **9**
Player, Willa B. **43**
Pleasant, Mary Ellen **9**
Plessy, Homer Adolph **31**
Poitier, Sidney **11, 36**
Powell, Adam Clayton, Jr. **3**
Price, Hugh B. **9, 54**
Ramaphosa, Cyril **3**
Randolph, A. Philip **3**
Reagon, Bernice Johnson **7**
Redding, Louis L. **26**
Riggs, Marlon **5, 44**
Robeson, Paul **2**
Robinson, Jackie **6**
Robinson, Rachel **16**
Robinson, Randall **7, 46**
Robinson, Sharon **22**
Robinson, Spottswood W., III **22**
Rowan, Carl T. **1, 30**
Rush, Bobby **26**
Rustin, Bayard **4**
Sadlier, Rosemary **62**
Sané, Pierre Gabriel **21**
Sanders, Malika **48**
Saro-Wiwa, Kenule **39**
Seale, Bobby **3**
Shabazz, Attallah **6**
Shabazz, Betty **7, 26**
Shakur, Assata **6**
Shinhoster, Earl **32**
Shuttlesworth, Fred **47**
Simone, Nina **15, 41**
Sisulu, Albertina **57**
Sisulu, Sheila Violet Makate **24**
Sleet, Moneta, Jr. **5**
Smith, Barbara **28**
Staupers, Mabel K. **7**
Sullivan, Leon H. **3, 30**
Sutton, Percy E. **42**
Sweet, Ossian **68**
Thompson, Bennie G. **26**
Thurman, Howard **3**
Till, Emmett **7**
Touré, Faya Ora Rose **56**
Trotter, Monroe **9**
Tsvangirai, Morgan **26, 72**
Turner, Henry McNeal **5**
Tutu, Desmond Mpilo **6, 44**
Underwood, Blair **7**
Walker, Rebecca **50**
Washington, Booker T. **4**
Washington, Fredi **10**
Watt, Melvin **26**
Weaver, Robert C. **8, 46**
Wells, James Lesesne **10**
Wells-Barnett, Ida B. **8**
West, Cornel **5**
White, Walter F. **4**
Wideman, John Edgar **5**
Wilkins, Roy **4**
Williams, Evelyn **10**
Williams, Fannie Barrier **27**
Williams, Hosea Lorenzo **15, 31**
Williams, Robert F. **11**
Williams, Walter E. **4**
Wilson, August **7, 33, 55**
Wilson, Sunnie **7, 55**

Wilson, William Julius **22**
Woodson, Robert L. **10**
Wright, Nathan, Jr. **56**
X, Malcolm **1**
Yoba, Malik **11**
Young, Andrew **3, 48**
Young, Jean Childs **14**
Young, Whitney M., Jr. **4**

Civilian Pilots Training Program
Brown, Willa **40**

Classical music
Adams, Leslie **39**
Baiocchi, Regina Harris **41**
Bonds, Margaret **39**
Brown, Uzee **42**
Burleigh, Henry Thacker **56**
Cook, Will Marion **40**
Dawson, William Levi **39**
DePriest, James **37**
Dixon, Dean **68**
Dunner, Leslie B. **45**
Freeman, Paul **39**
Kay, Ulysses **37**
Lewis, Henry **38**
McFerrin, Bobby **68**
Moore, Dorothy Rudd **46**
Murray, Tai **47**
Pratt, Awadagin **31**
Price, Florence **37**
Schuyler, Philippa **50**
Sowande, Fela **39**
Still, William Grant **37**
Tillis, Frederick **40**
Walker, George **37**
Wilkins, Thomas Alphonso **71**
Williams, Denise **40**

Classical singers
Anderson, Marian **2, 33**
Battle, Kathleen **70**
Bumbry, Grace **5**
Burleigh, Henry Thacker **56**
Hayes, Roland **4**
Hendricks, Barbara **3, 67**
Lister, Marquita **65**
Norman, Jessye **5**
Price, Leontyne **1**
Three Mo' Tenors **35**
Williams, Denise **40**

Clearview Golf Club
Powell, Renee **34**

Cleo Parker Robinson Dance Ensemble
Robinson, Cleo Parker **38**

Clergy
Agyeman, Jaramogi Abebe **10, 63**
Anthony, Wendell **25**
Austin, Junius C. **44**
Black, Barry C. **47**
Burgess, John **46**
Bynum, Juanita **31, 71**
Caesar, Shirley **19**
Caldwell, Kirbyjon **55**
Cleveland, James **19**
Cook, Suzan D. Johnson **22**
Dyson, Michael Eric **11, 40**
Falana, Lola **42**
Gilmore, Marshall **46**
Gomes, Peter J. **15**

Gregory, Wilton **37**
Howard, M. William, Jr. **26**
Jakes, Thomas "T. D." **17, 43**
James, Skip **38**
Jemison, Major L. **48**
Johns, Vernon **38**
Jones, Absalom **52**
Jones, Alex **64**
Jones, William A., Jr. **61**
Karim, Benjamin **61**
Kee, John P. **43**
Kelly, Leontine **33**
King, Barbara **22**
King, Bernice **4**
Kobia, Samuel **43**
Lincoln, C. Eric **38**
Long, Eddie L. **29**
Maxis, Theresa **62**
McClurkin, Donnie **25**
McKenzie, Vashti M. **29**
Morgan, Gertrude **63**
Okaalet, Peter **58**
Otunga, Maurice Michael **55**
Phipps, Wintley **59**
Reems, Ernestine Cleveland **27**
Reese, Della **6, 20**
Sentamu, John **58**
Shuttlesworth, Fred **47**
Thurman, Howard **3**
Thurston, Stephen J. **49**
Tillard, Conrad **47**
Tolton, Augustine **62**
Walker, John T. **50**
Washington, James Melvin **50**
Weeks, Thomas, III **70**
Weems, Renita J. **44**
White-Hammond, Gloria **61**
Williams, David Rudyard **50**
Williams, Frederick (B.) **63**
Williams, Preston Warren, II **64**
Winans, Marvin L. **17**
Wright, Nathan, Jr. **56**

Cleveland Browns football team
Brown, Jim **11**
Crennel, Romeo **54**
Hill, Calvin **19**
Motley, Marion **26**
Newsome, Ozzie **26**
Willis, Bill **68**

Cleveland Cavaliers basketball team
Brandon, Terrell **16**
Wilkens, Lenny **11**

Cleveland city government
Stokes, Carl **10, 73**
White, Michael R. **5**

Cleveland Foundation
Adams, Leslie **39**

Cleveland Indians baseball team
Belle, Albert **10**
Bonds, Bobby **43**
Carter, Joe **30**
Doby, Lawrence Eugene, Sr. **16, 41**
Justice, David **18**
Lofton, Kenny **12**
Murray, Eddie **12**
Paige, Satchel **7**

Robinson, Frank **9**

Cleveland Rockers basketball team
Jones, Merlakia **34**

CLIO Awards
Lewis, Emmanuel **36**

Clothing design
Aberra, Amsale **67**
Bailey, Xenobia **11**
Burrows, Stephen **31**
Gaskins, Eric **64**
Henderson, Gordon **5**
John, Daymond **23**
Jones, Carl **7**
Kani, Karl **10**
Kelly, Patrick **3**
Lars, Byron **32**
Malone, Maurice **32**
Pinkett Smith, Jada **10, 41**
Robinson, Patrick **19, 71**
Smith, Willi **8**
Walker, T. J. **7**
Williams, Serena **20, 41, 73**

CNBC
Epperson, Sharon **54**
Thomas-Graham, Pamela **29**

CNN
See Cable News Network

CNU
See Cameroon National Union

Coaching
Amaker, Tommy **62**
Anderson, Mike **63**
Ashley, Maurice **15, 47**
Baker, Dusty **8, 43, 72**
Baylor, Don **6**
Bickerstaff, Bernie **21**
Bonds, Bobby **43**
Campanella, Roy **25**
Carew, Rod **20**
Carter, Butch **27**
Carter, Kenneth **53**
Chaney, John **67**
Cheeks, Maurice **47**
Cooper, Michael **31**
Crennel, Romeo **54**
Davis, Mike **41**
Dorrell, Karl **52**
Dungy, Tony **17, 42, 59**
Dunn, Jerry **27**
Edwards, Herman **51**
Ellerbe, Brian **22**
Freeman, Marianna **23**
Gaines, Clarence E., Sr. **55**
Gaither, Alonzo Smith (Jake) **14**
Gaston, Cito **71**
Gentry, Alvin **23**
Gibson, Althea **8, 43**
Gibson, Bob **33**
Gorden, W. C. **71**
Gray, Yeshimbra "Shimmy" **55**
Green, Dennis **5, 45**
Greene, Joe **10**
Haskins, Clem **23**
Heard, Gar **25**
Johnson, Avery **62**
Keith, Floyd A. **61**
Lewis, Marvin **51**

Lofton, James **42**
Miller, Cheryl **10**
O'Neil, Buck **19, 59**
Parish, Robert **43**
Phillips, Teresa L. **42**
Rhodes, Ray **14**
Richardson, Nolan **9**
Rivers, Glenn "Doc" **25**
Robinson, Eddie G. **10, 61**
Robinson, Will **51, 69**
Russell, Bill **8**
Shell, Art **1, 66**
Silas, Paul **24**
Simmons, Bob **29**
Smith, Lovie **66**
Smith, Tubby **18**
Stringer, C. Vivian **13, 66**
Thomas, Emmitt **71**
Tunnell, Emlen **54**
White, Jesse **22**
Williams, Doug **22**
Willingham, Tyrone **43**
Wills, Maury **73**

Coalition of Black Trade Unionists
Lucy, William **50**
Wyatt, Addie L. **56**

Coca-Cola Company
Ware, Carl T. **30**

Coca-Cola Foundation
Jones, Ingrid Saunders **18**

COHAR
See Committee on Appeal for Human Rights

Collage
Andrews, Benny **22, 59**
Bearden, Romare **2, 50**
Driskell, David C. **7**
Pindell, Howardena **55**
Robinson, Aminah **50**
Thomas, Mickalene **61**
Verna, Gelsy **70**

College and university administration
Archie-Hudson, Marguerite **44**
Barnett, Marguerite **46**
Burnim, Mickey L. **48**
Christian, Barbara T. **44**
Davis, Erroll B., Jr. **57**
Ford, Nick Aaron **44**
Hill, Leslie Pinckney **44**
Hogan, Beverly Wade **50**
Horne, Frank **44**
Jackson, Edison O. **67**
King, Reatha Clark **65**
Lee, Joe A. **45**
Massey, Walter E. **5, 45**
Mell, Patricia **49**
Nance, Cynthia **71**
Newman, Lester C. **51**
Ribeau, Sidney **70**
Trueheart, William E. **49**

Colorado Rockies baseball team
Baylor, Don **6**

Colorado state government
Brown, George Leslie 62
Rogers, Joe 27

Columbia Broadcasting System (CBS)
Bradley, Ed 2, 59
Dourdan, Gary 37
Kellogg, Clark 64
Mabrey, Vicki 26
McEwen, Mark 5
Mitchell, Russ 21, 73
Olden, Georg(e) 44
Pinkston, W. Randall 24
Pitts, Byron 71
Rashad, Phylicia 21
Rodgers, Johnathan 6, 51
Taylor, Meshach 4
Ware, Andre 37

Columbia Records
Jackson, Randy 40
Knowles, Tina 61
Olatunji, Babatunde 36
Williams, Deniece 36

Columbia space shuttle
Anderson, Michael P. 40

Columbus city government
Bradley, Jennette B. 40
Coleman, Michael 28

Comedy
Allen, Byron 3, 24
Amos, John 8, 62
Anderson, Anthony 51
Anderson, Eddie "Rochester" 30
Anthony, Trey 63
Arnez J 53
Beaton, Norman 14
Bellamy, Bill 12
Berry, Bertice 8, 55
Brady, Wayne 32, 71
Bruce, Bruce 56
Campbell-Martin, Tisha 8, 42
Cannon, Nick 47, 73
Cedric the Entertainer 29, 60
Chappelle, Dave 50
Cosby, Bill 7, 26, 59
Curry, Mark 17
Davidson, Tommy 21
Davis, Sammy, Jr. 18
Dieudonné 67
Earthquake 55
Epps, Mike 60
Foxx, Jamie 15, 48
Foxx, Redd 2
Freeman, Aaron 52
Givens, Adele 62
Goldberg, Whoopi 4, 33, 69
Gregory, Dick 1, 54
Harris, Robin 7
Harvey, Steve 18, 58
Henry, Lenny 9, 52
Hughley, D. L. 23
Kirby, George 14
Lawrence, Martin 6, 27, 60
Mabley, Jackie "Moms" 15
Mac, Bernie 29, 61, 72
Mayo, Whitman 32
McEwen, Mark 5
Meadows, Tim 30
Mo'Nique 35

Mooney, Paul 37
Moore, Melba 21
Morgan, Tracy 61
Morris, Garrett 31
Moss, Preacher 63
Murphy, Eddie 4, 20, 61
Nash, Niecy 66
Perry, Tyler 40, 54
Pryor, Rain 65
Pryor, Richard 3, 24, 56
Rashad, Phylicia 21
Reese, Della 6, 20
Rock, Chris 3, 22, 66
Russell, Nipsey 66
Schultz, Michael A. 6
Shepherd, Sherri 55
Sinbad 1, 16
Slocumb, Jonathan 52
Smiley, Rickey 59
Smith, Will 8, 18
Sommore 61
Sykes, Wanda 48
Taylor, Meshach 4
Thompson, Kenan 52
Torry, Guy 31
Townsend, Robert 4, 23
Tucker, Chris 13, 23, 62
Tyler, Aisha N. 36
Warfield, Marsha 2
Wayans, Damon 8, 41
Wayans, Keenen Ivory 18
Wayans, Marlon 29
Wayans, Shawn 29
Wilson, Debra 38
Wilson, Flip 21
Witherspoon, John 38
Yarbrough, Cedric 51

Comer Method
Comer, James P. 6

Comerica Bank
Forte, Linda Diane 54

Commercial art
Freeman, Leonard 27

Commission for Racial Justice
Chavis, Benjamin 6

Committee on Appeal for Human Rights (COHAR)
Bond, Julian 2, 35

Communist Party
Brown, Lloyd Louis 42
Davis, Angela 5
Du Bois, W. E. B. 3
Jagan, Cheddi 16
Wright, Richard 5

Complete Energy Partners
Scott, Milton 51

Complexions dance troupe
Rhoden, Dwight 40
Richardson, Desmond 39
Tyson, Andre 40

Computer graphics
Coleman, Ken 57
Hannah, Marc 10

Computer science
Adkins, Rod 41
Auguste, Donna 29

Dean, Mark 35
Easley, Annie J. 61
Ellis, Clarence 38
Emeagwali, Philip 30
Hannah, Marc 10
Irvin, Vernon 65
Laryea, Thomas Davies, III 67
Mensah, Thomas 48
Millines Dziko, Trish 28
Zollar, Alfred 40

Conceptual art
Allen, Tina 22
Bailey, Xenobia 11
O'Grady, Lorraine 73
Piper, Adrian 71
Pope.L, William 72
Robinson, Aminah 50
Simpson, Lorna 4, 36

Concerned Parents Association (Uganda)
Atyam, Angelina 55

Conductors
Calloway, Cab 14
Cook, Will Marion 40
Dawson, William Levi 39
DePriest, James 37
Dixon, Dean 68
Dunner, Leslie B. 45
Freeman, Paul 39
Jackson, Isaiah 3
León, Tania 13
Lewis, Henry 38

Co-nect Schools
Fuller, Arthur 27

Congressional Black Caucus (CBC)
Christian-Green, Donna M. 17
Clay, William Lacy 8
Clyburn, James E. 21, 71
Collins, Cardiss 10
Conyers, John, Jr. 4, 45
Dellums, Ronald 2
Diggs, Charles C. 21
Fauntroy, Walter E. 11
Gray, William H., III 3
Hastings, Alcee L. 16
Hawkins, Augustus F. 68
Johnson, Eddie Bernice 8
Mfume, Kweisi 6, 41
Mitchell, Parren J. 42, 66
Owens, Major 6
Payton, John 48
Rangel, Charles 3, 52
Scott, Robert C. 23
Stokes, Louis 3
Thompson, Bennie G. 26
Towns, Edolphus 19

Congressional Black Caucus Higher Education Braintrust
Owens, Major 6

Congress of Racial Equality (CORE)
Dee, Ruby 8, 50, 68
Farmer, James 2, 64
Hobson, Julius W. 44
Innis, Roy 5
Jackson, Jesse 1, 27, 72
McKissick, Floyd B. 3

Rustin, Bayard 4

Contemporary Christian music
Griffin, LaShell 51
Tait, Michael 57

Continental Basketball Association (CBA)
Davis, Mike 41
Thomas, Isiah 7, 26, 65
Ussery, Terdema, II 29

Convention People's Party (Ghana; CPP)
Nkrumah, Kwame 3

Cook County Circuit Court
Sampson, Edith S. 4

Cooking
Brown, Warren 61
Chase, Leah 57
Clark, Patrick 14
Estes, Rufus 29
Evans, Darryl 22
Henderson, Jeff 72
Roker, Al 12, 49
Samuelsson, Marcus 53

Coppin State College
Blair, Paul 36

CORE
See Congress of Racial Equality

Coretta Scott King Awards
Haskins, James 36, 54

Coronet
Oliver, Joe "King" 42

Corporation for Public Broadcasting (CPB)
Brown, Tony 3

Cosmetology
Cottrell, Comer 11
Fuller, S. B. 13
McGrath, Pat 72
Morgan, Rose 11
Powell, Maxine 8
Roche, Joyce M. 17
Walker, A'lelia 14
Walker, Madame C. J. 7

Cotton Club Revue
Johnson, Buddy 36

Council for a Black Economic Agenda (CBEA)
Woodson, Robert L. 10

Council for the Economic Development of Black Americans (CEDBA)
Brown, Tony 3

Council on Legal Education Opportunities (CLEO)
Henderson, Wade J. 14
Henry, Aaron 19

Count Basie Orchestra
Eldridge, Roy 37
Johnson, J. J. 37
Rushing, Jimmy 37
Williams, Joe 5, 25

Young, Lester 37

Country music
Bailey, DeFord 33
Cowboy Troy 54
Palmer, Rissi 65
Pride, Charley 26
Randall, Alice 38

Covad Communications
Knowling, Robert 38

Cowboys
Love, Nat 9
Pickett, Bill 11

CPB
See Corporation for Public Broadcasting

CPDM
See Cameroon People's Democratic Movement

CPP
See Convention People's Party

Creative Artists Agency
Nelson Meigs, Andrea 48

Credit Suisse First Boston, Inc.
Ogunlesi, Adebayo 37

Creole music
Ardoin, Alphonse 65

Cress Theory of Color-Confrontation and Racism
Welsing, Frances Cress 5

Cricket
Adams, Paul 50

Crisis
Du Bois, W. E. B. 3
Fauset, Jessie 7
Wilkins, Roy 4

Critics' Choice Award
Channer, Colin 36

Cross Colours
Jones, Carl 7
Kani, Karl 10
Walker, T. J. 7

Crown Media
Corbi, Lana 42

Crucial Films
Henry, Lenny 9, 52

Crusader
Williams, Robert F. 11

CTRN
See Transitional Committee for National Recovery (Guinea)

Cuban League
Charleston, Oscar 39
Day, Leon 39

Cuban music
Ferrer, Ibrahim 41
Portuondo, Omara 53

Cubism
Bearden, Romare 2, 50
Green, Jonathan 54

Culinary arts
Clark, Patrick 14
Henderson, Jeff 72

Cultural Hangups
Ham, Cynthia Parker 58

Cultural pluralism
Locke, Alain 10

Cumulative voting
Guinier, Lani 7, 30

Curator/exhibition designer
Camp, Kimberly 19
Campbell, Mary Schmidt 43
Golden, Thelma 10, 55
Hoyte, Lenon 50
Hutson, Jean Blackwell 16
Pindell, Howardena 55
Sanders, Joseph R., Jr. 11
Sims, Lowery Stokes 27
Stewart, Paul Wilbur 12

Cycling
Taylor, Marshall Walter "Major" 62
Yeboah, Emmanuel Ofosu 53

Cytogenetics
Satcher, David 7, 57

Dallas city government
Johnson, Eddie Bernice 8
Kirk, Ron 11

Dallas Cowboys football team
Hill, Calvin 19
Irvin, Michael 64
Jones, Ed "Too Tall" 46
Sanders, Deion 4, 31
Smith, Emmitt 7
Wright, Rayfield 70

Dallas Mavericks basketball team
Ussery, Terdema 29

Dallas Police Department
Bolton, Terrell D. 25

Dance
LeTang, Henry 66

DanceAfrica
Davis, Chuck 33

Dance Theatre of Harlem
Johnson, Virginia 9
King, Alonzo 38
Mitchell, Arthur 2, 47
Nicholas, Fayard 20, 57
Nicholas, Harold 20
Tyson, Cicely 7, 51

Darkchild Records
Jerkins, Rodney 31

Darrell Green Youth Life Foundation
Green, Darrell 39

DAV
See Disabled American Veterans

David M. Winfield Foundation
Winfield, Dave 5

Daytona Institute
See Bethune-Cookman College

Dayton Philharmonic Orchestra
Jackson, Isaiah 3

D.C. Black Repertory Theater
Reagon, Bernice Johnson 7

D.C. sniper
Moose, Charles 40

Death Row Records
Dre, Dr. 10, 14, 30
Hammer, M. C. 20
Knight, Suge 11, 30
Shakur, Tupac 14

De Beers Botswana
See Debswana
Allen, Debbie 13, 42

Debswana
Masire, Quett 5

Decca Records
Hardin Armstrong, Lil 39

Def Jam Records
Brown, Foxy 25
DMX 28, 64
Gotti, Irv 39
Jay-Z 27, 69
Jordan, Montell 23
Liles, Kevin 42
LL Cool J 16, 49
Simmons, Russell 1, 30

Def Jam South Records
Ludacris 37, 60

Def Poetry Jam
Letson, Al 39

Defense Communications Agency
Gravely, Samuel L., Jr. 5, 49

Delta Sigma Theta Sorority
Rice, Louise Allen 54

Democratic National Committee (DNC)
Brown, Ron 5
Brown, Willie L., Jr. 7
Dixon, Sharon Pratt 1
Fattah, Chaka 11, 70
Hamer, Fannie Lou 6
Jackson, Maynard 2, 41
Jordan, Barbara 4
Joyner, Marjorie Stewart 26
Mallett, Conrad, Jr. 16
Martin, Louis E. 16
Moore, Minyon 45
Waters, Maxine 3, 67
Williams, Maggie 7, 71

Democratic National Convention
Allen, Ethel D. 13
Brown, Ron 5
Brown, Willie L., Jr. 7
Dixon, Sharon Pratt 1

Hamer, Fannie Lou 6
Herman, Alexis M. 15
Jordan, Barbara 4
Millender-McDonald, Juanita 21, 61
Waters, Maxine 3, 67
Williams, Maggie 7, 71

Democratic Socialists of America (DSA)
Marable, Manning 10
West, Cornel 5

Dentistry
Bluitt, Juliann S. 14
Delany, Bessie 12
Gray, Ida 41
Madison, Romell 45
Sinkford, Jeanne C. 13

Denver Broncos football team
Barnes, Ernie 16
Briscoe, Marlin 37
Davis, Terrell 20
Jackson, Tom 70

Denver city government
Webb, Wellington 3

Denver Nuggets basketball team
Bickerstaff, Bernie 21
Bynoe, Peter C. B. 40
Hardaway, Tim 35
Lee, Bertram M., Sr. 46
Mutombo, Dikembe 7

DePaul University
Braun, Carol Moseley 4, 42
Sizemore, Barbara A. 26

Depression/The Great Depression
Hampton, Henry 6

Dermatology
Taylor, Susan C. 62

Desert Shield
See Operation Desert Shield

Desert Storm
See Operation Desert Storm

Destiny's Child
Beyoncé 39, 70
Knowles, Tina 61
Luckett, Letoya 61
Williams, Michelle 73

Detective fiction
Bates, Karen Grigsby 40
Bland, Eleanor Taylor 39
DeLoach, Nora 30
Hayes, Teddy 40
Haywood, Gar Anthony 43
Himes, Chester 8
Holton, Hugh, Jr. 39
Mosley, Walter 5, 25, 68
Wesley, Valerie Wilson 18

Detroit Bible Institute
Patterson, Gilbert Earl 41

Detroit city government
Archer, Dennis 7, 36
Collins, Barbara-Rose 7
Crockett, George W., Jr. 10, 64

Garrett, Joyce Finley 59
Kilpatrick, Kwame 34, 71
Marshall, Bella 22
Young, Coleman 1, 20

Detroit College of Law
Archer, Dennis 7, 36

Detroit Golden Gloves
Wilson, Sunnie 7, 55

Detroit Lions football team
Barney, Lem 26
Farr, Mel 24
Johnson, Levi 48
Sanders, Barry 1, 53
Ware, Andre 37

Detroit Pistons basketball team
Bing, Dave 3, 59
Dumars, Joe 16, 65
Gentry, Alvin 23
Hill, Grant 13
Lanier, Bob 47
Lloyd, Earl 26
Lowe, Sidney 64
Mahorn, Rick 60
Mohammed, Nazr 64
Prince, Tayshaun 68
Robinson, Will 51, 69
Stackhouse, Jerry 30
Thomas, Isiah 7, 26, 65
Wallace, Ben 54
Webber, Chris 15, 30, 59

Detroit Police Department
Bully-Cummings, Ella 48
Gomez-Preston, Cheryl 9
McKinnon, Isaiah 9
Napoleon, Benny N. 23

Detroit Public Schools
Coleman, William F., III 61

Detroit Stars baseball team
Kaiser, Cecil 42

Detroit Tigers baseball team
Fielder, Cecil 2
Granderson, Curtis 66
Sheffield, Gary 16
Virgil, Ozzie 48

Detroit Wolves baseball team
Dandridge, Ray 36

Diabetes
Fennoy, Ilene 72
Wisdom, Kimberlydawn 57

Diamond mining
Masire, Quett 5

Dictators
Abacha, Sani 11, 70
Amin, Idi 42
Biya, Paul 28
Eyadéma, Gnassingbé 7, 52
Habré, Hissène 6
Kabila, Laurent 20
Meles Zenawi 3
Mengistu, Haile Mariam 65
Moi, Daniel Arap 1, 35
Mswati III 56
Mugabe, Robert 10, 71

Touré, Sekou 6

Digital divide
Adkins, Rod 41

Dillard University
Cook, Samuel DuBois 14
Lomax, Michael L. 58

Dime Savings Bank
Parsons, Richard Dean 11

Diner's Club
Gaines, Brenda 41

Diplomatic Corps
See U.S. Department of State

Directing
Akomfrah, John 37
Barclay, Paris 37
Branch, William Blackwell 39
Chong, Rae Dawn 62
Dixon, Ivan 69
Hines, Gregory 1, 42
Milner, Ron 39
Perry, Tyler 40, 54
Scott, Harold Russell, Jr. 61
Thompson, Tazewell 13
Ward, Douglas Turner 42
Warner, Malcolm-Jamal 22, 36
Whack, Rita Coburn 36
Wolfe, George C. 6, 43

Director's Guild of America
Barclay, Paris 37

Disabled American Veterans (DAV)
Brown, Jesse 6, 41

Disco
Gaynor, Gloria 36
Payne, Freda 58
Perren, Freddie 60
Staton, Candi 27
Summer, Donna 25

Distance running
Cheruiyot, Robert 69
Loroupe, Tegla 59
Tergat, Paul 59

Diving
Brashear, Carl 29

DJ
Alert, Kool DJ Red 32
Atkins, Juan 50
Bond, Beverly 53
DJ Jazzy Jeff 32
Grandmaster Flash 33, 60
Knuckles, Frankie 42
Love, Ed 58

DNC
See Democratic National Committee

Documentary film
Blackwood, Maureen 37
Branch, William Blackwell 39
Byrd, Robert 11
Dash, Julie 4
Davis, Ossie 5, 50
Gray, Darius 69
Greaves, William 38

Hampton, Henry 6
Henry, Lenny 9, 52
Hudlin, Reginald 9
Hudlin, Warrington 9
Hurt, Byron 61
Jean, Michaëlle; 70
Julien, Isaac 3
Lee, Spike 5, 19
Lynch, Shola 61
Peck, Raoul 32
Riggs, Marlon 5, 44
Roberts, Kimberly Rivers 72
Whack, Rita Coburn 36
Williams, Marco 53

Dollmaking
El Wilson, Barbara 35

Dominica government
Charles, Mary Eugenia 10, 55
Charles, Pierre 52
Skerrit, Roosevelt 72

Donald Byrd/The Group
Byrd, Donald 10

Donnaerobics
Richardson, Donna 39

Dove Award
Baylor, Helen 36
Winans, CeCe 14, 43

Down Beat Jazz Hall of Fame
Terry, Clark 39

Dr. Martin Luther King Boys and Girls Club
Gaines, Brenda 41

Drama Desk Awards
Carter, Nell 39
Taylor, Ron 35
Wesley, Richard 73

Drawing
Simmons, Gary 58

Dreamland Orchestra
Cook, Charles "Doc" 44

Drug abuse prevention
Brown, Les 5
Clements, George 2
Creagh, Milton 27
Hale, Lorraine 8
Harris, Alice 7
Lucas, John 7
Rangel, Charles 3, 52

Drug synthesis
Julian, Percy Lavon 6
Pickett, Cecil 39

Drums
Blakey, Art 37
Durham, Bobby 73
Güines, Tata 69
Jones, Elvin 14, 68
Locke, Eddie 44
Miles, Buddy 69
Williams, Tony 67
Young, Lee 72

DSA
See Democratic Socialists of America

Dub poetry
Breeze, Jean "Binta" 37
Johnson, Linton Kwesi 37

Duke Ellington School of Arts
Cooper Cafritz, Peggy 43

Duke Records
Bland, Bobby "Blue" 36

Dunham Dance Company
Dunham, Katherine 4, 59

DuSable Museum of African American History
Burroughs, Margaret Taylor 9
Wright, Antoinette 60

Dynegy
Scott, Milton 51

E Street Band
Clemons, Clarence 41

Earthquake Early Alerting Service
Person, Waverly 9, 51

East Harlem School at Exodus House
Hageman, Hans 36
Hageman, Ivan 36

East St. Louis city government
Powell, Debra A. 23

Ebonics
Cook, Toni 23

Ebony magazine
Bennett, Lerone, Jr. 5
Branch, William Blackwell 39
Cullers, Vincent T. 49
Fuller, Hoyt 44
Johnson, John H. 3, 54
Massaquoi, Hans J. 30
Rice, Linda Johnson 9, 41
Sleet, Moneta, Jr. 5

Ebony Museum of African American History
See DuSable Museum of African American History

E.C. Reems Women's International Ministries
Reems, Ernestine Cleveland 27

Economic Community of West African States (ECOWAS)
Sawyer, Amos 2

Economic Regulatory Administration
O'Leary, Hazel 6

Economics
Ake, Claude 30
Arthur, Owen 33
Boyd, T. B., III 6
Brimmer, Andrew F. 2, 48
Brown, Tony 3
Divine, Father 7
Fryer, Roland G. 56
Gibson, William F. 6
Hamer, Fannie Lou 6
Hampton, Henry 6

Juma, Calestous 57
Machel, Graca Simbine 16
Malveaux, Julianne 32, 70
Masire, Quett 5
Pitta, Celso 17
Raines, Franklin Delano 14
Robinson, Randall 7, 46
Sowell, Thomas 2
Spriggs, William 67
Sullivan, Leon H. 3, 30
Van Peebles, Melvin 7
Wallace, Phyllis A. 9
Wharton, Clifton R., Jr. 7
White, Michael R. 5
Williams, Walter E. 4

ECOWAS
See Economic Community of West
    African States

Edelman Public Relations
Barrett, Andrew C. 12

Editing
Aubert, Alvin 41
Bass, Charlotta Spears 40
Brown, Lloyd Louis 42
Curry, George E. 23
Delany, Martin R. 27
Dumas, Henry 41
Murphy, John H. 42
Schuyler, George Samuel 40

Edmonds Entertainment
Edmonds, Kenneth "Babyface" 10,
    31
Edmonds, Tracey 16, 64
Tillman, George, Jr. 20

Edmonton Oilers hockey team
Fuhr, Grant 1, 49
Grier, Mike 43
Laraque, Georges 48

Educational Testing Service
Stone, Chuck 9

EEC
See European Economic Commu-
    nity

EEOC
See Equal Employment Opportunity
    Commission

Egyptology
Diop, Cheikh Anta 4

Elder Foundation
Elder, Lee 6

Electronic music
Craig, Carl 31, 71

Elektra Records
McPherson, David 32

Emerge (Savoy) magazine
Ames, Wilmer 27
Curry, George E. 23

Emmy awards
Allen, Debbie 13, 42
Amos, John 8, 62
Ashe, Arthur 1, 18
Barclay, Paris 37
Belafonte, Harry 4, 65

Bradley, Ed 2, 59
Branch, William Blackwell 39
Brown, James 22
Brown, Les 5
Browne, Roscoe Lee 66
Carter, Nell 39
Clayton, Xernona 3, 45
Cosby, Bill 7, 26, 59
Curtis-Hall, Vondie 17
De Shields, André 72
Dee, Ruby 8, 50, 68
Foxx, Redd 2
Freeman, Al, Jr. 11
Goldberg, Whoopi 4, 33, 69
Gossett, Louis, Jr. 7
Guillaume, Robert 3, 48
Gumbel, Greg 8
Hunter-Gault, Charlayne 6, 31
Jones, James Earl 3, 49
La Salle, Eriq 12
Mabrey, Vicki 26
McQueen, Butterfly 6, 54
Moore, Shemar 21
Parks, Gordon 1, 35, 58
Pinkston, W. Randall 24
Quarles, Norma 25
Richards, Beah 30
Robinson, Max 3
Rock, Chris 3, 22, 66
Rolle, Esther 13, 21
St. John, Kristoff 25
Taylor, Billy 23
Thigpen, Lynne 17, 41
Tyson, Cicely 7, 51
Uggams, Leslie 23
Wayans, Damon 8, 41
Whack, Rita Coburn 36
Whitfield, Lynn 18
Williams, Montel 4, 57
Williams, Russell, II 70
Williams, Sherley Anne 25
Winfrey, Oprah 2, 15, 61
Woodard, Alfre 9

Emory University
Cole, Johnnetta B. 5, 43

Endocrinology
Elders, Joycelyn 6
Fennoy, Ilene 72

Energy studies
Cose, Ellis 5, 50
O'Leary, Hazel 6

Engineering
Alexander, Archie Alphonso 14
Anderson, Charles Edward 37
Auguste, Donna 29
Benson, Angela 34
Boyd, Gwendolyn 49
Burns, Ursula 60
Emeagwali, Philip 30
Ericsson-Jackson, Aprille 28
Gibson, Kenneth Allen 6
Gourdine, Meredith 33
Grooms, Henry R(andall) 50
Hannah, Marc 10
Henderson, Cornelius Langston 26
Howard, Ayanna 65
Jones, Wayne 53
Laryea, Thomas Davies, III 67
McCoy, Elijah 8
Miller, Warren F., Jr. 53

Mills, Joseph C. 51
Pierre, Percy Anthony 46
Price, Richard 51
Sigur, Wanda 44
Slaughter, John Brooks 53
Trotter, Lloyd G. 56
Wilkens, J. Ernest, Jr. 43
Williams, O. S. 13

Entertainment promotion
Lewis, Butch 71

Environmental issues
Chavis, Benjamin 6
Eugene-Richard, Margie 63
Hill, Bonnie Guiton 20
Jones, Van 70
Miller-Travis, Vernice 64
Osborne, Na'taki 54

Epic Records
McPherson, David 32
Mo', Keb' 36

Epidemiology
Gayle, Helene D. 3

**Episcopal Diocese of Massa-
chusetts**
Harris, Barbara 12

Episcopalian
Burgess, John 46
Jones, Absalom 52
Walker, John T. 50
Williams, Frederick (B.) 63

EPRDF
See Ethiopian People's Revolution-
    ary Democratic Front

**Equal Employment Opportu-
nity Commission (EEOC)**
Alexander, Clifford 26
Hill, Anita 5, 65
Lewis, Delano 7
Norton, Eleanor Holmes 7
Thomas, Clarence 2, 39, 65
Wallace, Phyllis A. 9

Equality Now
Jones, Sarah 39

Esalen Institute
Olatunji, Babatunde 36

ESPN
Jackson, Tom 70
Roberts, Robin 16, 54
Salters, Lisa 71
Scott, Stuart 34
Smith, Stephen A. 69
Tirico, Mike 68
Wilbon, Michael 68

Essence magazine
Bandele, Asha 36
Burt-Murray, Angela 59
Channer, Colin 36
De Veaux, Alexis 44
Ebanks, Michelle 60
Grant, Gwendolyn Goldsby 28
Greenwood, Monique 38
Lewis, Edward T. 21
Parks, Gordon 1, 35, 58
Smith, Clarence O. 21
Taylor, Susan L. 10

Wesley, Valerie Wilson 18

Essence Award
Broadbent, Hydeia 36
McMurray, Georgia L. 36

Essence Communications
Lewis, Edward T. 21
Smith, Clarence O. 21
Taylor, Susan L. 10

*Essence, the Television Pro-
gram*
Taylor, Susan L. 10

Ethiopian government
Haile Selassie 7
Meles Zenawi 3
Mengistu, Haile Mariam 65

Etiquette
Bates, Karen Grigsby 40

Eugene O'Neill Theater
Richards, Lloyd 2

**European Economic Commu-
nity (EEC)**
Diouf, Abdou 3

Event planning
Bailey, Preston 64

Executive Leadership Council
Jackson, Mannie 14

Exiled heads of state
Aristide, Jean-Bertrand 6, 45

Exploration
Henson, Matthew 2

Eyes on the Prize series
Hampton, Henry 6

F & M Schaefer Brewing Co.
Cooper, Andrew W. 36

Fairbanks city government
Hayes, James C. 10

FAIRR
See Foundation for the Advance-
    ment of Inmate Rehabilitation and
    Recreation

Fair Share Agreements
Gibson, William F. 6

Famine relief
See World hunger

**Famous Amos Cookie Corpo-
ration**
Amos, Wally 9

FAN
See Forces Armées du Nord
    (Chad)

Fannie Mae
Jackson, Maynard 2, 41

FANT
See Forces Amrées Nationales
    Tchadiennes

Fashion
Aberra, Amsale 67
Boateng, Ozwald 35

Boyd, Suzanne 52
Darego, Agbani 52
Delice, Ronald 48
Delice, Rony 48
Evans, Etu 55
Fine, Sam 60
Gaskins, Eric 64
Givhan, Robin Deneen 72
Hall, Kevan 61
Hendy, Francis 47
Knowles, Tina 61
Lars, Byron 32
Malone, Maurice 32
McGrath, Pat 72
Reese, Tracy 54
Sade 15
Simmons, Kimora Lee 51
Smaltz, Audrey 12
Steele, Lawrence 28
Stoney, Michael 50
Sy, Oumou 65
Talley, André Leon 56

Fashion Institute of Technology (FIT)
Brown, Joyce F. 25

Fast 50 Awards
Steward, David L. 36

FCC
See Federal Communications Commission

Federal Bureau of Investigation (FBI)
Gibson, Johnnie Mae 23
Harvard, Beverly 11

Federal Communications Commission (FCC)
Barrett, Andrew C. 12
Hooks, Benjamin L. 2
Hughes, Cathy 27
Kennard, William Earl 18
Powell, Michael 32
Russell-McCloud, Patricia A. 17

Federal Court of Canada
Isaac, Julius 34

Federal Energy Administration
O'Leary, Hazel 6

Federal Reserve Bank
Brimmer, Andrew F. 2, 48
Ferguson, Roger W. 25

Federal Set-Aside Program
Mitchell, Parren J. 42, 66

Federation of Nigeria
Sowande, Fela 39

Feed the Hungry program
Williams, Hosea Lorenzo 15, 31

Fellowship of Reconciliation (FOR)
Farmer, James 2, 64
Rustin, Bayard 4

Feminist studies
Carby, Hazel 27
Christian, Barbara T. 44
De Veaux, Alexis 44

Hull, Akasha Gloria 45
Smith, Barbara 28
Walker, Rebecca 50

Fencing
Westbrook, Peter 20

Fiction
Adams, Jenoyne 60
Adichie, Chimamanda Ngozi 64
Alexander, Margaret Walker 22
Ali, Mohammed Naseehu 60
Amadi, Elechi 40
Anthony, Michael 29
Ansa, Tina McElroy 14
Armah, Ayi Kwei 49
Ba, Mariama 30
Baiocchi, Regina Harris 41
Baisden, Michael 25, 66
Ballard, Allen Butler, Jr. 40
Bandele, Biyi 68
Barrett, Lindsay 43
Bates, Karen Grigsby 40
Beckham, Barry 41
Benson, Angela 34
Berry, James 41
Bland, Eleanor Taylor 39
Bolden, Tonya 32
Bradley, David Henry, Jr. 39
Brand, Dionne 32
Briscoe, Connie 15
Brown, Cecil M. 46
Brown, Lloyd Louis 42
Bunkley, Anita Richmond 39
Butler, Octavia 8, 43, 58
Campbell, Bebe Moore 6, 24, 59
Cartiér, Xam Wilson 41
Chase-Riboud, Barbara 20, 46
Cheney-Coker, Syl 43
Chesnutt, Charles 29
Clarke, Austin 32
Cleage, Pearl 17, 64
Cliff, Michelle 42
Creagh, Milton 27
Curtis, Christopher Paul 26
Danticat, Edwidge 15, 68
Dathorne, O.R. 52
Demby, William 51
Diop, Birago 53
Draper, Sharon Mills 16, 43
Due, Tananarive 30
Dumas, Henry 41
Dunbar-Nelson, Alice Ruth Moore 44
Duplechan, Larry 55
Emecheta, Buchi 30
Evans, Diana 72
Fair, Ronald L. 47
Farah, Nuruddin 27
Farley, Christopher John 54
Files, Lolita 35
Ford, Nick Aaron 44
Ford, Wallace 58
Forrest, Leon 44
Gomez, Jewelle 30
Gray, Darius 69
Greenlee, Sam 48
Harris, E. Lynn 12, 33
Haywood, Gar Anthony 43
Hercules, Frank 44
Hill, Donna 32
Holton, Hugh, Jr. 39
Horne, Frank 44

Jackson, Sheneska 18
Jakes, Thomas "T. D." 17, 43
Jasper, Kenji 39
Jenkins, Beverly 14
Johnson, Georgia Douglas 41
Johnson, Mat 31
Jones, Edward P. 43, 67
Jones, Gayl 37
Kamau, Kwadwo Agymah 28
Kay, Jackie 37
Kayira, Legson 40
Keene, John 73
Kendrick, Erika 57
Killens, John O. 54
Laferriere, Dany 33
LaGuma, Alex 30
Lamming, George 35
Marechera, Dambudzo 39
Markham, E.A. 37
Mason, Felicia 31
Mbaye, Mariétou 31
McCrary Anthony, Crystal 70
McFadden, Bernice L. 39
McKinney-Whetstone, Diane 27
McMillan, Terry 4, 17, 53
Memmi, Albert 37
Mengestu, Dinaw 66
Monroe, Mary 35
Mosley, Walter 5, 25, 68
Mossell, Gertrude Bustill 40
Mphalele, Es'kia 40
Mwangi, Meja 40
Naylor, Gloria 10, 42
Ngugi wa Thiong'o 29, 61
Nkosi, Lewis 46
Nugent, Richard Bruce 39
Nunez, Elizabeth 62
Okara, Gabriel 37
Ojikutu, Bayo 66
Packer, Z.Z. 64
Peters, Lenrie 43
Philip, Marlene Nourbese 32
Randall, Alice 38
Ridley, John 69
Saro-Wiwa, Kenule 39
Schuyler, George Samuel 40
Senior, Olive 37
Smith, Danyel 40
Smith, Zadie 51
Southgate, Martha 58
Tate, Eleanora E. 20, 55
Taylor, Mildred D. 26
Thomas, Michael 69
Thomas-Graham, Pamela 29
Tutuola, Amos 30
Vera, Yvonne 32
Verdelle, A. J. 26
Walker, Margaret 29
Weaver, Afaa Michael 37
Whitfield, Van 34
Williams, Sherley Anne 25
Williams, Stanley "Tookie" 29, 57
Woods, Teri 69
Yarbrough, Camille 40
Youngblood, Shay 32
Zane 71

Figure skating
Bonaly, Surya 7
Thomas, Debi 26

Film criticism
Mitchell, Elvis 67

Film direction
Akomfrah, John 37
Allain, Stephanie 49
Allen, Debbie 13, 42
Blackwood, Maureen 37
Burnett, Charles 16, 68
Byrd, Robert 11
Campbell-Martin, Tisha 8, 42
Cortez, Jayne 43
Curtis-Hall, Vondie 17
Dash, Julie 4
Davis, Ossie 5, 50
Dickerson, Ernest 6, 17
Diesel, Vin 29
Duke, Bill 3
Franklin, Carl 11
Freeman, Al, Jr. 11
Fuqua, Antoine 35
Gerima, Haile 38
Gray, Darius 69
Gray, F. Gary 14, 49
Greaves, William 38
Harris, Leslie 6
Hayes, Teddy 40
Henriques, Julian 37
Hines, Gregory 1, 42
Hudlin, Reginald 9
Hudlin, Warrington 9
Hughes, Albert 7
Hughes, Allen 7
Hurt, Byron 61
Jackson, George 19
Julien, Isaac 3
Lane, Charles 3
Lee, Spike 5, 19
Lemmons, Kasi 20
Lewis, Samella 25
Martin, Darnell 43
Micheaux, Oscar 7
Morton, Joe 18
Moses, Gilbert 12
Moss, Carlton 17
Mwangi, Meja 40
Onwurah, Ngozi 38
Peck, Raoul 32
Perry, Tyler 40, 54
Poitier, Sidney 11, 36
Prince-Bythewood, Gina 31
Riggs, Marlon 5, 44
Roberts, Darryl 70
St. Jacques, Raymond 8
Schultz, Michael A. 6
Sembène, Ousmane 13, 62
Singleton, John 2, 30
Smith, Roger Guenveur 12
Tillman, George, Jr. 20
Townsend, Robert 4, 23
Tyler, Aisha N. 36
Underwood, Blair 7
Van Peebles, Mario 2, 51
Van Peebles, Melvin 7
Ward, Douglas Turner 42
Wayans, Damon 8, 41
Wayans, Keenen Ivory 18
Whitaker, Forest 2, 49, 67

Film production
Allain, Stephanie 49
Chase, Debra Martin 49
Daniels, Lee Louis 36
Gerima, Haile 38
Greaves, William 38
Hines, Gregory 1, 42

Lewis, Emmanuel 36
Martin, Darnell 43
Onwurah, Ngozi 38
Packer, Will 71
Patton, Paula 62
Poitier, Sidney 11, 36
Randall, Alice 38
Robinson, Matt 69
Tyler, Aisha N. 36
Van Lierop, Robert 53
Ward, Douglas Turner 42
Whitaker, Forest 2, 49, 67
Williams, Marco 53
Williams, Russell, II 70
Williamson, Fred 67

Film scores
Blanchard, Terence 43
Crouch, Andraé 27
Hancock, Herbie 20, 67
Jean-Baptiste, Marianne 17, 46
Jones, Quincy 8, 30
Prince 18, 65

Finance
Adams, Eula L. 39
Banks, Jeffrey 17
Bell, James A. 50
Boston, Kelvin E. 25
Bryant, John 26
Chapman, Nathan A., Jr. 21
Doley, Harold, Jr. 26
Epperson, Sharon 54
Ferguson, Roger W. 25
Fletcher, Alphonse, Jr. 16
Funderburg, I. Owen 38
Gaines, Brenda 41
Griffith, Mark Winston 8
Harris, Carla A. 67
Hobson, Mellody 40
Jones, Thomas W. 41
Lawless, Theodore K. 8
Lewis, William M., Jr. 40
Louis, Errol T. 8
Marshall, Bella 22
O'Neal, Stanley 38, 67
Rogers, John W., Jr. 5, 52
Ross, Charles 27
Thompson, William C. 35

Firefighters
Barlow, Roosevelt 49
Bell, Michael 40

First Data Corporation
Adams, Eula L. 39

Fisk University
Harvey, William R. 42
Imes, Elmer Samuel 39
Johnson, Charles S. 12
Phillips, Teresa L. 42
Smith, John L. 22

Fitness
Richardson, Donna 39
Smith, Ian 62

Florida A & M University
Gaither, Alonzo Smith (Jake) 14
Humphries, Frederick 20
Meek, Kendrick 41

Florida International baseball league
Kaiser, Cecil 42

Florida Marlins baseball team
Mariner, Jonathan 41
Sheffield, Gary 16

Florida state government
Brown, Corrine 24
Meek, Carrie 6
Meek, Kendrick 41
Tribble, Israel, Jr. 8

Florida State Supreme Court
Quince, Peggy A. 69

Fluoride chemistry
Quarterman, Lloyd Albert 4

Focus Detroit Electronic Music Festival
May, Derrick 41

Folk music
Bailey, DeFord 33
Chapman, Tracy 26
Charlemagne, Manno 11
Cuney, William Waring 44
Davis, Gary 41
Dawson, William Levi 39
Harper, Ben 34, 62
Jenkins, Ella 15
Love, Laura 50
Odetta 37
Spence, Joseph 49
Williams, Denise 40
Wilson, Cassandra 16

Football
Alexander, Shaun 58
Allen, Marcus 20
Amos, John 8, 62
Anderson, Jamal 22
Barber, Ronde 41
Barber, Tiki 57
Barney, Lem 26
Bettis, Jerome 64
Briscoe, Marlin 37
Brooks, Aaron 33
Brooks, Derrick 43
Brown, James 22
Brown, Jim 11
Bruce, Isaac 26
Buchanan, Ray 32
Bush, Reggie 59
Butler, LeRoy, III 17
Carter, Cris 21
Cherry, Deron 40
Clemons, Michael "Pinball" 64
Crennel, Romeo 54
Croom, Sylvester 50
Culpepper, Daunte 32
Cunningham, Randall 23
Davis, Ernie 48
Davis, Terrell 20
Dickerson, Eric 27
Dorrell, Karl 52
Dungy, Tony 17, 42, 59
Edwards, Harry 2
Farr, Mel 24
Faulk, Marshall 35
Fowler, Reggie 51
Gaither, Alonzo Smith (Jake) 14
Gilliam, Frank 23

Gilliam, Joe 31
Gorden, W. C. 71
Green, Darrell 39
Green, Dennis 5, 45
Greene, Joe 10
Grier, Roosevelt 13
Hill, Calvin 19
Irvin, Michael 64
Johnson, Levi 48
Jones, Ed "Too Tall" 46
Keith, Floyd A. 61
Ladd, Ernie 64
Lanier, Willie 33
Lewis, Marvin 51
Lofton, James 42
Lott, Ronnie 9
McNair, Steve 22, 47
McNabb, Donovan 29
Monk, Art 38, 73
Moon, Warren 8, 66
Moss, Randy 23
Motley, Marion 26
Newsome, Ozzie 26
Owens, Terrell 53
Pace, Orlando 21
Page, Alan 7
Parker, Jim 64
Payton, Walter 11, 25
Perry, Lowell 30
Pollard, Fritz 53
Prince, Ron 64
Rashad, Ahmad 18
Rice, Jerry 5, 55
Robinson, Eddie G. 10, 61
Sanders, Barry 1, 53
Sanders, Bob 72
Sanders, Deion 4, 31
Sapp, Warren 38
Sayers, Gale 28
Sharper, Darren 32
Shell, Art 1, 66
Simmons, Bob 29
Simpson, O. J. 15
Singletary, Mike 4
Smith, Emmitt 7
Smith, Lovie 66
Smith, Rick 72
Stewart, Kordell 21
Stingley, Darryl 69
Strahan, Michael 35
Stringer, Korey 35
Swann, Lynn 28
Taylor, Lawrence 25
Thomas, Derrick 25
Thomas, Emmitt 71
Thrower, Willie 35
Tomlinson, LaDainian 65
Upshaw, Gene 18, 47, 72
Vick, Michael 39, 65
Walker, Herschel 1, 69
Ware, Andre 37
Watts, J. C., Jr. 14, 38
Weathers, Carl 10
White, Reggie 6, 50
Williams, Doug 22
Willingham, Tyrone 43
Willis, Bill 68
Wright, Rayfield 70

Football Hall of Fame, professional
Lofton, James 42
Sayers, Gale 28

Swann, Lynn 28
Upshaw, Gene 18, 47, 72
Willis, Bill 68
Wright, Rayfield 70

FOR
See Fellowship of Reconciliation

Forces Armées du Nord (Chad; FAN)
Déby, Idriss 30
Habré, Hissène 6

Ford Foundation
Franklin, Robert M. 13
Thomas, Franklin A. 5, 49

Ford Motor Company
Cherry, Deron 40
Dawson, Matel "Mat," Jr. 39
Goldsberry, Ronald 18
Hazel, Darryl B. 50
McMillan, Rosalynn A. 36

Fordham University
Blair, Paul 36
McMurray, Georgia L. 36

Foreign policy
Bunche, Ralph J. 5
Frazer, Jendayi 68
Rice, Condoleezza 3, 28, 72
Robinson, Randall 7, 46

Forensic science
Griffin, Bessie Blout 43

Forest Club
Wilson, Sunnie 7, 55

40 Acres and a Mule Filmworks
Dickerson, Ernest 6, 17
Lee, Spike 5, 19

Foster care
Hale, Clara 16
Hale, Lorraine 8

Foundation for the Advancement of Inmate Rehabilitation and Recreation (FAIRR)
King, B. B. 7

Fox Broadcasting Company
Corbi, Lana 42
McFarland, Roland 49
Oliver, Pam 54

FPI
See Ivorian Popular Front

Frank H. Williams Caribbean Cultural Center African Diaspora Institute
Vega, Marta Moreno 61

Freddie Mac Corporation
Baker, Maxine 28

Freddie Mac Foundation
Baker, Maxine 28

Frederick Douglass Caring Award
Broadbent, Hydeia 36

Frederick Douglass Memorial Hospital
Mossell, Gertrude Bustill 40

Freedom Farm Cooperative
Hamer, Fannie Lou 6

Free Southern Theater (FST)
Borders, James 9

FRELIMO
See Front for the Liberation of Mozambique

French West Africa
Diouf, Abdou 3

FRODEBU
See Front for Democracy in Burundi

FRONASA
See Front for National Salvation (Uganda)

Front for Democracy in Burundi (FRODEBU)
Ndadaye, Melchior 7
Ntaryamira, Cyprien 8

Front for National Salvation (Uganda; FRONASA)
Museveni, Yoweri 4

Front for the Liberation of Mozambique (FRELIMO)
Chissano, Joaquim 7, 55, 67
Machel, Graca Simbine 16
Machel, Samora Moises 8

FST
See Free Southern Theater

Full Gospel Baptist
Long, Eddie L. 29

FullerMusic
Fuller, Arthur 27

Fulton County Juvenile Court
Hatchett, Glenda 32

Funeral homes
March, William Carrington 56

Funk Brothers
Jamerson, James 59

Funk music
Ayers, Roy 16
Brown, James 15, 60
Clinton, George 9
Collins, Bootsy 31
Collins, Lyn 53
Love, Laura 50
Parker, Maceo 72
Richie, Lionel 27, 65
Watson, Johnny "Guitar" 18

Fusion
Davis, Miles 4
Jones, Quincy 8, 30
Williams, Tony 67

FWP Union
Nugent, Richard Bruce 39

Gambling
Ivey, Phil 72

Gangs
Taylor, Bo 72
Williams, Stanley "Tookie" 29, 57

Gary, Indiana, city government
Hatcher, Richard G. 55

Gary, Williams, Parenti, Finney, Lewis & McManus
Gary, Willie E. 12

Gary Enterprises
Gary, Willie E. 12

Gary Post-Tribune
Ross, Don 27

Gassaway, Crosson, Turner & Parsons
Parsons, James 14

Gay and Lesbian Activism
De Veaux, Alexis 44

Gay Men of Color Consortium
Wilson, Phill 9

Genealogy
Blockson, Charles L. 42
Dash, Julie 4
Haley, Alex 4

***General Hospital* TV series**
Cash, Rosalind 28

General Motors Corporation
O'Neal, Stanley 38, 67
Roberts, Roy S. 14
Welburn, Edward T. 50

Genetech
Potter, Myrtle 40

Genetics
Dunston, Georgia Mae 48
Harris, Mary Styles 31
Kittles, Rick 51
Olopade, Olufunmilayo Falusi 58

Geometric symbolism
Douglas, Aaron 7

Geophysics
Person, Waverly 9, 51

George Foster Peabody Broadcasting Award
Bradley, Ed 2, 59
Hunter-Gault, Charlayne 6, 31
Mac, Bernie 29, 61, 72
Shaw, Bernard 2

George Mason University
Dunn, Jerry 27

George Washington University
Carter, Joye Maureen 41

Georgia state government
Baker, Thurbert 22
Bishop, Sanford D., Jr. 24
Bond, Julian 2, 35
Brooks, Tyrone 59
Majette, Denise 41
McKinney, Cynthia Ann 11, 52
Scott, David 41

Williams, Hosea Lorenzo 15, 31

Georgia State Supreme Court
Sears-Collins, Leah J. 5

Ghanaian government
Awoonor, Kofi 37
Kufuor, John Agyekum 54

Girl Scouts of the USA
Thompson, Cynthia Bramlett 50

GLM Group
McMurray, Georgia L. 36

Goddard Space Flight Center
Ericsson-Jackson, Aprille 28

Gold Mind, Inc.
Elliott, Missy 31

Golden Globe awards
Allen, Debbie 13, 42
Bassett, Angela 6, 23, 62
Carroll, Diahann 9
Freeman, Morgan 2, 20, 62
Ross, Diana 8, 27
Taylor, Regina 9, 46

Golden Pen award
McFadden, Bernice L. 39

Golden State Warriors basketball team
Edwards, Harry 2
Lucas, John 7
Parish, Robert 43
Sprewell, Latrell 23

Golf
Elder, Lee 6
Gibson, Althea 8, 43
Gregory, Ann 63
Jackson, Fred James 25
Peete, Calvin 11
Richmond, Mitch 19
Shippen, John 43
Sifford, Charlie 4, 49
Spiller, Bill 64
Webber, Chris 15, 30, 59
Woods, Tiger 14, 31

Goodwill ambassador
Terry, Clark 39

Goodwill Games
Swoopes, Sheryl 12, 56

Gospel music
Adams, Oleta 18
Adams, Yolanda 17, 67
Armstrong, Vanessa Bell 24
Baylor Helen 36
Bonds, Margaret 39
Bradley, J. Robert 65
Caesar, Shirley 19
Cage, Byron 53
Clark, Mattie Moss 61
Clark-Cole, Dorinda 66
Clark-Sheard, Karen 22
Cleveland, James 19
Christie, Angella 36
Cooke, Sam 17
Crouch, Andraé 27
Davis, Gary 41
Dorsey, Thomas 15
Franklin, Aretha 11, 44

Franklin, Kirk 15, 49
Gaynor, Gloria 36
Green, Al 13, 47
Haddon, Dietrick 55
Hammond, Fred 23
Hawkins, Tramaine 16
Higginsen, Vy 65
Houston, Cissy 20
Jackson, Mahalia 5
Jakes, Thomas "T. D." 17, 43
Jones, Bobby 20
Kee, John P. 43
Kenoly, Ron 45
Killings, Debra 57
Knight, Gladys 16, 66
Lassiter, Roy 24
Little Richard 15
Majors, Jeff 41
Marrow, Queen Esther 24
Martin, Roberta 58
Mary Mary 34
Mayfield, Curtis 2, 43
McClendon, Lisa 61
McClurkin, Donnie 25
Mills, Stephanie 36
Monica 21
Moss, J 64
Mullen, Nicole C. 45
Peoples, Dottie 22
Phipps, Wintley 59
Preston, Billy 39, 59
Reagon, Bernice Johnson 7
Reese, Della 6, 20
Scott, George 55
Sheard, Kierra "Kiki" 61
Stampley, Micah 54
Staples, Mavis 50
Staples, "Pops" 32
Staton, Candi 27
Steinberg, Martha Jean "The Queen" 28
Tharpe, Rosetta 65
Tonex 54
Walker, Albertina 10, 58
Walker, Hezekiah 34
Washington, Dinah 22
West, Kanye 52
Whalum, Kirk 37, 64
Williams, Deniece 36
Williams, Michelle 73
Wilson, Natalie 38
Winans, Angie 36
Winans, BeBe 14
Winans, CeCe 14, 43
Winans, Debbie 36
Winans, Marvin L. 17
Winans, Ronald 54
Winans, Vickie 24

Gospel theater
Perry, Tyler 40, 54

Graffiti art
White, Dondi 34

Grambling State University
Favors, Steve 23

Grammy awards
Adams, Oleta 18
Adderley, Nat 29
Badu, Erykah 22
Battle, Kathleen 70
Belafonte, Harry 4, 65

Beyoncé **39, 70**
Blige, Mary J. **20, 34, 60**
Brandy **14, 34, 72**
Caesar, Shirley **19**
Chapman, Tracy **26**
Cleveland, James **19**
Cole, Natalie **17, 60**
Combs, Sean "Puffy" **17, 43**
Cosby, Bill **7, 26, 59**
Cray, Robert **30**
Crouch, Andraé **27**
Davis, Miles **4**
Dee, Ruby **8, 50, 68**
Edmonds, Kenneth "Babyface" **10, 31**
Ellington, Duke **5**
Ferrer, Ibrahim **41**
Fitzgerald, Ella **8**
Franklin, Aretha **11, 44**
Gaye, Marvin **2**
Gaynor, Gloria **36**
Gibson, Tyrese **27, 62**
Glover, Corey **34**
Goldberg, Whoopi **4, 33, 69**
Gray, Macy **29**
Guy, Buddy **31**
Hammer, M. C. **20**
Hathaway, Donny **18**
Hawkins, Tramaine **16**
Hayes, Isaac **20, 58, 73**
Hill, Lauryn **20, 53**
Holland-Dozier-Holland **36**
Hooker, John Lee **30**
Houston, Cissy **20**
Houston, Whitney **7, 28**
Isley, Ronald **25, 56**
Jackson, Janet **6, 30, 68**
Jackson, Michael **19, 53**
James, Etta **13, 52**
Jay-Z **27, 69**
Jean, Wyclef **20**
Jimmy Jam **13**
Jones, Bobby **20**
Jones, Quincy **8, 30**
Kee, John P. **43**
Kelly, R. **18, 44, 71**
Keys, Alicia **32, 68**
Knight, Gladys **16, 66**
Knuckles, Frankie **42**
LaBelle, Patti **13, 30**
Legend, John **67**
Lewis, Terry **13**
Lopes, Lisa "Left Eye" **36**
Mahal, Taj **39**
Makeba, Miriam **2, 50**
Marley, Ziggy **41**
Marsalis, Branford **34**
Mills, Stephanie **36**
Mo', Keb' **36**
Moore, LeRoi **72**
Murphy, Eddie **4, 20, 61**
Norman, Jessye **5**
Olatunji, Babatunde **36**
Perkins, Pinetop **70**
Poitier, Sidney **11, 36**
Price, Leontyne **1**
Pride, Charley **26**
Prince **18, 65**
Queen Latifah **1, 16, 58**
Reagon, Bernice Johnson **7**
Redding, Otis **16**
Reid, Vernon **34**
Richie, Lionel **27, 65**

Robinson, Smokey **3, 49**
Ross, Isaiah "Doc" **40**
Rucker, Darius **34**
Sade **15**
Shaggy **31**
Smith, Will **8, 18**
Summer, Donna **25**
Turner, Tina **6, 27**
Walker, Hezekiah **34**
Warwick, Dionne **18**
White, Barry **13, 41**
White, Maurice **29**
Whitfield, Norman **73**
Williams, Deniece **36**
Williams, Joe **5, 25**
Williams, Michelle **73**
Wilson, Nancy **10**
Winans, CeCe **14, 43**
Winans, Marvin L. **17**
Wonder, Stevie **11, 53**

Grand Ole Opry
Bailey, DeFord **33**

Graphic novels
Anderson, Ho Che **54**
McDuffie, Dwayne **62**
Tooks, Lance **62**

Green Bay Packers football team
Brooks, Aaron **33**
Butler, Leroy, III **17**
Howard, Desmond **16, 58**
Lofton, James **42**
Sharper, Darren **32**
White, Reggie **6, 50**

Green Belt Movement
Maathai, Wangari **43**

Grenadian government
Bishop, Maurice **39**

Groupe de Recherche Choréographique de
Dove, Ulysses **5**

Guardian
Trotter, Monroe **9**

Guggenheim fellowship
Pope.L, William **72**
Rollins, Sonny **37**
Taylor, Cecil **70**
Wilson, Ellis **39**

Guitar
Ade, King Sunny **41**
Barker, Danny **32**
Barnes, Roosevelt "Booba" **33**
Bibb, Eric **49**
Brown, Clarence Gatemouth **59**
Butler, Jonathan **28**
Burns, Eddie **44**
Burnside, R. L. **56**
Caymmi, Dorival **72**
Collins, Bootsy **31**
Cray, Robert **30**
Davis, Gary **41**
Diddley, Bo **39, 72**
Estes, Sleepy John **33**
Green, Grant **56**
Guy, Buddy **31**
Harris, Corey **39, 73**

Hemphill, Jessie Mae **33, 59**
Hendrix, Jimi **10**
House, Son **8**
Hooker, John Lee **30**
Howlin' Wolf **9**
Jean, Wyclef **20**
Johnson, Robert **2**
Jordan, Ronny **26**
Killings, Debra **57**
King, B. B. **7**
Klugh, Earl **59**
Kolosoy, Wendo **73**
Kravitz, Lenny **10, 34**
Lipscomb, Mance **49**
Marley, Bob **5**
Mayfield, Curtis **2, 43**
Ndegéocello, Me'Shell **15**
Ongala, Remmy **9**
Pena, Paul **58**
Seals, Son **56**
Spence, Joseph **49**
Staples, Mavis **50**
Staples, "Pops" **32**
Watson, Johnny "Guitar" **18**
Wilson, Cassandra **16**

Gulf War
Powell, Colin **1, 28**
Shaw, Bernard **2**
Von Lipsey, Roderick K. **11**

Gurdjieff Institute
Toomer, Jean **6**

Guyanese government
Burnham, Forbes **66**

Gymnastics
Dawes, Dominique **11**
Hilliard, Wendy **53**
White, Jesse **22**

Hair care
Cottrell, Comer **11**
Fuller, S. B. **13**
Gibson, Ted **66**
Johnson, George E. **29**
Joyner, Marjorie Stewart **26**
Malone, Annie **13**
Roche, Joyce M. **17**
Walker, Madame C. J. **7**

Haitian refugees
Ashe, Arthur **1, 18**
Dunham, Katherine **4, 59**
Jean, Wyclef **20**
Robinson, Randall **7, 46**

Hal Jackson's Talented Teens International
Jackson, Hal **41**

Hale House
Hale, Clara **16**
Hale, Lorraine **8**

Hallmark Channel
Corbi, Lana **42**

Hampton University
Harvey, William R. **42**

Handy Award
Hunter, Alberta **42**

Harlem Artist Guild
Nugent, Richard Bruce **39**
Wilson, Ellis **39**

Harlem Cultural Council
Nugent, Richard Bruce **39**

Harlem Globetrotters
Chamberlain, Wilt **18, 47**
Haynes, Marques **22**
Jackson, Mannie **14**
Woodward, Lynette **67**

Harlem Junior Tennis League
Blake, James **43**

Harlem Renaissance
Alexander, Margaret Walker **22**
Bennett, Gwendolyn B. **59**
Christian, Barbara T. **44**
Cullen, Countee **8**
Cuney, William Waring **44**
Dandridge, Raymond Garfield **45**
Davis, Arthur P. **41**
Delaney, Beauford **19**
Ellington, Duke **5**
Fauset, Jessie **7**
Fisher, Rudolph **17**
Frazier, E. Franklin **10**
Horne, Frank **44**
Hughes, Langston **4**
Hurston, Zora Neale **3**
Imes, Elmer Samuel **39**
Johnson, Georgia Douglas **41**
Johnson, James Weldon **5**
Johnson, William Henry **3**
Larsen, Nella **10**
Locke, Alain **10**
McKay, Claude **6**
Mills, Florence **22**
Nugent, Richard Bruce **39**
Petry, Ann **19**
Thurman, Wallace **16**
Toomer, Jean **6**
VanDerZee, James **6**
West, Dorothy **12, 54**
Wilson, Ellis **39**

Harlem Writers Guild
Guy, Rosa **5**
Killens, John O. **54**
Wesley, Valerie Wilson **18**

Harlem Youth Opportunities Unlimited (HARYOU)
Clark, Kenneth B. **5, 52**

Harmonica
Bailey, DeFord **33**
Barnes, Roosevelt "Booba" **33**
Burns, Eddie **44**
Howlin' Wolf **9**
Neal, Raful **44**
Ross, Isaiah "Doc" **40**

Harness racing
Minor, DeWayne **32**

Harp
Coltrane, Alice **70**
Majors, Jeff **41**

Harriet Tubman Home for Aged and Indigent Colored People
Tubman, Harriet **9**

Harrisburg Giants baseball team
Charleston, Oscar **39**

Harvard Law School
Bell, Derrick **6**
Dickerson, Debra J. **60**
Ogletree, Charles, Jr. **12, 47**

Harvard University
Amaker, Tommy **62**
Epps, Archie C., III **45**
Hammonds, Evelynn **69**
Huggins, Nathan Irvin **52**
Loury, Glenn **36**

HARYOU
See Harlem Youth Opportunities Unlimited

Hazelitt Award for Excellence in Arts
Bradley, David Henry, Jr. **39**

Head Start
Edelman, Marian Wright **5, 42**
Taylor, Helen (Lavon Hollingshed) **30**

Health care reform
Adams-Campbell, Lucille L. **60**
Berrysmith, Don Reginald **49**
Brown, Jesse **6, 41**
Carroll, L. Natalie **44**
Cole, Lorraine **48**
Cooper, Edward S. **6**
Davis, Angela **5**
Dirie, Waris **56**
Gibson, Kenneth A. **6**
Hughes, Ebony **57**
Kintaudi, Leon **62**
Lavizzo-Mourey, Risa **48**
Norman, Pat **10**
Potter, Myrtle **40**
Richardson, Rupert **67**
Satcher, David **7, 57**
Tuckson, Reed V. **71**
Vaughn, Viola **70**
Williams, Daniel Hale **2**
Williams, David Rudyard **50**

Heart disease
Cooper, Edward S. **6**
Grant, Augustus O. **71**

Heidelberg Project
Guyton, Tyree **9**

Heisman Trophy
Bush, Reggie **59**
Ware, Andre **37**

The Heritage Network
Mercado-Valdes, Frank **43**

HEW
See U.S. Department of Health, Education, and Welfare

HHS
See U.S. Department of Health and Human Services

Hip-hop music
Akon **68**
Ashanti **37**
Benjamin, Andre **45**

Fiasco, Lupe **64**
Garrett, Sean **57**
Jennings, Lyfe **56, 69**
K-Swift **73**
Lil Wayne **66**
Patton, Antwan **45**
Run **31, 73**
Smith, Danyel **40**
will.i.am **64**
Williams, Pharrell **47**

Historians
Ballard, Allen Butler, Jr. **40**
Benberry, Cuesta **65**
Berry, Mary Frances **7**
Blassingame, John Wesley **40**
Blockson, Charles L. **42**
Bogle, Donald **34**
Chase-Riboud, Barbara **20, 46**
Cooper, Afua **53**
Cooper, Anna Julia **20**
Cruse, Harold **54**
Diop, Cheikh Anta **4**
Dodson, Howard, Jr. **7, 52**
Du Bois, W. E. B. **3**
Franklin, John Hope **5**
Gates, Henry Louis, Jr. **3, 38, 67**
Giddings, Paula **11**
Gill, Gerald **69**
Hammonds, Evelynn **69**
Logan, Rayford W. **40**
Nash, Joe **55**
Hansberry, William Leo **11**
Harkless, Necia Desiree **19**
Hine, Darlene Clark **24**
Horton, James Oliver **58**
Huggins, Nathan Irvin **52**
Marable, Manning **10**
Painter, Nell Irvin **24**
Patterson, Orlando **4**
Quarles, Benjamin Arthur **18**
Reagon, Bernice Johnson **7**
Reddick, Lawrence Dunbar **20**
Rogers, Joel Augustus **30**
Sadlier, Rosemary **62**
Schomburg, Arthur Alfonso **9**
Skinner, Kiron K. **65**
Snowden, Frank M., Jr. **67**
van Sertima, Ivan **25**
Washington, James Melvin **50**
Williams, George Washington **18**
Woodson, Carter G. **2**

Hitman Records
Brae, C. Michael **61**

Hockey
Brashear, Donald **39**
Brathwaite, Fred **35**
Brown, James **22**
Brown, Sean **52**
Carnegie, Herbert **25**
Doig, Jason **45**
Fuhr, Grant **1, 49**
Grand-Pierre, Jean-Luc **46**
Grier, Mike **43**
Iginla, Jarome **35**
Mayers, Jamal **39**
McBride, Bryant **18**
McCarthy, Sandy **64**
McKegney, Tony **3**
O'Ree, Willie **5**
Salvador, Bryce **51**

Weekes, Kevin **67**

Homestead Grays baseball team
Charleston, Oscar **39**
Day, Leon **39**

Homosexuality
Carter, Mandy **11**
Clarke, Cheryl **32**
Delany, Samuel R., Jr. **9**
Gomes, Peter J. **15**
Harris, E. Lynn **12, 33**
Hemphill, Essex **10**
Julien, Isaac **3**
Lorde, Audre **6**
Norman, Pat **10**
Nugent, Richard Bruce **39**
Parker, Pat **19**
Riggs, Marlon **5, 44**
Rupaul **17**
Wilson, Phill **9**

Honeywell Corporation
Jackson, Mannie **14**

Horse racing
Harris, Sylvia **70**
St. Julien, Marlon **29**
Winkfield, Jimmy **42**

House music
Knuckles, Frankie **42**

House of Representatives
See U.S. House of Representatives

Housing Authority of New Orleans
Mason, Ronald **27**

Houston Astros baseball team
Morgan, Joe Leonard **9**
Watson, Bob **25**

Houston Comets basketball team
Perrot, Kim **23**
Thompson, Tina **25**

Houston Oilers football team
McNair, Steve **22, 47**
Moon, Warren **8, 66**

Houston Rockets basketball team
Lucas, John **7**
Olajuwon, Hakeem **2, 72**

Howard University
Adams-Campbell, Lucille L. **60**
Benjamin, Tritobia Hayes **53**
Cardozo, Francis L. **33**
Carter, Joye Maureen **41**
Cobb, W. Montague **39**
Davis, Arthur P. **41**
Dodson, Owen **38**
Gerima, Haile **38**
Jenifer, Franklyn G. **2**
Ladner, Joyce A. **42**
Locke, Alain **10**
Logan, Rayford W. **40**
Malveaux, Floyd **54**
Mays, Benjamin E. **7**
Neal, Larry **38**
Payton, Benjamin F. **23**

Porter, James A. **11**
Reid, Irvin D. **20**
Ribeau, Sidney **70**
Robinson, Spottswood W., III **22**
Snowden, Frank M., Jr. **67**
Sowande, Fela **39**
Spriggs, William **67**
Swygert, H. Patrick **22**
Wells, James Lesesne **10**
Wesley, Dorothy Porter **19**
White, Charles **39**
Young, Roger Arliner **29**

HRCF
See Human Rights Campaign Fund

Hubbard Hospital
Lyttle, Hulda Margaret **14**

HUD
See U.S. Department of Housing and Urban Development

Hugo awards
Butler, Octavia **8, 43, 58**
Delany, Samuel R., Jr. **9**

Hull-Ottawa Canadiens hockey team
O'Ree, Willie **5**

Human resources
Howroyd, Janice Bryant **42**

Human Rights Campaign Fund (HRCF)
Carter, Mandy **11**

Hunter College
DeCarava, Roy **42**
Mayhew, Richard **39**
Thomas, Michael **69**

Hurdle
Devers, Gail **7**

IBF
See International Boxing Federation

IBM
Adkins, Rod **41**
Blackwell, Robert D., Sr. **52**
Chenault, Kenneth I. **5, 36**
Dean, Mark **35**
Foster, Jylla Moore **45**
Thompson, John W. **26**
Zollar, Alfred **40**

IBM's National Black Family Technology Awareness
Adkins, Rod **41**

Ice Hockey in Harlem
Mayers, Jamal **39**

Ice skating
See Figure skating

Igbo people/traditions
Achebe, Chinua **6**

IHRLG
See International Human Rights Law Group

I-Iman Cosmetics
Iman **4, 33**

Ile Ife Films
Hall, Arthur 39

Illinois state government
Braun, Carol Moseley 4, 42
Burris, Roland W. 25
Colter, Cyrus J. 36
Obama, Barack 49
Raoul, Kwame 55
Trotter, Donne E. 28
Washington, Harold 6
White, Jesse 22

Illustrations
Anderson, Ho Che 54
Biggers, John 20, 33
Bryan, Ashley F. 41
Campbell, E. Simms 13
Fax, Elton 48
Honeywood, Varnette P. 54
Hudson, Cheryl 15
Kitt, Sandra 23
Pinkney, Jerry 15
Saint James, Synthia 12

Imani Temple
Stallings, George A., Jr. 6

IMF
See International Monetary Fund

Imhotep National Conference on Hospital Integration
Cobb, W. Montague 39

Indecorp, Inc.
Johnson, George E. 29

Indiana Fever basketball team
Catchings, Tamika 43

Indiana state government
Carson, Julia 23, 69
Carter, Pamela Lynn 67

Indianapolis ABCs baseball team
Charleston, Oscar 39

Indianapolis Clowns baseball team
Charleston, Oscar 39
Johnson, Mamie "Peanut" 40

Indianapolis Colts football team
Dickerson, Eric 27
Dungy, Tony 17, 42, 59
Sanders, Bob 72

Indianapolis Crawfords baseball team
Charleston, Oscar 39
Kaiser, Cecil 42

Indianapolis 500
Ribbs, Willy T. 2

Industrial design
Harrison, Charles 72

Information technology
Blackwell, Robert D., Sr. 52
Coleman, Ken 57
Pinkett, Randal 61
Smith, Joshua 10
Woods, Jacqueline 52

Zollar, Alfred 40

In Friendship
Baker, Ella 5

Inkatha
Buthelezi, Mangosuthu Gatsha 9

Inner City Broadcasting Corporation
Jackson, Hal 41
Sutton, Percy E. 42

Institute for Black Parenting
Oglesby, Zena 12

Institute for Research in African American Studies
Marable, Manning 10

Institute of Positive Education
Madhubuti, Haki R. 7

Institute of Social and Religious Research
Mays, Benjamin E. 7

Insurance
Hill, Jesse, Jr. 13
James, Donna A. 51
Kidd, Mae Street 39
Killingsworth, Cleve, Jr. 54
Procope, Ernesta 23
Procope, John Levy 56
Spaulding, Charles Clinton 9
Vaughns, Cleopatra 46
Williams, Ronald A. 57
Willie, Louis, Jr. 68

Interior design
Bridges, Sheila 36
De' Alexander, Quinton 57
Ham, Cynthia Parker 58
Hayes, Cecil N. 46
King, Robert Arthur 58
Myles, Kim 69
Steave-Dickerson, Kia 57
Taylor, Karin 34

Internal Revenue Service
Colter, Cyrus J. 36

International ambassadors
Davis, Ruth 37
Poitier, Sidney 11, 36
Smythe Haith, Mabel 61
Todman, Terence A. 55
Wharton, Clifton Reginald, Sr. 36

International Association of Fire Chiefs
Bell, Michael 40
Day, Leon 39

International Boxing Federation (IBF)
Ali, Muhammad 2, 16, 52
Hearns, Thomas 29
Hopkins, Bernard 35, 69
Lewis, Lennox 27
Moorer, Michael 19
Mosley, Shane 32
Tyson, Mike 28, 44
Whitaker, Pernell 10

International Federation of Library Associations and In-

stitutions
Wedgeworth, Robert W. 42

International Free and Accepted Masons and Eastern Star
Banks, William 11

International Human Rights Law Group (IHRLG)
McDougall, Gay J. 11, 43

International Ladies' Auxiliary
Tucker, Rosina 14

International law
Payne, Ulice 42

International Monetary Fund (IMF)
Babangida, Ibrahim 4
Chissano, Joaquim 7, 55, 67
Conté, Lansana 7
Diouf, Abdou 3
Patterson, P. J. 6, 20

International Workers Organization (IWO)
Patterson, Louise 25

Internet
Cooper, Barry 33
Gilliard, Steve 69
Knowling, Robert 38
Thomas-Graham, Pamela 29

Internet security
Thompson, John W. 26

Interpol
Noble, Ronald 46

Interscope Geffen A & M Records
Stoute, Steve 38

***In the Black* television show**
Jones, Caroline R. 29

Inventions
Johnson, Lonnie 32
Jones, Frederick McKinley 68
Julian, Percy Lavon 6
Latimer, Lewis H. 4
McCoy, Elijah 8
Morgan, Garrett 1
Woods, Granville T. 5

Investment management
Beal, Bernard B. 46
Bryant, John 26
Ford, Wallace 58
Gardner, Chris 65
Goings, Russell 59
Harris, Carla A. 67
Procope, Ernesta 23
Rogers, John W., Jr. 5, 52
Utendahl, John 23

Island Def Jam Music Group
Liles, Kevin 42

Ivorian Popular Front (FPI)
Gbagbo, Laurent 43

Ivory Coast government
Gbagbo, Laurent 43
Guéï, Robert 66

Jackie Robinson Foundation
Robinson, Rachel 16

Jackson Securities, Inc.
Jackson, Maynard 2, 41

Jackson University
Mason, Ronald 27

Jacksonville Jaguars football team
Cherry, Deron 40

Jamaican government
Simpson-Miller, Portia 62

Jazz
Adderley, Julian "Cannonball" 30
Adderley, Nat 29
Albright, Gerald 23
Anderson, Carl 48
Armstrong, Louis 2
Austin, Lovie 40
Austin, Patti 24
Ayers, Roy 16
Bailey, Buster 38
Bailey, Philip 63
Barker, Danny 32
Basie, Count 23
Batiste, Alvin 66
Bechet, Sidney 18
Belle, Regina 1, 51
Blakey, Art 37
Blanchard, Terence 43
Bolden, Buddy 39
Bridgewater, Dee Dee 32
Brooks, Avery 9
Butler, Jonathan 28
Calloway, Cab 14
Carter, Benny 46
Carter, Betty 19
Carter, Regina 23
Carter, Warrick L. 27
Cartiér, Xam Wilson 41
Charles, Ray 16, 48
Cheatham, Doc 17
Clarke, Kenny 27
Cole, Nat King 17
Coleman, Ornette 39, 69
Coltrane, Alice 70
Coltrane, John 19
Coltrane, Ravi 71
Cook, Charles "Doc" 44
Count Basie 23
Crawford, Randy 19
Crothers, Scatman 19
Crouch, Stanley 11
Crowder, Henry 16
Daemyon, Jerald 64
Dara, Olu 35
Davis, Anthony 11
Davis, Frank Marshall 47
Davis, Miles 4
Dickenson, Vic 38
Donegan, Dorothy 19
Downing, Will 19
Duke, George 21
Dumas, Henry 41
Durham, Bobby 73
Eckstine, Billy 28
Eldridge, Roy 37
Ellington, Duke 5
Ellison, Ralph 7
Eubanks, Kevin 15

Farmer, Art **38**
Ferrell, Rachelle **29**
Fitzgerald, Ella **8, 18**
Flanagan, Tommy **69**
Foster, George "Pops" **40**
Freelon, Nnenna **32**
Freeman, Yvette **27**
Fuller, Arthur **27**
Gillespie, Dizzy **1**
Golson, Benny **37**
Gordon, Dexter **25**
Green, Grant **56**
Griffin, Johnny **71**
Güines, Tata **69**
Hampton, Lionel **17, 41**
Hancock, Herbie **20, 67**
Hardin Armstrong, Lil **39**
Harris, Barry **68**
Hathaway, Lalah **57**
Hawkins, Coleman **9**
Henderson, Fletcher **32**
Higginbotham, J. C. **37**
Hill, Andrew **66**
Hines, Earl "Fatha" **39**
Hinton, Milt **30**
Holiday, Billie **1**
Horn, Shirley **32, 56**
Hyman, Phyllis **19**
Jackson, Milt **26**
Jacquet, Illinois **49**
Jamal, Ahmad **69**
James, Etta **13, 52**
Jarreau, Al **21, 65**
Johnson, Buddy **36**
Johnson, J. J. **37**
Jones, Elvin **14, 68**
Jones, Etta **35**
Jones, Hank **57**
Jones, Jonah **39**
Jones, Quincy **8, 30**
Jones, Thad **68**
Jordan, Ronny **26**
Kenyatta, Robin **54**
Klugh, Earl **59**
Ledisi **73**
Lewis, Ramsey **35, 70**
Lincoln, Abbey **3**
Locke, Eddie **44**
Lucien, Jon **66**
Madhubuti, Haki R. **7**
Marsalis, Branford **34**
Marsalis, Delfeayo **41**
Marsalis, Wynton **16**
McBride, James **35**
McGriff, Jimmy **72**
Mills, Florence **22**
Mingus, Charles **15**
Mitchell, Nicole **66**
Monk, Thelonious **1**
Moore, Melba **21**
Morton, Jelly Roll **29**
Muse, Clarence Edouard **21**
Nascimento, Milton **2, 64**
Oliver, Joe "King" **42**
Parker, Charlie **20**
Parker, Maceo **72**
Payne, Freda **58**
Peterson, Marvin "Hannibal" **27**
Peterson, Oscar **52**
Powell, Bud **24**
Redman, Joshua **30**
Reese, Della **6, 20**
Reeves, Dianne **32**

Roach, Max **21, 63**
Roberts, Marcus **19**
Rollins, Sonny **37**
Ross, Diana **8, 27**
Rushing, Jimmy **37**
Sample, Joe **51**
Scarlett, Millicent **49**
Scott, Hazel **66**
Scott, "Little" Jimmy **48**
Silver, Horace **26**
Simpson-Hoffman, N'kenge **52**
Sissle, Noble **29**
Smith, Bessie **3**
Smith, Cladys "Jabbo" **32**
Smith, Dr. Lonnie **49**
Smith, Lonnie Liston **49**
Smith, Stuff **37**
Staton, Dakota **62**
Strayhorn, Billy **31**
Sullivan, Maxine **37**
Sun Ra **60**
Swann, Lynn **28**
Tampa Red **63**
Taylor, Billy **23**
Taylor, Cecil **70**
Terry, Clark **39**
Tisdale, Wayman **50**
Vaughan, Sarah **13**
Waller, Fats **29**
Washington, Dinah **22**
Washington, Grover, Jr. **17, 44**
Waters, Benny **26**
Watson, Johnny "Guitar" **18**
Watts, Reggie **52**
Webster, Katie **29**
Wein, Joyce **62**
Whalum, Kirk **37, 64**
White, Maurice **29**
Williams, Joe **5, 25**
Williams, Mary Lou **15**
Williams, Tony **67**
Wilson, Cassandra **16**
Wilson, Gerald **49**
Wilson, Nancy **10**
York, Vincent **40**
Young, Lee **72**
Young, Lester **37**

Jazzistry
York, Vincent **40**

***Jet* magazine**
Bennett, Lerone, Jr. **5**
Johnson, John H. **3, 54**
Massaquoi, Hans J. **30**
Sleet, Moneta, Jr. **5**

Jive Records
McPherson, David **32**

Jockeys
Harris, Sylvia **70**
Lewis, Oliver **56**
Winkfield, Jimmy **42**

Johnson C. Smith University
Yancy, Dorothy Cowser **42**

Johnson Products
Johnson, George E. **29**

Johnson Publishing Company, Inc.
Bennett, Lerone, Jr. **5**
Booker, Simeon **23**

Johnson, John H. **3, 54**
Monroe, Bryan **71**
Rice, Linda Johnson **9, 41**
Sleet, Moneta, Jr. **5**

Joint Center for Political Studies
Williams, Eddie N. **44**

Joint Chiefs of Staff
See U.S. Joint Chiefs of Staff

Jones Haywood School of Ballet
Jones, Doris W. **62**

Journalism
Abbott, Robert Sengstacke **27**
Abrahams, Peter **39**
Abu-Jamal, Mumia **15**
Ansa, Tina McElroy **14**
Ashley-Ward, Amelia **23**
Asim, Jabari **71**
Auguste, Arnold A. **47**
Azikiwe, Nnamdi **13**
Bailey, Chauncey **68**
Baquet, Dean **63**
Barden, Don H. **9, 20**
Barnett, Amy Du Bois **46**
Barrett, Lindsay **43**
Bass, Charlotta Spears **40**
Bates, Karen Grigsby **40**
Bennett, Gwendolyn B. **59**
Bennett, Lerone, Jr. **5**
Blair, Jayson **50**
Blake, Asha **26**
Blow, Charles M. **73**
Bolden, Frank E. **44**
Booker, Simeon **23**
Borders, James **9**
Boyd, Gerald M. **32, 59**
Boyd, Suzanne **52**
Bradley, Ed **2, 59**
Britt, Donna **28**
Brower, William **49**
Brown, George Leslie **62**
Brown, Lloyd Louis **42**
Brown, Tony **3**
Buckley, Gail Lumet **39**
Burt-Murray, Angela **59**
Caldwell, Earl **60**
Campbell, Bebe Moore **6, 24, 59**
Cary, Mary Ann Shadd **30**
Cayton, Horace **26**
Chadiha, Jeffri **57**
Chideya, Farai **14, 61**
Ciara, Barbara **69**
Cooke, Marvel **31**
Cooper, Barry **33**
Cose, Ellis **5, 50**
Crouch, Stanley **11**
Crutchfield, James N. **55**
Cullen, Countee **8**
Cunningham, Evelyn **23**
Dash, Leon **47**
Datcher, Michael **60**
Davis, Belva **61**
Davis, Frank Marshall **47**
Davis, Thulani **61**
Dawkins, Wayne **20**
Deggans, Eric **71**
Drummond, William J. **40**
Due, Tananarive **30**
Dunbar, Paul Laurence **8**

Dunnigan, Alice Allison **41**
Edmonds, Terry **17**
Epperson, Sharon **54**
Farley, Christopher John **54**
Forman, James **7, 51**
Fortune, T. Thomas **6**
Fuller, Hoyt **44**
Giddings, Paula **11**
Gilliard, Steve **69**
Givhan, Robin Deneen **72**
Goode, Mal **13**
Gordon, Ed **10, 53**
Grimké, Archibald H. **9**
Gumbel, Bryant **14**
Gumbel, Greg **8**
Hansberry, Lorraine **6**
Hare, Nathan **44**
Harrington, Oliver W. **9**
Harris, Claire **34**
Harris, Jay **19**
Harris, Richard E. **61**
Haynes, Trudy **44**
Henriques, Julian **37**
Herbert, Bob **63**
Hickman, Fred **11**
Holt, Lester **66**
Huggins, Edie **71**
Hunter-Gault, Charlayne **6, 31**
Ifill, Gwen **28**
Jarrett, Vernon D. **42**
Jasper, Kenji **39**
Jealous, Benjamin **70**
Joachim, Paulin **34**
Johnson, Georgia Douglas **41**
Johnson, James Weldon **5**
Kaufman, Monica **66**
Kearney, Janis **54**
Khanga, Yelena **6**
Killens, John O. **54**
King, Colbert I. **69**
Knight, Etheridge **37**
LaGuma, Alex **30**
Lacy, Sam **30, 46**
Lampkin, Daisy **19**
Leavell, Dorothy R. **17**
Lewis, Edward T. **21**
Lowe, Herbert **57**
Mabrey, Vicki **26**
Mabry, Marcus **70**
Mabuza-Suttle, Felicia **43**
Madison, Paula **37**
Martin, Louis E. **16**
Martin, Roland S. **49**
Mason, Felicia **31**
Maynard, Nancy Hicks **73**
Maynard, Robert C. **7**
McBride, James **35**
McCall, Nathan **8**
McGruder, Robert **22, 35**
McKay, Claude **6**
Mickelbury, Penny **28**
Mitchell, Elvis **67**
Mitchell, Russ **21, 73**
Mkapa, Benjamin **16**
Monroe, Bryan **71**
Mossell, Gertrude Bustill **40**
Murphy, John H. **42**
Murray, Pauli **38**
Nelson, Jill **6, 54**
Neville, Arthel **53**
Newkirk, Pamela **69**
Nkosi, Lewis **46**
Oliver, Pam **54**

Olojede, Dele **59**
Page, Clarence **4**
Palmer, Everard **37**
Parham, Marjorie B. **71**
Parker, Star **70**
Parks, Gordon **1, 35, 58**
Payne, Ethel L. **28**
Perez, Anna **1**
Perkins, Tony **24**
Phillips, Joseph C. **73**
Pinkston, W. Randall **24**
Pitts, Byron **71**
Pitts, Leonard, Jr. **54**
Pressley, Condace L. **41**
Price, Hugh B. **9, 54**
Prince, Richard E. **71**
Quarles, Norma **25**
Raspberry, William **2**
Reed, Ishmael **8**
Reeves, Rachel J. **23**
Rhoden, William C. **67**
Riley, Rochelle **50**
Roberts, Robin **16, 54**
Robinson, Max **3**
Rodgers, Johnathan **6, 51**
Rowan, Carl T. **1, 30**
Salih, Al-Tayyib **37**
Salters, Lisa **71**
Sanders, Pharoah **64**
Schuyler, George Samuel **40**
Schuyler, Philippa **50**
Senior, Olive **37**
Shaw, Bernard **2, 28**
Shipp, E. R. **15**
Simpson, Carole **6, 30**
Smith, Clarence O. **21**
Smith, Danyel **40**
Smith, Stephen A. **69**
Sowell, Thomas **2**
Staples, Brent **8**
Stewart, Alison **13**
Stokes, Carl **10, 73**
Stone, Chuck **9**
Syler, Rene **53**
Tate, Eleanora E. **20, 55**
Taylor, Kristin Clark **8**
Taylor, Susan L. **10**
Thurman, Wallace **16**
Tolson, Melvin B. **37**
Trotter, Monroe **9**
Tucker, Cynthia **15, 61**
Wallace, Michele Faith **13**
Washington, Harriet A. **69**
Watson, Carlos **50**
Watts, Rolonda **9**
Webb, Veronica **10**
Wells-Barnett, Ida B. **8**
Wesley, Valerie Wilson **18**
Whitaker, Mark **21, 47**
Wilbekin, Emil **63**
Wilbon, Michael **68**
Wiley, Ralph **8**
Wilkerson, Isabel **71**
Wilkins, Roger **2**
Williams, Armstrong **29**
Williams, Clarence **70**
Williams, Juan **35**
Williams, Patricia **11, 54**
Wiwa, Ken **67**
Woods, Mattiebelle **63**
Yette, Samuel F. **63**

Zook, Kristal Brent **62**

Journal of Negro History
Woodson, Carter G. **2**

Judaism
Funnye, Capers C., Jr. **73**

Just Us Books
Hudson, Cheryl **15**
Hudson, Wade **15**

Kansas City Athletics baseball team
Paige, Satchel **7**

Kansas City Chiefs football team
Allen, Marcus **20**
Cherry, Deron **40**
Dungy, Tony **17, 42, 59**
Thomas, Derrick **25**
Thomas, Emmitt **71**

Kansas City (MO) government
Cleaver, Emanuel **4, 45, 68**

Kansas City Monarchs baseball team
Bell, James "Cool Papa" **36**
Brown, Willard **36**

Kansas State University
Prince, Ron **64**

KANU
See Kenya African National Union

Kappa Alpha Psi
Hamilton, Samuel C. **47**

Karl Kani Infinity
Kani, Karl **10**

KAU
See Kenya African Union

KCA
See Kikuyu Central Association

Kentucky Derby
Winkfield, Jimmy **42**

Kentucky Negro Educational Association
Cotter, Joseph Seamon, Sr. **40**

Kentucky state government
Kidd, Mae Street **39**

Kenya African National Union (KANU)
Kariuki, J. M. **67**
Kenyatta, Jomo **5**
Kibaki, Mwai **60**
Moi, Daniel Arap **1, 35**
Ngilu, Charity **58**
Odinga, Raila **67**

Kenya African Union (KAU)
Kenyatta, Jomo **5**

Kenya National Council of Churchs (NCCK)
Kobia, Samuel **43**

Kenyan government
Kariuki, J. M. **67**
Kibaki, Mwai **60**

Maathai, Wangari **43**
Moi, Daniel Arap **1, 35**
Ngilu, Charity **58**
Odinga, Raila **67**

Kikuyu Central Association (KCA)
Kenyatta, Jomo **5**

King Center
See Martin Luther King Jr. Center for Nonviolent Social Change

King Oliver's Creole Band
Armstrong, (Daniel) Louis **2**
Hardin Armstrong, Lil **39**
Oliver, Joe "King" **42**

King's Troop of the Royal Horse Artillery
Scantlebury, Janna **47**

Kitchen Table: Women of Color Press
Smith, Barbara **28**

Kmart Holding Corporation
Lewis, Aylwin **51**

Kraft General Foods
Fudge, Ann (Marie) **11, 55**
Sneed, Paula A. **18**

Kunta Kinte–Alex Haley Foundation
Blackshear, Leonard **52**

Kwanzaa
Karenga, Maulana **10, 71**

Kwazulu Territorial Authority
Buthelezi, Mangosuthu Gatsha **9**

Labour Party
Amos, Valerie **41**

Ladies Professional Golfers' Association (LPGA)
Gibson, Althea **8, 43**
Powell, Renee **34**

LaFace Records
Benjamin, Andre **45**
Edmonds, Kenneth "Babyface" **10, 31**
OutKast **35**
Patton, Antwan **45**
Reid, Antonio "L.A." **28**

Langston (OK) city government
Tolson, Melvin B. **37**

LAPD
See Los Angeles Police Department

Latin American folk music
Nascimento, Milton **2, 64**

Latin baseball leagues
Kaiser, Cecil **42**

Law enforcement
Alexander, Joyce London **18**
Barrett, Jacquelyn **28**
Bolton, Terrell D. **25**
Bradley, Thomas **2, 20**
Brown, Lee P. **1, 24**

Feemster, Herbert **72**
Freeman, Charles **19**
Gibson, Johnnie Mae **23**
Glover, Nathaniel, Jr. **12**
Gomez-Preston, Cheryl **9**
Harvard, Beverly **11**
Hillard, Terry **25**
Holton, Hugh, Jr. **39**
Hurtt, Harold **46**
Johnson, Norma L. Holloway **17**
Johnson, Robert T. **17**
Keith, Damon J. **16**
McKinnon, Isaiah **9**
Moose, Charles **40**
Napoleon, Benny N. **23**
Noble, Ronald **46**
Oliver, Jerry **37**
Parks, Bernard C. **17**
Ramsey, Charles H. **21, 69**
Robinson, Bishop L. **66**
Schmoke, Kurt **1, 48**
Smith, Richard **51**
Thomas, Franklin A. **5, 49**
Wainwright, Joscelyn **46**
Ward, Benjamin **68**
Williams, Willie L. **4**
Wilson, Jimmy **45**

Lawyers' Committee for Civil Rights Under Law
Arnwine, Barbara **28**
Hubbard, Arnette **38**
McDougall, Gay J. **11, 43**

LDF
See NAACP Legal Defense and Educational Fund

League of Nations
Haile Selassie **7**

League of Women Voters
Meek, Carrie **36**

"Leave No Child Behind"
Edelman, Marian Wright **5, 42**

Legal Defense Fund
See NAACP Legal Defense and Educational Fund

Lexicography
Major, Clarence **9**

Liberation theology
West, Cornel **5**

Liberian government
Henries, A. Doris Banks **44**
Sirleaf, Ellen Johnson **71**
Weah, George **58**

Liberians United for Reconciliation and Democracy (LURD)
Conneh, Sekou Damate, Jr. **51**

Library science
Bontemps, Arna **8**
Franklin, Hardy R. **9**
Harsh, Vivian Gordon **14**
Hutson, Jean Blackwell **16**
Jones, Clara Stanton **51**
Josey, E. J. **10**
Kitt, Sandra **23**
Larsen, Nella **10**

Morrison, Sam **50**
Owens, Major **6**
Rollins, Charlemae Hill **27**
Schomburg, Arthur Alfonso **9**
Smith, Jessie Carney **35**
Spencer, Anne **27**
Wedgeworth, Robert W. **42**
Wesley, Dorothy Porter **19**

Librettos
Chenault, John **40**

Lincoln University
Cuney, William Waring **44**
Randall, Dudley **8, 55**
Sudarkasa, Niara **4**

LISC
See Local Initiative Support Corporation

Listen Up Foundation
Jones, Quincy **8, 30**

Literacy Volunteers of America
Amos, Wally **9**

Literary criticism
Baker, Houston A., Jr. **6**
Braithwaite, William Stanley **52**
Brown, Sterling Allen **10, 64**
Broyard, Anatole **68**
Cartey, Wilfred **47**
Christian, Barbara T. **44**
Cook, Mercer **40**
De Veaux, Alexis **44**
Emanuel, James A. **46**
Fleming, Raymond **48**
Ford, Nick Aaron **44**
Fuller, Hoyt **44**
Joachim, Paulin **34**
Mugo, Micere Githae **32**
Ngugi wa Thiong'o **29, 61**
Redding, J. Saunders **26**
Reed, Ishmael **8**
Smith, Barbara **28**
Wesley, Valerie Wilson **18**
West, Cornel **5**

Literary Hall of Fame for Writers of African Descent
Colter, Cyrus J. **36**

Lithography
White, Charles **39**

Little Junior Project
Fuller, Arthur **27**

"Little Paris" group
Thomas, Alma **14**

"Little Rock Nine"
Bates, Daisy **13**

Liver research
Leevy, Carrol M. **42**

Lobbying
Boyd, John W., Jr. **20, 72**
Brooke, Edward **8**
Brown, Elaine **8**
Brown, Jesse **6, 41**
Brown, Ron **5**
Edelman, Marian Wright **5, 42**
Lee, Canada **8**

Mallett, Conrad, Jr. **16**
Reeves, Gregory **49**
Robinson, Randall **7, 46**

Los Angeles Angels baseball team
Baylor, Don **6**
Bonds, Bobby **43**
Carew, Rod **20**
Robinson, Frank **9**
Winfield, Dave **5**

Los Angeles city government
Bradley, Thomas **2, 20**
Evers, Myrlie **8**

Los Angeles Clippers basketball team
Brand, Elton **31**

Los Angeles Dodgers baseball team
Baker, Dusty **8, 43, 72**
Newcombe, Don **24**
Robinson, Frank **9**
Strawberry, Darryl **22**
Wills, Maury **73**

Los Angeles Lakers basketball team
Abdul-Jabbar, Kareem **8**
Bryant, Kobe **15, 31, 71**
Chamberlain, Wilt **18, 47**
Fox, Rick **27**
Green, A. C. **32**
Johnson, Earvin "Magic" **3, 39**
O'Neal, Shaquille **8, 30**
Worthy, James **49**

Los Angeles Philharmonic
Lewis, Henry **38**

Los Angeles Police Department (LAPD)
Parks, Bernard C. **17**
Smith, Richard **51**
Williams, Willie L. **4**

Los Angeles Raiders football team
Allen, Marcus **20**
Lofton, James **42**
Lott, Ronnie **9**
Shell, Art **1, 66**

Los Angeles Rams football team
Dickerson, Eric **27**
Washington, Kenny **50**

Los Angeles Sparks basketball team
Leslie, Lisa **16, 73**

Los Angeles Times newspaper
Baquet, Dean **63**
Drummond, William J. **40**

Lost-Found Nation of Islam
Ali, Muhammad **2, 16, 52**
Ellison, Keith **59**
Farrakhan, Louis **2, 15**
Heard, Nathan C. **45**
Karim, Benjamin **61**
Muhammad, Ava **31**
Muhammad, Elijah **4**

Muhammad, Jabir Herbert **72**
Muhammad, Khallid Abdul **10, 31**
Muhammed, W. Deen **27**
Sutton, Percy E. **42**
Tillard, Conrad **47**
X, Malcolm **1**
X, Marvin **45**

Louisiana Disaster Recovery Authority
Francis, Norman (C.) **60**

Louisiana state government
Fields, Cleo **13**
Jefferson, William J. **25, 72**
Morial, Ernest "Dutch" **26**
Pinchback, P. B. S. **9**
Richardson, Rupert **67**

LPGA
See Ladies Professional Golfers' Association

Lunar surface ultraviolet camera
See Ultraviolet camera/spectrograph (UVC)

Lynching (anti-lynching legislation)
Johnson, James Weldon **5**
Moore, Harry T. **29**
Till, Emmett **7**

Lyrics
Crouch, Andraé **27**
D'Angelo **27**
Dunbar, Paul Laurence **8**
Fitzgerald, Ella **8**
Jean, Wyclef **20**
Johnson, James Weldon **5**
KRS-One **34**
Lil' Kim **28**
MC Lyte **34**
Randall, Alice **38**
Run-DMC **31**

MacArthur Foundation Fellowship
Butler, Octavia **8, 43, 58**
Cooper, Lisa **73**
Hammons, David **69**
Harris, Corey **39, 73**
Jackson, Mary **73**
Olopade, Olufunmilayo Falusi **58**
Parks, Suzan-Lori **34**
Taylor, Cecil **70**

MacNeil/Lehrer NewsHour
Hunter-Gault, Charlayne **6, 31**

Mad TV
Jones, Orlando **30**
Wilson, Debra **38**

Madame C. J. Walker Manufacturing Company
Joyner, Marjorie Stewart **26**
Walker, A'lelia **14**
Walker, Madame C. J. **7**

Major League Baseball administration
Solomon, Jimmie Lee **38**

Maktub
Watts, Reggie **52**

Malaco Records
Bland, Bobby "Blue" **36**

Malawi Congress Party (MCP)
Banda, Hastings Kamuzu **6, 54**

Manhattan Project
Quarterman, Lloyd Albert **4**
Wilkens, J. Ernest, Jr. **43**

MARC Corp.
See Metropolitan Applied Research Center

March on Washington/Freedom March
Baker, Josephine **3**
Belafonte, Harry **4, 65**
Bunche, Ralph J. **5**
Davis, Ossie **5, 50**
Fauntroy, Walter E. **11**
Forman, James **7, 51**
Franklin, John Hope **5**
Hedgeman, Anna Arnold **22**
Horne, Lena **5**
Jackson, Mahalia **5**
King, Coretta Scott **3, 57**
King, Martin Luther, Jr. **1**
Lewis, John **2, 46**
Meredith, James H. **11**
Randolph, A. Philip **3**
Rustin, Bayard **4**
Sleet, Moneta, Jr. **5**
Wilkins, Roy **4**
Young, Whitney M., Jr. **4**

Marketing
DeVard, Jerri **61**
Edwards, Trevor **54**
Kaigler, Denise **63**
Kendrick, Erika **57**

Martial arts
Barnes, Steven **54**
Copeland, Michael **47**
Slice, Kimbo **73**

Martin Luther King Jr. Center for Nonviolent Social Change
Dodson, Howard, Jr. **7, 52**
Farris, Isaac Newton, Jr. **63**
King, Bernice **4**
King, Coretta Scott **3, 57**
King, Dexter **10**
King, Martin Luther, Jr. **1**
King, Yolanda **6**

Martin Luther King Jr. Drum Major Award
Broadbent, Hydeia **36**
Mfume, Kweisi **6, 41**

Martin Luther King Jr. National Memorial Project
Johnson, Harry E. **57**

Marxism
Baraka, Amiri **1, 38**
Bishop, Maurice **39**
Jagan, Cheddi **16**
Machel, Samora Moises **8**
Nkrumah, Kwame **3**
Sankara, Thomas **17**

Maryland Mustangs basketball team
Parish, Robert 43

Maryland state government
Brown, Anthony G. 72
Currie, Ulysses 73
Steele, Michael 38, 73

Massachusetts state government
Brooke, Edward 8

Masters Golf Tournament
Elder, Lee 6
Woods, Tiger 14, 31

Mathematics
Alcorn, George Edward, Jr. 59
Deconge-Watson, Lovenia 55
Emeagwali, Philip 30
Falconer, Etta Zuber 59
Gates, Sylvester James, Jr. 15
Johnson, Katherine (Coleman Goble) 61
Price, Richard 51
Wilkens, J. Ernest, Jr. 43

MAXIMA Corporation
Smith, Joshua 10

Maxwell House Coffee Company
Fudge, Ann (Marie) 11, 55

McCall Pattern Company
Lewis, Reginald F. 6

McDonald's Corporation
Thompson, Don 56

McGill University (Canada)
Elliott, Lorris 37

MCP
See Malawi Congress Party

Medical examiners
Carter, Joye Maureen 41

Medicine
Adams-Campbell, Lucille L. 60
Anderson, William G(ilchrist) 57
Atim, Julian 66
Banda, Hastings Kamuzu 6, 54
Bashir, Halima 73
Benjamin, Regina 20
Black, Keith Lanier 18
Callender, Clive O. 3
Canady, Alexa 28
Carroll, L. Natalie 44
Carson, Benjamin 1, 35
Carter, Joye Maureen 41
Chatard, Peter 44
Chinn, May Edward 26
Christian-Green, Donna M.17
Cobb, W. Montague 39
Cole, Rebecca 38
Comer, James P. 6
Coney, PonJola 48
Cooper, Edward S. 6
Cooper, Lisa 73
Cornwell, Edward E., III 70
Dickens, Helen Octavia 14, 64
Drew, Charles Richard 7
Edwards, Willarda V. 59

Elders, Joycelyn 6
Fennoy, Ilene 72
Fisher, Rudolph 17
Flowers, Sylester 50
Foster, Henry W., Jr. 26
Freeman, Harold P. 23
Fuller, Solomon Carter, Jr. 15
Gayle, Helene D. 3
Gibson, William F. 6
Grant, Augustus O. 71
Griffin, Anthony 71
Griffith, Patrick A. 64
Hinton, William Augustus 8
Hutcherson, Hilda Yvonne 54
Jemison, Mae C. 1, 35
Johnson, R. M. 36
Jones, Edith Mae Irby 65
Joseph, Kathie-Ann 56
Keith, Rachel Boone 63
Kenney, John A., Jr. 48
Kintaudi, Leon 62
Kong, B. Waine 50
Kountz, Samuel L. 10
Lavizzo-Mourey, Risa 48
Lawless, Theodore K. 8
Leffall, Lasalle 3, 64
Logan, Onnie Lee 14
Malveaux, Floyd 54
Maxey, Randall 46
Naki, Hamilton 63
Nour, Nawal M. 56
Okaalet, Peter 58
Olopade, Olufunmilayo Falusi 58
Pace, Betty 59
Pinn, Vivian Winona 49
Pitt, David Thomas 10
Poussaint, Alvin F. 5, 67
Rabb, Maurice F., Jr. 58
Randolph, Linda A. 52
Reece, E. Albert 63
Ross-Lee, Barbara 67
Satcher, David 7, 57
Scantlebury-White, Velma 64
Smith, Ian 62
Stewart, Ella 39
Sullivan, Louis 8
Sweet, Ossian 68
Taylor, Susan C. 62
Thomas, Claudia Lynn 64
Thomas, Vivien 9
Thornton, Yvonne S. 69
Tuckson, Reed V. 71
Washington, Harriet A. 69
Watkins, Levi, Jr. 9
Welsing, Frances Cress 5
White-Hammond, Gloria 61
Williams, Daniel Hale 2
Witt, Edwin T. 26
Wright, Charles H. 35
Wright, Louis Tompkins 4

Meharry Medical College
Coney, PonJola 48
Foster, Henry W., Jr. 26
Griffith, Patrick A. 64
Lyttle, Hulda Margaret 14

Melanin theory of racism
See Cress Theory of Color Confrontation and Racism

Melody Makers
Marley, Ziggy 41

Men's movement
Somé, Malidoma Patrice 10

Merce Cunningham Dance Company
Dove, Ulysses 5

Merrill Lynch & Co., Inc.
Ford, Harold E(ugene), Jr. 16, 70
Matthews Shatteen, Westina 51
O'Neal, Stanley 38, 67

Meteorology
Anderson, Charles Edward 37
Bacon-Bercey, June 38

Metropolitan Applied Research Center (MARC Corp.)
Clark, Kenneth B. 5, 52

Metropolitan Opera
Anderson, Marian 2, 33
Battle, Kathleen 70
Brown, Angela M. 54
Collins, Janet 33, 64
Dobbs, Mattiwilda 34
Phillips, Helen L. 63

Mexican baseball league
Bell, James "Cool Papa" 36
Dandridge, Ray 36

Miami Dolphins football team
Greene, Joe 10

Michigan state government
Brown, Cora 33
Collins, Barbara-Rose 7
Kilpatrick, Carolyn Cheeks 16
Kilpatrick, Kwame 34, 71
Reeves, Triette Lipsey 27

Michigan State Supreme Court
Archer, Dennis 7, 36
Mallett, Conrad, Jr. 16

Michigan State University
Wharton, Clifton R., Jr. 7
Willingham, Tyrone 43

Microsoft Corporation
Millines Dziko, Trish 28

Midwest Stamping
Thompson, Cynthia Bramlett 50

Midwifery
Logan, Onnie Lee 14
Robinson, Sharon 22

Military police
Cadoria, Sherian Grace 14

Millennium Digital Media
Westbrook, Kelvin 50

Miller Brewing Company
Colbert, Virgis William 17
Shropshire, Thomas B. 49

Millinery
Bailey, Xenobia 11

Million Man March
Farrakhan, Louis 2, 15
Hawkins, La-Van 17, 54

Worrill, Conrad 12

Milwaukee Braves baseball team
Aaron, Hank 5

Milwaukee Brewers baseball team
Aaron, Hank 5
Baylor, Don 6
Fielder, Prince Semien 68
Payne, Ulice 42
Sheffield, Gary 16

Milwaukee Bucks basketball team
Abdul-Jabbar, Kareem 8
Lucas, John 7
Robertson, Oscar 26

Mingo-Jones Advertising
Chisholm, Samuel J. 32
Jones, Caroline R. 29
Mingo, Frank 32

Minneapolis city government
Sayles Belton, Sharon 9, 16

Minneapolis Millers baseball team
Dandridge, Ray 36

Minnesota State Supreme Court
Page, Alan 7

Minnesota Timberwolves basketball team
Garnett, Kevin 14, 70

Minnesota Twins baseball team
Baylor, Don 6
Carew, Rod 20
Hunter, Torii 43
Puckett, Kirby 4, 58
Winfield, Dave 5

Minnesota Vikings football team
Carter, Cris 21
Culpepper, Daunte 32
Cunningham, Randall 23
Dungy, Tony 17, 42, 59
Fowler, Reggie 51
Gilliam, Frank 23
Green, Dennis 5, 45
Moon, Warren 8, 66
Moss, Randy 23
Page, Alan 7
Rashad, Ahmad 18
Stringer, Korey 35

Minority Business Enterprise Legal Defense and Education Fund
Mitchell, Parren J. 42, 66

Minority Business Resource Center
Hill, Jesse, Jr. 13

Minstrel shows
McDaniel, Hattie 5

Miracle Network Telethon
Warner, Malcolm-Jamal 22, 36

Miss America
Dunlap, Ericka 55
Harold, Erika 54
Vincent, Marjorie Judith 2
Williams, Vanessa L. 4, 17

Miss Collegiate African-American Pageant
Mercado-Valdes, Frank 43

Miss USA
Gist, Carole 1

Miss World
Darego, Agbani 52

Mississippi Freedom Democratic Party
Baker, Ella 5
Blackwell, Unita 17
Hamer, Fannie Lou 6
Henry, Aaron 19
Norton, Eleanor Holmes 7

Mississippi state government
Hamer, Fannie Lou 6

MLA
See Modern Language Association of America

Model Inner City Community Organization (MICCO)
Fauntroy, Walter E. 11

Modeling
Allen-Buillard, Melba 55
Banks, Tyra 11, 50
Beckford, Tyson 11, 68
Berry, Halle 4, 19, 57
Campbell, Naomi 1, 31
Darego, Agbani 52
Dirie, Waris 56
Ebanks, Selita 67
Gibson, Tyrese 27, 62
Hardison, Bethann 12
Hounsou, Djimon 19, 45
Houston, Whitney 7, 28
Iman 4, 33
Iman, Chanel 66
Johnson, Beverly 2
Kebede, Liya 59
Kodjoe, Boris 34
Langhart Cohen, Janet 19, 60
Leslie, Lisa 16, 73
LisaRaye 27
McKenzie, Jaunel 73
Michele, Michael 31
Niane, Katoucha 70
Onwurah, Ngozi 38
Powell, Maxine 8
Rochon, Lela 16
Simmons, Kimora Lee 51
Sims, Naomi 29
Smith, B(arbara) 11
Tamia 24, 55
Taylor, Karin 34
Tyson, Cicely 7, 51
Watley, Jody 54
Webb, Veronica 10
Wek, Alek 18, 63

Modern dance
Ailey, Alvin 8
Allen, Debbie 13, 42

Byrd, Donald 10
Collins, Janet 33, 64
Davis, Chuck 33
Diggs, Taye 25, 63
Dove, Ulysses 5
Fagan, Garth 18
Faison, George 16
Henson, Darrin 33
Jamison, Judith 7, 67
Jones, Bill T. 1, 46
King, Alonzo 38
Kitt, Eartha 16
Miller, Bebe 3
Pomare, Eleo 72
Primus, Pearl 6
Spears, Warren 52
Vereen, Ben 4
Williams, Dudley 60

Modern Language Association of America (MLA)
Baker, Houston A., Jr. 6

Modern Records
Brooks, Hadda 40

Monoprinting
Honeywood, Varnette P. 54

Montgomery bus boycott
Abernathy, Ralph David 1
Baker, Ella 5
Burks, Mary Fair 40
Carr, Johnnie 69
Jackson, Mahalia 5
Killens, John O. 54
King, Martin Luther, Jr. 1
Parks, Rosa 1, 35, 56
Rustin, Bayard 4

Montgomery County (MD) Police Department
Moose, Charles 40

Montreal Canadiens hockey team
Brashear, Donald 39

Montreal Expos baseball team
Doby, Lawrence Eugene, Sr. 16, 41

Morehouse College
Brown, Uzee 42
Hope, John 8
Mays, Benjamin E. 7

Morgan Stanley
Lewis, William M., Jr. 40

Morna
Evora, Cesaria 12

Morris Brown College
Cross, Dolores E. 23

Moscow World News
Khanga, Yelena 6
Sullivan, Louis 8

Motivational speaking
Bahati, Wambui 60
Baisden, Michael 66
Brown, Les 5
Bunkley, Anita Richmond 39
Creagh, Milton 27
Gardner, Chris 65
Grant, Gwendolyn Goldsby 28

Gray, Farrah 59
Jolley, Willie 28
July, William 27
Kimbro, Dennis 10
Russell-McCloud, Patricia 17
Tyson, Asha 39

Motor City Giants baseball team
Kaiser, Cecil 42

Motorcycle racing
Showers, Reggie 30
Stewart, James "Bubba," Jr. 60

Motown Records
Atkins, Cholly 40
Bizimungu, Pasteur 19
Busby, Jheryl 3
de Passe, Suzanne 25
Edwards, Esther Gordy 43
Gaye, Marvin 2
Gordy, Berry, Jr. 1
Harrell, Andre 9, 30
Holland-Dozier-Holland 36
Holloway, Brenda 65
Hutch, Willie 62
Jackson, George 19
Jackson, Michael 19, 53
Jamerson, James 59
Kendricks, Eddie 22
Knight, Gladys 16, 66
Massenburg, Kedar 23
Powell, Maxine 8
Richie, Lionel 27, 65
Robinson, Smokey 3, 49
Ross, Diana 8, 27
Terrell, Tammi 32
Wells, Mary 28
Whitfield, Norman 73
Wilson, Mary 28
Wonder, Stevie 11, 53

Mt. Holyoke College
Tatum, Beverly Daniel 42

Mouvement Revolutionnaire National pour la Developpement (Rwanda; MRND)
Habyarimana, Juvenal 8

MOVE
Goode, W. Wilson 4
Wideman, John Edgar 5

Movement for Assemblies of the People
Bishop, Maurice 39

Movement for Democratic Change (MDC)
Tsvangirai, Morgan 26, 72

Movement for the Survival of the Ogoni People
Saro-Wiwa, Kenule 39
Wiwa, Ken 67

Movimento Popular de Libertação de Angola (MPLA)
dos Santos, José Eduardo 43
Neto, António Agostinho 43

Mozambican government
Diogo, Luisa Dias 63

MPLA
See Movimento Popular de Libertação de Angola

MPS
See Patriotic Movement of Salvation

MRND
See Mouvement Revolutionnaire National pour la Developpement

MTV Jams
Bellamy, Bill 12

Multimedia art
Bailey, Xenobia 11
Robinson, Aminah 50
Simpson, Lorna 4, 36

Muppets, The
Clash, Kevin 14

Murals
Alston, Charles 33
Biggers, John 20, 33
Douglas, Aaron 7
Lee-Smith, Hughie 5
Walker, Kara 16

Murder Inc.
Ashanti 37
Gotti, Irv 39
Ja Rule 35

Museum of Modern Art
Pindell, Howardena 55

Music Critics Circle
Holt, Nora 38

Music One, Inc.
Majors, Jeff 41

Music publishing
Combs, Sean "Puffy" 17, 43
Cooke, Sam 17
Edmonds, Tracey 16, 64
Gordy, Berry, Jr. 1
Handy, W. C. 8
Holland-Dozier-Holland 36
Humphrey, Bobbi 20
Ice Cube 8, 30, 60
Jackson, George 19
Jackson, Michael 19, 53
James, Rick 17
Knight, Suge 11, 30
Lewis, Emmanuel 36
Master P 21
Mayfield, Curtis 2, 43
Otis, Clyde 67
Prince 18, 65
Redding, Otis 16
Ross, Diana 8, 27
Shakur, Afeni 67
Shorty, Ras, I 47

Music Television (MTV)
Bellamy, Bill 12
Chideya, Farai 14, 61
Norman, Christina 47
Powell, Kevin 31
Run 31, 73

Musical composition
Armatrading, Joan 32
Ashford, Nickolas 21

Baiocchi, Regina Harris **41**
Ballard, Hank **41**
Bebey, Francis **45**
Blanchard, Terence **43**
Blige, Mary J. **20, 34, 60**
Bonds, Margaret **39**
Bonga, Kuenda **13**
Braxton, Toni **15, 61**
Brown, Patrick "Sleepy" **50**
Brown, Uzee **42**
Burke, Solomon **31**
Burleigh, Henry Thacker **56**
Caesar, Shirley **19**
Carter, Warrick L. **27**
Chapman, Tracy **26**
Charlemagne, Manno **11**
Charles, Ray **16, 48**
Cleveland, James **19**
Cole, Natalie **17, 60**
Coleman, Ornette **39, 69**
Collins, Bootsy **31**
Combs, Sean "Puffy" **17, 43**
Cook, Will Marion **40**
Davis, Anthony **11**
Davis, Miles **4**
Davis, Sammy, Jr. **18**
Dawson, William Levi **39**
Diddley, Bo **39, 72**
Domino, Fats **20**
Ellington, Duke **5**
Elliott, Missy **31**
Europe, James Reese **10**
Evans, Faith **22**
Freeman, Paul **39**
Fuller, Arthur **27**
Garrett, Sean **57**
Gaynor, Gloria **36**
George, Nelson **12**
Gillespie, Dizzy **1**
Golson, Benny **37**
Gordy, Berry, Jr. **1**
Green, Al **13, 47**
Hailey, JoJo **22**
Hailey, K-Ci **22**
Hammer, M. C. **20**
Handy, W. C. **8**
Harris, Corey **39, 73**
Hathaway, Donny **18**
Hayes, Isaac **20, 58, 73**
Hayes, Teddy **40**
Hill, Lauryn **20, 53**
Holland-Dozier-Holland **36**
Holmes, Clint **57**
Holt, Nora **38**
Humphrey, Bobbi **20**
Hutch, Willie **62**
Isley, Ronald **25, 56**
Jackson, Fred James **25**
Jackson, Michael **19, 53**
Jackson, Randy **40**
James, Rick **17**
Jean, Wyclef **20**
Jean-Baptiste, Marianne **17, 46**
Jerkins, Rodney **31**
Johnson, Buddy **36**
Johnson, Georgia Douglas **41**
Jones, Jonah **39**
Jones, Quincy **8, 30**
Jones, Thad **68**
Joplin, Scott **6**
Jordan, Montell **23**
Jordan, Ronny **26**
Kay, Ulysses **37**

Kee, John P. **43**
Kelly, R. **18, 44, 71**
Keys, Alicia **32, 68**
Kidjo, Anjelique **50**
Killings, Debra **57**
King, B. B. **7**
León, Tania **13**
Lincoln, Abbey **3**
Little Milton **36, 54**
Little Walter **36**
Lopes, Lisa "Left Eye" **36**
Mahlasela, Vusi **65**
Majors, Jeff **41**
Marsalis, Delfeayo **41**
Marsalis, Wynton **16**
Martin, Roberta **58**
Master P **21**
Maxwell **20**
Mayfield, Curtis **2, 43**
McClurkin, Donnie **25**
McFerrin, Bobby **68**
Mills, Stephanie **36**
Mitchell, Brian Stokes **21**
Mo', Keb' **36**
Monica **21**
Moore, Chante **26**
Moore, Dorothy Rudd **46**
Moore, Undine Smith **28**
Muse, Clarence Edouard **21**
Nash, Johnny **40**
Ndegéocello, Me'Shell **15**
Osborne, Jeffrey **26**
Otis, Clyde **67**
Pratt, Awadagin **31**
Price, Florence **37**
Prince **18, 65**
Pritchard, Robert Starling **21**
Reagon, Bernice Johnson **7**
Redding, Otis **16**
Reed, A. C. **36**
Reid, Antonio "L.A." **28**
Roach, Max **21, 63**
Robinson, Reginald R. **53**
Run-DMC **31**
Rushen, Patrice **12**
Russell, Brenda **52**
Sangare, Oumou **18**
Shorty, Ras, I **47**
Silver, Horace **26**
Simone, Nina **15, 41**
Simpson, Valerie **21**
Sowande, Fela **39**
Still, William Grant **37**
Strayhorn, Billy **31**
Sundiata, Sekou **66**
Sweat, Keith **19**
Tillis, Frederick **40**
Usher **23, 56**
Van Peebles, Melvin **7**
Walker, George **37**
Warwick, Dionne **18**
Washington, Grover, Jr. **17, 44**
Williams, Deniece **36**
Williams, Tony **67**
Winans, Angie **36**
Winans, Debbie **36**
Withers, Bill **61**

Musicology
George, Zelma Watson **42**

Muslim Mosque, Inc.
X, Malcolm **1**

Mysteries
Bland, Eleanor Taylor **39**
Creagh, Milton **27**
DeLoach, Nora **30**
Himes, Chester **8**
Holton, Hugh, Jr. **39**
Mickelbury, Penny **28**
Mosley, Walter **5, 25, 68**
Thomas-Graham **29**
Wesley, Valerie Wilson **18**

The Mystery
Delany, Martin R. **27**

Mystic Seaport Museum
Pinckney, Bill **42**

NAACP
See National Association for the
Advancement of Colored People

NAACP Image Awards
Brandy **14, 34, 72**
Fields, Kim **36**
Lawrence, Martin **6, 27, 60**
Mac, Bernie **29, 61, 72**
Okonedo, Sophie **67**
Rhimes, Shonda Lynn **67**
Warner, Malcolm-Jamal **22, 36**
Wesley, Richard **73**

**NAACP Legal Defense and
Educational Fund (LDF)**
Bell, Derrick **6**
Carter, Robert L. **51**
Chambers, Julius **3**
Edelman, Marian Wright **5, 42**
Guinier, Lani **7, 30**
Jones, Elaine R. **7, 45**
Julian, Percy Lavon **6**
Marshall, Thurgood **1, 44**
Motley, Constance Baker **10, 55**
Rice, Constance LaMay **60**
Smith, Kemba **70**
Smythe Haith, Mabel **61**

NABJ
See National Association of Black
Journalists

NAC
See Nyasaland African Congress

NACGN
See National Association of Colored Graduate Nurses

NACW
See National Association of Colored Women

NAG
See Nonviolent Action Group

NASA
See National Aeronautics and
Space Administration

NASCAR
See National Association of Stock
Car Auto Racing

**NASCAR Craftsman Truck se-
ries**
Lester, Bill **42**

NASCAR Diversity Council
Lester, Bill **42**

Nation
Wilkins, Roger **2**

Nation of Islam
See Lost-Found Nation of Islam

National Academy of Design
White, Charles **39**

**National Action Council for
Minorities in Engineering**
Pierre, Percy Anthony **46**
Slaughter, John Brooks **53**

National Action Network
Sharpton, Al **21**

**National Aeronautics and
Space Administration (NASA)**
Anderson, Michael P. **40**
Bluford, Guy **2, 35**
Bolden, Charles F., Jr. **7**
Campbell, Donald J. **66**
Carruthers, George R. **40**
Drew, Alvin, Jr. **67**
Easley, Annie J. **61**
Gregory, Frederick **8, 51**
Jemison, Mae C. **1, 35**
Johnson, Katherine (Coleman
Goble) **61**
McNair, Ronald **3, 58**
Mills, Joseph C. **51**
Nichols, Nichelle **11**
Sigur, Wanda **44**
Wilson, Stephanie **72**

**National Afro-American Coun-
cil**
Fortune, T. Thomas **6**
Mossell, Gertrude Bustill **40**

**National Airmen's Association
of America**
Brown, Willa **40**

**National Alliance of Postal
and Federal Employees**
McGee, James Madison **46**

National Alliance Party (NAP)
Fulani, Lenora **11**

**National Association for the
Advancement of Colored
People (NAACP)**
Anderson, William G(ilchrist) **57**
Anthony, Wendell **25**
Austin, Junius C. **44**
Baker, Ella **5**
Ballance, Frank W. **41**
Bates, Daisy **13**
Bell, Derrick **6**
Bond, Julian **2, 35**
Bontemps, Arna **8**
Brooks, Gwendolyn **1**
Brown, Homer S. **47**
Bunche, Ralph J. **5**
Chambers, Julius **3**
Chavis, Benjamin **6**
Clark, Kenneth B. **5, 52**
Clark, Septima **7**
Cobb, W. Montague **39**
Colter, Cyrus, J. **36**
Cotter, Joseph Seamon, Sr. **40**
Creagh, Milton **27**
Days, Drew S., III **10**

Dee, Ruby **8, 50, 68**
Du Bois, W. E. B. **3**
DuBois, Shirley Graham **21**
Dukes, Hazel Nell **56**
Edelman, Marian Wright **5, 42**
Evers, Medgar **3**
Evers, Myrlie **8**
Farmer, James **2, 64**
Ford, Clyde W. **40**
Fuller, S. B. **13**
Gibson, William F. **6**
Grimké, Archibald H. **9**
Hampton, Fred **18**
Harrington, Oliver W. **9**
Hayes, Dennis **54**
Henderson, Wade **14**
Hobson, Julius W. **44**
Hollowell, Donald L. **57**
Hooks, Benjamin L. **2**
Horne, Lena **5**
Houston, Charles Hamilton **4**
Jackson, Vera **40**
Jealous, Benjamin **70**
Johnson, James Weldon **5**
Jordan, Vernon E. **3, 35**
Kidd, Mae Street **39**
Lampkin, Daisy **19**
Madison, Joseph E. **17**
Marshall, Thurgood **1, 44**
McKissick, Floyd B. **3**
McPhail, Sharon **2**
Meek, Carrie **36**
Meredith, James H. **11**
Mfume, Kweisi **6, 41**
Mitchell, Sharon **36**
Moore, Harry T. **29**
Morgan, Irene **65**
Moses, Robert Parris **11**
Motley, Constance Baker **10, 55**
Moyo, Yvette Jackson **36**
Owens, Major **6**
Payton, John **48**
Richardson, Rupert **67**
Rustin, Bayard **4**
Sutton, Percy E. **42**
Terrell, Mary Church **9**
Tucker, C. Delores **12, 56**
Van Lierop, Robert **53**
White, Walter F. **4**
Wilkins, Roger **2**
Wilkins, Roy **4**
Williams, Hosea Lorenzo **15, 31**
Williams, Robert F. **11**
Wright, Louis Tompkins **4**

National Association of Black Journalists (NABJ)
Curry, George E. **23**
Dawkins, Wayne **20**
Harris, Jay T. **19**
Jarrett, Vernon D. **42**
Lowe, Herbert **57**
Madison, Paula **37**
Pressley, Condace L. **41**
Rice, Linda Johnson **9, 41**
Shipp, E. R. **15**
Stone, Chuck **9**
Washington, Laura S. **18**

National Association of Colored Graduate Nurses (NACGN)
Staupers, Mabel K. **7**

National Association of Colored Women (NACW)
Bethune, Mary McLeod **4**
Cooper, Margaret J. **46**
Harper, Frances Ellen Watkins **11**
Lampkin, Daisy **19**
Stewart, Ella **39**
Terrell, Mary Church **9**

National Association of Negro Business and Professional Women's Clubs
Vaughns, Cleopatra **46**

National Association of Negro Musicians
Bonds, Margaret **39**
Brown, Uzee **42**

National Association of Regulatory Utility Commissioners
Colter, Cyrus, J. **36**

National Association of Social Workers
Jackson, Judith D. **57**
McMurray, Georgia L. **36**

National Association of Stock Car Auto Racing
Lester, Bill **42**

National Baptist Convention USA
Bradley, J. Robert **65**
Jones, E. Edward, Sr. **45**
Lyons, Henry **12**
Shaw, William J. **30**
Thurston, Stephen J. **49**

National Bar Association
Alexander, Joyce London **18**
Alexander, Sadie Tanner Mossell **22**
Archer, Dennis **7, 36**
Bailey, Clyde **45**
Hubbard, Arnette **38**
McPhail, Sharon **2**
Pincham, R. Eugene, Sr. **69**
Quince, Peggy A. **69**
Ray, Charlotte E. **60**
Robinson, Malcolm S. **44**
Thompson, Larry D. **39**
Walker, Cora T. **68**

National Basketball Association (NBA)
Abdul-Jabbar, Kareem **8**
Abdur-Rahim, Shareef **28**
Anthony, Carmelo **46**
Barkley, Charles **5, 66**
Bing, Dave **3, 59**
Bol, Manute **1**
Brandon, Terrell **16**
Bryant, Kobe **15, 31, 71**
Bynoe, Peter C. B. **40**
Carter, Vince **26**
Chamberlain, Wilt **18, 47**
Cheeks, Maurice **47**
Clifton, Nathaniel "Sweetwater" **47**
Cooper, Charles "Chuck" **47**
Dantley, Adrian **72**
Drexler, Clyde **4, 61**
Duncan, Tim **20**
Elliott, Sean **26**

Erving, Julius **18, 47**
Ewing, Patrick **17, 73**
Garnett, Kevin **14, 70**
Gourdine, Simon **11**
Green, A. C. **32**
Hardaway, Anfernee (Penny) **13**
Hardaway, Tim **35**
Heard, Gar **25**
Hill, Grant **13**
Howard, Juwan **15**
Hunter, Billy **22**
Johnson, Avery **62**
Johnson, Earvin "Magic" **3, 39**
Johnson, Larry **28**
Jordan, Michael **6, 21**
Lanier, Bob **47**
Lowe, Sidney **64**
Lucas, John **7**
Mahorn, Rick **60**
Mohammed, Nazr **64**
Mourning, Alonzo **17, 44**
Mutombo, Dikembe **7**
Olajuwon, Hakeem **2, 72**
O'Neal, Shaquille **8, 30**
Palmer, Violet **59**
Parish, Robert **43**
Pierce, Paul **71**
Pippen, Scottie **15**
Prince, Tayshaun **68**
Rivers, Glenn "Doc" **25**
Robertson, Oscar **26**
Robinson, David **24**
Rodman, Dennis **12, 44**
Russell, Bill **8**
Silas, Paul **24**
Sprewell, Latrell **23**
Stoudemire, Amaré **59**
Thomas, Isiah **7, 26, 65**
Tisdale, Wayman **50**
Wade, Dwyane **61**
Wallace, Ben **54**
Wallace, Rasheed **56**
Webber, Chris **15, 30, 59**
Wilkens, Lenny **11**
Worthy, James **49**

National Basketball Players Association
Erving, Julius **18, 47**
Ewing, Patrick **17, 73**
Gourdine, Simon **11**
Hunter, Billy **22**

National Black Arts Festival (NBAF)
Borders, James **9**
Brooks, Avery **9**

National Black College Hall of Fame
Dortch, Thomas W., Jr. **45**

National Black Farmers Association (NBFA)
Boyd, John W., Jr. **20, 72**

National Black Fine Art Show
Wainwright, Joscelyn **46**

National Black Gay and Lesbian Conference
Wilson, Phill **9**

National Black Gay and Lesbian Leadership Forum (NB-

GLLF)
Boykin, Keith **14**
Carter, Mandy **11**

National Black Theatre Festival
Hamlin, Larry Leon **49, 62**

National Black Women's Health Project
Avery, Byllye Y. **66**

National Book Award
Ellison, Ralph **7**
Haley, Alex **4**
Johnson, Charles **1**
Patterson, Orlando **4**

National Broadcasting Company (NBC)
Allen, Byron **3, 24**
Cosby, Bill **7, 26, 59**
Grier, David Alan **28**
Gumbel, Bryant **14**
Hinderas, Natalie **5**
Holt, Lester **66**
Ifill, Gwen **28**
Johnson, Rodney Van **28**
Madison, Paula **37**
Rashad, Phylicia **21**
Reuben, Gloria **15**
Reynolds, Star Jones **10, 27, 61**
Roker, Al **12, 49**
Simpson, Carole **6, 30**
Thomas-Graham, Pamela **29**
Williams, Montel **4, 57**
Wilson, Flip **21**

National Brotherhood of Skiers (NBS)
Horton, Andre **33**
Horton, Suki **33**

National Center for Neighborhood Enterprise (NCNE)
Woodson, Robert L. **10**

National Coalition of 100 Black Women (NCBW)
Mays, Leslie A. **41**
McCabe, Jewell Jackson **10**

National Coalition to Abolish the Dealth Penalty (NCADP)
Hawkins, Steven **14**

National Commission for Democracy (Ghana; NCD)
Rawlings, Jerry **9**

National Conference on Black Lawyers (NCBL)
McDougall, Gay J. **11, 43**

National Council of Churches
Howard, M. William, Jr. **26**

National Council of Negro Women (NCNW)
Bethune, Mary McLeod **4**
Blackwell, Unita **17**
Cole, Johnnetta B. **5, 43**
Hamer, Fannie Lou **6**
Height, Dorothy I. **2, 23**
Horne, Lena **5**
Lampkin, Daisy **19**

Sampson, Edith S. **4**
Smith, Jane E. **24**
Staupers, Mabel K. **7**

National Council of Nigeria and the Cameroons (NCNC)
Azikiwe, Nnamdi **13**

National Council of Teachers of Mathematics
Granville, Evelyn Boyd **36**

National Council on the Arts
Robinson, Cleo Parker **38**

National Cowboys of Color Museum and Hall of Fame
Austin, Gloria **63**
Austin, Jim **63**

National Defence Council (Ghana; NDC)
Rawlings, Jerry **9**

National Dental Association
Madison, Romell **45**

National Earthquake Information Center (NEIC)
Person, Waverly **9, 51**

National Education Association (NEA)
Futrell, Mary Hatwood **33**

National Endowment for the Arts (NEA)
Bradley, David Henry, Jr. **39**
Hall, Arthur **39**
Hemphill, Essex **10**
Pope.L, William **72**
Serrano, Andres **3**
Williams, John A. **27**
Williams, William T. **11**

National Endowment for the Arts Jazz Hall of Fame
Terry, Clark **39**

National Endowment for the Humanities
Gibson, Donald Bernard **40**

National Equal Rights League (NERL)
Trotter, Monroe **9**

National Football League (NFL)
Allen, Marcus **20**
Barber, Tiki **57**
Barney, Lem **26**
Bettis, Jerome **64**
Briscoe, Marlin **37**
Brooks, Aaron **33**
Brooks, Derrick **43**
Brown, Jim **11**
Bruce, Isaac **26**
Butler, Leroy, III **17**
Cherry, Deron **40**
Crennel, Romeo **54**
Croom, Sylvester **50**
Culpepper, Daunte **32**
Cunningham, Randall **23**
Davis, Terrell **20**
Dickerson, Eric **27**
Edwards, Herman **51**

Farr, Mel **24**
Faulk, Marshall **35**
Fowler, Reggie **51**
Gilliam, Frank **23**
Gilliam, Joe **31**
Green, Darrell **39**
Green, Dennis **5, 45**
Greene, Joe **10**
Hill, Calvin **19**
Howard, Desmond **16, 58**
Irvin, Michael **64**
Jackson, Tom **70**
Johnson, Levi **48**
Ladd, Ernie **64**
Lofton, James **42**
Lott, Ronnie **9**
Monk, Art **38, 73**
Moon, Warren **8, 66**
Moss, Randy **23**
Motley, Marion **26**
Newsome, Ozzie **26**
Oliver, Pam **54**
Owens, Terrell **53**
Pace, Orlando **21**
Page, Alan **7**
Payton, Walter **11, 25**
Peete, Rodney **60**
Rhodes, Ray **14**
Rice, Jerry **5, 55**
Sanders, Barry **1, 53**
Sanders, Bob **72**
Sanders, Deion **4, 31**
Sapp, Warren **38**
Sayers, Gale **28**
Sharper, Darren **32**
Shell, Art **1, 66**
Simpson, O.J. **15**
Singletary, Mike **4**
Smith, Emmitt **7**
Smith, Rick **72**
Stewart, Kordell **21**
Stingley, Darryl **69**
Strahan, Michael **35**
Stringer, Korey **35**
Swann, Lynn **28**
Taylor, Jason **70**
Taylor, Lawrence **25**
Thomas, Derrick **25**
Thomas, Emmitt **71**
Thrower, Willie **35**
Tomlinson, LaDainian **65**
Tunnell, Emlen **54**
Upshaw, Gene **18, 47, 72**
Vick, Michael **39, 65**
Walker, Herschel **1, 69**
Washington, Kenny **50**
Ware, Andre **37**
White, Reggie **6, 50**
Williams, Doug **22**
Williamson, Fred **67**
Wright, Rayfield **70**

National Heritage "Living Treasure" Fellowship
Jackson, John **36**

National Hockey League (NHL)
Brashear, Donald **39**
Brathwaite, Fred **35**
Brown, Sean **52**
Fuhr, Grant **1, 49**
Grier, Mike **43**

Iginla, Jarome **35**
Laraque, Georges **48**
Mayers, Jamal **39**
McBride, Bryant **18**
McCarthy, Sandy **64**
McKegney, Tony **3**
O'Ree, Willie **5**
Salvador, Bryce **51**
Weekes, Kevin **67**

National Immigration Forum
Jones, Sarah **39**

National Information Infrastructure (NII)
Lewis, Delano **7**

National Institute of Arts & Letters
Lewis, Norman **39**
White, Charles **39**

National Institute of Education
Baker, Gwendolyn Calvert **9**

National Institutes of Health (NIH)
Cargill, Victoria A. **43**
Dunston, Georgia Mae **48**
Pinn, Vivian Winona **49**

National Inventors Hall of Fame
Carruthers, George R. **40**

National Lawn & Garden Distributor Association
Donald, Arnold Wayne **36**

National Medical Association
Cole, Lorraine **48**
Maxey, Randall **46**
Ojikutu, Bisola **65**

National Minority Business Council
Leary, Kathryn D. **10**

National Museum of American History
Crew, Spencer R. **55**
Reagon, Bernice Johnson **7**

National Negro Congress
Bunche, Ralph J. **5**

National Negro Suffrage League
Trotter, Monroe **9**

National Network for African American Women and the Law
Arnwine, Barbara **28**

National Newspaper Publishers Association
Cooper, Andrew W. **36**
Jealous, Benjamin **70**
Oliver, John J., Jr. **48**

National Oceanic and Atmospheric Administration
Bacon-Bercey, June **38**
Fields, Evelyn J. **27**

National Organization for Women (NOW)
Hernandez, Aileen Clarke **13**
Kennedy, Florynce **12, 33**

Meek, Carrie **6, 36**
Murray, Pauli **38**

National Poetry Slam
Letson, Al **39**

National Political Congress of Black Women
Chisholm, Shirley **2, 50**
Tucker, C. Delores **12, 56**
Waters, Maxine **3, 67**

National Public Radio (NPR)
Abu-Jamal, Mumia **15**
Bates, Karen Grigsby **40**
Drummond, William J. **40**
Early, Gerald **15**
Lewis, Delano **7**
Mitchell, Elvis **67**
Smiley, Tavis **20, 68**
Zook, Kristal Brent **62**

National Resistance Army (Uganda; NRA)
Museveni, Yoweri **4**

National Resistance Movement
Museveni, Yoweri **4**

National Revolutionary Movement for Development
See Mouvement Revolutionnaire National pour la Developpment

National Rifle Association (NRA)
Williams, Robert F. **11**

National Science Foundation (NSF)
Massey, Walter E. **5, 45**

National Security Council
Frazer, Jendayi **68**
Powell, Colin **1, 28**
Rice, Condoleezza **3, 28, 72**

National Society of Black Engineers
Donald, Arnold Wayne **36**
Price, Richard **51**

National Underground Railroad Freedom Center
Crew, Spencer R. **55**

National Union for the Total Independence of Angola (UNITA)
Roberto, Holden **65**
Savimbi, Jonas **2, 34**

National Union of Mineworkers (South Africa; NUM)
Ramaphosa, Cyril **3**

National Urban Affairs Council
Cooper, Andrew W. **36**

National Urban Coalition (NUC)
Edelin, Ramona Hoage **19**

National Urban League
Brown, Ron **5**
Gordon, Bruce S. **41, 53**
Greely, M. Gasby **27**

Haynes, George Edmund **8**
Jacob, John E. **2**
Jordan, Vernon E. **3, 35**
Price, Hugh B. **9, 54**
Spriggs, William **67**
Young, Whitney M., Jr. **4**

National War College
Clemmons, Reginal G. **41**

National Wildlife Federation
Osborne, Na'taki **54**

National Women's Basketball League (NWBL)
Catchings, Tamika **43**

National Women's Hall of Fame
Kelly, Leontine **33**

National Women's Political Caucus
Hamer, Fannie Lou **6**

National Youth Administration (NYA)
Bethune, Mary McLeod **4**
Primus, Pearl **6**

Nationwide
James, Donna A. **51**

Nature Boy Enterprises
Yoba, Malik **11**

Naval Research Laboratory (NRL)
Carruthers, George R. **40**

NBA
See National Basketball Association

NBAF
See National Black Arts Festival

NBC
See National Broadcasting Company

NBGLLF
See National Black Gay and Lesbian Leadership Forum

NCBL
See National Conference on Black Lawyers

NCBW
See National Coalition of 100 Black Women

NCCK
See Kenya National Council of Churches

NCD
See National Commission for Democracy

NCNE
See National Center for Neighborhood Enterprise

NCNW
See National Council of Negro Women

NDC
See National Defence Council

NEA
See National Education Association; National Endowment for the

Arts

Nebula awards
Butler, Octavia **8, 43, 58**
Delany, Samuel R., Jr. **9**

Négritude
Césaire, Aimé **48, 69**
Damas, Léon-Gontran **46**

Negro American Labor Council
Randolph, A. Philip **3**

Negro American Political League
Trotter, Monroe **9**

Negro Digest magazine
Fuller, Hoyt **44**
Johnson, John H. **3, 54**

Negro Ensemble Company
Cash, Rosalind **28**
Rolle, Esther **13, 21**
Schultz, Michael A. **6**
Taylor, Susan L. **10**
Ward, Douglas Turner **42**

Negro History Bulletin
Woodson, Carter G. **2**

Negro Leagues
Banks, Ernie **33**
Barnhill, David **30**
Bell, James "Cool Papa" **36**
Brown, Willard **36**
Campanella, Roy **25**
Charleston, Oscar **39**
Dandridge, Ray **36**
Davis, Piper **19**
Day, Leon **39**
Gibson, Josh **22**
Hyde, Cowan F. "Bubba" **47**
Irvin, Monte **31**
Johnson, Clifford "Connie" **52**
Johnson, Mamie "Peanut" **40**
Kaiser, Cecil **42**
Kimbro, Henry A. **25**
Leonard, Buck **67**
Lloyd, John Henry "Pop" **30**
O'Neil, Buck **19, 59**
Paige, Satchel **7**
Pride, Charley **26**
Smith, Hilton **29**
Stearnes, Norman "Turkey" **31**
Stone, Toni **15**

Negro World
Fortune, T. Thomas **6**

NEIC
See National Earthquake Information Center

Neo-hoodoo
Reed, Ishmael **8**

NERL
See National Equal Rights League

Netherlands Antilles
Liberia-Peters, Maria Philomena **12**

Netherlands government
Ali, Ayaan Hirsi **58**

NetNoir Inc.
CasSelle, Malcolm **11**
Ellington, E. David **11**

Neurosurgery
Black, Keith Lanier **18**
Canady, Alexa **28**
Carson, Benjamin **1, 35**

Neustadt International Prize for Literature
Brathwaite, Kamau **36**

New Black Muslims
Muhammad, Khallid Abdul **10, 31**

New Black Panther Party
Muhammad, Khallid, Abdul **10, 31**

New Concept Development Center
Madhubuti, Haki R. **7**

New Dance Group
Primus, Pearl **6**

New Danish Dance Theatre
Spears, Warren **52**

New Edition
Bivins, Michael **72**
Gill, Johnny **51**

New Jack Swing music
Brown, Bobby **58**
Hall, Aaron **57**

New Jersey Family Development Act
Bryant, Wayne R. **6**

New Jersey General Assembly
Bryant, Wayne R. **6**
Payne, William D. **60**

New Jersey Nets
Doby, Lawrence Eugene, Sr. **16, 41**

New Jewel Movement
Bishop, Maurice **39**

New Life Community Choir
Kee, John P. **43**

New Negro movement
See Harlem Renaissance

New Orleans city government
Nagin, C. Ray **42, 57**

New Orleans Saints football team
Brooks, Aaron **33**
Mills, Sam **33**

New Patriotic Party (Ghana)
Kufuor, John Agyekum **54**

New York Age
Fortune, T. Thomas **6**

New York City government
Campbell, Mary Schmidt **43**
Crew, Rudolph F. **16**
Dinkins, David **4**
Fields, C. Virginia **25**
Ford, Wallace **58**
Hageman, Hans **36**

Paterson, Basil A. **69**
Sutton, Percy E. **42**
Thompson, William **35**

New York Coalition of 100 Black Woman
Wein, Joyce **62**

New York Daily News
Cose, Ellis **5, 50**

New York Drama Critics Circle Award
Hansberry, Lorraine **6**

New York Freeman
Fortune, T. Thomas **6**

New York Giants baseball team
Dandridge, Ray **36**
Mays, Willie **3**
Tunnell, Emlen **54**

New York Giants football team
Barber, Tiki **57**
Strahan, Michael **35**
Taylor, Lawrence **25**

New York Globe
Fortune, T. Thomas **6**

New York Hip Hop Theater Festival
Jones, Sarah **39**

New York Institute for Social Therapy and Research
Fulani, Lenora **11**

New York Jets football team
Lott, Ronnie **9**

New York Knicks basketball team
Ewing, Patrick **17, 73**
Johnson, Larry **28**
Sprewell, Latrell **23**

New York Mets baseball team
Clendenon, Donn **26, 56**

New York Philharmonic
DePriest, James **37**

New York Public Library
Baker, Augusta **38**
Dodson, Howard, Jr. **7, 52**
Schomburg, Arthur Alfonso **9**

New York Shakespeare Festival
Browne, Roscoe Lee **66**
Gunn, Moses **10**
Wolfe, George C. **6, 43**

New York state government
Brown, Byron W. **72**
McCall, H. Carl **27**
Motley, Constance Baker **10, 55**
Owens, Major **6**
Paterson, Basil A. **69**
Paterson, David A. **59**

New York State Supreme Court
Dudley, Edward R. **58**
Wright, Bruce McMarion **3, 52**

New York Stock Exchange
Doley, Harold, Jr. **26**

New York Sun
Fortune, T. Thomas **6**

New York Times
Blair, Jayson **50**
Blow, Charles M. **73**
Boyd, Gerald M. **32, 59**
Broyard, Anatole **68**
Caldwell, Earl **60**
Davis, George **36**
Hunter-Gault, Charlayne **6, 31**
Ifill, Gwen **28**
Mabry, Marcus **70**
Price, Hugh B. **9, 54**
Rhoden, William C. **67**
Wilkins, Roger **2**

New York University
Brathwaite, Kamau **36**
Campbell, Mary Schmidt **43**
Newkirk, Pamela **69**

New York Yankees baseball team
Baylor, Don **6**
Bonds, Bobby **43**
Jackson, Reggie **15**
Jeter, Derek **27**
Strawberry, Darryl **22**
Watson, Bob **25**
Winfield, Dave **5**

Newark city government
Booker, Cory Anthony **68**
Gibson, Kenneth Allen **6**
James, Sharpe **23, 69**

Newark Dodgers baseball team
Dandridge, Ray **36**

Newark Eagles baseball team
Dandridge, Ray, Sr. **16, 41**

Newark Housing Authority
Gibson, Kenneth Allen **6**

The News Hour with Jim Lehrer TV series
Ifill, Gwen **28**

Newsday
Olojede, Dele **59**

Newsweek
Mabry, Marcus **70**

NFL
See National Football League

NHL
See National Hockey League

Niagara movement
Du Bois, W. E. B. **3**
Hope, John **8**
Trotter, Monroe **9**

Nickelodeon
Thompson, Kenan **52**

Nigerian Armed Forces
Abacha, Sani **11, 70**
Abiola, Moshood **70**
Babangida, Ibrahim **4**

Obasanjo, Olusegun **5, 22**

Nigerian Association of Patriotic Writers and Artists
Barrett, Lindsay **43**

Nigerian government
Abiola, Moshood **70**
Abubakar, Abdulsalami **66**
Akunyili, Dora Nkem **58**
Yar'adua, Umaru **69**

Nigerian literature
Achebe, Chinua **6**
Akpan, Uwem **70**
Amadi, Elechi **40**
Bandele, Biyi **68**
Barrett, Lindsay **43**
Ekwensi, Cyprian **37**
Onwueme, Tess Osonye **23**
Rotimi, Ola **1**
Saro-Wiwa, Kenule **39**
Soyinka, Wole **4**

NIH
See National Institutes of Health

NII
See National Information Infrastructure

Nike, Inc.
Edwards, Trevor **54**
Miller, Larry G. **72**

1960 Masks
Soyinka, Wole **4**

Nobel Peace Prize
Annan, Kofi Atta **15, 48**
Bunche, Ralph J. **5**
King, Martin Luther, Jr. **1**
Luthuli, Albert **13**
Tutu, Desmond Mpilo **6, 44**

Nobel Prize for Literature
Morrison, Toni **2, 15**
Soyinka, Wole **4**
Walcott, Derek **5**

Noma Award for Publishing in African
Ba, Mariama **30**

Nonfiction
Abrahams, Peter **39**
Adams-Ender, Clara **40**
Ali, Hana Yasmeen **52**
Allen, Debbie **13, 42**
Allen, Robert L. **38**
Atkins, Cholly **40**
Baisden, Michael **66**
Ballard, Allen Butler, Jr. **40**
Bashir, Halima **73**
Beah, Ishmael **69**
Blassingame, John Wesley **40**
Blockson, Charles L. **42**
Bogle, Donald **34**
Brown, Cecil M. **46**
Brown, Lloyd Louis **42**
Broyard, Bliss **68**
Buckley, Gail Lumet **39**
Carby, Hazel **27**
Carter, Joye Maureen **41**
Cashin, Sheryll **63**
Cobb, William Jelani **59**

Cole, Johnnetta B. **5, 43**
Cook, Mercer **40**
Cox, Joseph Mason Andrew **51**
Crew, Spencer R. **55**
Cruse, Harold **54**
Datcher, Michael **60**
Davis, Arthur P. **41**
Davis, Thulani **61**
Dickerson, Debra J. **60**
Dunnigan, Alice Allison **41**
Edelman, Marian Wright **5, 42**
Elliott, Lorris **37**
Fax, Elton **48**
Fine, Sam **60**
Finner-Williams, Paris Michele **62**
Fisher, Antwone **40**
Fletcher, Bill, Jr. **41**
Ford, Clyde W. **40**
Foster, Cecil **32**
Gayle, Addison, Jr. **41**
Gibson, Donald Bernard **40**
Gladwell, Malcolm **62**
Greenwood, Monique **38**
Harrison, Alvin **28**
Harrison, Calvin **28**
Henderson, David **53**
Henries, A. Doris Banks **44**
Henriques, Julian **37**
Hercules, Frank **44**
Hernton, Calvin C. **51**
Hill, Errol **40**
Hobson, Julius W. **44**
Horne, Frank **44**
Ilibagiza, Immaculée **66**
Jakes, Thomas "T. D." **17, 43**
Jolley, Willie **28**
Jordan, Vernon E. **7, 35**
Kayira, Legson **40**
Kearney, Janis **54**
Kennedy, Randall **40**
Knight, Etheridge **37**
Kobia, Samuel **43**
Ladner, Joyce A. **42**
Lampley, Oni Faida **43, 71**
Lincoln, C. Eric **38**
Long, Eddie L. **29**
Mabuza-Suttle, Felicia **43**
Malveaux, Julianne **32, 70**
Manley, Ruth **34**
Matthews Shatteen, Westina **51**
McBride, James **35**
McKenzie, Vashti M. **29**
McKinney Hammond, Michelle **51**
McWhorter, John **35**
Mossell, Gertrude Bustill **40**
Murray, Pauli **38**
Myers, Walter Dean **8, 20**
Naylor, Gloria **10, 42**
Newkirk, Pamela **69**
Nissel, Angela **42**
Norton, Meredith **72**
Parks, Rosa **1, 35, 56**
Pitts, Leonard, Jr. **54**
Run **31, 73**
Rusesabagina, Paul **60**
Sadlier, Rosemary **62**
Smith, Jessie Carney **35**
Thornton, Yvonne S. **69**
Tillis, Frederick **40**
Wade-Gayles, Gloria Jean **41**
Walker, Rebecca **50**
Wambugu, Florence **42**
Wilkens, J. Ernest, Jr. **43**

Williams, Terrie **35**
Williams, Wendy **62**
Wiwa, Ken **67**
Wright, Nathan, Jr. **56**
Zook, Kristal Brent **62**

Nonviolent Action Group (NAG)
Al-Amin, Jamil Abdullah **6**

North Carolina Mutual Life Insurance
Spaulding, Charles Clinton **9**

North Carolina state government
Ballance, Frank W. **41**

North Carolina State University
Lowe, Sidney **64**

North Pole
Delany, Martin R. **27**
Henson, Matthew **2**
Hillary, Barbara **65**
McLeod, Gus **27**

Notre Dame Univeristy
Willingham, Tyrone **43**

NOW
See National Organization for Women

NPR
See National Public Radio

NRA
See National Resistance Army (Uganda); National Rifle Association

NRL
See Naval Research Laboratory

NSF
See National Science Foundation

Nuclear energy
O'Leary, Hazel **6**
Packer, Daniel **56**
Quarterman, Lloyd Albert **4**

Nuclear Regulatory Commission
Jackson, Shirley Ann **12**

Nucleus
King, Yolanda **6**
Shabazz, Attallah **6**

NUM
See National Union of Mineworkers (South Africa)

Nursing
Adams-Ender, Clara **40**
Auguste, Rose-Anne **13**
Hillary, Barbara **65**
Hughes, Ebony **57**
Hunter, Alberta **42**
Johnson, Eddie Bernice **8**
Johnson, Hazel **22**
Johnson, Mamie "Peanut" **40**
Larsen, Nella **10**
Lewis, Daurene **72**
Lyttle, Hulda Margaret **14**

Richards, Hilda 49
Riley, Helen Caldwell Day 13
Robinson, Rachel 16
Robinson, Sharon 22
Seacole, Mary 54
Shabazz, Betty 7, 26
Staupers, Mabel K. 7
Taylor, Susie King 13

Nursing agency
Daniels, Lee Louis 36

Nutrition
Clark, Celeste 15
Gregory, Dick 1, 54
Smith, Ian 62
Watkins, Shirley R. 17

Nuwaubianism
York, Dwight D. 71

NWBL
See National Women's Basketball
League

NYA
See National Youth Administration

**Nyasaland African Congress
(NAC)**
Banda, Hastings Kamuzu 6, 54

**Oakland Athletics baseball
team**
Baylor, Don 6
Henderson, Rickey 28
Jackson, Reggie 15
Morgan, Joe Leonard 9

Oakland Oaks baseball team
Dandridge, Ray 36

Oakland Raiders football team
Howard, Desmond 16, 58
Upshaw, Gene 18, 47, 72

Oakland Tribune
Bailey, Chauncey 68
Maynard, Nancy Hicks 73
Maynard, Robert C. 7

OAR
See Office of AIDS Research

OAU
See Organization of African Unity

Obie awards
Browne, Roscoe Lee 66
Carter, Nell 39
De Shields, André 72
Freeman, Yvette 27
Orlandersmith, Dael 42
Thigpen, Lynne 17, 41

OBSSR
See Office of Behavioral and Social
Sciences Research

OECS
See Organization of Eastern Caribbean States

**Office of AIDS Research
(OAR)**
Cargill, Victoria A. 43

**Office of Behavioral and So-
cial Science Research**
Anderson, Norman B. 45

Office of Civil Rights
See U.S. Department of Education

**Office of Management and
Budget**
Raines, Franklin Delano 14

Office of Public Liaison
Herman, Alexis M. 15

Ohio state government
Brown, Les 5
Ford, Jack 39
Stokes, Carl 10, 73
White, Michael R. 5
Williams, George Washington 18

Ohio Women's Hall of Fame
Craig-Jones, Ellen Walker 44
Stewart, Ella 39

OIC
See Opportunities Industrialization
Centers of America, Inc.

OKeh record label
Brooks, Hadda 40
Mo', Keb' 36

Oklahoma Eagle
Ross, Don 27

Oklahoma Hall of Fame
Mitchell, Leona 42

**Oklahoma House of Repre-
sentatives**
Ross, Don 27

**Olatunji Center for African
Culture**
Olatunji, Babatunde 36

Olympics
Ali, Muhammad 2, 16, 52
Beamon, Bob 30
Bolt, Usain 73
Bonaly, Surya 7
Bowe, Riddick 6
Christie, Linford 8
Clay, Bryan Ezra 57
Coachman, Alice 18
Davis, Shani 58
Dawes, Dominique 11
DeFrantz, Anita 37
Devers, Gail 7
Dibaba, Tirunesh 73
Edwards, Teresa 14
Ervin, Anthony 66
Eto'o, Samuel 73
Felix, Allyson 48
Flowers, Vonetta 35
Freeman, Cathy 29
Garrison, Zina 2
Gebrselassie, Haile 70
Gourdine, Meredith 33
Greene, Maurice 27
Griffith, Yolanda 25
Griffith-Joyner, Florence 28
Harrison, Alvin 28
Harrison, Calvin 28
Hines, Garrett 35

Holmes, Kelly 47
Holyfield, Evander 6
Howard, Sherri 36
Iginla, Jarome 35
Johnson, Ben 1
Johnson, Michael 13
Johnson, Rafer 33
Jones, Cullen 73
Jones, Lou 64
Jones, Randy 35
Joyner-Kersee, Jackie 5
Keflezighi, Meb 49
Lewis, Carl 4
Malone, Karl 18, 51
Metcalfe, Ralph 26
Miller, Cheryl 10
Montgomery, Tim 41
Moses, Edwin 8
Mutola, Maria 12
Owens, Jesse 2
Powell, Mike 7
Quirot, Ana 13
Richards, Sanya 66
Rudolph, Wilma 4
Scurry, Briana 27
Thomas, Debi 26
Thugwane, Josia 21
Ward, Andre 62
Ward, Lloyd 21, 46
Westbrook, Peter 20
Whitaker, Pernell 10
White, Willye 67
Whitfield, Mal 60
Wilkens, Lenny 11
Williams, Lauryn 58
Woodruff, John 68

On a Roll Radio
Smith, Greg 28

Oncology
Leffall, Lasalle 3, 64

100 Black Men of America
Dortch, Thomas W., Jr. 45

One Way-Productions
Naylor, Gloria 10, 42

Ontario Legislature
Curling, Alvin 34

Onyx Opera
Brown, Uzee 42

Onyx Theater Company
Banks, Michelle 59

OPC
See Ovambo People's Congress

Opera
Adams, Leslie 39
Anderson, Marian 2, 33
Arroyo, Martina 30
Battle, Kathleen 70
Brooks, Avery 9
Brown, Angela M. 54
Brown, Uzee 42
Bumbry, Grace 5
Davis, Anthony 11
Dobbs, Mattiwilda 34
Estes, Simon 28
Freeman, Paul 39
Graves, Denyce Antoinette 19, 57

Greely, M. Gasby 27
Hendricks, Barbara 3, 67
Joplin, Scott 6
Joyner, Matilda Sissieretta 15
Lister, Marquita 65
Maynor, Dorothy 19
McDonald, Audra 20, 62
Mitchell, Leona 42
Norman, Jessye 5
Phillips, Helen L. 63
Price, Leontyne 1
Simpson-Hoffman, N'kenge 52
Still, William Grant 37
Three Mo' Tenors 35
Verrett, Shirley 66
White, Willard 53

Operation Desert Shield
Powell, Colin 1, 28

Operation Desert Storm
Powell, Colin 1, 28

Operation HOPE
Bryant, John 26

Ophthalmology
Bath, Patricia E. 37

OPO
See Ovamboland People's Organization

**Opportunities Industrialization
Centers of America, Inc. (OIC)**
Sullivan, Leon H. 3, 30

Ora Nelle Records
Little Walter 36

Oracle Corporation
Phillips, Charles E., Jr. 57
Woods, Jacqueline 52

Organ
McGriff, Jimmy 72

Organization of African States
Museveni, Yoweri 4

**Organization of African Unity
(OAU)**
Diouf, Abdou 3
Haile Selassie 7
Kaunda, Kenneth 2
Kenyatta, Jomo 5
Nkrumah, Kwame 3
Nujoma, Samuel 10
Nyerere, Julius 5
Touré, Sekou 6

**Organization of Afro-American
Unity**
Feelings, Muriel 44
X, Malcolm 1

**Organization of Eastern Carib-
bean States (OECS)**
Charles, Mary Eugenia 10, 55

**Organization of Women Writ-
ers of African Descent**
Cortez, Jayne 43

Organization Us
Karenga, Maulana 10, 71

Orisun Repertory
Soyinka, Wole **4**

Orlando Magic basketball team
Erving, Julius **18, 47**
O'Neal, Shaquille **8, 30**
Rivers, Glenn "Doc" **25**

Orlando Miracle basketball team
Peck, Carolyn **23**

Osteopathy
Allen, Ethel D. **13**
Anderson, William G(ilchrist) **57**
Ross-Lee, Barbara **67**

Ovambo People's Congress (South Africa; OPC)
Nujoma, Samuel **10**

Ovamboland People's Organization (South Africa; OPO)
Nujoma, Samuel **10**

Overbrook Entertainment
Pinkett Smith, Jada **10, 41**

Page Education Foundation
Page, Alan **7**

PAIGC
See African Party for the Independence of Guinea and Cape Verde

Paine College
Lewis, Shirley A. R. **14**

Painting
Alston, Charles **33**
Amos, Emma **63**
Andrews, Benny **22, 59**
Bailey, Radcliffe **19**
Barthe, Richmond **15**
Basquiat, Jean-Michel **5**
Bearden, Romare **2, 50**
Beasley, Phoebe **34**
Biggers, John **20, 33**
Campbell, E. Simms **13**
Colescott, Robert **69**
Collins, Paul **61**
Cortor, Eldzier **42**
Cowans, Adger W. **20**
Crite, Alan Rohan **29**
Delaney, Beauford **19**
Delaney, Joseph **30**
Delsarte, Louis **34**
Douglas, Aaron **7**
Driskell, David C. **7**
Flood, Curt **10**
Freeman, Leonard **27**
Gilliam, Sam **16**
Goodnight, Paul **32**
Green, Jonathan **54**
Guyton, Tyree **9**
Harkless, Necia Desiree **19**
Hayden, Palmer **13**
Honeywood, Varnette P. **54**
Hunter, Clementine **45**
Jackson, Earl **31**
Johnson, William Henry **3**
Jones, Lois Mailou **13**
Knight, Gwendolyn **63**
Knox, Simmie **49**
Lawrence, Jacob **4, 28**

Lee, Annie Frances **22**
Lee-Smith, Hughie **5, 22**
Lewis, Norman **39**
Lewis, Samella **25**
Loving, Alvin, Jr. **35, 53**
Marshall, Kerry James **59**
Mayhew, Richard **39**
Major, Clarence **9**
McGee, Charles **10**
Mitchell, Corinne **8**
Motley, Archibald, Jr. **30**
Mutu, Wangechi **44**
Neals, Otto **73**
Nugent, Richard Bruce **39**
Ouattara **43**
Pierre, Andre **17**
Pindell, Howardena **55**
Pippin, Horace **9**
Porter, James A. **11**
Reid, Senghor **55**
Ringgold, Faith **4**
Ruley, Ellis **38**
Sallee, Charles **38**
Sebree, Charles **40**
Smith, Vincent D. **48**
Sudduth, Jimmy Lee **65**
Tanksley, Ann **37**
Tanner, Henry Ossawa **1**
Thomas, Alma **14**
Thomas, Mickalene **61**
Tolliver, Mose **60**
Tolliver, William **9**
Verna, Gelsy **70**
Washington, James, Jr. **38**
Wells, James Lesesne **10**
White, Charles **39**
Wiley, Kehinde **62**
Williams, Billy Dee **8**
Williams, William T. **11**
Wilson, Ellis **39**
Woodruff, Hale **9**

Pan African Congress
Logan, Rayford W. **40**

Pan African Orthodox Christian Church
Agyeman, Jaramogi Abebe **10, 63**

Pan-Africanism
Carmichael, Stokely **5, 26**
Clarke, John Henrik **20**
Du Bois, David Graham **45**
Du Bois, W. E. B. **3**
Garvey, Marcus **1**
Haile Selassie **7**
Kenyatta, Jomo **5**
Madhubuti, Haki R. **7**
Marshall, Paule **7**
Nkrumah, Kwame **3**
Nyerere, Julius **5**
Touré, Sekou **6**
Turner, Henry McNeal **5**

Papal Medal
Hampton, Lionel **17, 41**

Parents of Watts (POW)
Harris, Alice **7**

Parti Démocratique de la Côte d'Ivoire (Democratic Party of the Ivory Coast; PDCI)
Bedie, Henri Konan **21**
Houphouët-Boigny, Félix **4, 64**

Partido Africano da Independencia da Guine e Cabo Verde (PAIGC)
Vieira, Joao **14**

Party for Unity and Progress (Guinea; PUP)
Conté, Lansana **7**

PATC
See Performing Arts Training Center

Pathology
Fuller, Solomon Carter, Jr. **15**

Patriot Party
Fulani, Lenora **11**

Patriotic Alliance for Reconstruction and Construction (PARC)
Jammeh, Yahya **23**

Patriotic Movement of Salvation (MPS)
Déby, Idriss **30**

PBS
See Public Broadcasting Service

PDCI
See Parti Démocratique de la Côte d'Ivoire (Democratic Party of the Ivory Coast)

PDP
See People's Democratic Party

Peace and Freedom Party
Cleaver, Eldridge **5**

Peace Corps
See U.S. Peace Corps

Peck School of the Fine Arts
Tyson, Andre **40**

Pediatrics
Carson, Benjamin **1, 35**
Elders, Joycelyn **6**
Fennoy, Ilene **72**
Witt, Edwin T. **26**
Zuma, Nkosazana Dlamini **34**

Peg Leg Bates Country Club
Bates, Peg Leg **14**

PEN/Faulkner award
Bradley, David Henry, Jr. **39**
Mayhew, Richard **39**

Pennsylvania state government
Allen, Ethel D. **13**
Brown, Homer S. **47**
Fattah, Chaka **11, 70**
Irvis, K. Leroy **67**
Nix, Robert N. C., Jr. **51**

Pennsylvania State University
Dunn, Jerry **27**

People United to Serve Humanity (PUSH)
Jackson, Jesse **1, 27, 72**
Jackson, Jesse, Jr. **14, 45**

People's Association for Human Rights
Williams, Robert F. **11**

People's Choice Awards
Lewis, Emmanuel **36**

People's Democratic Party (Nigeria; PDP)
Obasanjo, Stella **32**
Yar'adua, Umaru **69**

People's Liberation Army of Namibia (PLAN)
Nujoma, Samuel **10**

People's National Party (Jamaica; PNP)
Patterson, P. J. **6, 20**

People's Progressive Party (PPP)
Jagan, Cheddi **16**
Jawara, Dawda Kairaba **11**

People's Revolutionary government
Bishop, Maurice **39**

PepsiCo Inc.
Banks, Paula A. **68**
Boyd, Edward **70**
Harvey, William R. **42**

Performing Arts Training Center (PATC)
Dunham, Katherine **4, 59**

Perkins Prize
Jones, Thomas W. **41**

PGA
See Professional Golfers' Association

Pharmaceutical research
Pickett, Cecil **39**

Pharmaceuticals
Flowers, Sylester **50**
Potter, Myrtle **40**

Pharmacist
Akunyili, Dora Nkem **58**
Flowers, Sylester **50**
Pickett, Cecil **39**
Stewart, Ella **39**

Phelps Stokes Fund
Patterson, Frederick Douglass **12**

Phi Beta Sigma Fraternity
Thomas, Arthur Ray **52**

Philadelphia city government
Allen, Ethel D. **13**
Goode, W. Wilson **4**
Nutter, Michael **69**
Street, John F. **24**

Philadelphia Eagles football team
Cunningham, Randall **23**
McNabb, Donovan **29**
Rhodes, Ray **14**

White, Reggie **6, 50**

Philadelphia Flyers hockey team
Brashear, Donald **39**
Charleston, Oscar **39**

Philadelphia Phillies baseball team
Howard, Ryan **65**
Morgan, Joe Leonard **9**
Rollins, Jimmy **70**

Philadelphia public schools
Clayton, Constance **1**

Philadelphia 76ers basketball team
Barkley, Charles **5, 66**
Bol, Manute **1**
Chamberlain, Wilt **18, 47**
Erving, Julius **18, 47**
Iverson, Allen **24, 46**
Lucas, John **7**
Stackhouse, Jerry **30**

Philadelphia Stars baseball team
Charleston, Oscar **39**

Philadelphia Warriors
Chamberlain, Wilt **18, 47**

Philanthropy
Banks, Paula A. **68**
Brown, Eddie C. **35**
Cooper, Evern **40**
Cosby, Bill **7, 26, 59**
Cosby, Camille **14**
Dawson, Matel "Mat," Jr. **39**
Edley, Christopher **2, 48**
Gardner, Chris **65**
Golden, Marita **19**
Gray, Willie **46**
Johnson, Kevin **70**
Johnson, Sheila Crump **48**
Lavizzo-Mourey, Risa **48**
Malone, Annie **13**
McCarty, Osceola **16**
Millines Dziko, Trish **28**
Pleasant, Mary Ellen **9**
Reeves, Rachel J. **23**
Thomas, Franklin A. **5, 49**
Waddles, Charleszetta "Mother" **10, 49**
Walker, Madame C. J. **7**
Wein, Joyce **62**
White, Reggie **6, 50**
Williams, Fannie Barrier **27**
Wonder, Stevie **11, 53**

Philosophy
Appiah, Kwame Anthony **67**
Baker, Houston A., Jr. **6**
Davis, Angela **5**
Piper, Adrian **71**
Toomer, Jean **6**
West, Cornel **5**

Phoenix Suns basketball team
Barkley, Charles **5, 66**
Heard, Gar **25**
Johnson, Kevin **70**

Photography
Andrews, Bert **13**
Barboza, Anthony **10**

Cowans, Adger W. **20**
Cox, Renée **67**
DeCarava, Roy **42**
Hinton, Milt **30**
Jackson, Vera **40**
Lester, Julius **9**
Moutoussamy-Ashe, Jeanne **7**
Parks, Gordon **1, 35, 58**
Pinderhughes, John **47**
Robeson, Eslanda Goode **13**
Roble, Abdi **71**
Serrano, Andres **3**
Simpson, Lorna **4, 36**
Sleet, Moneta, Jr. **5**
Smith, Marvin **46**
Smith, Morgan **46**
Tanner, Henry Ossawa **1**
Thomas, Mickalene **61**
VanDerZee, James **6**
Weems, Carrie Mae **63**
White, John H. **27**
Williams, Clarence **70**
Withers, Ernest C. **68**

Photojournalism
Ashley-Ward, Amelia **23**
DeCarava, Roy **42**
Jackson, Vera **40**
Moutoussamy-Ashe, Jeanne **7**
Parks, Gordon **1, 35, 58**
Sleet, Moneta, Jr. **5**
Van Lierop, Robert **53**
White, John H. **27**
Williams, Clarence **70**
Withers, Ernest C. **68**
Yette, Samuel F. **63**

Physical therapy
Elders, Joycelyn **6**
Griffin, Bessie Blout **43**

Physics
Adkins, Rutherford H. **21**
Carruthers, George R. **40**
Gates, Sylvester James, Jr. **15**
Gourdine, Meredith **33**
Imes, Elmer Samuel **39**
Jackson, Shirley Ann **12**
Massey, Walter E. **5, 45**
Tyson, Neil deGrasse **15, 65**

Piano
Adams, Leslie **39**
Austin, Lovie **40**
Basie, Count **23**
Bonds, Margaret **39**
Brooks, Hadda **40**
Cartiér, Xam Wilson **41**
Cole, Nat King **17**
Coltrane, Alice **70**
Cook, Charles "Doc" **44**
Domino, Fats **20**
Donegan, Dorothy **19**
Duke, George **21**
Ellington, Duke **5**
Flanagan, Tommy **69**
Hancock, Herbie **20, 67**
Hardin Armstrong, Lil **39**
Harris, Barry **68**
Hayes, Isaac **20, 58, 73**
Hinderas, Natalie **5**
Hines, Earl "Fatha" **39**
Horn, Shirley **32, 56**
Jamal, Ahmad **69**

Johnson, Johnnie **56**
Jones, Hank **57**
Joplin, Scott **6**
Keys, Alicia **32, 68**
Monk, Thelonious **1**
Perkins, Pinetop **70**
Peterson, Oscar **52**
Powell, Bud **24**
Pratt, Awadagin **31**
Preston, Billy **39, 59**
Price, Florence **37**
Pritchard, Robert Starling **21**
Roberts, Marcus **19**
Robinson, Reginald R. **53**
Sample, Joe **51**
Schuyler, Philippa **50**
Scott, Hazel **66**
Silver, Horace **26**
Simone, Nina **15, 41**
Sun Ra **60**
Swann, Lynn **28**
Southern, Eileen **56**
Sykes, Roosevelt **20**
Taylor, Billy **23**
Taylor, Cecil **70**
Turner, Ike **68**
Vaughan, Sarah **13**
Walker, George **37**
Waller, Fats **29**
Watts, Andre **42**
Webster, Katie **29**
Williams, Mary Lou **15**

Pittsburgh Crawfords
See Indianapolis Crawfords

Pittsburgh Homestead Grays baseball team
Charleston, Oscar **39**
Kaiser, Cecil **42**
Leonard, Buck **67**

Pittsburgh Pirates baseball team
Bonds, Barry **6, 34, 63**
Clendenon, Donn **26, 56**
Stargell, Willie **29**

Pittsburgh Steelers football team
Dungy, Tony **17, 42, 59**
Gilliam, Joe **31**
Greene, Joe **10**
Perry, Lowell **30**
Stargell, Willie **29**
Stewart, Kordell **21**
Swann, Lynn **28**

PLAN
See People's Liberation Army of Namibia

Planned Parenthood Federation of America Inc.
Wattleton, Faye **9**

Playboy
Brown, Robert **65**
Taylor, Karin **34**

Playwright
Allen, Debbie **13, 42**
Anthony, Trey **63**
Arkadie, Kevin **17**
Baldwin, James **1**

Bandele, Biyi **68**
Barrett, Lindsay **43**
Beckham, Barry **41**
Branch, William Blackwell **39**
Brown, Cecil M. **46**
Brown, Oscar, Jr. **53**
Bullins, Ed **25**
Caldwell, Benjamin **46**
Carroll, Vinnette **29**
Césaire, Aimé **48, 69**
Cheadle, Don **19, 52**
Chenault, John **40**
Childress, Alice **15**
Clark-Bekedermo, J. P. **44**
Clarke, George **32**
Cleage, Pearl **17, 64**
Corthron, Kia **43**
Cotter, Joseph Seamon, Sr. **40**
Cox, Joseph Mason Andrew **51**
Dadié, Bernard **34**
Davis, Eisa **68**
De Veaux, Alexis **44**
Dent, Thomas C. **50**
Dodson, Owen **38**
Elder, Larry, III **38**
Evans, Mari **26**
Farah, Nuruddin **27**
Franklin, J. E. **44**
Gordone, Charles **15**
Gurira, Danai **73**
Hansberry, Lorraine **6**
Harris, Bill **72**
Hayes, Teddy **40**
Hill, Errol **40**
Hill, Leslie Pinckney **44**
Holder, Laurence **34**
Hughes, Langston **4**
Jean-Baptiste, Marianne **17, 46**
Johnson, Georgia Douglas **41**
Johnson, Je'Caryous **63**
Jones, Sarah **39**
Kennedy, Adrienne **11**
Kente, Gibson **52**
King, Woodie, Jr. **27**
Lampley, Oni Faida **43, 71**
Long, Richard Alexander **65**
Marechera, Dambudzo **39**
Milner, Ron **39**
Mitchell, Loften **31**
Moss, Carlton **17**
Mugo, Micere Githae **32**
Nottage, Lynn **66**
Onwueme, Tess Osonye **23**
Orlandersmith, Dael **42**
Parks, Suzan-Lori **34**
Perry, Tyler **40, 54**
Rahman, Aishah **37**
Richards, Beah **30**
Salter, Nikkole **73**
Sanchez, Sonia **17, 51**
Schuyler, George Samuel **40**
Sebree, Charles **40**
Smith, Anna Deavere **6, 44**
Talbert, David **34**
Taylor, Regina **9, 46**
Thurman, Wallace **17**
Tolson, Melvin B. **37**
Walcott, Derek **5**
Ward, Douglas Turner **42**
Wesley, Richard **73**
Williams, Samm-Art **21**
Wilson, August **7, 33, 55**
Wolfe, George C. **6, 43**

Youngblood, Shay **32**

PNP
See People's National Party (Jamaica)

Podium Records
Patterson, Gilbert Earl **41**

Poet laureate (U.S.)
Dove, Rita **6**

Poetry
Adams, Jenoyne **60**
Alexander, Margaret Walker **22**
Allen, Samuel L. **38**
Angelou, Maya **1, 15**
Atkins, Russell **45**
Aubert, Alvin **41**
Baiocchi, Regina Harris **41**
Bandele, Asha **36**
Barrax, Gerald William **45**
Barrett, Lindsay **43**
Bell, James Madison **40**
Bennett, Gwendolyn B. **59**
Bennett, Louise **69**
Berry, James **41**
Bontemps, Arna **8**
Braithwaite, William Stanley **52**
Brand, Dionne **32**
Breeze, Jean "Binta" **37**
Brooks, Gwendolyn **1, 28**
Brown, Cecil M. **46**
Brutus, Dennis **38**
Burgess, Marjorie L. **55**
Carter, Martin **49**
Cartey, Wilfred **47**
Césaire, Aimé **48, 69**
Chenault, John **40**
Cheney-Coker, Syl **43**
Clark-Bekedermo, J. P. **44**
Clarke, Cheryl **32**
Clarke, George **32**
Cleage, Pearl **17, 64**
Cliff, Michelle **42**
Clifton, Lucille **14, 64**
Coleman, Wanda **48**
Cooper, Afua **53**
Cornish, Sam **50**
Cortez, Jayne **43**
Cotter, Joseph Seamon, Sr. **40**
Cox, Joseph Mason Andrew **51**
Cuney, William Waring **44**
Dabydeen, David **48**
Dadié, Bernard **34**
D'Aguiar, Fred **50**
Damas, Léon-Gontran **46**
Dandridge, Raymond Garfield **45**
Danner, Margaret Esse **49**
Datcher, Michael **60**
Davis, Charles T. **48**
Davis, Frank Marshall **47**
De Veaux, Alexis **44**
Dent, Thomas C. **50**
Dodson, Owen **38**
Dove, Rita **6**
Draper, Sharon Mills **16, 43**
Dumas, Henry **41**
Dunbar-Nelson, Alice Ruth Moore **44**
Emanuel, James A. **46**
Evans, Mari **26**
Fabio, Sarah Webster **48**
Fair, Ronald L. **47**

Figueroa, John J. **40**
Fisher, Antwone **40**
Fleming, Raymond **48**
Forbes, Calvin **46**
Ford, Nick Aaron **44**
Frazier, Oscar **58**
Gabre-Medhin, Tsegaye **64**
Gilbert, Christopher **50**
Goings, Russell **59**
Goodison, Lorna **71**
Harkless, Necia Desiree **19**
Harper, Frances Ellen Watkins **11**
Harper, Michael S. **34**
Harris, Bill **72**
Harris, Claire **34**
Hayden, Robert **12**
Henderson, David **53**
Herndon, Calvin C. **51**
Hill, Leslie Pinckney **44**
Hoagland, Everett H. **45**
Horne, Frank **44**
Hughes, Langston **7**
Jackson, Fred James **25**
Joachim, Paulin **34**
Johnson, Georgia Douglas **41**
Johnson, Linton Kwesi **37**
Jones, Sarah **39**
Kay, Jackie **37**
Keene, John **73**
Knight, Etheridge **37**
Laraque, Paul **67**
Letson, Al **39**
Lorde, Audre **6**
Manley, Ruth **34**
Marechera, Dambudzo **39**
Moore, Jessica Care **30**
Mugo, Micere Githae **32**
Mullen, Harryette **34**
Naylor, Gloria **10, 42**
Neto, António Agostinho **43**
Nugent, Richard Bruce **39**
Okara, Gabriel **37**
Parker, Pat **19**
Peters, Lenrie **43**
Philip, Marlene Nourbese **32**
Powell, Kevin **31**
Quigless, Helen G. **49**
Randall, Dudley **8, 55**
Redmond, Eugene **23**
Richards, Beah **30**
Sanchez, Sonia **17, 51**
Sapphire **14**
Senghor, Léopold Sédar **12**
Senior, Olive **37**
Smith, Mary Carter **26**
Spencer, Anne **27**
Sundiata, Sekou **66**
Tillis, Frederick **40**
Tolson, Melvin B. **37**
Touré, Askia (Muhammad Abu Bakr el) **47**
van Sertima, Ivan **25**
Walker, Margaret **29**
Washington, James, Jr. **38**
Weaver, Afaa Michael **37**
Williams, Saul **31**
Williams, Sherley Anne **25**
Woods, Scott **55**

Poetry Slam, Inc.
Woods, Scott **55**

Political science
Ake, Claude **30**
Dawson, Michael C. **63**
Skinner, Kiron K. **65**
Watson, Carlos **50**

Politics
Alexander, Archie Alphonso **14**
Allen, Claude **68**
Arthur, Owen **33**
Austin, Junius C. **44**
Baker, Thurbert **22**
Ballance, Frank W. **41**
Barrow, Dean **69**
Bass, Charlotta Spears **40**
Belton, Sharon Sayles **9, 16**
Bishop, Sanford D., Jr. **24**
Blackwell, Unita **17**
Boateng, Paul Yaw **56**
Booker, Cory Anthony **68**
Boye, Madior **30**
Brazile, Donna **25, 70**
Brown, Corrine **24**
Brown, Oscar, Jr. **53**
Buckley, Victoria (Vikki) **24**
Burris, Chuck **21**
Burris, Roland W. **25**
Butler, Jerry **26**
Césaire, Aimé **48, 69**
Chideya, Farai **14, 61**
Christian-Green, Donna M. **17**
Clayton, Eva M. **20**
Coleman, Mary **46**
Compton, John **65**
Connerly, Ward **14**
Cummings, Elijah E. **24**
Curling, Alvin **34**
Currie, Betty **21**
Davis, Artur **41**
Davis, James E. **50**
Dixon, Julian C. **24**
Dixon, Sheila **68**
dos Santos, José Eduardo **43**
Dymally, Mervyn **42**
Edmonds, Terry **17**
Ellison, Keith **59**
Fields, C. Virginia **25**
Fields, Julia **45**
Ford, Jack **39**
Gbagbo, Laurent **43**
Gordon, Pamela **17**
Greenlee, Sam **48**
Hatcher, Richard G. **55**
Henry, Aaron **19**
Herenton, Willie W. **24**
Hilliard, Earl F. **24**
Hobson, Julius W. **44**
Holmes, Amy **69**
Ingraham, Hubert A. **19**
Isaac, Julius **34**
Jackson, Mae **57**
Jackson Lee, Sheila **20**
James, Sharpe **23, 69**
Jammeh, Yahya **23**
Jarrett, Valerie **73**
Jarvis, Charlene Drew **21**
Jefferson, William J. **25, 72**
Johnson, Harvey, Jr. **24**
Kabbah, Ahmad Tejan **23**
Kabila, Joseph **30**
Kariuki, J. M. **67**
Kidd, Mae Street **39**
Lee, Barbara **25**

Maathai, Wangari **43**
Magloire, Paul Eugène **68**
Majette, Denise **41**
Mamadou, Tandja **33**
McGlowan, Angela **64**
Meek, Carrie **6, 36**
Meek, Kendrick **41**
Meeks, Gregory **25**
Metcalfe, Ralph **26**
Millender-McDonald, Juanita **21, 61**
Moore, Gwendolynne S. **55**
Moore, Harry T. **29**
Morial, Ernest "Dutch" **26**
Morial, Marc H. **20, 51**
Nagin, C. Ray **42, 57**
Obasanjo, Olusegun **22**
Pereira, Aristides **30**
Perry, Ruth **15**
Pitta, Celso **17**
Powell, Debra A. **23**
Rush, Bobby **26**
Saro-Wiwa, Kenule **39**
Scott, David **41**
Scott, Robert C. **23**
Simmons, Jamal **72**
Sisulu, Sheila Violet Makate **24**
Smith, Jennifer **21**
Spencer, Winston Baldwin **68**
Thompson, Bennie G. **26**
Touré, Amadou Toumani **18**
Watson, Diane **41**
Watt, Melvin **26**
Watts, J. C., Jr. **14, 38**
Wheat, Alan **14**
White, Jesse **22**
Williams, Anthony **21**
Williams, Eddie N. **44**
Williams, Eric Eustace **65**
Williams, George Washington **18**
Wiwa, Ken **67**
Wynn, Albert R. **25**
Yar'adua, Umaru **69**

Pop music
Ashanti **37**
Ashford, Nickolas **21**
Barrino, Fantasia **53**
Bassey, Shirley **25**
Bleu, Corbin **65**
Blige, Mary J. **20, 34, 60**
Brown, Bobby **58**
Brown, Melanie **73**
Butler, Jonathan **28**
Cannon, Nick **47, 73**
Carey, Mariah **32, 53, 69**
Cee-Lo **70**
Chanté, Keshia **50**
Checker, Chubby **28**
Cole, Nat King **17**
Combs, Sean "Puffy" **17, 43**
Cox, Deborah **28**
David, Craig **31, 53**
Duke, George **21**
Edmonds, Kenneth "Babyface" **10, 31**
Ferrell, Rachelle **29**
Franklin, Aretha **11, 44**
Franklin, Kirk **15, 49**
Gray, Macy **29**
Hailey, JoJo **22**
Hailey, K-Ci **22**
Hammer, M. C. **20**
Hathaway, Lalah **57**

Hawkins, Screamin' Jay **30**
Hayes, Isaac **20, 58, 73**
Hill, Lauryn **20, 53**
Holmes, Clint **57**
Houston, Cissy **20**
Houston, Whitney **7, 28**
Hudson, Jennifer **63**
Humphrey, Bobbi **20**
Isley, Ronald **25, 56**
Ja Rule **35**
Jackson, Janet **6, 30, 68**
Jackson, Michael **19, 53**
James, Rick **17**
Jarreau, Al **21, 65**
Jean, Wyclef **20**
Jones, Quincy **8, 30**
Jordan, Montell **23**
Kelis **58**
Kendricks, Eddie **22**
Keys, Alicia **32, 68**
Khan, Chaka **12, 50**
LaBelle, Patti **13, 30**
Love, Darlene **23**
Luckett, Letoya **61**
Massenburg, Kedar **23**
Mathis, Johnny **20**
McFerrin, Bobby **68**
Monica **21**
Moore, Chante **26**
Mumba, Samantha **29**
Mya **35**
Ne-Yo **65**
Neville, Aaron **21**
Noah, Yannick **4, 60**
Osborne, Jeffrey **26**
Otis, Clyde **67**
P.M. Dawn **54**
Palmer, Keke **68**
Preston, Billy **39, 59**
Prince **18, 65**
Reid, Antonio "L.A." **28**
Reid, Vernon **34**
Richie, Lionel **27, 65**
Rihanna **65**
Robinson, Smokey **3, 49**
Rucker, Darius **34**
Rupaul **17**
Sade **15**
Seal **14**
Senghor, Léopold Sédar **12**
Short, Bobby **52**
Simpson, Valerie **21**
Sisqo **30**
Staton, Candi **27**
Summer, Donna **25**
Supremes, The **33**
Sweat, Keith **19**
Temptations, The **33**
Thomas, Irma **29**
TLC **34**
Turner, Tina **6, 27**
Usher **23, 56**
Vanity **67**
Washington, Dinah **22**
Washington, Grover, Jr. **17, 44**
Washington, Val **12**
Welch, Elisabeth **52**
White, Barry **13, 41**
White, Josh, Jr. **52**
White, Maurice **29**
will.i.am **64**
Williams, Vanessa L. **4, 17**
Wilson, Jackie **60**

Wilson, Mary **28**
Wilson, Nancy **10**
Withers-Mendes, Elisabeth **64**
Wonder, Stevie **11, 53**

Portland (OR) Police Department
Moose, Charles **40**

Portland Trail Blazers basketball team
Drexler, Clyde **4, 61**
Miller, Larry G. **72**
Wilkens, Lenny **11**

POW
See Parents of Watts

PPP
See People's Progressive Party (Gambia)

Pratt Institute
Mayhew, Richard **39**

Presbyterianism
Cannon, Katie **10**

Pride Economic Enterprises
Barry, Marion S. **7, 44**

Princeton University
Blanks, Deborah K. **69**
Simmons, Ruth **13, 38**

Printmaking
Blackburn, Robert **28**
Neals, Otto **73**
Tanksley, Ann **37**
Thrash, Dox **35**
Wells, James Lesesne **10**

Printmaking Workshop
Blackburn, Robert **28**
Tanksley, Ann **37**

Prison ministry
Bell, Ralph S. **5**

Professional Golfers' Association (PGA)
Elder, Lee **6**
Powell, Renee **34**
Sifford, Charlie **4, 49**
Woods, Tiger **14, 31**

Professional Women's Club of Chicago
Gray, Ida **41**

Progressive Labour Party
Smith, Jennifer **21**

Progressive Party
Bass, Charlotta Spears **40**

Project Teen Aid
McMurray, Georgia L. **36**

Pro-Line Corp.
Cottrell, Comer **11**

Proposition 209
Connerly, Ward **14**

Provincial Freeman
Cary, Mary Ann Shadd **30**

Psychiatry
Cobbs, Price M. **9**
Comer, James P. **6**

Fanon, Frantz **44**
Fuller, Solomon Carter, Jr. **15**
Poussaint, Alvin F. **5, 67**
Welsing, Frances Cress **5**

Psychic health
Ford, Clyde W. **40**

Psychology
Anderson, Norman B. **45**
Archie-Hudson, Marguerite **44**
Brown, Joyce F. **25**
Finner-Williams, Paris Michele **62**
Fulani, Lenora **11**
Gilbert, Christopher **50**
Hare, Nathan **44**
Hilliard, Asa Grant, III **66**
Staples, Brent **8**
Steele, Claude Mason **13**
Tatum, Beverly Daniel **42**

Psychotheraphy
Berrysmith, Don Reginald **49**
Ford, Clyde W. **40**

Public Broadcasting Service (PBS)
Brown, Les **5**
Davis, Ossie **5, 50**
Duke, Bill **3**
Hampton, Henry **6**
Hunter-Gault, Charlayne **6, 31**
Lawson, Jennifer **1, 50**
Lynch, Shola **61**
Riggs, Marlon **5, 44**
Roker, Al **12, 49**
Wilkins, Roger **2**

Public housing
Hamer, Fannie Lou **6**
Lane, Vincent **5**
Reems, Ernestine Cleveland **27**

Public relations
Barden, Don H. **9, 20**
Edmonds, Terry **17**
Graham, Stedman **13**
Hedgeman, Anna Arnold **22**
McCabe, Jewell Jackson **10**
Perez, Anna **1**
Pritchard, Robert Starling **21**
Rowan, Carl T. **1, 30**
Taylor, Kristin Clark **8**
Williams, Maggie **7, 71**

Public speaking
Bell, James Madison **40**
Kennedy, Randall **40**

Public television
Brown, Tony **3**
Creagh, Milton **27**
Ifill, Gwen **28**
Long, Loretta **58**

Publishing
Abbott, Robert Sengstacke **27**
Achebe, Chinua **6**
Ames, Wilmer **27**
Ashley-Ward, Amelia **23**
Aubert, Alvin **41**
Auguste, Arnold A. **47**
Baisden, Michael **25, 66**
Barden, Don H. **9, 20**
Bass, Charlotta Spears **40**

Bates, Daisy **13**
Boston, Lloyd **24**
Boyd, T. B., III **6**
Brown, Marie Dutton **12**
Cary, Mary Ann Shadd **30**
Coombs, Orde M. **44**
Cox, William E. **68**
Dawkins, Wayne **20**
Driver, David E. **11**
Ducksworth, Marilyn **12**
Dumas, Henry **41**
Fuller, Hoyt **44**
Giddings, Paula **11**
Graves, Earl G. **1, 35**
Harris, Jay **19**
Harris, Monica **18**
Hill, Bonnie Guiton **20**
Hudson, Cheryl **15**
Hudson, Wade **15**
James, Juanita **13**
Johnson, John H. **3, 54**
Jones, Quincy **8, 30**
Kunjufu, Jawanza **3, 50**
Lawson, Jennifer **1, 50**
Leavell, Dorothy R. **17**
Lewis, Edward T. **21**
Lorde, Audre **6**
Madhubuti, Haki R. **7**
Maynard, Nancy Hicks **73**
Maynard, Robert C. **7**
McDonald, Erroll **1**
Moore, Jessica Care **30**
Morgan, Garrett **1**
Murphy, John H. **42**
Myers, Walter Dean **8, 20**
Parks, Gordon **1, 35, 58**
Perez, Anna **1**
Randall, Dudley **8, 55**
Scott, C. A. **29**
Sengstacke, John **18**
Smith, Clarence O. **21**
Stinson, Denise L. **59**
Stringer, Vickie **58**
Tyree, Omar Rashad **21**
Vanzant, Iyanla **17, 47**
Walker, Alice **1, 43**
Washington, Alonzo **29**
Washington, Laura S. **18**
Wells-Barnett, Ida B. **8**
Williams, Armstrong **29**
Williams, Patricia **11, 54**
Woods, Teri **69**

Pulitzer prize
Brooks, Gwendolyn **1, 28**
Dove, Rita **6**
Fuller, Charles **8**
Givhan, Robin Deneen **72**
Gordone, Charles **15**
Haley, Alex **4**
Komunyakaa, Yusef **9**
Lewis, David Levering **9**
McPherson, James Alan **70**
Morrison, Toni **2, 15**
Newkirk, Pamela **69**
Page, Clarence **4**
Parks, Suzan-Lori **34**
Shipp, E. R. **15**
Sleet, Moneta, Jr. **5**
Walker, Alice **1, 43**
Walker, George **37**
White, John H. **27**
Wilkins, Roger **2**

Wilson, August **7, 33, 55**

PUP

See Party for Unity and Progress (Guinea)

Puppeteer

Clash, Kevin **14**

PUSH

See People United to Serve Humanity

Quiltmaking

Benberry, Cuesta **65**
Ringgold, Faith **4**

Qwest Records

Jones, Quincy **8, 30**

Race car driving

Hamilton, Lewis **66**
Lester, Bill **42**
Ribbs, Willy T. **2**
Scott, Wendell Oliver, Sr. **19**

Race relations

Abbott, Diane **9**
Achebe, Chinua **6**
Alexander, Clifford **26**
Anthony, Wendell **25**
Asante, Molefi Kete **3**
Baker, Ella **5**
Baker, Houston A., Jr. **6**
Baldwin, James **1**
Beals, Melba Patillo **15**
Bell, Derrick **6**
Bennett, Lerone, Jr. **5**
Bethune, Mary McLeod **4**
Bobo, Lawrence **60**
Booker, Simeon **23**
Bosley, Freeman, Jr. **7**
Boyd, T. B., III **6**
Bradley, David Henry, Jr. **39**
Branch, William Blackwell **39**
Brown, Elaine **8**
Bunche, Ralph J. **5**
Butler, Paul D. **17**
Butts, Calvin O., III **9**
Carter, Stephen L. **4**
Cary, Lorene **3**
Cashin, Sheryll **63**
Cayton, Horace **26**
Chavis, Benjamin **6**
Clark, Kenneth B. **5, 52**
Clark, Septima **7**
Cobbs, Price M. **9**
Cochran, Johnnie **11, 39, 52**
Cole, Johnnetta B. **5, 43**
Comer, James P. **6**
Cone, James H. **3**
Conyers, John, Jr. **4, 45**
Cook, Suzan D. Johnson **22**
Cook, Toni **23**
Cosby, Bill **7, 26, 59**
Cunningham, Evelyn **23**
Darden, Christopher **13**
Davis, Angela **5**
Davis, Benjamin O., Jr. **2, 43**
Davis, Benjamin O., Sr. **4**
Dee, Ruby **8, 50, 68**
Delany, Martin R. **27**
Dellums, Ronald **2**
Diallo, Amadou **27**
Dickerson, Debra J. **60**

Divine, Father **7**
DuBois, Shirley Graham **21**
Dunbar, Paul Laurence **8**
Dunbar-Nelson, Alice Ruth Moore **44**
Dyson, Michael Eric **11, 40**
Edelman, Marian Wright **5, 42**
Elder, Lee **6**
Ellison, Ralph **7**
Esposito, Giancarlo **9**
Farmer, James **2, 64**
Farmer-Paellmann, Deadria **43**
Farrakhan, Louis **2**
Fauset, Jessie **7**
Franklin, John Hope **5**
Fuller, Charles **8**
Gaines, Ernest J. **7**
Gibson, William F. **6**
Goode, W. Wilson **4**
Graham, Lawrence Otis **12**
Gregory, Dick **1, 54**
Grimké, Archibald H. **9**
Guinier, Lani **7, 30**
Guy, Rosa **5**
Haley, Alex **4**
Hall, Elliott S. **24**
Hampton, Henry **6**
Hansberry, Lorraine **6**
Harris, Alice **7**
Hastie, William H. **8**
Haynes, George Edmund **8**
Hedgeman, Anna Arnold **22**
Henry, Aaron **19**
Henry, Lenny **9, 52**
Hill, Oliver W. **24, 63**
hooks, bell **5**
Hooks, Benjamin L. **2**
Hope, John **8**
Howard, M. William, Jr. **26**
Ingram, Rex **5**
Innis, Roy **5**
Jeffries, Leonard **8**
Johnson, James Weldon **5**
Jones, Elaine R. **7, 45**
Jordan, Vernon E. **3, 35**
Khanga, Yelena **6**
King, Bernice **4**
King, Coretta Scott **3, 57**
King, Martin Luther, Jr. **1**
King, Yolanda **6**
Lane, Charles **3**
Lee, Spike **5, 19**
Lee-Smith, Hughie **5, 22**
Lorde, Audre **6**
Mabuza-Suttle, Felicia **43**
Mandela, Nelson **1, 14**
Martin, Louis E. **16**
Mathabane, Mark **5**
Maynard, Robert C. **7**
Mays, Benjamin E. **7**
McDougall, Gay J. **11, 43**
McKay, Claude **6**
Meredith, James H. **11**
Micheaux, Oscar **7**
Moore, Harry T. **29**
Mosley, Walter **5, 25, 68**
Muhammad, Khallid Abdul **10, 31**
Norton, Eleanor Holmes **7**
Page, Clarence **4**
Perkins, Edward **5**
Pitt, David Thomas **10**
Poussaint, Alvin F. **5, 67**
Price, Frederick K.C. **21**

Price, Hugh B. **9, 54**
Robeson, Paul **2**
Robinson, Spottswood W., III **22**
Sampson, Edith S. **4**
Shabazz, Attallah **6**
Sifford, Charlie **4, 49**
Simpson, Carole **6, 30**
Sister Souljah **11**
Sisulu, Sheila Violet Makate **24**
Smith, Anna Deavere **6, 44**
Sowell, Thomas **2**
Spaulding, Charles Clinton **9**
Staples, Brent **8**
Steele, Claude Mason **13**
Taulbert, Clifton Lemoure **19**
Till, Emmett **7**
Tutu, Desmond Mpilo **6, 44**
Tutu, Nontombi Naomi **57**
Tyree, Omar Rashad **21**
Walcott, Derek **5**
Walker, Maggie **17**
Washington, Booker T. **4**
Washington, Harold **6**
Wells-Barnett, Ida B. **8**
Welsing, Frances Cress **5**
West, Cornel **5**
Wideman, John Edgar **5**
Wiley, Ralph **8**
Wilkins, Roger **2**
Wilkins, Roy **4**
Williams, Fannie Barrier **27**
Williams, Gregory **11**
Williams, Hosea Lorenzo **15, 31**
Williams, Patricia **11, 54**
Williams, Walter E. **4**
Wilson, Sunnie **7, 55**
Wright, Richard **5**
Young, Whitney M., Jr. **4**

Radio

Abrahams, Peter **39**
Abu-Jamal, Mumia **15**
Alert, Kool DJ Red **33**
Anderson, Eddie "Rochester" **30**
Banks, William **11**
Bates, Karen Grigsby **40**
Beasley, Phoebe **34**
Blayton, Jesse B., Sr. **55**
Booker, Simeon **23**
Branch, William Blackwell **39**
Crocker, Frankie **29**
Dee, Ruby **8, 50, 68**
Dre, Dr. **10, 14, 30**
Elder, Larry **25**
Fuller, Charles **8**
Gibson, Truman K., Jr. **60**
Goode, Mal **13**
Greene, Petey **65**
Gumbel, Greg **8**
Hamblin, Ken **10**
Haynes, Trudy **44**
Holt, Nora **38**
Hughes, Cathy **27**
Jackson, Hal **41**
Jarrett, Vernon D. **42**
Joe, Yolanda **21**
Joyner, Tom **19**
Keyes, Alan L. **11**
Lewis, Delano **7**
Lewis, Ramsey **35, 70**
Ligging, Alfred, III **43**
Love, Ed **58**
Lover, Ed **10**

Ludacris **37, 60**
Madison, Joseph E. **17**
Majors, Jeff **41**
Mickelbury, Penny **28**
Moss, Carlton **17**
Parr, Russ **51**
Pressley, Condace L. **41**
Quivers, Robin **61**
Samara, Noah **15**
Smiley, Rickey **59**
Smiley, Tavis **20, 68**
Smith, Greg **28**
Steinberg, Martha Jean "The Queen" **28**
Taylor, Billy **23**
Tirico, Mike **68**
Whack, Rita Coburn **36**
Williams, Armstrong **29**
Williams, Juan **35**
Williams, Wendy **62**
Woods, Georgie **57**
Yarbrough, Camille **40**

Radio Jamaica

Abrahams, Peter **39**

Radio One Inc.

Hughes, Cathy **27**
Ligging, Alfred, III **43**
Majors, Jeff **41**

Radio-Television News Directors Association

Pressley, Condace L. **41**

Ragtime

Blake, Eubie **29**
Europe, James Reese **10**
Joplin, Scott **6**
Robinson, Reginald R. **53**
Sissle, Noble **29**

Rainbow Coalition

Chappell, Emma **18**
Jackson, Jesse **1, 27, 72**
Jackson, Jesse, Jr. **14, 45**
Moore, Minyon **45**

Rap music

Alert, Kool DJ Red **33**
Baker, Houston A., Jr. **6**
Bambaataa, Afrika **34**
Banner, David **55**
Benjamin, Andre **45**
Black Thought **63**
Blow, Kurtis **31**
Bow Wow **35**
Brown, Foxy **25**
Butts, Calvin O., III **9**
Cee-Lo **70**
Chuck D. **9**
Combs, Sean "Puffy" **17, 43**
Common **31, 63**
Deezer D **53**
DJ Jazzy Jeff **32**
DMX **28, 64**
Dre, Dr. **10, 14, 30**
Dupri, Jermaine **13, 46**
Dyson, Michael Eric **11, 40**
Elliott, Missy **31**
Eve **29**
50 Cent **46**
Flavor Flav **67**
Gotti, Irv **39**
Grae, Jean **51**

Grandmaster Flash **33, 60**
Gray, F. Gary **14, 49**
Hammer, M. C. **20**
Harrell, Andre **9, 30**
Heavy, D **58**
Hill, Lauryn **20, 53**
Ice Cube **8, 30, 60**
Ice-T **6, 31**
Ja Rule **35**
Jay-Z **27, 69**
Jean, Wyclef **20**
Jones, Quincy **8, 30**
Knight, Suge **11, 30**
KRS-One **34**
Lil' Kim **28**
Lil Wayne **66**
Liles, Kevin **42**
Lopes, Lisa "Left Eye" **36**
Lover, Ed **10**
Ludacris **37, 60**
Mase **24**
Master P **21**
MC Lyte **34**
Mos Def **30**
Nelly **32**
Notorious B.I.G. **20**
Ol' Dirty Bastard **52**
O'Neal, Shaquille **8, 30**
OutKast **35**
Queen Latifah **1, 16, 58**
Rhymes, Busta **31**
Roberts, Kimberly Rivers **72**
Run-DMC **31**
Shakur, Afeni **67**
Shakur, Tupac **14**
Simmons, Russell **1, 30**
Sister Souljah **11**
Smith, Will **8, 18, 53**
Snoop Dogg **35**
Timbaland **32**
T-Pain **73**
West, Kanye **52**
Yarbrough, Camille **40**
Young Jeezy **63**

Rassemblement Démocratique Africain (African Democratic Rally; RDA)
Houphouët-Boigny, Félix **4, 64**
Touré, Sekou **6**

Rastafarianism
Haile Selassie **7**
Marley, Bob **5**
Marley, Rita **32, 70**
Tosh, Peter **9**

RDA
See Rassemblement Démocratique Africain (African Democratic Rally)

Reader's Choice Award
Holton, Hugh, Jr. **39**

Reading Is Fundamental
Trueheart, William E. **49**

Real estate development
Barden, Don H. **9, 20**
Brooke, Edward **8**
Holmes, Larry **20, 68**
Lane, Vincent **5**
Marshall, Bella **22**
Russell, Herman Jerome **17**

Toote, Gloria E.A. **64**

"Real Men Cook"
Moyo, Karega Kofi **36**

Record producer
Albright, Gerald **23**
Ayers, Roy **16**
Bambaataa, Afrika **34**
Bivins, Michael **72**
Blige, Mary J. **20, 34, 60**
Butler, George, Jr. **70**
Coleman, Ornette **39, 69**
Combs, Sean "Puffy" **17, 43**
de Passe, Suzanne **25**
DJ Jazzy Jeff **32**
Dre, Dr. **10, 14, 30**
Duke, George **21**
Dupri, Jermaine **13, 46**
Edmonds, Kenneth "Babyface" **10, 31**
Elliott, Missy **31**
Gotti, Irv **39**
Hailey, JoJo **22**
Hailey, K-Ci **22**
Hammond, Fred **23**
Hill, Lauryn **20, 53**
Ice Cube **8, 30, 60**
Ja Rule **35**
Jackson, George **19**
Jackson, Michael **19, 53**
Jackson, Randy **40**
Jean, Wyclef **20**
Jerkins, Rodney **31**
Jimmy Jam **13**
Jones, Quincy **8, 30**
Kelly, R. **18, 44, 71**
Lewis, Terry **13**
Liles, Kevin **42**
Marley, Rita **32, 70**
Master P **21**
Mayfield, Curtis **2, 43**
Osborne, Jeffrey **26**
Prince **18, 65**
Queen Latifah **1, 16, 58**
Reid, Antonio "L.A." **28**
Sweat, Keith **19**
Timbaland **32**
Turner, Ike **68**
Vandross, Luther **13, 48, 59**
White, Barry **13, 41**
Whitfield, Norman **73**
Williams, Pharrell **47**
Young, Lee **72**

Recording executives
Avant, Clarence **19**
Busby, Jheryl **3**
Butler, George, Jr. **70**
Combs, Sean "Puffy" **17, 43**
de Passe, Suzanne **25**
Dupri, Jermaine **13, 46**
Gordy, Berry, Jr. **1**
Gotti, Irv **39**
Harrell, Andre **9, 30**
Jackson, George **19**
Jackson, Randy **40**
Jimmy Jam **13**
Jones, Quincy **8, 30**
Knight, Suge **11, 30**
Lewis, Terry **13**
Liles, Kevin **42**
Massenburg, Kedar **23**
Master P **21**

Mayfield, Curtis **2, 43**
Queen Latifah **1, 16, 58**
Reid, Antonio "L.A." **28**
Rhone, Sylvia **2**
Robinson, Smokey **3, 49**
Simmons, Russell **1, 30**

Reform Party
Foster, Ezola **28**

Reggae
Beenie Man **32**
Blondy, Alpha **30**
Cliff, Jimmy **28**
Griffiths, Marcia **29**
Hammond, Lenn **34**
Johnson, Linton Kwesi **37**
Marley, Bob **5**
Marley, Rita **32, 70**
Marley, Ziggy **41**
Mowatt, Judy **38**
Perry, Ruth **19**
Rhoden, Wayne **70**
Shaggy **31**
Sly & Robbie **34**
Tosh, Peter **9**

Republic of New Africa (RNA)
Williams, Robert F. **11**

Republican Party
Allen, Ethel D. **13**
Steele, Michael **38, 73**
Toote, Gloria E. A. **64**

Resource Associates International
Moyo, Karega Kofi **36**
Moyo, Yvette Jackson **36**

Restaurants
Cain, Herman **15**
Daniels-Carter, Valerie **23**
Hawkins, La-Van **17, 54**
James, Charles H., III **62**
Otis, Clarence, Jr. **55**
Rodriguez, Jimmy **47**
Samuelsson, Marcus **53**
Smith, B(arbara) **11**
Thompson, Don **56**
Washington, Regynald G. **44**

Restitution Study Group, Inc.
Farmer-Paellmann, Deadria **43**

Revolutionary Party of Tanzania
See Chama cha Mapinduzi

Revolutionary People's Communication Network
Cleaver, Kathleen Neal **29**

Rheedlen Centers for Children and Families
Canada, Geoffrey **23**

Rhode Island School of Design
Prophet, Nancy Elizabeth **42**

Rhodes scholar
Kennedy, Randall **40**

Rhythm and blues/soul music
Aaliyah **30**
Ace, Johnny **36**

Adams, Johnny **39**
Adams, Oleta **18**
Akon **68**
Amerie **52**
Ashanti **37**
Ashford, Nickolas **21**
Austin, Patti **24**
Ayers, Roy **16**
Badu, Erykah **22**
Bailey, Philip **63**
Baker, Anita **21, 48**
Baker, LaVern **26**
Ballard, Hank **41**
Baylor, Helen **36**
Belle, Regina **1, 51**
Benét, Eric **28**
Berry, Chuck **29**
Beverly, Frankie **25**
Beyoncé **39, 70**
Bivins, Michael **72**
Blige, Mary J. **20, 34, 60**
Brandy **14, 34, 72**
Braxton, Toni **15, 61**
Brooks, Hadda **40**
Brown, Bobby **58**
Brown, Charles **23**
Brown, Clarence Gatemouth **59**
Brown, James **15, 60**
Brown, Nappy **73**
Brown, Oscar, Jr. **53**
Burke, Solomon **31**
Busby, Jheryl **3**
Butler, Jerry **26**
Campbell-Martin, Tisha **8, 42**
Carey, Mariah **32, 53, 69**
Charles, Ray **16, 48**
Ciara **56**
Clinton, George **9**
Cole, Keyshia **63**
Combs, Sean "Puffy" **17, 43**
Cooke, Sam **17**
Cox, Deborah **28**
D'Angelo **27**
David, Craig **31, 53**
Davis, Tyrone **54**
Diddley, Bo **39, 72**
Domino, Fats **20**
Dorsey, Lee **65**
Downing, Will **19**
Dre, Dr. **14, 30**
Dupri, Jermaine **13, 46**
Edmonds, Kenneth "Babyface" **10, 31**
Elliott, Missy **31**
Escobar, Damien **56**
Escobar, Tourie **56**
Evans, Faith **22**
Feemster, Herbert **72**
Foxx, Jamie **15, 48**
Franklin, Aretha **11, 44**
Garrett, Sean **57**
Gaye, Marvin **2**
Gaynor, Gloria **36**
Gibson, Tyrese **27, 62**
Gill, Johnny **51**
Ginuwine **35**
Goapele **55**
Gotti, Irv **39**
Gray, Macy **29**
Green, Al **13, 47**
Hailey, JoJo **22**
Hailey, K-Ci **22**
Hamilton, Anthony **61**

Hammer, M. C. **20**
Harris, Corey **39, 73**
Hart, Alvin Youngblood **61**
Hathaway, Donny **18**
Hathaway, Lalah **57**
Hayes, Isaac **20, 58, 73**
Hendryx, Nona **56**
Henry, Clarence "Frogman" **46**
Hall, Aaron **57**
Hill, Lauryn **20, 53**
Holloway, Brenda **65**
Houston, Cissy **20**
Houston, Whitney **7**
Hyman, Phyllis **19**
India.Arie **34**
Isley, Ronald **25, 56**
Ja Rule **35**
Jackson, Janet **6, 30, 68**
Jackson, Michael **19, 53**
Jackson, Millie **25**
Jaheim **58**
Jamelia **51**
James, Etta **13, 52**
James, Rick **17**
Jarreau, Al **21, 65**
Jean, Wyclef **20**
Jennings, Lyfe **56, 69**
Johnson, Robert **2**
Jones, Donell **29**
Jones, Quincy **8, 30**
Jordan, Montell **23**
Kelly, R. **18, 44, 71**
Kem **47**
Kendricks, Eddie **22**
Keys, Alicia **32, 68**
Knight, Gladys **16, 66**
LaBelle, Patti **13, 30**
Larrieux, Amel **63**
Lattimore, Kenny **35**
Ledisi **73**
Legend, John **67**
Levert, Eddie **70**
Levert, Gerald **22, 59**
Little Richard **15**
Lopes, Lisa "Left Eye" **36**
Luckett, Letoya **61**
Mario **71**
Massenburg, Kedar **23**
Master P **21**
Maxwell **20**
Mayfield, Curtis **2, 43**
McCoo, Marilyn **53**
McKnight, Brian **18, 34**
Miles, Buddy **69**
Monica **21**
Moore, Chante **26**
Moore, Melba **21**
Musiq **37**
Mya **35**
Nash, Johnny **40**
Ndegéocello, Me'Shell **15**
Ne-Yo **65**
Neale, Haydain **52**
Neville, Aaron **21**
Notorious B.I.G. **20**
Otis, Clyde **67**
Parker, Maceo **72**
Pendergrass, Teddy **22**
Preston, Billy **39, 59**
Price, Kelly **23**
Prince **18, 65**
Record, Eugene **60**
Redding, Otis **16**

Reed, A. C. **36**
Richie, Lionel **27, 65**
Rihanna **65**
Riperton, Minnie **32**
Robinson, Smokey **3, 49**
Ross, Diana **8, 27**
Russell, Brenda **52**
Sade **15**
Sample, Joe **51**
Scott, Jill **29**
Scott, "Little" Jimmy **48**
Siji **56**
Simpson, Valerie **21**
Sisqo **30**
Sledge, Percy **39**
Sparks, Jordin **66**
Staples, Mavis **50**
Staples, "Pops" **32**
Staton, Candi **27**
Steinberg, Martha Jean "The
  Queen" **28**
Stone, Angie **31**
Studdard, Ruben **46**
Supremes, The **33**
Sweat, Keith **19**
Tamia **24, 55**
Temptations, The **33**
Terrell, Tammi **32**
Thomas, Irma **29**
Thomas, Rufus **20**
TLC **34**
Tresvant, Ralph **57**
Turner, Ike **68**
Turner, Tina **6, 27**
Usher **23, 56**
Valentino, Bobby **62**
Vandross, Luther **13, 48, 59**
West, Kanye **52**
Watley, Jody **54**
Watts, Reggie **52**
Wells, Mary **28**
White, Barry **13, 41**
Williams, Michelle **73**
Williams, Vanessa L. **4, 17**
Wilson, Cassandra **16**
Wilson, Charlie **31**
Wilson, Mary **28**
Wilson, Nancy **10**
Withers, Bill **61**
Womack, Bobby **60**
Wonder, Stevie **11, 53**

Richmond city government
Marsh, Henry **32**

RNA
See Republic of New Africa

**Robert C. Maynard Institute
for Journalism Education**
Harris, Jay T. **19**
Maynard, Nancy Hicks **73**
Maynard, Robert C. **7**

Roberts Companies, The
Roberts, Mike **57**

Roc-A-Fella Films
Dash, Damon **31**

Roc-A-Fella Records
Dash, Damon **31**
Jay-Z **27, 69**

Roc-A-Wear
Dash, Damon **31**

Rock and Roll Hall of Fame
Ballard, Hank **41**
Bland, Bobby "Blue" **36**
Brown, Charles **23**
Diddley, Bo **39, 72**
Franklin, Aretha **11, 44**
Holland-Dozier-Holland **36**
Hooker, John Lee **30**
Isley, Ronald **25, 56**
Jamerson, James **59**
James, Etta **13, 52**
Johnson, Johnnie **56**
Knight, Gladys **16, 66**
Mayfield, Curtis **2, 43**
Steinberg, Martha Jean "The
  Queen" **28**
Toussaint, Allen **60**
Turner, Ike **68**
Turner, Tina **6, 27**
Wilson, Jackie **60**
Wilson, Mary **28**
Wonder, Stevie **11, 53**

Rock music
Ballard, Hank **41**
Berry, Chuck **29**
Clemons, Clarence **41**
Clinton, George **9**
Diddley, Bo **39, 72**
Domino, Fats **20**
Edwards, Esther Gordy **43**
Glover, Corey **34**
Hendrix, Jimi **10**
Ice-T **6, 31**
Johnson, Johnnie **56**
Kravitz, Lenny **10, 34**
Little Richard **15**
Lymon, Frankie **22**
Mayfield, Curtis **2, 43**
Miles, Buddy **69**
Moore, LeRoi **72**
Preston, Billy **39, 59**
Prince **18, 65**
Reid, Vernon **34**
Run-DMC **31**
Stew **69**
Tait, Michael **57**
Tamar-kali **63**
Tinsley, Boyd **50**
Toussaint, Allen **60**
Turner, Ike **68**
Turner, Tina **6, 27**
will.i.am **64**
Wilson, Jackie **60**

Rockefeller Foundation
Price, Hugh B. **9, 54**

Rockets
Williams, O. S. **13**

Rodeo
Nash, Johnny **40**
Pickett, Bill **11**
Sampson, Charles **13**
Whitfield, Fred **23**

Roman Catholic Church
Akpan, Uwem **70**
Arinze, Francis Cardinal **19**
Aristide, Jean-Bertrand **6, 45**
Clements, George **2**

DeLille, Henriette **30**
Fabre, Shelton **71**
Gantin, Bernardin **70**
Gregory, Wilton D. **37**
Guy, Rosa **5**
Healy, James Augustine **30**
Jones, Alex **64**
Marino, Eugene Antonio **30**
Otunga, Maurice Michael **55**
Rugambwa, Laurean **20**
Senghor, Augustin Diamacoune **66**
Stallings, George A., Jr. **6**

Romance fiction
Bunkley, Anita Richmond **39**
Hill, Donna **32**

Royal Ballet
Jackson, Isaiah **3**

Royalty
Christophe, Henri **9**
Ka Dinizulu, Mcwayizeni **29**
Mswati III **56**
Mutebi, Ronald **25**

RPT
See Togolese People's Rally

Ruff Ryders Records
Eve **29**

Rugby
Mundine, Anthony **56**

Rush Artists Management Co.
Simmons, Russell **1, 30**

Rutgers University
Davis, George **36**
Gibson, Donald Bernard **40**

Rwandan government
Kagame, Paul **54**

Rwandese Patriotic Front
Kagame, Paul **54**

SAA
See Syndicat Agricole Africain

SACC
See South African Council of
  Churches

**Sacramento Kings basketball
team**
Russell, Bill **8**
Webber, Chris **15, 30, 59**

**Sacramento Monarchs basket-
ball team**
Griffith, Yolanda **25**

SADCC
See Southern African Development
  Coordination Conference

Sailing
Pinckney, Bill **42**

**St. Kitts and Nevis govern-
ment**
Douglas, Denzil Llewellyn **53**

St. Louis Blues hockey team
Brathwaite, Fred **35**
Mayers, Jamal **39**

St. Louis Browns baseball team
Brown, Willard **36**
Paige, Satchel **7**

St. Louis Cardinals baseball team
Baylor, Don **6**
Bonds, Bobby **43**
Brock, Lou **18**
Flood, Curt **10**
Gibson, Bob **33**
Lankford, Ray **23**

St. Louis city government
Bosley, Freeman, Jr. **7**
Harmon, Clarence **26**

St. Louis Giants baseball team
Charleston, Oscar **39**

St. Louis Hawks basketball team
See Atlanta Hawks basketball team

St. Louis Rams football team
Bruce, Isaac **26**
Faulk, Marshall **35**
Pace, Orlando **21**

St. Louis Stars baseball team
Bell, James "Cool Papa" **36**

St. Louis' Twenty-Third Street Theater
Leggs, Kingsley **62**

Sainte Beuve Prize
Beti, Mongo **36**

Salvation Army
Gaither, Israel L. **65**

SAMM
See Stopping AIDS Is My Mission

Sammy Davis Jr. National Liver Institute University Hospital
Leevy, Carrol M. **42**

San Antonio Spurs basketball team
Duncan, Tim **20**
Elliott, Sean **26**
Lucas, John **7**
Mohammed, Nazr **64**
Robinson, David **24**

San Diego Chargers football team
Barnes, Ernie **16**
Lofton, James **42**
Tomlinson, LaDainian **65**

San Diego Conquistadors
Chamberlain, Wilt **18, 47**

San Diego Gulls hockey team
O'Ree, Willie **5**

San Diego Hawks hockey team
O'Ree, Willie **5**

San Diego Padres baseball team
Carter, Joe **30**
Gwynn, Tony **18**

McGriff, Fred **24**
Sheffield, Gary **16**
Winfield, Dave **5**

San Francisco 49ers football team
Edwards, Harry **2**
Green, Dennis **5, 45**
Lott, Ronnie **9**
Rice, Jerry **5, 55**
Simpson, O. J. **15**
Washington, Gene **63**

San Francisco Giants baseball team
Baker, Dusty **8, 43, 72**
Bonds, Barry **6, 34, 63**
Bonds, Bobby **43**
Carter, Joe **30**
Mays, Willie **3**
Morgan, Joe Leonard **9**
Robinson, Frank **9**
Strawberry, Darryl **22**

San Francisco Opera
Mitchell, Leona **42**

San Francisco public schools
Coleman, William F., III **61**

Sankofa Film and Video
Blackwood, Maureen **37**
Julien, Isaac **3**

Sankofa Video and Bookstore
Gerima, Haile **38**

Saturday Night Live
Meadows, Tim **30**
Morgan, Tracy **61**
Morris, Garrett **31**
Murphy, Eddie **4, 20, 61**
Rock, Chris **3, 22, 66**
Rudolph, Maya **46**
Thompson, Kenan **52**

Savoy Ballroom
Johnson, Buddy **36**

Saxophone
Adderley, Julian "Cannonball" **30**
Albright, Gerald **23**
Bechet, Sidney **18**
Clemons, Clarence **41**
Coltrane, John **19**
Coltrane, Ravi **71**
Golson, Benny **37**
Gordon, Dexter **25**
Griffin, Johnny **71**
Hawkins, Coleman **9**
Jacquet, Illinois **49**
Kay, Ulyssess **37**
Kenyatta, Robin **54**
Moore, LeRoi **72**
Parker, Charlie **20**
Parker, Maceo **72**
Redman, Joshua **30**
Rollins, Sonny **37**
Sanders, Pharoah **64**
Washington, Grover, Jr. **17, 44**
Waters, Benny **26**
Whalum, Kirk **37, 64**
York, Vincent **40**

Young, Lester **37**

Schomburg Center for Research in Black Culture
Andrews, Bert **13**
Dodson, Howard, Jr. **7, 52**
Hutson, Jean Blackwell **16**
Morrison, Sam **50**
Reddick, Lawrence Dunbar **20**
Schomburg, Arthur Alfonso **9**

School desegregation
Chestnut, J. L., Jr. **73**
Fortune, T. Thomas **6**
Hamer, Fannie Lou **6**
Hobson, Julius W. **44**

Science fiction
Barnes, Steven **54**
Bell, Derrick **6**
Butler, Octavia **8, 43, 58**
Delany, Samuel R., Jr. **9**

SCLC
See Southern Christian Leadership Conference

Score One for Kids
Cherry, Deron **40**

Scotland Yard
Griffin, Bessie Blout **43**

Screen Actors Guild
Dixon, Ivan **69**
Fields, Kim **36**
Howard, Sherri **36**
Lewis, Emmanuel **36**
Poitier, Sidney **11, 36**

Screenplay writing
Akil, Mara Brock **60**
Brown, Cecil M. **46**
Campbell-Martin, Tisha **8, 42**
Chong, Rae Dawn **62**
Clack, Zoanne **73**
Davis, Thulani **61**
Elder, Lonne, III **38**
Fisher, Antwone **40**
Greaves, William **38**
Ice Cube **8, 30, 60**
Jones, Orlando **30**
Martin, Darnell **43**
Nissel, Angela **42**
Prince-Bythewood, Gina **31**
Rhimes, Shonda Lynn **67**
Ridley, John **69**
Robinson, Matt **69**
Singleton, John **2, 30**
Wesley, Richard **73**

Sculpture
Allen, Tina **22**
Amos, Emma **63**
Bailey, Radcliffe **19**
Barthe, Richmond **15**
Biggers, John **20, 33**
Biggers, Sanford **62**
Brown, Donald **19**
Burke, Selma **16**
Catlett, Elizabeth **2**
Chase-Riboud, Barbara **20, 46**
Cortor, Eldzier **42**
Dwight, Edward **65**
Edwards, Melvin **22**
Fuller, Meta Vaux Warrick **27**

Guyton, Tyree **9**
Hammons, David **69**
Hathaway, Isaac Scott **33**
Hunt, Richard **6**
Lewis, Edmonia **10**
Lewis, Samella **25**
Manley, Edna **26**
Marshall, Kerry James **59**
McCullough, Geraldine **58**
McGee, Charles **10**
Moody, Ronald **30**
Neals, Otto **73**
Perkins, Marion **38**
Prophet, Nancy Elizabeth **42**
Puryear, Martin **42**
Ringgold, Faith **4**
Saar, Alison **16**
Savage, Augusta **12**
Scott, John T. **65**
Shabazz, Attallah **6**
Simmons, Gary **58**
Stout, Renee **63**
Washington, James, Jr. **38**

Sean John clothing line
Combs, Sean "Puffy" **17, 43**

Seattle city government
Rice, Norm **8**

Seattle Mariners baseball team
Griffey, Ken, Jr. **12, 73**

Seattle Supersonics basketball team
Bickerstaff, Bernie **21**
Lucas, John **7**
Russell, Bill **8**
Silas, Paul **24**
Wilkens, Lenny **11**

Second District Education and Policy Foundation
Burke, Yvonne Braithwaite **42**

Second Republic (Nigeria)
Obasanjo, Olusegun **5**

Seismology
Person, Waverly **9, 51**

Selma, Alabama, city government
Perkins, James, Jr. **55**

Senate Confirmation Hearings
Ogletree, Charles, Jr. **12, 47**

Senate Judiciary Subcommittee on the Consitution
Hageman, Hans **36**

Senegalese government
Senghor, Léopold Sédar **66**
Wade, Abdoulaye **66**

Sesame Street
Byrd, Eugene **64**
Clash, Kevin **14**
Glover, Savion **14**
Long, Loretta **58**
Orman, Roscoe **55**

Robinson, Matt **69**

Sexual harassment
Gomez-Preston, Cheryl **9**
Hill, Anita **5, 65**
Thomas, Clarence **2, 39, 65**

Share
Auguste, Arnold A. **47**

Sheila Bridges Design Inc.
Bridges, Sheila **36**

Shell Oil Company
Mays, Leslie A. **41**

Shrine of the Black Madonna
Agyeman, Jaramogi Abebe **10, 63**

Sickle cell anemia
Edwards, Willarda V. **59**
Pace, Betty **59**
Satcher, David **7, 57**

Sierra Leone People's Party (SLPP)
Kabbah, Ahmad Tejan **23**

Silicon Graphics Incorporated
Coleman, Ken **57**
Hannah, Marc **10**

Siméus Foods International
Siméus, Dumas M. **25**

Skateboarding
Williams, Stevie **71**

Sketches
Crite, Alan Rohan **29**
Sallee, Charles **38**

Skiing
Horton, Andre **33**
Horton, Suki **33**

Skillman Foundation
Goss, Carol A. **55**

Slavery
Asante, Molefi Kete **3**
Bennett, Lerone, Jr. **5**
Bibb, Henry and Mary **54**
Blackshear, Leonard **52**
Blassingame, John Wesley **40**
Chase-Riboud, Barbara **20, 46**
Cooper, Anna Julia **20**
Douglas, Aaron **7**
Du Bois, W. E. B. **3**
Dunbar, Paul Laurence **8**
Farmer-Paellmann, Deadria **43**
Gaines, Ernest J. **7**
Haley, Alex **4**
Harper, Frances Ellen Watkins **11**
Huggins, Nathan Irvin **52**
Johnson, Charles **1**
Jones, Edward P. **43, 67**
Morrison, Toni **2, 15**
Muhammad, Elijah **4**
Patterson, Orlando **4**
Pleasant, Mary Ellen **9**
Stephens, Charlotte Andrews **14**
Stewart, Maria W. Miller **19**
Tancil, Gladys Quander **59**
Taylor, Susie King **13**
Tubman, Harriet **9**

X, Malcolm **1**

Small Business Association Hall of Fame
Steward, David L. **36**

Smart Books
Pinkett Smith, Jada **10, 41**

Smith College
Mayhew, Richard **39**
Simmons, Ruth **13, 38**

SNCC
See Student Nonviolent Coordinating Committee

Soccer
Adu, Freddy **67**
Anderson, Viv **58**
Barnes, John **53**
Beasley, Jamar **29**
Crooks, Garth **53**
dos Santos, Manuel Francisco **65**
Eto'o, Samuel **73**
Henry, Thierry **66**
Jones, Cobi N'Gai **18**
Kanouté, Fred **68**
Mello, Breno **73**
Milla, Roger **2**
Nakhid, David **25**
Onyewu, Oguchi **60**
Pelé **7**
Regis, Cyrille **51**
Ronaldinho **69**
Scurry, Briana **27**
Weah, George **58**

Social disorganization theory
Frazier, E. Franklin **10**

Social science
Berry, Mary Frances **7**
Black, Albert **51**
Bobo, Lawrence **60**
Bunche, Ralph J. **5**
Cayton, Horace **26**
Clark, Kenneth B. **5, 52**
Cobbs, Price M. **9**
Collins, Patricia Hill **67**
Frazier, E. Franklin **10**
George, Zelma Watson **42**
Hare, Nathan **44**
Harris, Eddy L. **18**
Haynes, George Edmund **8**
Ladner, Joyce A. **42**
Lawrence-Lightfoot, Sara **10**
Marable, Manning **10**
Steele, Claude Mason **13**
Williams, David Rudyard **50**
Woodson, Robert L. **10**

Social Service Auxiliary
Mossell, Gertrude Bustill **40**

Social work
Auguste, Rose-Anne **13**
Berry, Bertice **8, 55**
Berrysmith, Don Reginald **49**
Brown, Cora **33**
Canada, Geoffrey **23**
Colston, Hal **72**
Dunham, Katherine **4, 59**
Fields, C. Virginia **25**
Finner-Williams, Paris Michele **62**
Hale, Clara **16**

Hale, Lorraine **8**
Harris, Alice **7**
Haynes, George Edmund **8**
Jackson, Judith D. **57**
Jackson, Mae **57**
King, Barbara **22**
Lewis, Thomas **19**
Little, Robert L. **2**
Robinson, Rachel **16**
Sears, Stephanie **53**
Smith, Damu **54**
Vaughn, Viola **70**
Waddles, Charleszetta "Mother" **10, 49**
Walker, Bernita Ruth **53**
Wallace, Joaquin **49**
Wells, Henrietta Bell **69**
White-Hammond, Gloria **61**
Williams, Fannie Barrier **27**
Thrower, Willie **35**
Young, Whitney M., Jr. **4**

Socialist Party of Senegal
Diouf, Abdou **3**

Soft Sheen Products
Gardner, Edward G. **45**

Soledad Brothers
Jackson, George **14**

Soul City, NC
McKissick, Floyd B. **3**

Soul Train
Baylor, Helen **36**
Cornelius, Don **4**
D'Angelo **27**
Lil' Kim **28**
Winans, CeCe **14, 43**

Source music awards
Nelly **32**

South African Communist Party
Hani, Chris **6**
Mhlaba, Raymond **55**

South African Council of Churches (SACC)
Tutu, Desmond Mpilo **6, 44**

South African Defence Force (SADF)
Nujoma, Samuel **10**

South African government
Mhlaba, Raymond **55**
Sisulu, Walter **47**
Zuma, Nkosazana Dlamini **34**

South African literature
Abrahams, Peter **39**
Brutus, Dennis **38**
Head, Bessie **28**
Mathabane, Mark **5**
Mofolo, Thomas **37**
Mphalele, Es'kia **40**

South African Students' Organization
Biko, Steven **4**

South Carolina state government
Cardozo, Francis L. **33**

South West African People's Organization (SWAPO)
Nujoma, Samuel **10**

Southeastern University
Jarvis, Charlene Drew **21**

Southern African Development Community (SADC)
Mbuende, Kaire **12**

Southern African Development Coordination Conference (SADCC)
Masire, Quett **5**
Numjoma, Samuel **10**

Southern African Project
McDougall, Gay J. **11, 43**

Southern Christian Leadership Conference (SCLC)
Abernathy, Ralph **1**
Angelou, Maya **1, 15**
Baker, Ella **5**
Brooks, Tyrone **59**
Chavis, Benjamin **6**
Dee, Ruby **8, 50, 68**
Fauntroy, Walter E. **11**
Hooks, Benjamin L. **2**
Jackson, Jesse **1, 27, 72**
Jones, William A., Jr. **61**
King, Martin Luther, Jr. **1**
King, Martin Luther, III **20**
Lowery, Joseph **2**
Moses, Robert Parris **11**
Moss, Otis, Jr. **72**
Nash, Diane **72**
Rustin, Bayard **4**
Shuttlesworth, Fred **47**
Williams, Hosea Lorenzo **15, 31**
Young, Andrew **3, 48**

Southern Syncopated Orchestra
Cook, Will Marion **40**

Space shuttle
Anderson, Michael **40**
Bluford, Guy **2, 35**
Bolden, Charles F., Jr. **7**
Gregory, Frederick **8, 51**
Jemison, Mae C. **1, 35**
McNair, Ronald **3, 58**
Wilson, Stephanie **72**

Special Olympics
Clairborne, Loretta **34**

Spectroscopy
Quarterman, Lloyd Albert **4**

Speedskating
Davis, Shani **58**

Spelman College
Cobb, William Jelani **59**
Cole, Johnnetta B. **5, 43**
Falconer, Etta Zuber **59**
Price, Glenda **22**
Simmons, Ruth **13, 38**
Tatum, Beverly Daniel **42**
Wade-Gayles, Gloria Jean **41**

Sphinx Organization
Dworkin, Aaron P. **52**

Spingarn medal
Aaron, Hank **5**
Ailey, Alvin **8**
Anderson, Marian **2, 33**
Angelou, Maya **1, 15**
Bates, Daisy **13**
Bethune, Mary McLeod **4**
Bradley, Thomas **2, 20**
Brooke, Edward **8**
Bunche, Ralph J. **5**
Carver, George Washington **4**
Chesnutt, Charles **29**
Clark, Kenneth B. **5, 52**
Cosby, Bill **7, 26, 59**
Davis, Sammy, Jr. **18**
Drew, Charles Richard **7**
Du Bois, W. E. B. **3**
Ellington, Duke **5**
Evers, Medgar **3**
Franklin, John Hope **5**
Grimké, Archibald H. **9**
Haley, Alex **4**
Hastie, William H. **8**
Hayes, Roland **4**
Height, Dorothy I. **2, 23**
Higginbotham, A. Leon, Jr. **13, 25**
Hinton, William Augustus **8**
Hooks, Benjamin L. **2**
Horne, Lena **5**
Houston, Charles Hamilton **4**
Hughes, Langston **4**
Jackson, Jesse **1, 27, 72**
Johnson, James Weldon **5**
Johnson, John H. **3, 54**
Jordan, Barbara **4**
Julian, Percy Lavon **6**
Just, Ernest Everett **3**
Keith, Damon **16**
King, Martin Luther, Jr. **1**
Lawless, Theodore K. **8**
Lawrence, Jacob **4**
Logan, Rayford **40**
Marshall, Thurgood **1, 44**
Mays, Benjamin E. **7**
Moore, Harry T. **29**
Parks, Gordon **1, 35, 58**
Parks, Rosa **1, 35, 56**
Powell, Colin **1, 28**
Price, Leontyne **1**
Randolph, A. Philip **3**
Robeson, Paul **2**
Robinson, Jackie **6**
Staupers, Mabel K. **7**
Sullivan, Leon H. **3, 30**
Weaver, Robert C. **8, 46**
White, Walter F. **4**
Wilder, L. Douglas **3, 48**
Wilkins, Roy **4**
Williams, Paul R. **9**
Woodson, Carter G. **2**
Wright, Louis Tompkins **4**
Wright, Richard **5**
Young, Andrew **3, 48**
Young, Coleman **1, 20**

Spiral Group
Mayhew, Richard **39**

Spirituals
Anderson, Marian **2, 33**
Carr, Kurt **56**
Hayes, Roland **4**
Jackson, Mahalia **5**

Joyner, Matilda Sissieretta **15**
Norman, Jessye **5**
Reese, Della **6, 20**
Robeson, Paul **2**
Williams, Denise **40**

Sports administration
Fuller, Vivian **33**
Kerry, Leon G. **46**
Lee, Bertram M., Sr. **46**
Mills, Steve **47**
Phillips, Teresa L. **42**
Randolph, Willie **53**

Sports agent
Holland, Kimberly N. **62**

Sports psychology
Edwards, Harry **2**

Stanford University
Bobo, Lawrence **60**
Rice, Condoleezza **3, 28, 72**
Washington, Gene **63**
Willingham, Tyrone **43**

Starcom
McCann, Renetta **44**

State University of New York System
Ballard, Allen Butler, Jr. **40**
Baraka, Amiri **1, 38**
Wharton, Clifton R., Jr. **7**

Stay Fit Plus
Richardson, Donna **39**

Stellar Awards
Baylor, Helen **36**

Stonewall 25
Norman, Pat **10**

Stop the Violence Movement
KRS-One **34**
MC Lyte **34**

Stopping AIDS Is My Mission (SAMM)
Cargill, Victoria A. **43**

Storytelling
Baker, Augusta **38**
Bennett, Louise **69**

Structural Readjustment Program
Babangida, Ibrahim **4**

Student Nonviolent Coordinating Committee (SNCC)
Al-Amin, Jamil Abdullah **6**
Anderson, William G(ilchrist) **57**
Baker, Ella **5**
Barry, Marion S. **7, 44**
Blackwell, Unita **17**
Bond, Julian **2, 35**
Carmichael, Stokely **5, 26**
Clark, Septima **7**
Crouch, Stanley **11**
Davis, Angela **5**
Forman, James **7, 51**
Hamer, Fannie Lou **6**
Holland, Endesha Ida Mae **3, 57**
Lester, Julius **9**
Lewis, John **2, 46**

Moses, Robert Parris **11**
Nash, Diane **72**
Norton, Eleanor Holmes **7**
Poussaint, Alvin F. **5, 67**
Reagon, Bernice Johnson **7**
Touré, Askia (Muhammad Abu Bakr el) **47**

Subway rescue
Autrey, Wesley **68**

Sugarfoots
El Wilson, Barbara **35**

Sun Microsystems
Tademy, Lalita **36**

Sundance Film Festival
Harris, Leslie **6**

Sunni Muslim
Muhammed, W. Deen **27**

Sunny Alade Records
Ade, King Sunny **41**

Supreme Court
See U.S. Supreme Court

Supreme Court of Haiti
Pascal-Trouillot, Ertha **3**

Surfing
Corley, Tony **62**

Surgeon General of the State of Michigan
Wisdom, Kimberlydawn **57**

Surrealism
Ellison, Ralph **7**
Lee-Smith, Hughie **5, 22**

SWAPO
See South West African People's Organization

Swaziland government
Mswati III **56**

Sweet Honey in the Rock
Reagon, Bernice Johnson **7**

Swimming
Jones, Cullen **73**

Sylvia's Restaurant
Washington, Regynald G. **44**
Woods, Sylvia **34**

Syndicat Agricole Africain (SAA)
Houphouët-Boigny, Félix **4, 64**

Talk Soup
Tyler, Aisha N. **36**

Talladega College
Archie-Hudson, Marguerite **44**

Tampa Bay Buccaneers football team
Barber, Ronde **41**
Brooks, Derrick **43**
Dungy, Tony **17, 42, 59**
Sapp, Warren **38**

Williams, Doug **22**

Tanga Consultative Congress (Tanzania)
Nujoma, Samuel **10**

Tanganyikan African National Union (TANU)
Kikwete, Jakaya Mrisho **73**
Nyerere, Julius **5**

TANU
See Tanganyikan African National Union

Tanzanian African National Union (TANU)
See Tanganyikan African National Union

Tap dancing
Atkins, Cholly **40**
Bates, Peg Leg **14**
Glover, Savion **14**
Hines, Gregory **1, 42**
Robinson, LaVaughn **69**
Sims, Howard "Sandman" **48**
Slyde, Jimmy **70**
Walker, Dianne **57**

TBS
See Turner Broadcasting System

Teacher of the Year Award
Draper, Sharon Mills **16, 43**
Oliver, Kimberly **60**

Teachers Insurance and Annuity Association and the College Retirement Equities Fund (TIAA-CREF)
Wharton, Clifton R., Jr. **7**

Teaching
Adams-Ender, Clara **40**
Alexander, Margaret Walker **22**
Amadi, Elechi **40**
Archie-Hudson, Marguerite **44**
Aubert, Alvin **41**
Baiocchi, Regina Harris **41**
Ballard, Allen Butler, Jr. **40**
Bibb, Henry and Mary **54**
Blassingame, John Wesley **40**
Branch, William Blackwell **39**
Brawley, Benjamin **44**
Brown, Uzee **42**
Brown, Willa **40**
Bryan, Ashley F. **41**
Campbell, Mary Schmidt **43**
Cardozo, Francis L. **33**
Carruthers, George R. **40**
Carter, Joye Maureen **41**
Chenault, John **40**
Cheney-Coker, Syl **43**
Clarke, John Henrik **20**
Clemmons, Reginal G. **41**
Cobb, Jewel Plummer **42**
Cobb, W. Montague **39**
Cole, Johnnetta B. **5, 43**
Colescott, Robert **69**
Collins, Patricia Hill **67**
Cook, Mercer **40**
Cooper Cafritz, Peggy **43**
Cortez, Jayne **43**
Cortor, Eldzier **42**
Cotter, Joseph Seamon, Sr. **40**

Davis, Arthur P. 41
Davis, Gary 41
De Veaux, Alexis 44
Dennard, Brazeal 37
Draper, Sharon Mills 16, 43
Drummond, William J. 40
Dumas, Henry 41
Dunnigan, Alice Allison 41
Dymally, Mervyn 42
Early, Gerald 15
Falconer, Etta Zuber 59
Feelings, Muriel 44
Figueroa, John J. 40
Fletcher, Bill, Jr. 41
Ford, Nick Aaron 44
Forrest, Leon 44
Fuller, A. Oveta 43
Fuller, Arthur 27
Fuller, Howard L. 37
Gates, Sylvester James, Jr. 15
Gayle, Addison, Jr. 41
George, Zelma Watson 42
Gibson, Donald Bernard 40
Gill, Gerald 69
Hall, Arthur 39
Hammonds, Evelynn 69
Harding, Vincent 67
Hare, Nathan 44
Harris, Barry 68
Harvey, William R. 42
Henries, A. Doris Banks 44
Hill, Errol 40
Hill, Leslie Pinckney 44
Horne, Frank 44
Humphries, Frederick 20
Imes, Elmer Samuel 39
Jackson, Fred James 25
Jarrett, Vernon D. 42
Jarvis, Erich 67
Kennedy, Randall 40
Ladner, Joyce A. 42
Leevy, Carrol M. 42
Lewis, Norman 39
Lindsey, Tommie 51
Logan, Rayford W. 40
Maathai, Wangari 43
McCullough, Geraldine 58
Mitchell, Parren J. 42, 66
Moore, Harry T. 29
Mphalele, Es'kia 40
Naylor, Gloria 10, 42
Norman, Maidie 20
Oliver, Kimberly 60
Owens, Helen 48
Palmer, Everard 37
Patterson, Mary Jane 54
Peters, Margaret and Matilda 43
Player, Willa B. 43
Prophet, Nancy Elizabeth 42
Puryear, Martin 42
Ray, Charlotte E. 60
Redmond, Eugene 23
Reid, Senghor 55
Ross-Lee, Barbara 67
Simpson-Hoffman, N'kenge 52
Smith, Anna Deavere 6, 44
Smith, John L. 22
Tatum, Beverly Daniel 42
Tillis, Frederick 40
Tutu, Nontombi Naomi 57
Tyson, Andre 40
Wambugu, Florence 42
Watson, Diane 41

Wells, Henrietta Bell 69
Wesley, Richard 73
Wilkens, J. Ernest, Jr. 43
Yancy, Dorothy Cowser 42
Yarbrough, Camille 40
York, Vincent 40

Techno music
Atkins, Juan 50
Craig, Carl 31, 71
May, Derrick 41

Technology Access Foundation
Millines Dziko, Trish 28

TEF
See Theological Education Fund

Telecommunications
Gordon, Bruce S. 41, 53
Ibrahim, Mo 67
Irvin, Vernon 65
Wilkins, Ray 47

Telemat Incorporated
Bynoe, Peter C. B. 40
Bynum, Juanita 31, 71

Television
Akil, Mara Brock 60
Alexander, Khandi 43
Anderson, Eddie "Rochester" 30
Arkadie, Kevin 17
Arnold, Tichina 63
Banks, Tyra 11, 50
Barclay, Paris 37
Barrino, Fantasia 53
Beach, Michael 26
Bentley, Lamont 53
Blacque, Taurean 58
Blake, Asha 26
Bonet, Lisa 58
Bowser, Yvette Lee 17
Brady, Wayne 32, 71
Branch, William Blackwell 39
Bridges, Todd 37
Brooks, Golden 62
Brooks, Hadda 40
Brooks, Mehcad 62
Brown, Bobby 58
Brown, Joe 29
Brown, Vivian 27
Burnett, Charles 16, 68
Carson, Lisa Nicole 21
Carter, Nell 39
Cash, Rosalind 28
Cedric the Entertainer 29, 60
Cheadle, Don 19, 52
Clack, Zoanne 73
Coleman, Gary 35
Corbi, Lana 42
Cosby, Bill 7, 26, 59
Creagh, Milton 27
Curtis-Hall, Vondie 17
Davis, Viola 34
de Passe, Suzanne 25
Deezer D 53
Diggs, Taye 25, 63
Dourdan, Gary 37
Dungey, Merrin 62
Earthquake 55
Elba, Idris 49
Elder, Larry 25
Ephriam, Mablean 29

Eubanks, Kevin 15
Evans, Harry 25
Faison, Donald 50
Falana, Lola 42
Fields, Kim 36
Flavor Flav 67
Fox, Rick 27
Frazier, Kevin 58
Freeman, Yvette 27
Givens, Robin 4, 25, 58
Gray, Willie 46
Greely, M. Gasby 27
Greene, Petey 65
Grier, David Alan 28
Hall, Arsenio 58
Hardison, Kadeem 22
Harewood, David 52
Hatchett, Glenda 32
Haynes, Trudy 44
Haysbert, Dennis 42
Hemsley, Sherman 19
Henriques, Julian 37
Hill, Lauryn 20, 53
Houston, Whitney 7, 28
Hughley, D. L. 23
Hyman, Earle 25
Jackson, George 19
Jackson, Randy 40
Jackson, Tom 70
Jarrett, Vernon D. 42
Joe, Yolanda 21
Johnson, Rodney Van 28
Jones, Bobby 20
Kodjoe, Boris 34
Lathan, Sanaa 27
Lesure, James 64
Lewis, Emmanuel 36
Long, Loretta 58
Lumbly, Carl 47
Mabuza-Suttle, Felicia 43
Mac, Bernie 29, 61, 72
Mahorn, Rick 60
Manigault-Stallworth, Omarosa 69
Marsalis, Branford 34
Martin, Helen 31
Martin, Jesse L. 31
Mathis, Greg 26
McCrary Anthony, Crystal 70
McFarland, Roland 49
McGlowan, Angela 64
McKenzie, Vashti M. 29
McKinney, Nina Mae 40
Meadows, Tim 30
Mercado-Valdes, Frank 43
Merkerson, S. Epatha 47
Michele, Michael 31
Mitchell, Brian Stokes 21
Mitchell, Russ 21, 73
Moss, Carlton 16
Nash, Johnny 40
Nash, Niecy 66
Neal, Elise 29
Neville, Arthel 53
Nissel, Angela 42
Norman, Christina 47
Orman, Roscoe 55
Palmer, Keke 68
Parker, Nicole Ari 52
Perry, Tyler 40, 54
Phifer, Mekhi 25
Pickens, James, Jr. 59
Pitts, Byron 71
Pratt, Kyla 57

Premice, Josephine 41
Price, Frederick K. C. 21
Quarles, Norma 25
Ray, Gene Anthony 47
Reddick, Lance 52
Reynolds, Star Jones 10, 27, 61
Rhimes, Shonda Lynn 67
Richards, Beah 30
Richardson, Salli 68
Ridley, John 69
Roberts, Deborah 35
Robinson, Shaun 36
Rock, Chris 3, 22, 66
Rodrigues, Percy 68
Roker, Al 12, 49
Roker, Roxie 68
Rollins, Howard E., Jr. 17
Russell, Nipsey 66
St. Patrick, Mathew 48
Salters, Lisa 71
Sanford, Isabel 53
Shepherd, Sherri 55
Simmons, Henry 55
Smiley, Tavis 20, 68
Snipes, Wesley 3, 24, 67
Sykes, Wanda 48
Taylor, Jason 70
Taylor, Karin 34
Taylor, Regina 9, 46
Thigpen, Lynne 17, 41
Thompson, Kenan 52
Torres, Gina 52
Tyler, Aisha N. 36
Union, Gabrielle 31
Usher 23, 56
Vaughn, Countess 53
Wainwright, Joscelyn 46
Warner, Malcolm-Jamal 22, 36
Warren, Michael 27
Watson, Carlos 50
Wayans, Damon 8, 41
Wayans, Marlon 29
Wayans, Shawn 29
Whitaker, Forest 2, 49, 67
Williams, Armstrong 29
Williams, Clarence, III 26
Williams, Serena 20, 41, 73
Williams, Vanessa A. 32, 66
Williams, Wendy 62
Williamson, Mykelti 22
Wilson, Chandra 57
Wilson, Dorien 55

Temple of Hip-Hop
KRS-One 34

Tennessee state government
Ford, Harold E(ugene) 42

Tennessee State University
Phillips, Teresa L. 42

Tennessee Titans football team
McNair, Steve 22, 47

Tennis
Ashe, Arthur 1, 18
Blake, James 43
Garrison, Zina 2
Gibson, Althea 8, 43
Jackson, Jamea 64
Lucas, John 7
McNeil, Lori 1

Noah, Yannick **4, 60**
Peters, Margaret and Matilda **43**
Rubin, Chanda **37**
Washington, MaliVai **8**
Williams, Samm-Art **21**
Williams, Serena **20, 41, 73**
Williams, Venus **17, 34, 62**
Young, Donald, Jr. **57**

Texas House of Representatives
Delco, Wilhemina **33**
Johnson, Eddie Bernice **8**

Texas Rangers baseball team
Bonds, Bobby **43**
Cottrell, Comer **11**

Texas State Senate
Johnson, Eddie Bernice **8**
Jordan, Barbara **4**

Theatre Owner's Booking Association (TOBA)
Austin, Lovie **40**
Cox, Ida **42**

Theatrical direction
Hall, Juanita **62**
Hayes, Teddy **40**

Theatrical production
Hayes, Teddy **40**
Perry, Tyler **40, 54**

Thelonius Monk Institute of Jazz Performance
Blanchard, Terence **43**

Theological Education Fund (TEF)
Gordon, Pamela **17**
Tutu, Desmond Mpilo **6, 44**

Theology
Franklin, Robert M. **13**
Harding, Vincent **67**
Wright, Jeremiah A., Jr. **45, 69**

They All Played Baseball Foundation
Johnson, Mamie "Peanut" **40**

Third World Press
Madhubuti, Haki R. **7**
Moyo, Karega Kofi **36**

Threads 4 Life
Jones, Carl **7**
Kani, Karl **10**
Walker, T. J. **7**

Three Fifths Productions
Marsalis, Delfeayo **41**

TIAA-CREF
See Teachers Insurance and Annuity Association and the College Retirement Equities Fund

Tiger Woods Foundation
Woods, Tiger **14, 31**

Time-Warner Inc.
Ames, Wilmer **27**
Parsons, Richard Dean **11, 33**

TLC Beatrice International Holdings, Inc.
Lewis, Reginald F. **6**

TLC Group L.P.
Lewis, Reginald F. **6**

TOBA
See Theatre Owner's Booking Association

Today show
Gumbel, Bryant **14**

Togolese Army
Eyadéma, Gnassingbé **7, 52**

Togolese People's Rally (RPT)
Eyadéma, Gnassingbé **7, 52**
Gnassingbé, Faure **67**

Toledo city government
Bell, Michael **40**

Toledo Civic Hall of Fame
Stewart, Ella **39**

The Tonight Show
Eubanks, Kevin **15**

Tony awards
Allen, Debbie **13, 42**
Belafonte, Harry **4, 65**
Carroll, Diahann **9**
Carter, Nell **39**
Clarke, Hope **14**
Davis, Viola **34**
Faison, George **16**
Falana, Lola **42**
Fishburne, Laurence **4, 22, 70**
Hall, Juanita **62**
Horne, Lena **5**
Hyman, Phyllis **19**
Jones, James Earl **3, 49**
McDonald, Audra **20, 62**
Moore, Melba **21**
Premice, Josephine **41**
Richards, Lloyd **2**
Rose, Anika Noni **70**
Thigpen, Lynne **17, 41**
Uggams, Leslie **23**
Vereen, Ben **4**
Wilson, August **7, 33, 55**
Wolfe, George C. **6, 43**

Toronto Blue Jays baseball team
Carter, Joe **30**
Gaston, Cito **71**
McGriff, Fred **24**
Winfield, Dave **5**

Toronto Raptors basketball team
Carter, Butch **27**
Carter, Vince **26**
Olajuwon, Hakeem **2, 72**
Thomas, Isiah **7, 26, 65**

Tourism
Edmunds, Gladys **48**
Roker, Al **12, 49**

Track and field
Ashford, Evelyn **63**
Beamon, Bob **30**
Bolt, Usain **73**

Christie, Linford **8**
Clay, Bryan Ezra **57**
Devers, Gail **7**
Dibaba, Tirunesh **73**
Felix, Allyson **48**
Freeman, Cathy **29**
Gebrselassie, Haile **70**
Greene, Maurice **27**
Griffith-Joyner, Florence **28**
Harrison, Alvin **28**
Harrison, Calvin **28**
Holmes, Kelly **47**
Jacobs, Regina **38**
Johnson, Michael **13**
Johnson, Rodney Van **28**
Jones, Lou **64**
Jones, Marion **21, 66**
Joyner-Kersee, Jackie **5**
Keflezighi, Meb **49**
Lewis, Carl **4**
Metcalfe, Ralph **26**
Montgomery, Tim **41**
Moses, Edwin **8**
Mutola, Maria **12**
Owens, Jesse **2**
Pollard, Fritz **53**
Powell, Mike **7**
Quirot, Ana **13**
Richards, Sanya **66**
Rudolph, Wilma **4**
Thugwane, Josia **21**
White, Willye **67**
Whitfield, Mal **60**
Williams, Lauryn **58**
Woodruff, John **68**

TransAfrica Forum, Inc.
Fletcher, Bill, Jr. **41**
Robinson, Randall **7, 46**

Transition
Soyinka, Wole **4**

Transitional Committee for National Recovery (Guinea; CTRN)
Conté, Lansana **7**

Transplant surgery
Callender, Clive O. **3**
Kountz, Samuel L. **10**

Transport and General Workers' Union
Morris, William "Bill" **51**

Trans-Urban News Service
Cooper, Andrew W. **36**

"Trial of the Century"
Cochran, Johnnie **11, 39, 52**
Darden, Christopher **13**
Simpson, O. J. **15**

Trombone
Marsalis, Delfeayo **41**

Trumpet
Adderley, Nat **29**
Armstrong, Louis **2**
Blanchard, Terence **43**
Dara, Olu **35**
Davis, Miles **4**
Eldridge, Roy **37**
Ellison, Ralph **7**

Farmer, Art **38**
Gillespie, Dizzy **1**
Jones, Jonah **39**
Jones, Thad **68**
Smith, Cladys "Jabbo" **32**
Terry, Clark **39**
Wilson, Gerald **49**

Tulane University
Mason, Ronald **27**

Turner Broadcasting System (TBS)
Clayton, Xernona **3, 45**

Tuskegee Airmen
Brown, Willa **40**
Davis, Benjamin O., Jr. **2, 43**
James, Daniel, Jr. **16**
Patterson, Frederick Douglass **12**

Tuskegee Experiment Station
Carver, George Washington **4**

Tuskegee Institute School of Music
Dawson, William Levi **39**

Tuskegee University
Harvey, William R. **42**
Payton, Benjamin F. **23**

TV One
Ligging, Alfred, III **43**

UAW
See United Auto Workers

UCC
See United Church of Christ

UFBL
See Universal Foundation for Better Living

UGA
See United Golf Association

Ugandan government
Amin, Idi **42**
Obote, Milton **63**

Ultraviolet camera/spectrograph (UVC)
Carruthers, George R. **40**

Umkhonto we Sizwe
Hani, Chris **6**
Mandela, Nelson **1, 14**
Zuma, Jacob **33**

UN
See United Nations

UNCF
See United Negro College Fund

Uncle Nonamé Cookie Company
Amos, Wally **9**

Underground Railroad
Blockson, Charles L. **42**
Cohen, Anthony **15**
DeBaptiste, George **32**

Unemployment and Poverty Action Committee
Forman, James **7, 51**

UNESCO
See United Nations Educational, Scientific, and Cultural Organization

UNESCO Medals
Dadié, Bernard 34

UNIA
See Universal Negro Improvement Association

UNICEF
See United Nations Children's Fund

Unions
Brown, Lloyd Louis 42
Clay, William Lacy 8
Crockett, George W., Jr. 10, 64
Europe, James Reese 10
Farmer, James 2, 64
Fletcher, Bill, Jr. 41
Hilliard, David 7
Holt Baker, Arlene 73
Lucy, William 50
Morris, William "Bill" 51
Ramaphosa, Cyril 3
Randolph, A. Philip 3
Smith, Nate 49
Touré, Sekou 6
Wyatt, Addie L. 56

UNIP
See United National Independence Party

UNITA
See National Union for the Total Independence of Angola

United Auto Workers (UAW)
Dawson, Matel "Mat," Jr. 39
Fletcher, Bill, Jr. 41

United Bermuda Party
Gordon, Pamela 17

United Church of Christ (UCC)
Chavis, Benjamin 6
Forbes, James A., Jr. 71
Moss, Otis, III 72

United Democratic Front (UDF)
Muluzi, Bakili 14

United Golf Association (UGA)
Elder, Lee 6
Sifford, Charlie 4, 49

United Methodist Church
Caldwell, Kirbyjon 55
Lewis, Shirley A. R. 14
Stith, Charles R. 73

United National Independence Party (UNIP)
Kaunda, Kenneth 2

United Nations (UN)
Annan, Kofi Atta 15, 48
Bunche, Ralph J. 5
Cleaver, Emanuel 4, 45, 68
Diouf, Abdou 3
Juma, Calestous 57
Lafontant, Jewel Stradford 3, 51
McDonald, Gabrielle Kirk 20

Mongella, Gertrude 11
Perkins, Edward 5
Sampson, Edith S. 4
Young, Andrew 3, 48

United Nations Children's Fund (UNICEF)
Baker, Gwendolyn Calvert 9
Belafonte, Harry 4, 65
Machel, Graca Simbine 16
Weah, George 58

United Nations Educational, Scientific, and Cultural Organization (UNESCO)
Diop, Cheikh Anta 4
Frazier, E. Franklin 10
Machel, Graca Simbine 16
Smythe Haith, Mabel 61

United Negro College Fund (UNCF)
Boyd, T. B., III 6
Bunkley, Anita Richmond 39
Creagh, Milton 27
Dawson, Matel "Mat," Jr. 39
Edley, Christopher 2, 48
Gray, William H., III 3
Jordan, Vernon E. 3, 35
Lomax, Michael L. 58
Mays, Benjamin E. 7
Patterson, Frederick Douglass 12
Tillis, Frederick 40

United Parcel Service
Cooper, Evern 40
Darden, Calvin 38
Washington, Patrice Clarke 12

United Parcel Service Foundation
Cooper, Evern 40

United Somali Congress (USC)
Ali Mahdi Mohamed 5

United States Delegations
Shabazz, Ilyasah 36

United States Football League (USFL)
White, Reggie 6, 50
Williams, Doug 22

United Way
Donald, Arnold Wayne 36
Steward, David L. 36

United Workers Union of South Africa (UWUSA)
Buthelezi, Mangosuthu Gatsha 9

Universal Foundation for Better Living (UFBL)
Colemon, Johnnie 11
Reese, Della 6, 20

Universal Negro Improvement Association (UNIA)
Austin, Junius C. 44
Garvey, Marcus 1

University of Alabama
Davis, Mike 41
Lucy Foster, Autherine 35

University of California–Berkeley
Drummond, William J. 40
Edley, Christopher F., Jr. 48

University of Cape Town
Ramphele, Mamphela 29

University of Chicago Hospitals
Obama, Michelle 61

University of Colorado administration
Berry, Mary Frances 7

University of Delaware's Center for Counseling and Student Development
Mitchell, Sharon 36

University of Florida
Haskins, James 36, 54

University of Michigan
Amaker, Tommy 62
Dillard, Godfrey J. 45
Fuller, A. Oveta 43
Goss, Tom 23
Gray, Ida 41
Imes, Elmer Samuel 39

University of Missouri
Anderson, Mike 63
Floyd, Elson S. 41

University of North Carolina
Floyd, Elson S. 41

University of Texas
Granville, Evelyn Boyd 36

University of the West Indies
Brathwaite, Kamau 36
Hill, Errol 40

University of Virginia
Littlepage, Craig 35

UniverSoul Circus
Walker, Cedric "Ricky" 19

Upscale magazine
Bronner, Nathaniel H., Sr. 32

Uptown Music Theater
Marsalis, Delfeayo 41

Urban Bush Women
Zollar, Jawole 28

Urban League (regional)
Adams, Sheila J. 25
Clayton, Xernona 3, 45
Jacob, John E. 2
Mays, Benjamin E. 7
Young, Whitney M., Jr. 4

Urban renewal
Archer, Dennis 7, 36
Barry, Marion S. 7, 44
Bosley, Freeman, Jr. 7
Collins, Barbara-Rose 7
Harris, Alice 7
Lane, Vincent 5

Waters, Maxine 3, 67

Urban theater
Perry, Tyler 40, 54

Urbancrest, Ohio, government
Craig-Jones, Ellen Walker 44

U.S. Air Force
Anderson, Michael P. 40
Carter, Joye Maureen 41
Davis, Benjamin O., Jr. 2, 43
Drew, Alvin, Jr. 67
Dwight, Edward 65
Gregory, Frederick 8, 51
Harris, Marcelite Jordan 16
James, Daniel, Jr. 16
Johnson, Lonnie 32
Jones, Wayne 53
Lyles, Lester 31

U.S. Armed Forces Nurse Corps
Staupers, Mabel K. 7

U.S. Army
Adams-Ender, Clara 40
Baker, Vernon Joseph 65
Brown, Anthony G. 72
Cadoria, Sherian Grace 14
Clemmons, Reginal G. 41
Davis, Benjamin O., Sr. 4
Delany, Martin R. 27
Flipper, Henry O. 3
Greenhouse, Bunnatine "Bunny" 57
Honoré, Russel L. 64
Jackson, Fred James 25
Johnson, Hazel 22
Johnson, Shoshana 47
Matthews, Mark 59
Powell, Colin 1, 28
Rogers, Alan G. 72
Snow, Samuel 71
Stanford, John 20
Watkins, Perry 12
West, Togo D., Jr. 16

U.S. Army Air Corps
Anderson, Charles Edward 37

U.S. Atomic Energy Commission
Nabrit, Samuel Milton 47

U.S. Attorney's Office
Lafontant, Jewel Stradford 3, 51

U.S. Basketball League (USBL)
Lucas, John 7

USBL
See U.S. Basketball League

U.S. Bureau of Engraving and Printing
Felix, Larry R. 64

USC
See United Somali Congress

U.S. Cabinet
Brown, Ron 5
Elders, Joycelyn 6
Espy, Mike 6
Harris, Patricia Roberts 2
Herman, Alexis M. 15

O'Leary, Hazel 6
Powell, Colin 1, 28
Rice, Condoleezza 3, 28, 72
Slater, Rodney E. 15
Sullivan, Louis 8
Weaver, Robert C. 8, 46

U.S. Circuit Court of Appeals
Hastie, William H. 8
Keith, Damon J. 16

U.S. Coast Guard
Brown, Erroll M. 23

U.S. Commission on Civil Rights
Berry, Mary Frances 7
Edley, Christopher 2, 48
Fletcher, Arthur A. 63

U.S. Conference of Catholic Bishops
Gregory, Wilton D. 37

U.S. Court of Appeals
Higginbotham, A. Leon, Jr. 13, 25
Kearse, Amalya Lyle 12
Ogunlesi, Adebayo 37

U.S. Department of Agriculture (USDA)
Espy, Mike 6
Vaughn, Gladys Gary 47
Watkins, Shirley R. 17
Williams, Hosea Lorenzo 15, 31

U.S. Department of Commerce
Brown, Ron 5
Irving, Larry, Jr. 12
Person, Waverly 9, 51
Shavers, Cheryl 31
Wilkins, Roger 2

U.S. Department of Defense
Greenhouse, Bunnatine "Bunny" 57
Tribble, Israel, Jr. 8

U.S. Department of Education
Hill, Anita 5, 65
Hill, Bonnie Guiton 20
Paige, Rod 29
Purnell, Silas 59
Thomas, Clarence 2, 39, 65
Tribble, Israel, Jr. 8
Velez-Rodriguez, Argelia 56

U.S. Department of Energy
O'Leary, Hazel 6

U.S. Department of Health and Human Services (HHS)
See also U.S. Department of Health, Education, and Welfare
Gaston, Marilyn Hughes 60

U.S. Department of Health, Education, and Welfare (HEW)
Bell, Derrick 6
Berry, Mary Frances 7
Harris, Patricia Roberts 2
Johnson, Eddie Bernice 8
Randolph, Linda A. 52
Sullivan, Louis 8

U.S. Department of Housing and Urban Development

(HUD)
Blackwell, J. Kenneth, Sr. 61
Gaines, Brenda 41
Harris, Patricia Roberts 2
Jackson, Alphonso R. 48
Weaver, Robert C. 8, 46

U.S. Department of Justice
Bell, Derrick 6
Campbell, Bill 9
Days, Drew S., III 10
Guinier, Lani 7, 30
Holder, Eric H., Jr. 9
Lafontant, Jewel Stradford 3, 51
Lewis, Delano 7
Patrick, Deval 12, 61
Payton, John 48
Thompson, Larry D. 39
Wilkins, Roger 2

U.S. Department of Labor
Crockett, George W., Jr. 10, 64
Fletcher, Arthur A. 63
Herman, Alexis M. 15

U.S. Department of Social Services
Little, Robert L. 2

U.S. Department of State
Baltimore, Richard Lewis, III 71
Bethune, Mary McLeod 4
Bunche, Ralph J. 5
Davis, Ruth 37
Dougherty, Mary Pearl 47
Frazer, Jendayi 68
Garrett, Joyce Finley 59
Grimké, Archibald H. 9
Haley, George Williford Boyce 21
Harris, Patricia Roberts 2
Keyes, Alan L. 11
Lafontant, Jewel Stradford 3, 51
Perkins, Edward 5
Powell, Colin 1, 28
Rice, Condoleezza 3, 28, 72
Stokes, Carl 10, 73
Van Lierop, Robert 53
Wharton, Clifton R., Jr. 7
Wharton, Clifton Reginald, Sr. 36

U.S. Department of the Interior
Person, Waverly 9, 51

U.S. Department of the Treasury
Morton, Azie Taylor 48

U.S. Department of Transportation
Davis, Benjamin O., Jr. 2, 43

U.S. Department of Veterans Affairs
Brown, Jesse 6, 41

U.S. Diplomatic Corps
See U.S. Department of State

U.S. District Attorney
Harris, Kamala D. 64
Lloyd, Reginald 64

U.S. District Court judge
Bryant, William Benson 61
Carter, Robert L. 51

Cooke, Marcia 60
Diggs-Taylor, Anna 20
Henderson, Thelton E. 68
Keith, Damon J. 16
Parsons, James 14

U.S. Dream Academy
Phipps, Wintley 59

U.S. Foreign Service
See U.S. Department of State

U.S. Geological Survey
Person, Waverly 9, 51

U.S. House of Representatives
Archie-Hudson, Marguerite 44
Ballance, Frank W. 41
Bishop, Sanford D., Jr. 24
Brown, Corrine 24
Burke, Yvonne Braithwaite 42
Carson, André 69
Carson, Julia 23, 69
Chisholm, Shirley 2, 50
Clay, William Lacy 8
Clayton, Eva M. 20
Cleaver, Emanuel 4, 45, 68
Clyburn, James E. 21, 71
Collins, Barbara-Rose 7
Collins, Cardiss 10
Conyers, John, Jr. 4, 45
Crockett, George W., Jr. 10, 64
Cummings, Elijah E. 24
Davis, Artur 41
Dellums, Ronald 2
Diggs, Charles C. 21
Dixon, Julian C. 24
Dymally, Mervyn 42
Ellison, Keith 59
Espy, Mike 6
Fattah, Chaka 11, 70
Fauntroy, Walter E. 11
Fields, Cleo 13
Flake, Floyd H. 18
Ford, Harold E(ugene) 42
Ford, Harold E(ugene), Jr. 16, 70
Franks, Gary 2
Gray, William H., III 3
Hastings, Alcee L. 16
Hawkins, Augustus F. 68
Hilliard, Earl F. 24
Jackson, Jesse, Jr. 14, 45
Jackson Lee, Sheila 20
Jefferson, William J. 25, 72
Johnson, Eddie Bernice 8
Jordan, Barbara 4
Kilpatrick, Carolyn Cheeks 16
Lee, Barbara 25
Leland, Mickey 2
Lewis, John 2, 46
Majette, Denise 41
McKinney, Cynthia Ann 11, 52
Meek, Carrie 6
Meek, Kendrick 41
Meeks, Gregory 25
Metcalfe, Ralph 26
Mfume, Kweisi 6, 41
Millender-McDonald, Juanita 21, 61
Mitchell, Parren J. 42, 66
Moore, Gwendolynne S. 55
Norton, Eleanor Holmes 7
Owens, Major 6
Payne, Donald M. 2, 57

Pinchback, P. B. S. 9
Powell, Adam Clayton, Jr. 3
Rangel, Charles 3, 52
Rush, Bobby 26
Scott, David 41
Scott, Robert C. 23
Stokes, Louis 3
Towns, Edolphus 19
Tubbs Jones, Stephanie 24, 72
Washington, Harold 6
Waters, Maxine 3, 67
Watson, Diane 41
Watt, Melvin 26
Watts, J. C., Jr. 14, 38
Wheat, Alan 14
Wynn, Albert R. 25
Young, Andrew 3, 48

U.S. Information Agency
Allen, Samuel 38

U.S. Joint Chiefs of Staff
Howard, Michelle 28
Powell, Colin 1, 28
Rice, Condoleezza 3, 28, 72

U.S. Marines
Bolden, Charles F., Jr. 7
Brown, Jesse 6, 41
Petersen, Franke E. 31
Von Lipsey, Roderick K. 11

U.S. Navy
Black, Barry C. 47
Brashear, Carl 29
Brown, Jesse Leroy 31
Doby, Lawrence Eugene, Sr. 16, 41
Fields, Evelyn J. 27
Gravely, Samuel L., Jr. 5, 49
Howard, Michelle 28
Miller, Dorie 29
Pinckney, Bill 42
Reason, J. Paul 19
Wright, Lewin 43

U.S. Open golf tournament
Shippen, John 43
Woods, Tiger 14, 31

U.S. Open tennis tournament
Williams, Venus 17, 34, 62

U.S. Peace Corps
Days, Drew S., III 10
Johnson, Rafer 33
Lewis, Delano 7

U.S. Register of the Treasury
Bruce, Blanche Kelso 33

U.S. Senate
Black, Barry C. 47
Bowman, Bertie 71
Braun, Carol Moseley 4, 42
Brooke, Edward 8
Bruce, Blanche Kelso 33
Obama, Barack 49
Pinchback, P. B. S. 9

U.S. State Department
See U.S. Department of State

U.S. Supreme Court
Marshall, Thurgood 1, 44
Thomas, Clarence 2, 39, 65

U.S. Surgeon General
Elders, Joycelyn **6**
Satcher, David **7, 57**

U.S. Virgin Islands government
Hastie, William H. **8**
Turnbull, Charles Wesley **62**

USDA
See U.S. Department of Agriculture

USFL
See United States Football League

U.S.S. *Constitution*
Wright, Lewin **43**

UVC
See Ultraviolet camera/spectrograph

UWUSA
See United Workers Union of South Africa

Vancouver Canucks hockey team
Brashear, Donald **39**

Vancouver Grizzlies basketball team
Abdur-Rahim, Shareef **28**

Vaudeville
Anderson, Eddie "Rochester" **30**
Austin, Lovie **40**
Bates, Peg Leg **14**
Cox, Ida **42**
Davis, Sammy, Jr. **18**
Johnson, Jack **8**
Martin, Sara **38**
McDaniel, Hattie **5**
Mills, Florence **22**
Robinson, Bill "Bojangles" **11**
Waters, Ethel **7**

Verizon Communication
DeVard, Jerri **61**
Gordon, Bruce S. **41, 53**

Veterinary science
Jawara, Dawda Kairaba **11**
Lushington, Augustus Nathaniel **56**
Maathai, Wangari **43**
Patterson, Frederick Douglass **12**
Thomas, Vivien **9**

Vibe
Jones, Quincy **8, 30**
Smith, Danyel **40**
Wilbekin, Emil **63**

Vibraphone
Hampton, Lionel **17, 41**

Victim's Bill of Rights
Dee, Merri **55**

Video direction
Barclay, Paris **37**
Fuqua, Antoine **35**
Pinkett Smith, Jada **10, 41**

Vietnam Veterans of America
Duggins, George **64**

Village Voice
Cooper, Andrew W. **36**
Crouch, Stanley **11**

Violin
Daemyon, Jerald **64**
Dworkin, Aaron P. **52**
Escobar, Damien **56**
Escobar, Tourie **56**
Murray, Tai **47**
Smith, Stuff **37**
Tinsley, Boyd **50**

***VIP Memphis* magazine**
McMillan, Rosalynn A. **36**

Virgin Records
Brooks, Hadda **40**
Sledge, Percy **39**

Virginia state government
Marsh, Henry **32**
Martin, Ruby Grant **49**
Wilder, L. Douglas **3, 48**

Virgina State Supreme Court
Hassell, Leroy Rountree, Sr. **41**

Virginia Tech University
Vick, Michael **39, 65**

Virology
Fuller, A. Oveta **43**

***Vogue* magazine**
Talley, André Leon **56**

Volleyball
Blanton, Dain **29**

Voodoo
Dunham, Katherine **4, 59**
Guy, Rosa **5**
Hurston, Zora Neale **3**
Pierre, Andre **17**

Voting rights
Cary, Mary Ann Shadd **30**
Chestnut, J. L., Jr. **73**
Clark, Septima **7**
Forman, James **7, 51**
Guinier, Lani **7, 30**
Hamer, Fannie Lou **6**
Harper, Frances Ellen Watkins **11**
Hill, Jesse, Jr. **13**
Johnson, Eddie Bernice **8**
Lampkin, Daisy **19**
Mandela, Nelson **1, 14**
Moore, Harry T. **29**
Moses, Robert Parris **11**
Terrell, Mary Church **9**
Touré, Faya Ora Rose **56**
Trotter, Monroe **9**
Tubman, Harriet **9**
Wells-Barnett, Ida B. **8**
Williams, Fannie Barrier **27**
Williams, Hosea Lorenzo **15, 31**
Woodard, Alfre **9**

Vulcan Realty and Investment Company
Gaston, Arthur George **3, 38, 59**

WAAC (Women's Auxiliary Army Corps)
See Women's Army Corps (WAC)

WAC
See Women's Army Corp

Wall Street
Lewis, William M., Jr. **40**
McGuire, Raymond J. **57**
Phillips, Charles E., Jr. **57**

War Resister's League (WRL)
Carter, Mandy **11**

Washington Capitols basketball team
Lloyd, Earl **26**

Washington Capitols hockey team
Grier, Mike **43**

Washington Color Field group
Thomas, Alma **14**

Washington, D.C., city government
Barry, Marion S. **7, 44**
Cooper Cafritz, Peggy **43**
Dixon, Sharon Pratt **1**
Fauntroy, Walter E. **11**
Fenty, Adrian **60**
Hobson, Julius W. **44**
Jarvis, Charlene Drew **21**
Norton, Eleanor Holmes **7**
Washington, Walter **45**
Williams, Anthony **21**

Washington, D.C., Commission on the Arts and Humanities
Neal, Larry **38**

Washington Mystics basketball team
McCray, Nikki **18**

Washington Post
Britt, Donna **28**
Davis, George **36**
Givhan, Robin Deneen **72**
Ifill, Gwen **28**
King, Colbert I. **69**
Maynard, Robert C. **7**
McCall, Nathan **8**
Nelson, Jill **6, 54**
Raspberry, William **2**
Wilkins, Roger **2**

Washington Redskins football team
Green, Darrell **39**
Monk, Art **38, 73**
Sanders, Deion **4, 31**

Washington State Higher Education Coordinating Board
Floyd, Elson S. **41**

Washington Week in Review
TV Series
Ifill, Gwen **28**

Washington Wizards basketball team
Bickerstaff, Bernie **21**
Heard, Gar **25**
Howard, Juwan **15**
Lucas, John **7**
Unseld, Wes **23**

Webber, Chris **15, 30, 59**

Watts Repetory Theater Company
Cortez, Jayne **43**

WBA
See World Boxing Association

WBC
See World Boxing Council

WCC
See World Council of Churches

Weather
Brown, Vivian **27**
Christian, Spencer **15**
McEwen, Mark **5**

Welfare reform
Bryant, Wayne R. **6**
Carson, Julia **23, 69**
Parker, Star **70**
Wallace, Joaquin **49**
Williams, Walter E. **4**

Wellspring Gospel
Winans, CeCe **14, 43**

WERD (radio station)
Blayton, Jesse B., Sr. **55**

West Indian folk songs
Belafonte, Harry **4, 65**
Rhoden, Wayne **70**

West Indian literature
Coombs, Orde M. **44**
Guy, Rosa **5**
Kincaid, Jamaica **4**
Markham, E.A. **37**
Marshall, Paule **7**
McKay, Claude **6**
Walcott, Derek **5**

West Point
Davis, Benjamin O., Jr. **2, 43**
Flipper, Henry O. **3**

West Side Preparatory School
Collins, Marva **3, 71**

Western Michigan University
Floyd, Elson S. **41**

White House Conference on Civil Rights
Randolph, A. Philip **3**

Whitney Museum of American Art
Golden, Thelma **10, 55**
Simpson, Lorna **4, 36**

WHO
See Women Helping Offenders

"Why Are You on This Planet?"
Yoba, Malik **11**

William Morris Talent Agency
Amos, Wally **9**

WillieWear Ltd.
Smith, Willi **8**

Wilmington 10
Chavis, Benjamin 6

Wimbledon
Williams, Venus 17, 34, 62

Wine and Winemaking
Allen-Buillard, Melba 55
Rideau, Iris 46

Wisconsin State Supreme Court
Butler, Louis 70

WOMAD
See World of Music, Arts, and Dance

Women Helping Offenders (WHO)
Holland, Endesha Ida Mae 3, 57

Women's Army Corps (WAC)
Adams Earley, Charity 13, 34
Cadoria, Sherian Grace 14

Women's Auxiliary Army Corps
See Women's Army Corps

Women's issues
Allen, Ethel D. 13
Angelou, Maya 1, 15
Avery, Byllye Y. 66
Ba, Mariama 30
Baker, Ella 5
Bashir, Halima 73
Berry, Mary Frances 7
Brown, Elaine 8
Campbell, Bebe Moore 6, 24, 59
Cannon, Katie 10
Cary, Mary Ann Shadd 30
Charles, Mary Eugenia 10, 55
Chinn, May Edward 26
Christian, Barbara T. 44
Christian-Green, Donna M. 17
Clark, Septima 7
Cole, Johnnetta B. 5, 43
Cooper, Anna Julia 20
Cunningham, Evelyn 23
Dash, Julie 4
Davis, Angela 5
Edelman, Marian Wright 5, 42
Elders, Joycelyn 6
Evans, Diana 72
Fauset, Jessie 7
Giddings, Paula 11
Goldberg, Whoopi 4, 33, 69
Gomez, Jewelle 30
Grimké, Archibald H. 9
Guy-Sheftall, Beverly 13
Hale, Clara 16
Hale, Lorraine 8
Hamer, Fannie Lou 6
Harper, Frances Ellen Watkins 11
Harris, Alice 7
Harris, Leslie 6
Harris, Patricia Roberts 2
Height, Dorothy I. 2, 23
Hernandez, Aileen Clarke 13
Hill, Anita 5, 65
Hine, Darlene Clark 24
Holland, Endesha Ida Mae 3, 57
hooks, bell 5
Hughes, Ebony 57

Jackson, Alexine Clement 22
Joe, Yolanda 21
Jordan, Barbara 4
Jordan, June 7, 35
Lampkin, Daisy 19
Larsen, Nella 10
Lorde, Audre 6
Maathai, Wangari 43
Marshall, Paule 7
Mbaye, Mariétou 31
McCabe, Jewell Jackson 10
McKenzie, Vashti M. 29
McMillan, Terry 4, 17, 53
Meek, Carrie 6
Millender-McDonald, Juanita 21, 61
Mongella, Gertrude 11
Morrison, Toni 2, 15
Mossell, Gertrude Bustill 40
Naylor, Gloria 10, 42
Nelson, Jill 6, 54
Niane, Katoucha 70
Nichols, Nichelle 11
Norman, Pat 10
Norton, Eleanor Holmes 7
Ormes, Jackie 73
Painter, Nell Irvin 24
Parker, Pat 19
Rawlings, Nana Konadu Agyeman 13
Ringgold, Faith 4
Shange, Ntozake 8
Simpson, Carole 6, 30
Smith, Jane E. 24
Terrell, Mary Church 9
Tubman, Harriet 9
Vanzant, Iyanla 17, 47
Walker, Alice 1, 43
Walker, Maggie Lena 17
Wallace, Michele Faith 13
Waters, Maxine 3, 67
Wattleton, Faye 9
Williams, Fannie Barrier 27
Winfrey, Oprah 2, 15, 61
Xuma, Madie Hall 59

Women's Leadership Forum
Shabazz, Ilyasah 36

Women's National Basketball Association (WNBA)
Bolton-Holifield, Ruthie 28
Cash, Swin 59
Catchings, Tamika 43
Cooper, Cynthia 17
Edwards, Teresa 14
Ford, Cheryl 45
Griffith, Yolanda 25
Holdsclaw, Chamique 24
Jones, Merlakia 34
Lennox, Betty 31
Leslie, Lisa 16, 73
McCray, Nikki 18
Milton, DeLisha 31
Peck, Carolyn 23
Perrot, Kim 23
Swoopes, Sheryl 12, 56
Thompson, Tina 25
Williams, Natalie 31
Woodward, Lynette 67

Women's Political Council
Burks, Mary Fair 40

Women's United Soccer Association (WUSA)
Scurry, Briana 27

Worker's Party (Brazil)
da Silva, Benedita 5

Workplace equity
Clark, Septima 7
Hill, Anita 5, 65
Nelson, Jill 6, 54
Simpson, Carole 6, 30

Works Progress (Projects) Administration (WPA)
Alexander, Margaret Walker 22
Baker, Ella 5
Blackburn, Robert 28
DeCarava, Roy 42
Douglas, Aaron 7
Dunham, Katherine 4, 59
Hall, Juanita 62
Lawrence, Jacob 4, 28
Lee-Smith, Hughie 5, 22
Murray, Pauli 38
Sallee, Charles 38
Sebree, Charles 40
Winkfield, Jimmy 42
Wright, Richard 5

World African Hebrew Israelite Community
Ben-Israel, Ben Ami 11

World Bank
Soglo, Nicéphore 15

World beat
Belafonte, Harry 4, 65
Fela 1, 42
Maal, Baaba 66
N'Dour, Youssou 1, 53
Okosuns, Sonny 71
Ongala, Remmy 9

World Boxing Association (WBA)
Ellis, Jimmy 44
Hearns, Thomas 29
Hopkins, Bernard 35, 69
Lewis, Lennox 27
Tyson, Mike 28, 44
Whitaker, Pernell 10

World Boxing Council (WBC)
Mosley, Shane 32
Tyson, Mike 28, 44
Whitaker, Pernell 10

World Council of Churches (WCC)
Kobia, Samuel 43
Mays, Benjamin E. 7
Tutu, Desmond Mpilo 6, 44

World Cup
dos Santos, Manuel Francisco 65
Milla, Roger 2
Pelé 7
Scurry, Briana 27

World hunger
Belafonte, Harry 4, 65
Iman 4, 33
Jones, Quincy 8, 30
Leland, Mickey 2

Masire, Quett 5
Obasanjo, Olusegun 5

World of Music, Arts, and Dance (WOMAD)
Ongala, Remmy 9

World Wide Technology
Steward, David L. 36

World Wrestling Entertainment (WWE) Hall of Fame
Ladd, Ernie 64

World Wrestling Federation (WWF)
Ladd, Ernie 64
Lashley, Bobby 63
Rock, The 29, 66

WPA
See Works Progress Administration

Wrestling
Ladd, Ernie 64
Lashley, Bobby 63
Rock, The 29, 66

WRL
See War Resister's League

WSB Radio
Pressley, Condace L. 41

WWF
See World Wrestling Federation

Xavier University of Louisiana
Francis, Norman (C.) 60

Xerox Corp.
Burns, Ursula 60
Rand, A. Barry 6

Yab Yum Entertainment
Edmonds, Tracey 16, 64

Yale Child Study Center
Comer, James P. 6

Yale Repertory Theater
Dutton, Charles S. 4, 22
Richards, Lloyd 2
Wilson, August 7, 33, 55

Yale School of Drama
Dutton, Charles S. 4, 22
Richards, Lloyd 2

Yale University
Blassingame, John Wesley 40
Carby, Hazel 27
Davis, Charles T. 48
Hill, Errol 40
Neal, Larry 38

Ybor City Boys and Girls Club
Brooks, Derrick 43

YMCA
See Young Men's Christian Associations

Yoruban folklore
Soyinka, Wole 4
Vanzant, Iyanla 17, 47

Young adult literature
Anderson, Ho Che **54**
Bolden, Tonya **32**
Ekwensi, Cyprian **37**
Johnson, Angela **52**

Young and Rubicam Brands
Fudge, Ann (Marie) **11, 55**

Young British Artists
Shonibare, Yinka **58**

Young Men's Christian Association (YMCA)
Butts, Calvin O., III **9**
Goode, Mal **13**
Hope, John **8**
Mays, Benjamin E. **7**

Young Negroes' Cooperative League
Baker, Ella **5**

Young Women's Christian Association (YWCA)
Baker, Ella **5**
Baker, Gwendolyn Calvert **9**
Clark, Septima **7**
Claytor, Helen **14, 52**
Hedgeman, Anna Arnold **22**
Height, Dorothy I. **2, 23**
Jackson, Alexine Clement **22**
Jenkins, Ella **15**
Sampson, Edith S. **4**
Stewart, Ella **39**

Xuma, Madie Hall **59**

Youth Services Administration
Little, Robert L. **2**

YWCA
See Young Women's Christian Association

Zairian government
Mobutu Sese Seko **1, 56**

Zambian government
Chiluba, Frederick Jacob Titus **56**
Mwanawasa, Levy **72**

ZCTU
See Zimbabwe Congress of Trade Unions

Zimbabwe Congress of Trade Unions (ZCTU)
Tsvangirai, Morgan **26, 72**
Young, Roger Arliner **29**

Zimbabwean government
Mugabe, Robert **10, 71**
Nkomo, Joshua **4, 65**

Zouk music
Lefel, Edith **41**

ZTA
See Zululand Territorial Authority

Zululand Territorial Authority (ZTA)
Buthelezi, Mangosuthu Gatsha **9**

Cumulative Name Index

Volume numbers appear in **bold**

Aaliyah 1979-2001 **30**

Aaron, Hank 1934— **5**

Aaron, Henry Louis *See Aaron, Hank*

Abacha, Sani 1943—1998 **11, 70**

Abbott, Diane (Julie) 1953— **9**

Abbott, Robert Sengstacke 1868-1940 **27**

Abdul-Jabbar, Kareem 1947— **8**

Abdullah, Imaam Isa *See York, Dwight D.*

Abdulmajid, Iman Mohamed *See Iman*

Abdur-Rahim, Shareef 1976— **28**

Abele, Julian 1881-1950 **55**

Abernathy, Ralph David 1926-1990 **1**

Aberra, Amsale 1954— **67**

Abiola, Moshood 1937–1998 **70**

Abrahams, Peter 1919— **39**

Abu-Jamal, Mumia 1954— **15**

Abubakar, Abdulsalami 1942— **66**

Ace, Johnny 1929-1954 **36**

Achebe, (Albert) Chinua(lumogu) 1930— **6**

Acogny, Germaine 1944— **55**

Adams, Eula L. 1950— **39**

Adams, Floyd, Jr. 1945— **12**

Adams, H. Leslie *See Adams, Leslie*

Adams, Jenoyne (?)— **60**

Adams, Johnny 1932-1998 **39**

Adams, Leslie 1932— **39**

Adams, Oleta 19(?)(?)— **18**

Adams, Osceola Macarthy 1890-1983 **31**

Adams, Paul 1977— **50**

Adams, Sheila J. 1943— **25**

Adams, Yolanda 1961— **17, 67**

Adams-Campbell, Lucille L. 1953— **60**

Adams Earley, Charity (Edna) 1918— **13, 34**

Adams-Ender, Clara 1939— **40**

Adderley, Julian "Cannonball" 1928-1975 **30**

Adderley, Nat 1931-2000 **29**

Adderley, Nathaniel *See Adderley, Nat*

Ade, Sunny King 1946— **41**

Adeniyi, Sunday *See Ade, Sunny King*

Adichie, Chimamanda Ngozi 1977— **64**

Adjaye, David 1966— **38**

Adkins, Rod 1958— **41**

Adkins, Rutherford H. 1924-1998 **21**

Adu, Freddy 1989— **67**

Adu, Fredua Koranteng *See Adu, Freddy*

Adu, Helen Folasade *See Sade*

Agyeman Rawlings, Nana Konadu 1948— **13**

Agyeman, Jaramogi Abebe 1911-2000 **10, 63**

Aidoo, Ama Ata 1942— **38**

Aiken, Loretta Mary *See Mabley, Jackie "Moms"*

Ailey, Alvin 1931-1989 **8**

Ake, Claude 1939-1996 **30**

Akil, Mara Brock 1970— **60**

Akinnuoye-Agbaje, Adewale 1967— **56**

Akinola, Peter Jasper 1944— **65**

Akomfrah, John 1957— **37**

Akon 1973(?)— **68**

Akpan, Uwem 1971— **70**

Akunyili, Dora Nkem 1954— **58**

Al-Amin, Jamil Abdullah 1943— **6**

Albright, Gerald 1947— **23**

Alcindor, Ferdinand Lewis *See Abdul-Jabbar, Kareem*

Alcorn, George Edward, Jr. 1940— **59**

Alert, Kool DJ Red 19(?)(?)— **33**

Alexander, Archie Alphonso 1888-1958 **14**

Alexander, Clifford 1933— **26**

Alexander, John Marshall *See Ace, Johnny*

Alexander, Joyce London 1949— **18**

Alexander, Khandi 1957— **43**

Alexander, Margaret Walker 1915-1998 **22**

Alexander, Sadie Tanner Mossell 1898-1989 **22**

Alexander, Shaun 1977— **58**

Ali, Ayaan Hirsi 1969— **58**

Ali, Hana Yasmeen 1976— **52**

Ali, Laila 1977— **27, 63**

Ali, Mohammed Naseehu 1971— **60**

Ali, Muhammad 1942— **2, 16, 52**

Ali, Tatyana 1979— **73**

Ali Mahdi Mohamed 1940— **5**

Allain, Stephanie 1959— **49**

Allen, Byron 1961— **3, 24**

Allen, Claude 1960— **68**

Allen, Debbie 1950— **13, 42**

Allen, Ethel D. 1929-1981 **13**

Allen, Marcus 1960— **20**

Allen, Richard 1760-1831 **14**

Allen, Robert L. 1942— **38**

Allen, Samuel W. 1917— **38**

Allen, Tina 1955— **22**

Allen-Buillard, Melba 1960— **55**

Alston, Charles Henry 1907-1997 **33**

Amadi, Elechi 1934— **40**

Amaker, Harold Tommy, Jr. *See Amaker, Tommy*

Amaker, Norman 1935-2000 **63**

Amaker, Tommy 1965— **62**

Amerie 1980— **52**

Ames, Wilmer 1950-1993 **27**

Amin, Idi 1925-2003 **42**

Amos, Emma 1938— **63**

Amos, John 1941— **8, 62**

Amos, Valerie 1954— **41**

Amos, Wally 1937— **9**

Anderson, Anthony 1970— **51**

Anderson, Carl 1945-2004 **48**

Anderson, Charles Edward 1919-1994 **37**

Anderson, Eddie "Rochester" 1905-1977 **30**

Anderson, Elmer 1941— **25**

Anderson, Ho Che 1969— **54**

Anderson, Jamal 1972— **22**

Anderson, Lauren 1965— **72**

Anderson, Marian 1902— **2, 33**

Anderson, Michael P. 1959-2003 **40**

Anderson, Mike 1959— **63**

Anderson, Norman B. 1955— **45**

Anderson, Viv 1956— **58**

Anderson, William G(ilchrist), D.O. 1927— **57**

Andre 3000 *See Benjamin, Andre*

Andrews, Benny 1930-2006 **22, 59**

Andrews, Bert 1929-1993 **13**

Andrews, Mark *See Sisqo*

Andrews, Raymond 1934-1991 **4**

Angelou, Maya 1928— **1, 15**

Anna Marie *See Lincoln, Abbey*

Annan, Kofi Atta 1938— **15, 48**

Ansa, Tina McElroy 1949— **14**

Anthony, Carmelo 1984— **46**

Anthony, Crystal *See McCrary Anthony, Crystal*

Anthony, Michael 1930(?)— **29**

Anthony, Trey 1974— **63**

Anthony, Wendell 1950— **25**

Appiah, Kwame Anthony 1954— **67**

Arac de Nyeko, Monica 1979— **66**

Arach, Monica *See Arac de Nyeko, Monica*

Archer, Dennis (Wayne) 1942— **7, 36**

Archer, Michael D'Angelo *See D'Angelo*

Archer, Osceola *See Adams, Osceola Macarthy*

Archie-Hudson, Marguerite 1937— **44**

Ardoin, Alphonse 1915-2007 **65**

Arinze, Francis Cardinal 1932— **19**

Aristide, Jean-Bertrand 1953— **6, 45**

Arkadie, Kevin 1957— **17**

Armah, Ayi Kwei 1939— **49**

Armatrading, Joan 1950— **32**

Armstrong, (Daniel) Louis 1900-1971 **2**

Armstrong, Robb 1962— **15**

Armstrong, Vanessa Bell 1953— **24**

Arnez J, 1966(?)— **53**

Arnold, Monica *See Monica*

Arnold, Tichina 1971— **63**

Arnwine, Barbara 1951(?)— **28**

Arrington, Richard 1934— **24**

Arroyo, Martina 1936— **30**

Artest, Ron 1979— **52**

Arthur, Owen 1949— **33**

Asante, Molefi Kete 1942— **3**

Ashanti 1980— **37**

Ashe, Arthur Robert, Jr. 1943-1993 **1, 18**

Ashford, Emmett 1914-1980 **22**

Ashford, Evelyn 1957— **63**

Ashford, Nickolas 1942— **21**

Ashley, Maurice 1966— **15, 47**

Ashley-Ward, Amelia 1957— **23**

Asim, Jabari 1962— **71**

Atim, Julian 1980(?)— **66**

Atkins, Cholly 1930-2003 **40**

Atkins, David *See Sinbad*

Atkins, Erica 1972(?)— *See Mary Mary*

Atkins, Jeffrey *See Ja Rule*

Atkins, Juan 1962— **50**

Atkins, Russell 1926— **45**

Atkins, Tina 1975(?)— *See Mary Mary*

Atyam, Angelina 1946— **55**

Aubert, Alvin 1930— **41**

Auguste, Arnold A. 1946— **47**

Auguste, Donna 1958— **29**

Auguste, (Marie Carmele) Rose-Anne 1963— **13**

Augustine, Jean 1937— **53**

Austin, Gloria 1956— **63**

Austin, Jim 1951— **63**

Austin, Junius C. 1887-1968 **44**

Austin, Lovie 1887-1972 **40**

Austin, Patti 1948— **24**

Autrey, Wesley 1956— **68**

Avant, Clarence 19(?)(?)— **19**

Avery, Byllye Y. 1937— **66**

Awoonor, Kofi 1935— **37**

Awoonor-Williams, George *See Awoonor, Kofi*

Awoyinka, Adesiji *See Siji*

Ayers, Roy 1940— **16**

Azikiwe, Nnamdi 1904-1996 **13**

Ba, Mariama 1929-1981 **30**

Babangida, Ibrahim (Badamasi) 1941— **4**

Babatunde, Obba 19(?)(?)— **35**

Babyface *See Edmonds, Kenneth "Babyface"*

Bacon-Bercey, June 1942— **38**

Badu, Erykah 1971(?)— **22**

Bahati, Wambui 1950(?)— **60**

Bailey, Buster 1902-1967 **38**

Bailey, Chauncey 1949–2007 **68**

Bailey, Clyde 1946— **45**

Bailey, DeFord 1899-1982 **33**

Bailey, Pearl Mae 1918-1990 **14**

Bailey, Philip 1951— **63**

Bailey, Preston 1948(?)— **64**

Bailey, Radcliffe 1968— **19**

Bailey, William C. *See Bailey, Buster*

Bailey, Xenobia 1955(?)— **11**

Baines, Harold 1959— **32**

Baiocchi, Regina Harris 1956— **41**

Baisden, Michael 1963— **25, 66**

Baker, Anita 1957— **21, 48**

Baker, Arlene Holt *See Holt Baker, Arlene*

Baker, Augusta 1911-1998 **38**

Baker, Constance *See Motley, Constance Baker*

Baker, Dusty 1949— **8, 43, 72**

Baker, Ella 1903-1986 **5**

Baker, George *See Divine, Father*

Baker, Gwendolyn Calvert 1931— **9**

Baker, Houston A(lfred), Jr. 1943— **6**

Baker, Johnnie B., Jr. *See Baker, Dusty*

Baker, Josephine 1906-1975 **3**

Baker, LaVern 1929-1997 **26**

Baker, Maxine 1952— **28**

Baker, Thurbert 1952— **22**

Baker, Vernon Joseph 1919— **65**

Balance, Frank W. 1942— **41**

Baldwin, James 1924-1987 **1**

Ballard, Allen B(utler), Jr. 1930— **40**

Ballard, Hank 1927-2003 **41**

Baltimore, Richard Lewis, III 1946— **71**

Bambaataa, Afrika 1958— **34**

Bambara, Toni Cade 1939— **10**

Banda, Hastings Kamuzu 1898(?)-1997 **6, 54**

Bandele, Asha 1970(?)— **36**

Bandele, Biyi 1967— **68**

Bandele-Thomas, Biyi *See Bandele, Biyi*

Banks, A. Doris *See Henries, A. Doris Banks*

Banks, Ernie 1931— **33**

Banks, Jeffrey 1953— **17**

Banks, Michelle 1968(?)— **59**

Banks, Paula A. 1950— **68**

Banks, Tyra 1973— **11, 50**

Banks, William (Venoid) 1903-1985 **11**

Banner, David 1975(?)— **55**

Baquet, Dean 1956— **63**

Baraka, Amiri 1934— **1, 38**

Barbee, Lloyd Augustus 1925–2002 **71**

Barber, Atiim Kiambu *See Barber, Tiki*

Barber, Ronde 1975— **41**

Barber, Tiki 1975— **57**

Barboza, Anthony 1944— **10**

Barclay, Paris 1957— **37**

Barden, Don H. 1943— **9, 20**

Barker, Danny 1909-1994 **32**

Barkley, Charles 1963— **5, 66**

Barlow, Roosevelt 1917-2003 **49**

Barnes, Ernie 1938— **16**

Barnes, John 1963— **53**

Barnes, Roosevelt "Booba" 1936-1996 **33**

Barnes, Steven 1952— **54**

Barnett, Amy Du Bois 1969— **46**

Barnett, Etta Moten 1901-2004 **18, 56**

Barnett, Marguerite 1942-1992 **46**

Barney, Lem 1945— **26**

Barnhill, David 1914-1983 **30**

Barrax, Gerald William 1933— **45**

Barrett, Andrew C. 1942(?)— **12**

Barrett, Jacqueline 1950— **28**

Barrett, Lindsay 1941— **43**

Barrett, Mario Dewar *See Mario*

Barrino, Fantasia 1984— **53**

Barrow, Dean 1951— **69**

Barrow, Joseph Louis *See Louis, Joe*

Barry, Marion S(hepilov, Jr.) 1936— **7, 44**

Barthe, Richmond 1901-1989 **15**

Bashir, Halima 1979— **73**

Basie, William James *See Count Basie*

Basquiat, Jean-Michel 1960-1988 **5**

Bass, Charlotta Amanda Spears 1874-1969 **40**

Bass, Karen 1953— **70**

Bassett, Angela 1958— **6, 23, 62**

Bassey, Shirley 1937— **25**

Bates, Clayton *See Bates, Peg Leg*

Bates, Daisy (Lee Gatson) 1914(?)— **13**

Bates, Elias *See Diddley, Bo*

Bates, Karen Grigsby 19(?)(?)— **40**

Bates, Peg Leg 1907— **14**

Bath, Patricia E. 1942— **37**

Batiste, Alvin 1932-2007 **66**

Battle, Kathleen 1948— **70**

Baugh, David 1947— **23**

Baylor, Don(ald Edward) 1949— **6**

Baylor, Helen 1953— **36**

Beach, Michael 1963— **26**

Beah, Ishmael 1980— **69**

Beal, Bernard B. 1954(?)— **46**

Beals, Jennifer 1963— **12**

Beals, Melba Patillo 1941— **15**

Beamon, Bob 1946— **30**

Bearden, Romare 1912–1988 **2, 50**

Beasley, Jamar 1979— **29**

Beasley, Myrlie *See Evers, Myrlie*

Beasley, Phoebe 1943— **34**

Beaton, Norman Lugard 1934-1994 **14**

Beatty, Talley 1923(?)-1995 **35**

Beauvais, Garcelle 1966— **29**

Bebey, Francis 1929-2001 **45**

Bechet, Sidney 1897-1959 **18**

Beck, Robert *See Iceberg Slim*

Beckford, Tyson 1970— **11, 68**

Beckham, Barry 1944— **41**

Bedie, Henri Konan 1934— **21**

Beenie Man 1973— **32**

Belafonte, Harold George, Jr. *See Belafonte, Harry*

Belafonte, Harry 1927— **4, 65**

Bell, Derrick (Albert, Jr.) 1930— **6**

Bell, James "Cool Papa" 1901-1991 **36**

Bell, James A. 1948— **50**

Bell, James Madison 1826-1902 **40**

Bell, Michael 1955— **40**

Bell, Ralph S. 1934— **5**

Bell, Robert Mack 1943— **22**

Bellamy, Bill 1967— **12**

Bellamy, Terry 1972— **58**

Belle, Albert (Jojuan) 1966— **10**

Belle, Regina 1963— **1, 51**

Belton, Sharon Sayles 1951— **9, 16**

Benberry, Cuesta 1923-2007 **65**

Benét, Eric 1970— **28**

Ben-Israel, Ben Ami 1940(?)— **11**

Benjamin, Andre 1975— **45**

Benjamin, Andre (3000) 1975(?)— *See OutKast*

Benjamin, Regina 1956— **20**

Benjamin, Tritobia Hayes 1944— **53**

Bennett, George Harold "Hal" 1930— **45**

Bennett, Gwendolyn B. 1902-1981 **59**

Bennett, Lerone, Jr. 1928— **5**

Bennett, Louise 1919–2006 **69**

Benson, Angela 19(?)(?)— **34**

Bentley, Lamont 1973-2005 **53**

Berry, Bertice 1960— **8, 55**

Berry, Charles Edward Anderson *See Berry, Chuck*

Berry, Chuck 1926— **29**

Berry, Fred "Rerun" 1951-2003 **48**

Berry, Halle 1966— **4, 19, 57**

Berry, James 1925— **41**

Berry, Mary Frances 1938— **7**

Berry, Theodore M. 1905-2000 **31**

Berrysmith, Don Reginald 1936— **49**

Betha, Mason Durrell 1977(?)— **24**

Bethune, Mary (Jane) McLeod 1875-1955 **4**

Beti, Mongo 1932-2001 **36**

Betsch, MaVynee 1935— **28**

Bettis, Jerome 1972— **64**

Beverly, Frankie 1946— **25**

Beyoncé 1981— **39, 70**

Beze, Dante Terrell *See Mos Def*

Bibb, Eric 1951— **49**

Bibb, Henry 1815-1854 **54**

Bibb, Mary 1820-1877 **54**

Bickerstaff, Bernard Tyrone 1944— **21**

Big Boi *See Patton, Antwan*

Biggers, John 1924-2001 **20, 33**

Biggers, Sanford 1970— **62**

Biko, Stephen *See Biko, Steven (Bantu)*

Biko, Steven (Bantu) 1946-1977 **4**

Bing, Dave 1943— **3, 59**

Birch, Glynn R. 195(?)— **61**

Bishop, Eric *See Foxx, Jamie*

Bishop, Maurice 1944-1983 **39**

Bishop, Sanford D. Jr. 1947— **24**

Bivins, Michael 1968— **72**

Biya, Paul 1933— **28**

Biyidi-Awala, Alexandre *See Beti, Mongo*

Bizimungu, Pasteur 1951— **19**

Black, Albert 1940— **51**

Black, Barry C. 1948— **47**

Black, Keith Lanier 1955— **18**

Black Kold Madina *See Roberts, Kimberly Rivers*

Black Thought 1972— **63**

Blackburn, Robert 1920— **28**

Blackmon, Brenda 1952— **58**

Blackshear, Leonard 1943— **52**

Blackwell, Kenneth, Sr. 1948— **61**

Blackwell, Robert D., Sr. 1937— **52**

Blackwell, Unita 1933— **17**

Blackwood, Maureen 1960— **37**

Blacque, Taurean 1941— **58**

Blair, Jayson 1976— **50**

Blair, Maxine *See Powell, Maxine*

Blair, Paul 1944— **36**

Blake, Asha 1961(?)— **26**

Blake, Eubie 1883-1983 **29**

Blake, James 1979— **43**

Blake, James Hubert *See Blake, Eubie*

Blakey, Art(hur) 1919-1990 **37**

Blanchard, Terence 1962— **43**

Bland, Bobby "Blue" 1930— **36**

Bland, Eleanor Taylor 1944— **39**

Bland, Robert Calvin *See Bland, Bobby "Blue"*

Blanks, Billy 1955(?)— **22**

Blanks, Deborah K. 1958— **69**

Blanton, Dain 1971— **29**

Blassingame, John Wesley 1940-2000 **40**

Blayton, Jesse B., Sr. 1897-1977 **55**

Bleu, Corbin 1989— **65**

Blige, Mary J. 1971— **20, 34, 60**

Blockson, Charles L. 1933— **42**

Blondy, Alpha 1953— **30**

Blow, Charles M. 1968(?)— **73**

Blow, Kurtis 1959— **31**

Bluford, Guion Stewart, Jr. *See Bluford, Guy*

Bluford, Guy 1942— **2, 35**

Bluitt, Juliann Stephanie 1938— **14**

Boateng, Ozwald 1968— **35**

Boateng, Paul Yaw 1951— **56**

Bobo, Lawrence 1958— **60**

Bogle, Donald 19(?)(?)— **34**

Bogues, Tyrone "Muggsy" 1965— **56**

Bol, Manute 1963— **1**

Bolden, Buddy 1877-1931 **39**

Bolden, Charles F(rank), Jr. 1946—
7

Bolden, Charles Joseph See
Bolden, Buddy

Bolden, Frank E. 1913-2003 44

Bolden, Tonya 1959— 32

Bolin, Jane 1908-2007 22, 59

Bolt, Usain 1986— 73

Bolton, Terrell D. 1959(?)— 25

Bolton-Holifield, Ruthie 1967— 28

Bonaly, Surya 1973— 7

Bond, Beverly 1970— 53

Bond, (Horace) Julian 1940— 2, 35

Bonds, Barry 1964— 6, 34, 63

Bonds, Bobby 1946— 43

Bonds, Margaret 1913-1972 39

Bonet, Lisa 1967— 58

Boney, Lisa Michelle See Bonet,
Lisa

Bonga, Kuenda 1942— 13

Bongo, Albert-Bernard See Bongo,
(El Hadj) Omar

Bongo, (El Hadj) Omar 1935— 1

Bontemps, Arna(ud Wendell) 1902-
1973 8

Booker, Cory Anthony 1969— 68

Booker, Simeon 1918— 23

Borders, James (Buchanan, IV)
1949— 9

Bosley, Freeman (Robertson), Jr.
1954— 7

Boston, Kelvin E. 1955(?)— 25

Boston, Lloyd 1970(?)— 24

Bow Wow 1987— 35

Bowe, Riddick (Lamont) 1967— 6

Bowman, Bertie 1931— 71

Bowman, Herbert See Bowman,
Bertie

Bowser, Yvette Lee 1965(?)— 17

Boyd, Edward 1914–2007 70

Boyd, Gerald M. 1950-2006 32, 59

Boyd, Gwendolyn 1955— 49

Boyd, John W., Jr. 1965— 20, 72

Boyd, Suzanne 1963— 52

Boyd, T(heophilus) B(artholomew),
III 1947— 6

Boye, Madior 1940— 30

Boykin, Keith 1965— 14

Bradley, David Henry, Jr. 1950— 39

Bradley, Ed 1941-2006 2, 59

Bradley, J. Robert 1919-2007 65

Bradley, Jennette B. 1952— 40

Bradley, Thomas 1917— 2, 20

Brady, Wayne 1972— 32, 71

Brae, C. Michael 1963(?)— 61

Braithwaite, William Stanley 1878-
1962 52

Branch, William Blackwell 1927—
39

Brand, Dionne 1953— 32

Brand, Elton 1979— 31

Brandon, Barbara 1960(?)— 3

Brandon, Thomas Terrell 1970— 16

Brandy 1979— 14, 34, 72

Branham, George, III 1962— 50

Brashear, Carl Maxie 1931— 29

Brashear, Donald 1972— 39

Brathwaite, Fred 1972— 35

Brathwaite, Kamau 1930— 36

Brathwaite, Lawson Edward See
Kamau Brathwaite

Braugher, Andre 1962— 13, 58

Braun, Carol (Elizabeth) Moseley
1947— 4, 42

Brawley, Benjamin 1882-1939 44

Braxton, Toni 1968(?)— 15, 61

Brazile, Donna 1959— 25, 70

Breedlove, Sarah See Walker, Madame C. J.

Breeze, Jean "Binta" 1956— 37

Bridges, Christopher See Ludacris

Bridges, Sheila 1964— 36

Bridges, Todd 1965— 37

Bridgewater, Dee Dee 1950— 32

Bridgforth, Glinda 1952— 36

Brimmer, Andrew F. 1926— 2, 48

Briscoe, Connie 1952— 15

Briscoe, Marlin 1946(?)— 37

Britt, Donna 1954(?)— 28

Broadbent, Hydeia 1984— 36

Brock, Louis Clark 1939— 18

Bronner, Nathaniel H., Sr. 1914-
1993 32

Brooke, Edward (William, III)
1919— 8

Brooks, Aaron 1976— 33

Brooks, Avery 1949— 9

Brooks, Derrick 1973— 43

Brooks, Golden 1970— 62

Brooks, Gwendolyn 1917-2000 1,
28

Brooks, Hadda 1916-2002 40

Brooks, Mehcad 1980— 62

Brooks, Tyrone 1945— 59

Brower, William 1916-2004 49

Brown, Andre See Dre, Dr.

Brown, Angela M. 1964(?)— 54

Brown, Anthony G. 1961— 72

Brown, Bobby 1969— 58

Brown, Buck See Brown, Robert

Brown, Byrd 1930-2001 49

Brown, Byron W. 1958— 72

Brown, Cecil M. 1943— 46

Brown, Charles 1922-1999 23

Brown, Clarence Gatemouth 1924-
2005 59

Brown, Claude 1937-2002 38

Brown, Cora 1914-1972 33

Brown, Corrine 1946— 24

Brown, Cupcake 1964— 63

Brown, Donald 1963— 19

Brown, Eddie C. 1940— 35

Brown, Elaine 1943— 8

Brown, Erroll M. 1950(?)— 23

Brown, Foxy 1979— 25

Brown, George Leslie 1926-2006
62

Brown, H. Rap See Al-Amin, Jamil
Abdullah

Brown, Homer S. 1896-1977 47

Brown, Hubert Gerold See Al-Amin,
Jamil Abdullah

Brown, James 1933-2006 15, 60

Brown, James 1951— 22

Brown, James Nathaniel See
Brown, Jim

Brown, James Willie, Jr. See Komunyakaa, Yusef

Brown, Janice Rogers 1949— 43

Brown, Jesse 1944-2003 6, 41

Brown, Jesse Leroy 1926-1950 31

Brown, Jim 1936— 11

Brown, Joe 19(?)(?)— 29

Brown, Joyce F. 1946— 25

Brown, Lee P(atrick) 1937— 1, 24

Brown, Les(lie Calvin) 1945— 5

Brown, Lloyd Louis 1913-2003 42

Brown, Melanie 1975— 73

Brown, Nappy 1929–2008 73

Brown, Oscar, Jr. 1926-2005 53

Brown, Patrick "Sleepy" 1970— 50

Brown, Robert 1936-2007 65

Brown, Ron(ald Harmon) 1941— 5

Brown, Rosemary 1930-2003 62

Brown, Sean 1976— 52

Brown, Sterling Allen 1901-1989
10, 64

Brown, Tony 1933— 3

Brown, Uzee 1950— 42

Brown, Vivian 1964— 27

Brown, Warren 1971(?)— 61

Brown, Wesley 1945— 23

Brown, Willa Beatrice 1906-1992
40

Brown, Willard 1911(?)-1996 36

Brown, William Anthony See
Brown, Tony

Brown, Willie L., Jr. 1934— 7

Brown, Zora Kramer 1949— 12

Brown Bomber, The See Louis, Joe

Browne, Roscoe Lee 1925-2007 66

Broyard, Anatole 1920–1990 68

Broyard, Bliss 1966— 68

Bruce, Blanche Kelso 1849-1898
33

Bruce, Bruce 19(?)(?)— 56

Bruce, Isaac 1972— 26

Brunson, Dorothy 1938— 1

Brutus, Dennis 1924— 38

Bryan, Ashley F. 1923— 41

Bryant, John 1966— 26

Bryant, John R. 1943— 45

Bryant, Kobe 1978— 15, 31, 71

Bryant, Wayne R(ichard) 1947— 6

Bryant, William Benson 1911-2005
61

Buchanan, Ray 1971— 32

Buckley, Gail Lumet 1937— 39

Buckley, Victoria (Vikki) 1947-1999
24

Bullard, Eugene Jacques 1894-
1961 12

Bullins, Ed 1935— 25

Bullock, Anna Mae See Turner,
Tina

Bullock, Steve 1936— 22

Bully-Cummings, Ella 1957(?)— 48

Bumbry, Grace (Ann) 1937— 5

Bunche, Ralph J(ohnson) 1904-
1971 5

Bunkley, Anita Richmond 19(?)(?)—
39

Burgess, John 1909-2003 46

Burgess, Marjorie L. 1929— 55

Burke, Selma Hortense 1900-1995
16

Burke, Solomon 1936— 31

Burke, Yvonne Braithwaite 1932—
42

Burks, Mary Fair 1920-1991 40

Burleigh, Henry Thacker 1866-1949
56

Burley, Mary Lou See Williams,
Mary Lou

Burnett, Charles 1944— 16, 68

Burnett, Chester Arthur See Howlin'
Wolf

Burnett, Dorothy 1905-1995 19

Burnham, Forbes 1923-1985 66

Burnim, Mickey L. 1949— 48

Burns, Eddie 1928— 44

Burns, Jesse Louis See Jackson,
Jesse

Burns, Ursula 1958— 60

Burnside, R. L. 1926-2005 56

Burrell, Orville Richard See Shaggy

Burrell, Stanley Kirk See Hammer,
M. C.

Burrell, Tom 1939— 21, 51

Burris, Chuck 1951— 21

Burris, Roland W. 1937— 25

Burroughs, Margaret Taylor 1917—
9

Burrows, Stephen 1943— 31

Burrus, William Henry "Bill" 1936—
45

Burt-Murray, Angela 1970— 59

Burton, LeVar(dis Robert Martyn)
1957— 8

Busby, Jheryl 1949(?)— 3

Bush, Reggie 1985— 59

Buthelezi, Mangosuthu Gatsha
1928— 9

Butler, George, Jr. 1931–2008 70

Butler, Jerry 1939— 26

Butler, Jonathan 1961— 28

Butler, Leroy, III 1968— 17

Butler, Louis 1952— 70

Butler, Octavia 1947-2006 8, 43, 58

Butler, Paul D. 1961— 17

Butts, Calvin O(tis), III 1950— 9

Bynoe, Peter C. B. 1951— 40

Bynum, Juanita 1959— 31, 71

Byrd, Donald 1949— 10

Byrd, Eugene 1975— 64

Byrd, Michelle 1965— 19

Byrd, Robert (Oliver Daniel, III)
1952— 11

Byron, JoAnne Deborah See
Shakur, Assata

Cade, Toni See Bambara, Toni
Cade

Cadoria, Sherian Grace 1940— 14

Caesar, Shirley 1938— 19

Cage, Byron 1965(?)— 53

Cain, Herman 1945— 15

Caldwell, Benjamin 1937— 46

Caldwell, Earl 1941(?)— 60

Caldwell, Kirbyjon 1953(?)— 55

Calhoun, Cora See Austin, Lovie

Callaway, Thomas DeCarlo See
Cee-Lo

Callender, Clive O(rville) 1936— 3

Calloway, Cabell, III 1907-1994 14

Cameron, Earl 1917— 44

Camp, Georgia Blanche Douglas
See Johnson, Georgia Douglas

Camp, Kimberly 1956— 19

Campanella, Roy 1921-1993 25

Campbell, Bebe Moore 1950-2006
6, 24, 59

Campbell, Bill 1954— 9

Campbell, Charleszetta Lena See
Waddles, Charleszetta (Mother)

Campbell, Donald J. 1935— 66

Campbell, E(lmer) Simms 1906-
1971 13

Campbell, Mary Schmidt 1947— 43

Campbell, Milton See Little Milton

Campbell, Naomi 1970— 1, 31

Campbell, Tisha See Campbell-
Martin, Tisha

Campbell-Martin, Tisha 1969— 8,
42

Canada, Geoffrey 1954— 23

Canady, Alexa 1950— **28**

Canegata, Leonard Lionel Cornelius See Lee, Canada

Cannon, Katie 1950— **10**

Cannon, Nick 1980— **47, 73**

Cannon, Reuben 1946— **50**

Carby, Hazel 1948— **27**

Cardozo, Francis L. 1837-1903 **33**

Carew, Rod 1945— **20**

Carey, Mariah 1970— **32, 53, 69**

Cargill, Victoria A. 19(?)(?)— **43**

Carmichael, Stokely 1941-1998 **5, 26**

Carnegie, Herbert 1919— **25**

Carr, Johnnie 1911–2008 **69**

Carr, Kurt 196(?)— **56**

Carr, Leroy 1905-1935 **49**

Carroll, Diahann 1935— **9**

Carroll, L. Natalie 1950— **44**

Carroll, Vinnette 1922— **29**

Carruthers, George R. 1939— **40**

Carson, André 1974— **69**

Carson, Benjamin 1951— **1, 35**

Carson, Josephine See Baker, Josephine

Carson, Julia 1938–2007 **23, 69**

Carson, Lisa Nicole 1969— **21**

Carter, Anson 1974— **24**

Carter, Ben See Ben-Israel, Ben Ami

Carter, Benny 1907-2003 **46**

Carter, Betty 1930— **19**

Carter, Butch 1958— **27**

Carter, Cris 1965— **21**

Carter, Dwayne Michael, Jr. See Lil Wayne

Carter, Joe 1960— **30**

Carter, Joye Maureen 1957— **41**

Carter, Kenneth 1959(?)— **53**

Carter, Mandy 1946— **11**

Carter, Martin 1927-1997 **49**

Carter, Nell 1948-2003 **39**

Carter, Pamela Lynn 1949— **67**

Carter, Regina 1966(?)— **23**

Carter, Robert L. 1917— **51**

Carter, Rubin 1937— **26**

Carter, Shawn See Jay-Z

Carter, Stephen L(isle) 1954— **4**

Carter, Vince 1977— **26**

Carter, Warrick L. 1942— **27**

Cartey, Wilfred 1931-1992 **47**

Cartiér, Xam Wilson 1949— **41**

Carver, George Washington 1861(?)-1943 **4**

Cary, Lorene 1956— **3**

Cary, Mary Ann Shadd 1823-1893 **30**

Cash, Rosalind 1938-1995 **28**

Cash, Swin 1979— **59**

Cashin, Sheryll 1962— **63**

CasSelle, Malcolm 1970— **11**

Catchings, Tamika 1979— **43**

Catlett, Elizabeth 1919— **2**

Caymmi, Dorival 1914–2008 **72**

Cayton, Horace 1903-1970 **26**

Cedric the Entertainer 1964— **29, 60**

Cee-Lo 1974— **70**

Césaire, Aimé 1913–2008 **48, 69**

Chadiha, Jeffri 1970— **57**

Chamberlain, Wilt 1936-1999 **18, 47**

Chambers, James See Cliff, Jimmy

Chambers, Julius (LeVonne) 1936— **3**

Chaney, John 1932— **67**

Channer, Colin 1963— **36**

Chanté, Keshia 1988— **50**

Chapman, Nathan A., Jr. 1957— **21**

Chapman, Tracy 1964— **26**

Chappell, Emma C. 1941— **18**

Chappelle, Dave 1973— **50**

Charlemagne, Emmanuel See Charlemagne, Manno

Charlemagne, Manno 1948— **11**

Charles, Mary Eugenia 1919-2005 **10, 55**

Charles, Pierre 1954-2004 **52**

Charles, Ray 1930-2004 **16, 48**

Charleston, Oscar 1896-1954 **39**

Chase, Debra Martin 1956(?)— **49**

Chase, Leah 1923— **57**

Chase-Riboud, Barbara 1939— **20, 46**

Chatard, Peter 1936— **44**

Chavis, Benjamin (Franklin, Jr.) 1948— **6**

Cheadle, Don 1964— **19, 52**

Cheatham, Doc 1905-1997 **17**

Checker, Chubby 1941— **28**

Cheeks, Maurice 1956— **47**

Chenault, John 1952— **40**

Chenault, Kenneth I. 1952— **4, 36**

Cheney-Coker, Syl 1945— **43**

Cheruiyot, Robert 1978— **69**

Cherry, Deron 1959— **40**

Chesimard, JoAnne (Deborah) See Shakur, Assata

Chesnutt, Charles 1858-1932 **29**

Chestnut, J. L., Jr. 1930–2008 **73**

Chestnut, Morris 1969— **31**

Chideya, Farai 1969— **14, 61**

Chief Black Thunderbird Eagle See York, Dwight D.

Childress, Alice 1920-1994 **15**

Chiluba, Frederick Jacob Titus 1943— **56**

Chinn, May Edward 1896-1980 **26**

Chisholm, Samuel J. 1942— **32**

Chisholm, Shirley 1924-2005 **2, 50**

Chissano, Joaquim 1939— **7, 55, 67**

Chong, Rae Dawn 1961— **62**

Christian, Barbara T. 1946-2000 **44**

Christian, Spencer 1947— **15**

Christian-Green, Donna M. 1945— **17**

Christie, Angella **36**

Christie, Linford 1960— **8**

Christie, Perry Gladstone 1944— **53**

Christophe, Henri 1767-1820 **9**

Chuck D 1960— **9**

Church, Bruce See Bruce, Bruce

Chweneyagae, Presley 1984— **63**

Ciara 1985— **56**

Ciara, Barbara 195(?)— **69**

Clack, Zoanne 1968(?)— **73**

Claiborne, Loretta 1953— **34**

Clark, Celeste (Clesteen) Abraham 1953— **15**

Clark, Joe 1939— **1**

Clark, John Pepper See Clark-Bekedermo, J. P.

Clark, Kenneth B. 1914-2005 **5, 52**

Clark, Kristin See Taylor, Kristin Clark

Clark, Mattie Moss 1925-1994 **61**

Clark, Patrick 1955— **14**

Clark, Septima (Poinsette) 1898-1987 **7**

Clark-Bekedermo, J. P. 1935— **44**

Clark-Cole, Dorinda 1957— **66**

Clarke, Austin C. 1934— **32**

Clarke, Cheryl 1947— **32**

Clarke, George Elliott 1960— **32**

Clarke, Hope 1943(?)— **14**

Clarke, John Henrik 1915-1998 **20**

Clarke, Kenny 1914-1985 **27**

Clarke, Patrice Francise See Washington, Patrice Clarke

Clark-Sheard, Karen 19(?)(?)— **22**

Clash, Kevin 1961(?)— **14**

Clay, Bryan Ezra 1980— **57**

Clay, Cassius Marcellus, Jr. See Ali, Muhammad

Clay, William Lacy 1931— **8**

Clayton, Constance 1937— **1**

Clayton, Eva M. 1934— **20**

Clayton, Mayme Agnew 1923-2006 **62**

Clayton, Xernona 1930— **3, 45**

Claytor, Helen 1907-2005 **14, 52**

Cleage, Albert B., Jr. See Agyeman, Jaramogi Abebe

Cleage, Pearl 1948— **17, 64**

Cleaver, (Leroy) Eldridge 1935— **5, 45**

Cleaver, Emanuel (II) 1944— **4, 68**

Cleaver, Kathleen Neal 1945— **29**

Clements, George (Harold) 1932— **2**

Clemmons, Reginal G. 19(?)(?)— **41**

Clemons, Clarence 1942— **41**

Clemons, Michael "Pinball" 1965— **64**

Clendenon, Donn 1935-2005 **26, 56**

Cleveland, James 1932(?)-1991 **19**

Cliff, Jimmy 1948— **28**

Cliff, Michelle 1946— **42**

Clifton, Lucille 1936— **14, 64**

Clifton, Nathaniel "Sweetwater" 1922(?)-1990 **47**

Clinton, George (Edward) 1941— **9**

Clyburn, James E. 1940— **21, 71**

Coachman, Alice 1923— **18**

Cobb, Jewel Plummer 1924— **42**

Cobb, Monty See Cobb, W. Montague

Cobb, W. Montague 1904-1990 **39**

Cobb, William Jelani 1969— **59**

Cobbs, Price M(ashaw) 1928— **9**

Cochran, Johnnie 1937-2005 **11, 39, 52**

Cohen, Anthony 1963— **15**

Colbert, Virgis William 1939— **17**

Cole, Johnnetta B(etsch) 1936— **5, 43**

Cole, Keyshia 1983— **63**

Cole, Lorraine 195(?)— **48**

Cole, Nat King 1919-1965 **17**

Cole, Natalie 1950— **17, 60**

Cole, Rebecca 1846-1922 **38**

Coleman, Bessie 1892-1926 **9**

Coleman, Donald 1952— **24, 62**

Coleman, Gary 1968— **35**

Coleman, Ken 1942— **57**

Coleman, Leonard S., Jr. 1949— **12**

Coleman, Mary 1946— **46**

Coleman, Michael B. 1955(?)— **28**

Coleman, Ornette 1930— **39, 69**

Coleman, Troy See Cowboy Troy

Coleman, Wanda 1946— **48**

Coleman, William F., III 1955(?)— **61**

Colemon, Johnnie 1921(?)— **11**

Colescott, Robert 1925— **69**

Collins, Albert 1932-1993 **12**

Collins, Barbara-Rose 1939— **7**

Collins, Bootsy 1951— **31**

Collins, Cardiss 1931— **10**

Collins, Janet 1917-2003 **33, 64**

Collins, Lyn 1948-2005 **53**

Collins, Marva 1936— **3, 71**

Collins, Patricia Hill 1948— **67**

Collins, Paul 1936— **61**

Collins, William See Collins, Bootsy

Colston, Hal 1953(?)— **72**

Colter, Cyrus J. 1910-2002 **36**

Coltrane, Alice 1937–2007 **70**

Coltrane, John William 1926-1967 **19**

Coltrane, Ravi 1965— **71**

Combs, Sean "Puffy" 1969— **17, 43**

Comer, James P(ierpont) 1934— **6**

Common 1972— **31, 63**

Compton, John 1925-2007 **65**

Cone, James H. 1938— **3**

Coney, PonJola 1951— **48**

Conneh, Sekou Damate, Jr. 1960— **51**

Connerly, Ward 1939— **14**

Conté, Lansana 1944(?)— **7**

Conyers, John, Jr. 1929— **4, 45**

Conyers, Nathan G. 1932— **24**

Cook, Charles "Doc" 1891-1958 **44**

Cook, (Will) Mercer 1903-1987 **40**

Cook, Sam 1931-1964 **17**

Cook, Samuel DuBois 1928— **14**

Cook, Suzan D. Johnson 1957— **22**

Cook, Toni 1944— **23**

Cook, Victor Trent 19(?)(?)— See Three Mo' Tenors

Cook, Wesley See Abu-Jamal, Mumia

Cook, Will Marion 1869-1944 **40**

Cooke, Charles L. See Cook, Charles "Doc"

Cooke, Marcia 1954— **60**

Cooke, Marvel 1901(?)-2000 **31**

Cooks, Patricia 1944-1989 **19**

Cool Papa Bell See Bell, James "Cool Papa"

Cools, Anne 1943— **64**

Coombs, Orde M. 1939-1984 **44**

Cooper, Afua 1957— **53**

Cooper, Andrew Lewis See Cooper, Andy "Lefty"

Cooper, Andrew W. 1928-2002 **36**

Cooper, Andy "Lefty" 1898-1941 **63**

Cooper, Anna Julia 1858-1964 **20**

Cooper, Barry 1956— **33**

Cooper, Charles "Chuck" 1926-1984 **47**

Cooper, Cynthia 1963— **17**

Cooper, Edward S(awyer) 1926— **6**

Cooper, Evern 19(?)(?)— **40**

Cooper, J. California 19(?)(?)— **12**

Cooper, Lisa 1963— **73**

Cooper, Margaret J. 194(?)— **46**

Cooper, Michael 1956— **31**

Cooper Cafritz, Peggy 1947— **43**
Copeland, Michael 1954— **47**
Corbi, Lana 1955— **42**
Corley, Tony 1949— **62**
Cornelius, Don 1936— **4**
Cornish, Sam 1935— **50**
Cornwell, Edward E., III 1956— **70**
Cortez, Jayne 1936— **43**
Corthron, Kia 1961— **43**
Cortor, Eldzier 1916— **42**
Cosby, Bill 1937— **7, 26, 59**
Cosby, Camille Olivia Hanks 1944— **14**
Cosby, William Henry, Jr. *See Cosby, Bill*
Cose, Ellis 1951— **5, 50**
Cotter, Joseph Seamon, Sr. 1861-1949 **40**
Cottrell, Comer 1931— **11**
Count Basie 1904-1984 **23**
Couto, Mia 1955— **45**
Coverley, Louise Bennett *See Bennett, Louise*
Cowans, Adger W. 1936— **20**
Cowboy Troy, 1970— **54**
Cox, Deborah 1974(?)— **28**
Cox, Ida 1896-1967 **42**
Cox, Joseph Mason Andrew 1930— **51**
Cox, Renée 1960— **67**
Cox, William E. 1942— **68**
Craig, Carl 1969— **31, 71**
Craig-Jones, Ellen Walker 1906-2000 **44**
Crawford, Randy 1952— **19**
Crawford, Veronica *See Crawford, Randy*
Cray, Robert 1953— **30**
Creagh, Milton 1957— **27**
Crennel, Romeo 1947— **54**
Crew, Rudolph F. 1950(?)— **16**
Crew, Spencer R. 1949— **55**
Crite, Alan Rohan 1910— **29**
Crocker, Frankie 1937-2000 **29**
Crockett, George W., Jr. 1909-1997 **10, 64**
Crooks, Garth 1958— **53**
Croom, Sylvester 1954— **50**
Cross, Dolores E. 1938— **23**
Crothers, Benjamin Sherman *See Crothers, Scatman*
Crothers, Scatman 1910-1986 **19**
Crouch, Andraé 1942— **27**
Crouch, Stanley 1945— **11**
Crowder, Henry 1895-1954(?) **16**
Crump, Lavell *See Banner, David*
Cruse, Harold 1916-2005 **54**
Crutchfield, James N. 1947— **55**
Cullen, Countee 1903-1946 **8**
Cullers, Vincent T. 1924(?)-2003 **49**
Culp, Napoleon Brown Goodson *See Brown, Nappy*
Culpepper, Daunte 1977— **32**
Cummings, Elijah E. 1951— **24**
Cuney, William Waring 1906-1976 **44**
Cunningham, Evelyn 1916— **23**
Cunningham, Randall 1963— **23**
Curling, Alvin 1939— **34**
Currie, Betty 1939(?)— **21**
Currie, Ulysses 1937— **73**
Curry, George E. 1947— **23**
Curry, Mark 1964— **17**

Curtis, Christopher Paul 1954(?)— **26**
Curtis-Hall, Vondie 1956— **17**
da Silva, Benedita 1942— **5**
da Silva, Jorge Mário *See Jorge, Seu*
Dabydeen, David 1956— **48**
Dadié, Bernard 1916— **34**
Daemyon, Jerald 1970(?)— **64**
D'Aguiar, Fred 1960— **50**
Daly, Marie Maynard 1921— **37**
Damas, Léon-Gontran 1912-1978 **46**
Dandridge, Dorothy 1922-1965 **3**
Dandridge, Ray 1913-1994 **36**
Dandridge, Raymond Garfield 1882-1930 **45**
D'Angelo 1974— **27**
Daniels, Gertrude *See Haynes, Trudy*
Daniels, Lee Louis 1959— **36**
Daniels-Carter, Valerie 19(?)(?)— **23**
Danner, Margaret Esse 1915-1986 **49**
Danticat, Edwidge 1969— **15, 68**
Dantley, Adrian 1956— **72**
Dara, Olu 1941— **335**
Darden, Calvin 1950— **38**
Darden, Christopher 1957— **13**
Darego, Agbani 1982— **52**
Dash, Damon 19(?)(?)— **31**
Dash, Darien 1972(?)— **29**
Dash, Julie 1952— **4**
Dash, Leon 1944— **47**
Datcher, Michael 1967— **60**
Dathorne, O. R. 1934— **52**
Davenport, Arthur *See Fattah, Chaka*
David, Craig 1981— **31, 53**
David, Keith 1954— **27**
Davidson, Jaye 1967(?)— **5**
Davidson, Tommy 1963(?)— **21**
Davis, Allison 1902-1983 **12**
Davis, Angela (Yvonne) 1944— **5**
Davis, Anthony 1951— **11**
Davis, Anthony Moses *See Beenie Man*
Davis, Arthur P. 1904-1996 **41**
Davis, Artur 1967— **41**
Davis, Belva 1932— **61**
Davis, Benjamin O(liver), Jr. 1912-2002 **2, 43**
Davis, Benjamin O(liver), Sr. 1877-1970 **4**
Davis, Charles T. 1918-1981 **48**
Davis, Chuck 1937— **33**
Davis, Danny K. 1941— **24**
Davis, Ed 1911-1999 **24**
Davis, Eisa 1971— **68**
Davis, Ernie 1939-1963 **48**
Davis, Erroll B., Jr. 1944— **57**
Davis, Frank Marshall 1905-1987 **47**
Davis, Gary 1896-1972 **41**
Davis, George 1939— **36**
Davis, Guy 1952— **36**
Davis, Jamelia Niela *See Jamelia*
Davis, James E. 1962-2003 **50**
Davis, Lorenzo "Piper" 1917-1997 **19**
Davis, Mike 1960— **41**
Davis, Miles (Dewey, III) 1926-1991 **4**

Davis, Nolan 1942— **45**
Davis, Ossie 1917-2005 **5, 50**
Davis, Ruth 1943— **37**
Davis, Sammy, Jr. 1925-1990 **18**
Davis, Shani 1982— **58**
Davis, Terrell 1972— **20**
Davis, Thulani 1948— **61**
Davis, Tyrone 1938-2005 **54**
Davis, Viola 1965— **34**
Dawes, Dominique (Margaux) 1976— **11**
Dawkins, Wayne 1955— **20**
Dawson, Matel "Mat," Jr. 1921-2002 **39**
Dawson, Michael C. 1951— **63**
Dawson, Rosario 1979— **72**
Dawson, William Levi 1899-1900 **39**
Day, Leon 1916-1995 **39**
Days, Drew S(aunders, III) 1941— **10**
De' Alexander, Quinton 19??— **57**
de Assís Moreira, Ronaldo *See Ronaldinho*
de Carvalho, Barcelo *See Bonga, Kuenda*
de Passe, Suzanne 1948(?)— **25**
De Shields, André 1946— **72**
De Veaux, Alexis 1948— **44**
"Deadwood Dick" *See Love, Nat*
Dean, Mark E. 1957— **35**
DeBaptiste, George 1814(?)-1875 **32**
Déby, Idriss 1952— **30**
DeCarava, Roy 1919— **42**
Deconge-Watson, Lovenia 1933— **55**
Dee, Merri 1936— **55**
Dee, Ruby 1924— **8, 50, 68**
Deezer D 1965— **53**
DeFrantz, Anita 1952— **37**
Deggans, Eric 1965— **71**
Delaney, Beauford 1901-1979 **19**
Delaney, Joseph 1904-1991 **30**
Delany, Annie Elizabeth 1891-1995 **12**
Delany, Martin R. 1812-1885 **27**
Delany, Samuel R(ay), Jr. 1942— **9**
Delany, Sarah (Sadie) 1889— **12**
Delco, Wilhemina R. 1929— **33**
Delice, Ronald 1966— **48**
Delice, Rony 1966— **48**
DeLille, Henriette 1813-1862 **30**
Dellums, Ronald (Vernie) 1935— **2**
DeLoach, Nora 1940-2001 **30**
Delsarte, Louis 1944— **34**
Demby, William 1922— **51**
Dennard, Brazeal 1929— **37**
Dent, Thomas C. 1932-1998 **50**
Dent, Tom *See Dent, Thomas C.*
DePriest, James 1936— **37**
DeVard, Jerri 1957(?)— **61**
Devers, (Yolanda) Gail 1966— **7**
Devine, Loretta 1953— **24**
Devine, Major J. *See Divine, Father*
DeWese, Mohandas *See Kool Moe Dee*
Diallo, Amadou 1976-1999 **27**
Dibaba, Tirunesh 1985— **73**
Dickens, Helen Octavia 1909-2001 **14, 64**
Dickenson, Vic 1906-1984 **38**
Dickerson, Debra J. 1959— **60**

Dickerson, Eric 1960— **27**
Dickerson, Ernest 1952(?)— **6, 17**
Dickey, Eric Jerome 1961— **21, 56**
Diddley, Bo 1928-2008 **39, 72**
Diesel, Vin 1967(?)— **29**
Dieudonné 1966— **67**
Diggs, Charles C. 1922-1998 **21**
Diggs, Scott *See Diggs, Taye*
Diggs, Taye 1972— **25, 63**
Diggs-Taylor, Anna 1932— **20**
Dillard, Godfrey J. 1948— **45**
Dinkins, David (Norman) 1927— **4**
Diogo, Luisa Dias 1958— **63**
Diop, Birago 1906-1989 **53**
Diop, Cheikh Anta 1923-1986 **4**
Diouf, Abdou 1935— **3**
Dirie, Waris 1965(?)— **56**
Divine, Father 1877(?)-1965 **7**
Dixon, Dean 1915—1976 **68**
Dixon, George 1870-1909 **52**
Dixon, Ivan 1931–2008 **69**
Dixon, Julian C. 1934— **24**
Dixon, Margaret 192(?)— **14**
Dixon, Rodrick 19(?)(?)— *See Three Mo' Tenors*
Dixon, Sharon Pratt 1944— **1**
Dixon, Sheila 1953— **68**
Dixon, Willie (James) 1915-1992 **4**
DJ Jazzy Jeff 1965— **32**
DJ Red Alert *See Alert, Kool DJ Red*
DMC 1964— **31**
DMX 1970— **28, 64**
do Nascimento, Edson Arantes *See Pelé*
Dobbs, Mattiwilda 1925— **34**
Doby, Larry *See Doby, Lawrence Eugene, Sr.*
Doby, Lawrence Eugene, Sr. 1924-2003 **16, 41**
Dodson, Howard, Jr. 1939— **7, 52**
Dodson, Owen 1914-1983 **38**
Doig, Jason 1977— **45**
Doley, Harold, Jr. 1947— **26**
Domini, Rey *See Lorde, Audre (Geraldine)*
Domino, Fats 1928— **20**
Donald, Arnold Wayne 1954— **36**
Donaldson, Jeff 1932-2004 **46**
Donegan, Dorothy 1922-1998 **19**
Donovan, Kevin *See Bambaataa, Afrika*
Dorrell, Karl 1963— **52**
Dorsey, Lee 1926-1986 **65**
Dorsey, Thomas Andrew 1899-1993 **15**
Dortch, Thomas W., Jr. 1950— **45**
dos Santos, José Eduardo 1942— **43**
dos Santos, Manuel Francisco 1933 **65**
Dougherty, Mary Pearl 1915-2003 **47**
Douglas, Aaron 1899-1979 **7**
Douglas, Ashanti *See Ashanti*
Douglas, Denzil Llewellyn 1953— **53**
Douglas, Lizzie *See Memphis Minnie*
Dourdan, Gary 1966— **37**
Dove, Rita (Frances) 1952— **6**
Dove, Ulysses 1947— **5**
Downing, Will 19(?)(?)— **19**

Dozier, Lamont See Holland-Dozier-Holland

Dr. J See Erving, Julius

Draper, Sharon Mills 1952— **16, 43**

Drayton, William Jonathan, Jr. See Flavor Flav

Dre, Dr. 1965(?)— **10, 14, 30**

Drew, Alvin, Jr. 1962— **67**

Drew, Charles Richard 1904-1950 **7**

Drexler, Clyde 1962— **4, 61**

Driskell, David C(lyde) 1931— **7**

Driver, David E. 1955— **11**

Drummond, William J. 1944— **40**

Du Bois, David Graham 1925— **45**

Du Bois, W(illiam) E(dward) B(urghardt) 1868-1963 **3**

DuBois, Shirley Graham 1907-1977 **21**

Duchemin, Alamaine See Maxis, Theresa

Duchemin, Marie See Maxis, Theresa

Duchemin, Theresa Maxis See Maxis, Theresa

Ducksworth, Marilyn 1957— **12**

Dudley, Edward R. 1911-2005 **58**

Due, Tananarive 1966— **30**

Duggins, George 1943-2005 **64**

Duke, Bill 1943— **3**

Duke, George 1946— **21**

Dukes, Hazel Nell 1932— **56**

Dumars, Joe 1963— **16, 65**

Dumas, Henry 1934-1968 **41**

Dunbar, Alice See Dunbar-Nelson, Alice Ruth Moore

Dunbar, Paul Laurence 1872-1906 **8**

Dunbar, Sly 1952— See Sly & Robbie

Dunbar-Nelson, Alice Ruth Moore 1875-1935 **44**

Duncan, Michael Clarke 1957— **26**

Duncan, Tim 1976— **20**

Dungey, Merrin 1971— **62**

Dungy, Tony 1955— **17, 42, 59**

Dunham, Katherine 1910-2006 **4, 59**

Dunlap, Ericka 1982(?)— **55**

Dunn, Jerry 1953— **27**

Dunner, Leslie B. 1956— **45**

Dunnigan, Alice Allison 1906-1983 **41**

Dunston, Georgia Mae 1944— **48**

Duplechan, Larry 1956— **55**

Dupri, Jermaine 1972— **13, 46**

Durham, Bobby 1937–2008 **73**

Durham, Robert Joseph See Durham, Bobby

Dutton, Charles S. 1951— **4, 22**

Dutton, Marie Elizabeth 1940— **12**

Dwight, Edward 1933— **65**

Dworkin, Aaron P. 1970— **52**

Dye, Jermaine 1974— **58**

Dymally, Mervyn 1926— **42**

Dyson, Michael Eric 1958— **11, 40**

Early, Deloreese Patricia See Reese, Della

Early, Gerald (Lyn) 1952— **15**

Earthquake, 1963— **55**

Easley, Annie J. 1933— **61**

Ebanks, Michelle 1962— **60**

Ebanks, Selita 1983— **67**

Eckstein, William Clarence See Eckstine, Billy

Eckstine, Billy 1914-1993 **28**

Edelin, Ramona Hoage 1945— **19**

Edelman, Marian Wright 1939— **5, 42**

Edgerton, Khia Danielle See K-Swift

Edley, Christopher 1928-2003 **2, 48**

Edley, Christopher F., Jr. 1953— **48**

Edmonds, Kenneth "Babyface" 1958(?)— **10, 31**

Edmonds, Terry 1950(?)— **17**

Edmonds, Tracey 1967— **16, 64**

Edmunds, Gladys 1951(?)— **48**

Edwards, Eli See McKay, Claude

Edwards, Esther Gordy 1920(?)— **43**

Edwards, Harry 1942— **2**

Edwards, Herman 1954— **51**

Edwards, Melvin 1937— **22**

Edwards, Teresa 1964— **14**

Edwards, Trevor 1962— **54**

Edwards, Willarda V. 1951— **59**

Ejiofor, Chiwetel 1977(?)— **67**

Ekwensi, Cyprian 1921— **37**

El Wilson, Barbara 1959— **35**

Elba, Idris 1972— **49**

Elder, Larry 1952— **25**

Elder, (Robert) Lee 1934— **6**

Elder, Lonne, III 1931-1996 **38**

Elders, Joycelyn (Minnie) 1933— **6**

Eldridge, Roy 1911-1989 **37**

El-Hajj Malik El-Shabazz See X, Malcolm

Elise, Kimberly 1967— **32**

Ellerbe, Brian 1963— **22**

Ellington, Duke 1899-1974 **5**

Ellington, E. David 1960— **11**

Ellington, Edward Kennedy See Ellington, Duke

Ellington, Mercedes 1939— **34**

Elliott, Lorris 1931-1999 **37**

Elliott, Missy "Misdemeanor" 1971— **31**

Elliott, Sean 1968— **26**

Ellis, Clarence A. 1943— **38**

Ellis, Jimmy 1940— **44**

Ellison, Keith 1963— **59**

Ellison, Ralph (Waldo) 1914-1994 **7**

Elmore, Ronn 1957— **21**

El-Shabazz, El-Hajj Malik See X, Malcolm

Emanuel, James A. 1921— **46**

Emeagwali, Dale 1954— **31**

Emeagwali, Philip 1954— **30**

Emecheta, Buchi 1944— **30**

Emmanuel, Alphonsia 1956— **38**

Ensley, Carol Denis See Nash, Niecy

Ephriam, Mablean 1949(?)— **29**

Epperson, Sharon 1969(?)— **54**

Epps, Archie C., III 1937-2003 **45**

Epps, Mike 1970— **60**

Epps, Omar 1973— **23, 59**

Ericsson-Jackson, Aprille 19(?)(?)— **28**

Ervin, Anthony 1981— **66**

Erving, Julius 1950— **18, 47**

Escobar, Damien 1987— **56**

Escobar, Tourie 1985— **56**

Esposito, Giancarlo (Giusseppi Alessandro) 1958— **9**

Espy, Alphonso Michael See Espy, Mike

Espy, Mike 1953— **6**

Estes, Rufus 1857-19(?)(?) **29**

Estes, Simon 1938— **28**

Estes, Sleepy John 1899-1977 **33**

Eto'o, Samuel 1981— **73**

Eubanks, Kevin 1957— **15**

Eugene-Richard, Margie 1941— **63**

Europe, (William) James Reese 1880-1919 **10**

Evans, Darryl 1961— **22**

Evans, Diana 1972(?)— **72**

Evans, Ernest See Checker, Chubby

Evans, Etu 1969— **55**

Evans, Faith 1973(?)— **22**

Evans, Harry 1956(?)— **25**

Evans, Mari 1923— **26**

Eve 1979— **29**

Everett, Francine 1917-1999 **23**

Everett, Ronald McKinley See Karenga, Maulana

Evers, Medgar (Riley) 1925-1963 **3**

Evers, Myrlie 1933— **8**

Evora, Cesaria 1941— **12**

Ewing, Patrick 1962— **17, 73**

Eyadéma, Gnassingbé 1937-2005 **7, 52**

Fabio, Sarah Webster 1928-1979 **48**

Fabre, Shelton 1963— **71**

Fagan, Garth 1940— **18**

Fair, Ronald L. 1932— **47**

Faison, Donald 1974— **50**

Faison, Frankie 1949— **55**

Faison, George William 1946— **16**

Falana, Lola 1942— **42**

Falconer, Etta Zuber 1933-2002 **59**

Fanon, Frantz 1925-1961 **44**

Farah, Nuruddin 1945— **27**

Fargas, Antonio 1946(?)— **50**

Farley, Christopher John 1966— **54**

Farmer, Art(hur Stewart) 1928-1999 **38**

Farmer, Forest J(ackson) 1941— **1**

Farmer, James 1920-1999 **2, 64**

Farmer-Paellmann, Deadria 1966— **43**

Farr, Mel 1944— **24**

Farrakhan, Louis 1933— **2, 15**

Farris, Isaac Newton, Jr. 1962— **63**

Father Goose See Rhoden, Wayne

Fattah, Chaka 1956— **11, 70**

Faulk, Marshall 1973— **35**

Fauntroy, Walter E(dward) 1933— **11**

Fauset, Jessie (Redmon) 1882-1961 **7**

Favors, Steve 1948— **23**

Fax, Elton 1909-1993 **48**

Feaster, Robert Franklin See Sundiata, Sekou

Feelings, Muriel 1938— **44**

Feelings, Tom 1933-2003 **11, 47**

Feemster, Herbert 1942— **72**

Fela 1938-1997 **1, 42**

Felix, Allyson 1985— **48**

Felix, Larry R. (?)— **64**

Fennoy, Ilene 1947— **72**

Fenty, Adrian 1970— **60**

Fentry, Robyn See Rihanna

Ferguson, Kevin See Slice, Kimbo

Ferguson, Roger W. 1951— **25**

Ferrell, Rachelle 1961— **29**

Ferrer, Ibrahim 1927— **41**

Fetchit, Stepin 1892-1985 **32**

Fiasco, Lupe 1982— **64**

Fielder, Cecil (Grant) 1963— **2**

Fielder, Prince Semien 1984— **68**

Fields, C. Virginia 1946— **25**

Fields, Cleo 1962— **13**

Fields, Evelyn J. 1949— **27**

Fields, Felicia P. (?)— **60**

Fields, Julia 1938— **45**

Fields, Kim 1969— **36**

50 Cent 1976— **46**

Figueroa, John J. 1920-1999 **40**

Files, Lolita 1964(?)— **35**

Fine, Sam 1969— **60**

Finner-Williams, Paris Michele 1951— **62**

Fishburne, Larry See Fishburne, Laurence

Fishburne, Laurence 1961— **4, 22, 70**

Fisher, Antwone Quenton 1959— **40**

Fisher, Rudolph John Chauncey 1897-1934 **17**

Fitzgerald, Ella 1918-1996 **8, 18**

Flack, Roberta 1940— **19**

Flake, Floyd H. 1945— **18**

Flanagan, Tommy 1930–2001 **69**

Flash, Grandmaster See Grandmaster Flash

Flavor Flav 1959— **67**

Fleming, Raymond 1945— **48**

Fletcher, Alphonse, Jr. 1965— **16**

Fletcher, Arthur A. 1924-2005 **63**

Fletcher, Bill, Jr. 1954— **41**

Flipper, Henry O(ssian) 1856-1940 **3**

Flood, Curt(is) 1963— **10**

Flowers, Sylester 1935— **50**

Flowers, Vonetta 1973— **35**

Floyd, Elson S. 1956— **41**

Folks, Byron See Allen, Byron

Forbes, Audrey Manley 1934— **16**

Forbes, Calvin 1945— **46**

Forbes, James A., Jr. 1935— **71**

Ford, Cheryl 1981— **45**

Ford, Clyde W. 1951— **40**

Ford, Harold E(ugene) 1945— **42**

Ford, Harold E(ugene), Jr. 1970— **16, 70**

Ford, Jack 1947— **39**

Ford, Johnny 1942— **70**

Ford, Nick Aaron 1904–1982 **44**

Ford, Wallace 1950— **58**

Foreman, George 1948— **1, 15**

Forman, James 1928-2005 **7, 51**

Forrest, Leon 1937–1997 **44**

Forrest, Vernon 1971— **40**

Forte, Linda Diane 1952— **54**

Fortune, T(imothy) Thomas 1856-1928 **6**

Foster, Cecil (A.) 1954— **32**

Foster, Ezola 1938— **28**

Foster, George "Pops" 1892-1969 **40**

Foster, Henry W., Jr. 1933— **26**

Foster, Jylla Moore 1954— **45**

Foster, Marie 1917-2003 **48**

Fowler, Reggie 1959— **51**

Fowles, Gloria See Gaynor, Gloria

Fox, Rick 1969— **27**

Fox, Ulrich Alexander See Fox, Rick

Fox, Vivica A. **15, 53**

Foxx, Jamie 1967— **15, 48**
Foxx, Redd 1922-1991 **2**
Francis, Norman (C.) 1931— **60**
Franklin, Aretha 1942— **11, 44**
Franklin, C. L. 1915–1984 **68**
Franklin, Carl 1949— **11**
Franklin, Hardy R. 1929— **9**
Franklin, J.E. 1937— **44**
Franklin, John Hope 1915— **5**
Franklin, Kirk 1970(?)— **15, 49**
Franklin, Robert M(ichael) 1954— **13**
Franklin, Shirley 1945— **34**
Franks, Gary 1954(?)— **2**
Frazer, Jendayi 196(?)— **68**
Frazier, Edward Franklin 1894-1962 **10**
Frazier, Joe 1944— **19**
Frazier, Kevin 1964— **58**
Frazier, Oscar 1956-2005 **58**
Frazier-Lyde, Jacqui 1961— **31**
Fredericks, Henry Saint Claire See Mahal, Taj
Freelon, Nnenna 1954— **32**
Freeman, Aaron 1956— **52**
Freeman, Al(bert Cornelius), Jr. 1934— **11**
Freeman, Cathy 1973— **29**
Freeman, Charles Eldridge 1933— **19**
Freeman, Harold P. 1933— **23**
Freeman, Leonard 1950— **27**
Freeman, Marianna 1957— **23**
Freeman, Morgan 1937— **2, 20, 62**
Freeman, Paul 1936— **39**
Freeman, Yvette **27**
French, Albert 1943— **18**
Fresh Prince, The See Smith, Will
Friday, Jeff 1964(?)— **24**
Fryer, Roland G. 1977— **56**
Fudge, Ann (Marie) 1951— **11, 55**
Fuhr, Grant 1962— **1, 49**
Fulani, Lenora (Branch) 1950— **11**
Fuller, A. Oveta 1955— **43**
Fuller, Arthur 1972— **27**
Fuller, Charles (Henry) 1939— **8**
Fuller, Howard L. 1941— **37**
Fuller, Hoyt 1923-1981 **44**
Fuller, Meta Vaux Warrick 1877-1968 **27**
Fuller, S. B. 1895-1988 **13**
Fuller, Solomon Carter, Jr. 1872-1953 **15**
Fuller, Vivian 1954— **33**
Funderburg, I. Owen 1924-2002 **38**
Funnye, Capers C., Jr. 1952(?)— **73**
Fuqua, Antoine 1966— **35**
Futch, Eddie 1911-2001 **33**
Gabre-Medhin, Tsegaye 1936-2006 **64**
Gaines, Brenda 19(?)(?)— **41**
Gaines, Clarence E., Sr. 1923-2005 **55**
Gaines, Ernest J(ames) 1933— **7**
Gaines, Grady 1934— **38**
Gaither, Israel L. 1944— **65**
Gaither, Jake 1903-1994 **14**
Gantin, Bernardin 1922–2008 **70**
Gantt, Harvey (Bernard) 1943— **1**
Gardner, Chris 1954— **65**
Gardner, Edward G. 1925— **45**
Garnett, Kevin (Maurice) 1976— **14, 70**

Garrett, Joyce Finley 1931-1997 **59**
Garrett, Sean 1979— **57**
Garrincha See dos Santos, Manuel Francisco
Garrison, Zina 1963— **2**
Garvey, Marcus 1887-1940 **1**
Gary, Willie Edward 1947— **12**
Gaskins, Eric 1958— **64**
Gaston, Arthur George 1892-1996 **3, 38, 59**
Gaston, Cito 1944— **71**
Gaston, Clarence Edwin See Gaston, Cito
Gaston, Marilyn Hughes 1939— **60**
Gates, Henry Louis, Jr. 1950— **3, 38, 67**
Gates, Sylvester James, Jr. 1950— **15**
Gay, Marvin Pentz, Jr. See Gaye, Marvin
Gaye, Marvin 1939-1984 **2**
Gaye, Nona 1974— **56**
Gayle, Addison, Jr. 1932-1991 **41**
Gayle, Helene D. 1955— **3, 46**
Gaynor, Gloria 1947— **36**
Gbagbo, Laurent 1945— **43**
Gebrselassie, Haile 1973— **70**
Gentry, Alvin 1954— **23**
George, Nelson 1957— **12**
George, Zelma Watson 1903-1994 **42**
Gerima, Haile 1946— **38**
Gibson, Althea 1927-2003 **8, 43**
Gibson, Bob 1935— **33**
Gibson, Donald Bernard 1933— **40**
Gibson, Johnnie Mae 1949— **23**
Gibson, Josh 1911-1947 **22**
Gibson, Kenneth Allen 1932— **6**
Gibson, Ted 1965— **66**
Gibson, Truman K., Jr. 1912-2005 **60**
Gibson, Tyrese 1978— **27, 62**
Gibson, William F(rank) 1933— **6**
Giddings, Paula (Jane) 1947— **11**
Gidron, Richard D. 1939–2007 **68**
Gil, Gilberto 1942— **53**
Gilbert, Christopher 1949— **50**
Gill, Gerald 1948–2007 **69**
Gill, Johnny 1966— **51**
Gilles, Ralph 1970— **61**
Gillespie, Dizzy 1917-1993 **1**
Gillespie, John Birks See Gillespie, Dizzy
Gilliam, Frank 1934(?)— **23**
Gilliam, Joe, Jr. 1950-2000 **31**
Gilliam, Sam 1933— **16**
Gilliard, Steve 1964–2007 **69**
Gilmore, Marshall 1931— **46**
Ginuwine 1975(?)— **35**
Giovanni, Nikki 1943— **9, 39**
Giovanni, Yolande Cornelia, Jr. See Giovanni, Nikki
Gist, Carole 1970(?)— **1**
Givens, Adele 19(?)(?)— **62**
Givens, Robin 1964— **4, 25, 58**
Givhan, Robin Deneen 1964— **72**
Gladwell, Malcolm 1963— **62**
Glover, Corey 1964— **34**
Glover, Danny 1948— **1, 24**
Glover, Nathaniel, Jr. 1943— **12**
Glover, Savion 1974— **14**
Gnassingbé, Faure 1966— **67**
Goapele 1977— **55**

"The Goat" See Manigault, Earl "The Goat"
Godbolt, James Titus See Slyde, Jimmy
Goines, Donald 1937(?)-1974 **19**
Goings, Russell 1932(?)— **59**
Goldberg, Whoopi 1955— **4, 33, 69**
Golden, Marita 1950— **19**
Golden, Thelma 1965— **10, 55**
Goldsberry, Ronald 1942— **18**
Golson, Benny 1929— **37**
Golston, Allan C. 1967(?)— **55**
Gomes, Peter J(ohn) 1942— **15**
Gomez, Jewelle 1948— **30**
Gomez-Preston, Cheryl 1954— **9**
Goode, Mal(vin Russell) 1908-1995 **13**
Goode, W(oodrow) Wilson 1938— **4**
Gooden, Dwight 1964— **20**
Gooden, Lolita See Roxanne Shante
Gooding, Cuba, Jr. 1968— **16, 62**
Goodison, Lorna 1947— **71**
Goodnight, Paul 1946— **32**
Gorden, W. C. 1930— **71**
Gorden, William C. See Gorden, W. C.
Gordon, Bruce S. 1946— **41, 53**
Gordon, Dexter 1923-1990 **25**
Gordon, Ed 1960— **10, 53**
Gordon, Pamela 1955— **17**
Gordone, Charles 1925-1995 **15**
Gordy, Berry, Jr. 1929— **1**
Goreed, Joseph See Williams, Joe
Goss, Carol A. 1947— **55**
Goss, Tom 1946— **23**
Gossett, Louis, Jr. 1936— **7**
Gotti, Irv 1971— **39**
Gourdine, Meredith 1929-1998 **33**
Gourdine, Simon (Peter) 1940— **11**
Grace, George H. 1948— **48**
Grae, Jean 1976— **51**
Graham, Lawrence Otis 1962— **12**
Graham, Lorenz 1902-1989 **48**
Graham, Stedman 1951(?)— **13**
Granderson, Curtis 1981— **66**
Grandmaster Flash 1958— **33, 60**
Grand-Pierre, Jean-Luc 1977— **46**
Grant, Augustus O. 1946(?)— **71**
Grant, Bernie 1944-2000 **57**
Grant, Gwendolyn Goldsby 19(?)(?)— **28**
Granville, Evelyn Boyd 1924— **36**
Gravely, Samuel L., Jr. 1922-2004 **5, 49**
Graves, Denyce Antoinette 1964— **19, 57**
Graves, Earl G(ilbert) 1935— **1, 35**
Gray, Darius 1945— **69**
Gray, F. Gary 1969— **14, 49**
Gray, Farrah 1984— **59**
Gray, Fred Sr. 1930— **37**
Gray, Frizzell See Mfume, Kweisi
Gray (Nelson Rollins), Ida 1867-1953 **41**
Gray, Macy 1970— **29**
Gray, William H., III 1941— **3**
Gray, Willie 1947— **46**
Gray, Yeshimbra "Shimmy" 1972— **55**
Greaves, William 1926— **38**
Greely, M. Gasby 1946— **27**

Greely, Margaret Gasby See Greely, M. Gasby
Green, A. C. 1963— **32**
Green, Al 1946— **13, 47**
Green, Cee-Lo See Cee-Lo
Green, Darrell 1960— **39**
Green, Dennis 1949— **5, 45**
Green, Grant 1935-1979 **56**
Green, Jonathan 1955— **54**
Greene, Joe 1946— **10**
Greene, Maurice 1974— **27**
Greene, Petey 1931-1984 **65**
Greene, Ralph Waldo See Greene, Petey
Greene, Richard Thaddeus, Sr. 1913–2006 **67**
Greenfield, Eloise 1929— **9**
Greenhouse, Bunnatine "Bunny" 1944— **57**
Greenlee, Sam 1930— **48**
Greenwood, Monique 1959— **38**
Gregg, Eric 1951— **16**
Gregory, Ann 1912-1990 **63**
Gregory, Dick 1932— **1, 54**
Gregory, Frederick 1941— **8, 51**
Gregory, Wilton 1947— **37**
Grier, David Alan 1955— **28**
Grier, Mike 1975— **43**
Grier, Pam(ela Suzette) 1949— **9, 31**
Grier, Roosevelt (Rosey) 1932— **13**
Griffey, Ken, Jr. 1969— **12, 73**
Griffin, Anthony 1960— **71**
Griffin, Bessie Blout 1914— **43**
Griffin, John Arnold, III See Griffin, Johnny
Griffin, Johnny 1928–2008 **71**
Griffin, LaShell 1967— **51**
Griffith, Mark Winston 1963— **8**
Griffith, Patrick A. 1944— **64**
Griffith, Yolanda 1970— **25**
Griffith-Joyner, Florence 1959-1998 **28**
Griffiths, Marcia 1948(?)— **29**
Grimké, Archibald H(enry) 1849-1930 **9**
Grooms, Henry R(andall) 1944— **50**
Guarionex See Schomburg, Arthur Alfonso
Guéï, Robert 1941-2002 **66**
Guillaume, Robert 1927— **3, 48**
Güines, Tata 1930–2008 **69**
Guinier, (Carol) Lani 1950— **7, 30**
Gumbel, Bryant Charles 1948— **14**
Gumbel, Greg 1946— **8**
Gunn, Moses 1929-1993 **10**
Gurira, Danai 1978(?)— **73**
Guy, (George) Buddy 1936— **31**
Guy, Jasmine 1964(?)— **2**
Guy, Rosa 1925(?)— **5**
Guy-Sheftall, Beverly 1946— **13**
Guyton, Tyree 1955— **9**
Gwynn, Anthony Keith 1960— **18**
Habré, Hissène 1942— **6**
Habyarimana, Juvenal 1937-1994 **8**
Haddon, Dietrick 1973(?)— **55**
Hageman, Hans 19(?)(?)— **36**
Hageman, Ivan 19(?)(?)— **36**
Haile Selassie 1892-1975 **7**
Hailey, JoJo 1971— **22**
Hailey, K-Ci 1969— **22**
Hale, Clara 1902-1992 **16**

Hale, Lorraine 1926(?)— **8**
Haley, Alex (Palmer) 1921-1992 **4**
Haley, George Williford Boyce 1925— **21**
Hall, Aaron 1963— **57**
Hall, Arsenio 1955— **58**
Hall, Arthur 1943-2000 **39**
Hall, Elliott S. 1938(?)— **24**
Hall, Juanita 1901-1968 **62**
Hall, Kevan 19(?)(?)— **61**
Hall, Lloyd A(ugustus) 1894-1971 **8**
Halliburton, Warren J. 1924— **49**
Ham, Cynthia Parker 1970(?)— **58**
Hamblin, Ken 1940— **10**
Hamer, Fannie Lou (Townsend) 1917-1977 **6**
Hamilton, Anthony 1971— **61**
Hamilton, Lewis 1985— **66**
Hamilton, Lisa Gay 1964— **71**
Hamilton, Samuel C. 19(?)(?)— **47**
Hamilton, Virginia 1936— **10**
Hamlin, Larry Leon 1948-2007 **49, 62**
Hammer *See Hammer, M. C.*
Hammer, M. C. 1963— **20**
Hammond, Fred 1960— **23**
Hammond, Lenn 1970(?)— **34**
Hammonds, Evelynn 1953— **69**
Hammons, David 1943— **69**
Hampton, Fred 1948-1969 **18**
Hampton, Henry (Eugene, Jr.) 1940— **6**
Hampton, Lionel 1908(?)-2002 **17, 41**
Hancock, Herbie 1940— **20, 67**
Handy, W(illiam) C(hristopher) 1873-1937 **8**
Hani, Chris 1942-1993 **6**
Hani, Martin Thembisile *See Hani, Chris*
Hannah, Marc (Regis) 1956— **10**
Hansberry, Lorraine (Vivian) 1930-1965 **6**
Hansberry, William Leo 1894-1965 **11**
Hardaway, Anfernee (Deon) *See Hardaway, Anfernee (Penny)*
Hardaway, Anfernee (Penny) 1971— **13**
Hardaway, Penny *See Hardaway, Anfernee (Penny)*
Hardaway, Tim 1966— **35**
Hardin Armstrong, Lil 1898-1971 **39**
Hardin, Lillian Beatrice *See Hardin Armstrong, Lil*
Harding, Vincent 1931— **67**
Hardison, Bethann 19(?)(?)— **12**
Hardison, Kadeem 1966— **22**
Hardy, Nell *See Carter, Nell*
Hare, Nathan 1934— **44**
Harewood, David 1965— **52**
Harkless, Necia Desiree 1920— **19**
Harmon, Clarence 1940(?)— **26**
Harold, Erika 1980(?)— **54**
Harper, Ben 1969— **34, 62**
Harper, Frances E(llen) W(atkins) 1825-1911 **11**
Harper, Frank *See Harper, Hill*
Harper, Hill 1966— **32, 65**
Harper, Michael S. 1938— **34**
Harrell, Andre (O'Neal) 1962(?)— **9, 30**
Harrington, Oliver W(endell) 1912— **9**

Harris, Alice 1934— **7**
Harris, Barbara 1930— **12**
Harris, Barry 1929— **68**
Harris, Bill 1941— **72**
Harris, Carla A. 1962— **67**
Harris, Ciara Princess *See Ciara*
Harris, Claire 1937— **34**
Harris, Corey 1969— **39, 73**
Harris, E. Lynn 1957— **12, 33**
Harris, Eddy L. 1956— **18**
Harris, James, III *See Jimmy Jam*
Harris, Jay **19**
Harris, Kamala D. 1964— **64**
Harris, Leslie 1961— **6**
Harris, Marcelite Jordon 1943— **16**
Harris, Mary Styles 1949— **31**
Harris, Monica 1968— **18**
Harris, Naomie 1976— **55**
Harris, Patricia Roberts 1924-1985 **2**
Harris, Richard E. 1912(?)— **61**
Harris, Robin 1953-1990 **7**
Harris, "Sweet" Alice *See Harris, Alice*
Harris, Sylvia 1967(?)— **70**
Harris, William Anthony *See Harris, Bill*
Harrison, Alvin 1974— **28**
Harrison, Calvin 1974— **28**
Harrison, Charles 1931— **72**
Harrison, Mya *See Mya*
Harsh, Vivian Gordon 1890-1960 **14**
Hart, Alvin Youngblood 1963— **61**
Hart, Gregory Edward *See Hart, Alvin Youngblood*
Harvard, Beverly (Joyce Bailey) 1950— **11**
Harvey, Steve 1956— **18, 58**
Harvey, William R. 1941— **42**
Haskins, Clem 1943— **23**
Haskins, James 1941-2005 **36, 54**
Hassell, Leroy Rountree, Sr. 1955— **41**
Hastie, William H(enry) 1904-1976 **8**
Hastings, Alcee Lamar 1936— **16**
Hatcher, Richard G. 1933— **55**
Hatchett, Glenda 1951(?)— **32**
Hathaway, Donny 1945-1979 **18**
Hathaway, Isaac Scott 1874-1967 **33**
Hathaway, Lalah 1969— **57**
Haughton, Aaliyah *See Aaliyah*
Hawkins, "Screamin'" Jay 1929-2000 **30**
Hawkins, Adrienne Lita *See Kennedy, Adrienne*
Hawkins, Augustus F. 1907–2007 **68**
Hawkins, Coleman 1904-1969 **9**
Hawkins, Erskine Ramsey 1914-1993 **14**
Hawkins, Jamesetta *See James, Etta*
Hawkins, La-Van 1960— **17, 54**
Hawkins, Steven Wayne 1962— **14**
Hawkins, Tramaine Aunzola 1951— **16**
Hayden, Carla D. 1952— **47**
Hayden, Palmer 1890-1973 **13**
Hayden, Robert Earl 1913-1980 **12**
Hayes, Cecil N. 1945— **46**
Hayes, Dennis 1951— **54**

Hayes, Isaac 1942–2008 **20, 58, 73**
Hayes, James C. 1946— **10**
Hayes, Roland 1887-1977 **4**
Hayes, Teddy 1951— **40**
Haynes, Cornell, Jr. *See Nelly*
Haynes, George Edmund 1880-1960 **8**
Haynes, Marques 1926— **22**
Haynes, Trudy 1926— **44**
Haysbert, Dennis 1955— **42**
Haywood, Gar Anthony 1954— **43**
Haywood, Jimmy 1993(?)— **58**
Haywood, Margaret A. 1912— **24**
Hazel, Darryl B. 1949— **50**
Head, Bessie 1937-1986 **28**
Healy, James Augustine 1830-1900 **30**
Heard, Gar 1948— **25**
Heard, Nathan C. 1936-2004 **45**
Hearne, John Edgar Caulwell 1926-1994 **45**
Hearns, Thomas 1958— **29**
Heavy, D 1967— **58**
Hedgeman, Anna Arnold 1899-1990 **22**
Hedgeman, Peyton Cole *See Hayden, Palmer*
Height, Dorothy I(rene) 1912— **2, 23**
Hemphill, Essex 1957— **10**
Hemphill, Jessie Mae 1923-2006 **33, 59**
Hemsley, Sherman 1938— **19**
Henderson, Cornelius Langston 1888(?)-1976 **26**
Henderson, David 1942— **53**
Henderson, Fletcher 1897-1952 **32**
Henderson, Gordon 1957— **5**
Henderson, Jeff 1964— **72**
Henderson, Natalie Leota *See Hinderas, Natalie*
Henderson, Rickey 1958— **28**
Henderson, Stephen E. 1925-1997 **45**
Henderson, Thelton E. 1933— **68**
Henderson, Wade 1944(?)— **14**
Henderson, Zelma 1920–2008 **71**
Hendricks, Barbara 1948— **3, 67**
Hendrix, James Marshall *See Hendrix, Jimi*
Hendrix, Jimi 1942-1970 **10**
Hendrix, Johnny Allen *See Hendrix, Jimi*
Hendryx, Nona 1944— **56**
Hendy, Francis 195(?)— **47**
Henries, A. Doris Banks 1913-1981 **44**
Henriques, Julian 1955(?)— **37**
Henry, Aaron Edd 1922-1997 **19**
Henry, Clarence "Frogman" 1937— **46**
Henry, Lenny 1958— **9, 52**
Henson, Darrin 1970(?)— **33**
Henson, Matthew (Alexander) 1866-1955 **2**
Henson, Taraji 1971— **58**
Henry, Thierry 1977— **66**
Herbert, Bob 1945— **63**
Hercules, Frank 1911-1996 **44**
Herenton, Willie W. 1940— **24**
Herman, Alexis Margaret 1947— **15**
Hernandez, Aileen Clarke 1926— **13**
Hernton, Calvin C. 1932-2001 **51**

Hickman, Fred(erick Douglass) 1951— **11**
Hicks Maynard, Nancy *See Maynard, Nancy Hicks*
Higginbotham, A(loyisus) Leon, Jr. 1928-1998 **13, 25**
Higginbotham, Jack *See Higginbotham, Jay C.*
Higginbotham, Jay C. 1906-1973 **37**
Higginsen, Vy 1945(?)— **65**
Hightower, Dennis F(owler) 1941— **13**
Hill, Andrew 1931-2007 **66**
Hill, Anita 1956— **5, 65**
Hill, Beatrice *See Moore, Melba*
Hill, Bonnie Guiton 1941— **20**
Hill, Calvin 1947— **19**
Hill, Donna 1955— **32**
Hill, Dulé 1975(?)— **29**
Hill, Errol 1921— **40**
Hill, Grant (Henry) 1972— **13**
Hill, Janet 1947— **19**
Hill, Jesse, Jr. 1927— **13**
Hill, Lauryn 1975— **20, 53**
Hill, Leslie Pinckney 1880-1960 **44**
Hill, Oliver W. 1907-2007 **24, 63**
Hill, Tamia *See Tamia*
Hillard, Terry 1954— **25**
Hillary, Barbara 1923(?)— **65**
Hilliard, Asa Grant, III 1933-2007 **66**
Hilliard, David 1942— **7**
Hilliard, Earl F. 1942— **24**
Hilliard, Wendy 196(?)— **53**
Himes, Chester 1909-1984 **8**
Hinderas, Natalie 1927-1987 **5**
Hine, Darlene Clark 1947— **24**
Hines, Earl "Fatha" 1905-1983 **39**
Hines, Garrett 1969— **35**
Hines, Gregory (Oliver) 1946-2003 **1, 42**
Hinton, Milt 1910-2000 **30**
Hinton, William Augustus 1883-1959 **8**
Hoagland, Everett H. 1942— **45**
Hoagland, Jaheim *See Jaheim*
Hobson, Julius W. 1919-1977 **44**
Hobson, Mellody 1969— **40**
Hogan, Beverly Wade 1951— **50**
Holder, Eric H., Jr. 1951(?)— **9**
Holder, Laurence 1939— **34**
Holdsclaw, Chamique 1977— **24**
Holiday, Billie 1915-1959 **1**
Holland, Brian *See Holland-Dozier-Holland*
Holland, Eddie *See Holland-Dozier-Holland*
Holland, Endesha Ida Mae 1944-2006 **3, 57**
Holland, Kimberly N. 19(?)(?)— **62**
Holland, Robert, Jr. 1940— **11**
Holland-Dozier-Holland **36**
Holloway, Brenda 1946— **65**
Hollowell, Donald L. 1917-2004 **57**
Holmes, Amy 1973— **69**
Holmes, Clint 1946— **57**
Holmes, Kelly 1970— **47**
Holmes, Larry 1949— **20, 68**
Holmes, Shannon 1973(?)— **70**
Holt, Lester 1959— **66**
Holt, Nora 1885(?)-1974 **38**
Holt Baker, Arlene 1951— **73**

Holte, Patricia Louise *See LaBelle, Patti*

Holton, Hugh, Jr. 1947-2001 **39**

Holyfield, Evander 1962— **6**

Honeywood, Varnette P. 1950— **54**

Honoré, Russel L. 1947— **64**

Hooker, John Lee 1917-2000 **30**

hooks, bell 1952— **5**

Hooks, Benjamin L(awson) 1925— **2**

Hope, John 1868-1936 **8**

Hopgood, Hadda *See Brooks, Hadda*

Hopkins, Bernard 1965— **35, 69**

Horn, Shirley 1934-2005 **32, 56**

Horne, Frank 1899-1974 **44**

Horne, Lena (Mary Calhoun) 1917— **5**

Horton, Andre 1979— **33**

Horton, James Oliver 1943— **58**

Horton, (Andreana) "Suki" 1982— **33**

Hounsou, Djimon 1964— **19, 45**

Houphouët, Dia *See Houphouët-Boigny, Félix*

Houphouët-Boigny, Félix 1905-1993 **4, 64**

House, Eddie James, Jr. *See House, Son*

House, Eugene *See House, Son*

House, Son 1902-1988 **8**

Houston, Charles Hamilton 1895-1950 **4**

Houston, Cissy 19(?)(?)— **20**

Houston, Whitney 1963— **7, 28**

Howard, Ayanna 1972— **65**

Howard, Corinne *See Mitchell, Corinne*

Howard, Desmond 1970— **16, 58**

Howard, Juwan Antonio 1973— **15**

Howard, M. William, Jr. 1946— **26**

Howard, Michelle 1960— **28**

Howard, Ryan 1979— **65**

Howard, Sherri 1962— **36**

Howard, Terrence Dashon 1969— **59**

Howlin' Wolf 1910-1976 **9**

Howroyd, Janice Bryant 1953— **42**

Hoyte, Lenon 1905-1999 **50**

Hrabowski, Freeman A., III 1950— **22**

Hubbard, Arnette 19(?)(?)— **38**

Hudlin, Reginald 1962(?)— **9**

Hudlin, Warrington, Jr. 1953(?)— **9**

Hudson, Cheryl 19(?)(?)— **15**

Hudson, Ernie 1945— **72**

Hudson, Jennifer 1981— **63**

Hudson, Wade 1946— **15**

Huggins, Edie 1935–2008 **71**

Huggins, Larry 1950— **21**

Huggins, Nathan Irvin 1927-1989 **52**

Hughes, Albert 1972— **7**

Hughes, Allen 1972— **7**

Hughes, Cathy 1947(?)— **27**

Hughes, Ebony 1948— **57**

Hughes, (James Mercer) Langston 1902-1967 **4**

Hughley, Darryl Lynn 1964— **23**

Hull, Akasha Gloria 1944— **45**

Humphrey, Bobbi 1950— **20**

Humphries, Frederick 1935— **20**

Hunt, Richard (Howard) 1935— **6**

Hunter, Alberta 1895-1984 **42**

Hunter, Billy 1943— **22**

Hunter, Charlayne *See Hunter-Gault, Charlayne*

Hunter, Clementine 1887-1988 **45**

Hunter, George William *See Hunter, Billy*

Hunter, Torii 1975— **43**

Hunter-Gault, Charlayne 1942— **6, 31**

Hurston, Zora Neale 1891-1960 **3**

Hurt, Byron 1970— **61**

Hurtt, Harold 1947(?)— **46**

Hutch, Willie 1944-2005 **62**

Hutcherson, Hilda Yvonne 1955— **54**

Hutchinson, Earl Ofari 1945— **24**

Hutson, Jean Blackwell 1914— **16**

Hyde, Cowan F. "Bubba" 1908-2003 **47**

Hyman, Earle 1926— **25**

Hyman, Phyllis 1949(?)-1995 **19**

Ibrahim, Mo 1946— **67**

Ice Cube 1969— **8, 30, 60**

Iceberg Slim 1918-1992 **11**

Ice-T 1958(?)— **6, 31**

Ifill, Gwen 1955— **28**

Iginla, Jarome 1977— **35**

Ilibagiza, Immaculée 1972(?)— **66**

Iman 1955— **4, 33**

Iman, Chanel 1989— **66**

Imes, Elmer Samuel 1883-1941 **39**

India.Arie 1975— **34**

Ingraham, Hubert A. 1947— **19**

Ingram, Rex 1895-1969 **5**

Innis, Roy (Emile Alfredo) 1934— **5**

Irvin, Michael 1966— **64**

Irvin, (Monford Merrill) Monte 1919— **31**

Irvin, Vernon 1961— **65**

Irving, Clarence (Larry) 1955— **12**

Irvis, K. Leroy 1917(?)–2006 **67**

Isaac, Julius 1928— **34**

Isley, Ronald 1941— **25, 56**

Iverson, Allen 1975— **24, 46**

Ivey, Phil 1976— **72**

Ja Rule 1976— **35**

Jackson Lee, Sheila 1950— **20**

Jackson, Alexine Clement 1936— **22**

Jackson, Alphonso R. 1946— **48**

Jackson, Earl 1948— **31**

Jackson, Edison O. 1943(?)— **67**

Jackson, Fred James 1950— **25**

Jackson, George 1960(?)— **19**

Jackson, George Lester 1941-1971 **14**

Jackson, Hal 1915— **41**

Jackson, Isaiah (Allen) 1945— **3**

Jackson, Jamea 1986— **64**

Jackson, Janet 1966— **6, 30, 68**

Jackson, Jesse 1941— **1, 27, 72**

Jackson, Jesse Louis, Jr. 1965— **14, 45**

Jackson, John 1924-2002 **36**

Jackson, Judith D. 1950— **57**

Jackson, Mae 1941-2005 **57**

Jackson, Mahalia 1911-1972 **5**

Jackson, Mannie 1939— **14**

Jackson, Mary 1945— **73**

Jackson, Maynard (Holbrook, Jr.) 1938-2003 **2, 41**

Jackson, Michael 1958— **19, 53**

Jackson, Millie 1944— **25**

Jackson, Milt 1923-1999 **26**

Jackson, O'Shea *See Ice Cube*

Jackson, Randy 1956— **40**

Jackson, Reginald Martinez 1946— **15**

Jackson, Samuel 1948— **8, 19, 63**

Jackson, Sheneska 1970(?)— **18**

Jackson, Shirley Ann 1946— **12**

Jackson, Tom 1951— **70**

Jackson, Vera 1912— **40**

Jackson, Zelda Mavin *See Ormes, Jackie*

Jaco, Wasalu Muhammad *See Fiasco, Lupe*

Jacob, John E(dward) 1934— **2**

Jacobs, Marion Walter *See Little Walter*

Jacobs, Regina 1963— **38**

Jacquet, Illinois 1922(?)-2004 **49**

Jagan, Cheddi 1918-1997 **16**

Jaheim 1978— **58**

Jakes, Thomas "T.D." 1957— **17, 43**

Jam, Jimmy *See Jimmy Jam*

Jamal, Ahmad 1930— **69**

Jamelia 1981— **51**

Jamerson, James 1936-1983 **59**

James, Charles H., III 1959(?)— **62**

James, Daniel "Chappie," Jr. 1920-1978 **16**

James, Donna A. 1957— **51**

James, Etta 1938— **13, 52**

James, Juanita (Therese) 1952— **13**

James, LeBron 1984— **46**

James, Sharpe 1936— **23, 69**

James, Skip 1902-1969 **38**

Jamison, Judith 1943— **7, 67**

Jammeh, Yahya 1965— **23**

Jarreau, Al 1940— **21, 65**

Jarrett, Valerie 1956— **73**

Jarrett, Vernon D. 1921— **42**

Jarvis, Charlene Drew 1941— **21**

Jarvis, Erich 1965— **67**

Jasper, Kenji 1976(?)— **39**

Jawara, Dawda Kairaba 1924— **11**

Jay, Jam Master 1965— **31**

Jay-Z 1970— **27, 69**

Jealous, Benjamin 1973— **70**

Jean, Michaëlle 1957— **70**

Jean, Wyclef 1970— **20**

Jean-Baptiste, Marianne 1967— **17, 46**

Jeffers, Eve Jihan *See Eve*

Jefferson, William J. 1947— **25, 72**

Jeffries, Leonard 1937— **8**

Jemison, Mae C. 1957— **1, 35**

Jemison, Major L. 1955(?)— **48**

Jenifer, Franklyn G(reen) 1939— **2**

Jenkins, Beverly 1951— **14**

Jenkins, Ella (Louise) 1924— **15**

Jenkins, Fergie 1943— **46**

Jenkins, Jay *See Young Jeezy*

Jennings, Chester *See Jennings, Lyfe*

Jennings, Lyfe 1973— **56, 69**

Jerkins, Rodney 1978(?)— **31**

Jeter, Derek 1974— **27**

Jimmy Jam 1959— **13**

Joachim, Paulin 1931— **34**

Joe, Yolanda 19(?)(?)— **21**

John, Daymond 1969(?)— **23**

Johns, Vernon 1892-1965 **38**

Johnson, Angela 1961— **52**

Johnson, Arnez *See Arnez J*

Johnson, Avery 1965— **62**

Johnson, Ben 1961— **1**

Johnson, Beverly 1952— **2**

Johnson, Buddy 1915-1977 **36**

Johnson, Carol Diann *See Carroll, Diahann*

Johnson, Caryn E. *See Goldberg, Whoopi*

Johnson, Charles 1948— **1**

Johnson, Charles Arthur *See St. Jacques, Raymond*

Johnson, Charles Spurgeon 1893-1956 **12**

Johnson, Clifford "Connie" 1922-2004 **52**

Johnson, Dwayne *See Rock, The*

Johnson, Earvin "Magic" 1959— **3, 39**

Johnson, Eddie Bernice 1935— **8**

Johnson, George E. 1927— **29**

Johnson, Georgia Douglas 1880-1966 **41**

Johnson, Harry E. 1954— **57**

Johnson, Harvey Jr. 1947(?)— **24**

Johnson, Hazel 1927— **22**

Johnson, J. J. 1924-2001 **37**

Johnson, Jack 1878-1946 **8**

Johnson, James Louis *See Johnson, J. J.*

Johnson, James Weldon 1871-1938 **5**

Johnson, James William *See Johnson, James Weldon*

Johnson, Je'Caryous 1977— **63**

Johnson, Jeh Vincent 1931— **44**

Johnson, John Arthur *See Johnson, Jack*

Johnson, John H. 1918-2005 **3, 54**

Johnson, Johnnie 1924-2005 **56**

Johnson, Katherine (Coleman Goble) 1918— **61**

Johnson, Kevin 1966— **70**

Johnson, Larry 1969— **28**

Johnson, Levi 1950— **48**

Johnson, Linton Kwesi 1952— **37**

Johnson, Lonnie G. 1949— **32**

Johnson, "Magic" *See Johnson, Earvin "Magic"*

Johnson, Mamie "Peanut" 1932— **40**

Johnson, Marguerite *See Angelou, Maya*

Johnson, Mat 1971(?)— **31**

Johnson, Michael (Duane) 1967— **13**

Johnson, Norma L. Holloway 1932— **17**

Johnson, R. M. 1968— **36**

Johnson, Rafer 1934— **33**

Johnson, Robert 1911-1938 **2**

Johnson, Robert L. 1946(?)— **3, 39**

Johnson, Robert T. 1948— **17**

Johnson, Rodney Van 19(?)(?)— **28**

Johnson, Sheila Crump 1949(?)— **48**

Johnson, Shoshana 1973— **47**

Johnson, Taalib *See Musiq*

Johnson, Virginia (Alma Fairfax) 1950— **9**

Johnson, William Henry 1901-1970 **3**

Johnson, Woodrow Wilson *See Johnson, Buddy*
Johnson-Brown, Hazel W. *See Johnson, Hazel*
Jolley, Willie 1956— **28**
Jones, Absalom 1746-1818 **52**
Jones, Alex 1941— **64**
Jones, Anthony *See Jones, Van*
Jones, Bill T. 1952— **1, 46**
Jones, Bobby 1939(?)— **20**
Jones, Carl 1955(?)— **7**
Jones, Caroline R. 1942— **29**
Jones, Clara Stanton 1913— **51**
Jones, Cobi N'Gai 1970— **18**
Jones, Cullen 1984— **73**
Jones, Donell 1973— **29**
Jones, Doris W. 1914(?)–2006 **62**
Jones, E. Edward, Sr. 1931— **45**
Jones, Ed "Too Tall" 1951— **46**
Jones, Edith Mae Irby 1927— **65**
Jones, Edward P. 1950— **43, 67**
Jones, Elaine R. 1944— **7, 45**
Jones, Elvin 1927–2004 **14, 68**
Jones, Etta 1928-2001 **35**
Jones, Frederick McKinley 1893–1961 **68**
Jones, Frederick Russell *See Jamal, Ahmad*
Jones, Gayl 1949— **37**
Jones, Hank 1918— **57**
Jones, Ingrid Saunders 1945— **18**
Jones, James Earl 1931— **3, 49**
Jones, Jonah 1909-2000 **39**
Jones, Kelis *See Kelis*
Jones, Kimberly Denise *See Lil' Kim*
Jones, Le Roi *See Baraka, Amiri*
Jones, Lillie Mae *See Carter, Betty*
Jones, Lois Mailou 1905— **13**
Jones, Lou 1932-2006 **64**
Jones, Marion 1975— **21, 66**
Jones, Merlakia 1973— **34**
Jones, Monty 1951(?)— **66**
Jones, Nasir *See Nas*
Jones, Orlando 1968— **30**
Jones, Quincy (Delight) 1933— **8, 30**
Jones, Randy 1969— **35**
Jones, Robert Elliott *See Jones, Jonah*
Jones, Roy Jr. 1969— **22**
Jones, Russell *See Ol' Dirty Bastard*
Jones, Ruth Lee *See Washington, Dinah*
Jones, Sarah 1974— **39**
Jones, Sissieretta *See Joyner, Matilda Sissieretta*
Jones, Star *See Reynolds, Star Jones*
Jones, Thad 1923–1986 **68**
Jones, Thomas W. 1949— **41**
Jones, Van 1968— **70**
Jones, Wayne 1952— **53**
Jones, William A., Jr. 1934-2006 **61**
Joplin, Scott 1868-1917 **6**
Jordan, Barbara (Charline) 1936— **4**
Jordan, Eric Benét *See Benét, Eric*
Jordan, June 1936— **7, 35**
Jordan, Michael (Jeffrey) 1963— **6, 21**
Jordan, Montell 1968(?)— **23**

Jordan, Ronny 1962— **26**
Jordan, Vernon E(ulion, Jr.) 1935— **3, 35**
Jorge, Seu 1970— **73**
Joseph, Kathie-Ann 1970(?)— **56**
Josey, E. J. 1924— **10**
Joyner, Jacqueline *See Joyner-Kersee, Jackie*
Joyner, Marjorie Stewart 1896-1994 **26**
Joyner, Matilda Sissieretta 1869(?)-1933 **15**
Joyner, Tom 1949(?)— **19**
Joyner-Kersee, Jackie 1962— **5**
Julian, Percy Lavon 1899–1975 **6**
Julien, Isaac 1960— **3**
July, William II 19(?)(?)— **27**
Juma, Calestous 1953— **57**
Just, Ernest Everett 1883-1941 **3**
Justice, David Christopher 1966— **18**
Ka Dinizulu, Israel *See Ka Dinizulu, Mcwayizeni*
Ka Dinizulu, Mcwayizeni 1932-1999 **29**
Kabbah, Ahmad Tejan 1932— **23**
Kabila, Joseph 1968(?)— **30**
Kabila, Laurent 1939— **20**
Kagame, Paul 1957— **54**
Kaigler, Denise 1962— **63**
Kaiser, Cecil 1916— **42**
Kamau, Johnstone *See Kenyatta, Jomo*
Kamau, Kwadwo Agymah 1960(?)— **28**
Kani, Karl 1968(?)— **10**
Kanouté, Fred 1977— **68**
Karenga, Maulana 1941— **10, 71**
Karim, Benjamin 1932-2005 **61**
Kariuki, J. M. 1929–1975 **67**
Katoucha *See Niane, Katoucha*
Kaufman, Monica 1948(?)— **66**
Kaunda, Kenneth (David) 1924— **2**
Kay, Jackie 1961— **37**
Kay, Ulysses 1917-1995 **37**
Kayira, Legson 1942— **40**
Kearney, Janis 1953— **54**
Kearse, Amalya Lyle 1937— **12**
Kebede, Liya 1978— **59**
Kee, John P. 1962— **43**
Keene, John 1965— **73**
Keflezighi, Meb 1975— **49**
Keith, Damon Jerome 1922— **16**
Keith, Floyd A. 1948— **61**
Keith, Rachel Boone 1924-2007 **63**
Kelis 1979— **58**
Kelley, Elijah 1986— **65**
Kelley, Malcolm David 1992— **59**
Kellogg, Clark 1961— **64**
Kelly, Leontine 1920— **33**
Kelly, Patrick 1954(?)-1990 **3**
Kelly, R. 1967— **18, 44, 71**
Kelly, Robert Sylvester *See Kelly, R.*
Kelly, Sharon Pratt *See Dixon, Sharon Pratt*
Kem 196(?)— **47**
Kendrick, Erika 1975— **57**
Kendricks, Eddie 1939-1992 **22**
Kennard, William Earl 1957— **18**
Kennedy, Adrienne 1931— **11**
Kennedy, Florynce Rae 1916-2000 **12, 33**

Kennedy, Lelia McWilliams Robinson 1885-1931 **14**
Kennedy, Randall 1954— **40**
Kennedy-Overton, Jayne Harris 1951— **46**
Kenney, John A., Jr. 1914-2003 **48**
Kenoly, Ron 1944— **45**
Kente, Gibson 1932-2004 **52**
Kenyatta, Jomo 1891(?)-1978 **5**
Kenyatta, Robin 1942-2004 **54**
Kerekou, Ahmed (Mathieu) 1933— **1**
Kerry, Leon G. 1949(?)— **46**
Keyes, Alan L(ee) 1950— **11**
Keys, Alicia 1981— **32, 68**
Khan, Chaka 1953— **12, 50**
Khanga, Yelena 1962— **6**
Khumalo, Leleti 1970— **51**
Kibaki, Mwai 1931— **60**
Kidd, Mae Street 1904-1995 **39**
Kidjo, Anjelique 1960— **50**
Kikwete, Jakaya Mrisho 1950— **73**
Killens, John O. 1967-1987 **54**
Killings, Debra 196(?)— **57**
Killingsworth, Cleve, Jr. 1952— **54**
Kilpatrick, Carolyn Cheeks 1945— **16**
Kilpatrick, Kwame 1970— **34, 71**
Kimbro, Dennis (Paul) 1950— **10**
Kimbro, Henry A. 1912-1999 **25**
Kincaid, Bernard 1945— **28**
Kincaid, Jamaica 1949— **4**
King, Alonzo 19(?)(?)— **38**
King, B. B. 1925— **7**
King, Barbara 19(?)(?)— **22**
King, Bernice (Albertine) 1963— **4**
King, Colbert I. 1939— **69**
King, Coretta Scott 1927-2006 **3, 57**
King, Dexter (Scott) 1961— **10**
King, Don 1931— **14**
King, Gayle 1956— **19**
King, Martin Luther, III 1957— **20**
King, Martin Luther, Jr. 1929-1968 **1**
King, Oona 1967— **27**
King, Preston 1936— **28**
King, Reatha Clark 1938— **65**
King, Regina 1971— **22, 45**
King, Riley B. *See King, B. B.*
King, Robert Arthur 1945— **58**
King, Woodie Jr. 1937— **27**
King, Yolanda (Denise) 1955— **6**
Kintaudi, Leon 1949(?)— **62**
Kintaudi, Ngoma Miezi *See Kintaudi, Leon*
Kirby, George 1924-1995 **14**
Kirk, Ron 1954— **11**
Kitt, Eartha Mae 1928(?)— **16**
Kitt, Sandra 1947— **23**
Kittles, Rick 1976(?)— **51**
Klugh, Earl 1953— **59**
Knight, Etheridge 1931-1991 **37**
Knight, Gladys 1944— **16, 66**
Knight, Gwendolyn 1913-2005 **63**
Knight, Marion, Jr. *See Knight, Suge*
Knight, Suge 1966— **11, 30**
Knowles, Beyoncé *See Beyoncé*
Knowles, Tina 1954(?)— **61**
Knowling, Robert Jr. 1955(?)— **38**
Knox, Simmie 1935— **49**
Knuckles, Frankie 1955— **42**

Kobia, Samuel 1947— **43**
Kodjoe, Boris 1973— **34**
Kolosoy, Wendo 1925–2008 **73**
Komunyakaa, Yusef 1941— **9**
Kone, Seydou *See Blondy, Alpha*
Kong, B. Waine 1943— **50**
Kool DJ Red Alert *See Alert, Kool DJ Red*
Kool Moe Dee 1963— **37**
Kotto, Yaphet (Fredrick) 1944— **7**
Kountz, Samuel L(ee) 1930-1981 **10**
Kravitz, Lenny 1964— **10, 34**
Kravitz, Leonard *See Kravitz, Lenny*
KRS-One 1965— **34**
Krute, Fred *See Alert, Kool DJ Red*
K-Swift 1978–2008 **73**
Kufuor, John Agyekum 1938— **54**
Kunjufu, Jawanza 1953— **3, 50**
Kuti, Fela Anikulapo *See Fela*
Kuti, Femi 1962— **47**
Kuzwayo, Ellen 1914–2006 **68**
Kyles, Cedric *See Cedric the Entertainer*
La Menthe, Ferdinand Joseph *See Morton, Jelly Roll*
La Salle, Eriq 1962— **12**
LaBelle, Patti 1944— **13, 30**
Lacy, Sam 1903-2003 **30, 46**
Ladd, Ernie 1938-2007 **64**
Ladner, Joyce A. 1943— **42**
Laferriere, Dany 1953— **33**
Lafontant, Jewel Stradford 1922-1997 **3, 51**
Lafontant-MANkarious, Jewel Stradford *See Lafontant, Jewel Stradford*
LaGuma, Alex 1925-1985 **30**
Lamming, George 1927— **35**
Lampkin, Daisy 1883(?)-1965 **19**
Lampley, Oni Faida 1959–2008 **43, 71**
Lampley, Vera *See Lampley, Oni Faida*
Lane, Charles 1953— **3**
Lane, Vincent 1942— **5**
Langhart Cohen, Janet 1941— **19, 60**
Lanier, Bob 1948— **47**
Lanier, Willie 1945— **33**
Lankford, Raymond Lewis 1967— **23**
Laraque, Georges 1976— **48**
Laraque, Paul 1920–2007 **67**
Larkin, Barry 1964— **24**
Larrieux, Amel 1973(?)— **63**
Lars, Byron 1965— **32**
Larsen, Nella 1891-1964 **10**
Laryea, Thomas Davies III 1979— **67**
Lashley, Bobby 1976— **63**
Lashley, Franklin Roberto *See Lashley, Bobby*
Lassiter, Roy 1969— **24**
Lathan, Sanaa 1971— **27**
Latimer, Lewis H(oward) 1848-1928 **4**
Lattimore, Kenny 1970(?)— **35**
Lavizzo-Mourey, Risa 1954— **48**
Lawal, Kase L. 19(?)(?)— **45**
Lawless, Theodore K(enneth) 1892-1971 **8**

Lawrence, Jacob (Armstead) 1917-2000 **4, 28**

Lawrence, Martin 1965— **6, 27, 60**

Lawrence, Robert Henry, Jr. 1935-1967 **16**

Lawrence-Lightfoot, Sara 1944— **10**

Lawson, Jennifer 1946— **1, 50**

Leary, Kathryn D. 1952— **10**

Leavell, Dorothy R. 1944— **17**

Ledisi 197(?)— **73**

Lee, Annie Frances 1935— **22**

Lee, Barbara 1946— **25**

Lee, Bertram M., Sr. 1939-2003 **46**

Lee, Canada 1907-1952 **8**

Lee, Debra L. 1954— **62**

Lee, Don L(uther) See Madhubuti, Haki R.

Lee, Gabby See Lincoln, Abbey

Lee, Joe A. 1946(?)— **45**

Lee, Joie 1962(?)— **1**

Lee, Shelton Jackson See Lee, Spike

Lee, Spike 1957— **5, 19**

Lee-Smith, Hughie 1915— **5, 22**

Leevy, Carrol M. 1920— **42**

Lefel, Edith 1963-2003 **41**

Leffall, Lasalle, Jr. 1930— **3, 64**

Legend, John 1978— **67**

Leggs, Kingsley 196(?)— **62**

Leland, George Thomas See Leland, Mickey

Leland, Mickey 1944-1989 **2**

Lemmons, Kasi 1961— **20**

Lennox, Betty 1976— **31**

LeNoire, Rosetta 1911-2002 **37**

Lenox, Adriane 1956— **59**

Leon, Kenny 1957(?)— **10**

León, Tania 1943— **13**

Leonard, Buck 1907— **67**

Leonard, Sugar Ray 1956— **15**

Leonard, Walter Fenner See Leonard, Buck

Leslie, Lisa 1972— **16, 73**

Lester, Adrian 1968— **46**

Lester, Bill 1961— **42**

Lester, Julius 1939— **9**

Lesure, James 1975— **64**

LeTang, Henry 1915-2007 **66**

Letson, Al 1972— **39**

Levert, Eddie 1942— **70**

Levert, Gerald 1966-2006 **22, 59**

Lewellyn, J(ames) Bruce 1927— **13**

Lewis, Aylwin 1954(?)— **51**

Lewis, Butch 1946— **71**

Lewis, Byron E(ugene) 1931— **13**

Lewis, (Frederick) Carl(ton) 1961— **4**

Lewis, Daurene 194(?)— **72**

Lewis, David Levering 1936— **9**

Lewis, Delano (Eugene) 1938— **7**

Lewis, Denise 1972— **33**

Lewis, (Mary) Edmonia 1845(?)-1911(?) **10**

Lewis, Edward T. 1940— **21**

Lewis, Emmanuel 1971— **36**

Lewis, Henry 1932-1996 **38**

Lewis, John 1940— **2, 46**

Lewis, Lennox 1965— **27**

Lewis, Marvin 1958— **51**

Lewis, Norman 1909-1979 **39**

Lewis, Oliver 1856-1924 **56**

Lewis, Ramsey 1935— **35, 70**

Lewis, Ray 1975— **33**

Lewis, Reginald F. 1942-1993 **6**

Lewis, Ronald See Lewis, Butch

Lewis, Samella 1924— **25**

Lewis, Shirley Ann Redd 1937— **14**

Lewis, Terry 1956— **13**

Lewis, Thomas 1939— **19**

Lewis, William M., Jr. 1956— **40**

Lewis-Thornton, Rae 1962— **32**

Ligging, Alfred III 1965— **43**

Lil' Bow Wow See Bow Wow

Lil' Kim 1975— **28**

Lil Wayne 1979— **66**

Lilakoi Moon See Bonet, Lisa

Liles, Kevin 1968— **42**

Lincoln, Abbey 1930— **3**

Lincoln, C(harles) Eric 1924-2000 **38**

Lindo, Delroy 1952— **18, 45**

Lindsey, Tommie 1951— **51**

Lipscomb, Mance 1895-1976 **49**

LisaRaye 1967— **27**

Lister, Marquita 1965(?) **65**

Liston, (Charles) Sonny 1928(?)-1970 **33**

Little Milton 1934-2005 **36, 54**

Little Richard 1932— **15**

Little Walter 1930-1968 **36**

Little, Benilde 1958— **21**

Little, Malcolm See X, Malcolm

Little, Robert L(angdon) 1938— **2**

Littlepage, Craig 1951— **35**

LL Cool J 1968— **16, 49**

Lloyd, Earl 1928(?)— **26**

Lloyd, John Henry "Pop" 1884-1965 **30**

Lloyd, Reginald 1967— **64**

Locke, Alain (LeRoy) 1886-1954 **10**

Locke, Eddie 1930— **44**

Lofton, James 1956— **42**

Lofton, Kenneth 1967— **12**

Lofton, Ramona 1950— **14**

Logan, Onnie Lee 1910(?)-1995 **14**

Logan, Rayford W. 1897-1982 **40**

Lomax, Michael L. 1947— **58**

Long, Eddie L. 19(?)(?)— **29**

Long, Loretta 1940— **58**

Long, Nia 1970— **17**

Long, Richard Alexander 1927— **65**

Lopes, Lisa " Left Eye" 1971-2002 **36**

Lord Pitt of Hampstead See Pitt, David Thomas

Lorde, Audre (Geraldine) 1934-1992 **6**

Lorenzo, Irving See Gotti, Irv

Loroupe, Tegla 1973— **59**

Lott, Ronnie 1959— **9**

Louis, Errol T. 1962— **8**

Louis, Joe 1914-1981 **5**

Loury, Glenn 1948— **36**

Love, Darlene 1941— **23**

Love, Ed 1932(?)— **58**

Love, Laura 1960— **50**

Love, Nat 1854-1921 **9**

Lover, Ed **10**

Loving, Alvin, Jr., 1935-2005 **35, 53**

Loving, Mildred 1939–2008 **69**

Lowe, Herbert 1962— **57**

Lowe, Sidney 1960— **64**

Lowery, Joseph E. 1924— **2**

Lowry, A. Leon 1913-2005 **60**

Lucas, John 1953— **7**

Lucien, Jon 1942-2007 **66**

Luckett, Letoya 1981— **61**

Lucy, William 1933— **50**

Lucy Foster, Autherine 1929— **35**

Ludacris, 1978— **37, 60**

Luke, Derek 1974— **61**

Lumbly, Carl 1952— **47**

Lumpkin, Elgin Baylor See Ginuwine

Lumumba, Patrice 1925-1961 **33**

Lushington, Augustus Nathaniel 1869-1939 **56**

Luthuli, Albert (John Mvumbi) 1898(?)-1967 **13**

Lyfe See Jennings, Lyfe

Lyle, Marcenia See Stone, Toni

Lyles, Lester Lawrence 1946— **31**

Lymon, Frankie 1942-1968 **22**

Lynch, Shola 1969— **61**

Lynn, Lonnie Rashid See Common

Lyons, Henry 1942(?)— **12**

Lyttle, Hulda Margaret 1889-1983 **14**

Maal, Baaba 1953— **66**

Maathai, Wangari 1940— **43**

Mabley, Jackie "Moms" 1897(?)-1975 **15**

Mabrey, Vicki 1957(?)— **26**

Mabry, Marcus 1967— **70**

Mabuza, Lindiwe 1938— **18**

Mabuza-Suttle, Felicia 1950— **43**

Mac, Bernie 1957–2008 **29, 61, 72**

Machel, Graca Simbine 1945— **16**

Machel, Samora Moises 1933-1986 **8**

Madhubuti, Haki R. 1942— **7**

Madikizela, Nkosikazi Nobandle Nomzamo Winifred See Mandela, Winnie

Madison, Joseph E. 1949— **17**

Madison, Paula 1952— **37**

Madison, Romell 1952— **45**

Magloire, Paul Eugène 1907–2001 **68**

Mahal, Taj 1942— **39**

Mahlasela, Vusi 1965— **65**

Mahorn, Rick 1958— **60**

Mainor, Dorothy Leigh 1910(?)-1996 **19**

Majette, Denise 1955— **41**

Major, Clarence 1936— **9**

Majors, Jeff 1960(?)— **41**

Makeba, Miriam 1932— **2, 50**

Malco, Romany 1968— **71**

Malcolm X See X, Malcolm

Mallett, Conrad, Jr. 1953— **16**

Mallory, Mark 1962— **62**

Malone, Annie (Minerva Turnbo Pope) 1869-1957 **13**

Malone, Karl 1963— **18, 51**

Malone, Maurice 1965— **32**

Malone Jones, Vivian 1942-2005 **59**

Malveaux, Floyd 1940— **54**

Malveaux, Julianne 1953— **32, 70**

Mamdou, Tandja 1938— **33**

Mandela, Nelson (Rolihlahla) 1918— **1, 14**

Mandela, Winnie 1934— **2, 35**

Manigault, Earl "The Goat" 1943— **15**

Manigault-Stallworth, Omarosa 1974— **69**

Manley, Audrey Forbes 1934— **16**

Manley, Edna 1900-1987 **26**

Manley, Ruth 1947— **34**

Marable, Manning 1950— **10**

March, William Carrington 1923-2002 **56**

Marchand, Inga See Foxy Brown

Marechera, Charles William See Marechera, Dambudzo

Marechera, Dambudzo 1952-1987 **39**

Marechera, Tambudzai See Marechera, Dambudzo

Mariner, Jonathan 1954(?)— **41**

Marino, Eugene Antonio 1934-2000 **30**

Mario 1986— **71**

Markham, E(dward) A(rchibald) 1939— **37**

Marley, Bob 1945-1981 **5**

Marley, David See Marley, Ziggy

Marley, Rita 1947— **32, 70**

Marley, Robert Nesta See Marley, Bob

Marley, Ziggy 1968— **41**

Marrow, Queen Esther 1943(?)— **24**

Marrow, Tracey See Ice-T

Marsalis, Branford 1960— **34**

Marsalis, Delfeayo 1965— **41**

Marsalis, Wynton 1961— **16**

Marsh, Henry L., III 1934(?)— **32**

Marshall, Bella 1950— **22**

Marshall, Gloria See Sudarkasa, Niara

Marshall, Kerry James 1955— **59**

Marshall, Paule 1929— **7**

Marshall, Thurgood 1908-1993 **1, 44**

Marshall, Valenza Pauline Burke See Marshall, Paule

Martha Jean "The Queen" See Steinberg, Martha Jean

Martin, Darnell 1964— **43**

Martin, Helen 1909-2000 **31**

Martin, Jesse L. 19(?)(?)— **31**

Martin, Louis Emanuel 1912-1997 **16**

Martin, Roberta 1907-1969 **58**

Martin, Roland S. 1969(?)— **49**

Martin, Ruby Grant 1933-2003 **49**

Martin, Sara 1884-1955 **38**

Marvin X See X, Marvin

Mary Mary **34**

Mase 1977(?)— **24**

Masekela, Barbara 1941— **18**

Masekela, Hugh (Ramopolo) 1939— **1**

Masire, Quett (Ketumile Joni) 1925— **5**

Mason, Felicia 1963(?)— **31**

Mason, Ronald 1949— **27**

Massaquoi, Hans J. 1926— **30**

Massenburg, Kedar 1964(?)— **23**

Massey, Brandon 1973— **40**

Massey, Walter E(ugene) 1938— **5, 45**

Massie, Samuel Proctor, Jr. 1919— **29**

Master P 1970— **21**

Mathabane, Johannes See Mathabane, Mark

Mathabane, Mark 1960— **5**

Mathis, Greg 1960— **26**

Mathis, Johnny 1935— **20**

Matthews, Denise *See Vanity*

Matthews, Mark 1894-2005 **59**

Matthews Shatteen, Westina 1948— **51**

Mauldin, Jermaine Dupri *See Dupri, Jermaine*

Maxey, Randall 1941— **46**

Maxis, Theresa 1810-1892 **62**

Maxwell 1973— **20**

May, Derrick 1963— **41**

Mayers, Jamal 1974— **39**

Mayfield, Curtis (Lee) 1942-1999 **2, 43**

Mayhew, Richard 1924— **39**

Maynard, Nancy Hicks 1946–2008 **73**

Maynard, Robert C(lyve) 1937-1993 **7**

Maynor, Dorothy 1910-1996 **19**

Mayo, Whitman 1930-2001 **32**

Mays, Benjamin E(lijah) 1894-1984 **7**

Mays, Leslie A. 19(?)(?)— **41**

Mays, William G. 1946— **34**

Mays, William Howard, Jr. *See Mays, Willie*

Mays, Willie 1931— **3**

Mayweather, Floyd, Jr. 1977— **57**

Mazrui, Ali Al'Amin 1933— **12**

M'bala M'bala, Dieudonné *See Dieudonné*

Mbaye, Mariétou 1948— **31**

Mbeki, Thabo 1942— **14, 73**

Mboup, Souleymane 1951— **10**

Mbuende, Kaire Munionganda 1953— **12**

MC Lyte 1971— **34**

McAnulty, William E., Jr. 1947-2007 **66**

McBride, Bryant Scott 1965— **18**

McBride, Chi 1961— **73**

McBride, James C. 1957— **35**

McCabe, Jewell Jackson 1945— **10**

McCall, H. Carl 1938(?)— **27**

McCall, Nathan 1955— **8**

McCann, Renetta 1957(?)— **44**

McCarthy, Sandy 1972— **64**

McCarty, Osceola 1908— **16**

McClendon, Lisa 1975(?)— **61**

McClurkin, Donnie 1961— **25**

McCoo, Marilyn 1943— **53**

McCoy, Elijah 1844-1929 **8**

McCrary, Crystal *See McCrary Anthony, Crystal*

McCrary Anthony, Crystal 1969— **70**

McCray, Nikki 1972— **18**

McCullough, Bernard Jeffrey *See Mac, Bernie*

McCullough, Geraldine 1922— **58**

McDaniel, Hattie 1895-1952 **5**

McDaniels, Darryl *See DMC*

McDonald, Audra 1970— **20, 62**

McDonald, Erroll 1954(?)— **1**

McDonald, Gabrielle Kirk 1942— **20**

McDougall, Gay J. 1947— **11, 43**

McDuffie, Dwayne 1962— **62**

McEwen, Mark 1954— **5**

McFadden, Bernice L. 1966— **39**

McFarlan, Tyron 1971(?)— **60**

McFarland, Roland 1940— **49**

McFerrin, Bobby 1950— **68**

McFerrin, Robert, Jr. *See McFerrin, Bobby*

McGee, Charles 1924— **10**

McGee, James Madison 1940— **46**

McGlowan, Angela 1970(?)— **64**

McGrath, Pat 1970— **72**

McGriff, Fred 1963— **24**

McGriff, James Harrell *See McGriff, Jimmy*

McGriff, Jimmy 1936–2008 **72**

McGruder, Aaron 1974— **28, 56**

McGruder, Robert 1942— **22, 35**

McGuire, Raymond J. 1957(?)(—) **57**

McIntosh, Winston Hubert *See Tosh, Peter*

McIntyre, Natalie *See Gary, Macy*

McKay, Claude 1889–1948 **6**

McKay, Festus Claudius *See McKay, Claude*

McKay, Nellie Yvonne 19(?)(?)–2006 **17, 57**

McKee, Lonette 1952— **12**

McKegney, Tony 1958— **3**

McKenzie, Jaunel 1986— **73**

McKenzie, Vashti M. 1947— **29**

McKinney Hammond, Michelle 1957— **51**

McKinney, Cynthia Ann 1955— **11, 52**

McKinney, Nina Mae 1912-1967 **40**

McKinney-Whetstone, Diane 1954(?)— **27**

McKinnon, Ike *See McKinnon, Isaiah*

McKinnon, Isaiah 1943— **9**

McKissick, Floyd B(ixler) 1922-1981 **3**

McKnight, Brian 1969— **18, 34**

McLeod, Gus 1955(?)— **27**

McLeod, Gustavus *See McLeod, Gus*

McMillan, Rosalynn A. 1953— **36**

McMillan, Terry 1951— **4, 17, 53**

McMurray, Georgia L. 1934-1992 **36**

McNabb, Donovan 1976— **29**

McNair, Ronald 1950-1986 **3, 58**

McNair, Steve 1973— **22, 47**

McNeil, Lori 1964(?)— **1**

McPhail, Sharon 1948— **2**

McPherson, David 1968— **32**

McPherson, James Alan 1943— **70**

McQueen, Butterfly 1911-1995 **6, 54**

McQueen, Thelma *See McQueen, Butterfly*

McWhorter, John 1965— **35**

Meadows, Tim 1961— **30**

Meek, Carrie (Pittman) 1926— **6, 36**

Meek, Kendrick 1966— **41**

Meeks, Gregory 1953— **25**

Meles Zenawi 1955(?)— **3**

Mell, Patricia 1953— **49**

Mello, Breno 1931–2008 **73**

Memmi, Albert 1920— **37**

Memphis Minnie 1897-1973 **33**

Mengestu, Dinaw 1978— **66**

Mengistu, Haile Mariam 1937— **65**

Mensah, Thomas 1950— **48**

Mercado-Valdes, Frank 1962— **43**

Meredith, James H(oward) 1933— **11**

Merkerson, S. Epatha 1952— **47**

Messenger, The *See Divine, Father*

Metcalfe, Ralph 1910-1978 **26**

Meyer, June *See Jordan, June*

Mfume, Kweisi 1948— **6, 41**

Mhlaba, Raymond 1920-2005 **55**

Micheaux, Oscar (Devereaux) 1884-1951 **7**

Michele, Michael 1966— **31**

Mickelbury, Penny 1948— **28**

Milla, Roger 1952— **2**

Miles, Buddy 1947–2008 **69**

Miles, George Allen, Jr. *See Miles, Buddy*

Millender-McDonald, Juanita 1938-2007 **21, 61**

Miller, Bebe 1950— **3**

Miller, Cheryl 1964— **10**

Miller, Dorie 1919-1943 **29**

Miller, Doris *See Miller, Dorie*

Miller, Larry G. 1950(?)— **72**

Miller, Maria 1803-1879 **19**

Miller, Percy *See Master P*

Miller, Reggie 1965— **33**

Miller, Warren F., Jr. 1943— **53**

Miller-Travis, Vernice 1959— **64**

Millines Dziko, Trish 1957— **28**

Mills, Florence 1896-1927 **22**

Mills, Joseph C. 1946— **51**

Mills, Sam 1959— **33**

Mills, Stephanie 1957— **36**

Mills, Steve 1960(?)— **47**

Milner, Ron 1938— **39**

Milton, DeLisha 1974— **31**

Mingo, Frank L. 1939-1989 **32**

Mingus, Charles Jr. 1922-1979 **15**

Minor, DeWayne 1956— **32**

Mitchell, Arthur 1934— **2, 47**

Mitchell, Brian Stokes 1957— **21**

Mitchell, Corinne 1914-1993 **8**

Mitchell, Elvis 1958— **67**

Mitchell, Kel 1978— **66**

Mitchell, Leona 1949— **42**

Mitchell, Loften 1919-2001 **31**

Mitchell, Nicole 1967(?)— **66**

Mitchell, Parren J. 1922-2007 **42, 66**

Mitchell, Russ 1960— **21, 73**

Mitchell, Sharon 1962— **36**

Mizell, Jason *See Jay, Jam Master*

Mkapa, Benjamin William 1938— **16**

Mo', Keb' 1952— **36**

Mobutu Sese Seko 1930-1997 **1, 56**

Mofolo, Thomas (Mokopu) 1876-1948 **37**

Mogae, Festus Gontebanye 1939— **19**

Mohamed, Ali Mahdi *See Ali Mahdi Mohamed*

Mohammed, Nazr 1977— **64**

Mohammed, W. Deen 1933— **27**

Mohammed, Warith Deen *See Mohammed, W. Deen*

Mohlabane, Goapele *See Goapele*

Moi, Daniel Arap 1924— **1, 35**

Mollel, Tololwa 1952— **38**

Mongella, Gertrude 1945— **11**

Monica 1980— **21**

Mo'Nique 1967— **35**

Monk, Art 1957— **38, 73**

Monk, Thelonious (Sphere, Jr.) 1917-1982 **1**

Monroe, Bryan 1965— **71**

Monroe, Mary 19(?)(?)— **35**

Montgomery, Tim 1975— **41**

Moody, Ronald 1900-1984 **30**

Moon, Warren 1956— **8, 66**

Mooney, Paul 19(?)(?)— **37**

Moore, Alice Ruth *See Dunbar-Nelson, Alice Ruth Moore*

Moore, Barbara C. 1949— **49**

Moore, Bobby *See Rashad, Ahmad*

Moore, Chante 1970(?)— **26**

Moore, Dorothy Rudd 1940— **46**

Moore, Gwendolynne S. 1951— **55**

Moore, Harry T. 1905-1951 **29**

Moore, Jessica Care 1971— **30**

Moore, Johnny B. 1950— **38**

Moore, Kevin *See Mo', Keb'*

Moore, LeRoi 1961–2008 **72**

Moore, Melba 1945— **21**

Moore, Minyon 19(?)(?)— **45**

Moore, Shemar 1970— **21**

Moore, Undine Smith 1904-1989 **28**

Moorer, Lana *See MC Lyte*

Moorer, Michael 1967— **19**

Moose, Charles 1953— **40**

Morgan, Garrett (Augustus) 1877-1963 **1**

Morgan, Gertrude 1900-1986 **63**

Morgan, Irene 1917-2007 **65**

Morgan, Joe Leonard 1943— **9**

Morgan, Rose (Meta) 1912(?)— **11**

Morgan, Tracy 1968— **61**

Morganfield, McKinley *See Muddy Waters*

Morial, Ernest "Dutch" 1929-1989 **26**

Morial, Marc H. 1958— **20, 51**

Morris, Garrett 1937— **31**

Morris, Greg 1934-1996 **28**

Morris, William "Bill" 1938— **51**

Morris, Stevland Judkins *See Wonder, Stevie*

Morrison, Keith 1942— **13**

Morrison, Mary Thelma *See Washington, Mary T.*

Morrison, Sam 1936— **50**

Morrison, Toni 1931— **2, 15**

Morton, Azie Taylor 1936-2003 **48**

Morton, Jelly Roll 1885(?)-1941 **29**

Morton, Joe 1947— **18**

Mos Def 1973— **30**

Moseka, Aminata *See Lincoln, Abbey*

Moseley-Braun, Carol *See Braun, Carol (Elizabeth) Moseley*

Moses, Edwin 1955— **8**

Moses, Gilbert, III 1942-1995 **12**

Moses, Robert Parris 1935— **11**

Mosley, "Sugar" Shane 1971— **32**

Mosley, Tim *See Timbaland*

Mosley, Walter 1952— **5, 25, 68**

Moss, Bryant *See Moss, Preacher*

Moss, Carlton 1909-1997 **17**

Moss, J. (?)— **64**

Moss, Otis, Jr. 1935— **72**

Moss, Otis, III 1971(?)— **72**

Moss, Preacher 1967— **63**

Moss, Randy 1977— **23**

Moss, Shad Gregory *See Lil' Bow Wow*

Mossell, Gertrude Bustill 1855-1948 40

Moten, Etta See Barnett, Etta Moten

Motley, Archibald, Jr. 1891-1981 30

Motley, Constance Baker 1921-2005 10, 55

Motley, Marion 1920-1999 26

Mourning, Alonzo 1970— 17, 44

Moutoussamy-Ashe, Jeanne 1951— 7

Mowatt, Judy 1952(?)— 38

Mowry, Jess 1960— 7

Moyo, Karega Kofi 19(?)(?)— 36

Moyo, Yvette Jackson 1953— 36

Mphalele, Es'kia (Ezekiel) 1919— 40

Mswati III 1968— 56

Mudimbe, V. Y. 1941— 61

Mugabe, Robert 1924— 10, 71

Mugo, Madeleine See Mugo, Micere Githae

Mugo, Micere Githae 1942— 32

Muhajir, El See X, Marvin

Muhammad, Ava 1951— 31

Muhammad, Elijah 1897-1975 4

Muhammad, Jabir Herbert 1929–2008 72

Muhammad, Khallid Abdul 1951(?)— 10, 31

Mullen, Harryette 1953— 34

Mullen, Nicole C. 1967— 45

Muluzi, Elson Bakili 1943— 14

Mumba, Samantha 1983— 29

Mundine, Anthony 1975— 56

Murphy, Eddie 1961— 4, 20, 61

Murphy, Edward Regan See Murphy, Eddie

Murphy, John H. 1916— 42

Murphy, Laura M. 1955— 43

Murphy McKenzie, Vashti See McKenzie, Vashti M.

Murray, Albert L. 1916— 33

Murray, Cecil 1929— 12, 47

Murray, Eddie 1956— 12

Murray, Lenda 1962— 10

Murray, Pauli 1910-1985 38

Murray, Tai 1982— 47

Murrell, Sylvia Marilyn 1947— 49

Muse, Clarence Edouard 1889-1979 21

Museveni, Yoweri (Kaguta) 1944(?)— 4

Musiq 1977— 37

Mutebi, Ronald 1956— 25

Mutola, Maria de Lurdes 1972— 12

Mutombo, Dikembe 1966— 7

Mutu, Wangechi 19(?)(?)— 44

Mwanawasa, Levy 1948–2008 72

Mwangi, Meja 1948— 40

Mwinyi, Ali Hassan 1925— 1

Mya 1979— 35

Myers, Dwight See Heavy D

Myers, Walter Dean 1937— 8, 70

Myers, Walter Milton See Myers, Walter Dean

Myles, Kim 1974— 69

Nabrit, Samuel Milton 1905-2003 47

Nagin, C. Ray 1956— 42, 57

Nagin, Ray See Nagin, C. Ray

Najm, Faheem Rasheed See T-Pain

Nakhid, David 1964— 25

Naki, Hamilton 1926-2005 63

Nance, Cynthia 1958— 71

Nanula, Richard D. 1960— 20

Napoleon, Benny N. 1956(?)— 23

Nas 1973— 33

Nascimento, Milton 1942— 2, 64

Nash, Diane 1938— 72

Nash, Joe 1919-2005 55

Nash, Johnny 1940— 40

Nash, Niecy 1970— 66

Naylor, Gloria 1950— 10, 42

Nazario, Zoe Yadira Zaldaña See Saldana, Zoe

Ndadaye, Melchior 1953-1993 7

Ndegeocello, Me'Shell 1968— 15

N'Dour, Youssou 1959— 1, 53

Ndungane, Winston Njongonkulu 1941— 16

Ne-Yo 1982— 65

Neal, Elise 1970— 29

Neal, Larry 1937-1981 38

Neal, Raful 1936— 44

Neale, Haydain 1970— 52

Neals, Otto 1930— 73

Nelly 1978— 32

Nelson, Jill 1952— 6, 54

Nelson, Prince Rogers See Prince

Nelson Meigs, Andrea 1968— 48

Neto, António Agostinho 1922— 43

Nettles, Marva Deloise See Collins, Marva

Neville, Aaron 1941— 21

Neville, Arthel 1962— 53

Newcombe, Don 1926— 24

Newkirk, Pamela 1957— 69

Newman, Lester C. 1952— 51

Newsome, Ozzie 1956— 26

Newton, Huey (Percy) 1942-1989 2

Newton, Thandie 1972— 26

Ngengi, Kamau wa See Kenyatta, Jomo

Ngilu, Charity 1952— 58

Ngubane, (Baldwin Sipho) Ben 1941— 33

Ngugi wa Thiong'o 1938— 29, 61

Ngugi, James wa Thiong'o See Ngugi wa Thiong'o

Niane, Katoucha 1960–2008 70

Nicholas, Fayard 1914-2006 20, 57, 61

Nicholas, Harold 1921— 20

Nichols, Grace See Nichols, Nichelle

Nichols, James Thomas See Bell, James "Cool Papa"

Nichols, Nichelle 1933(?)— 11

Nissel, Angela 1974— 42

Nix, Robert N.C., Jr. 1928-2003 51

Njongonkulu, Winston Ndungane 1941— 16

Nkoli, Simon 1957-1998 60

Nkomo, Joshua 1917-1999 4, 65

Nkosi, Lewis 1936— 46

Nkrumah, Kwame 1909-1972 3

N'Namdi, George R. 1946— 17

Noah, Yannick 1960— 4, 60

Noble, Ronald 1957— 46

Norman, Christina 1960(?)— 47

Norman, Jessye 1945— 5

Norman, Maidie 1912-1998 20

Norman, Pat 1939— 10

Norton, Eleanor Holmes 1937— 7

Norton, Meredith 1970(?)— 72

Norwood, Brandy See Brandy

Notorious B.I.G. 1972-1997 20

Nottage, Cynthia DeLores See Tucker, C. DeLores

Nottage, Lynn 1964— 66

Nour, Nawal M. 1965(?)— 56

Ntaryamira, Cyprien 1955-1994 8

Ntshona, Winston 1941— 52

Nugent, Richard Bruce 1906-1987 39

Nujoma, Samuel 1929— 10

Nunez, Elizabeth 1944(?)— 62

Nunn, Annetta 1959— 43

Nutter, Michael 1958— 69

Nuttin' but Stringz See Escobar, Tourie, and Escobar, Damien

Nyanda, Siphiwe 1950— 21

Nyerere, Julius (Kambarage) 1922— 5

Nzo, Alfred (Baphethuxolo) 1925— 15

Obama, Barack 1961— 49

Obama, Michelle 1964— 61

Obasanjo, Olusegun 1937— 5, 22

Obasanjo, Stella 1945-2005 32, 56

Obote, Milton 1925-2005 63

ODB See Ol' Dirty Bastard

Odetta 1939 37

Odinga, Raila 1945— 67

Oglesby, Zena 1947— 12

Ogletree, Charles, Jr. 1952— 12, 47

O'Grady, Lorraine 1934— 73

Ogunlesi, Adebayo O. 19(?)(?)— 37

Ojikutu, Bayo 1971— 66

Ojikutu, Bisola 1974— 65

Okaalet, Peter 1953— 58

Okara, Gabriel 1921— 37

Okonedo, Sophie 1969— 67

Okosuns, Sonny 1947–2008 71

Olajuwon, Akeem See Olajuwon, Hakeem

Olajuwon, Hakeem 1963— 2, 72

Olatunji, Babatunde 1927— 36

Olden, Georg(e) 1920-1975 44

O'Leary, Hazel (Rollins) 1937— 6

Oliver, Jerry 1947— 37

Oliver, Joe "King" 1885-1938 42

Oliver, John J., Jr. 1945— 48

Oliver, Kimberly 1976— 60

Oliver, Pam 1961— 54

Olojede, Dele 1961— 59

Olopade, Olufunmilayo Falusi 1957(?)— 58

O'Neal, Ron 1937-2004 46

O'Neal, Shaquille (Rashaun) 1972— 8, 30

O'Neal, Stanley 1951— 38, 67

O'Neil, Buck 1911-2006 19, 59

O'Neil, John Jordan See O'Neil, Buck

Ongala, Ramadhani Mtoro See Ongala, Remmy

Ongala, Remmy 1947— 9

Onwueme, Tess Osonye 1955— 23

Onwurah, Ngozi 1966(?)— 38

Onyewu, Oguchi 1982— 60

O'Ree, William Eldon See O'Ree, Willie

O'Ree, Willie 1935— 5

Orlandersmith, Dael 1959— 42

Orman, Roscoe 1944— 55

Ormes, Jackie 1911–1985 73

Ortiz, David 1975— 52

Osborne, Jeffrey 1948— 26

Osborne, Na'taki 1974— 54

Otis, Clarence, Jr. 1956— 55

Otis, Clyde 1924— 67

Otunga, Maurice Michael 1923-2003 55

Ouattara 1957— 43

Ousmane, Sembène See Sembène, Ousmane

OutKast 35

Owens, Dana See Queen Latifah

Owens, Helen 1937— 48

Owens, J. C. See Owens, Jesse

Owens, Jack 1904-1997 38

Owens, James Cleveland See Owens, Jesse

Owens, Jesse 1913-1980 2

Owens, Major (Robert) 1936— 6

Owens, Terrell 1973— 53

Oyono, Ferdinand 1929— 38

P. Diddy See Combs, Sean "Puffy"

P.M. Dawn, 54

Pace, Betty 1954— 59

Pace, Orlando 1975— 21

Packer, Daniel 1947— 56

Packer, Will 1974(?)— 71

Packer, Z. Z. 1973— 64

Page, Alan (Cedric) 1945— 7

Page, Clarence 1947— 4

Paige, Leroy Robert See Paige, Satchel

Paige, Rod 1933— 29

Paige, Satchel 1906-1982 7

Painter, Nell Irvin 1942— 24

Palmer, Everard 1930— 37

Palmer, Keke 1993— 68

Palmer, Rissi 1981— 65

Palmer, Violet 1964— 59

Papa Wendo See Kolosoy, Wendo

Parham, Marjorie B. 1918— 71

Parish, Robert 1953— 43

Parker, Charlie 1920-1955 20

Parker, Jim 1934-2005 64

Parker, Kellis E. 1942-2000 30

Parker, (Lawrence) Kris(hna) See KRS-One

Parker, LarStella Irby See Parker, Star

Parker, Maceo 1943— 72

Parker, Nicole Ari 1970— 52

Parker, Star 1956— 70

Parks, Bernard C. 1943— 17

Parks, Gordon 1912-2006 1, 35, 58

Parks, Rosa 1913-2005 1, 35, 56

Parks, Suzan-Lori 1964— 34

Parr, Russ 196(?)— 51

Parsons, James Benton 1911-1993 14

Parsons, Richard Dean 1948— 11, 33

Pascal-Trouillot, Ertha 1943— 3

Paterson, Basil A. 1926— 69

Paterson, David A. 1954— 59

Patillo, Melba Joy 1941— 15

Patrick, Deval 1956— 12, 61

Patterson, Floyd 1935-2006 19, 58

Patterson, Frederick Douglass 1901-1988 12

Patterson, Gilbert Earl 1939— 41

Patterson, Louise 1901-1999 25

Patterson, Mary Jane 1840-1894 **54**
Patterson, Orlando 1940— **4**
Patterson, P(ercival) J(ames) 1936(?)— **6, 20**
Patton, Antwan 1975— **45**
Patton, Antwan "Big Boi" 1975(?)— *See OutKast*
Patton, Paula 1975— **62**
Payne, Allen 1962(?)— **13**
Payne, Donald M. 1934— **2, 57**
Payne, Ethel L. 1911-1991 **28**
Payne, Freda 1942— **58**
Payne, Ulice 1955— **42**
Payne, William D. 1932— **60**
Payton, Benjamin F. 1932— **23**
Payton, John 1946— **48**
Payton, Walter (Jerry) 1954–1999 **11, 25**
Pearman, Raven-Symone Christina *See Raven*
Peck, Carolyn 1966(?)— **23**
Peck, Raoul 1953— **32**
Peete, Calvin 1943— **11**
Peete, Holly Robinson 1965— **20**
Peete, Rodney 1966— **60**
Pelé 1940— **7**
Pena, Paul 1950-2005 **58**
Pendergrass, Teddy 1950— **22**
Penniman, Richard Wayne *See Little Richard*
Peoples, Dottie 19(?)(?)— **22**
Pereira, Aristides 1923— **30**
Perez, Anna 1951— **1**
Perkins, Anthony 1959(?)— **24**
Perkins, Edward (Joseph) 1928— **5**
Perkins, James, Jr. 1953(?)— **55**
Perkins, Joe Willie *See Perkins, Pinetop*
Perkins, Marion 1908-1961 **38**
Perkins, Pinetop 1913— **70**
Perren, Freddie 1943-2004 **60**
Perrineau, Harold, Jr. 1968— **51**
Perrot, Kim 1967-1999 **23**
Perry, Emmitt, Jr. *See Perry, Tyler*
Perry, Laval 195(?)— **64**
Perry, Lee "Scratch" 1936— **19**
Perry, Lincoln *See Fetchit, Stepin*
Perry, Lowell 1931-2001 **30**
Perry, Rainford Hugh *See Perry, Lee "Scratch"*
Perry, Ruth 1936— **19**
Perry, Ruth Sando 1939— **15**
Perry, Tyler 1969— **40, 54**
Perry, Warren 1942(?)— **56**
Person, Waverly 1927— **9, 51**
Peters, Lenrie 1932— **43**
Peters, Margaret 1915— **43**
Peters, Maria Philomena 1941— **12**
Peters, Matilda 1917— **43**
Petersen, Frank E. 1932— **31**
Peterson, Hannibal *See Peterson, Marvin "Hannibal"*
Peterson, James 1937— **38**
Peterson, Marvin "Hannibal" 1948— **27**
Peterson, Oscar 1925— **52**
Petry, Ann 1909-1997 **19**
Phifer, Mekhi 1975— **25**
Philip, M. Nourbese *See Philip, Marlene Nourbese*
Philip, Marlene Nourbese 1947— **32**

Phillips, Charles E., Jr. 1959— **57**
Phillips, Helen L. 1919-2005 **63**
Phillips, Joseph C. 1962— **73**
Phillips, Teresa L. 1958— **42**
Phipps, Wintley 1955— **59**
Pickens, James, Jr. 1954— **59**
Pickett, Bill 1870-1932 **11**
Pickett, Cecil 1945— **39**
Pierce, Paul 1977— **71**
Pierre, Andre 1915— **17**
Pierre, Percy Anthony 1939— **46**
Pincham, R. Eugene, Sr. 1925–2008 **69**
Pinchback, P(inckney) B(enton) S(tewart) 1837-1921 **9**
Pinckney, Bill 1935— **42**
Pinckney, Sandra 194(?)— **56**
Pindell, Howardena 1943— **55**
Pinderhughes, John 1946— **47**
Pinkett, Jada *See Pinkett Smith, Jada*
Pinkett, Randal 1971— **61**
Pinkett Smith, Jada 1971— **10, 41**
Pinkney, Jerry 1939— **15**
Pinkston, W. Randall 1950— **24**
Pinn, Vivian Winona 1941— **49**
Piper, Adrian 1948— **71**
Pippen, Scottie 1965— **15**
Pippin, Horace 1888-1946 **9**
Pitt, David Thomas 1913-1994 **10**
Pitta (do Nascimento), Celso (Roberto) 19(?)(?)— **17**
Pitts, Byron 1960— **71**
Pitts, Leonard, Jr. 1957— **54**
Player, Willa B. 1909-2003 **43**
Pleasant, Mary Ellen 1814-1904 **9**
Plessy, Homer Adolph 1862-1925 **31**
Poitier, Sidney 1927— **11, 36**
Poitier, Sydney Tamiia 1973— **65**
Pollard, Fritz 1894-1986 **53**
Pomare, Eleo 1937–2008 **72**
Poole, Elijah *See Muhammad, Elijah*
Pope.L, William 1955— **72**
Porter, Countee Leroy *See Cullin, Countee*
Porter, Dorothy *See Wesley, Dorothy Porter*
Porter, James A(mos) 1905-1970 **11**
Portuondo, Omara 1930— **53**
Potter, Myrtle 1958— **40**
Pough, Terrell 1987(?)-2005 **58**
Pounder, Carol Christine Hilaria *See Pounder, CCH*
Pounder, CCH 1952— **72**
Poussaint, Alvin F. 1934— **5, 67**
Powell, Adam Clayton, Jr. 1908-1972 **3**
Powell, Bud 1924-1966 **24**
Powell, Colin (Luther) 1937— **1, 28**
Powell, Debra A. 1964— **23**
Powell, Kevin 1966— **31**
Powell, Maxine 1924— **8**
Powell, Michael Anthony *See Powell, Mike*
Powell, Michael K. 1963— **32**
Powell, Mike 1963— **7**
Powell, Renee 1946— **34**
Pratt Dixon, Sharon *See Dixon, Sharon Pratt*
Pratt, Awadagin 1966— **31**
Pratt, Geronimo 1947— **18**

Pratt, Kyla 1986— **57**
Premice, Josephine 1926-2001 **41**
Pressley, Condace L. 1964— **41**
Preston, Billy 1946-2006 **39, 59**
Preston, William Everett *See Preston, Billy*
Price, Florence 1887-1953 **37**
Price, Frederick K.C. 1932— **21**
Price, Glenda 1939— **22**
Price, Hugh B. 1941— **9, 54**
Price, Kelly 1973(?)— **23**
Price, Leontyne 1927— **1**
Price, Richard 1930(?)— **51**
Pride, Charley 1938(?)— **26**
Primus, Pearl 1919— **6**
Prince 1958— **18, 65**
Prince, Richard E. 1947— **71**
Prince, Ron 1969— **64**
Prince, Tayshaun 1980— **68**
Prince-Bythewood, Gina 1968— **31**
Pritchard, Robert Starling 1927— **21**
Procope, Ernesta 19(?)(?)— **23**
Procope, John Levy 1925-2005 **56**
Prophet, Nancy Elizabeth 1890-1960 **42**
Prothrow, Deborah Boutin *See Prothrow-Stith, Deborah*
Prothrow-Stith, Deborah 1954— **10**
Pryor, Rain 1969— **65**
Pryor, Richard 1940-2005 **3, 24, 56**
Puckett, Kirby 1960-2006 **4, 58**
Puff Daddy *See Combs, Sean "Puffy"*
Purnell, Silas 1923-2003 **59**
Puryear, Martin 1941— **42**
Quarles, Benjamin Arthur 1904-1996 **18**
Quarles, Norma 1936— **25**
Quarterman, Lloyd Albert 1918-1982 **4**
Queen Latifah 1970— **1, 16, 58**
Quigless, Helen G. 1944-2004 **49**
Quince, Peggy A. 1948— **69**
Quirot, Ana (Fidelia) 1963— **13**
Quivers, Robin 1952— **61**
Rabb, Maurice F., Jr. 1932-2005 **58**
Rabia, Aliyah *See Staton, Dakota*
Rahman, Aishah 1936— **37**
Raines, Franklin Delano 1949— **14**
Rainey, Ma 1886-1939 **33**
Ralph, Sheryl Lee 1956— **18**
Ramaphosa, (Matamela) Cyril 1952— **3**
Rambough, Lori Ann *See Sommore*
Ramphele, Mamphela 1947— **29**
Ramsey, Charles H. 1948— **21, 69**
Rand, A(ddison) Barry 1944— **6**
Randall, Alice 1959— **38**
Randall, Dudley 1914-2000 **8, 55**
Randle, Theresa 1967— **16**
Randolph, A(sa) Philip 1889-1979 **3**
Randolph, Linda A. 1941— **52**
Randolph, Willie 1954— **53**
Rangel, Charles 1930— **3, 52**
Rankin Don *See Rhoden, Wayne*
Raoul, Kwame 1964— **55**
Ras Tafari *See Haile Selassie*
Rashad, Ahmad 1949— **18**
Rashad, Phylicia 1948— **21**
Raspberry, William 1935— **2**
Raven, 1985— **44**
Raven-Symone *See Raven*

Rawlings, Jerry (John) 1947— **9**
Rawls, Lou 1936-2006 **17, 57**
Ray, Charlotte E. 1850-1911 **60**
Ray, Gene Anthony 1962-2003 **47**
Raymond, Usher, IV *See Usher*
Razaf, Andy 1895-1973 **19**
Razafkeriefo, Andreamentania Paul *See Razaf, Andy*
Ready, Stephanie 1975— **33**
Reagon, Bernice Johnson 1942— **7**
Reason, Joseph Paul 1943— **19**
Record, Eugene 1940-2005 **60**
Reddick, Lance 19(?)(?)— **52**
Reddick, Lawrence Dunbar 1910-1995 **20**
Redding, J. Saunders 1906-1988 **26**
Redding, Louis L. 1901-1998 **26**
Redding, Otis, Jr. 1941— **16**
Redman, Joshua 1969— **30**
Redmond, Eugene 1937— **23**
Reece, E. Albert 1950— **63**
Reed, A. C. 1926— **36**
Reed, Ishmael 1938— **8**
Reed, Jimmy 1925-1976 **38**
Reems, Ernestine Cleveland 1932— **27**
Reese, Calvin *See Reese, Pokey*
Reese, Della 1931— **6, 20**
Reese, Milous J., Jr. 1904— **51**
Reese, Pokey 1973— **28**
Reese, Tracy 1964— **54**
Reeves, Dianne 1956— **32**
Reeves, Gregory 1952— **49**
Reeves, Rachel J. 1950(?)— **23**
Reeves, Triette Lipsey 1963— **27**
Regis, Cyrille 1958— **51**
Reid, Antonio "L.A." 1958(?)— **28**
Reid, Irvin D. 1941— **20**
Reid, L.A. *See Reid, Antonio "L.A."*
Reid, Senghor 1976— **55**
Reid, Tim 1944— **56**
Reid, Vernon 1958— **34**
Reivers, Corbin Bleu *See Corbin Bleu*
Reuben, Gloria 19(?)(?)— **15**
Rev Run *See Run*
Reynolds, Star Jones 1962(?)— **10, 27, 61**
Rhames, Ving 1959— **14, 50**
Rhimes, Shonda Lynn 1970— **67**
Rhoden, Dwight 1962— **40**
Rhoden, Wayne 1966— **70**
Rhoden, William C. 1950(?)— **67**
Rhodes, Ray 1950— **14**
Rhone, Sylvia 1952— **2**
Rhymes, Busta 1972— **31**
Ribbs, William Theodore, Jr. *See Ribbs, Willy T.*
Ribbs, Willy T. 1956— **2**
Ribeau, Sidney 1947(?)— **70**
Ribeiro, Alfonso 1971— **17**
Rice, Condoleezza 1954— **3, 28, 72**
Rice, Constance LaMay 1956— **60**
Rice, Jerry 1962— **5, 55**
Rice, Linda Johnson 1958— **9, 41**
Rice, Louise Allen 1941— **54**
Rice, Norm(an Blann) 1943— **8**
Richards, Beah 1926-2000 **30**
Richards, Hilda 1936— **49**
Richards, Lloyd 1923(?)— **2**
Richards, Sanya 1985— **66**

Richardson, Desmond 1969— **39**
Richardson, Donna 1962— **39**
Richardson, Elaine Potter *See Kincaid, Jamaica*
Richardson, LaTanya 1949— **71**
Richardson, Nolan 1941— **9**
Richardson, Pat *See Norman, Pat*
Richardson, Rupert 1930–2008 **67**
Richardson, Salli 1967— **68**
Richie, Leroy C. 1941— **18**
Richie, Lionel 1949— **27, 65**
Richmond, Mitchell James 1965— **19**
Rideau, Iris 1940(?)— **46**
Ridenhour, Carlton *See Chuck D.*
Ridley, John 1965— **69**
Riggs, Marlon 1957–1994 **5, 44**
Rihanna 1988— **65**
Riley, Helen Caldwell Day 1926— **13**
Riley, Rochelle 1959(?)— **50**
Ringgold, Faith 1930— **4**
Riperton, Minnie 1947-1979 **32**
Rivers, Glenn "Doc" 1961— **25**
Rivers, Kim *See Roberts, Kimberly Rivers*
Roach, Max 1924-2007 **21, 63**
Roberto, Holden 1923-2007 **65**
Roberts, Darryl 1962(?)— **70**
Roberts, Deborah 1960— **35**
Roberts, James *See Lover, Ed*
Roberts, Kimberly Rivers 1981(?)— **72**
Roberts, Kristina LaFerne *See Zane*
Roberts, Marcus 1963— **19**
Roberts, Marthaniel *See Roberts, Marcus*
Roberts, Mike 1948— **57**
Roberts, Robin 1960— **16, 54**
Roberts, Roy S. 1939(?)— **14**
Robertson, Oscar 1938— **26**
Robeson, Eslanda Goode 1896-1965 **13**
Robeson, Paul (Leroy Bustill) 1898-1976 **2**
Robinson, Aminah 1940— **50**
Robinson, Bill "Bojangles" 1878-1949 **11**
Robinson, Bishop L. 1927— **66**
Robinson, Cleo Parker 1948(?)— **38**
Robinson, David 1965— **24**
Robinson, Eddie G. 1919-2007 **10, 61**
Robinson, Fatima 19(?)(?)— **34**
Robinson, Fenton 1935-1997 **38**
Robinson, Frank 1935— **9**
Robinson, Jack Roosevelt *See Robinson, Jackie*
Robinson, Jackie 1919-1972 **6**
Robinson, LaVaughn 1927–2008 **69**
Robinson, Luther *See Robinson, Bill "Bojangles"*
Robinson, Malcolm S. 1948— **44**
Robinson, Matt 1937–2002 **69**
Robinson, Matthew, Jr. *See Robinson, Matt*
Robinson, Max 1939-1988 **3**
Robinson, Patrick 1966— **19, 71**
Robinson, Rachel 1922— **16**
Robinson, Randall 1941— **7, 46**
Robinson, Reginald R. 1972— **53**
Robinson, Sharon 1950— **22**

Robinson, Shaun 19(?)(?)— **36**
Robinson, Smokey 1940— **3, 49**
Robinson, Spottswood W., III 1916-1998 **22**
Robinson, Sugar Ray 1921— **18**
Robinson, Will 1911–2008 **51, 69**
Robinson, William, Jr. *See Robinson, Smokey*
Roble, Abdi 1964— **71**
Roche, Joyce M. 1947— **17**
Rochester *See Anderson, Eddie "Rochester"*
Rochon, Lela 1965(?)— **16**
Rock, Chris 1967(?)— **3, 22, 66**
Rock, The 1972— **29, 66**
Rodgers, Johnathan 1946— **6, 51**
Rodgers, Rod 1937-2002 **36**
Rodman, Dennis 1961— **12, 44**
Rodrigues, Percy 1918–2007 **68**
Rodriguez, Jimmy 1963(?)— **47**
Rodriguez, Cheryl 1952— **64**
Rogers, Alan G. 1967–2008 **72**
Rogers, Jimmy 1924-1997 **38**
Rogers, Joe 1964— **27**
Rogers, Joel Augustus 1883(?)-1996 **30**
Rogers, John W., Jr. 1958— **5, 52**
Rogers, Kelis *See Kelis*
Rojas, Don 1949— **33**
Roker, Al 1954— **12, 49**
Roker, Roxie 1929–1995 **68**
Rolle, Esther 1920-1998 **13, 21**
Rollins, Charlemae Hill 1897-1979 **27**
Rollins, Howard E., Jr. 1950-1996 **16**
Rollins, Ida Gray Nelson *See Gray (Nelson Rollins), Ida*
Rollins, James Calvin, III *See Rollins, Jimmy*
Rollins, Jimmy 1978— **70**
Rollins, Sonny 1930— **37**
Ronaldinho 1980— **69**
Rooakhptah, Amunnubi *See York, Dwight D.*
Rose, Anika Noni 1972— **70**
Rose, Lionel 1948— **56**
Ross, Araminta *See Tubman, Harriet*
Ross, Charles 1957— **27**
Ross, Diana 1944— **8, 27**
Ross, Don 1941— **27**
Ross, Isaiah "Doc" 1925-1993 **40**
Ross, Tracee Ellis 1972— **35**
Ross-Lee, Barbara 1942— **67**
Rotimi, (Emmanuel Gladstone) Ola-(wale) 1938— **1**
Roundtree, Richard 1942— **27**
Rowan, Carl T(homas) 1925— **1, 30**
Rowell, Victoria 1960— **13, 68**
Roxanne Shante 1969— **33**
Roy, Kenny 1990(?)— **51**
Rubin, Chanda 1976— **37**
Rucker, Darius 1966(?)— **34**
Rudolph, Maya 1972— **46**
Rudolph, Wilma (Glodean) 1940— **4**
Rugambwa, Laurean 1912-1997 **20**
Ruley, Ellis 1882-1959 **38**
Run 1964— **31, 73**
Run-DMC **31**
Rupaul 1960— **17**
Rusesabagina, Paul 1954— **60**

Rush, Bobby 1946— **26**
Rush, Otis 1934— **38**
Rushen, Patrice 1954— **12**
Rushing, Jimmy 1903-1972 **37**
Russell, Bill 1934— **8**
Russell, Brenda 1944(?)— **52**
Russell, Herman Jerome 1931(?)— **17**
Russell, Nipsey 1924-2005 **66**
Russell, William Felton *See Russell, Bill*
Russell-McCloud, Patricia 1946— **17**
Rustin, Bayard 1910-1987 **4**
Saar, Alison 1956— **16**
Sade 1959— **15**
Sadler, Joseph *See Grandmaster Flash*
Sadlier, Rosemary 19(?)(?)— **62**
St. Jacques, Raymond 1930-1990 **8**
Saint James, Synthia 1949— **12**
St. John, Kristoff 1966— **25**
St. Julien, Marlon 1972— **29**
St. Patrick, Mathew 1969— **48**
Saldana, Zoe 1978— **72**
Salih, Al-Tayyib 1929— **37**
Sallee, Charles 1911— **38**
Salter, Nikkole 1979(?)— **73**
Salters, Alisia *See Salters, Lisa*
Salters, Lisa 1966(?)— **71**
Salvador, Bryce 1976— **51**
Samara, Noah 1956— **15**
SAMO *See Basquiat, Jean-Michel*
Sample, Joe 1939— **51**
Sampson, Charles 1957— **13**
Sampson, Edith S(purlock) 1901-1979 **4**
Samuel, Sealhenry Olumide 1963— **14**
Samuelsson, Marcus 1970— **53**
Sanchez, Sonia 1934— **17, 51**
Sanders, Barry 1968— **1, 53**
Sanders, Bob 1981— **72**
Sanders, Deion (Luwynn) 1967— **4, 31**
Sanders, Demond *See Sanders, Bob*
Sanders, Dori(nda) 1935— **8**
Sanders, Joseph R(ichard, Jr.) 1954— **11**
Sanders, Malika 1973— **48**
Sanders, Pharoah 1940— **64**
Sanders, Rose M. *See Touré, Faya Ora Rose*
Sané, Pierre Gabriel 1948-1998 **21**
Sanford, Isabel 1917-2004 **53**
Sanford, John Elroy *See Foxx, Redd*
Sangare, Oumou 1968— **18**
Sankara, Thomas 1949-1987 **17**
Sapp, Warren 1972— **38**
Saro-Wiwa, Kenule 1941-1995 **39**
Satcher, David 1941— **7, 57**
Satchmo *See Armstrong, (Daniel) Louis*
Savage, Augusta Christine 1892(?)-1962 **12**
Savimbi, Jonas (Malheiro) 1934-2002 **2, 34**
Sawyer, Amos 1945— **2**
Sayers, Gale 1943— **28**
Sayles Belton, Sharon 1952(?)— **9, 16**

Scantlebury, Janna 1984(?)— **47**
Scantlebury-White, Velma 1955— **64**
Scarlett, Millicent 1971— **49**
Schmoke, Kurt 1949— **1, 48**
Schomburg, Arthur Alfonso 1874-1938 **9**
Schomburg, Arturo Alfonso *See Schomburg, Arthur Alfonso*
Schultz, Michael A. 1938— **6**
Schuyler, George Samuel 1895-1977 **40**
Schuyler, Philippa 1931-1967 **50**
Scott, C. A. 1908-2000 **29**
Scott, Coretta *See King, Coretta Scott*
Scott, Cornelius Adolphus *See Scott, C. A.*
Scott, David 1946— **41**
Scott, George 1929-2005 **55**
Scott, Harold Russell, Jr. 1935-2006 **61**
Scott, Hazel 1920-1981 **66**
Scott, Jill 1972— **29**
Scott, John T. 1940-2007 **65**
Scott, "Little" Jimmy 1925— **48**
Scott, Milton 1956— **51**
Scott, Robert C. 1947— **23**
Scott, Stuart 1965— **34**
Scott, Wendell Oliver, Sr. 1921-1990 **19**
Scruggs, Mary Elfrieda *See Williams, Mary Lou*
Scurry, Briana 1971— **27**
Seacole, Mary 1805-1881 **54**
Seal **14**
Seale, Bobby 1936— **3**
Seale, Robert George *See Seale, Bobby*
Seals, Frank *See Seals, Son*
Seals, Son 1942-2004 **56**
Sears, Stephanie 1964— **53**
Sears-Collins, Leah J(eanette) 1955— **5**
Sebree, Charles 1914-1985 **40**
Seele, Pernessa 1954— **46**
Selassie, Haile *See Haile Selassie*
Sembène, Ousmane 1923-2007 **13, 62**
Senghor, Augustin Diamacoune 1928-2007 **66**
Senghor, Léopold Sédar 1906-2001 **12, 66**
Sengstacke, John Herman Henry 1912-1997 **18**
Senior, Olive 1941— **37**
Sentamu, John 1949— **58**
Serrano, Andres 1951(?)— **3**
Shabazz, Attallah 1958— **6**
Shabazz, Betty 1936-1997 **7, 26**
Shabazz, Ilyasah 1962— **36**
Shaggy 1968— **31**
Shakespeare, Robbie 1953— *See Sly & Robbie*
Shakur, Afeni 1947— **67**
Shakur, Assata 1947— **6**
Shakur, Tupac Amaru 1971-1996 **14**
Shange, Ntozake 1948— **8**
Sharper, Darren 1975— **32**
Sharpton, Al 1954— **21**
Shavers, Cheryl 19(?)(?)— **31**
Shaw, Bernard 1940— **2, 28**
Shaw, William J. 1934— **30**

Sheard, Kierra "Kiki" 1987— **61**

Sheffey, Asa Bundy *See Hayden, Robert Earl*

Sheffield, Gary Antonian 1968— **16**

Shell, Art 1946— **1, 66**

Shepherd, Sherri 1970— **55**

Sherrod, Clayton 1944— **17**

Shinhoster, Earl 1950(?)-2000 **32**

Shipp, E. R. 1955— **15**

Shippen, John 1879-1968 **43**

Shirley, George I. 1934— **33**

Shonibare, Yinka 1962— **58**

Short, Bobby 1924-2005 **52**

Shorty, Ras, I 1941-2000 **47**

Showers, Reggie 1964— **30**

Shropshire, Thomas B. 1925-2003 **49**

Shuttlesworth, Fred 1922— **47**

Sifford, Charlie 1922— **4, 49**

Sigur, Wanda 1958— **44**

Siji 1971(?)— **56**

Silas, Paul 1943— **24**

Silver, Horace 1928— **26**

Siméus, Dumas M. 1940— **25**

Simmons, Bob 1948— **29**

Simmons, Gary 1964— **58**

Simmons, Henry 1970— **55**

Simmons, Jamal 1971— **72**

Simmons, Joseph *See Run*

Simmons, Kimora Lee 1975— **51**

Simmons, Russell 1957(?)— **1, 30**

Simmons, Ruth J. 1945— **13, 38**

Simone, Nina 1933-2003 **15, 41**

Simpson, Carole 1940— **6, 30**

Simpson, Lorna 1960— **4, 36**

Simpson, O. J. 1947— **15**

Simpson, Valerie 1946— **21**

Simpson-Hoffman, N'kenge 1975(?)— **52**

Simpson-Miller, Portia 1945— **62**

Sims, Howard "Sandman" 1917-2003 **48**

Sims, Lowery Stokes 1949— **27**

Sims, Naomi 1949— **29**

Sinbad 1957(?)— **1, 16**

Singletary, Michael *See Singletary, Mike*

Singletary, Mike 1958— **4**

Singleton, John 1968— **2, 30**

Sinkford, Jeanne C. 1933— **13**

Sirleaf, Ellen Johnson 1938— **71**

Sisqo 1976— **30**

Sissle, Noble 1889-1975 **29**

Sister Souljah 1964— **11**

Sisulu, Albertina 1918— **57**

Sisulu, Sheila Violet Makate 1948(?)— **24**

Sisulu, Walter 1912-2003 **47**

Sizemore, Barbara A. 1927— **26**

Skerrit, Roosevelt 1972— **72**

Skinner, Kiron K. 1962(?) **65**

Sklarek, Norma Merrick 1928— **25**

Slater, Rodney Earl 1955— **15**

Slaughter, John Brooks 1934— **53**

Sledge, Percy 1940— **39**

Sleet, Moneta (J.), Jr. 1926— **5**

Slice, Kimbo 1974— **73**

Slocumb, Jonathan 19(?)(?)— **52**

Sly & Robbie **34**

Slyde, Jimmy 1927–2008 **70**

Smaltz, Audrey 1937(?)— **12**

Smiley, Rickey 1968— **59**

Smiley, Tavis 1964— **20, 68**

Smith, Anjela Lauren 1973— **44**

Smith, Anna Deavere 1950— **6, 44**

Smith, Arthur Lee, *See Asante, Molefi Kete*

Smith, B. *See Smith, B(arbara)*

Smith, B(arbara) 1949(?)— **11**

Smith, Barbara 1946— **28**

Smith, Bessie 1894-1937 **3**

Smith, Bruce W. 19(?)(?)— **53**

Smith, Cladys "Jabbo" 1908-1991 **32**

Smith, Clarence O. 1933— **21**

Smith, Damu 1951— **54**

Smith, Danyel 1966(?)— **40**

Smith, Dr. Lonnie 1942— **49**

Smith, Emmitt (III) 1969— **7**

Smith, Greg 1964— **28**

Smith, Hezekiah Leroy Gordon *See Smith, Stuff*

Smith, Hilton 1912-1983 **29**

Smith, Ian 1970(?)— **62**

Smith, Jabbo *See Smith, Cladys "Jabbo"*

Smith, Jane E. 1946— **24**

Smith, Jennifer 1947— **21**

Smith, Jessie Carney 1930— **35**

Smith, John L. 1938— **22**

Smith, Joshua (Isaac) 1941— **10**

Smith, Kemba 1971— **70**

Smith, Lonnie Liston 1940— **49**

Smith, Lovie 1958— **66**

Smith, Mamie 1883-1946 **32**

Smith, Marie F. 1939— **70**

Smith, Marvin 1910-2003 **46**

Smith, Mary Carter 1919— **26**

Smith, Morgan 1910-1993 **46**

Smith, Nate 1929— **49**

Smith, Orlando *See Smith, Tubby*

Smith, Richard 1957— **51**

Smith, Rick 1969— **72**

Smith, Roger Guenveur 1960— **12**

Smith, Shaffer Chimere *See Ne-Yo*

Smith, Stephen A. 1967— **69**

Smith, Stuff 1909-1967 **37**

Smith, Tasha 1971— **73**

Smith, Trevor, Jr. *See Rhymes, Busta*

Smith, Trixie 1895-1943 **34**

Smith, Tubby 1951— **18**

Smith, Vincent D. 1929-2003 **48**

Smith, Walker, Jr. *See Robinson, Sugar Ray*

Smith, Will 1968— **8, 18, 53**

Smith, Willi (Donnell) 1948-1987 **8**

Smith, Zadie 1975— **51**

Smythe Haith, Mabel 1918-2006 **61**

Sneed, Paula A. 1947— **18**

Snipes, Wesley 1962— **3, 24, 67**

Snoop Dogg 1972— **35**

Snow, Samuel 1923–2008 **71**

Snowden, Frank M., Jr. 1911–2007 **67**

Soglo, Nicéphore 1935— **15**

Solomon, Jimmie Lee 1947(?)— **38**

Somé, Malidoma Patrice 1956— **10**

Sommore, 1966— **61**

Sosa, Sammy 1968— **21, 44**

Soto Alejo, Federico Arístides *See Güines, Tata*

Soulchild, Musiq *See Musiq*

Southern, Eileen 1920-2002 **56**

Southgate, Martha 1960(?)— **58**

Sowande, Fela 1905-1987 **39**

Sowande, Olufela Obafunmilayo *See Sowande, Fela*

Sowell, Thomas 1930— **2**

Soyinka, (Akinwande Olu) Wole 1934— **4**

Sparks, Corinne Etta 1953— **53**

Sparks, Jordin 1989— **66**

Spaulding, Charles Clinton 1874-1952 **9**

Spears, Warren 1954-2005 **52**

Spence, Joseph 1910-1984 **49**

Spencer, Anne 1882-1975 **27**

Spencer, Winston Baldwin 1948— **68**

Spikes, Dolores Margaret Richard 1936— **18**

Spiller, Bill 1913-1988 **64**

Sprewell, Latrell 1970— **23**

Spriggs, William 195(?)— **67**

Stackhouse, Jerry 1974— **30**

Staley, Dawn 1970— **57**

Stallings, George A(ugustus), Jr. 1948— **6**

Stampley, Micah 1971— **54**

Stanford, John 1938— **20**

Stanford, Olivia Lee Dilworth 1914-2004 **49**

Stanton, Robert 1940— **20**

Staples, Brent 1951— **8**

Staples, Mavis 1939(?)— **50**

Staples, "Pops" 1915-2000 **32**

Staples, Roebuck *See Staples, "Pops"*

Stargell, Willie "Pops" 1940(?)–2001 **29**

Staton, Candi 1940(?)— **27**

Staton, Dakota 1930(?)-2007 **62**

Staupers, Mabel K(eaton) 1890-1989 **7**

Stearnes, Norman "Turkey" 1901-1979 **31**

Steave-Dickerson, Kia 1970— **57**

Steele, Claude Mason 1946— **13**

Steele, Lawrence 1963— **28**

Steele, Michael 1958— **38, 73**

Steele, Shelby 1946— **13**

Steinberg, Martha Jean 1930(?)-2000 **28**

Stephens, Charlotte Andrews 1854-1951 **14**

Stephens, John *See Legend, John*

Stephens, Myrtle *See Potter, Myrtle*

Stevens, Yvette *See Khan, Chaka*

Stew 1961— **69**

Steward, David L. 19(?)(?)— **36**

Steward, Emanuel 1944— **18**

Stewart, Alison 1966(?)— **13**

Stewart, Ella 1893-1987 **39**

Stewart, James "Bubba," Jr. 1985— **60**

Stewart, Kordell 1972— **21**

Stewart, Mark *See Stew*

Stewart, Paul Wilbur 1925— **12**

Still, William Grant 1895-1978 **37**

Stingley, Darryl 1951–2007 **69**

Stinson, Denise L. 1954— **59**

Stith, Charles R. 1949— **73**

Stokes, Carl 1927–1996 **10, 73**

Stokes, Louis 1925— **3**

Stone, Angie 1965(?)— **31**

Stone, Charles Sumner, Jr. *See Stone, Chuck*

Stone, Chuck 1924— **9**

Stone, Toni 1921-1996 **15**

Stoney, Michael 1969— **50**

Stott, Dorothy M. *See Stout, Renee*

Stott, Dot *See Stout, Renee*

Stoudemire, Amaré 1982— **59**

Stout, Juanita Kidd 1919-1998 **24**

Stout, Renee 1958— **63**

Stoute, Steve 1971(?)— **38**

Strahan, Michael 1971— **35**

Strawberry, Darryl 1962— **22**

Strayhorn, Billy 1915-1967 **31**

Street, John F. 1943(?)— **24**

Streeter, Sarah 1953— **45**

Stringer, C. Vivian 1948— **13, 66**

Stringer, Korey 1974-2001 **35**

Stringer, Vickie 196(?)— **58**

Stroman, Nathaniel *See Earthquake*

Studdard, Ruben 1978— **46**

Sudarkasa, Niara 1938— **4**

Sudduth, Jimmy Lee 1910-2007 **65**

Sullivan, Leon H(oward) 1922— **3, 30**

Sullivan, Louis (Wade) 1933— **8**

Sullivan, Maxine 1911-1987 **37**

Summer, Donna 1948— **25**

Sun Ra, 1914-1993 **60**

Sundiata, Sekou 1948-2007 **66**

Supremes, The **33**

Sutton, Percy E. 1920— **42**

Swann, Lynn 1952— **28**

Sweat, Keith 1961(?)— **19**

Sweet, Ossian 1895–1960 **68**

Swoopes, Sheryl 1971— **12, 56**

Swygert, H. Patrick 1943— **22**

Sy, Oumou 1952— **65**

Sykes, Roosevelt 1906-1984 **20**

Sykes, Wanda 1964— **48**

Syler, Rene 1963— **53**

Tademy, Lalita 1948— **36**

Tafari Makonnen *See Haile Selassie*

Tait, Michael 1966— **57**

Talbert, David 1966(?)— **34**

Talley, André Leon 1949(?)— **56**

Tamar-kali 1973(?)— **63**

Tamia 1975— **24, 55**

Tampa Red 1904(?)-1980 **63**

Tancil, Gladys Quander 1921-2002 **59**

Tanksley, Ann (Graves) 1934— **37**

Tanner, Henry Ossawa 1859-1937 **1**

Tate, Eleanora E. 1948— **20, 55**

Tate, Larenz 1975— **15**

Tatum, Art 1909-1956 **28**

Tatum, Beverly Daniel 1954— **42**

Taulbert, Clifton Lemoure 1945— **19**

Taylor, Billy 1921— **23**

Taylor, Bo 1966–2008 **72**

Taylor, Cecil 1929— **70**

Taylor, Charles 1948— **20**

Taylor, Darren *See Taylor, Bo*

Taylor, Ephren W., II 1982— **61**

Taylor, Helen (Lavon Hollingshed) 1942-2000 **30**

Taylor, Jason 1974— **70**

Taylor, Jermain 1978— **60**

Taylor, John (David Beckett) 1952— **16**

Taylor, Karin 1971— **34**

Taylor, Koko 1935— **40**

Taylor, Kristin Clark 1959— **8**

Taylor, Lawrence 1959— **25**
Taylor, Marshall Walter "Major" 1878-1932 **62**
Taylor, Meshach 1947(?)— **4**
Taylor, Mildred D. 1943— **26**
Taylor, Natalie 1959— **47**
Taylor, Regina 1959(?)— **9, 46**
Taylor, Ron 1952-2002 **35**
Taylor, Susan C. 1957— **62**
Taylor, Susan L. 1946— **10**
Taylor, Susie King 1848-1912 **13**
Temptations, The **33**
Tergat, Paul 1969— **59**
Terrell, Dorothy A. 1945— **24**
Terrell, Mary (Elizabeth) Church 1863-1954 **9**
Terrell, Tammi 1945-1970 **32**
Terry, Clark 1920— **39**
Tharpe, Rosetta 1915-1973 **65**
The Artist *See Prince*
Thiam, Aliaune Akon *See Akon*
Thigpen, Lynne 1948-2003 **17, 41**
Thomas, Alma Woodsey 1891-1978 **14**
Thomas, Arthur Ray 1951— **52**
Thomas, Clarence 1948— **2, 39, 65**
Thomas, Claudia Lynn 1950— **64**
Thomas, Debi 1967— **26**
Thomas, Derrick 1967-2000 **25**
Thomas, Emmitt 1943— **71**
Thomas, Frank 1968— **12, 51**
Thomas, Franklin A. 1934— **5, 49**
Thomas, Irma 1941— **29**
Thomas, Isiah 1961— **7, 26, 65**
Thomas, Michael 1967— **69**
Thomas, Mickalene 1971— **61**
Thomas, Rozonda "Chilli" 1971— *See TLC*
Thomas, Rufus 1917— **20**
Thomas, Sean Patrick 1970— **35**
Thomas, Trisha R. 1964— **65**
Thomas, Vivien (T.) 1910-1985 **9**
Thomas-Graham, Pamela 1963(?)— **29**
Thomason, Marsha 1976— **47**
Thompson, Bennie G. 1948— **26**
Thompson, Cynthia Bramlett 1949— **50**
Thompson, Dearon *See Deezer D*
Thompson, Don 1963— **56**
Thompson, John W. 1949— **26**
Thompson, Kenan 1978— **52**
Thompson, Larry D. 1945— **39**
Thompson, Tazewell (Alfred, Jr.) 1954— **13**
Thompson, Tina 1975— **25**
Thompson, William C. 1953(?)— **35**
Thoms, Tracie 1975— **61**
Thornton, Big Mama 1926-1984 **33**
Thornton, Yvonne S. 1947— **69**
Thrash, Dox 1893-1965 **35**
Three Mo' Tenors **35**
Thrower, Willie 1930-2002 **35**
Thugwane, Josia 1971— **21**
Thurman, Howard 1900-1981 **3**
Thurman, Wallace Henry 1902-1934 **16**
Thurston, Stephen J. 1952— **49**
Till, Emmett (Louis) 1941-1955 **7**
Tillard, Conrad 1964— **47**
Tillis, Frederick 1930— **40**
Tillman, George, Jr. 1968— **20**
Timbaland 1971— **32**

Tinsley, Boyd 1964— **50**
Tirico, Michael *See Tirico, Mike*
Tirico, Mike 1966— **68**
Tisdale, Wayman 1964— **50**
TLC **34**
Todman, Terence A. 1926— **55**
Tolliver, Mose 1915(?)-2006 **60**
Tolliver, William (Mack) 1951— **9**
Tolson, Melvin B(eaunorus) 1898-1966 **37**
Tolton, Augustine 1854-1897 **62**
Tomlinson, LaDainian 1979— **65**
Tonex, 1978(?)— **54**
Tooks, Lance 1962— **62**
Toomer, Jean 1894-1967 **6**
Toomer, Nathan Pinchback *See Toomer, Jean*
Toote, Gloria E. A. 1931— **64**
Torres, Gina 1969— **52**
Torry, Guy 19(?)(?)— **31**
Tosh, Peter 1944-1987 **9**
Touré, Amadou Toumani 1948(?)— **18**
Touré, Askia (Muhammad Abu Bakr el) 1938— **47**
Touré, Faya Ora Rose 1945— **56**
Touré, Sekou 1922-1984 **6**
Toussaint, Allen 1938— **60**
Toussaint, Lorraine 1960— **32**
Townes, Jeffrey Allan *See DJ Jazzy Jeff*
Towns, Edolphus 1934— **19**
Townsend, Robert 1957— **4, 23**
T-Pain 1985— **73**
Trammell, Kimberly N. *See Holland, Kimberly N.*
Tresvant, Ralph 1968— **57**
Tribble, Israel, Jr. 1940— **8**
Trotter, Donne E. 1950— **28**
Trotter, Lloyd G. 1945(?)— **56**
Trotter, (William) Monroe 1872-1934 **9**
Trotter, Tariq Luqmaan *See Black Thought*
Trouillot, Ertha Pascal *See Pascal-Trouillot, Ertha*
Trueheart, William E. 1942— **49**
Tsvangirai, Morgan 1952— **26, 72**
Tubbs Jones, Stephanie 1949-2008 **24, 72**
Tubman, Harriet 1820(?)-1913 **9**
Tucker, C. Delores 1927-2005 **12, 56**
Tucker, Chris 1972— **13, 23, 62**
Tucker, Cynthia 1955— **1561**
Tucker, Rosina Budd Harvey Corrothers 1881-1987 **14**
Tuckson, Reed V. 1951(?)— **71**
Tunie, Tamara 1959— **63**
Tunnell, Emlen 1925-1975 **54**
Ture, Kwame *See Carmichael, Stokely*
Turnbull, Charles Wesley 1935— **62**
Turnbull, Walter 1944— **13, 60**
Turner, Henry McNeal 1834-1915 **5**
Turner, Ike 1931-2007 **68**
Turner, Izear *See Turner, Ike*
Turner, Tina 1939— **6, 27**
Tutu, Desmond (Mpilo) 1931— **6, 44**
Tutu, Nontombi Naomi 1960— **57**
Tutuola, Amos 1920-1997 **30**
Tyler, Aisha N. 1970— **36**

Tyree, Omar Rashad 1969— **21**
Tyrese *See Gibson, Tyrese*
Tyson, Andre 1960— **40**
Tyson, Asha 1970— **39**
Tyson, Cicely 1933— **7, 51**
Tyson, Mike 1966— **28, 44**
Tyson, Neil deGrasse 1958— **15, 65**
Uggams, Leslie 1943— **23**
Underwood, Blair 1964— **7, 27**
Union, Gabrielle 1973— **31**
Unseld, Wes 1946— **23**
Upshaw, Gene 1945–2008 **18, 47, 72**
Usher 1978— **23, 56**
Usry, James L. 1922— **23**
Ussery, Terdema Lamar, II 1958— **29**
Utendahl, John 1956— **23**
Valentino, Bobby 1980— **62**
Van Lierop, Robert 1939— **53**
Van Peebles, Mario 1957— **2, 51**
Van Peebles, Melvin 1932— **7**
van Sertima, Ivan 1935— **25**
Vance, Courtney B. 1960— **15, 60**
VanDerZee, James (Augustus Joseph) 1886-1983 **6**
Vandross, Luther 1951-2005 **13, 48, 59**
Vanity 1959— **67**
Vann, Harold Moore *See Muhammad, Khallid Abdul*
Vanzant, Iyanla 1953— **17, 47**
Vaughan, Sarah (Lois) 1924-1990 **13**
Vaughn, Countess 1978— **53**
Vaughn, Gladys Gary 1942(?)— **47**
Vaughn, Mo 1967— **16**
Vaughn, Viola 1947— **70**
Vaughns, Cleopatra 1940— **46**
Vega, Marta Moreno 1942(?)— **61**
Velez-Rodriguez, Argelia 1936— **56**
Vera, Yvonne 1964— **32**
Verdelle, A. J. 1960— **26**
Vereen, Ben(jamin Augustus) 1946— **4**
Verna, Gelsy 1961–2008 **70**
Verrett, Shirley 1931— **66**
Vick, Michael 1980— **39, 65**
Vieira, Joao 1939— **14**
Vincent, Marjorie Judith 1965(?)— **2**
Vincent, Mark *See Diesel, Vin*
Virgil, Ozzie 1933— **48**
Von Lipsey, Roderick 1959— **11**
wa Ngengi, Kamau *See Kenyatta, Jomo*
Waddles, Charleszetta "Mother" 1912-2001 **10, 49**
Waddles, Mother *See Waddles, Charleszetta "Mother"*
Wade, Abdoulaye 1926— **66**
Wade, Dwyane 1982— **61**
Wade-Gayles, Gloria Jean 1937(?)— **41**
Wagner, Annice 1937— **22**
Wainwright, Joscelyn 1941— **46**
Walcott, Derek (Alton) 1930— **5**
Walcott, Louis Eugene 1933— **2, 15**
Walker, Albertina 1929— **10, 58**
Walker, Alice 1944— **1, 43**
Walker, Bernita Ruth 1946— **53**
Walker, Cedric "Ricky" 1953— **19**

Walker, Cora T. 1922–2006 **68**
Walker, Dianne 1951— **57**
Walker, Eamonn 1961(?)— **37**
Walker, George 1922— **37**
Walker, Herschel 1962— **1, 69**
Walker, Hezekiah 1962— **34**
Walker, John T. 1925–1989 **50**
Walker, Kara 1969— **16**
Walker, Kurt *See Blow, Kurtis*
Walker, Madame C. J. 1867-1919 **7**
Walker, Maggie Lena 1867(?)-1934 **17**
Walker, Margaret 1915-1998 **29**
Walker, Nellie Marian *See Larsen, Nella*
Walker, Rebecca 1969— **50**
Walker, T. J. 1961(?)— **7**
Walker, Thomas "T. J." *See Walker, T. J.*
Wallace, Ben 1974— **54**
Wallace, Joaquin 1965— **49**
Wallace, Michele Faith 1952— **13**
Wallace, Perry E. 1948— **47**
Wallace, Phyllis A(nn) 1920(?)-1993 **9**
Wallace, Rasheed 1974— **56**
Wallace, Ruby Ann *See Dee, Ruby*
Wallace, Sippie 1898-1986 **1**
Waller, Fats 1904-1943 **29**
Waller, Thomas Wright *See Waller, Fats*
Walton, Cora *See Taylor, Koko*
Wambugu, Florence 1953— **42**
Wamutombo, Dikembe Mutombo Mpolondo Mukamba Jean Jacque *See Mutombo, Dikembe*
Ward, Andre 1984— **62**
Ward, Benjamin 1926–2002 **68**
Ward, Douglas Turner 1930— **42**
Ward, Lloyd 1949— **21, 46**
Ware, Andre 1968— **37**
Ware, Carl H. 1943— **30**
Warfield, Marsha 1955— **2**
Warner, Malcolm-Jamal 1970— **22, 36**
Warren, Michael 1946— **27**
Warren, Mike *See Warren, Michael*
Warwick, Dionne 1940— **18**
Washington, Alonzo 1967— **29**
Washington, Booker T(aliaferro) 1856-1915 **4**
Washington, Denzel 1954— **1, 16**
Washington, Dinah 1924-1963 **22**
Washington, Fred(er)i(cka Carolyn) 1903-1994 **10**
Washington, Gene 1947— **63**
Washington, Grover, Jr. 1943-1999 **17, 44**
Washington, Harold 1922–1987 **6**
Washington, Harriet A. 1951— **69**
Washington, Isaiah 1963— **62**
Washington, James, Jr. 1909(?)–2000 **38**
Washington, James Melvin 1948-1997 **50**
Washington, Kenny 1918-1971 **50**
Washington, Kerry 1977— **46**
Washington, Laura S. 1956(?)— **18**
Washington, MaliVai 1969— **8**
Washington, Mary T. 1906-2005 **57**
Washington, Patrice Clarke 1961— **12**
Washington, Regynald G. 1954(?)— **44**

Washington, Tamia Reneé *See Tamia*

Washington, Valores James 1903-1995 **12**

Washington, Walter 1915-2003 **45**

Washington Wylie, Mary T. *See Washington, Mary T.*

Wasow, Omar 1970— **15**

Waters, Benny 1902-1998 **26**

Waters, Ethel 1895-1977 **7**

Waters, Maxine 1938— **3, 67**

Waters, Muddy 1915-1983 **34**

Watkins, Donald 1948— **35**

Watkins, Frances Ellen *See Harper, Frances Ellen Watkins*

Watkins, Gloria Jean *See hooks, bell*

Watkins, Levi, Jr. 1945— **9**

Watkins, Perry James Henry 1948-1996 **12**

Watkins, Shirley R. 1938— **17**

Watkins, Tionne "T-Boz" 1970— *See TLC*

Watkins, Walter C. 1946— **24**

Watley, Jody 1959— **54**

Watson, Bob 1946— **25**

Watson, Carlos 1970— **50**

Watson, Diane 1933— **41**

Watson, Johnny "Guitar" 1935-1996 **18**

Watt, Melvin 1945— **26**

Wattleton, (Alyce) Faye 1943— **9**

Watts, Andre 1946— **42**

Watts, J(ulius) C(aesar), Jr. 1957— **14, 38**

Watts, Reggie 1972(?)— **52**

Watts, Rolonda 1959— **9**

Wayans, Damon 1961— **8, 41**

Wayans, Keenen Ivory 1958— **18**

Wayans, Marlon 1972— **29**

Wayans, Shawn 1971— **29**

Waymon, Eunice Kathleen *See Simone, Nina*

Weah, George 1966— **58**

Weathers, Carl 1948— **10**

Weaver, Afaa Michael 1951— **37**

Weaver, Michael S. *See Weaver, Afaa Michael*

Weaver, Robert C. 1907-1997 **8, 46**

Webb, Veronica 1965— **10**

Webb, Wellington, Jr. 1941— **3**

Webber, Chris 1973— **15, 30, 59**

Webster, Katie 1936-1999 **29**

Wedgeworth, Robert W. 1937— **42**

Weekes, Kevin 1975— **67**

Weeks, Thomas, III 1967— **70**

Weems, Carrie Mae 1953— **63**

Weems, Renita J. 1954— **44**

Wein, Joyce 1928-2005 **62**

Wek, Alek 1977— **18, 63**

Welburn, Edward T. 1950— **50**

Welch, Elisabeth 1908-2003 **52**

Wells, Henrietta Bell 1912–2008 **69**

Wells, James Lesesne 1902-1993 **10**

Wells, Mary 1943-1992 **28**

Wells-Barnett, Ida B(ell) 1862-1931 **8**

Welsing, Frances (Luella) Cress 1935— **5**

Wendo *See Kolosoy, Wendo*

Wesley, Dorothy Porter 1905-1995 **19**

Wesley, Richard 1945— **73**

Wesley, Valerie Wilson 194(?)— **18**

West, Cornel (Ronald) 1953— **5, 33**

West, Dorothy 1907-1998 **12, 54**

West, Kanye 1977— **52**

West, Togo Dennis, Jr. 1942— **16**

Westbrook, Kelvin 1955— **50**

Westbrook, Peter 1952— **20**

Westbrooks, Bobby 1930(?)-1995 **51**

Whack, Rita Coburn 1958— **36**

Whalum, Kirk 1958— **37, 64**

Wharton, Clifton R(eginald), Jr. 1926— **7**

Wharton, Clifton Reginald, Sr. 1899-1990 **36**

Wheat, Alan Dupree 1951— **14**

Whitaker, "Sweet Pea" *See Whitaker, Pernell*

Whitaker, Forest 1961— **2, 49, 67**

Whitaker, Mark 1957— **21, 47**

Whitaker, Pernell 1964— **10**

White, Barry 1944-2003 **13, 41**

White, Bill 1933(?)— **1, 48**

White, Charles 1918-1979 **39**

White, (Donald) Dondi 1961-1998 **34**

White, Jesse 1934— **22**

White, John H. 1945— **27**

White, Josh, Jr. 1940— **52**

White, Linda M. 1942— **45**

White, Lois Jean 1938— **20**

White, Maurice 1941— **29**

White, Michael Jai 1967— **71**

White, Michael R(eed) 1951— **5**

White, Reggie 1961-2004 **6, 50**

White, Reginald Howard *See White, Reggie*

White, Walter F(rancis) 1893-1955 **4**

White, Willard 1946— **53**

White, William DeKova *See White, Bill*

White, Willye 1939— **67**

White-Hammond, Gloria 1951(?)— **61**

Whitfield, Fred 1967— **23**

Whitfield, Lynn 1954— **18**

Whitfield, Mal 1924— **60**

Whitfield, Norman 1940–2008 **73**

Whitfield, Van 1960(?)— **34**

Whittaker, Hudson *See Tampa Red*

Wideman, John Edgar 1941— **5**

Wilbekin, Emil 1968— **63**

Wilbon, Michael 1958— **68**

Wilder, L. Douglas 1931— **3, 48**

Wiley, Kehinde 1977— **62**

Wiley, Ralph 1952— **8**

Wilkens, J. Ernest, Jr. 1923— **43**

Wilkens, Lenny 1937— **11**

Wilkens, Leonard Randolph *See Wilkens, Lenny*

Wilkerson, Isabel 1961— **71**

Wilkins, Ray 1951— **47**

Wilkins, Roger (Wood) 1932— **2**

Wilkins, Roy 1901-1981 **4**

Wilkins, Thomas Alphonso 1956— **71**

will.i.am 1975— **64**

Williams, Alice Faye *See Shakur, Afeni*

Williams, Anthony 1951— **21**

Williams, Anthony Charles *See Tonex*

Williams, Armstrong 1959— **29**

Williams, Bert 1874-1922 **18**

Williams, Billy Dee 1937— **8**

Williams, Carl *See Kani, Karl*

Williams, Clarence 1893(?)-1965 **33**

Williams, Clarence 1967— **70**

Williams, Clarence, III 1939— **26**

Williams, Daniel Hale (III) 1856-1931 **2**

Williams, David Rudyard 1954— **50**

Williams, Deniece 1951— **36**

Williams, Denise 1958— **40**

Williams, Doug 1955— **22**

Williams, Dudley 1938— **60**

Williams, Eddie N. 1932— **44**

Williams, Eric Eustace 1911-1981 **65**

Williams, Evelyn 1922(?)— **10**

Williams, Fannie Barrier 1855-1944 **27**

Williams, Frederick (B.) 1939-2006 **63**

Williams, George Washington 1849-1891 **18**

Williams, Gertrude *See Morgan, Gertrude*

Williams, Gregory (Howard) 1943— **11**

Williams, Hosea Lorenzo 1926— **15, 31**

Williams, Joe 1918-1999 **5, 25**

Williams, John A. 1925— **27**

Williams, Juan 1954— **35**

Williams, Ken 1964— **68**

Williams, Lauryn 1983— **58**

Williams, Maggie 1954— **7, 71**

Williams, Malinda 1975— **57**

Williams, Marco 1956— **53**

Williams, Margaret Ann *See Williams, Maggie*

Williams, Mary Lou 1910-1981 **15**

Williams, Michelle 1980— **73**

Williams, Montel 1956— **4, 57**

Williams, Natalie 1970— **31**

Williams, O(swald) S. 1921— **13**

Williams, Patricia 1951— **11, 54**

Williams, Paul R(evere) 1894-1980 **9**

Williams, Paulette Linda *See Shange, Ntozake*

Williams, Pharrell 1973— **47**

Williams, Preston Warren, II 1939(?)— **64**

Williams, Robert F(ranklin) 1925— **11**

Williams, Robert Peter *See Guillaume, Robert*

Williams, Ronald A. 1949— **57**

Williams, Russell, II 1952— **70**

Williams, Samuel Arthur 1946— **21**

Williams, Saul 1972— **31**

Williams, Serena 1981— **20, 41, 73**

Williams, Sherley Anne 1944-1999 **25**

Williams, Stanley "Tookie" 1953-2005 **29, 57**

Williams, Stevie 1979— **71**

Williams, Terrie M. 1954— **35**

Williams, Tony 1945–1997 **67**

Williams, Vanessa A. 1963— **32, 66**

Williams, Vanessa L. 1963— **4, 17**

Williams, Venus 1980— **17, 34, 62**

Williams, Walter E(dward) 1936— **4**

Williams, Wendy 1964— **62**

Williams, William December *See Williams, Billy Dee*

Williams, William T(homas) 1942— **11**

Williams, Willie L(awrence) 1943— **4**

Williamson, Fred 1938— **67**

Williamson, Lisa *See Sister Souljah*

Williamson, Mykelti 1957— **22**

Willie, Louis, Jr. 1923–2007 **68**

Willingham, Tyrone 1953— **43**

Willis, Bill 1921–2007 **68**

Willis, Cheryl *See Hudson, Cheryl*

Willis, Dontrelle 1982— **55**

Willis, William Karnet *See Willis, Bill*

Wills, Maury 1932— **73**

Wilson, August 1945-2005 **7, 33, 55**

Wilson, Cassandra 1955— **16**

Wilson, Chandra 1969— **57**

Wilson, Charlie 1953— **31**

Wilson, Debra 1970(?)— **38**

Wilson, Dorien 1962(?)— **55**

Wilson, Ellis 1899-1977 **39**

Wilson, Flip 1933-1998 **21**

Wilson, Gerald 1918— **49**

Wilson, Jackie 1934-1984 **60**

Wilson, Jimmy 1946— **45**

Wilson, Mary 1944 **28**

Wilson, Nancy 1937— **10**

Wilson, Natalie 1972(?)— **38**

Wilson, Phill 1956— **9**

Wilson, Stephanie 1966— **72**

Wilson, Sunnie 1908-1999 **7, 55**

Wilson, William Julius 1935— **22**

Wilson, William Nathaniel *See Wilson, Sunnie*

Winans, Angie 1968— **36**

Winans, Benjamin 1962— **14**

Winans, CeCe 1964— **14, 43**

Winans, Debbie 1972— **36**

Winans, Marvin L. 1958— **17**

Winans, Ronald 1956-2005 **54**

Winans, Vickie 1953(?)— **24**

Winfield, Dave 1951— **5**

Winfield, David Mark *See Winfield, Dave*

Winfield, Paul (Edward) 1941-2004 **2, 45**

Winfrey, Oprah 1954— **2, 15, 61**

Winkfield, Jimmy 1882-1974 **42**

Wisdom, Kimberlydawn 1956— **57**

Withers, Bill 1938— **61**

Withers, Ernest C. 1922–2007 **68**

Withers-Mendes, Elisabeth 1973(?)— **64**

Witherspoon, John 1942— **38**

Witt, Edwin T. 1920— **26**

Wiwa, Ken 1968— **67**

Wofford, Chloe Anthony *See Morrison, Toni*

Wolfe, George C. 1954— **6, 43**

Womack, Bobby 1944— **60**

Wonder, Stevie 1950— **11, 53**

Woodard, Alfre 1953— **9**

Woodbridge, Hudson *See Tampa Red*

Woodruff, Hale (Aspacio) 1900-1980 **9**

Woodruff, John 1915–2007 **68**

Woods, Eldrick *See Woods, Tiger*

Woods, Georgie 1927-2005 **57**

Woods, Granville T. 1856-1910 **5**

Woods, Jacqueline 1962— **52**

Woods, Mattiebelle 1902-2005 **63**

Woods, Scott 1971— **55**

Woods, Sylvia 1926— **34**

Woods, Teri 1968— **69**

Woods, Tiger 1975— **14, 31**

Woodson, Carter G(odwin) 1875-1950 **2**

Woodson, Robert L. 1937— **10**

Woodward, Lynette 1959— **67**

Wooldridge, Anna Marie *See Lincoln, Abbey*

Worrill, Conrad 1941— **12**

Worthy, James 1961— **49**

Wright, Antoinette 195(?)— **60**

Wright, Bruce McMarion 1918-2005 **3, 52**

Wright, Charles H. 1918-2002 **35**

Wright, Deborah C. 1958— **25**

Wright, Jeffrey 1966— **54**

Wright, Jeremiah A., Jr. 1941— **45, 69**

Wright, Lewin 1962— **43**

Wright, Louis Tompkins 1891-1952 **4**

Wright, Nathan, Jr. 1923-2005 **56**

Wright, Rayfield 1945— **70**

Wright, Richard 1908-1960 **5**

Wyatt, Addie L. 1924— **56**

Wynn, Albert R. 1951— **25**

X, Malcolm 1925-1965 **1**

X, Marvin 1944— **45**

Xuma, Madie Hall 1894-1982 **59**

Yancy, Dorothy Cowser 1944— **42**

Yar'adua, Umaru 1951— **69**

Yarbrough, Camille 1938— **40**

Yarbrough, Cedric 1971— **51**

Yeboah, Emmanuel Ofosu 1977— **53**

Yette, Samuel F. 1929— **63**

Yoba, (Abdul-)Malik (Kashie) 1967— **11**

York, Dwight D. 1945— **71**

York, Malachi Z. *See York, Dwight D.*

York, Vincent 1952— **40**

Young, Andre Ramelle *See Dre, Dr.*

Young, Andrew 1932— **3, 48**

Young, Coleman 1918-1997 **1, 20**

Young, Donald, Jr. 1989— **57**

Young, Jean Childs 1933-1994 **14**

Young, Jimmy 1948-2005 **54**

Young, Ledisi Anibade *See Ledisi*

Young, Lee 1914–2008 **72**

Young, Leonidas Raymond *See Young, Lee*

Young, Roger Arliner 1899-1964 **29**

Young, Thomas 194(?)— *See Three Mo' Tenors*

Young, Whitney M(oore), Jr. 1921-1971 **4**

Young Jeezy 1977— **63**

Youngblood, Johnny Ray 1948— **8**

Youngblood, Shay 1959— **32**

Zane 1967(?)— **71**

Zollar, Alfred 1955(?)— **40**

Zollar, Jawole Willa Jo 1950— **28**

Zook, Kristal Brent 1966(?)— **62**

Zulu, Princess Kasune 1977— **54**

Zuma, Jacob G. 1942— **33**

Zuma, Nkosazana Dlamini 1949— **34**

For Reference

Not to be taken from this room